Management Consultancy and Skills

A Pearson Custom Publication

Management Consultancy and Skills

Compiled from:

Management Consulting: Delivering an Effective Project
Second Edition
by Philip A. Wickham

Developing Management Skills for Europe
Second Edition
by David A. Whetten, Kim S. Cameron and
Mike Woods

PEARSON
Custom
Publishing

Pearson Education Limited
Edinburgh Gate
Harlow
Essex CM20 2JE

And associated companies throughout the world

Visit us on the World Wide Web at:
www.pearsoned.co.uk

First published 2006

This Custom Book Edition © 2006 Published by Pearson Education Limited

Taken from:

Management Consulting: Delivering an Effective Project
Second Edition
by Philip A. Wickham
ISBN 0 273 68347 0

Copyright © Pearson Education Limited 1999, 2004

Developing Management Skills for Europe
Second Edition
by David A. Whetten, Kim S. Cameron and Mike Woods
ISBN 0 201 34276 6

Copyright © Pearson Education Limited 2000

ISBN-10   1 84658 047 1
ISBN-13   978 1 84658 047 5

Printed and bound in Great Britain by Henry Ling Limited at the Dorset Press, Dorchester,
DT1 1HD

Contents

Part 2
Developing Management Skills 147

Chapters from
Developing Management Skills for Europe
Second Edition
by David A. Whetten, Kim S. Cameron and
Mike Woods

Instructions

Management Consultancy and Skills online registration.

The access card included with your textbook provides access to an online CourseCompass course.

You must register before you can access your online product for the first time.

Before you register you will need:
- A valid email address.
- A student access code. This consists of a six 'word' printed code and will have been shrink wrapped with your text book

The Course ID for your CourseCompass is: leedsmet40804

How to register:

Click the Register button for Students on the CourseCompass home page at www.coursecompass.com and follow the on-screen instructions.

Step 1 Access Information
- Do you have a Pearson Education account?
    Select **No, I am a New User** if you have never registered for any Pearson Education CourseCompass product before.

- Access code

    Type your six "word" student access code, one word in each box. Don't type the dashes.

- School location

    Enter your school Post code and select Country from the drop-down list

Select the Next button to move to the next screen.

Step2: Course ID

Next enter the Course ID for your CourseCompass course :
- For Management Consultancy and Skills - this is **leedsmet40804**

Step 3 Account Information

This step of the registration requires you to:

- Enter your contact information

- Add your School/Institution

- Create a unique Login name and Password

- Provide an answer to a security question

Step 3 Confirmation and summary

You will be presented with a screen summarising your account information. This information will also be e-mailed to you.

To access your course please return to www.coursecompass.com and select the Students Log In option.

Part 1
Management Consultancy

The nature of management consulting

The main learning outcomes from this chapter are:

■ to understand the nature of management consulting as a managerial role;

■ to appreciate the nature of the client–consultant role relationship;

■ to recognise the responsibilities of the consultant.

1.1 What a management consultant does

Management consulting is, as its title suggests, a management *activity*. But it is a special form of management. Many would regard it as one of the most exciting of management challenges. It is certainly one of the most demanding. The upside of this is that it can also be one of the most rewarding – not just financially (though the rewards here can be high indeed for good consultants) but also in terms of task enjoyment, satisfaction with achievements and intellectual stimulation.

A management consultant is rewarded for going into an organisation and undertaking a special project on its behalf. Usually the organisation is a profit-motivated commercial venture. But it does not have to be. Consultants are also (and increasingly) called upon to offer their services to non-profit organisations such as charities. Governmental and non-governmental organisations, whether local, national or international, also make frequent calls on the skills of management consultants.

The types of project undertaken by consultants are as varied as management itself. They may involve the proffering of technical expertise, such as the development of information technology systems. They may be 'softer' and aim at generating cultural change within the organisation. In some cases they may have the objective of resolving internal conflicts within the organisation. They may be concerned with helping the organisation build relationships with outside parties. In other instances, they may aim to help the organisation gain some critical resource. Often they will be focused on some specific issue that has been recognised by the organisation's management and has been well defined. In many instances though they are of a broad 'business development' nature. Most will involve gathering and analysing information and sharing discoveries with the organisation. Usually the management consulting project is undertaken over a relatively short time scale – say weeks or, at most, a few months. Increasingly, however, projects with a longer time scale (up to a year or more) are in demand.

In short, a management consultant offers his or her management abilities, expertise and insights to the client business in order to *create value for it*. Consulting activity is something that the client business decides to buy in. It represents a *factor* that managers decide they need in order to progress their business and improve its performance. As a factor that is bought in, consulting activity competes with all the other factors a business must buy in if it is to grow: money for investment, people and their skills, raw materials and the equipment necessary to deliver what the business offers. The client will find the service the consultant is offering attractive only if it is something that the business cannot provide for itself. Further, it must be the *best* investment option on offer given all the other things the business could buy in.

This means a consultant must understand a number of things from the outset. Clearly, the consultant must know why what he or she is offering will be of value to the client business. Although important, this is not enough. Consultants must also know why what they are offering represents a good *investment opportunity* for the business given all the other investment opportunities available. This forms the basis of what the consultant can 'sell' to the business. As with any form of selling to organisations, the selling is most effective when the underlying *buying process* is appreciated. Organisations do not buy – individuals within them do. The way in which individuals react, interact and influence each other must be taken into account when delivering a consulting exercise. In short, the consultant must recognise what he or she will enable the business to do in its marketplace, why the business cannot do this for itself and how the individuals who make up the business can unify around the project.

Although management consultancy is seen as a specialist management role, the consultant must have the skills of a general manager. He or she must not only be able to undertake specific (and often technical) projects, he or she must also be able to market what they offer (not forgetting that marketing includes the development of the actual consulting 'product' as well as its promotion), sell the product to clients and manage a relationship with them. This is a challenge. But if it is met effectively the rewards can be great. Consultants often enjoy fast-track careers. Experience in consulting provides such a fast 'learning curve' that they quickly mature as managers and can take on high-level roles, even when quite young. For the ambitious manager, investing in developing the skills that make a consultant effective offers the potential of considerable rewards.

1.2   Consulting and management roles

Given that consulting represents a special form of management, it is necessary to have a preliminary understanding of what management is. The nature of management is subject to a great deal of discussion. A traditional approach defines management in terms of the *functions* the manager undertakes. For example, Henri Fayol, a management thinker of the early twentieth century, decided there were five such basic functions: planning, organising, staffing, directing and controlling.

Planning

Planning is concerned with deciding a future direction for the business and defining the courses of action and projects needed to move the organisation in that direction. Planning varies greatly in its formality. A simple project with few tasks and low resource requirements will demand only a minimum of consideration and documentation. A major project with complex, and perhaps risky, outcomes will require a considerable degree of time and effort in its planning. Its implementation will involve complex communication networks drawing together a large number of managers.

Formal planning techniques may be advantageous if project organisation is to be effective. Different businesses differ in their approach to planning and the degree to which it is formalised as a management activity. As well as the nature and complexity of the project and the significance of its outcomes, organisational style, culture and individual management traits will be important determinants in the approach to planning.

Organising

The organising function relates to the overall structure of the business. Roles, responsibilities and reporting relationships are defined for individuals and sub-groups. In strategic terms this means ensuring that the organisation's structure is appropriate for its strategy and environmental situation. The organisation's structure dictates the way in which it will work and how it will use its capabilities. This is sometimes referred to as the strategy-structure-process fit. This topic is reviewed well by Van de Ven and Drazin (1985).

Staffing

Staffing is the function concerned with making sure that the business has the right people in place. It ensures that its people have the right skills in order to undertake the projects the business needs to carry out to be successful. In modern organisations the staffing function is often integrated into a broader human resource management function. Key elements of the human resource strategy are recruitment and training. Additional elements will include establishing remuneration, career development and staff motivation policies.

Directing

Directing relates to the process of encouraging people to undertake the tasks necessary to deliver the project outcomes the business needs. Originally it referred to the management function of instruction or delegation to subordinates. A modern interpretation would be broader and would include a manager's responsibilities as a leader and motivator of individuals and teams and the creator of a supportive organisational culture.

Management Consultancy and Skills

Controlling

Managers use resources. Resources, be they money, people or productive assets, must be utilised in the best way possible. Controlling is the function that is concerned with making sure that the right resources are in place, that they are being used effectively and that their use is properly accounted for.

Traditionally, controlling was largely about *budgeting*, that is financial control. Now a broader interpretation would regard it as the process of focusing the business towards its goals through the implementation of an appropriate *strategy*. This strategy will direct the utilisation of all the business's resources and the development of its capabilities.

This traditional approach to the nature of management has been criticised because it offers an idealised image of what the manager actually does. It pictures the manager as 'above' the organisation, co-ordinating its activities in a detached way, progressing it towards some well-defined, rational end. In fact, most organisations are not like this at all. Managers cannot detach themselves from their organisations; they are very much part of them. The organisation defines the manager as much as the manager defines the organisation. They must work with limited information and make decisions using intuition as much as formal analysis. The ends they work towards may be motivated as much by implicit and emotional drives as explicit and rational ones.

The Canadian management theorist Henry Mintzberg spent a long period observing how managers actually worked. In his groundbreaking 1973 book, *The Nature of Managerial Work*, he suggested that a more productive approach was to look at the *roles* managers actually undertake rather than the *functions* they are supposed to undertake. He suggested that there are ten such roles, which fall into three groups: *interpersonal* roles, *informational* roles and *decisional* roles.

Interpersonal roles relate to the ways in which managers interact with other organisational members. It is through interpersonal roles that managers draw their power and authority. The three key interpersonal roles are the figurehead, the leader and the liaison.

The figurehead

The figurehead role is the one in which the manager represents his or her organisation, or the part of it for which he or she is responsible, in a formal manner. This role draws on the responsibilities defined in a job description, though traditional activities, informal elements and unwritten expectations may also play an important part in characterising the figurehead role. The figurehead role is very important for entrepreneurs and the manager of a small business.

The leader

The leader role refers to the manager's interaction with subordinates. It is the role the manager is playing when he or she is delegating tasks, motivating people to undertake these tasks and supporting them in achieving them. Leadership is different to authority. Authority arises from a position within an organisational hierarchy. This position makes leadership possible, but it does not guarantee it.

The liaison

Many managers have a responsibility for representing the business to the outside world. Sales people, procurement managers and finance specialists in particular have important responsibilities in this way. The liaison role is the one in which managers interact with people from other organisations. The critical responsibility is one of gaining some resource for the business such as, for the management roles noted, customer goodwill, essential productive factors or investment capital.

Managers must make decisions on behalf of their organisations. Indeed it might be argued that decision-making is a manager's fundamental responsibility. To do so they must make use of available information on both the internal state of the business and what is happening in its environment. *Informational roles* are concerned with obtaining and manipulating the information the business needs. The three critical informational roles are the monitor, the disseminator and the spokesperson.

The monitor

The monitor role is that which leads the manager to identify and acquire information on behalf of the organisation. It may also involve the processing and storage of that information so that it is readily available for use by decision-makers. Analysis is a critical task for the monitor. The production of sales statistics, accounts and market intelligence are important tasks for the monitor.

The disseminator

Managers do not work in isolation. Information must be shared with others in the organisation. The disseminator role is concerned with making sure that available information is passed on within the organisation to information processors and decision-makers. Dissemination occurs through a variety of means. Reports, meetings and presentations represent formal means of dissemination. Unofficial 'grapevines' are often a very influential way of disseminating information informally. Monitors may also take on disseminator roles, but this is far from inevitable, especially in larger organisations.

The spokesperson

The spokesperson is also involved in disseminating information, but to the outside world rather than internally. Important spokesperson roles are taken on by sales and marketing staff who tell customers about what the company has on offer, purchasing managers, who let suppliers know what the company needs, and financial managers, who let investors know about the company's status and prospects.

The third class of roles, *decisional roles,* are involved in identifying a future direction for the organisation, defining the projects needed in order to get it there and dealing with the crises that tend to knock it off the path it must follow while getting there.

The entrepreneur

The entrepreneur role is concerned with shaping and making decisions that lead the organisation forward in a significant way. Mintzberg uses the term entrepreneurial in a broader sense than it is used in traditional management theory. In Mintzberg's sense, the entrepreneur need not be an owner or founder of the organisation. Any manager can take on the entrepreneurial role, not just those who set up and own businesses. An entrepreneurial decision is one that aims to exploit an opportunity or address a threat. Such a decision may be significant, but it is not usually pressing at the time. It encompasses the activities of conventional entrepreneurs and what have come to be known as *intrapreneurs*, managers who take an entrepreneurial approach within an established business.

The entrepreneurial role demands that information be taken from those undertaking the informational roles and then used to identify new opportunities and new ways of doing things. To make entrepreneurial decisions really happen will demand effective use of the interpersonal roles. The entrepreneurial decision-maker takes resources and makes good use of them, even if it means that decision-maker may be exposed to risk. Critically, the entrepreneurial role is concerned with driving change. The organisation is not the same after the entrepreneurial decision-maker has finished with it.

The disturbance handler

Organisations tend to establish and then follow set patterns of behaviour. They find their own ways of doing things and stick to them. This is known as organisational inertia. A fixed pattern of working will produce satisfactory results provided that there is no change in either the organisation's internal state or its external condition. If change does occur, the organisation's way of doing things may no longer produce the desired results. Such a change is known as a disturbance.

Disturbances can arise from internal events such as intergroup conflicts or the loss of a critical person from the organisation. External disturbances usually result from the organisation losing access to an essential resource. This might be loss in sales income from an important customer or group of customers. The cause of this may be a customer moving to a competitor or going out of business. The loss of an important input from a supplier also represents a disturbance. Disturbances can also arise if an investor loses faith in the business and pulls out investment capital. This can be critical for fast-growing entrepreneurial businesses.

The opportunities and threats the entrepreneurial decision-maker addresses are long term. Disturbances, on the other hand, demand immediate attention. The business will suffer a reduced performance or even fail if they are not dealt with promptly. A disturbance is often referred to as a management crisis. Organisational inertia conditions management's response to a crisis. Often, the first reaction of managers when faced with a crisis is to try to replace the missing resource and so keep the organisation in its original state. Maintaining the status quo when the organisation has been knocked off track by a disturbance is the responsibility of the disturbance handler.

The kinds of project the disturbance handler undertakes will depend on the type of disturbance affecting the organisation. Disturbance handlers may attempt to resolve intergroup conflicts. If a critical resource such as a customer, supplier or investor is lost, they will lead the search for a suitable replacement.

Disturbance handling is not a continuous role. It comes into play only when a crisis happens. Some managers may be predisposed to deal with certain crises as a consequence of their roles: sales managers, for example, will be in the front line if an important customer is lost; purchasing managers will lead the way in finding a new supplier. If the crisis is significant enough, conventional relationships can be driven into a state of flux. Recrimination and organisational politics can arise. Eventually new roles and even new leaders may emerge. Leaders often come to the fore in a crisis.

Sometimes the projects undertaken to deal with disturbances will be successful. The organisation may be able to return to its original state. Often, though, the crisis will be too great and the organisation's ability to respond too limited. In this case the organisation will need to make functional and structural changes in order to survive in the changed circumstances it faces.

The resource allocator

Businesses consume resources. They do so in order to pursue the opportunities that present themselves. These resources are valuable and must be used in the best way possible if the business is to be successful. Few businesses face a simple yes or no answer when considering future possibilities. It is not the cost of investing in a project that matters so much as its opportunity cost: the returns that might have been gained if the resources invested in the project had been invested elsewhere.

Managers must decide which of the opportunities that offer themselves is the best one at a particular time. In practice this means that managers must decide how to allocate the resources they have to hand across a variety of projects. This consideration resolves itself into a series of immediate and practical tasks. For example, should the business invest in that advertising campaign or would the money be better spent on a new sales representative? Should export efforts be directed at the Far East or are the developing economies of central Europe likely to offer a better return? Should investment be directed at a new product, or might it be more profitable to acquire that competitor? It is questions like these that managers must address every day. In doing so they are taking on the resource allocator role.

As with the entrepreneurial role, the resource allocator is dependent on the informational role in order to make good decisions about where resources are best placed.

The negotiator

People come together and work in organisations because value can be created by differentiating and co-ordinating tasks. The extra value created must, however, be shared both within organisations and between the different organisations that come into contact with each other.

Individuals and organisations must be active in advocating their right to a particular share of resources available. This advocacy is reflected in the negotiator role. Sometimes this role is concerned with sharing resources with outside organisations. The sales manager will negotiate with customers. The purchasing manager will negotiate with suppliers. Finance managers will negotiate with

investors and lenders. Sometimes it will be concerned with the internal allocation of resources. Personnel managers will negotiate remuneration packages with
employees. Managers will negotiate with resource allocators in order to gain a
budget for investment in the projects they wish to see happen.

Not all negotiations are so formal. Many negotiations take on an informal
character. They may manifest themselves as unofficial 'understandings' between
managers about how resources will be shared. Organisational politics is often
both a consequence of, and limited by, unofficially negotiated outcomes. It
should not be thought that all negotiations are a 'zero-sum' game: that if one
party wins, the other must lose. Effective negotiators look for win-win solutions.
Nor is effective negotiation about taking a stance and holding to it. It is more
about identifying what is wanted out of a situation and then being flexible in
finding ways to achieve what is wanted.

Any one management role will have a profile that combines some or even all of
these ten pure roles in a particular way. The way in which these roles define the
profile of management responsibilities within the organisation will depend on a
range of factors. The organisation's size will be a critical determinant. The
bigger the business and the more managers it employs, the greater will be the
latitude for managers to specialise. In a small business, a single entrepreneur
may take on most, if not all, the roles at some time or other. In a large multinational corporation, managers may be in a position where their roles will be
more narrowly defined.

The complexity of the organisation and its environment will also be important. Complexity refers to the amount of information managers must process
before making a decision. If complexity is high, informational roles will be
important and it may be necessary to have managers dedicated to these roles. A
fast-growing organisation undergoing rapid change may present a special leadership challenge and demand that particular attention be paid to interpersonal
roles. The profile of management roles will reflect the organisation, the stage in
its evolution and its environmental situation.

1.3   The client–consultant interaction

The consultant *is* a manager. We must understand the nature of the consultant's
tasks in terms of them being *management* tasks. Like any manager, the consultant
will at times take on many if not all of the ten roles defined by Mintzberg. The
consultant's role parallels and integrates with that of managers within the client
organisation. It is through the interaction of these roles that the client–consultant
relationship is built.

The managers who make up organisations work in a network of relationships.
These relationships exist between managers working within a particular organisation and between the managers in different organisations who come into
contact with each other. The consultant who moves into an organisation must
define the relationship he or she wishes to create with the managers who already
work in the client business, and, often, with some of those in other organisations

with which the client comes into contact. Two considerations will determine what sort of relationship this will be. These are:

■ the nature and structure of management roles in the client organisation; and
■ the objectives of the consulting exercise.

Every organisation is different and so is every manager. However, it is possible to see consistent patterns in the way in which managerial roles take shape. Different organisations will require a different profile of management roles. But every organisation will demand that managers carry out the interpersonal, informational and decisional roles in a way that is right for the business. These roles must be carried out with the correct degree of competence and in balance with each other.

The motivation to call in a consultant (a topic discussed fully in Chapter 2) arises because managers have identified a project that they think will benefit the organisation but they recognise that they are not in a position to deliver it themselves. The reason for their inability to deliver may be articulated in the form of resource or skill gaps. In entering to fill these gaps the consultant is offering to complement and develop the role profile within the organisation.

The managerial roles described by Henry Mintzberg provide a clue to the kind of interaction that will take place between the consultant and the client organisation's management team. We can use a visual metaphor to picture the ways in which a consultant can interact with and develop the business management role profile.

Think of the role profile as a triangle, with each apex representing one of the groups of roles. This is illustrated in Figure 1.1.

Using this simple diagram we can create a visual depiction of the five primary types of consultant–management role interaction: supplementing, complementing, differentiating, integrating and enhancing.

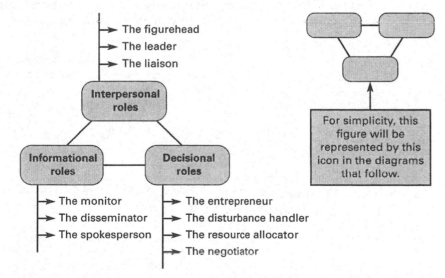

Figure 1.1 The managerial role profile

Management Consultancy and Skills

Supplementing

Supplementing involves the consultant adding to the existing skill profile to increase its capability but not alter its overall shape. The consultant is an additional resource who takes on a project that could well have been taken on by an existing manager had time been available. An example might be a business with a local sales base using a consultant with sales experience to test the possibility of expanding into a new area. Had a sales manager from within the company been available then he or she would have done the job in exactly the same way. In principle, the consultant could be recruited into the organisation and there would be little change in the way in which he or she operates with and interacts with the rest of the organisation.

This type of consulting role offers a way of enabling the business to manage demand fluctuations in a low-risk way. The consultant allows the business to add and subtract human resources in a flexible manner. The consultant is neutral in development terms and does not aim to make any fundamental changes in the organisation. We can picture the supplementing role as a simple addition to the existing role profile (*see* Figure 1.2).

Complementing

Complementing occurs when the organisation notices a gap in its profile of management roles and asks the consultant to fill that role. This may require the consultant to specialise in any one of the basic role types.

For example, a consultant may be required to complement the organisation's liaison role and develop the way it represents itself to the outside world. Projects that enhance the business's marketing approach or develop presentations to financial backers are important examples. Consultants can play an important role in supporting existing managers to improve leadership, through, say, the development of a unifying organisational mission.

A wide range of projects can involve the consultant complementing the informational role. Important examples might include marketing research and the setting up of management information systems. These projects will make

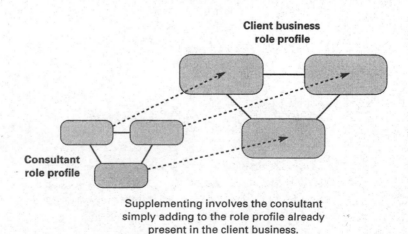

Supplementing involves the consultant
simply adding to the role profile already
present in the client business.

Figure 1.2 The consultant–manager role supplementing interaction

Management Consultancy and Skills

demands on both the monitoring and disseminating aspects of the informational role. The consultant may also be active in supporting the spokesperson role. Developing communications aimed at customers and investors is the task of the public relations expert. Lobbyists may be employed to communicate and influence decision-makers in government.

The consultant can contribute to the decisional role in a variety of ways. Speculative business development projects, which explore a range of possibilities for the business in the future, complement the *entrepreneurial role*. A consultant may be called in as a *disturbance handler* to help the business's management deal with a crisis. The setting up of budgeting management control systems is an example of the consultant complementing the work of the *resource allocator*. Some consultants specialise in *negotiating* and can contribute to the way in which the business approaches important customers, suppliers or investors.

The complementing role can be pictured as the consultant filling in a gap in the management's existing role profile. Figure 1.3 shows how this may be illustrated.

Differentiating

The overall profile of management roles will depend on a number of factors. The size of the organisation will be critical. The larger the business, the greater the latitude for allowing managers to specialise their roles. One aspect of the process of organisational growth will be an increasing tendency towards role specialisation. For example, a small business will tend to have a leading entrepreneur (perhaps with a high level of ownership) undertaking the decisional and the spokesperson roles. He or she may also have responsibility for the informational roles. As the business grows the entrepreneur can allow other managers to take on more responsibility. A sales and marketing function may emerge to take on the spokesperson roles and promote the product to customers. A management information system can be set up to monitor financial data and so supplement the informational role. The entrepreneur can also delegate certain areas of decision-making to subordinate managers.

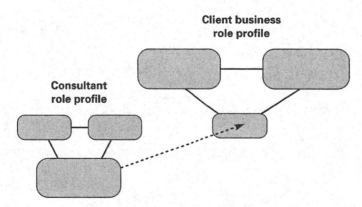

**Client business
role profile**

**Consultant
role profile**

Complementing involves the consultant bringing
along a role specialism to complement a
weakness in the client business role profile.

Figure 1.3 The consultant–manager role complementing interaction

Management Consultancy and Skills

This process of role differentiation is critical if the organisation is to grow successfully. It is only through such specialisation that the business can not only grow but also improve its performance as it grows. However, such differentiation is not always easy. Managers (not least successful entrepreneurs) often resist giving away areas of responsibility. They would rather use the organisation's growth to 'build their empire'. This can result in the manager having too large an area of responsibility, too much information to analyse and not enough time. Invariably, the quality of decision-making suffers.

Consultants can help facilitate the process of role differentiation. At one level this involves designing appropriate organisation structures, defining managerial responsibilities and setting up communication systems. But this is just the 'hardware' of the organisation. Managers must feel comfortable with their new responsibilities, be motivated to work within them and interact positively with colleagues. Changing the 'software' is a change management process calling upon a specialist type of consulting. This type of role differentiation can be illustrated as in Figure 1.4.

Integrating

Mature organisations are characterised by well-defined organisation structure and role responsibilities. These become established and are subject to organisational inertia. They may persist even when they are no longer appropriate. If the business's environment and competitive situation change then an evolution in the way the business does things may be called for. If environmental change is particularly fast, the occasional revolution may be called for. Such changes demand that the old role profile be broken down and a new profile allowed to emerge. The new roles may combine or integrate a number of aspects of the old roles.

An important recent trend in organisational change has been the shift from vertically ordered functions to horizontally ordered teams. Traditional departments such as marketing, finance, operations and the like have been supplemented, or even replaced, by small, multidisciplinary teams. The focus shifts to the team

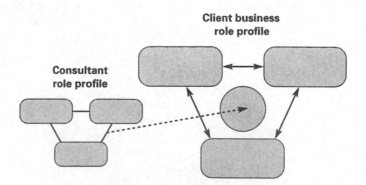

Differentiating involves the consultant helping the
client business to differentiate its management
roles and allow managers to specialise.

Figure 1.4 The consultant–manager role differentiating interaction

Management Consultancy and Skills

undertaking specific tasks rather than the department fulfilling fixed roles. This allows a more flexible response to the shifting needs of the marketplace.

This process makes a number of demands on managers. Of course, team working must be made effective (a topic discussed in Chapter 20), but there are more subtle demands as well. The hierarchical department offers a traditional path for promotion in the organisation. If it goes, managers may see no clear way for advancing and may become demotivated. If the team structure is combined with traditional functions (a structure known as a matrix organisation), managers may become disorientated at having two bosses (the team leader and the departmental manager). Such 'challenges' to the departmental manager's authority may also be a recipe for political infighting.

As with differentiating, the consultant called in to integrate roles into a new, more flexible structure must address both hardware and software issues. A new structure must be invented and the change management issues needed to motivate managers to work within it must be addressed. Role integrating may be illustrated as in Figure 1.5.

Enhancing

Enhancing is the most general type of role development process. It demands not so much that the role profile of the organisation be changed but that the manager's overall level of performance be improved. There are a variety of ways this might be achieved. Training of individual managers is usually an important part. This training may be directed towards improving technical and functional skills or may develop interpersonal skills such as motivation and leadership. Training may be supplemented through structural changes such as improved communication systems and attention to overall strategic understanding. The process of role enhancement is illustrated in Figure 1.6.

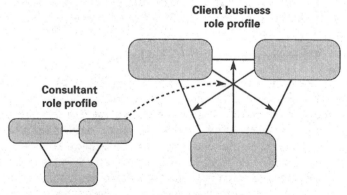

Integrating involves the consultant helping the client business to reorganise its management roles and build a new set of manager relationships and responsibilities.

Figure 1.5 The consultant–manager role integrating interaction

Management Consultancy and Skills

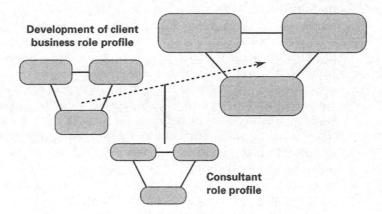

Enhancing involves the consultant helping the client
management team improve the effectiveness
of their overall management role profile.

Figure 1.6 The consultant–manager role enhancing interaction

1.4 The responsibilities of the management consultant

All managers have responsibilities. They have responsibilities both to organisations and to the individuals who work in them. At one level, organisations are
collections of individuals, so it is individual managers who must take on responsibilities on behalf of the organisations they work for. The consultant is in a
special position. He or she must take on the responsibilities of being a manager,
not just for the organisation they work for but also for the organisation they
work with.

It has been suggested (by Archie Carroll in an article in 1979) that managerial
and organisational responsibilities operate at four levels. These may be referred
to as the economic, the legal, the moral and the discretionary.

Economic responsibilities

The fundamental economic responsibility of the manager is to act in a way which
is consistent with the long-term health of their business, and maximise its value
for its investors. This is not to suggest that the manager, like the economist's perfect entrepreneur, simply tries to maximise short-term profits. Real-world
managers do not have the information to behave like this. Short-term profits to
investors may be diverted in order to fund reinvestment projects aimed to achieve
growth and so deliver more profits in the future. Potential profits may be compromised if other responsibilities are given priority. An area of economics called
agency theory suggests that the interests of managers and investors differ and that,
under certain circumstances, managers will act in their own best interests.

Given these constraints, it may still be properly said that the consultant's economic responsibility is to advocate only projects which genuinely seem, in light

of the information available, to be in the best interests of the business as a whole, given its stated strategic objectives and the concerns of the stakeholders who have an interest in it.

Legal responsibilities

All businesses have a responsibility to operate within the rule of law. Laws provide the official 'rules of the game' through which businesses interact with each other. Legal systems around the world differ, but generally have two codes: the *criminal*, which the state takes responsibility for implementing, and the *civil*, in which the responsibility for initiating proceedings lies with individuals. Business activity is subject to both codes.

Nowadays, most governments try to minimise the impact of legislation on business. In that legal restrictions impede business activity, they are seen as an evil, albeit a necessary one. Consideration of the impact of a new law on business is, these days, usually taken into account in the legislative process. This means that the laws that remain are usually there for a good reason.

The consultant has a legal responsibility to ensure that the activities of the organisation he or she is working for, and any activities he or she may advocate on its behalf, are legitimate in light of the criminal and civil laws to which the business is subject. The exact nature of this legal responsibility, and the extent to which the consultant may face recrimination if it is breached, will depend on the law involved, the consultant's contractual obligations and the degree of culpability for outcomes.

Ensuring that this condition is met, especially when the business is operating in a highly technical area, or in a part of the world with a different legal system, can be quite challenging. In this case, taking legal advice from experts (not least about one's own responsibilities) may be an important part of the consulting exercise.

Moral responsibilities

Moral responsibilities go one step beyond legal ones. The societies in which businesses operate function on the basis of a whole complex of rules, norms and expectations. Some of these rules are written down in the form of laws or contractual agreements (which are often subject to civil law). But many are unwritten. They may not even be spoken. They are merely an understanding about what is 'right' and what is 'wrong'. They are expectations about how people should behave towards each other. These rules may not even be noticed – until they are broken!

Though it is not always made explicit, every society, and to some extent every distinct grouping within a society, has its own code of morality. These codes often relate to the way in which stakeholders will be treated, above and beyond simple contractual rights. For example, most managers feel a higher degree of responsibility to employees than their contracts of employment dictate. This can manifest itself in many ways. Losing people is painful: a business may retain people who are not absolutely necessary. Entrepreneurs who own their business may allow family members a greater performance latitude than non-family members.

Many cultures have their own distinct rule systems. In displaced ethnic groups, networking may be supported by moral expectations about the responsibilities of members of the community towards each other. Edicts on the way in which debt is structured are common, as are rules about reciprocity of favours. Recognising such moral codes is an important aspect of the consultant's job.

The consultant must recognise that he or she is as subject to these moral responsibilities as to the legal ones. Moral responsibilities are not merely 'nice to have'. Ignoring them will limit the effectiveness of the consulting exercise. Outcomes which go against the moral expectations of the client will, at best, not be implemented. Outright rejection can often occur.

Discretionary responsibilities

Discretionary responsibilities are those the consultant decides to take on as part of a personal moral order. They are not responsibilities the industry would normally be expected to observe.

Discretionary responsibilities usually relate to a refusal to work in certain project areas, or to work towards project outcomes of which the consultant does not approve. This may mean avoiding certain industry sectors or types of project. Typically, such discretionary responsibilities arise as a result of the consultant's personal concerns about a range of domestic political issues, the environment or business activity in the developing world.

Although this may mean that the consultant must occasionally turn down valuable projects, it can also be a means of differentiation from the values other (perhaps competing) consultants advocate. Discretionary values may make a consultant more attractive to certain individuals and organisations. There is nothing inconsistent in using discretionary responsibilities as a means of gaining an edge in the marketplace. Where discretionary values offer an edge they may eventually set the standard for consulting as a whole.

1.5 Types of client

In a 1997 paper, Edgar Schein suggested that process consulting can be enhanced by an appreciation of the different types of client involved. He suggested that the consultant interacts with a number of individuals within the client organisation and that the concept of the individual client may be problematic. Rather, the consultant interacts with a network of individuals who play subtly different roles. Schein proposed six such client types.

Contact clients

The contact client is the person, or persons, who first approach the consultant and propose the consultant addresses a problem or issue on behalf of the organisation.

Intermediate clients

Intermediate clients are members of the organisation who become involved in the consulting project. They will work with the consultant and provide information. They will sit in on meetings and influence the way the project unfolds. Intermediate clients may be the actual recipients of the final report.

Primary clients

The primary client is the person or persons who have identified the problem or issue the consultant has been called in to address and who are most immediately affected by it. It is they who will be willing to pay in order to have the issue resolved.

Unwitting clients

Unwitting clients are members of the organisation who will be affected by the intervention of the consultant. They do not initiate the project and have no direct or formal control over it. They are not aware that they will be affected by the project.

Indirect clients

Indirect clients are members of the organisation who will be affected by the intervention of the consultant and who are aware that they will be affected. However, the consultant is not aware that the project will have an impact on them. Indirect clients may feel either positive or negative about the consultant's intervention. They can be very influential behind the scenes and, unbeknown to the consultant, can facilitate or hinder the progress of the project.

Ultimate clients

Ultimate clients are the total community that will be affected by the consultant's intervention. This will include members of the organisation and, possibly, members of the organisations which come into contact with the client organisation. The ultimate client group forms the universe of whose interests the consultant must take account when progressing the project.

1.6   Modes of consulting

All managers have their own approach to the tasks they face and the way they deal with people. This is an important factor in determining the manager's style. A critical element here is the perception the manager has about his or her fundamental role in the organisation. Consulting is also characterised by different approaches which reflect fundamental assumptions about the role of the consultant. These are referred to as *modes*. In his 1987 book *Process Consultation*, Edgar Schein characterised three basic modes based on the relationship between the consultant and client: the expert, the doctor–patient and the process consulting modes.

The expert mode

In the expert mode the client identifies a particular problem with the business, analyses the problem and articulates it to the consultant. The consultant then uses his or her expertise to identify a solution to the problem. This form of consulting is often found in areas where the consultant has a specialist knowledge which the client organisation recognises that it lacks.

The doctor–patient mode

The doctor–patient mode is also characterised by the consultant acting as an expert. In this mode, however, the consultant also takes responsibility for diagnosing the problem in the first place. The client may just express an opinion that the business 'could be better' in some way or that 'something is not quite right'. Again, the consultant is expected to contribute specialist knowledge and insights to the business.

The process consulting mode

Both the expert mode and the doctor–patient mode demand that the consultant, an outsider, offers a solution – a prescription – to address the problems that the business faces. Process consulting takes a different stance. It is based on the premise that the only people who can, ultimately, help the business are the people who made it up. The consultant, as an outsider, cannot impose a solution on the organisation. What the consultant can do, however, is assist those who make up the organisation with the process of recognising problems and then discovering the solutions to them. The consultant is not so much an expert, more a facilitator of change.

Schein makes a strong case of the process mode. This is for good reasons. Consultants can recommend better ways of doing things but these will become reality only if the people who make up the organisation feel that they have ownership of the new approach, that they have had a part in creating it and that it will work for them. A process approach to consulting helps ensure that the client organisation feels it is coming up with its own solutions to its own problems and so solutions which are right for its business. A note of caution is in order though. Consultants do bring along expertise and should not be frightened to recognise that they are doing so. Further, the client will often expect the consultant to show evidence of expertise and to 'take charge' of the issues the business faces. 'After all,' it is often heard said, 'that's what they are being paid for!' An over-reliance on a process approach can sometimes leave clients feeling that they have done all the work themselves. Indeed, by the very nature of the process mode, the more proficient the consultant is in using it, the greater the risk that the client will feel that the consultant has not made a 'real' contribution.

Rather than advocate one mode as right in all circumstances the effective consultant recognises the advantages of flexibility. He or she learns when, and under what circumstances, to adopt each mode.

Team discussion point

1 Most consulting teams differentiate individual roles within the team. In this way they get the best out of a team effort. The exact profile of roles varies. Often the following roles make an appearance:

- a team co-ordinator;
- an information gatherer;
- an information analyser;
- a report writer;
- a report presenter;
- a client contactor;
- a team councillor.

These roles are discussed more fully in Section 15.1.

Allocate each of these consulting roles to one of the ten types of management role defined by Mintzberg. Note that more than one may be involved.

2 In private, consider the types of project on which, as consultant, you would not wish to work. Think in terms of business sectors and project outcomes you feel would go against your personal moral code of discretionary responsibilities. Present your discretionary responsibilities, with a brief rationale, to the rest of the group.

◆ Summary of key ideas

- Consulting is a special type of management activity.

- The consultant can be understood to provide ten types of managerial role to the client business. These are placed into three groups:
  - the interpersonal (featuring the roles of the figurehead, the liaison and the leader);
  - the informational (featuring the roles of the monitor, the disseminator and the spokesperson); and
  - the decisional (featuring the roles of the entrepreneur, the disturbance handler and the resource allocator).

- The consultant must integrate these roles with those already operating in the client business. This can happen in one of five ways:
  - supplementary (adding extra skills to those already present);
  - complementary (adding a missing role);
  - differentiating (helping managers distinguish roles among themselves);
  - integrating (helping managers build a new order of roles and individual responsibilities);
  - enhancing (helping managers make their existing roles more effective).

- The consultant must operate with four levels of managerial responsibility. These are:
  - economic (a responsibility to ensure that the projects advocated are in the best interests of the client business);
  - legal (a responsibility to ensure that projects operate within the law);
  - moral (a responsibility to ensure that project outcomes meet with the moral and ethical expectations of the client); and
  - discretionary (the right of the consultant to select or reject projects on the basis of personal ethical considerations).

Key reading

Bell, C.R. and Nadler, L. (1979) *Clients and Consultants*. Houston, TX: Gulf Publishing.

Canback, S. (1999) 'The logic of management consulting', *Journal of Management Consulting*, Vol. 10, No. 3, pp. 190–220.

Carroll, A. (1979) 'A three dimensional model of corporate performance', *Academy of Management Review*, 4 (4), 497–505.

Drucker, P.F. (1954) *The Practice of Management*. New York: Harper & Row.

Exton, W. (1982) 'Ethical and moral considerations and the principle of excellence in management consulting', *Journal of Business Ethics*, Vol. 1, No. 3, pp. 211–18.

Gallessich, J. (1985) 'Towards a meta-theory of consultation', *Counselling Psychologist*, 13 (3), 336–54.

Golembiewski, R.T. (ed.) (1993) *Handbook of Organizational Consultation*. New York: Marcell Decker.

Lundberg, C.C. (1997) 'Towards a general model of consultancy', *Journal of Organisational Change Management*, 10 (3), 193–201.

Lundberg, C.C. and Finney, M. (1987) 'Emerging models of consultancy', *Consultation* 6, (1).

Mintzberg, H. (1973) *The Nature of Managerial Work*. New York: Harper & Row.

Mintzberg, H. (1975) 'The manager's job: folklore and fact', *Harvard Business Review*, July–August, 49–61.

Schein, E.H. (1985) *Organizational Culture and Leadership*. San Francisco: Jossey-Bass.

Schein, E.H. (1987) *Process Consultation*, Vol. II. Reading, MA: Addison-Wesley.

Schein, E.H. (1988) *Process Consultation*, Vol. I (revised edn). Reading, MA: Addison-Wesley.

Schein, E.H. (1997) 'The concept of "client" from a process consultation perspective: A guide for change agents', *Journal of Organisational Change Management*, 10 (3), 202–16.

Van de Ven, A.H. and Drazin, R. (1985) 'The concept of fit in contingency theory', *Research of Organizational Behaviour*, 7, 333–65.

Discussion point

IBM's new chief executive is betting that the company's future lies in the acquisition of a consulting arm and on-demand computing

10 October 2003

By **Simon London**

The future of information technology can be found in central Cincinnati, Ohio, where Procter & Gamble has its headquarters. The 166-year-old maker of soaps and snacks has this year outsourced not only management of its IT infrastructure but also business processes including relocation services and employee benefits administration.

From next year, it will also attach tiny microchips to every pallet and carton that leaves its warehouses in order to mesh with a supply chain system being developed by Wal-Mart, its largest customer. Technology is being used to redraw corporate boundaries by building closer links with customers and suppliers.

P&G is not alone. If the 1990s were about automating functions and departments, the next decade will be about trying to integrate these 'islands of automation' so that information flows more easily through, and between, corporations.

For companies selling computers, software and related services, however, this new era raises uncomfortable questions. How do technology companies add value in a world where integration is being made possible by industry standards, rather than their own proprietary technologies? What skills are required now that clients are less interested in bits and bytes than in processes and payback?

While every company in the technology sector is facing these questions, none seems more sure of its answers than International Business Machines. Under Sam Palmisano, chairman and chief executive, IBM is investing billions of dollars in research and acquisitions under the banner of 'e-business on demand'.

The scope of Big Blue's ambition is breathtaking. Executives admit that IBM now sees itself as competing not only for the $1,000bn a year that companies spend each year on IT but also for the billions spent on processes of the kind outsourced by P&G – which last month signed a $400m, 10-year contract with IBM.

'IBM made a big bet on the 360 series [of mainframe computers] in the 1960s and by the end of it people were talking about "IBM and the seven dwarfs". If they get this right, we could have the same thing all over again,' says Charles O'Reilly, professor of organisational behaviour at Stanford business school.

When Mr Palmisano took the top job last year from Lou Gerstner, he wasted no time in putting his stamp on the company he had joined in 1973. He disbanded the 12-strong management committee that had ruled IBM for close to 100 years. He voluntarily surrendered a large slice of his annual bonus so that the money could be used to reward senior managers.

His avuncular personal style – a direct contrast to the gruff, combative Mr Gerstner – underlined the change.

Early in his tenure, however, it was unclear in which direction the 51-year-old insider would take the company. The answer came a year ago with two high-profile moves.

First, Mr Palmisano paid $3.5bn for the management consulting business of PwC, the professional services firm. The deal brought 30,000 consultants on to IBM's payroll and took it into the nascent market for 'business process outsourcing'.

Second, in a speech given razzmatazz billing as The Sam Palmisano Event, he laid out his vision for computer systems that are self-healing or 'autonomic', linked in giant 'grids' and available 'on demand', like water or electric utilities. This, he declared, was IBM's future.

At first blush, the two events seemed barely related. But IBM-ers say the combination of consulting skills and technology leadership is the essence of Mr Palmisano's strategy.

"On demand" is a statement of flexibility. It doesn't start with technology, it starts with business model and operations,' says Steve Mills, head of IBM's software division. 'The aim is to achieve smoothness of processing, from demand to delivery.'

IBM is hardly alone in promoting the opportunity for companies to take advantage of the internet, grid computing and other technologies to rethink the way they do business. Hewlett-Packard, IBM's biggest competitor in selling computer systems to corporations, calls its strategy 'the adaptive enterprise'. Peoplesoft, the software group, talks about 'real time enterprise'.

Consulting firms of all stripes are advising companies to redesign business processes to become more flexible.

Paul Horn, head of IBM's research labs, concedes: 'We are not unique in having this thought. It is all about giving companies the tools and technologies they need to be responsive and flexible.'

Mr Palmisano, in an e-mail exchange with the Financial Times, argues that even if some of the words are the same, IBM's 'understanding of their meaning goes deeper than most'.

The message would matter less if IBM had an undisputed lead in terms of technology. But it does not. Forrester, the market research group, this summer judged HP to have a narrow lead in 'organic IT' – Forrester's catch-all for the technologies required to implement the 'on-demand' or 'adaptive enterprise' agenda.

Alan Ganek, vice-president of autonomic computing at IBM, bristles at the suggestion that HP is ahead: 'In terms of rolling out the product features we are competitive with anyone – and on a trajectory to have a big lead.'

The truth is that many of the technologies required to implement the 'on-demand' or 'adaptive enterprise' agenda are still under development. Examples include software to automate the management of corporate data centres, 'web services' standards to enable computers to share data, and software to link computing resources in giant grids.

Whether IBM can out-engineer its competitors in the field remains to be seen. There is one dimension, however, in which IBM has without doubt differentiated itself from the competition: its business model. No other technology company has married so many elements within the same corporate entity.

IBM now encompasses financial services; software in a multitude of flavours (operating systems, databases, collaboration tools and middleware); hardware, ranging from mainframes to notebook computers; and the design and manufacture of microprocessors. Now Mr Palmisano's move into management consulting and business process outsourcing has taken IBM into activities that are not one step but two steps removed from the old, core business of building computers.

There is more to this than empire-building. Bruce Harreld, the former Boston

Chicken executive hired by Mr Gerstner to head IBM's strategy unit, points out that profits in the IT industry have been migrating away from makers of components – such as disc drives, microchips and operating systems – towards suppliers of software, services and consultancy.

The only notable exceptions to this trend are the two manufacturers with tremendous market power: Microsoft and Intel.

This analysis explains not only why IBM has moved up the IT value chain into services and consulting but also why it has been shedding component businesses where sustained profits look out of reach. In the latest such move, IBM last year hived off its disc drive business into a joint venture with Hitachi.

So far, IBM has executed this port-folio shuffle with remarkable efficiency. Mr Gerstner proved wrong those who said IBM's services division would be blighted by suspicions that it was a marketing front for the hardware side. Mr Palmisano is out to repeat the success as he pushes into management consulting and business process outsourcing. He must outflank competitors, convince customers and mobilise IBM's own resources.

As a result of its huge scope, IBM now competes against almost every company of note in the technology sector. In services it competes not only against outsourcers such as Electronic Data Systems and Computer Sciences Corporation but now also against IT consultants Accenture and Cap Gemini Ernst & Young. Rivals argue that trying to compete against everyone will be Big Blue's undoing in an industry where strategic partnerships remain important. 'It will be difficult for them to collaborate [with other technology companies] when there are whole groups of people within IBM trying to put their competitors out of business. There is too much baggage,' says Nora Denzel, head of HP's software business.

IBM's response is the classic defence of the vertically integrated: operating at every level from microprocessors to management consulting will become a competitive advantage as its products and services converge on the vision of 'on-demand' business.

'A few years ago you could have made the argument that services, software and servers worked independently of each other [within IBM]. Now we are working in concert. We really do get advantages from working with these folks. Growth is being unlocked,' says Bill Zeitler, head of IBM's server business. One example is co-operation between IBM's chip designers and server engineers to produce computers with the kind of security features demanded by their colleagues in services.

A further question is how many customers there are for utility-style computing, business process outsourcing and other exotic dishes on IBM's on-demand menu.

While chief executives everywhere would like their companies to be more flexible and responsive, one of the lessons of the 1990s is that technology-driven programmes of corporate change can take much longer, and cost much more, than expected. Incremental investment and a measured pace of change are the order of the day. Even companies wanting to push foward quickly are often handicapped by the complexity of modern corporate IT systems. 'The on-demand concept is going to be very important eventually. The trouble is that I don't think most companies have [IT] architectures mature enough to take advantage of it,' says Jeanne Ross, principal research scientist at the Massachusetts Institute of Technology's Centre for Information Systems Research.

Even if a significant proportion of customers are ready to embrace the 'on-demand' agenda, and Mr Palmisano can compete effectively against everyone from Intel to Accenture, a further challenge remains: how to mobilise IBM's 315,000 employees in common cause.

Mr Gerstner did this by first imposing common processes across Big Blue's previously semi-autonomous divisions and then by sheer force of personality. As is clear from *Who Says Elephants Can't Dance?*, his memoir of the turnround, the fact that IBM came close to insolvency also helped to instil discipline.

Mr Palmisano starts in a more comfortable position. IBM's revenue and earnings have held up well during the technology recession. Its balance sheet is sound. Yet the sheer scope of his empire – now ranging from consulting, which requires almost no capital investment and has planning horizons measured in months, to semiconductors, in which multi-billion-dollar investment decisions demand a five-to-10-year view – makes his job in some ways more difficult.

Herein may lie the real significance of 'e-business on demand'. The initiative gives IBM-ers a common frame of reference and a reason to co-operate, rather than squabble, across divisional boundaries. In 1993, Mr Gerstner famously declared that the last thing IBM needed at that moment was a vision. In 2003, a vision is precisely what Mr Palmisano is working hard to articulate.

Like so much of what passes for technology vision, 'e-business on demand' is about organisational change. For customers that means reinventing themselves in more a flexible, less bureaucratic guise. For IBM it means much the same.

Sam Palmisano wants to re-engineer your business. While the chairman and chief execu-tive of International Business Machines does not state it so bluntly, his lieutenants are direct.

'The leap to the next level of productivity won't come from just making the same business processes more efficient. It will involve another wave of process re-engineering, no question,' says Doug Elix, who runs IBM's global services division, including its 60,000-strong management consulting unit.

Managers who lived through the last wave of business process re-engineering might be forgiven for thinking: 'Not again.' What started in the late 1980s as an attempt to streamline and automate ended in cost-cutting and recrimination.

But it is important to separate the original idea from the pejorative term that re-engineering became.

Looking at companies as collections of business processes (order entry, fulfilment or billing) rather than functional departments (marketing, manufacturing or customer care) makes sense. Breaking down boundaries between departments to ensure smooth operations is also a legitimate goal.

The first re-engineering wave was pioneered in the early 1990s by CSC Index, the consulting arm of Computer Sciences Corporation, the information technology services and outsourcing group. The aim was to enable companies to take full advantage of powerful but enormously complex 'enterprise resource planning' (ERP) software suites.

The objective now is to use industry standard technologies – such as the internet and XML, a kind of lingua franca that enables computers to understand each other regardless of the software they run – to bring more flexibility and transparency to companies' operations.

But how can technology companies earn decent profits in a world dominated by industry standards? IBM's answer can be seen partly in its investment in software to enable companies to model the way work flows through their organisations. 'Information technology is becoming the language in which you describe business. Business design is becoming a computer science problem,' says Paul Horn, head of IBM research.

Once business processes have been described, re-engineered and automated, of course, who better to supply the equipment on which they run than IBM? Big Blue will even operate the processes for you.

But are corporations as eager to buy business process re-engineering as IBM is to sell? And if they do take the plunge, will they do so with Big Blue?

Q1 Why does IBM see its future lies in acquiring a consulting arm?

Q2 How might consulting add value to what IBM does?

Q3 What would you look for in a consulting firm that might make a good acquisition for IBM?

2 How consulting adds value

Learning outcomes

The main learning outcomes from this chapter are:

■ to understand what *motivates* a business manager to bring in a consultant;

■ to recognise the ways in which a consultant can *add value* for a business;

■ to understand the things a consultant can *offer* a business by way of valuable support.

2.1 The decision to use a consultant

Why should a business manager ask the advice of an independent consultant? The decision is a significant one for a number of reasons. There may be an immediate financial cost. Leading management consulting firms have daily rates that are well into four figures. Even if the consulting is 'free' because it is being undertaken through an undergraduate consulting team, or the cost is being borne by a small business support agency, there may still be significant indirect costs. The consultant team may need money from the client to undertake marketing research, for example.

There will also be a cost due to the need to dedicate management time to the consulting exercise. If a consulting project is to be successful, the consultant team must be supported in their activities. They will need briefing sessions and regular review meetings. The management time that must be dedicated to this is valuable, especially in a small business. Also, the activities of consultants can be upsetting to the business as a whole. Consultants will disrupt a manager's routines. If not managed effectively their involvement can raise suspicions and lead to political infighting between managers.

The decision to call in consultants is like the decision to buy anything else for the business. It happens after a consideration of the costs and benefits involved and a conclusion that the benefits outweigh the costs. This is not a one-off decision. It is something that the client business constantly assesses. Maintaining the client's confidence and the belief that the consultancy exercise has something of value to offer is a critical responsibility for the consultant.

This presents a particular challenge for *management* consultants. Consultants who work in highly technical areas such as computing and engineering clearly offer the business an expertise the business itself does not have. That they offer something different and valuable is evident. However, every business, without fail, will have *management* expertise. And the chances are (or at least the business will *feel*) that this expertise is greater than that offered by outsiders who have no knowledge of the business, its customers and its markets. In any case, even if the business recognises the need for additional management resources, why should consultants be used? Why not just employ more managers?

In short, the management consultant must constantly ask three fundamental questions:

1 What can I offer the client business that will enhance its performance and help it achieve its objectives?

2 Why will my contribution be more valuable than that which existing managers, and potential recruits, can contribute?

3 How can I communicate to the client business that what I offer is valuable?

Answering these three questions involves the application of analytical, project management and relationship-building skills. This chapter aims to set the scene for discussion of how these skills may be developed and applied by considering what a management consultant has to offer the client business.

The actual outputs of a consulting exercise centre on providing one or more of six things: information, specialist expertise, a new perspective on problems, support with internal arguments, support in gaining a critical resource and the creation of organisational change. Each of these will now be examined in depth.

2.2 Provision of information

Managers make decisions. If those decisions are to be good ones, they must be based on a full and proper understanding of the business and its situation. Information is needed if decision-making is to be effective.

Some areas of information that are critical to a business include:

■ the business's customers: their needs and buying behaviour;

■ the business's products: their design, technology and development;

■ the markets in which the business operates: their size, growth and dynamics;

■ outside organisations (including suppliers) that can offer support: who they are, what they offer and how they can be contacted;

■ the business's competitors: who they are, their strengths and the threat they pose.

Information is valuable to a business. As a result it has a cost. Information is a resource that must be managed. Much information has a direct cost – that obtained from market researchers, for example – while if there is no direct cost there may be a hidden cost in the management time and effort in gathering information. Even if managers are willing to face this cost they can do so only if they know what information is available, where it is stored and how it can be accessed. There is no guarantee they can do this.

The consultant can offer the small business manager a service in providing him or her with information which can help the business. However, this is only the start of the consultant's service. Decisions are not made on the basis of hard data alone – those data must first be processed and interpreted. The consultant can add value by analysing and presenting information in a way that enables the business manager to make effective decisions from it. To do this requires the analysis skills that will be considered in Part Two of this book.

2.3 Provision of specialist expertise

Some managers, especially those running small businesses, must be generalists. The demands of managing a small business are such that managers cannot afford to specialise in a narrow area of management such as marketing, operations or finance. They must do all these things at once. This means that at times they will seek the advice of people with specialist knowledge.

Some important areas of management that can benefit from the insights and ideas of a specialist are:

- business strategy: its development, evaluation and planning;
- marketing strategy development: defining a successful marketing mix;
- marketing research studies: utilising sophisticated research methodologies;
- promotional campaign development: how to ensure that promotional drives are well designed and cost effective;
- new product development programmes: converting customer needs into a successful product offering;
- developing proposals for financial support: identifying and approaching backers and making a good case for their support;
- information systems development: enabling managers to get the information they need to make decisions;
- planning exporting and international marketing: providing the business with a valuable route to growth.

Projects such as these benefit from the application of technical knowledge and an ability to use specialist analysis techniques. Rather than have to learn these themselves managers will often call upon the support of consultants.

The key to successful consulting in this area is not to make decisions on behalf of the manager but to *help* the manager in making their own. It is their business, they have a detailed knowledge of what it is about and know what it aims to achieve. This knowledge of the business is much greater than any the consultant can develop in the short time he or she will be working with the business. The consultant adds value by bringing along a 'tool-kit' of conceptual frameworks and idea-generating models that can be used to make sense of the information and knowledge the manager already has. This then enables the manager to make better decisions. The management of projects involving the provision of specialist expertise will be discussed further in Chapter 3.

2.4 Provision of a new perspective

Managers are not decision-making automata. They are human beings who must analyse complex environments, use well-developed but necessarily limited cognitive skills and then make decisions in the face of uncertainty.

Managers use 'cognitive maps', 'mindsets' or 'dominant logics' through which they see their managerial world. These act to focus the manager's attention on certain aspects of their environment, select particular facts as relevant, link causes to effects and then suggest courses of action. Such cognitive schema are not rational decision-making devices. They manifest themselves as the manager's interests, priorities, prejudices and judgement. Cognitive schema become established and resist change. They determine the way managers see their organisations and competitors. They have a bearing on the way joint ventures are managed, for example. Interested students are referred to the articles by Caloris, Johnson and Sarnin (1994), Daniels, Johnson and de Chernatony (1994) and Prahalad and Bettis (1986) for illuminating discussions of these issues. In a study of what he refers to as 'groupthink', Irvin L. Janis examined in great depth decisions by US Presidents and close advisory groups that led to far-reaching policy errors in international affairs (such as the Bay of Pigs invasion of Cuba and the escalation of the Korean War). He concluded that seven defects in decision-making can arise when a group becomes over-coherent and begins to share expectations and norms:

1 The group's considerations are limited to a narrow range of options – possibilities outside this set are rejected out of hand or not considered at all.

2 The initial objectives to be fulfilled by the course of action are not reviewed or challenged.

3 Newly discovered risks are not used to challenge the initially preferred course of action.

4 Courses of action initially rejected by the group are not reconsidered in the light of new information.

5 The experience and expertise of external experts are not sought or considered.

6 When new information comes to light, the group emphasises and prioritises information that backs its initial hypotheses and ignores information that contradicts them – this is sometimes referred to as a 'myside bias'.

7 The group spends little time considering how bureaucratic inertia or organisational resistance might inhibit the implementation of chosen policies.

While Janis's examples are drawn from political decision-making, their relevance to organisational decision-making in general is not in doubt. The effective consultant should be aware of these factors and be prepared to challenge group thinking.

In simple terms, managers, and close managerial groups, limit their problem-solving ability because they often get too close to an issue. They see it only in terms of their existing expectations, understanding and 'way of doing things'. The consultant can add value by helping the manager to step back from a problem, to see it in a different way and to see new means to its solution. Indeed, the consultant should ultimately aim to help managers see 'problems' really as opportunities to do things differently and perhaps better.

To do this the consultant may simply offer a fresh mind to an issue. Better still, the consultant can contribute some conceptual frameworks that open up thinking and aid the development of the manager's cognitive schema. Consultants can also offer support in helping individuals and groups become more innovative in their thinking by using the creativity techniques described in Chapter 10.

2.5 Provision of support for internal arguments

Managers do not always agree with each other. Disagreements arise over a wide range of issues. Conflicts of opinion take a variety of form. They range from open, honest exploration of different options to often quite nefarious political intriguing. They can be seen as a refreshing opening of possibilities or they may lead to smouldering resentment.

A manager may be tempted to use a consultant not so much to provide an impartial view but to back up his or her position in a debate. A consultant's opinion is of clear value here. It can be presented as 'independent' and as coming from an 'expert'. How should a consultant react to being used in this way?

The first thing to note is that the existence of different perspectives and a tolerance of dissent that allows them to be expressed is a healthy thing. Managers should be paid to think and express themselves and must be free to do so. In a competitive environment (in which ideas compete for resources) they should also be free to marshal whatever resources they can to make their case. This may include external consultants.

A consultant must recognise that he or she is not employed by a company in the abstract but rather by *individuals* within a company. The decision to use consultants is made by a group or 'decision-making unit' within the business. (This idea is covered in detail in Chapter 13.) The consultant is responsible for delivering findings and advice to individuals, and must be sensitive to the interests of those individuals and what their objectives are. This may involve supporting them in internal debates. However, the consultant must be careful.

If the consultant is too obviously in the camp of a particular manager, his or her impartiality will be impaired. Other management groups may become suspicious and will find grounds on which to reject the consultant's advice. If the consultant is seen to be twisting facts to fit a particular position, his or her credibility will be damaged. At a minimum the consultant will lose the support and goodwill of other managers. This can make the consultant's job difficult and uncomfortable. So being called upon to support a particular position, especially when it is contentious, demands sensitive management on the part of the consultant.

Management Consultancy and Skills

A few useful ground rules are as follows:

- Understand the 'politics' of the consulting exercise.
- Be sensitive to who is supporting different positions in the organisation.
- Recognise who will benefit and who will lose from the different options under discussion.
- Make sure the objectives of the consulting exercise are clear and in the open.
- Make sure any information used can be legitimated and any analysis undertaken justified.
- Build rapport with the client (a skill discussed in Chapter 19) and be honest with the client about the strengths and weaknesses of his or her argument.
- Introduce and explore options which reconcile different positions in a win-win way.
- Provide the client manager with information and insights but allow him or her to make a particular case within the business – don't be tempted to advocate it on his or her behalf.
- If put in a position where credibility might be lost, remind the manager that a loss of impartiality and credibility will defeat the point of using independent consultants in the first place!

2.6 Provision of support in gaining a critical resource

An organisation must attract resources in order to survive. One of the manager's most critical functions is attracting resources on behalf of the firm. Some important resources for the business include:

- the goodwill of customers;
- capital from investors;
- capital from government support agencies;
- people with particular skills and knowledge;
- specialist materials, equipment and services.

The consultant can offer the client business valuable support in gaining these resources. Key tasks involve identifying who can supply the particular resources, how they might be contacted and the issues involved in working with them. The consultant can be particularly valuable by working with the client and developing a communication strategy, which helps the business be successful in its approach to suppliers of critical resources.

Gaining the goodwill of customers is the function of marketing in its broadest sense. The consultant can assist in the developing of marketing plans, communication strategies and promotional campaigns. There are a number of support programmes provided by government and non-governmental organisations to businesses, especially small businesses. They take a variety of forms and change regularly. They often demand that a specific, well-organised proposal be made.

The consultant can be of great value in structuring a proposal and advising on how it might be delivered.

People, especially those with special knowledge and skills, are a critical – if not *the* critical – resource for businesses. Consultants can add much value by advising a business on its people requirements, developing an understanding of the market for such people and developing advertisements to attract them. The consultant may also advise on the interview and selection procedures.

A business may have identified suppliers of the materials and services it needs to undertake its activities. It is increasingly recognised that a business can improve its performance by actively *reverse marketing* itself to suppliers. This ensures that suppliers are aware of the business's needs and are responsive to them. It may, for example, encourage suppliers to innovate and make their offerings more suited to the buyer's requirements. This demands communication with both existing and potential suppliers, a process a consultant can assist greatly.

Many businesses will benefit from further cash injection by investors. Different stages of growth create different capital requirements. An important, and exciting, type of consulting activity is the assistance given in helping businesses gain the support of investors such as banks and venture capitalists. This involves developing a picture of the potential of the firm and why it might offer an exciting investment opportunity, identifying suitable investment organisations, preparing a business plan and perhaps even formally presenting it.

The different types of output consulting projects aim to acquire are not mutually exclusive. A consulting exercise may combine elements from a number of them. Each project should be considered on its own merit: how it adds value for the client and helps his or her business achieve its objectives.

2.7   Facilitating organisational change

All organisations are undergoing change all the time. Sometimes this is a 'natural' response to the internal dynamics of organisational growth. At other times it may be in response to an external impetus or shock that forces the organisation to modify the way in which it does things. All of the types of project above may, if they are to be implemented successfully, demand some degree of change in the structures and operating practices of the business. They may also demand that managers change their roles and responsibilities.

Change usually meets resistance. Managers, like most human beings, tend to be conservative when it comes to altering the way things are done. This is only to be expected. Although change may offer new possibilities, it also presents uncertainties. It is only natural that a manager tries to hold on to what he or she knows to be reliable and rewarding. How can he or she be certain that a different future will offer the satisfactions achieved at present? Are the changes in his or her best interest? Even if change *seems* to offer the possibility of greater satisfaction, what are the risks? What happens if the manager is dissatisfied with the outcomes? What 'insurance' against unwanted consequences can he or she call on? It is concerns such as these which can lead to distrust of consultants operating in a business.

The effective management of organisational change demands that these questions be addressed. Sometimes organisations call for change as the primary goal of the consulting exercise. In response to this, *change management* has developed as a specialist consulting area. More often, though, change management is required as a subsidiary area in order to effect the implementation of more specific organisational projects, such as business expansion or structural reorganisation. Whatever the motive and source of the change, the effective consultant must be aware of the human dimensions to the change he or she is advocating and be competent in addressing the issues it creates.

Team discussion point	Read the following short case study.

Natural Beauty Ltd is a business which manufactures and markets a range of premium-priced toiletries and beauty products with a 'no animal testing – natural ingredients' positioning. Distribution is direct to the customer via catalogue ordering. The business was started some eight years ago and after enjoying early success now employs 11 people. It recognises its success and is ambitious for growth.

Maggie, a member of the firm's 'commercial team' (the business is run on a co-operative basis and prefers not to define formal management roles), has approached an undergraduate consulting team to assist the business and help it formulate its expansion plans.

During an introductory meeting with the consulting team, Maggie explains that the business feels it has a worthwhile product with good potential in the marketplace. There is a general feeling, however, that the present approach of the business – direct marketing in the UK – is largely saturated: there is no room for further growth. If the business is to grow further it must take a different approach. There is a lot of debate within the commercial team as to the best way forward. Two options are emerging from the discussions.

The first is a move from direct marketing into retailing in the UK, possibly on a franchise basis. The second option is to expand the direct marketing approach into continental and eastern Europe. Maggie admits to preferring this option. Despite the fact it will mean finding partners in Europe to act as agents, she feels it is the lower-risk option.

She asks the consulting team to evaluate both options on behalf of the business and make a recommendation as to the best way forward.

With your team, consider which of the outputs discussed in this chapter might be involved in the final consulting project which can add value for Maggie and Natural Beauty Ltd.

◆ Summary of key ideas

- Consultants must be able to do something for a business that it is unable to do for itself.
- This must genuinely offer new value to the client business.
- Important areas of value addition include the provision of:
  - information;
  - specialist expertise;
  - a new and innovative perspective;
  - support with internal arguments;

> – support in gaining critical resources such as capital, people or productive factors;
>
> – driving organisational change.

- Many consulting projects involve a combination of a number of these elements.
- The consultant must constantly communicate to the client the new value he or she is creating through these outputs.

Key reading

Blake, R.R. and Mouton, J.S. (1976) *Consultation*. Reading, MA: Addison-Wesley.

Caloris, R., Johnson, G. and Sarnin, P. (1994) 'CEO's cognitive maps and the scope of the organisation', *Strategic Management Journal*, 15, 437–57.

Daniels, K., Johnson, G. and de Chernatony, L. (1994) 'Differences in managerial cognitions of competition', *British Journal of Management*, 5 Special Issue, S21–S29.

Dawes, P.L., Dowling, G.R. and Patterson, P.G. (1993) 'Determinants of pre-purchase search effort for management consulting services', *Journal of Business-to-Business Marketing*, Vol. 1, No. 1, pp. 31–61.

Kumar, V. and Simon, A. (2000) 'Strategic capabilities which lead to management consulting success in Australia', *Management Decision*, Vol. 38, No. 1/2, pp. 24–33.

Patterson, P.G. (2000) 'A contingency approach to modelling satisfaction with management consulting services', *Journal of Service Research*, Vol. 3, No. 2, pp. 138–52.

Prahalad, C.K. and Bettis, R.A. (1986) 'The dominant logic: A new linkage between diversity and performance', *Strategic Management Journal*, 7 (6), 485–501.

Janis, I.L. (1982) *Groupthink*. Boston, MA: Houghton Mifflin Company.

Discussion point

Why are the fads fading away?

By **Simon London**

FT

12 June 2003

Don't look now, but the zeitgeist has changed. While the last two decades of the 20th century produced wave after wave of new management ideas – total quality management, business process re-engineering, knowledge management, e-commerce – the first few years of the new millennium have been, for want of a better word, fadless.

This is bad news for the publishers, consultants and academics who profit from the spread of new management techniques.

Sales of management books have fallen by at least 30 per cent since the late 1990s, according to publishers. The few titles now achieving blockbuster status make a point of eschewing big ideas.

Examples include *Good to Great*, Jim Collins' folksy examination of established companies that make the transition to industry leadership, and *Execution: The Discipline of Getting Things Done*, Larry Bossidy's tutorial on line management.

Similarly, the management consulting firms that prospered by selling companies on the latest management concepts are facing lean times. After growing at a compound rate of 20 per cent a year through the 1980s and 1990s, consulting revenues are in decline. 'Companies have retrenched not only financially but also intellectually,' says Gary Hamel, the academic, author and consultant.

So why the change of mood? The obvious explanation is that managers are too busy dealing with the combined threats of recession, global terrorism and an equity bear market to take much interest in new ideas. Yet economic downturns have in the past been fertile times for management fads to take root. The brutal recession of the early 1980s spurred companies to adopt first 'quality circles' and then TQM. From the slump of the early 1990s arose business process re-engineering.

If history is any guide, then, it should be possible even in this dour economic climate to identify the Next Big Thing. Yet those active in the market for management ideas admit that there are no obvious contenders.

'When one fad fades it usually creates a void that gets filled by a lot of new ideas. Right now I'm not sure what comes next,' admits Eric Abrahamson, a management professor at Columbia University business school in New York.

While there is no standard definition of what constitutes a management fad, faddish ideas tend to be simple, prescriptive and transient. They are adopted widely by companies but quickly fall from favour when the hoped-for benefits fail to emerge.

Prof Abrahamson, a noted student of management fashions, adds that fads tend to be accompanied by 'emotionally charged, enthusiastic and unreasoned discourse'. For example, *Re-engineering the Corporation*, the 1993 book that stoked the business process re-engineering movement, was a self-described 'manifesto for business revolution', brimming with rhetoric about 'blowing up the old and replacing it with something new'.

Even bolder claims were made in the late 1990s by supporters of e-commerce: rethink your business model or face extinction.

Judged against these benchmarks, no management idea currently in circulation makes the grade. The closest contender is Six Sigma, the quality improvement technique developed by Motorola in the late 1980s and popularised by General Electric. But while Six Sigma has some faddish attributes – overblown claims, widespread adoption, impenetrable jargon – it is a little long in the tooth to be characterised as a fad. There are also welcome signs that interest in Six Sigma is waning (see below).

If cyclical factors do not account for the lack of interest in new ideas, what does? 'Indigestion,' is Prof Abrahamson's explanation. He argues that companies are still working on initiatives started under the influence of previous fads.

The collapse in late 2001 of Enron also left a sour taste. The Houston-based energy trading company was lionised by management writers for winning the *War for Talent* (2001), *Leading the Revolution* (2000) and embracing *Creative Destruction* (2001). Yet what was once the world's most faddist company turned out to be built on wishful thinking, accounting illusions and, quite possibly, fraud.

However, it would be easy to overestimate the Enron effect. The reaction against management ideas, fads and fashions started several years before Enron became a byword for failure.

The first signs of a backlash came in the mid-1990s, when re-engineering was blamed for the loss of thousands of jobs and the

'hollowing out' of companies in the name of efficiency. Michael Hammer and James Champy, authors of *Re-engineering the Corporation*, were vilified.

There followed a spate of books bemoaning the faddish nature of management theory. Bestsellers in this reactionary genre included *The Witch Doctors*, a 1996 dissection of fads by Economist editors John Micklethwait and Adrian Wooldridge. Fadbashing became something of a fad.

At around the same time, business schools started drawing the attention of students to the danger of being transfixed by endless new ideas. A favourite case study was AT&T, the telecommunications group, which spent an estimated $100m (£61m) a year on consulting services through the 1990s yet still destroyed shareholder value at an alarming rate.

Against this background, the current ambivalent attitude of managers towards big ideas looks like more than a mild case of indigestion. Consumers of management ideas, it appears, have become less gluttonous and more refined in their tastes.

This can only be good news, right?

Well, yes and no, says Tom Davenport, director of Accenture's Institute for Strategic Change. He argues that the capacity to innovate using management techniques is an important competitive advantage.

Thus Jack Welch, GE's recently retired chief executive, cultivated the public persona of a hard-nosed line manager. Yet he took care to surround himself with business intellectuals such as Noel Tichy, hired from the University of Michigan, and Steve Kerr, former dean of University of Southern California's Marshall School of Business.

Both academics were hired to run GE's Crotonville management training centre. Using Crotonville as a stronghold, Mr Welch launched initiatives such as 'boundarylessness', Six Sigma and 'digitisation' on his way to making GE one of the world's most respected companies.

In contrast, consider Westinghouse, the conglomerate that once rivalled GE. Mr Davenport says: 'Westinghouse was always run by scientists and engineers. It had innovative products but the only business notions it pursued involved financial analysis, acquisitions and a late-in-the-game approach to quality.'

Management Consultancy and Skills

This failure to innovate in management was one reason, he concludes, why Westinghouse was broken up in the 1990s following a string of disappointing financial results.

If Mr Davenport is correct, the hope must be that after the bull phase of the 1980s and 1990s, and the bear phase of the past few years, the market for management ideas will reach equilibrium – a state in which good ideas are fairly valued and bad ideas ignored.

This is not as utopian as it sounds. The first management blockbuster, *In Search of Excellence*, written by Tom Peters and Bob Waterman, the first modern management gurus, was published only in 1982. Before then even the most successful business books sold only a few thousand copies.

To be sure, ideas came in and out of fashion, but without the bluster and ballyhoo we have come to expect. In the pre-*In Search of Excellence* era, influential management thinkers such as Joseph Juran, the pioneer of quality control, and Bruce Henderson, strategy seer and founder of Boston Consulting Group, were hardly known outside their field. Management consulting was a cottage industry.

Is this the world to which we are now returning? Or will 'fadlessness' turn out to be just another fad? It is hard to believe that the market for management ideas will never again go through a period of irrational exuberance.

Mr Davenport says: 'We need some of the energy that management gurus and their ideas can create. We just need to be a lot smarter about managing expectations.'

The cult of Six Sigma is so last business cycle

You read it here first: Six Sigma quality, the closest thing to a management fad to have surfaced since the dotcom bust, has passed its peak. Academics measure the progress of management ideas by conducting 'bibliometric' studies: surveys of how often ideas are mentioned in magazines, journals and newspapers. This inexact science provides an insight into the prevalence of an idea in business discourse. An electronic search of US magazines and newspapers, including the Financial Times, reveals that Six Sigma garnered its first media mention in 1988. The technique had just been developed by Motorola, the electronics group.

Like all management fads, Six Sigma has cult-like aspects. Companies adopting the system commit to retraining a proportion of senior managers as 'black belts' and 'master black belts', responsible for spreading the technique through the organisation. Implementation involves breaking processes down into small steps and examining each in turn, in order to reduce defects and errors. The goal is to reduce defects to no more than 3.4 per million – the statistical meaning of Six Sigma. Six Sigma had a low profile until the mid 1990s, when it began to spread from Motorola to manufacturers such as AlliedSignal and Siebe, the UK-based engineering group.

Only when it was adopted in 1996 by General Electric, one of the world's most closely watched companies, did the buzz start to build. The peak came in 2001, when former GE executives such as James McNerney, now chief executive of 3M, and Bob Nardelli, now in charge at Home Depot, carried it to their new companies. Sun Microsystems, Bank of America and Merrill Lynch also adopted Six Sigma at about that time. Since then, however, the system's media profile has been on the wane.

Anecdotal evidence from consultants suggests that the rate of adoption by large corporations has also started to slow. Organisations now arriving late at the Six Sigma party tend to be smaller companies and public sector institutions, such as the city of St Paul, Minnesota. This slow build-up, following by a brief flowering, is typical of the life cycle of management fads. While the fads of the 1980s – such as total quality management and benchmarking – lasted for six years or more, bibliometric studies suggest that fads became shorter and more intense through the 1990s. If Six Sigma continues to follow past patterns, the next stage will be disenchantment, as companies find that the technique often achieves less than expected, followed by decline.

The seeds for such a backlash have already been sown. Six Sigma has been adopted in sectors such as banking and retailing that are far from the manufacturing environment in which it was developed. Moreover, plenty of high-profile management gurus are itching to point out its shortcomings. 'Six Sigma is good for execution problems but not for design problems. It doesn't help you if you've got a process that needs fixing,' says Michael Hammer, the consultant and *de facto* leader of the business process re-engineering movement, which favours a more radical approach. Larry Bossidy, former chairman and chief executive of AlliedSignal and Honeywell, and an early devotee, believes the technique can be applied by almost any company prepared to take it seriously. Even so, research indicates that a high proportion of management initiatives of all stripes fall short of expectations. It is difficult to see why Six Sigma should buck the trend. Says Mr Hammer: 'My leading indicator of business sentiment is Dilbert. The latest Dilbert book has a whole series of cartoons on Six Sigma.'

Q1	Detail the reasons why managers might be suspicious of consulting as a service.
Q2	'Consultants must use jargon – otherwise clients will not believe they are experts.' Comment on this statement.
Q3	Can (should?) consulting change its approach to deal with the new issues managers face?

Types of management consulting project

Learning outcomes

The learning outcomes from this chapter are:

■ to recognise the types of project consultants are called upon to undertake;

■ to appreciate the ways in which those projects add value.

3.1 Business planning and development

The discussion about the management role of consultants (Chapter 1) and the ways in which they add value (Chapter 2) makes it clear that the challenges consultants face are as wide as management itself. However, when consultants are called in to undertake work on behalf of a business, it is with a specific project in mind.

One of the broadest project types is 'business planning' or 'business development'. This is a phrase often encountered in businesses that have ambitions to grow and develop. A project of this type is a great opportunity. It offers the consultant a broad remit to contribute to the development of the business. However, some care is called for in interpretation.

Business development is a very broad term. It can mean different things to different people. The first task the consultant faces is to establish exactly what the client wants from a business development project. Sometimes the client has something specific in mind. Common outcomes desired from business development include:

■ growth of the business within its core markets by capitalising on market growth or market share increase;

■ expansion of the business into new market sectors;

■ development of new products;

■ increasing profits through cost-reduction programmes;

■ internal structural reorganisations.

The client may simply state that he or she wants to 'grow the business'. If this is so then the consultant will need to step back, evaluate the possible options for growth and propose the best path to the client. At this stage many business development projects resolve themselves into one or more of the project types listed below. The effective consultant can use the project proposal to establish exactly what the client wants and to manage his or her expectations about what can realistically be achieved.

3.2   Marketing research

Marketing research is the process through which managers discover the nature of the competitive environment in which they are operating. The objective of marketing research is to obtain information which managers can use to support their decision-making. Information reduces risk and enables managers to dedicate valuable resources in a more reliable way. Marketing research falls into two types, based on the sort of questions it aims to answer and the source of the answers. First there is *primary research* that is information collected for the specific project. This is further subdivided as follows:

■ *Quantitative research* provides answers to questions when those answers need to be expressed in statistical or numerical form. It aims to answer the 'how much, how often and how many' questions that managers pose.

■ *Qualitative research* provides answers to questions that do not demand a quantified answer. It provides the insights that answer managers' 'who, what and why' questions.

Secondary research is based on information that has been collated earlier for reasons other than the project at hand. It takes the form of existing reports, articles and commentaries that just prove to be relevant to the project.

These approaches to answering managers' questions about business opportunities are reviewed more fully in Chapter 12.

Marketing research takes a number of forms. At one level it is market 'intelligence': an ongoing review of articles, reports and customer gossip about a market. At another level it might be a cognitive study aimed at consolidating the experience of a group of managers and insights into their working environment. Ultimately, it can demand the use of complex statistical techniques or sophisticated psychometric methodologies to develop a complete picture of how customers see and buy a product category and the details of their expenditure. At this level marketing research demands a high degree of expertise on the part of the researcher.

Good consultants recognise their limitations. They know when it is time to call in the expert marketing researcher. This does not mean they cannot add value for the client. A consultant is in a better position to develop a brief for a professional marketing research exercise and can help the client understand what the results mean. For this reason, consultants often subcontract marketing research when necessary.

3.3   Marketing strategy development

Marketing research is a powerful approach to identifying business opportunities. Exploiting them, though, requires a *marketing strategy*. A marketing strategy defines the approach the business will take in order to get the customers' attention and – critically – get them to spend their money on the business's products or services.

The key elements of a marketing strategy are dictated by the marketing mix. The marketing strategy will be built on the answers to the following questions:

- What products do customers want from a sector's producers?
- In what way are competitors failing to provide these products?
- What price are customers expecting or willing to pay?
- What channels are available for getting the product to the customer?
- Who might be the partners in the distribution process?
- How might they be approached?
- In what ways can customers be informed that the product is available?
- How can the customers' interest be stimulated through promotion?

In developing a marketing strategy the consultant is answering these questions. Often, getting the answers will demand the contribution of experts such as marketing researchers and advertising specialists. If this is the case the consultant can be involved in a number of ways. He or she might simply be asked to highlight these needs so that the client can pick up the project. Alternatively he or she may be invited in to support the client in working with such experts. In some cases, the client may give the consultant complete control and have him or her subcontract work with specialists as an integral part of the consulting project.

Implementing a marketing strategy involves a range of activities. The implementation can resolve itself into the product development, promotional and sales activity projects detailed below. Clearly, an effective, well-presented marketing strategy project creates follow-up opportunities for the consultant.

3.4   Developing promotional campaigns

A promotional campaign is any programme of activities dedicated to informing customers about a product, stimulating their interest and encouraging purchase. Examples include advertising and public relations campaigns, sales drives, direct mailings, exhibitions and in-store demonstrations.

Though each of these approaches is different, the consultant faces a common profile of tasks when developing such campaigns. The key questions the client will be asking will be:

- What methods will prove to be cost effective?
- What will be the mechanics of running the campaign?
- How can it be monitored?

The consultant must develop an understanding of how much it will cost, using each technique available, to contact a potential customer, the impact each is likely to have on the potential customer, the likelihood that they will make a purchase, how much they will spend if they do and over what period. A comparison of the techniques can then be made which, in light of the client's promotional objectives and available budget, provides the basis for designing an effective promotional plan.

3.5 Planning sales force activity

For many businesses, especially small and medium-sized ones, the sales team is the primary promotional tool. Expenditure on sales force activity is one of the most important investments the firm will make. Detailed and thoughtful planning of sales force activity is a process which offers real returns. This is an area in which the consultant can offer valuable support. Some of the key issues that might be addressed include the following.

Overall organisation of the team

How should the team be organised? For what should individual sales people have responsibility? Options include a geographic area, a group of customers or a product category. The answer will depend on the size of the team, the type and range of products sold and the nature and size of customers.

Sales team training

What skills do the sales team need in order to be effective? How might they be encouraged to focus on customer service rather than 'short-term' sales? How might they become more active in obtaining market intelligence while out selling? Might the sales team use their knowledge of customers to contribute more directly to new product development?

Sales team motivation

Most sales people are motivated by a combination of fixed salary and a performance-based bonus. This bonus element is critical in directing and motivating the sales team. Some important issues to be addressed when designing the bonus scheme include:

- What level of expenditure do managers wish to invest in the bonus scheme?
- How can the bonus be used to align the thrust of the sales with the firm's overall strategic objectives?
- Will the sales team find the scheme transparent and easy to understand?
- Will it be seen as 'fair'?
- Does it leave latitude for managers to deal with contingencies and conflicts?
- How will the bonus scheme fit with the organisation's broader motivational and development strategy?

Planning sales campaigns

A sales campaign is a plan detailing how the sales team will be used. It may reflect ongoing activity or it may be a short-term period of special activity to support, say, a new product launch, the firm's entry into a new geographic area or a move into a new customer sector. The important decision elements of a sales campaign include:

- which members of the sales force will be involved;
- what products will be given priority;
- which customers will be targeted;
- in what geographic area;
- the sales literature that will be used;
- the special prices and deals that can be used to motivate purchase;
- bonuses and rewards for sales performance;
- other marketing and PR activity that will support the sales drive.

The decision about each of these elements will affect not only the cost of the promotion but also its overall success. Insights may be gained from both the qualitative management experience and quantitative management science methods. Clearly, there is an opportunity for the consultant to add considerable value here.

3.6 New product development

It is a business's products (which can include services as well as tangible products) that the customer ultimately buys. They are the basis on which a business is built. A well-designed product that addresses the customer's needs in an effective manner is only part of a business success story: but it is an *essential* part. New product development represents a complex project that draws in most, if not all, of the firm's functions. Research and development, marketing and sales, production, purchasing and human resources will all be called upon to make a contribution. New product development is often undertaken by interdisciplinary teams, which cut across departmental boundaries.

The consultant can offer support to the new product development programme in a number of ways. The most important include:

- understanding the customer's needs through market research;
- technical advice on product development;
- identifying and contacting suppliers of critical components;
- development of marketing and PR campaigns to support the launch;
- developing promotion campaigns to get distributors on board;
- financial planning and evaluation of the return on new product investment.

In a broader sense, the consultant may be invited in to facilitate change management programmes designed to integrate the new product development team and enhance its performance.

3.7   Developing proposals for financial support

Businesses often need injections of capital. New start-ups and high-growth businesses in particular need funds – in addition to those provided by customers – in order to ensure they reach their potential. Investment capital can be obtained from a number of sources. Banks and venture capital companies are important to new and high-growth businesses. Government grants may be available to small businesses in some areas. More mature firms can obtain funds from stock market flotation.

Consultants are often called in to offer advice in four critical areas:

■ evaluation of the business's investment needs;

■ identification of funding providers and how they might be contacted;

■ developing an understanding of the criteria employed by funding providers and how these might be addressed;

■ developing communications with funding providers, particularly in relation to proposals and business plans.

Though general in form, these project areas will vary in their details according to the business and the fund provider it is approaching.

3.8   Staff recruitment

People, it is often said, are a business's most important resource. Attracting the right sort of people to contribute to the business is certainly an important challenge managers must address, especially those in high-growth businesses.

A consultant can be of value in this area in several ways. Important contributions to recruitment projects might include:

■ assessing the firm's human resource requirement and identifying skill and knowledge gaps, both currently and predicting for the future;

■ creating advertisements (with insights into both message and medium) to attract the right people;

■ developing assessment criteria, interview procedures and, possibly, psychometric testing of candidates;

■ advice on the reimbursement packages new recruits will expect.

Successful recruitment can demand a degree of specialist knowledge. As a result it is often an area in which dedicated consultants operate.

3.9   Information systems development

Managers need information if they are to make good decisions. They need information on both the business's external situation – its competitive environment – and its internal state. Information is, as Paul Tom points out in his 1987 book, a

Management Consultancy and Skills

corporate resource. Management information systems aim to collect and organise such information and present it to managers in a usable form. Nowadays management information systems are usually based on computer technology. They therefore require a good deal of technical expertise to implement. However, even the non-technical consultant can add value, particularly in developing an understanding of the information needs of the business, the way in which information flows around the organisation and the competitive advantage that might be gained through investment in information technology. Such a consulting exercise provides a sound basis on which to progress the technical implementation and helps ensure that it will be rewarding.

3.10 Exporting and international marketing

Most large firms have an international if not a truly global dimension to their operations. Many high-growth firms soon recognise the opportunity the international stage offers them as a route for expansion. For most businesses, moving into the international arena is a step into the unknown. They lack experience of the competitive and regulatory environment. Their understanding of the customers will be limited. They must deal with distributors and partners they have not dealt with before. The most successful moves into international operations are those which are based on sound preliminary research and a thorough understanding of what to expect. The consultant can assist this process of discovery.

In particular the consultant can supply:

- an overall insight into regional, social and macroeconomic development;
- an analysis of the growth and evolution of specific markets;
- an evaluation of consumer needs and requirements and how these are being satisfied currently;
- information on regulatory and legal issues;
- details of the existing supply structure and competitors present;
- an investigation into distribution channels and possible partners;
- information on advertising and promotional opportunities.

These insights can be used to develop an overall strategy of entry into international markets, including decisions such as whether to rely on exporting or to set up permanent international operations.

A consultant may be called in to address any one of these projects in a 'pure' form. The boundaries between the projects are somewhat arbitrary, though. Many real projects combine aspects of these project types. International marketing will involve marketing research. A new product development or management information project may demand the recruitment of specialist staff. Business development may demand that financing be obtained from external investors. However, planning of such hybrid projects is usually helped by resolving them into their core aspects. This clarifies both the setting of objectives and the monitoring of their delivery.

3.11 Creative consulting in arts, media and design

A great deal of consulting activity involves the application of specialist technical expertise. Even within technologically orientated organisations it is important to draw a distinction between consulting that aims to contribute to technical know-how, expertise and outputs and management consulting that aims to facilitate managerial structures that enhance such activity.

Design is of increasing importance to businesses. *Exogenous* technological advances – those that a group of firms share rather than being the property of a single firm – mean that few businesses have access to a unique technology that makes a core product different to its competitors. In many categories most offerings from different firms perform in pretty much the same way (think of mid-price cars, airlines and personal computers!). To ensure differentiation from competitors – ensuring the buyer feels the product is different in a substantive way – means that producers must turn to aesthetic and emotional benefits rather than core performance benefits. Those with an expertise in the arts, media and design are in a position to add value directly by providing technical support to such projects. Specialist consulting agencies exist to undertake this. Typical projects include product and packaging design, the development of communication strategies (increasingly via the Internet) and general advertising.

However, the general management consultant, who does not have such technical knowledge, should never be intimidated by the technical nature of the task in hand. General consultants can still add value by refining and clarifying what managers want from creative consulting. They can facilitate the development of managerial processes and structures that make best use of the opportunities creative design offers. More immediately, they can help managers develop specific and clear-sighted briefings for creative designers.

3.12 Technical consulting in science and engineering

A major boost to technical consulting in science and engineering has been the rapid growth in science parks, often associated with universities, that aim to provide a commercial conduit between the university's fundamental – 'blue-sky' – research and the application of that technology to practical products. Many major advances in medicine, electronics, chemical engineering and information technology have arisen through this route.

An interesting example is the firm set up by three mathematicians based at the Massachusetts Institute of Technology – Adi Shamir, Ron Rivest and Leonard Adleman – to promote a cryptographic encryption key based on prime numbers known as RSA. Their work started in number theory, which is concerned with the basic properties, perhaps the most abstract and, ostensively at least, practically, applicable area of mathematics. However, it was found that their mathematical algorithm could be used to provide a high degree of security for credit card transactions on the Internet, an application of enormous commercial value.

Management Consultancy and Skills

The importance of the distinction between providing direct technical assistance and the provision of managerial advice in how to make best use of technology applies as much to consulting in science and engineering as it does to consulting in the creative arts. Technical innovations do not promote themselves. The experts who develop ideas are not usually equipped with the managerial skills necessary to set up firms to produce and promote them effectively in a competitive marketplace. Often venture capitalists and other financial backers will wish to see a high degree of managerial expertise complementing the technical ability of the innovation team. Consultants have a clear role to play here.

Team discussion point	Chapter 2 discussed the mechanisms by which consultants can create value for their clients. In summary, these were:

- the provision of information;
- the provision of specialist expertise;
- the provision of a new perspective;
- the provision of support for internal arguments;
- the provision of support in gaining a critical resource;
- the creation of organisational change.

Each member of the team should select one of the project types listed in this chapter. Using the framework in Chapter 2, each team member should prepare and deliver a short (one-page) presentation detailing how each means of value creation can support the project type selected and ensure that its outcomes will be satisfactory for the client.

◆ Summary of key ideas

Consultants take on a variety of projects on behalf of their clients. The most common include:

- business planning and development;
- marketing research;
- marketing strategy development;
- developing promotional campaigns;
- planning sales activity;
- new product development;
- developing proposals for financial support;
- staff recruitment;
- information systems development;
- exporting and international marketing.

Some projects may combine one or more of these pure types.

Key reading

Czerniawska, F. (2002) *The Intelligent Client: Managing Your Management Consultant*. London: Hodder Arnold H&S.

Floyd, C. (1997) *Managing Technology for Corporate Success*. Aldershot: Gower.

Kotler, P. (2001) *Principles of Marketing: European Edition*. Harlow, Essex: FT Prentice Hall.

Tom, P.L. (1987) *Managing Information as a Corporate Resource*. Glenview, IL: Scott, Foresman and Co.

Discussion point

Positive prognosis from HR health check

By **Richard Donkin**

22 May 2003

Companies pay management consultants big bucks in the belief that the fees will soon be recovered as a result of the strategies, cost savings and efficiencies that the consultants have identified.

Business understands this relationship. If you need external expertise, you pay for it. The saying 'The best things in life are free' is counter-intuitive to the principles of capitalism.

Perhaps this explains why Bath University's school of management had the devil of a job persuading companies to let them take an in-depth look at their human resources systems. John Purcell, the school's professor of human resource management, believes the reluctance in some cases came down to control of the findings.

'A management consultant's report would be to the company and the company alone. Our objective is to publish our findings. We gave the co-operating employers absolute control over factual information but we reserved the right to interpret the findings,' he says.

Good for him – and good for the 12 companies and public sector employers who buried their anxieties and let in the academics. Three years later, these employers have the benefit of some first-rate analysis that cost them no more than the time expended by staff in co-operating with the researchers.

The result of this co-operation, according to findings published at a London-based seminar last week, is a much sharper focus on the human resources policies that make a difference to their businesses.

The three-year research project by the management school, funded by the Chartered Institute of Personnel and Development, worked as a health check on HR policies: the researchers were able to identify those policies that worked best, allowing companies to install or improve the ones that made a big difference.

In fact the number of policies, the researchers found, was less critical than the way they were executed. A well administered appraisal system, for example, achieves positive results. But poorly run appraisals can prove more harmful to staff morale than the absence of any system, says Prof Purcell.

Tesco, the supermarket chain, tested the methodology by asking the researchers to assess four stores in very similar towns. One was a high-performing store, two were average and one was performing comparatively poorly; but the researchers were not told where the stores stood in terms of their profitability.

Using interviews covering a series of HR policies, the team was able to identify one store that was out of line with the others. It was rated comparatively poorly for its training provision, pay and knowledge-sharing. It also scored badly on areas connected with job satisfaction. Its ratings for allowing staff to influence their jobs and for responding to staff suggestions were markedly lower than the other stores in the survey.

These areas of job influence, what the report describes as 'controlling dimensions of discretion', tend to be directly connected with the quality of management. This was particularly discernible at Tesco, which operates its stores under highly standardised and centralised policies and procedures.

In theory, therefore, each store should operate much like another. In practice, however, the role of the store manager and the senior management team and the way they relate to the section managers (whose work rate scored the highest among all the case studies) is crucial.

The manager of the poorly performing store was exposed as over-controlling in his methods. It was clear that he did not give his section managers enough latitude and did not respond effectively to comments from staff. It should surprise no one to learn that he no longer works for Tesco.

The problem of bad managers may be more widespread in the UK than this one example suggests. In a survey of 700 senior HR professionals featured in the magazine Personnel Today last week, three-quarters of those questioned were concerned at the capabilities of line managers, highlighting leadership and people management among the skills found wanting.

In the past, such comments have been dismissed as a product of HR antipathy to the hierarchy. But the Bath research has demonstrated that HR not only is in a position to point out problems but can also provide the remedies. The research has created a model of employee performance that relies on a combination of ability, motivation and opportunity.

Motivation, organisational commitment and the chance to shine, says Prof Purcell, are all important if employees are to exercise the kind of discretionary behaviour that makes the difference between excellent and ordinary performance.

This is particularly significant among line managers, he believes. 'Line managers' behaviour bringing policies to life does make a very big difference,' he says. Yet the tacit knowledge that this has always been the case was ignored in the re-engineering of the 1990s that swept through business like a revolutionary class war.

At Selfridges, the department store that was another of the featured companies, the HR team had succeeded in securing a more central role under former chief executive Vittorio Radice, who led the store's transformation from dull Oxford Street retailer to the innovative and expanding 'house of brands' it is today.

The way the store runs its branded departments means that a high proportion of sales staff are not employed by Selfridges but by the various brand-owners. These so-called 'concessionary staff' undergo the same training as their Selfridges counterparts, with opportunities to gain job qualifications and in-store promotion. Staff training has a long history at Selfridges, which was talking about its valued 'human resources' as long ago as 1920.

Selfridges must be doing something right. A few weeks ago, when 600 people took off their clothes in the Oxford Street store to be photographed on the escalators by Spencer Tunick, an installation artist, a third of them were staff. Now that's what I call commitment.

Understanding The People and Performance Link: Unlocking the Black Box is published by the Chartered Institute of Personnel and Development, price £50,
www.cipdpublishing.co.uk tel 0870 800 3366 ..
richard.donkin@ft.com

Q1 Why might managers be suspicious of consulting projects offered 'for free'?

Q2 Select three different types of project from those listed in this chapter and detail a selling strategy for them offered on a no-fee basis.

Q3 How would your selling strategy change if you were offering them on a full-fee basis?

The consulting process

4.1 Overview of the process

A *process* is a sequence of events directed towards achieving some overall outcome. When we recognise a process we recognise the interconnectedness and interrelatedness of independent actions. It is not just *what* we do that matters. It is the *order* in which we do things.

A consulting project will be successful only if the right actions are carried out in the right order. A client will not accept a solution to a problem he or she does not yet recognise exists. It is premature to decide on the best options for a business if no analysis of what that business is about has been carried out. It is no good presenting the customer with a bill if he or she has not received any advice yet!

Most consulting projects go through nine stages. The process starts with an initial contact between the consultant and the client. This is followed by a recognition that the consultant can help the business in some way and a project is initiated. In the third stage the consultant will suggest further investigation into and analysis of the issues facing the client's business before proposing a set of formal objectives that both should work towards. Fourthly, the consultant will then document those objectives in a formal proposal. This

Management Consultancy and Skills

constitutes the 'contract' between the consultant and client. The fifth stage requires developing a project charter that supports this contract. The development of the project can only be undertaken on the basis of a sound understanding of the business and its context. The sixth stage of the project involves undertaking this analysis. This stage never really ends, as further analysis may be required as the project progresses, even in the final follow-up stage.

The seventh stage is the implementation of the project. This stage will demand further information gathering, evaluation of the business issues, analysis and evaluation of options and formulation of recommendations. When this is complete, the eighth stage involves communicating those findings and recommendations back to the client in some way. This communication will aim to encourage and facilitate implementation. In the final stage, the consultant may maintain contact with the client if this can in some way benefit one or preferably both parties. This process is illustrated in Figure 4.1.

Every consulting project is different. The nine stages of different consulting exercises will vary in length and complexity. The consultant's approach to each stage will differ depending on the nature of the consulting project and the client with whom he or she is working. This said, every successful consulting project achieves its aims because the consultant has managed each stage effectively. We will now examine each stage in detail.

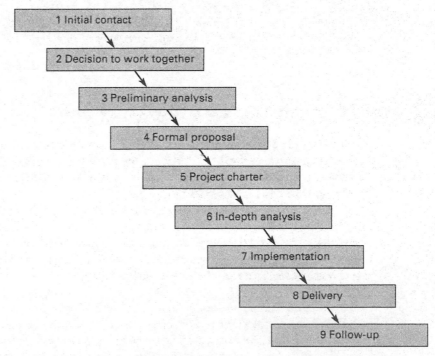

Figure 4.1 Dynamics of the consulting project

Management Consultancy and Skills

4.2 Initial contact

Consultants meet with potential clients in a great number of forums. In principle, there are four mechanisms by which the consultant and client meet and decide they should work together.

- The consultant and client meet in an impromptu way.
- The consultant proposes his or her services to a client.
- The client seeks out the services of a particular consultant.
- A third party brings the consultant and client together.

Project initiation may occur with both consultant and client sharing a clear understanding of what the client wants. Quite often, though, the client is unclear as to specific objectives. He or she may just feel that things could be better with the business. In this case, the consultant must be adept at probing the client and getting him or her to reveal something about the business. Such probing must be undertaken with subtlety if it is not to be seen as obvious and invasive. This demands effective use of the questioning techniques detailed in Section 19.3.

Business networks bring many people together seeking ways to help each other. This is often an important forum for consultants to make contact and present what they have to offer. Business networks exist in and between business sectors. They may be stimulated by professional bodies, which will set up conferences and seminars. An example is the *Marketing Network* associated with the Chartered Institute of Marketing.

Consultants, like any other business service providers, are responsible for promoting the service they offer to their customers. This may be through professional bodies that offer some endorsement for the service on offer and support its promotion. Consultants can also promote themselves via advertising, particularly in specialist industry publications. Direct marketing to potential clients may also be a useful tool.

Clients may sometimes approach a consultant in search of advice. This may be in response to the consultant's promotional activities or be a result of recommendations from another satisfied customer.

4.3 Initiating the project

The decision to work together is a significant one for both the client and the consultant. The client is making the decision to invest in his or her business through buying the insights and advice of an outside expert. The consultant is deciding to offer his or her expertise to the client. This demands a considerable commitment and means the consultant cannot pursue other projects. Taking on a particular project represents an *opportunity cost* to the consultant.

Both client and consultant must be clear on exactly what is being initiated. It could be the entire project. It is more likely, though, that it is actually an invitation by the client to the consultant to make a *formal proposal* for the project (stage 4 of the process). This will certainly be the case if the consultant is being invited to make a proposal or pitch in competition with other consultants. Even if no competition is involved and the client is inviting the consultant to move straight on to the full project, an interim proposal is still a good idea. As discussed below, it is an effective means of managing the client's expectations about the project's outcomes.

The actual initiation of the project can take a variety of forms. The degree of formality that the initiation takes is particularly important. It may be a simple verbal agreement to go ahead. It may take the form of an informal note or letter. In other cases the project may be initiated by a formal and detailed contract.

The formality of the initiation will reflect the interests of both client and consultant. A number of factors will affect this, the most important of which are as follows.

How well the consultant and client know each other

If the consultant and client know each other very well, the project can be initiated with a low degree of formality. If there is a good deal of trust between both parties to the exercise then both will rely on the fact that the details of the project can be adjusted through mutual agreement as understanding develops.

Expectations from the project

The agreement to initiate the project will reflect the expectations of the client as to the outcomes of the project. If those expectations have been thoroughly thought through by the client and have been well defined, the client may use the initiation of the project as an opportunity to articulate those outcomes and communicate them to the consultant. In this case the initiation may take a more formal guise.

Level of resources committed to the project by the client

The more the client is likely to invest in the consulting exercise (by way of money, people and time), the more likely it is that he or she will want to document the decision in some way and to formalise the initiation.

Investment by the consultant in making the formal proposal

As noted below, preparing the formal proposal demands time, energy and possibly direct expenditure on the part of the consultant. How much commitment is made here will depend on the nature (and value) of the project, the need to collect information, the level of detail in the proposal and the mechanism of delivering it to the client. A great deal of preparation may be needed, especially if the pitch for the project is a competitive one. In this case, the consultant may require the client to offer a degree of commitment to undertaking the project and to make this commitment explicit in the terms of the proposal.

The need to communicate within the client business

If the client business is quite large, a manager in the middle of the organisational hierarchy may initiate the consulting exercise. If so, such a person may want to record the decision to initiate a consulting exercise. He or she may need to do so in order to inform superiors and to comply with internal decision-control procedures.

The need to inform third parties

The delivery of the exercise may be of interest to a number of people outside the client organisation. Often institutional investors such as banks and venture capitalists will demand the opinions of outside experts before committing capital. If the business is the subject of a possible acquisition, the acquirer may require that a consultant evaluate the business. In these cases the initiation may be formalised so as to keep the third party informed.

4.4 Preliminary analysis of the issues

The consultant must make a decision about what can be achieved by the consulting exercise. It is this that will be offered to the client in the formal proposal. This decision must be based on an understanding of the business and its situation. Background research and an evaluation of the business will be called for. This stage calls on the analytical approaches discussed in Chapter 10.

There are three key questions to be answered by this preliminary analysis:

1 What are the major opportunities and issues the business faces?

2 What prevents the business capitalising on the opportunity or dealing with the issues?

3 How can the consultant's service help the business overcome this block?

The formal proposal will be made around the answers to these questions.

It should not be forgotten that this is a *preliminary* analysis. Any analysis demands an investment of time and effort (and possibly direct expenditure) in developing an understanding. This investment must be of the right order for the project. On the one hand it should be sufficient so that a proposal can be made which is relevant, meaningful and, critically, attractive to the client. If the consultant is in a competitive situation, then investing in this understanding may offer good dividends. On the other hand, the investment should not be too high in relation to the final scope of the project. Clients rarely pay the consultant for making the initial proposal. The costing of this preliminary evaluation must, ultimately, be included in the overall bill for the exercise. If the pitch is competitive, the consultant will not see any return on the investment if the proposal is not successful.

Management Consultancy and Skills

53

A simple test can be applied before a consultant dedicates resources to gaining new information at this stage. This is to ask how the information will be used. If it is needed to develop an understanding of how the client *potentially* may be helped, it may be useful. If it will be used only for *delivering* that help, it can safely be left until a commitment has been made to the full project.

4.5 Defining objectives

A management project of any significance should be defined around its *objectives*; that is, what it aims to achieve. Objectives provide a means of communicating the reason the project exists, provide a common focal point for all involved and act as an indication of what level of investment is appropriate, given the options available for other projects.

Defining proper objectives is a very important part of the project. A critical element in the success of the consulting exercise is that its objectives are well defined and understood by all involved. It is the objectives of the project that the client is 'buying'. At this stage it should be noted that objectives represent the link between where the business is now and where it might be with the consultant's help. It is also useful to note that objectives are different from *outcomes*. An objective is what the consulting project will achieve. An outcome is what the business will be able to do as a result of the consulting exercise.

4.6 Making a formal proposal

The formal proposal is a pivotal point in the consulting exercise. It represents the consultant's statement of what he or she can achieve on behalf of the client business. The proposal defines what the client will be paying for. Investing time and effort in the preparation and communication of a good proposal always pays dividends.

A full exploration of the details to be included in and the structuring and writing of a formal proposal is given in Chapter 6. An important point to be made at this stage is that the proposal operates at a number of levels.

The key functions of the proposal are as follows. The proposal:

- provides a concise and efficient means of communicating the objectives of the project to the client;
- guides analysis and ensures that investment in information gathering is at an appropriate level;
- gives the consulting team a common focus when differentiating tasks and organising the project delivery;
- provides a fixed point of reference which can be referred back to if it is felt the project is drifting;
- can be used to manage the expectations of the client.

Management Consultancy and Skills

This last point is very important. If properly written and presented, the proposal prevents expectations of the outcomes becoming unrealistic. This can easily happen and if expectations get too high, even a good project will disappoint the client.

4.7 The project charter

This is discussed in more detail in Section 8.1. This provides the key document for the project and the 'ground rules' for the team. The project charter is a very useful document, not just for the client but for the consulting team as well. It acts as an anchor for the project and manages the expectations of both parties. It is often kept to one page and is always agreed by the project team at the start. It can change only if all members of the team agree and they have very strong reasons for changing it.

4.8 Project progression

Progression represents the actual undertaking of the project. At this stage the consultant applies his or her insights, expertise and knowledge to create a new understanding for the client. Every consulting project has its own character but also includes some essential activities, which are common to most projects. The important ones are as follows.

Information gathering

An understanding of the business and its context must be developed. Information is needed to understand the opportunities and issues the business faces and its capabilities in relation to them. Information gathering is an ongoing activity that is assisted by the techniques discussed in Chapter 12. A crucial point that will be developed in this discussion is that the need for information must always be challenged in relation to its cost and the objectives of the project.

Analysis and interpretation

Information on its own is of little use. It is the *sense* that the consultant can make of it that is valuable for the client. The consultant must interpret the information and create a new perspective from it. Developing this new perspective can be aided by the creative approaches described in Chapter 10 and the auditing techniques in Chapter 11. Analysis does not occur in isolation from information gathering: it is iterative with it. Information prompts analysis and analysis highlights information gaps.

Interaction with the client business

The consultant team, or a representative of it, will usually maintain contact with a manager, or managers, in the client business. This may be driven by the need to keep the client informed of the progression of the project. It may also be a consequence of the need to obtain further information about the business. Contact can be through meetings, telephone calls, written and electronic communications. Whatever the motivation, or the means, interacting with the client is an opportunity not just to give and obtain information but also to build a relationship with the client, which can lead to a more effective project. Approaches to building this relationship are discussed in Chapter 19.

Project management and monitoring

The project proposal and charter commit the consultant to three things. These are a set of *agreed objectives* that will be delivered at a *specified time* for a *given budget*. Slippage in any one of these aspects can lead to unsatisfactory outcomes for the client, the consultant or both. Monitoring is the activity dedicated to ensuring that the project is progressing in a satisfactory manner. It will involve ensuring that key events are happening on time and that expenditure is in line with that anticipated. Effective monitoring procedures ensure that if slippage does occur, remedial action can be taken to get the project back on track.

Keeping records

Effective consultants invest time in keeping a good record of the progression of a project. As a minimum, this will be a file of important documents and notes on communications. This may be supplemented by a project log such as that discussed in Chapter 6. It may involve more formal records such as plans and budgets.

Keeping records is good practice for several reasons. It enables progression of the project to be monitored. Queries may be resolved quickly by reference back to communications. Most important, though, is the fact that a good set of records allows the consultant to reflect on the project, learn from the experience in an active way and so enhance performance in the future.

4.9   Communicating the findings

Consulting is an activity which can build value through interaction with the client. The benefits of the exercise are delivered over time, especially if a process consulting approach is taken. Even so, the client will see the final communication of the results of the consulting exercise as an important event. This is often seen as the delivery of the actual consulting 'product' – the tangible item the client has actually paid for.

4.10   Following up

There are a variety of reasons why the client and consultant might want to keep in touch after the formal outputs of the project have been delivered. Some of the more important are as follows.

Advice on implementation

The final report will make a series of recommendations to the client. It is usually up to the client to put those recommendations into practice. However, the client may feel the need to call further upon the skills and insights of the consultant for clarification of points in the final report and for guidance on how implementation might be effected. An agreement to support the client in this way may be a feature of the project proposal.

Preparing ground for new project

Even if the consultant has not made an explicit agreement to support the client after the final report has been delivered, it may be judicious to do so. If the client is satisfied with the outputs of the project then there is the possibility that the client and consultant may both gain by working together on a future project.

Seeking an endorsement

A consultant builds his or her career on reputation. If a project has been undertaken well, that is something the consultant might use in the future. The endorsement of a satisfied client, a statement that he or she has benefited from the advice of the consultant, can be very valuable, particularly if the client represents a well-known business which is challenging in the demands it makes on its suppliers. Of course, confidentiality is important. Some circumspection may be needed in referring to a particular project. But this is an issue that can usually be resolved.

Project review and evaluation

As noted in the point about record keeping, effective consultants engage in active learning. They are always alert to the possibility of improving their performance. This demands that they learn from their experiences. Reviewing how the project went, in terms of both positives to be repeated and negatives to learn from, is an important part of this. The views of the client may be sought, either through informal discussion or by means of a more formal questionnaire.

Networking

The consultant may seek to maintain a relationship with the client merely to build his or her presence in the business network. The benefits may not be immediately clear, but awareness of the consultant and what he or she can offer is built. There is always the possibility that new business will emerge if the client recommends the consultant to a contact.

Team discussion point	Most consulting teams differentiate individual roles within the team. In this way they get the best out of a team effort. The exact profile of roles varies. Often the following roles make an appearance:

- a team co-ordinator;
- an information gatherer;
- an information analyser;
- a report writer;
- a report presenter;
- a client contactor;
- a team councillor.

These roles are discussed more fully in Section 13.2.

Discuss, as a group, how each role might contribute to each stage of the consulting process. You may care to set up a grid summarising your ideas (stages vertically and roles horizontally). Retain this for planning individual involvement in the project when the project charter is developed.

Summary of key ideas

A consulting exercise is a project that moves through a number of distinct stages. The key stages are:

- initiation: the consultant and client meet and decide to work together;
- preliminary analysis: development of an understanding of what the consultant can do for the client;
- formal proposal: a statement by the consultant to the client of what the project will achieve for the business;
- progression of project: actual undertaking of the project;
- delivery of results: communicating the findings to the client;
- following up: post-delivery activities.

Different projects move through these stages in different ways but each represents a distinct management challenge that can be met by using analysis, project management and relationship-building skills.

Key reading

Coster, R.A. and Dalton, D.R. (1993) 'Management Consulting: Planning, entry and performance', *Journal of Counseling and Development*, Vol. 72, No. 2, pp. 191–8.

Dougherty, A.M. (1990) *Consultation; Practice and Perspectives*. Pacific Grove, CA: Brookes Cole.

Kakabadse, A., Ludlow, R. and Vinnicombe, S. (1988) *Working in Organizations*. London: Penguin.

Lippitt, G. and Lippitt, R. (1994) *The Consulting Process in Action*. Chichester, West Sussex: Pfeiffer Wiley.

Robbins, S.P. (1988) *Essentials of Organizational Behaviour* (2nd edn). Upper Saddle River, NJ: Prentice-Hall.

Sturdy, A. (1997) 'The consultancy process – an insecure business', *Journal of Management Studies*, 34 (3), 389–413.

Discussion point

A flair for stating the obvious

By **Michael Skapinker**

29 January 2003

A reader sends the following story. A shepherd is tending his flock when a Jeep screeches to a halt beside him. The driver hops out and says: 'If I tell you how many sheep you've got, will you give me one?' The shepherd looks him up and down. 'OK,' he shrugs. The stranger takes out his laptop, plugs it into his mobile phone and, after a little work involving Nasa websites and satellite readings, says: 'The answer is 931.' The shepherd nods. 'Choose your sheep,' he says. The stranger bundles the animal into his Jeep.

'Now,' says the shepherd. 'If I tell you what job you do, can I have it back?' Sure, the stranger replies. 'You're a management consultant,' the shepherd says. 'How did you know?' the astonished stranger asks. 'Easy,' the shepherd says. 'First, you charged me a fortune. Second, you told me something I already knew. And third, you know nothing about my business. Now please give me back my dog.'

Michael Porter, the celebrated Harvard Business School professor, is not charging his client, the UK government, a fortune to tell it what to do with British business. His fee is £50,000 – a pittance by consulting standards. But, when he breezed into London last week, much of what he told us we already knew. He spelt out his conclusions in an interview with the Financial Times and then spoke at the London School of Economics. The UK has made enormous strides in the past 20 years, he said, but is now suffering from underinvestment in its infrastructure, particularly its trains, roads and universities.

Any taxi driver, wedged in the unmoving London traffic, would tell you the same, although he might leave out the bit about enormous strides in the past 20 years.

So why did the LSE have to provide an overflow room for those who could not squeeze into the main hall? And why did the audience sit rapt throughout Prof Porter's 90-minute talk and give him an enthusiastic ovation at the end? Why does this month's edition of Outlook, Accenture's journal, conclude, after examining Google hits, academic citations and media mentions, that Prof Porter is the world's most admired business guru? What is it that makes him so successful when other management consultants are floundering? Here, after watching Prof Porter at work, is my consultant-style, bullet point guide to being a winning consultant.

■ Respect your audience. Whatever cynicism you harbour about Prof Porter dissolves when he walks into the room. He is courteous, friendly without being over-familiar, and never forgets that he is talking to people who know something about their business.

■ Identify with the client. Early in his LSE speech, Prof Porter, talking about the UK's success in stemming decades of decline, said: 'You've achieved a level of performance that is quite unusual.' But as his talk went on, a subtle change occurred. The second person plural became the first; 'you' became 'we'. So, observing the relatively poor level of investment in UK companies, he said: 'We have a low capital stock and we're not growing it very rapidly.' However, the country was still heading in the right direction. 'We are on the way up,' he said.

This sort of empathy is probably not for every consultant because, unless genuinely felt, it sounds utterly contrived. What helps in Prof Porter's case is that his connections with the UK go back

years. The affection he feels for the country is unforced. He remembers how bad things used to be. 'This was a nation in decline,' he said in his interview with the FT. 'And really, doing business has been transformed. It's just palpable.'

If one of your parents worked for your client company, or if you grew up in its home town, you may want to try this sort of thing. Otherwise, it is probably best to rely on the other Porter techniques.

■ Make sure your spiel has a respectable provenance. Every consultancy has its favourite schema for understanding the world, into which it tries to squeeze its client's particular circumstances. Readers of Prof Porter's work know that one of his themes is 'clusters', the collections of businesses, universities and chambers of commerce that support particular industries, whether Italian footwear or Silicon Valley start-ups. There is little point trying to argue with Prof Porter on the subject; his knowledge of the area is vast.

Not every consultant can be a top business school professor, of course, but you could forge links with one, or perhaps with a whole business school. This will help with your next trick:

■ Throw in some nuggets. While much of Prof Porter's speech covered familiar terrain, it was punctuated with facts that made his audience sit up. For example, he put up a slide showing which UK organisations scored highest in registering US patents. Many of the companies on the list were foreign-owned. More important, only one was an institution: the Ministry of Defence. In France, the organisations that registered the most patents were a mixture of companies and research institutes; in the US, they were companies and universities. This bolstered Prof Porter's point: the UK lacks the links between companies and institutions that other successful economies have.

■ Leave interesting questions unanswered. Having whetted his audience's appetite, Prof Porter said, after many of his most enticing points, that his research was still at an early stage. There was much more to discover. This is the final key to successful consulting: leave them begging for more.

Q1 Detail each stage of the consulting process for Professor Michael Porter's project.

Q2 How would you go about managing such a process?

Q3 Is the anecdote at the beginning of the article fair? Discuss.

5 The skills of the consultant

Learning outcomes

The learning outcomes from this chapter are:

- to appreciate the skills effective management consultants bring to the job; and in particular:

- to recognise the importance of the *project management skills* necessary to keep the consulting project on schedule and on budget;

- to recognise the importance of the *analysis skills* needed to understand the client business, identify the opportunities it faces and develop strategies to exploit them;

- to recognise the importance of the *relationship-building skills* needed to relate ideas to positively influence decision-makers and to make the project happen in real organisations.

5.1 The effective consultant's skill profile

Consulting represents a particularly challenging management task for a number of reasons. First, the consultant is not working within his or her 'own' organisation. He or she is, in the first stages of the consulting exercise at least, an 'outsider'. In some ways this offers advantages. It may allow the consultant to ask questions and make recommendations that an 'insider' feels they cannot. Managers within a business tend to adopt the organisation's way of seeing things – a kind of 'groupthink', which limits the way both problems and opportunities are seen. A consultant may view things in a different way. He or she might well see opportunities in a fresher, more responsive way. Because the consultant ultimately leaves the organisation, he or she can afford a more dispassionate approach. Painful 'home truths' may be recognised more readily (or at least not denied!) by the consultant. For this reason, the consultant will be in a stronger position to advocate difficult courses than someone who does not wish to compromise an open-ended and long-term position within the business.

However, being an outsider presents some challenges. It means that the consultant must actively build relationships and create a sense of trust. Established managers can often take these for granted. Consultants may formally be employed by an organisation, but often they must operate some distance from it. The employing organisation offers support in a variety of ways but the consultant is 'out on his or her own' in a way the conventional manager is not. The consultant must be both self-supporting and self-starting.

The consultant is often involved in projects which are 'strategic'. Strategic projects have significant consequences and affect the future of the whole business. They can cut across the interests of the managers of established parts or functions within the business. Managers may resist what they see as interference in 'their' areas and challenges to 'their' interests. (These issues are explored at length in the studies by Guth and MacMillan (1986) and Wooldridge and Floyd (1990).) Managing such projects demands an ability to deal with such organisational politics in a firm, sensitive and responsible way.

All managers must offer a value-adding service to their organisations. However, a consultant is able to offer a service in a way that is *explicit*. What a consultant offers is subject to scrutiny which is much more intense and continuous than the scrutiny to which an established manager is exposed. An effective (and politically astute) consultant must be willing to let the client management take credit for successes while often being prepared to take the blame for mistakes.

In order to meet the challenge of managing the consulting project the consultant must develop a skill profile that allows him or her to call upon abilities in three key areas:

- an ability to manage the consulting exercise as a *formal project*;
- an ability to manage the *analytical skills* necessary to gain an understanding of the client business and the possibilities it faces;
- an ability to *communicate ideas* and *positively influence* others.

These three areas represent distinct types of management skill. Learning and using them can be supported by a variety of concepts and techniques. These concepts and techniques are drawn from a wide range of management disciplines and traditions. However, it should not be forgotten that the effective consultant can not only call upon skills in each of these areas but integrate them into a seamless whole of management practice.

We can picture these three skill areas working together as illustrated in Figure 5.1.

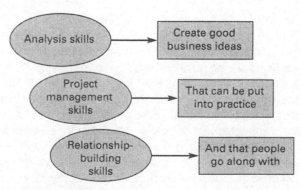

Figure 5.1 The skills of the consultant

Management Consultancy and Skills

The next three sections provide an overview of these consulting skill areas. These reviews are an introduction. They will leave unanswered many questions about the type of challenges these skills can be used to address, how the skills may be developed and how they can be used. It will be the task of the following sections in this book to explore these questions in depth.

5.2 Project management skills

A consulting exercise is a self-contained project within a business environment. The best results are achieved if the consulting exercise is managed as such. Important project management skills include the following.

An ability to define objectives and outcomes

An objective states what the project is going to achieve for the client. However, not every statement is a good objective. A stated objective must be subject to a critical review. Is it well defined? Will the organisation know when it has achieved the objective? Is the objective achievable, given the external market conditions that face the business? Is it realistic, given the business's internal resources?

How is the objective to be phrased? Will those who will play a part in achieving it readily and clearly understand it? Is the objective one that all involved in the business can commit to? If not, why not? How will this matter? These questions will be explored fully in Chapter 7.

An ability to develop formal plans

A plan is a course of action specified in order to achieve a certain objective. Critical aspects of planning include defining tasks, ordering them and understanding the resource implications of the task sequence; in particular, identifying who will be responsible for carrying out the tasks and the financial implications of their activities.

A plan must be properly articulated and communicated if it is to work. A variety of project planning techniques are discussed in Chapter 15.

An ability to sequence and prioritise tasks

Even a simple plan will demand that different people carry out a number – often a considerable number – of tasks at different times. Those tasks must be co-ordinated within the shape of the overall project. Timetabling will be important. It will be possible to carry out some tasks only after others have been carried out first. Some tasks may be performed alongside each other. Some tasks must be given priority over others if resources are to be used effectively. Prioritisation must be undertaken both *by* individuals and *between* individuals on the project team.

A project in which task order and priority have been well defined will be delivered in a shorter time period and at lower cost than one where they have not. A number of formal (though practical and quite easy to use) methods have been developed to assist managers in organising complex task sequences. These are reviewed in Chapter 15.

An ability to manage the financial resources that are to be invested in the consulting project

All management activity demands that money be spent. As a minimum, managers and other workers must be paid for their work. The purchase of external goods (market research, for example) may also be required. With some projects capital expenditure may be expected. For example, the consultant may take responsibility for the purchase of a major piece of equipment or building or investment in an expensive promotional campaign. Keeping track of that expenditure is a critical management responsibility. Profiles of expected expenditure – budgets – must be set before the project starts so that the resource requirements may be understood. These budgets must be managed. Actual expenditure must be monitored against anticipated expenditure. A project, no matter how good its outcomes, runs the risk of disappointing the client if it turns out to be more expensive than anticipated.

Most consulting projects undertaken by students do not demand the management of large financial sums. However, clients have been known to make money available to the student team, especially if a project is going well and they are keen to expand its possibilities. It is far from uncommon for a client who is pleased with the outcomes of a consulting exercise to ask members of the student team who have delivered it to come in on a full-time basis and implement its recommendations.

For these reasons developing an awareness of budget management issues and recognising the skills necessary for managing them are valuable parts of the consulting learning experience. An effective approach to managing the budget for a consulting project is discussed in Section 15.4.

An ability to recognise the human expertise necessary to deliver the project

A particularly important aspect of recognising the human expertise necessary to deliver a project is to understand how the various members of the consulting team can specialise their roles. It is often said that people are a business's greatest asset. After all, it is only people who can make one business different from another. Consultants must work as part of a team. At any one time professional consultants will be members of at least two teams: one based with their own employing business and one at the client business. Student consultants are also likely to be members of a team made up of other students. This team will be an adjunct to the management team at the client business.

Productive team working is crucial for consulting success. (This issue is discussed in detail in Chapter 20.) One area where team working and project management skills meet is in deciding who will do what. Not every member of the team can or should attempt to undertake every task. It is unlikely, given people's individual preferences, that they would wish to. A lot of value can be created by differentiation activities and allowing an individual in the team an opportunity to specialise his or her contribution. The range of individual roles in the project is considered in Section 13.2.

An ability to manage personal time

Time is the most precious of resources. We never seem to have enough of it. All managers must learn to use their time well. This is no less so for the student consultant. The consulting exercise will not be the only thing on the agenda. Other courses must be attended, tutorials prepared for and examinations revised for. A little time for a social life would also be nice!

The management of personal time is an important aspect of project management. Time management skills are discussed in detail in Chapter 17. They are worth investing in. Not only do they allow time to be used productively, they also mean that last-minute panics are avoided. This reduces stress. Relaxed management is more effective, engenders confidence, and makes learning easier and much more enjoyable.

5.3 Analysis skills

A consulting exercise must do something for the client business. It must offer the business the chance of moving from where it is 'now' to somewhere 'new and better'. This demands both an analysis of the business's current situation and an analysis of the opportunities open to it. Analysis involves taking information about the business and its situation and processing that information so that effective decisions may be made from it.

The management consultant's analysis skills may be considered at two levels. At one level there are skills that enable information in general to be manipulated and used. These are skills which all people use all the time. However, a consultant must hone them to a high level. At a more technical level there are skills that facilitate the analysis of business activity. Consultants must be specialists in understanding a business, its strengths and weaknesses, its situation and the opportunities and threats it presents. To do so requires the application of more specific concepts and techniques.

General analysis skills are often subsumed into management 'intuition'. They are just what experienced managers do on the basis of what they know. Just because they are not necessarily explicit does not mean they are not important. In fact, this is evidence of *deep learning* (a technique that can be mastered). General analysis skills include the following.

An ability to identify what information is available in a particular situation

Decision-makers demand information. The more information that is taken into account, the more confidence there can be in the decision made. A good decision-maker is active in auditing the information that is available to be used in a decision-making situation. In many cases this will involve background research and reviews of published information. However, at an immediate level it will demand effective questioning of those with experience of the business and its situation to get them to share the information they have (and which they may not even know they have!). This process involves both problem definition and questioning skills. Problem definition is reviewed in Chapter 7. Questioning skills are critical to communication and are considered in Section 19.3.

An ability to identify what information is needed in a particular situation

Often in a decision-making situation it is not a lack of information that presents a problem. Quite the reverse in fact: it is that too much is available. The consultant always walks a tightrope between not gaining enough information and so making uninformed decisions and having so much that focused decision-making is impaired – between what two of the founders of modern systems thinking, Kast and Rosenzweig (1985), have called 'extinction by instinct' and 'paralysis by analysis'. Anne Langley explores the practical implications of this issue in a 1995 paper.

Having identified what information is available in a situation a consultant must decide which information is pertinent to the decision in hand. The information that is needed to make the decision an effective one must be distinguished from that which is merely a distraction. The balance will lie in the nature of the decision, its significance to the consulting project and the business, and the type of information available.

An ability to process that information to identify the important relationships within it

Information on its own is not much use. It must be processed in order to identify the important relationships within it. Critically, what the information is really saying about the business and the opportunities open to it must be revealed. For instance, consumer demand figures suggest a market is growing. Does this present an opportunity for your client's business? Or does it just make life easier for competitors? Will it attract new ones into your client's market? For example, a report in the *Financial Times* suggests an important competitor of your client is failing. Does this suggest an easier time for your client or does it herald a tougher time for your client's sector as a whole? An innovative product of the client business is making a real impact in the market. Good. But will it lead to cash flow problems? Drawing conclusions such as these demands an understanding of patterns of relationships and causal linkages that connect businesses, their customers and their environments. Creative approaches to analysis are discussed in Chapter 10.

An ability to draw meaning from that information and use it to support decision-making

Once connections have been made and conclusions drawn it is necessary to identify the impact of those conclusions on the courses of action open to the client business and their significance to the consulting project.

This processing of information has both 'private' and 'public' aspects. The private aspect involves a detached and reflective consideration of what the information means and what, in consequence, is the best option for the business. The public aspect demands using information to make the case for a particular course of action, to advocate particular options, to convince others of the correctness of that course and to meet objections. These two aspects do, of course, go hand in hand.

The 'intuitive' side of analysis is often supplemented by the use of formal techniques that can help business decision-making. Some of the more important consulting analysis skills are in the areas dealt with in the following sections.

An ability to recognise the business's profile of strengths, weaknesses and capabilities

All businesses are different. They develop strengths that allow them to deliver certain sorts of value to particular customers in a special and valuable way. They have weaknesses that leave them open to attack by competitors. A variety of conceptual frameworks can be used to guide the exploration of a firm's strengths, capabilities and weaknesses.

An ability to recognise the opportunities and challenges the environment offers the business

A business's environment presents a constantly shifting kaleidoscope of possibilities. Some offer new opportunities to serve customers better and so grow and develop the business. Others expose weaknesses which at best leave the business in a position where it will fail to reach its potential and at worst will cause its decline. An ability to evaluate the opportunities and threats its markets offer the business is a fundamental prerequisite to devising rewarding consulting projects and defining their objectives.

An ability to assess the business's financial situation

Financial performance is not the only measure of a business's success. But it is fundamental. It is only through a sound financial performance that a business can reward its stakeholders. An analysis of a company's financial situation offers a route to understanding its performance in its marketplace, the risks to which it is exposed and the resources it has available to invest in the future. Financial analysis is easiest and most rewarding when undertaken with the guidance of formal ratio methods.

All of these methods of analysis will be considered in detail in Chapter 11.

An ability to evaluate the business's markets and how they are developing

A market is the total of demand for a particular good or service. A particular business gains sales through having a share of that market. The growth of the business will be sensitive to the development of its markets. If the market is growing, new business opportunities may present themselves. But new competitors may be attracted to them as well. If the market is in decline, business pressures may be building. If the market is fragmenting, new niches may be opening up and innovation may be rewarded.

An analysis of trends in the business's markets, combined with a consideration of the firm's capabilities, can be used to define consulting project outcomes that make a real contribution to the business's development.

The techniques that can be used to explore market conditions and the opportunities they present will be considered in Chapter 11.

An ability to assess the business's internal conditions

A business is able to exploit market opportunities only if it has the internal conditions that allow it to meet them head-on. The business must have internal conditions that are flexible and responsive to new possibilities and have the resources needed to innovate in an appropriate way. The business must have the capacity to grow in response to those possibilities or be able to get hold of the resources it will need to invest in growth. These resources include human skills as well as productive capacity.

An ability to analyse the way in which decision-making occurs within the business

Understanding the possibilities open to a business and devising ways in which those possibilities can be exploited is only the first half of the consultant's responsibilities. If the consultant is to offer real value to a business, he or she must also help the business make those possibilities a reality.

One of the few, perhaps the only, unquestionable truth about organisational life is that businesses rarely recognise good ideas instantly and pursue them without question. Usually a consultant must convince the client business that what he or she is suggesting is a real opportunity. To do this an effective consultant must understand decision-making in the business and use this knowledge to his or her advantage. This demands knowing who is involved in the decision-making process and the roles different individuals play. It also means a sensitivity to who will gain (and who might lose) if particular ideas are put into practice. The consultant must be aware that not all objections are purely rational. Analysing the decision-making processes in the client business is a first stage in building relationships with individuals in the business. Models that assist in this analysis are discussed in Chapters 10 and 11.

5.4   Relationship-building skills

Analysis skills offer an insight into where the client business might go. Project management skills offer an ability to deliver the project necessary to move the business forward. However, these skills are of only very limited use if the client firm's management and influential outsiders cannot be convinced that this is the right way to go and that they should give their support to the project and the direction it offers. Gaining this support demands relationship-building skills.

Some critical relationship-building skills include the following.

An ability to build rapport and trust with the client

Rapport is hard to define – but it is easy to recognise. Two people have a rapport when they communicate with ease and work together effectively. It is clear that they have a trust in each other and a commitment to each other. Rapport is not confined to face-to-face communication. It is a feature of all communication. Rapport can be built through written and verbal communications as well. It is not just subject to what is said. How things are said matters as well.

Rapport is very important in 'lubricating' the consultant's activities within the organisation. Developing rapport demands practice. It is a skill that can be developed through active learning. Guidance and some hints on how to build rapport are given in Chapter 19.

An ability to question effectively

Questioning is one of the fundamental communication skills. Questioning is not only a way to get information (though this is important). It is also a way to build rapport and to control the direction of a conversation. Effective questioning skills are an important plank in any manager's leadership strategy. They are especially important for the consultant. Questioning is so important that it is discussed in a separate section (19.3).

An ability to communicate ideas succinctly and precisely

A consultant brings a special level of expertise to a business. He or she must offer something the business cannot offer itself. This may mean that the consultant is working in an area with a high technical content, for example finance or marketing. Areas such as these and many others have a language all their own. The consultant must be cautious about using this language directly to the client. After all, the client is not interested in the consultant's knowledge of a technical area but in his or her ability to use that knowledge in a way which creates value for the business.

A consultant has most impact when he or she talks the same language as the client. Ideas must be related in a way that is succinct and precise and uses no more technical jargon than the client is comfortable with. Converting technical ideas into plain language is not always easy. But it is important and is a skill of its own which can be developed with practice.

An ability to negotiate objectives and outcomes

A consulting project must have definite objectives and outcomes. The value the project is expected to deliver to the client business must be explicit. However, the consultant and the client do not always agree, in the first instance at least, on what those outcomes should be. The client may not have a clear idea of what is wanted for the business. If he or she does have a definite idea it may be beyond the scope of what the consultant is in a position to offer realistically. It may be that the consultant is not convinced that what the client is demanding as an outcome is absolutely right for the business. Such disagreements can often occur with student consulting projects where the client's expectations are very high and there is a need to reconcile commercial with educational outcomes.

Whatever the source of any disagreement, the project outcomes must be defined and agreed by consultant and client. This is a process of negotiation that results in the formal project brief.

The need to negotiate is not an admission that there is necessarily a conflict between the client and the consultant. Rather, it is a recognition that the consultancy exercise will work best when both client and consultant have clear expectations as to what will result from the consulting exercise and what the responsibility of both parties will be in achieving them. The consultant must be aware that disappointment in consultancy (for both client and consultant team) results more from unclear expectations than from poor outcomes.

Ways to approach negotiating the outcomes of the project are considered in Chapter 7.

An ability to convince through verbal, written and visual mediums

In business, having good ideas is not enough. Ideas must be used to encourage people to follow them as courses of action. They must be used to encourage the business's managers to implement plans and its backers to make supportive investment decisions. Ideas must be communicated in a way that convinces people that they are good and are worth implementing. This conviction comes as much from the 'how' of communication as from the 'what', that is, from the form of the communication as well as its content.

Conviction results if ideas are communicated in a manner that is appropriate to the audience; for example if the communication uses the right language, is of the right length and adopts a proper style. This applies to communication in any situation and whether the medium is verbal, visual or written.

An ability to use information to make a case for a particular course of action

Of course, ideas must have some substance if they are to deliver real value. Communication of ideas must be backed up with information. This includes both facts and interpretation of facts. The logic of that interpretation must be clear. Different people in the client business will seek and will be convinced by different corroborating information, at different levels and presented in different ways. Some information will be included in an initial communication. Other parts may be kept back as a response to questions and challenges.

Knowing when to use particular information, and how to use it to convince, is an important communication skill for the consultant, especially as a consultant's ideas are likely to be under close scrutiny by the client business, certainly more so than those of internal managers. Convincing with information and well-structured, well-communicated arguments is a theme developed in Chapter 18.

Management Consultancy and Skills

An ability to develop selling strategies

Effective selling calls for a definite, well-developed and quite well-understood set of skills. Selling of goods and services is a specialist management activity. However, all managers are involved in selling their ideas all the time. Consultants must certainly sell their ideas. But they must also sell themselves and their own organisations as *providers* of ideas. This is a particular challenge for consultants involved in general management rather than some specialist area. A business may readily accept that it lacks technical knowledge in product development, information technology or finance. However, few businesses will readily admit to being deficient in general management skills.

The consultant can draw on a variety of formal selling skills. These must be used appropriately though. Consultancy, as a 'product', does not usually respond to a 'hard sell' approach. Rather, a formal selling approach should be used as the tactic in a well-thought-through selling strategy. This strategy should aim to communicate what the consultant can genuinely offer the client and be used to build a long-term, mutually rewarding relationship.

An ability to work effectively as a member of a team

Many consulting tasks (especially those of major significance) require a team effort. As a minimum they will demand that the consultant and client work together. Usually they will involve an extended management team in the client business. Often the consulting task will have significant resource implications and will be complex to deliver. The scope of its demands will go beyond the capabilities of one individual, certainly in time and perhaps in technical knowledge. Delivering the project will require the consultant to work as part of a team.

Good team working is essential for business success and not just in consulting. It is a skill in itself. It demands many things. It requires, for example, a careful definition of individual roles in relation to the team as a whole. It also requires well-honed interpersonal, motivation and conflict-resolution skills. Most of all, perhaps, it demands a willingness to align the interests of the individuals who make up the team with the overall task the team must address. This requires an ability to advocate individual interests and yet, when necessary, to compromise individual concerns for the interests of the group as a whole.

If the team is to develop a productive coherence through which its members can make individual contributions, it must be actively managed. Chapter 20 considers the issues involved in and the skills needed for team working. These will be considered with the support of conceptual thinking about the dynamics of team working.

An ability to demonstrate leadership

Leadership is an ability to focus and direct the individuals in an organisation in a way that brings the whole organisation benefits. Leadership is perhaps the most valuable commodity a senior manager can offer his or her organisation. Leadership draws together a variety of relationship skills – not least articulation of vision, motivation and communication – into a coherent behavioural strategy.

It should not be thought that a consulting team can have only one, permanent leader and that the remainder of the team must be followers. Such an assumption lies behind many intragroup conflicts. Leadership is not an inherent and fixed property of an individual. It is situational; that is, it arises out of the conditions of a particular situation in which people interact in a particular way. Leadership may shift between members as the project evolves and the situation changes. The individual who shows leadership for the team may not be the same person who shows leadership towards the client business or towards people from outside the team offering support to the project. In professional consulting, as in business generally, leadership up the formal reporting hierarchy, from subordinate to superior, may be as important as traditional leadership down it.

A consulting project is one of the best opportunities a student will be given to recognise the nature and value of leadership, and to develop leadership skills. The nature of leadership skills important for the consultant is discussed in Chapter 21.

The project management, analysis and relationship skill areas do not work in isolation. They must operate in conjunction and in balance with each other. Relationship building must be based on a proficient analysis of the business and the people in it. Project management must be aimed at delivering negotiated outcomes. Good project management skills offer a base on which can be built a trust that outcomes will be delivered. And so on.

Team discussion point

You have undertaken a consulting exercise with a local travel firm. The firm is very pleased with the outcomes of the project and by way of thanks offers your group a free holiday together. Consider this holiday as a project. What project management, analysis and relationship-building skills must the group use if you are to make the holiday enjoyable for all?

Hint

Consider the various stages of the 'project':

- deciding where to go, when to go and how long to stay;
- ~~deciding what needs to be taken and packing your luggage;~~
- travelling to your destination;
- enjoying the activities available on the holiday;
- returning home.

What skills will be called on at each stage?

 Summary of key ideas

The effective consultant offers the client firm a way to add value that it cannot do on its own. To do this the consultant must call on three areas of management skill:

- *analysis skills* – an ability to know where to go and how to get there;
- *relationship-building skills* – an ability to take people along with you;
- *project management skills* – an ability to make it happen!

Figure 5.2 The consultant must always convince the client that the service on offer is of real value!

Source: copyright © 1998 United Feature Syndicate, Inc. Reproduction by permission

These are general management skills. Consulting presents a steep learning curve. This means it is a challenge. However, the rewards are high. An effective consultant can expect to take on highly responsible roles at an early stage in his or her career.

Key reading

Creplet, F., Dupouet, O., Kern, F., Mehmanpazir, B. and Munier, F. (2001) 'Consultants and experts in management consulting firms', *Research Policy*, Vol. 30, No. 9, pp. 1517–35.

Guth, W.D. and MacMillan, I.C. (1986) 'Strategy implementation versus middle management self-interest', *Strategic Management Journal*, 7, 313–27.

Kast, F.G. and Rosenzweig, J.G. (1985) *Organization and Management* (4th edn). New York: McGraw Hill.

Langley, A. (1995) 'Between "paralysis by analysis" and "extinction by instinct"', *Sloan Management Review*, Spring, 63–76.

Schaffer, R.H. (1997) 'Looking at the 5 fatal flaws of management consulting', *Journal for Quality and Participation*, Vol. 20, No. 3, pp. 44–50.

Simon, A. and Kumar, V. (2001) 'Client's views on strategic capabilities which lead to management consulting success', *Management Decision*, Vol. 39, No. 5, pp. 362–72.

Wooldridge, W. and Floyd, S.W. (1990) 'The strategy process, middle management involvement and organisational performance', *Strategic Management Journal*, 11, 231–41.

Young, J. and Jinloo, L. (1998) 'Factors influencing the success of management consulting projects', *International Journal of Project Management*, Vol. 16, No. 2, pp. 67–72.

Helping hand of experience

By **Kathy Harvey**

FT

12 May 2003

MBA students do not need any reminding that times are tough. Most accept that their dream job may not materialise in the current economic gloom, and business schools are responding by expanding their career services to include everything from mock interviews to seminars on how to write a good curriculum vitae.

Now Manchester Business School, which runs an 18-month MBA programme, is going a step further by offering a selected handful of students the chance to compete for a corporate 'mentor' to guide them from the first term to the final job search. Alison Edmonds, director of career services at MBS, says the scheme, called 'Manchester Gold', is an extension of an idea first tried at undergraduate level.

'As far as I know, no other business school in the UK is running anything quite like this. Among all the different messages about career choices, it is invaluable to have an independent, external view which is anchored in the marketplace.'

The selection process for the scheme starts a few weeks into the first term of the MBA, when students are invited to apply online, arguing their case to be included in the scheme. A shortlist for potential mentors to choose from is then drawn up. This year, about half the 150-strong cohort applied, for only 20 places. Although the small number of mentors makes an element of competition inevitable, Ms Edmonds believes it is a useful way to assess motivation and need.

'Some people are disappointed when they aren't chosen but not everyone would benefit from this process. It's important that a suitable match is found for both parties.'

The mentors are all MBS alumni – offering experience of post-MBA life and an understanding of the difficulties students face in combining a job search with study.

Rob Elliot, a business improvement consultant with BT Group, had been looking for ways to maintain his links with the school when he was asked to act as a mentor.

'I looked at the shortlist and tried to choose someone I felt I could help – someone who had a clear focus about his or her own intentions.'

He was paired with Peris Roberts, a former software consultant who is hoping to change direction, looking possibly at jobs in finance.

As someone who had used his own MBA as a way of moving from commercial man-

agement in the pharmaceuticals sector to consultancy, Mr Elliot could identify with his 'mentee'. 'I suppose I could see myself in him. I hope I can be of help – and of course this keeps me plugged into the business school world.'

As well as acting as a sounding board, the corporate mentors can nudge students into thinking ahead – even when the workload of the MBA is uppermost in their mind. Mr Roberts believes the process has also made him more realistic about his options once he graduates.

Mr Roberts is researching several career options discussed during the last mentoring meeting. 'It's a motivating process. I sense that Rob is giving me a lot of his time and the benefit of his experience a few years down the line,' he says.

While pleased that students seem to be benefiting so much from the scheme, MBS careers staff say mentors are not expected to act as unpaid headhunters. Before the mentoring begins, both parties are issued with guidelines on how to manage expectations, how often to meet during the MBA course and what to do if the student and mentor find they are unsuited. Nevertheless, many of the alumni appear to be happy to go the extra mile, passing on names of business contacts who could form a useful network in the final hunt for jobs.

Andy Katz, now working for Corven, the consultancy firm, is mentoring an MBS student who has worked as an engineer in the oil industry and as an English teacher in Japan.

'I do feel as though I can be something of a Mr Fixit when it comes to extending his network,' says Mr Katz. 'I've also introduced him to an MBS alumnus working at Shell and suggested ways he could extend his own contacts.'

His mentoring partner, Gavin Hepburn, had not expected to have as much help in his first year on the course. 'Andy is helping me to analyse the process of looking for a job and to think of ways around simply approaching human resources departments.' They have also discussed the possibility of Mr Hepburn working for himself, with Mr Katz offering

advice on how to choose electives to maximise his understanding of entrepreneurship.

The MBS mentors are also proving their worth in the company internship.

'The commercial reality,' says Mr Katz, 'is that it is difficult to get what you want. It is vital to talk to as many potential sponsors as you can.'

Careers advice from mentors may not always be in line with the received wisdom. 'Students are often told that a one-page CV is the best way of grabbing attention,' he says, 'but I see and expect a bit more detail, perhaps two pages from most people.'

While the benefit for the students is obvious, the MBS careers team points out that the advantages are not all one-sided. Coaching experience is a valuable asset in many companies, especially where a system of internal mentoring is in place. While some alumni taking part have reached very senior positions, they believe that they need to gain extra skills that will stand them in good stead in the marketplace.

Failure to be picked for the scheme has – in some cases – brought home the importance of starting early when it comes to thinking about networking.

'I suppose I didn't realise how much effort some students were putting into their application for a mentor,' admits Andy Brown, a first-year MBA student.

'I'm not against the competitive element; my failure to get on the scheme has spurred me on to find my own mentor – a friend of a friend who is a management consultant.'

Over the next five years the business school hopes to expand the programme, perhaps recruiting mentors who are not alumni. Once MBA students realise the benefits, Ms Edmonds expects pressure to grow to offer everyone a corporate mentor.

'The better career service you provide for people, the more they rely on it,' she says. And, as the MBS students struggle through another night catching up on coursework, their mentors provide an optimistic reality check.

Q1 'The skills of the consultant cannot be taught in the classroom.' Comment on this statement.

Q2 What value might the process of mentoring offer in the development of consulting skills?

Q3 What skills do you think are important for an effective consulting mentor?

CHAPTER 6

The project proposal and the project log

The learning outcomes from this chapter are:

- to recognise the key elements of the project proposal and how they may be articulated in order to have an impact and to influence the recipient;
- to recognise how a *project log* can help the effective delivery of the consulting project;
- to know what to *include* in the log;
- to be able to select a log *format* that is right for you and your project.

6.1 The function of the project proposal

The project proposal is a short, straightforward document. It has two simple aims. These are to state what the consulting exercise aims to achieve and to get the client to commit to it. Despite its brevity the project proposal is very important. It is the pivot about which the whole project revolves. A good proposal gets the project off to a good start. A weak one will hinder the project from the outset.

The proposal is a statement to the client of what the project is about and what it will do for the business. The proposal is what the client is *buying* from the consultant. It needs to present what the consultant has to offer in a positive light. It has to make the consultant's offering appear as an attractive investment given all the other things the business has an opportunity to invest in. If the consultant's pitch is a competitive one, the proposal has to present the consultant as the best available.

A further and equally important function of the proposal is to manage the client's *expectations*. An individual's satisfaction with a product or service is not usually based on the absolute utility of what he or she receives. More often it is based on outcomes relative to expectations. If expectations are met or exceeded, then satisfaction will occur. If expectations are not met, disappointment will inevitably result. If the client recognises the proposal as what he or she is buying then it is against this that the final project delivery will be compared.

Some managers have an unrealistic idea of what a consultant is capable of, or at least capable of given the resources the manager is able to invest in the consulting project, both in terms of the money the client is putting forward and the time and capabilities of the consultant. If this is so then the manager is likely to be dissatisfied with the results of a consulting exercise *even if, in absolute terms, that project is a good one*. However, a manager who has doubts about the ability of a consultant to offer anything of value may well be pleasantly satisfied with the results of a quite mediocre project. (Though, of course, such a manager may resist using a consultant in the first place!)

The proposal must serve a twofold function. On the one hand, it must 'sell' what the consultant has to offer. On the other, it must manage the expectations of the client manager so that he or she does not make an unreasonable demand on the consultant given the resources that are available. The project proposal demands a balanced approach from the consultant. The temptation to 'get a sale' by offering a lot must be tempered by a care not to raise the client's expectations so high that they cannot be met. There are a few simple rules which will allow this balance to be struck.

First, understand what the client would *really* like for his or her business. Do not fall into the trap of assuming that he or she will want what the 'textbooks' suggest they *should* have, or that they must take what you think is best for them. Managers often reject the obvious answers for very good reasons. Second, enquire into, and gain a thorough understanding of, the extent to which the client expects the consulting exercise to contribute to the overall goal for the business. It is particularly important to ensure that the client makes the distinction between the consulting project offering a *means* to achieve the business's goals and its actually *implementing* them: between the consultant pointing out a *direction* for the business and actually *taking* it there. This is an issue about which the consultant and client can easily develop different expectations.

Developing this understanding of the client's needs and expectations must take place at the preliminary analysis stage of the project. It is best done through a personal meeting between the manager and the consulting team or a representative of it. At this stage the objective of the meeting should be to gather information about the business and what might be done for it. It is not a time to start negotiating on outcomes.

It is better to wait until the written proposal has been presented before starting negotiating on precisely what can and cannot be achieved. The proposal helps here. It provides something tangible around which discussions can centre. The initial proposal can always be modified in light of further discussion. How to approach these negotiations will be dealt with fully in Chapter 7. If the proposal is modified, however, do produce a written version so that finalised aims, objectives and outcomes are clear to all and can be referred back to.

6.2 What to include in the proposal

The proposal needs to be succinct and must make an impact. It must speak for itself; you cannot rely on having an opportunity to explain it in person. Typically it will be one to two pages long. If it is longer than this it will risk losing its impact.

As with any business communication, the proposal should always be approached with a fresh mind. There are always new ways of doing things to be discovered. However, there are some key elements which, when included in the proposal, do add to its impact and help it communicate effectively within the constraints described above. These will now be described in detail.

A title

All that is necessary is a short title for the project, perhaps the client company's name and a brief descriptive phrase. This provides a reference for the project in the future and helps locate it in the minds of all involved.

Client's requirements

This should be a brief statement about the company, the opportunities or issues it faces and the scope of the project. The scope may be drawn from the types of consulting project described in Chapter 3. The background statement should aim to convey the fact that the consultant understands the key issue or issues and is committed to addressing them. It should not be a complete description of the business and its situation. This would be far too long and as the client possesses this information they would not be interested.

Overall aim

This is a statement of what the project aims to achieve, in broad terms. This might be thought of as the mission for the project from which definite objectives might be drawn.

Objectives

This is a list of the detailed objectives for the project. Objectives should be active; they are statements of what the project will do. A good way of starting the list is to use the phrase:

This consulting exercise aims to . . .

Outcomes

Outcomes are subtly different from objectives. They are a statement of what the business *will be able to do* as a result of receiving the consulting exercise and the delivery of its objectives. Again, they should be active. A good way of starting the list is to use the phrase:

As a result of this consulting exercise the business will be able to . . .

Both objectives and outcomes are best summarised in the form of a bullet-point list. Objectives and outcomes should be complete in themselves. Do not be tempted to expand on them or qualify them with subsidiary paragraphs. If the consulting exercise is long and complex it may be proper to develop interim objectives and outcomes for the intermediate stages of the project. The development and articulation of good objectives and outcomes is discussed in Chapter 7.

Our approach

This section provides an opportunity for the consulting group to describe how it will address the exercise. It should highlight the approach in broad terms. It might detail activities such as market research, analysis and guidance with implementation. It should not give a detailed exposition of the methodologies that might be adopted. This section is an opportunity for the consulting team to indicate what it has to offer. The emphasis should be on why what the group can offer is different or special. It is a further opportunity to manage the client's expectations and in particular to emphasise the distinction between developing a plan for the business and actually implementing it.

Time plan

The time plan is an indication of when the outcomes of the exercise will be delivered and identifies important milestones *en route*. Milestones are key events along the way to the final delivery and might include things like meetings with the client and information providers, interim reports and presentations.

The amounts of detail in the time plan will reflect the length and complexity of the project.

Costings

Costings are statements of how much the project will cost the client. Important elements are the consultant's fees, the consultant's expenses (often just a *pro rata* cost on top of fees) and any direct expenditure needed. Direct expenditure might be needed for buying market research or undertaking surveys.

What not to include in the proposal

It is as important to know what *not* to include in the project proposal as to know what to put in. A lot of background on the business does not usually help. It 'pads out' the proposal, making it longer than it need be. It tells the client things he or she already knows and runs the risk of losing his or her interest before the important aspects of the proposal are reached. The temptation to discuss the methodology that will be adopted should also be avoided. The formal business analysis techniques used by the consultant in developing an understanding of the business and how it might be moved forward are the consultant's concern – not the client's! A simple analogy with the repairing of your car makes the point. If you take your car to the garage for repair, you are not particularly interested in what tools the mechanic will use. Management consulting is the same. The consultant is an expert who is brought in because he or she knows how to call upon a range of tools to deal with business issues. There is no reason to reveal those tools to the client before the project starts.

The project proposal should be prepared after an initial meeting to discuss the client's business and requirements. Initial proposals can always be modified after discussion with the client to produce a final proposal. An initial proposal can be used as a basis for detailed negotiations with the client.

6.3   An example of a project proposal

Exhibit 6.1 presents an example of a project proposal along the lines discussed in this chapter.

Exhibit 6.1 Consulting proposal

Greyline Printers: support for a business expansion programme

Your requirements

Greyline Printers is a small but ambitious and fast-growing firm offering a range of printing and reprographic services. The consulting team has been invited to work with the senior management team and explore the opportunities for growth the business might successfully capitalise upon, given the business's current resources.

Overall aim

The main aim of the consulting project is to give Greyline Printers a clear sense of direction for the way in which the business might be expanded into new market sectors.

Objectives

The consulting project aims to:

1 evaluate the market context of Greyline Printers;
2 identify high-growth customer segments;
3 develop an understanding of what those customers require from a good print and reprographics supplier – in terms of both products and service support;
4 identify major competitors of the business;
5 evaluate what those competitors offer and identify how Greyline Printers might develop a competitive edge;
6 summarise the findings in the form of a brief for the business's sales team;
7 make recommendations on a PR campaign to increase awareness of the company and its products among target customers.

Outcomes

As a result of this consulting exercise Greyline Printers will be able to:

1 develop an understanding of the market sectors that are most attractive for new business development;
2 dedicate valuable resources towards the exploitation of those market sectors;
3 position itself in a way which is competitive given the current profile of competitors.

In particular the business will be able to:

4 refine its product range and service offering to increase competitiveness;
5 initiate a sales campaign dedicated to gaining new customers in those sectors;
6 support sales activity with a well-focused PR campaign.

Our approach

Our approach will emphasise the importance of reliable information to the decision-makers of Greyline Printers. Secondary marketing research will be used to establish

---

▶

a picture of the dynamics of the print and reprographics market and the competitive situation. Building on this, primary market research will be used to investigate customer needs and expectations. The findings will be used to give a clear direction for new product development. Market intelligence will be summarised in a form that makes it accessible to the sales team. A review of publications which reach important customers will be undertaken. This will be used to develop for Greyline Printers an awareness-building communication plan.

Time plan

Key events in the project will be as follows:

October 2003:	Initial meeting with client to discuss requirements.
November 2003:	Initial proposal presented to client and reviewed.
November 2003:	Final proposal based on review: agreement to go ahead.
December 2003:	Progression of project. Further meetings with client (three expected over period).
May 2004:	Secondary marketing research.
June 2004:	Primary research with buyers.
June 2004:	Preparation of final report. Sales brief and PR plan appended.
July 2004:	Presentation of findings to client.

6.4 The function of the project log

A log is a day-by-day record of the consulting project. It summarises the activities, analysis, observations and experiences that occur as the project unfolds. Most professional consultants keep a private log of the consulting projects they undertake. Keeping a log may be part of the assessment procedure for a student consulting exercise. Even if it is not, the fact that professional consultants use one suggests there may be advantages in keeping a personal log in any case.

Why should this be so? Keeping a log takes time. It requires a commitment on the part of the consultant. We should always ask the same questions about any activity that demands a significant input on the part of the manager. First: what value is this activity adding? Second: is the value added worth the effort?

These questions must be demanded of the keeping of a consulting project log. This section will make the case that the value created through the keeping of a project log more than justifies the effort needed for its upkeep. This does, of course, depend on exactly how much information goes into keeping the log. This is subject to its format. We will deal with the question of what format to use in detail in Section 6.6.

The main benefits the log offers are as follows.

It aids project planning activities

A consulting project, like any other project, needs managing in its own terms. Formal project management techniques are valuable. (These are discussed in detail in Chapter 15.) The consultant must have a detailed and up-to-date schedule of the tasks that need to be undertaken. This demands an understanding of how activities support each other and depend on each other. Once this schedule is in place it provides a series of milestones or benchmarks against which the delivery of the project can be monitored. These benchmarks have a 'what' and 'when' aspect: *what* must have been done and *when* it must have been done by. The log offers a ready device for monitoring the what and when of these outcomes and for triggering remedial action if an expected outcome does not happen.

It provides a summary for information collected

In order to deliver the consulting exercise effectively it will be necessary to collect information. The amount of information needed will depend on the nature of the project. This information can often be quite extensive. It is not likely that it will be in the form of a neat summary. Articles and reports will be sourced. Statistics and facts will be identified. The log provides a good place to keep key data, a summary of the information collected and references back to primary sources. Ready access to this will make analysis and compiling the final report much easier.

It provides a secure location for notes taken when communicating

A consulting exercise demands both extensive and wide-ranging communications. As the exercise is undertaken a large number of notes will need to be taken as a result of these communications. These will arise from taking minutes in meetings, taking details from telephone conversations and recording the details of interviews.

It is tempting not to take detailed notes when engaging in communication with others. It is quite natural to assume that we will retain all the points made during communication in our memory. This is illusory. Our memories are not particularly good. Although we think we can retain everything, details are quickly forgotten. Important and valuable points slip from our grasp. Taking written notes helps in two ways. First, the very act of writing something down helps reinforce it in our memory. Second, it provides a hard source to refer back to when our memories need refreshing. Using the log as a place to keep these notes means they can be found later (odd scraps of paper are always lost). It should also be added that taking notes is a good way to assist in *active listening* (*see* Section 19.4).

It provides a forum for analysis

Analysis is an important part of decision-making. Approaches to analysis are discussed in Chapter 10. Analysis acts on information. Information must be processed before it becomes meaningful. Analysis takes a number of forms. It can be calculations performed on numerical data. It might be statistical manipulation aimed at identifying trends. It could be developing a visual representation, such as a graph, so that relationships become clear. It might be generation of a mind map to aid inventiveness and encourage innovation. Whatever its form, analysis must be an active process.

Active analysis is best undertaken in a written or visual form. The project log provides a good place to undertake analysis notes. First, using the log encourages analysis to be undertaken where and when it is necessary. This is better than leaving it until later. Doing analysis as the opportunity arises means that its insights are immediately available to guide the project and direct the need for more information. Analysis is usually more productive if the information to be processed is fresh in the mind and the motives for performing the analysis are clear and pressing. The motive for undertaking is the need to know something. If the analysis is sophisticated and is better left to a later time, the log can still be used to make a note about the need to do the analysis.

If a piece of analysis is undertaken by the group as a whole, or by one group member on behalf of the group as a whole, copies may be included in other group members' logs.

You should not forget that any analysis performed may well be included in the final report to the client. If it is included in the log it will act as at least a first draft that can be accessed easily. This will mean that you will not need to redraft it when writing the final report.

It encourages reflection on the consulting experience

The consulting project is an opportunity to learn. Learning is most effective (and easiest) if it is undertaken actively. Active learning involves a cycle of analysis, practice and reflection. The log, if used properly, can help the development of an active learning strategy. It does this by encouraging reflection and facilitating analysis.

A few questions that you might consider reflecting on within the log include the following:

- What outcomes have been achieved at this stage of the project?
- How do these compare to the project plan?
- How did they compare with my own expectations? (The answer to this question may not be the same as that to the previous one!)
- How might they compare with other people's expectations? (In particular: other members of the group; the client; the project assessors.)
- What has gone well to this stage?
- What made it a positive experience?
- What might have gone better?
- Why were these aspects not such a positive experience?
- How might this experience be improved in the future?

It acts as a permanent record of the consulting exercise

Our memories are not perfect. In some instances it is useful to be able to refer back and find out when something happened, what was undertaken or what was said or agreed at a particular point. The log can be used to store this information. This enables quick and productive review of the project as an aid to reflection on it. The log can be used to establish how much time was spent on a particular activity undertaken on behalf of the project. This can be useful for planning new projects. Information in the log can be used to resolve some of the disputes that inevitably occur when working in teams.

Management Consultancy and Skills

It provides a long-term learning resource

Active learning never ends. The future tends to throw new situations at us. But this does not, of course, mean that our learning from previous situations is of no value. Far from it. We can only build on the experience we have. The project log can provide us with information that we might use to plan our responses to new challenges. It can offer a guide to personal strengths and the areas that might be developed in the future. It can offer insights into what types of task we enjoy doing (and why). In this respect, many students for example, find it very useful as a source of points to discuss at job interviews.

6.5 What to include in the project log

The discussion in the previous section gives an indication of the kind of information that can feature in the log. At this stage it is useful to summarise what might be included. Key headings include:

- the date;
- the stage of the project;
- the status of the project (actual outcomes relative to objectives);
- a summary of activities undertaken since the last entry;
- the objectives of those activities;
- minutes of meetings held;
- details of information gathered;
- notes from communications;
- details of analysis undertaken.

And, in addition to these 'routine' headings:

- active learning reflections on the consulting experience.

Of course, the length of the inclusions under each heading will vary. Not every heading will be needed for every day's entry. Detailed reflection on active learning may not be a priority for *every* entry, especially if the project is at a very busy stage and entries are being made every day. Time should be taken at a convenient point to reflect on what has been learned.

Text is the main form of written communication and is very useful. However, many people also like to explore ideas using mind maps and other creative devices. The log is a good place to develop and keep these.

6.6 Suggested formats for the project log

The project log is a working tool that the consultant uses to assist in delivering the consulting project. It is a private document. It is not intended to be shown to the client. It is a flow of ideas, comments, notes and reflections. It does not

Management Consultancy and Skills

matter if it is rough and untidy in appearance. What matters is that it works as a store of notes on the project and a stimulus to reflection, not that it be polished and presentable.

The project log should not be completely lacking in organisation, though. You want to be able to find ideas later. A variety of formats have proved to be effective for organising the project log. You should select one that works for you. You may like the idea of a standardised form that prompts entries under the points discussed above. An example of how this might be filled in is given (*see* Figure 6.1). The blank form may be photocopied when needed. This approach is good because it disciplines thinking about the project. A loose-leaf binder allows pages to be inserted as they are required. It also allows other pieces of information such as notes from meetings to be included. You can add pages if you need more room for later reflection.

However, you may feel that the standardised format is restrictive. You might prefer the latitude to create entries as and when they are necessary in the way you think fit. In this case a bound notebook is best. It is permanent and pages cannot be lost. Notes from meetings can be added as the meetings happen. Leave some room for later reflection though. Odd pages can always be glued in between the bound leaves.

Increasingly, some people like the idea of using an electronic notebook for the project log. These are good for generating presentable versions of the log. However, they may tempt one to revise and refine notes to produce a polished document rather than let them stand as honest and immediate reflection on experienced events (which is what they are meant to be). Electronic notebooks can also prove to be slow and may be quite invasive as a way of making notes in a meeting.

Whatever format you choose, remember the function of the log is to aid active learning, not to be a history of the project.

Team discussion point	In private, consider the formats available for a project log. Decide on one which you think will work for you.
	Present your format to the rest of the group. Say what you think are its strong points. Invite (positive!) criticism to identify what might be its weak points. After each group member has done this, consider your choice of format. Can it be improved by making some modification? Does another format look better?
	Select the format you will use for the project. Don't forget, it is an individual choice. It is not necessary that every member of the group use the same format.
	The project log is an invaluable tool for the consultant.

Project Log – Date: 13 June 2004

Key achievements to date:
- *first meeting with client;*
- *initial analysis undertaken;*
- *team have met to develop first draft of proposal*

Objectives for next stage:
- *agree proposal with client;*
- *move on to next stage of analysis.*

Note: Meeting to be held next Wednesday – make sure all team know about it. Especially John, who missed last meeting!

Analysis
Client does not seem clear on what he wants. We must get a clear idea by the end of the meeting. Two strategies: (1) we explore options fully and hope that a decision comes out of the meeting; (2) we need to put forward clear proposals – tell him what he needs. It seems we must choose between the 'expert' and 'doctor-patient' modes described by Edgar Schein – task for self: get book out of library tonight to review. After this we must decide who will be doing what.

John
John is starting to be a bit of a problem. He has missed meetings and when he has attended he has not been prepared. I think I need to apply a bit of leadership!

Mind map on how to deal with John

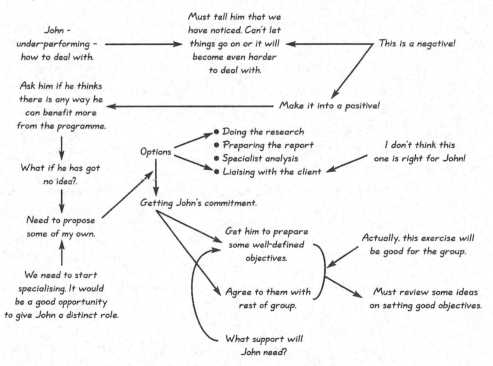

Figure 6.1 An example of a page from a project log

◆ Summary of key ideas

The project proposal is a critical part of the consulting project. It does two things:

- It sells what the consultant has to offer.
- It can be used to manage the client's expectations about the outcomes of the consulting exercise.

The proposal should be a short, impactful document. The key elements to include are:

1 a title;
2 a brief statement of the client's requirements;
3 an overall aim for the consulting project;
4 a list of specific objectives – what the project aims to do;
5 a list of specific outcomes – what the business will be able to do as a result of the project;
6 a statement about your approach to the project – how you intend to tackle the project and why this will be effective.

If appropriate, the following may be added:

7 a time plan detailing key events; and
8 a costing for the project, detailing fees and expenditure.

The project log serves a number of valuable functions:

- It provides a summary for information collected.
- It provides a secure location for notes taken when communicating.
- It acts as a permanent record of the consulting exercise.
- It encourages reflection on the consulting experience.
- It provides a forum for analysis.

The log should include details on the stages of the project, events and communications that take place. It should consider these in relation to the objectives set and the outcomes achieved. It is also a place where information important for the project may be noted and analysis undertaken. Critically, the log is a place where reflection on outcomes, both positive and negative, may be made.

The log is a private document. It need not be polished for presentation. Experiment with formats and find one that works for you.

Key reading

Markham, C. (1997) *Practical Management Consultancy* (3rd edn). Milton Keynes: Accountancy Books.
Noakes, S. (2003) *The Definitive Guide to Project Management*. Harlow, Essex: FT Prentice Hall.

Management Consultancy and Skills

Rackman, N. (1995) *Spin selling®*. Aldershot, Hampshire: Gower.
Wortman, M.S. and Forst, L.I. (eds) (1979) *The Academic Consultant Connection*. New York: Kendal-Hunt.

Discussion point

Keep a cool head in times of rising costs

FT

By **Anthony Hopwood**   **21 August 2003**

Costs are a strategic consideration for most companies. With pressure mounting on prices, volumes and margins, business leaders are having to give renewed consideration to their cost management strategies. With low-cost outsourcing becoming more widespread, concerns about costs are more intense than ever.

In times of slowing growth, increasing competition and the risk of deflation, costs take on a new significance in the management of profitability. As control of price starts to slip away, retailers and distributors demand an ever greater share of margins. Companies that are ill-prepared for the consequences can slip into crisis.

However, immediate cost-cutting in practice tends to be a crude and simplistic exercise. Redundancies and the elimination of overheads usually take priority. Investment in marketing and research and development is sacrificed for immediate gains. Goodwill can be lost both inside and outside the company to save short-term cash flow. In times of crisis, there is usually little investment in analysis and reflection. The meat-cleaver approach takes priority over putting the brain to work.

But in such difficult times it pays to be analytical. Even in the short term, cost management should never be merely an accountant's exercise. Accountants only record costs: they do not incur them. All functions – operations, distribution, marketing, human resources and finance – have a role to play in identifying targets for saving, and managers should establish interdisciplinary teams to co-ordinate their actions.

Managers tend to be inward-looking when thinking about costs, yet ideas for reducing costs are as likely to come from outside the company as inside. It is vital to benchmark against competitors and study developments in the wider economy. Germs of imaginative ideas that challenge the status quo should be welcomed. What is being done elsewhere? Can it be done here, or modified for application here?

Reducing costs requires them to become what they were not. In the process of transforming its supply chain systems, for example, a retail organisation is likely to reduce its costs of inventory. If managers have to conceive costs differently, this can be as much an act of imagination as a crude process of elimination. 'Can this be done without that?' ought to be the daily refrain.

Cost management should not be an isolated exercise but should sit alongside the disciplines of value creation and revenue management. Knowing when to incur additional costs for additional return is as important as knowing how to eliminate them when necessary. In the longer term, companies should be more interested in spending money to create profitable products – premium, high-quality products – than in cutting costs now.

Consider the example of Wedgwood, manufacturer of fine pottery. The company has been in the news this year for drastic cost-cutting, redundancies and – the ultimate irony – outsourcing manufacturing to Asia, where the techniques for producing its wares originated centuries ago. Its approach is strikingly different from that of the 18th-century founder, Josiah Wedgwood. He invested heavily in research and development, in management and in design. He was at pains to understand the emerging culture of eating and entertainment. As a result, he was able to create a range of high-quality products at premium prices that attracted attention – and profits.

How different has been the Wedgwood of recent years. No longer noted for its commitment to technical innovation or management expertise, it now trades largely on tradition, thus denying itself real possibilities for branding and product differentiation. Without that, prices are in turn under pressure and costs become more vital.

In the company's defence, it faces strong foreign competition and is one of many UK industries that have struggled with overcapacity inherited from the glory days. Wedgwood

has started to rediscover the value of investing in design, with a new range by Jasper Conran, the British designer. Yet this may be too little, too late.

Companies that lose control of their market see the importance of costs rise and the possibility of dealing with them in clever ways eliminated. Any significant change in a company's cost structure needs to be accompanied by a change in strategy, so that it can compete more effectively on the basis of its product.

Should Wedgwood expand further and promote its contemporary range alongside the classic Wedgwood of old? Should it invest in design, by creating a range that recalls the highlights of the Art Deco period, the 1950s and so on? Would such a strategy allow it to transform the production process using smaller-scale technologies? And how could the latest research on materials science and ceramics production enable it to restructure its costs more radically?

Such questions make it apparent that cost control cannot be considered outside the context of product, marketing and distribution strategies. Cost management is a knowledge-intensive pursuit. It requires information on much more than current costs, which on this view are only the benchmark for radical change. Wedgwood needs the stimulus that knowledge of radical alternative production techniques and modes of operations management could bring.

The latest thinking on ceramic materials would enable it to gauge whether niche product innovations could attract higher prices and bring in different production technologies. An informed decision on this requires the involvement of scientists, operations specialists, marketing experts and designers, as well as accountants. A successful cost management company, it follows, requires a strategy for bringing in fresh knowledge that includes a process for efficiently capturing the results and distributing them around the business.

This cannot be achieved overnight. There is no doubt that the Josiah Wedgwood of old would be comfortable in such an enterprise. He used his links with such bodies as the Royal Society and the Lunar Society to contact the top applied scientists of the late 18th century, and also to the artistic elite of his time – Stubbs, Flaxman and others. How would the Wedgwood of today attempt to replicate such a dense circle of knowledge and understanding?

First, he would be cautious of consultants. The knowledge they offer is often second-hand and sometimes dated. What is needed is the contextual understanding of people who know a sector and can see what it might become. When there is a need to be at the forefront of ideas it is best to look directly at internal talent and the centres of new expertise – companies in other industries, universities, research institutions and design schools. Use student project teams; they are cheap. Invite in a wider range of contacts and open the enterprise to new ideas. Travel, visit, read and reflect. Then act.

Today's most innovative companies are doing just that. Intel has set up a series of mini 'lablets' next to universities to draw in ideas. Eli Lilly continues to refine InnoCentive, its online knowledge broker, posting problems and inviting solutions from individuals and companies around the world.

Drastic though some of today's cost-cutting may need to become, its real pay-off can only come from a deeply informed strategic examination of the cost management agenda, one that is intertwined with a careful examination of other vital aspects of the business. Cost management is not an isolated art, or one that should be confined to the accountants' floor. It should involve the whole business. It also has the potential to change the whole business.

The writer is Peter Moores dean and professor of management studies at Said Business School, University of Oxford.

Q1 Imagine that you have been offered the Wedgwood project. Review the article and make a series of key points in your log for discussion at an initial meeting with the client.

Q2 What challenges and objections might the client raise about a consulting project? Detail about four in your log and plan responses.

Q3 What is the general learning from this article about your consulting in the future? Detail about four key points in the log.

CHAPTER 7

The consultant-organisational interaction I: setting goals

Learning outcomes

The learning outcomes from this chapter are:

- to recognise the *rational, cognitive* and *political* dimensions of a business problem;
- to understand how a problem may be *defined* to make it amenable to resolution;
- to understand the distinction between the aim, objectives and outcomes of the consulting project;
- to be able to define an effective aim, objectives and outcomes for the project;
- to be able to articulate the aim, objectives and outcomes in a convincing and influential way.

7.1 Identification of opportunities and issues by the client organisation

Evaluating the problem

Consultants are usually called in to the client business in order to address some 'problem' the business has, or at least that its managers perceive to have. The problem will be defined as something that stops the business reaching the potential that it feels it should have. The word 'problem' has a negative connotation. To a consultant and the client business, a problem may actually be *positive*. A problem might well be an opportunity the business could potentially exploit as much as an issue that restricts the business.

Problems do not present themselves. The firm's managers identify them. Managers interpret problems and decide to address them. A problem has three facets that determine the way in which it will be understood and acted upon by managers (*see* Figure 7.1). We may label these the *rational*, the *cognitive* and the *political*.

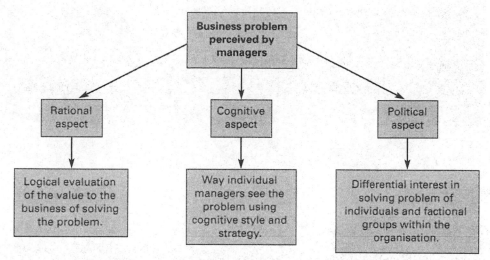

Figure 7.1 The facets of a business problem

The *rational* facet refers to the way in which the problem is seen in a logical manner. It reflects a formal or semi-formal evaluation of the way in which resolution of the problem might affect the business. It will be based on a dispassionate consideration of the economic 'value' or cost of the problem and the business's capability to deal with it or, if it is an opportunity, to exploit it.

The *cognitive* facet refers to the way in which individual managers see a problem. It reflects the way in which the problem is processed by a manager's mental faculties. Cognitive style and strategy determine the way in which managers see the world, process information about it and deal with challenges. The manager's cognitive style and strategy will influence the way in which the problem appears in the manager's mental landscape and determine the priority the manager will give it.

Ultimately, the problems that a firm faces must be dealt with by the business as a whole. The *political* facet reflects the way in which a problem is received and processed by the individuals who make up the organisation. Not all managers have the same objectives. Different individuals and groups have different interests. A particular problem will affect different managers in different ways, and some more than others. Some issues may be problems for some managers and opportunities for others. These differences will affect the way in which the managers work together as a team to address the problem. Ultimately, if the organisation's politics become pernicious, managers may actually work against each other.

The astute consultant recognises each of these facets. The rational is important because it determines the value the consultant can create by resolving the problem. The cognitive is relevant because it affects the way in which the consultant communicates with the client and can positively influence him or her. The political is significant because the success or otherwise of a project will depend on getting the whole organisation to see the benefits of a particular course of action and to unite behind it.

Four dimensions of a problem will be relevant to its definition (*see* Figure 7.2). These are the *current situation* of the business, the *goals* of the business (that is the state it aspires to achieve), the *assistors* (things which help the business achieve its goals) and the *inhibitors* (those things which limit the firm and stop it achieving its goals).

Assistors and inhibitors may be internal to the firm (that is, under the direct control of the firm's managers) or external to it (that is, *not* directly under the control of the firm's managers). Some important assistors and inhibitors are listed in Table 7.1.

Table 7.1 Assistors and inhibitors

	Internal	External
Assistors	Cost advantages (scale/experience) Unique resources Innovative products Knowledge of products Knowledge of markets Business location (especially for distributors)	Relationships with customers Investor's goodwill Location in business network Expanding market potential High profit margins
Inhibitors	Lack of management experience Lack of capital Lack of knowledge about products Limited knowledge about the environment	Limited market potential (market decline) Competitor activity Changes in customer interest (particularly for fashion-sensitive products) High entry costs

The challenge for the consultant is to define the business problem in the following terms.

How can assistors be used and developed to achieve the set objectives?

The key issues are how the business can capitalise on internal assistors and how the firm's managers can take advantage of external assistors. It is important to ask whether the problem can be defined to enable managers to take control of external assistors and bring them in: turning external assistors into internal ones. An example is taking control of customer demand through an effective marketing campaign. Here the external assistor of customer goodwill is converted into an internal assistor of marketing capability.

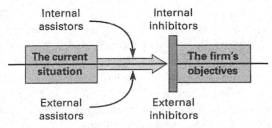

Figure 7.2 Framework for analysing business problems

Management Consultancy and Skills

How can inhibitors be overcome or avoided so that the business can move forward?

Inhibitors limit the business. An internal inhibitor is the responsibility of the firm's managers. It is they who must take the initiative and address the problem. The priority given to this will depend on the business's plans and the significance of the inhibitor. An external inhibitor is a given. It is outside the control of the firm's managers. The firm must develop strategies that take account of the external inhibitors in the environment and avoid their impact. For example, a lack of knowledge must be addressed through organisational learning. Sectors in which competitors (especially stronger competitors) are active should be given lower priority than those in which absence of competitors creates an opportunity.

A problem is best defined in relation to these four facets. They can be used to guide investigation of the problem and to specify the information that is required in order to define it. This framework works well as the basis of a brainstorming session. This is best undertaken with members of the consulting team and with key information providers from the client business.

Reinterpreting problems as opportunities

Problems, by their very nature, are negative. They demand to be solved, but they do not inspire. Opportunities, however, are positive. They call to be exploited. Problems, especially when their resolution is difficult, tend to be divisive. Managers may work at devising solutions. However, energy will also be diverted into avoiding recrimination. After all, a problem is 'internal' to the business. Someone, somewhere must have caused it. A problem is someone's *fault*. Rather than solve the problem, a manager may think it a better strategy to ensure that someone else gets the blame for it. This is a self-defence mechanism. Problems get caught up in the internal politics of the organisation and can exacerbate them.

An opportunity, however, is external to the firm. It comes from 'outside'. It is there to be exploited. It is not anyone's fault. Managers will resist identification of problems. They will minimise them or even deny their existence. Yet they will queue up to take credit for identifying an opportunity. Managers can rally round and work together to take advantage of an opportunity. In general, people are constrained to deal with problems; they are motivated to capitalise on opportunities. For these reasons it is better, whenever possible, to talk about taking advantage of opportunities rather than addressing problems.

In many respects problems and opportunities are the two sides of one coin. It depends on whether one looks towards what has been achieved from the perspective of what might have been achieved or from the starting-point. Translating one to the other is often a matter of rhetorical approach. The old adage of the half-filled glass applies: is it half-full or half-empty?

For example, a new product launch has not gone as well as expected. This is a problem: the return on the investment is not as good as expected. However, it represents an opportunity to understand customer demand better and come up with an improved product. A competitor moves into a market. This is a problem – it will increase competition – but it confirms that the sector is an attractive one for the player who can get it right.

A word of caution here: although it is better, for the reasons given, to talk about opportunities rather than problems, it is important to be realistic. Too much emphasis on the positives can make someone seem glib and unable to come to terms with the real world. People may begin to doubt the decision-making ability of the person. If the person cannot see the problem, how can his or her decisions address it? If the person does not allow himself or herself to talk about problems, this limits the call to action he or she can make to others. Further, individuals who tend to see problems rather than opportunities (and this is to some extent a part of the cognitive perspective discussed in Section 8.5) may feel that those who emphasise the positive are ignoring their concerns.

Turning problems into opportunities – negatives into positives – should not be a mantra; it should be a tool used as part of an overall communication strategy. It should not be used to deny problems but to put them into context. Revealing the opportunity makes the problem seem tractable and tackling it even enjoyable. It also takes the sting out of responsibility (real or imagined) for the problem in the first place.

7.2 Problem analysis, specification and quantification

The consultant is presented with a 'problem' by member(s) of the client organisation. Before he or she can start to solve this problem, they need to analyse it and discover whether the client has correctly identified the problem and its 'root cause'. Ideally this should be done before any formal proposal is given to the client.

Stage 1: Brainstorm the causes

Using members of the consulting team and, if possible, clients as well, you need to explore some of the causes of the problem. You need to clearly state the chosen problem and follow the rules of *brainstorming* (*see* Section 10.6) to answer the question.

For example, the question could be: *why is the response to my questionnaire too low*? *See* Table 7.2 for some responses to the question.

Table 7.2 Possible causes of a poor response rate

Not going to a named person

Survey is too long

The language used is too complicated

The incentives are not large enough

It is not clear on how the interviewee should respond

The person to whom the completed questionnaire should be sent is not obvious

It has not been sent to enough people

The mailing list details are out of date

The information requested is confidential or too personal

The target is too busy

The respondent is suspicious of the survey's motives

Our organisation has failed to process the completed questionnaire

Stage 2: Group the causes into major categories

This is often a helpful way to sort a lot of ideas that have come from the brainstorming session. Kerri Simon [www.isixsigma.com/library/content/t000827] describes two sets of categories for service and manufacturing which may prove a useful guide (*see* Table 7.3).

Table 7.3 Suggested categories for service and manufacturing

Service industries *(The 4 Ps)*	Manufacturing industries *(The 6 Ms)*
■ Policies	■ Machines
■ Procedures	■ Methods
■ People	■ Materials
■ Plant/Technology	■ Measurements
	■ Mother nature (environment)
	■ Manpower (people)

So using our example from above, we could group our responses in the way described in Table 7.4.

Table 7.4 Major causes of poor response

Not getting to the right person	Not going to a named person It has not been sent to enough people The mailing list details are out of date
Target not completing the survey	Survey is too long The language used is too complicated The incentives are not large enough The information requested is confidential or too personal The target is too busy The respondent is suspicious of the survey's motives
Survey completed but not processed	It is not clear on how the interviewee should respond The person to whom the completed questionnaire should be sent is not obvious Our organisation has failed to process the completed questionnaire

Stage 3: Construct a 'cause and effect' diagram

This useful tool (often called a 'fishbone diagram') was developed by Kaoru Ishikawa, a Japanese management guru who was particularly concerned with the achievement of total quality within the workplace. For this and other problem-solving techniques, you should refer to Ishikawa's book *What is Total Quality Control?: the Japanese Way*.

Here it provides a picture of the problem ('effect') and the likely causes. By using this, you can challenge further the groupings and identify the *major* causes. The minor causes should be ones that are easily resolved or do not have a significant impact on the problem. Figure 7.3 takes our example and uses the cause and effect tool.

Stage 4: Getting to the root cause of the major problems

Having established the major causes of the problem, it is important to determine the *root* causes. The '5 Whys' tool is useful here to challenge thinking and undercover the true root of the problem. It keeps asking 'why' until a meaningful answer to the root cause is uncovered. Sometimes it takes less than 5 Whys and sometimes more to reach an answer.

An example of this process using the 5 Whys approach follows. This example is based on the analysis of an unsuccessful sales call.

Problem statement: The last sales call was not successful.

1 **Why?** Because the customer did not buy.

2 **Why did the customer not buy?** Because the product did not seem right for her.

3 **Why was the product not right for her?** Because it did not address any needs she had.

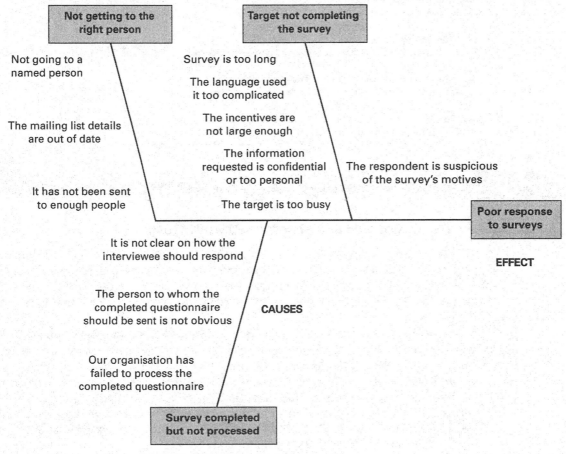

Figure 7.3 Fishbone diagram of the causes of low response to surveys

4 **Why did the product not address any need she had?** Because it was too complex for her business.

5 **Why did you not know this before the call?** Because I did not know about the business she was running.

6 **Why did you not know about the business she was running?** Because no research had been done in advance.

The solution to this problem is clear!

In our example, if we decide that the mailing list being out of date is a major cause of the problem, we can explore the root cause of this (Table 7.5). In this example, it is the last answer that gives us something to work on as including an update of the mailing list *is* within our control and therefore can be fixed. In comparison, if we had stopped at answer 4, we would be trying to change the budget we were given, which is harder or impossible to achieve.

Table 7.5 Root cause of why the mailing list is out of date

1 **Why** is the mailing list out of date?
   ■ Because we haven't updated it

2 **Why** did you not update it?
   ■ Because we cannot afford it

3 **Why** can you not afford it?
   ■ Because we did not put it in our budget for the year

4 **Why** did you not put it in our budget for the year?
   ■ Because we had no room in the budget we were given

5 **Why** did you have no room in the budget you were given?
   ■ Because we thought it was not necessary

7.3 Objective setting: defining the desired end state

Aims, objectives, outcomes and actions

When we engage in conscious action we do so with a view of what the future will be like. We anticipate future conditions when we make a decision and act on it. For example, an investor is not just interested in the current profitability of a company. He or she is also interested in what the company's profitability in the *future* will be.

Managers do not simply accept what the future conditions might be like. They try to control them. Good managers actively *shape* the future. Managers operate with a conscious picture of the state they wish to create: where they want their organisation to be, what they want the organisation to do, what they want it to be like. This desire colours management language. Managers talk in explicit terms about what they and their organisations wish to achieve. They use a variety of words to describe these ambitions. They will talk, for example, about their *goals, aims, objectives, missions* and *outcomes*.

Sometimes these words are taken to be synonymous with each other. At other times, users imply subtle distinctions between them. It is useful for the consultant to recognise differences in meaning between such terms. This aids thinking about the rationale for the consulting project and makes communication more efficient and likely to have an impact.

Appropriate and well-defined aims, objectives and outcomes are the cornerstone of effective project management. They are worth investing in. They provide the solid platform on which a successful project can be built. The consultant develops aims, objectives and outcomes in the preliminary analysis phase of the consulting project. They are communicated to the client through the proposal. They function to keep the project on track and help the consulting team maintain focus during the process of delivery. They can then be used to assess what the project has actually achieved at delivery. The following discussion highlights the differences between aims, objectives and outcomes and how that difference might be used to aid the consultant in analysis and communication with the client at the different stages of the project.

Aims

The aim of the project is its *overall goal*. It is the *broad* scope of what that project aspires to achieve. An aim is the starting-point of a project. It is first articulated as a desire: a sense that things might be different and better. Most businesses share a set of common desires. For example to grow, to be more profitable, to be more secure, to compete more effectively and so on. It is from these general desires that the aim of a consulting project can be distilled. In defining an aim, a consultant is refining the desires of the firm's managers. The way in which this will be done will depend on a number of factors. Some of those the consultant needs to take into account include the following.

The extent to which managers have already articulated their desires for the business

Some managers have a clear view of what they want to achieve. Others only harbour a vague sense of the direction they want to take their business. The consultant may obtain a well-specified project. Often, though, the consultant must help the client comprehend and articulate what he or she wants to achieve on behalf of the firm. This does not mean that the consultant imposes an aim and objectives on the client. Rather the consultant must *facilitate* the client's articulation of what he or she wishes to do.

The level of detail in that articulation

As a business moves forward to pursue its aims, it changes. It modifies its internal processes. It must adjust the structures that give the business its form. It develops its relationships with external stakeholders. Sometimes managers have thought these things through in detail. At other times they will have given them little thought. Consideration must be given to the *detailed* implications of pursuing and achieving particular goals for the firm as a whole. If managers have not

Management Consultancy and Skills

done this, the consultant must encourage them to do so and support them to appreciate these changes.

How appropriate the aims are for the business

Not all aims are appropriate for a business. A detailed consideration of what will happen if the business actually achieves the aims that managers are specifying may indicate that the outcomes might not help, and could even damage, the business. The outcomes may, for example, move the business into an area where competitive pressures are unsustainable. They may expose the business to too high a level of risk. In short, they may reduce rather than increase its ability to reward its stakeholders.

In this case, the consultant is obliged to inform the client that, in his or her opinion, the aim is not appropriate for the business. This will usually result in a reconsideration of the aims.

The extent to which aims are realistic, given the firm and its situation

Even if the aims are *appropriate* for the business, consideration must be given to how *realistic* they are. Can the business *really* deliver them? Two factors are important to this consideration. First: can the aims realistically be achieved given the situation in the market in which the firm operates? Aims must reflect the reality of the demand of the firm's customers. It is pointless having an aim of achieving sales of £10 million with a product whose total market is worth only £5 million. Second: are the aims reasonable given the resources the firm has available to pursue them? It is not usually realistic for a small firm to aspire to market leadership using just its own cash flow. It might do so if sufficient new investment capital can be found. If this is the course decided upon, acquiring this additional capital will need to be incorporated in the project.

The way in which the desires are particular to the firm and are distinguished from the general desires all firms have

All firms have ambitions of some sort. 'Generic aims' include a desire to grow, to increase profits, to make cash flow more stable and so on. These are common to most, if not all, businesses. The consultant must be careful to distinguish between those aims the firm will share with all other firms in its sector and those that can properly be said to be exclusive to the business. The distinction is important because businesses pursuing shared aims tend to meet in head-to-head competition. Aims which are exclusive may be a way of differentiating the firm and so reducing competitive pressures.

The scope of the consulting project relative to the business as a whole

Some aims are general. They relate to what the business as a whole wishes to achieve. Other aims may be more localised. They will relate to a limited part of the firm only. There are three dimensions along which aims usually become specific to a part of the business. If the firm is large enough, they may relate to one particular part of the business or business unit within the firm as a whole. In addition, they may refer to the development of a particular product range out of the firm's entire product scope. Finally, they may refer to a particular functional activity within the firm, such as marketing, production or human resource management. These three dimensions are illustrated in Figure 7.4.

A project should be summarised by a *single* aim, not a list. The important thing is that the aim summarises the project in a succinct way so that all involved can recognise it. It might even be thought of as the *mission* for the project. It is not necessary that the aim quantifies the project or gives away all the details. That is the job of objectives and outcomes, discussed below.

The best way to start the aim is with a phrase like:

It is the aim of this project to ...

or:

This project aims to ...

For example:

This consulting project aims to give New Firm Ltd an analysis of its main competitors to aid decision-making about competitive positioning.

Or:

It is the aim of this consulting project to develop a promotional plan for the effective launch of the Ideal product range.

Mission

In many ways, a business may be thought of as a permanent and ongoing project. Certainly, an entrepreneur will see the development of his or her venture as a project of great importance. In the case of the whole business as a project the overall aim of the business may be defined in terms of the business's *mission*. A mission is the reason for the firm's existence. It is a statement of *what* it will

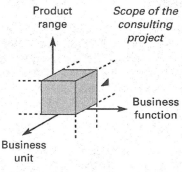

Figure 7.4 The scope of a consulting project

achieve and *how*. A mission can include a statement of what the firm offers, to whom it is offering it, the source of its advantages in the marketplace, its aspirations and the ethical values it will uphold. (*See* Wickham (1997) for a review of business missions.) If a business has a stated mission it is a good idea to test the aims of a particular consulting project against it. They should resonate. The consulting project should help the firm achieve its mission. If it is recognised that it does, it can be a positive selling point for the project.

Objectives

An aim is a *broad* statement. It is a *wish*. Objectives provide the details of how this wish will be made into reality. A single aim may be split into a number of objectives. These may be listed. A good way to start the objective list is with the phrase:

The objectives of the consulting project are to ...

The specific objectives may be put into a bullet-point list after this statement.

A number of tests should be applied to an objective list to ensure that the objectives provide the basis for a good project. Good objectives must meet the following criteria.

Consistency

Consistency is the first and most fundamental test. Are the objectives consistent with the agreed aim? Will they deliver it? If not, they must be revised.

Definition

An objective must be well defined: it should not be ambiguous. A great number of problems can arise if the consultant and the client (or different members of the consulting team) read objectives in different ways. Avoid words that mean different things to different people. For example, the word 'profitability' often appears in objectives. Improving it would certainly seem to be a good thing to do. Yet what does the word refer to? Is it profit margin? Or return on capital employed? Or cash flow? The simple rule is: if in doubt – spell it out!

Desirability

The test of desirability relates to the point about the appropriateness of aims discussed above. Will achieving the objectives actually be good for the firm? If the aim is appropriate and the objectives are consistent, then logically they should also be desirable. This allows a double check that what the consultant is doing for the firm is worthwhile.

Feasibility

Feasibility asks whether the objectives are likely to be achieved given the environmental conditions the firm faces. For example, can sales be achieved given the size of markets, product advantages and competitive pressures? Always ask challenging questions. For example, if the business is to grow, can margins be sustained given the strengths of suppliers and buyers? Can new business be delivered in the face of competitor responses?

Achievability

If an objective is feasible, it can be achieved in *principle*. For an objective to be achievable in *practice*, the firm must dedicate resources to pursuing it. Does the firm have the necessary resources? If it has, is this project the best available use for them? Account must be taken of productive resources and people as well as money. If the firm does not have the resources to hand, can it obtain them? Is obtaining these additional resources part of the consulting project or is it a separate project? Care needs to be taken to clarify and agree whether the project is just about identifying and recommending a direction for the business or actually implementing the project and taking the business there.

Quantified

Ideally, objectives should be quantified. To 'grow the business' does not mean very much. To 'grow the business by 20 per cent' does. Whenever possible, objectives should be quantified by numbers. It is not just *what* will be achieved, but *when* it will be achieved and, critically, *what it will be worth when it is.*

Not all objectives can easily be quantified. Objectives such as 'to make our human resource management more effective' or 'to make employees' working time happier' do not offer easy numerical targets. Some would argue that they can, ultimately, be quantified. A starting-point might be the actual costs of the human resource management function and staff turnover. Others may argue for the inherently qualitative nature of such objectives. Quantitative information may be difficult (that is, expensive) to obtain. In any case, they may argue, forcing artificial numerical targets on such objectives robs them of their essence.

If objectives are left unquantified it is particularly important that the client's expectations are carefully managed and not allowed to become unrealistic. Some understanding of what these objectives mean for the firm must be found. It is important that what the project can achieve is communicated in an unambiguous way.

Signposted

An objective is *signposted* if it will be clear when it has been achieved. As the word implies, a signpost indicates that the project is going, or has gone, in the right direction. Signposts take a number of forms. They may be a physical output (a report presented, for example) or may be indicated by a numerical measure (say, an increase in sales). Occasionally they may be revealed through qualitative information, for example a survey of employee satisfaction. Quantified objectives have inherent signposts. Qualitative objectives need signposts to be assigned to them. Good signposts are definite, are easily recognised and are agreed by all who have an interest in the consulting project. Do not assume that signposts are recognised and accepted by all involved. If in doubt, highlight the signpost and make sure it is agreed to.

Clearly, aims and objectives are involved in describing the same thing: the direction the business wishes to move in. They say this in different ways, though. In a 1977 article, James Brian Quinn makes a powerful case as to why broad goals and specific objectives should be separately articulated. Three reasons are important.

First, goals can be used to give a sense of direction without over-centralising decision-making. Individuals contributing to the project can set their own objectives or subobjectives and check them against the goal rather than have them set by the project leadership. For example, a goal might be set to generate sales from a new product. If so, decisions must be made about what the product will be like, its features, its price and so on. But the goal does not set these as specified objectives. The managers launching the product are free to use their experiences and local knowledge to set these themselves. An aim offers direction without dictating individual contribution.

Second, goals, being broad and unquantified, do not allow conflict over detail. It is details people often object to. For example, an objective to increase sales by 15 per cent might easily start an argument. Should it be 10 per cent or 20 per cent? Such a debate obscures the fact that there is unanimity on the central point: that growth is wanted. Recognising this as a general aim is a starting-point for agreement on the detail.

Third, goals define broad 'spaces' for achievement whereas objectives are narrow. Objectives are rigid, especially when they have agreed signposts attached to them. The point about objectives is that they be strived for. An objective is of little use if it can be changed easily. However, there are circumstances in which it might be legitimate to change objectives. The client may alter the requirements of the project. There may be a change in the resources available for the project. New information may become available which indicates a change in direction is judicious.

Situations in which objectives might be changed are discussed in Chapter 16. In such cases the best move is to go back to the original aim and use it to devise new objectives in light of the new situation. This is much easier, and prone to less disagreement than starting from scratch and establishing entirely new objectives in the absence of an overall goal.

Actions

Good objectives inspire managers to follow them through. They are a *call to action*. Actions are what managers actually do in order to achieve objectives. A collection of co-ordinated actions is a *plan*. It is implementing a plan of actions that actually consumes resources.

Plans organise actions in two dimensions. The first is linearly, as a *sequence in time*. Actions follow one another. Some actions can be undertaken only after others have been completed. Actions must be properly sequenced. The stages of the consulting project reviewed in Chapter 4 are an example. The second dimension is *co-ordination*, the ordering of actions between individuals. The advantage of team working is that it allows individuals to distinguish and differentiate the contribution they make. If the value this potentially offers is to be realised then individual contributions must be properly integrated. Planning will be dealt with in more detail in Chapter 15.

Outcomes

Outcomes are what will be *made possible* if the objectives are achieved. Outcomes are the difference that is made by achieving the objectives. An outcome is something that takes the business along the road to achieving its organisational mission. It is the outcomes of a project that really sell it to the client. The outcomes define the value of the project to the client.

A good way to start an outcome statement is:

As a result of this project the business will be able to ...

Defining outcomes gives the consultant a chance to check the value of what is being offered to the client. Three important aspects to question are as follows.

Are outcomes consistent with aims?

Are the outcomes of the project in line with the aims agreed for the project? Is the outcome the fulfilment of an aim? Will the outcomes take the business along the road that it wants to go? Critically, will the outcomes help the business deliver its mission?

Are outcomes attractive?

Will the client business and the decision-making unit involved in bringing in the consultant recognise the outcomes as ones which are right for the business and which they desire to see happen? Don't forget, managers are not always rational. They don't always do what the consultant might see as being in the best interests of the firm. Consultants drive change and change is usually political. Different managers see the benefits of change in different ways. If there is an issue, question how different individuals and groups might see the project outcomes. One approach is to consider the different types of client involved in the project (*see* Section 1.5).

Will the client recognise the value created by the consultant?

If managers find the outcomes attractive, do they recognise the contribution the consultant is making to their delivery? Do they feel that they can achieve them unaided? If not, why not? The process consulting mode (*see* Section 1.6) can be particularly prone to leaving managers feeling that the consultant has not made a contribution, especially when process consulting is at its most effective!

Understanding your own objectives

People work together because this allows greater value to be created. In working together, they agree to the aims and objectives of a project. However, individuals will have their own personal objectives that are distinct from those of others involved in the project. Managers pursue their own interests as well as the interests of the organisations they work for and with. The consulting project is no different. The consultant will have objectives that are distinct from those of the client. This does not detract from the potential for working together. Far from it. It is the fact that the client and consultant have distinct objectives that allows them to work together and create value for each other.

Gaining a valuable managerial experience

A consulting project is an opportunity to engage in a high-profile, senior-level managerial experience. If it is to be a valuable part of an overall management education, it needs to be an experience of a particular sort. It should involve contact with senior managers. It should demand that a strategic perspective be taken. It should require that initiative and innovation be brought to bear. Formal managerial skills should be used and developed. If any of these things are missing, the value of the consulting experience will be reduced. Ensuring that the project will have these elements should be an objective for any student undertaking a consulting project.

Practising particular skills

The consulting project provides an opportunity to apply in a real business situation the ideas and skills developed throughout a formal business education. It calls in equal measure on all of the skill areas that mark the effective manager: *analysis skills* which enable opportunities to be spotted, *project management* which can be used to exploit those opportunities and the *relationship-building skills* which enable the value of those opportunities to be communicated and used to motivate others. The consulting project is a chance to see that these skills are of value and to refine their use. It is a proper personal objective that the project be pursued in such a way that these skills are called on in a meaningful and balanced way.

Gaining evidence of achievement

The consulting experience also provides an opportunity to demonstrate managerial ability. The skills used in consulting are transferable to a variety of managerial roles. Successfully completed, the consulting project is something that can be used to enhance the curriculum vitae when applying for positions in the future. It is something that can be related at interviews. It is a very reasonable objective to view the consulting exercise as a way of gaining real and visible evidence of managerial competence. How this can be done is discussed fully in Chapter 23.

Understanding the client's objectives

Clearly, the main objective of the client is to develop the business in a particular direction. However, this is not the client's only objective. They may also have a number of subsidiary objectives that will colour the way he or she approaches the project. Whereas the formal objectives of the project will be explicit, discussed and documented, the client's subsidiary objectives will usually be implicit. It is worthwhile to develop an understanding of them. Recognising the client's subsidiary objectives gives the consultant an insight into how a good working relationship can be developed.

Some important subsidiary objectives for the client might be as follows.

An opportunity to develop general understanding

Consultants are experts. Experts have interesting things to say. The manager may regard working with consultants as an opportunity to explore and develop his or her understanding of management in general and the specific management tasks he or she faces. This general understanding will develop in areas that go well beyond the bounds of the particular project.

An opportunity to explore the business in general terms

Managers must be close to their businesses. Their success depends on an intimate knowledge of and sensitivity to the details of the business they are managing and the specific features of the sector in which it is operating. However, by being so close the manager may not find it easy to stand back and view the business as a whole. It is, as the saying goes, easy to lose sight of the wood for the trees. Working with a consultant is an opportunity to redress this situation.

An opportunity to talk about the business

Managers are usually proud of the businesses they work for. An entrepreneur will be very pleased with what he or she has achieved. The interest the consultant shows is flattering. The consulting project gives the manager a chance to talk about the business in which he or she is involved. This is something most will relish. It is something the consultant can use. Asking the manager to talk about the business will be the first step in building a positive relationship and engendering rapport. It will give the manager the confidence to be open and provide the consultant with the information needed to do the project well. As will be discussed in Section 19.3, rapport can be built and openness encouraged through an effective questioning technique.

Reconciling your own objectives with those of the client

In a good consulting exercise, the client and the consulting group work together as part of a team. This does not mean that the client and consultant share every objective, however. As discussed above, the client and consultant bring along their own, distinct objectives to the project. Usually these will be compatible: the client and the consultant team can agree on a set of co-ordinated actions and common outcomes which will deliver the objectives desired by both parties. Occasionally, however, there will be a misalignment and the consultant and client must negotiate the objectives of the project so that they are reconciled. This process is illustrated in Figure 7.5.

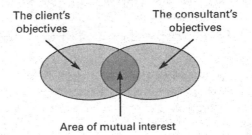

Figure 7.5 Negotiating objectives

Misalignments occur for a number of reasons. Some of the most common are as follows.

The client expects too much of the consulting team

The client may harbour unrealistic expectations about what the consulting team can achieve. The kind of problem that is highlighted may be of a highly technical nature. The project may require specific industry knowledge to be applied. Often, the client will expect the consulting team to build relationships with outside agencies (particularly customers and investors) in a way that the team simply does not have the experience or time to manage properly.

Projects which demand that the consulting team go out and act as a sales force selling products to customers (rather than just develop and advise on a marketing or selling strategy) are examples of this kind of demand.

The client expects too much of the project

The outcomes expected may be unrealistic given the resources the client is willing to put into the project. Unfortunately, whereas most managers recognise their own resource limitations, some think that consultants either have access to an unlimited supply or are superhumanly efficient with those they have!

Typical here are market research projects. The client may be quite clear about the market information wanted but may not recognise the cost involved in gaining that information. It is not unknown for a market research company to be approached and, after its quotation has been found to be too expensive, for a consulting team to be offered the same project without resources made available. The cost of promotional campaigns may also be underestimated.

The project does not have sufficient scope

It is easy for the client manager to look upon the consulting team as an additional, low-cost resource rather than as partners in the development of the business. It is tempting for client managers to hand over jobs that are important, but of low level. Such jobs may involve repetitive tasks. They will not demand that interpretive skills be brought to bear on information obtained. They will not challenge at a sufficiently intellectual level. Such jobs are of such limited scope that they do not demand the full range of skills and insights that would be expected of a consulting challenge. Such jobs should really be undertaken by the business itself.

An example would be a project which involves simply creating a list of potential customers rather than developing an understanding of a new customer segment.

The client is not willing to define specific outcomes

Not everybody works to objectives. Some managers simply don't bother. Others make a policy of not setting them. They prefer to deal with things on a contingency basis as they arise. They may present this as 'flexibility'. Problems will arise if the client resists setting objectives for the project. Without clear objectives, the consulting team has no idea of what to aim for. Expectations cannot be managed properly. It will be tempting for the client to simply see the consultant team as extra resource, to be called upon to do jobs that should be done by the business itself. If objectives are not set, the quality of the consulting exercise as a learning experience must be in doubt.

With a little thought, it is quite easy to deal with these situations. Some useful rules of thumb are as follows.

Agree on aims before discussing objectives

As noted above, aims, because they are broad in scope, tend to be less contentious than detailed objectives. It is better to agree on the overall aim of the project before moving on to specifics. If there is any debate about objectives, either within the consulting team or with the client, then the agreed aim can be used as a reference point.

Break down projects into subprojects

If the client is too ambitious about the project, or expects too much from it, then expectations must be managed. Don't reject the idea for the project out of hand. Rather, get the manager to explore the project he or she is proposing. Break the project down into relevant subprojects. It may be that one of these will present a more realistic project.

Get the client to prioritise outcomes

Having broken the project down, assign objectives to each subproject. Get the client to prioritise. If they must choose, which is most important to them? The argument to use is that it will be better for a realistic project to be done well rather than risk disappointment at the outcomes of one that is too ambitious.

Use the proposal

The proposal documents the project's aims, objectives and outcomes (*see* Section 6.2). If these are written and communicated, the client must recognise them. The aims and objectives of the project must reflect the interests of the manager. However, it is the consultancy team that will actually articulate and document them. This is an advantage, which might be used positively. In the preliminary discussions with the manager it is likely that a lot of ideas will come out. In distilling these into the proposal, the consultant has an opportunity to emphasise and prioritise. Avoid the temptation to impose ideas on the client though. The latitude available here should not be used simply as an opportunity for the team to present the project they believe to be appropriate. The best projects are those to which the client has a genuine commitment.

Understand the client's desired outcomes

Ultimately, it is the project's *outcomes* – the things that the business will be able to do as a result of the project – that are important. This is the difference that the project will make to the business. It is these that the client ultimately 'buys'.

Emphasise the importance of this. Understand what it is that the client wants the business to do. Once this understanding is in place the project can be designed to achieve the outcomes. If the client has unrealistic ambitions, break the outcomes down and get the client to prioritise. Again, a good small project is better than a large mediocre one.

Focus on win-win outcomes

Ultimately, the client and consulting team must work together. The manager will be getting insights of value to his or her business. The consulting team will be gaining a valuable learning experience. There is mutual benefit, not conflict. The consulting team should not hesitate to explain that they are seeking a project which will add to their experience in a meaningful way. The team should make it plain that the manager's knowledge and experience will be an important part of this. Most managers will be flattered that their insights are valuable in this way. It will certainly encourage them to shape the project so that it will provide a good learning experience. A general point: focusing on win-win scenarios like this is the essence of good negotiating practice.

Negotiating objectives is about aligning the project so that the outcomes desired by the client and those desired by the consulting team are achieved.

Team discussion point

Read the following short case study.

Exconom is a company specialising in cable and small-bore pipe laying technology. The company started life as a technical division of a major utility. It gained its independence as the result of a venture capital backed management buyout (MBO) three years ago. The company now has 21 employees and a turnover of just over £4 million. The company's competitive edge comes from its technological capabilities with 'mole' excavating tools. This is equipment that can lay cables and pipes underground without the need to dig a trench first. This reduces cost and disruption. Exconom contracts its services to companies which need to lay cables. Electrical and gas utilities provide the core of business. This business is largely based on historical relationships with these customers developed prior to the MBO. Marketing activities are limited. An as yet small but high-growth sector which is expected to be important in the future is cable television, though the company has not won any contracts here yet.

Alan, the business development manager, explains that the business is sound and has a lot of potential. However, the rest of the management team are limited in their ambitions. While they talk about the business moving into new areas, in practice they resist practical moves. They prefer to stick to the business applications they know and understand. The attitude tends to be one of not taking unnecessary risks while the company is under the 'control' of venture capitalists. In fact, Alan explains, although the venture capitalists will see a reasonable return on their investment (they have a five-year exit plan), they are a little disappointed that the company has not grown as much as initially suggested by the original business plan.

So far, Alan has argued for diversification of the customer base on an ad hoc basis in meetings. This has not really worked. Now he wants to put forward a proposal in the form of a cohesive plan. He wants the team to undertake the research necessary to develop this plan. His brief includes the comment that the management team tend to focus on details. They will make a move only if all implications have been considered. If he is to get his plan implemented he will need a lot of reliable information which makes the opportunities clear and unambiguous. Also, the emphasis should be on why the company's technology will work in the new application and will be attractive to customers.

Alan also mentions in passing the fact that he has heard of a couple of new companies in the sector using the same technology as Exconom. He would be interested in anything the team can pick up on these competitors.

As a team, analyse the problem presented by the client. Can Alan's problem(s) be presented as opportunities?

◆ Summary of key ideas

- The problem: a consultant has been called in to address has three facets:

  - the rational: the value the resolution of the problem will create for the business;
  - the cognitive: the way the problem is perceived by individual managers;
  - the political: the way the organisation as a whole reacts to the problem and the impact it (and its resolution) will have on different individuals.

- The consultant must be aware of each of these facets.
- When defining the problem it is useful to consider four dimensions:

  - the *current state* of the business;
  - the *desired goals* of the business;
  - *assistors*: those things which will help the business achieve its goals;
  - *inhibitors*: those things which will restrict the business and stop it achieving its goals.

- Assistors and inhibitors may both be further divided into internal and external dimensions. Those that are *internal* are part of the firm and are under the control of managers. Those that are *external* are given by the environment and must be accepted by managers.
- On being presented with the 'problem' by the client, it is important to go through a process to get to the root causes.
- Getting to the root causes involves challenging the reasons why there is a problem, uncovering the *major* causes and then asking 'why' until the answer is able to be 'solved' by the consulting team.
- A consulting project is defined in terms of its *aim, objectives* and *outcomes*.
- The aim of the project is a single statement of the project's broad goal, what it aims to achieve. The aim need not be quantified or have a lot of detail. It is important that all involved in the project recognise the aim and agree to it.
- A statement of an aim might start: '*It is the aim of this project to ...*'
- The objectives of the project are a detailed list of the things the project aims to achieve.
- Good objectives are:

  - consistent: they will lead to the aim being fulfilled;
  - well defined: they are unambiguous; they can be read only one way;
  - desirable: they will lead to outcomes wanted by all involved;
  - feasible: they are realistic given the firm's environment;

Management Consultancy and Skills

- achievable: they can be delivered given the firm's resources;
- quantified: it is agreed when they will be delivered and what it will be worth when they are delivered;
- signposted: it will be recognised when the objective has been achieved.

■ The list of objectives can be started with the statement: '*The objectives of this project are to ...*'

■ Objectives are a call to action and to initiate a plan.

■ The outcomes of a project are what the business will be able to do if the objectives are delivered. Outcomes are the *difference* the project will make to the client business.

■ The statement of outcomes can be started with the phrase: '*As a result of this project the business will be able to ...*'

Key reading

Ishikawa, K. (1988) *What is Total Quality Control?: the Japanese Way*. Harlow, Essex: Prentice Hall.

Kluckler, J. and Armbruster, T. (2003) 'Bridging uncertainty in management consulting: The mechanisms of trust and networked reputation', *Organization Studies*, Vol. 24, No. 2, pp. 787–94.

Quinn, J.B. (1977) 'Strategic goals: Process and politics', *Sloan Management Review*, Fall, 21–37.

Silberman, M. (ed.) (2000) *Consultant's Tool Kit: 50 High-impact questionnaires, Activities and How-to Guides for Diagnosing and Solving Client Problems*. New York: McGraw-Hill Education.

Wickham, P.A. (1997) 'Developing a mission for an entrepreneurial venture', *Management Decision*, 35 (5), 373–81.

New risks put scenario planning in favour

By Awi Federgruen and Garrett van Ryzin

FT

19 August 2003

Who could have predicted the horrific events of September 11, 2001? A 1999 US congressional commission led by former senators Gary Hart and Warren Rudman came close. It warned that the US was 'increasingly vulnerable to attack on our homeland' and that 'rapid advances in information and biotechnologies will create new vulnerabilities'.

But perhaps more important than the commission's prophetic messages was its approach. Instead of forecasting a specific future, it set out a collection of possible attack scenarios. It then evaluated national security by analysing possible policies to prepare for, or respond to them.

This approach – known as scenario planning – has gained renewed popularity among public and private decision-makers.

In January this year, the New England Journal of Medicine published a scenario planning analysis on whether US health workers or the whole nation should be vaccinated against smallpox to counter the threat of bio-terrorism. President George W. Bush decided to inoculate 500,000 military personnel and 439,000 health workers.

But what is scenario planning? How does it differ from conventional planning? It is based on a different notion. Rather than adopting a single, 'most likely' outcome, it advocates describing the future by a collection of possible eventualities. It encourages 'contingent thinking' rather than plans based on single predictions.

Introduced in the 1940s by the futurist Herman Kahn, it was used to analyse cold war threats. Since the work of academics Duncan Luce and Howard Raiffa in the 1950s, MBA students have been taught decision trees as a pictorial way of representing problems. And Richard Bellman showed how 'decision tree analysis' could be undertaken algebraically.

In the context of investment decisions, scenario planning has more recently re-emerged as real options analysis.

This shift leads to different decisions. Consider the example of a product launch. The product's price is \$1, but demand is uncertain. Different scenarios for macroeconomic and competitive factors produce demand of between 200 and 1,400 units. Generating the necessary production capacity requires developing land at a cost of \$100. The plant can be built either immedi-

ately for \$600, or later – after sales volumes are known – for \$660.

There are three possible strategies: (1) forego the venture; (2) develop the land and build the plant immediately; or (3) develop the land, but postpone the plant decision until demand is known.

Traditional planning starts with a forecast of demand. The midpoint of the range, 800, is a natural choice. This forecast is then used to evaluate the three options.

The second strategy looks best, yielding a projected profit of \$100 (\$800 in revenue, less the \$100 land cost and \$600 plant costs). But \$700 is a lot to wager on a guess about future demand. So a careful planner performs a complete 'sensitivity analysis' to determine the best option under different forecasts. This shows the second strategy is optimal if demand is more than 700, but the first (do nothing) is best if demand falls below this break-even value. While the recommendation is no longer clear-cut, at least the third strategy can be discarded as inferior, irrespective of future demand.

But while sensitivity analysis does determine the best response to each scenario, it fails to account for the fact that some options are available only before demand is known. That is the primary difference between scenario and traditional planning.

Consider the outcomes of each of the strategies. Doing nothing (strategy 1) always results in zero profits. The second and third strategies generate some profit. Under strategy 3, the \$100 development cost is a sunk cost. The plant should therefore be built as long as revenue exceeds the \$660 building cost, that is, demand (D) exceeds 660, with a resulting profit of D-660-100. If D falls below 660, we do not build the plant and profit equals -\$100. In contrast, strategy 2's profit is always D-600-100.

The develop-and-wait strategy now appears quite attractive, because although its profits are somewhat lower when demand is high, its losses when demand is low are capped at \$100. By postponing our decision to build, we are able to avoid the plant construction costs when demand is low, while still generating profits (albeit lower ones) when demand is high.

The value of such 'contingent decisions' is what scenario planning highlights. Indeed,

if each scenario is equally likely, the average profit under the develop-and-wait strategy is \$140, 40 per cent more than under the 'develop-and-build-immediately' strategy.

This is startling. The decision that is never appropriate in any scenario is optimal (in terms of average profit), in the face of uncertainty.

How does it work in real life? Consider the smallpox study. It identified six attack scenarios, varying from a small laboratory release to terrorists simultaneously spraying the virus at the 10 biggest US airports. The study evaluated the expected number of deaths in each case and concluded that the vaccination of health workers was desirable if the likelihood of a single, high-impact airport attack in, say, the next 10 years was bigger than 0.2 per cent.

Scenario planners face three challenges. The first is constructing meaningful scenarios. This requires expert analysis of the factors that affect the outcomes.

A second challenge is determining the likelihoods of the scenarios.

Finally, planners must decide on a good criterion for selecting strategies. Most individuals and institutions are risk-averse: they value an uncertain reward at a level significantly below the average level the reward in fact reaches. Strategies with higher average pay-offs often entail greater risks. Hence, scenario planning often involves analysing the reward at different levels of risk – much as is done in financial planning.

What explains the recent interest in scenario planning? For one thing, we live in turbulent times. Terrorism, political instability and threats of war make scenarios of extreme price fluctuations in commodity and energy markets more likely. Severe acute respiratory syndrome, 'mad cow disease' and foot-and-mouth disease have rekindled awareness of the natural biological threats we face. Accounting scandals force us to second-guess what used to be considered accurate information about suppliers and customers. In short, companies face far greater risks than before. Indeed, when Mattel used scenario planning to formulate its 2002 strategy, it considered scenarios with several big customers (such as Kmart, FAO and eToys) going bankrupt and others (Wal-Mart) starting to make their own toys.

Second, new analysis tools ranging from spreadsheet to enterprise software systems now allow managers to analyse efficiently large-scale scenario planning problems.

Many 'new' risks have preoccupied earlier generations. Two centuries ago the dilemma whether to vaccinate against small-pox was a principal catalyst for the early development of probability theory, which underlies most of modern-day risk management and scenario planning. One of its founding fathers, Daniel Bernoulli, engaged in a debate with Jean Le Rond d'Alembert. Bernoulli applied probability formulae to compare the risks of vaccination against non-vaccination. D'Alembert agreed with Bernoulli's recommendation but disagreed with assumptions in his analysis about life expectancies, the risk of dying from small-pox, and his disregard for ethical issues.

Scenario planning is like old wine in new bottles. But, as with wine, it does get better over time – and new bottles certainly help.

Awi Federgruen is the Charles E. Exley professor of management at Columbia Business School. Garrett van Ryzin is the Paul M. Montrone professor of private enterprise at Columbia Business School.

Q1 How might scenario planning help in defining objectives for a consulting project?

Q2 What sort of information would you look for in order to develop an effective and accurate scenario plan? (You may care to look ahead to the section on Delphi analysis here – Section 10.9.)

Q3 How would you manage a session with client managers aimed at developing scenarios? Give full details.

The consultant-organisational interaction II: making the journey

Learning outcomes

The learning outcomes from this chapter are:

- to develop a project charter;
- to use the principles from the Six Sigma DMAIC process;
- to understand the levels of client–consultant interaction depending on the type of consulting project undertaken.

8.1 Developing a strategy for the destination

As discussed in Chapter 7, clarifying the causes of the problem is vital. This is also true for the end-point or destination. You need to understand what you are trying to improve or change and when you have achieved your aim.

A good way to start is to develop a 'project charter'. An example is given in Table 8.1.

Table 8.1 Example of a project charter

Project information	Case for project
Leader:	(why are we doing this?)
Project start:	
Project end:	
Brief description:	
Team members	**Problem to be solved**
Sponsor:	(What will be the benefit to us?)
Leader:	
Core team:	
Ad hoc members:	
Scope of the project	**Project goals**
(What should and should not be included)	(What are your objectives?)
Project time frame	**Project measurements**
(Key milestones and dates)	(What tools will you use to know whether you are successful?)

Project information

This provides a quick summary such as the name of the leader, in case someone needs to contact them, the timing of the product and a brief description.

Team members

As well as a team leader, it is often useful to have a sponsor for the project. This person usually is someone senior within the organisation who can help if there are issues in delivering the project and who can ultimately influence upwards to gain implementation. Team size should be as restricted as possible (no more than six) but it may be necessary to involve others on an ad hoc basis, particularly if expert guidance is required.

Scope of the project

Sometimes an issue may be part of a larger problem within the organisation. For example, poor sales may be down to ineffective sales technique (which a project could address) but it may also be due to the wrong type of sales people being recruited, which may be beyond the control of the team. It is therefore important that it is clearly stated what is part of the project and what is not. However, at the end recommendations could be made if such wider issues were highlighted.

Project time frame

This should detail the date of the final delivery of the project outputs together with key events along the way. Pay attention to events that will entail a lot of involvement with the client managers so that they can timetable this into their schedules. Also detail any points at which the client managers will be expected to make expenditure so that they can manage their budgets. Finally consider any events, such as interim reports and presentations, that will reassure the client managers that the project is on track.

Case for project

It is rare that a consulting project is done for its own sake as it usually has wider implications. For example, a project to improve the effectiveness of your advertising will have the ultimate aim of increasing your sales and profits.

Problem to be solved

This is a detailed description of the problem and its root causes that are to be investigated. By solving this problem, it will bring benefits to the organisation that should be articulated.

Project goals

This is a clear statement of what you are trying to achieve that is measurable.

Project measurements

In general all objectives should be measurable but it is sometimes difficult to put hard numbers on everything or the cost of doing so may be prohibitive. In these circumstances, you look for tools that will give you some indication of whether you are successful or not. This also links back to the case for the project.

8.2 Developing the strategy for the journey

No two consulting projects are alike but there are some common processes which consultants can adopt to form the basis of a framework. The most popular of these at the time of writing is the 'Six Sigma' methodology.

Six Sigma

This was originated by Bill Smith at Motorola who developed a means of increasing profitability by reducing defects in manufacturing and services. He said that there should not be more than 3.4 million defects per million opportunities to achieve 'Six Sigma', with defects being defined as anything outside customer specifications.

In order to achieve this, the Six Sigma methodology is a measurement-based strategy that looks at process improvement through defined projects. Bill Smith's ideas were first adopted by Allied Signal (now Honeywell) and General Electric. The latter has estimated benefits of $10 billion in the first five years of operation [source: www.isixsigma.com/sixsigma/six_sigma.asp]. For more information, please refer to *Six Sigma Way* by Peter S. Panda and *The New Six Sigma* by Matt Barney and Tom McCarty.

At the heart of these are two methodologies: the DMAIC (define, measure, analyse, improve and control) process and the DMADV (define, measure, analyse, design and verify) process. The first is for existing processes and is the most widely used. We will concentrate on this one. The latter is for new processes or products.

DMAIC process

Figure 8.1 shows the outline process.

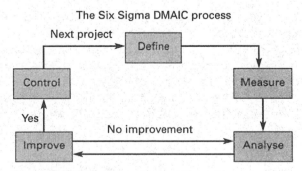

Figure 8.1 The Six Sigma DMAIC process

Management Consultancy and Skills

Define

The requirements for this phase include understanding the real problem and its causes and the objectives of the consulting exercise. These have been described in Sections 7.2 and 7.3. Also any current processes may be mapped out to get a common view of the 'way things are done now'. Consultants often refer to this as the 'as is' processes. The project charter outlined in Section 8.1 is the document issued after the 'define' phase has been completed.

Measure

Having defined in your project charter what measurements you are going to use, you need to start collecting some historical data to use as a benchmark. When doing this, you need to challenge whether the data:

- continue to be key to the project;
- are reliable and not liable to interpretation;
- are cost effective to collect;
- are able to be collected in the future.

Is the measure sensitive enough to answer whether you are making proper progress? Ask how the measure will change if the project goes off schedule. Will it change a lot or only a little for minor delays, moderate delays or major delays?

Analyse

This is the critical phase as you assess what is wrong with the current process and what you need to do in order to improve things. Consultants often call the resulting improved process the 'to be' process. Key questions that you need to ask are:

- Who do we need to involve to make the changes happen?
- What other resources do we need?
- What are the potential pitfalls we may face?
- What are the downsides if we fail to implement?
- What are the risks to the other parts of the business in implementation?

Improve

Here you draw up an implementation plan of how you will introduce the improved processes. This plan would include the breakdown of work required by subproject if necessary. The implementation plan would then be carried out and the results of the improved process monitored using the measurement tools described in the 'measure' phase. If the initial results were not as expected, it may be necessary to go back to the 'analyse' phase to ensure that the correct problems with the current process and solutions have been identified.

Control

This is the final phase where the consultant will usually hand control back to the process owner within the client company. In order for this to be done, the consultant (and his or her team) needs to ensure that the changes in the process are well embedded in the client organisation and all relevant personnel are trained in the new process. Any auditing of the process will now be the responsibility of the client process owner and this is critical to ensure that the improvements are maintained.

It is often at this stage that the next project is defined which relates to further improvements in this process or related processes. In this case a lot of the learning in the original project should be used, so as not to reinvent the wheel.

8.3 Consultant–client engagement for project implementation

As no two consulting projects are alike, nor is the level of engagement that a consultant has with a client. Figure 8.2 looks at the spectrum of consultant–client relationships, depending on the level of intimacy the consultant has with the client.

When the consultant is briefed and delivers a report at the end, the level of intimacy with the client is low. An example of this would be a market research brief. In this case the client would tell the consultant what information they required, agree the questions and the next interaction would be the findings from the research.

A more traditional view of a consulting project would be where the external consultants do most of the work but they have regular contact with the client. An example of this type of project would be a commercial due diligence. This is a review of a business that is for sale and a prospective purchaser wants to ensure that they are making a good investment. The brief is clear and the view from the consultant has to be independent, but a buyer wants to be kept informed of progress in case the consultant uncovers any major issues that would prevent the sale.

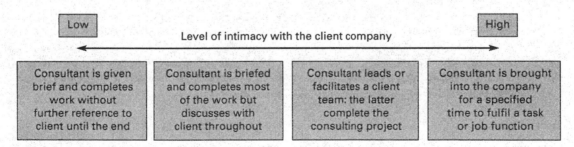

Figure 8.2 Spectrum of consultant–client interactions

The bulk of the work that many professional management consultants undertake would fall into the third category where the consultant would lead or facilitate a client team. The reasons for this are:

■ cost – external management consultants do not come cheap;
■ a better knowledge of the issues that the client company faces;
■ any solutions are likely to be better imbedded and therefore implemented;
■ it is a good training for the members of the client team;
■ the client has more control over the project.

The last category, where effectively the consultant becomes a full-time member of the client organisation, is often called interim management. There may be a role or specific project for a limited time that the client needs someone to fulfil but at the same time wants him or her to be part of the organisation. In cases where the client company is in dire straits, specialists called 'company doctors' are brought in to try to rescue the company.

8.4 Benchmarking project progression

Benchmarking is a process through which specific achievements are predicted, defined and evidenced. A consulting project will have an overall set of objectives. However, these may be broken down into a series of intermediate and subsidiary objectives, based on the objectives and outcomes specified in the project charter. This is particularly useful if the project is a long or complex one.
Benchmarking involves:

1 indentifying the relevant intermediate stages of the project;
2 defining specific objectives for each intermediate stage;
3 anticipating what will be appropriate evidence that each subsidiary objective has been achieved. This will be related to the means of measurement specified in the project charter;
4 delivering on the objective and producing the evidence.

What constitutes evidence will vary depending on the project and the nature of the subsidiary objective. It may be of a qualitative, numerical nature that is formally measured. It may take the form of the production of a particular document or the obtaining of a particular piece of evidence. It may be that a particular meeting has taken place, in which case notes from the meeting will constitute the evidence. The production of the evidence is a good discipline in that it substantiates progression of the project.

8.5 Handing over ownership of the project

In Section 8.2 we discussed the importance of the 'control' phase where the ownership of the project is handed over to the client. The handing over of the project to client management is an important step. It represents the final delivery of the project. It is at this stage that the client receives what he or she feels has been paid for. Hence it is the stage at which expectations are met or, better, exceeded. If this is to happen satisfactorily, it must have been clear from the outset the degree to which the responsibility of the project is about making recommendations or about *implementing* those recommendations. Even if the project is primarily concerned with making recommendations, it is important that these recommendations are presented in an actionable way, so that the client has a clear plan of action to put them into effect and is motivated to do so.

Team discussion point	Hold a brainstorming session to identify the types of evidence that demonstrate progression of the consulting project through delivery of its subsidiary objectives. Once ideas dry up on the types of evidence, move on to classify them (say in quantitative–qualitative/documentary/non-documentary, etc.).
	Finally, consider how these different types of evidence will work given the spectrum of consultant–client interactions. Do some types of evidence work better with one type of interaction or another?

◆ Summary of key ideas

- A consulting project has both a destination and a journey.
- The destination can be defined through the use of a project charter.
- The project charter includes information on the team members, project goals and scope, the problem the project sets out to resolve, and how outcomes will be measured.
- The project journey can be defined using the Six Sigma DMAIC process.
- Benchmarking involves anticipating and generating evidence that the journey is progressing to plan.
- Handing over ownership of the project is a critical step. Recommendations should be motivational and action orientated.

Key reading

Barney, M. and McCarty, T. (2003) *The New Six Sigma*. Harlow, Essex: Prentice Hall.

Panda, P.S. (2000) *Six Sigma Way*. Maidenhead, Berkshire: McGraw-Hill Education Europe.

Pyzdek, T. (2003) *The Six Sigma Project Handbook*. New York: McGraw-Hill Education.

Silberman, M. (ed.) (2002) *Consultant's Big Book of Organizational Development Tools*. New York: McGraw-Hill Education.

Why don't they understand our strategy?

20 August 2003

When running executive education programmes, interviewing executives and sitting as a board member, I have heard one statement recur with surprising regularity: 'I don't understand our strategy.'

Strategies come in many shapes and sizes and every chief executive has to have one. The media, institutional investors and the clamour of the annual meeting demand a concerted plan of action, never a simple declaration of business as usual.

Yet those further down the organisation often fail to see the relevance of the strategy to their own activities. Chief executives typically respond: 'They've been briefed a hundred times – they should understand it by now.'

Good strategies that differentiate a company and create value are not easily found. Managers work hard to identify opportunities, find new ways to compete and make sure they have the resources they need to execute the strategy. But it is usually focus and execution that make or break the company.

The strategy of US retailer Wal-Mart is not complex but its operation is extraordinary. Its competitor K-Mart failed to execute its strategy and went bankrupt. In the airline business, Ryanair in Europe and Southwest in the US have simple business models that they are adept at carrying out.

Competitors tempted to pursue more than one strategy, such as both full-service and discount offerings within the same corporate structure, usually fail, not because the ideas are bad but because employees get confused about their priorities and execution suffers. Think of US airline Continental's creation of Continental Lite, British Airways' launch of Go, or US Airways' cut-price MetroJet.

Multiple strategies conceal a lack of focus and are often couched in terms that merely exhort employees to try hard to overcome their inherent conflicts. Corporate wordsmiths massage the communication of the strategy until it becomes all things to all people, belying its true complexity and meaning nothing to the person trying to do his or her job every day.

Making the connection

Strategy can come alive for every employee but for this to happen managers have to give up some control Long before the fad for empowerment of the late 1980s, Kenwyn Smith of the University of Pennsylvania advised: 'To gain power, give up control.'

Prof Smith meant that for managers to be really effective they must draw a range of people into situations where they have both an incentive and authority for action. When this works, managers will have gained power through the actions of others but lost some immediate control in the process.

For strategy, this means giving individuals some flexibility to figure out what the strategy means in the context of the execution of their daily job, and encouraging and allowing them to take appropriate action without checking every step.

This does not mean every employee should develop a strategy. It means one must look for ways to communicate the strategy in a way that will mean something – perhaps something different – to everyone. If a person understands what has been communicated, she will ask herself how she can personalise it for her situation and then look for ways to take action.

Problems can result if the individual either does not see a personal link or feels no freedom to act. Employees who understand the communication but do not believe it are unlikely to follow it up with action.

How, then, do you make it personal? Colleen Barrett, president of Southwest Airlines, writes: 'When we began flying 32 years ago, our goal was to make affordable travel available to every American barred from exercising their freedom to fly by other airlines' high fares.'

At Southwest, people learn to do their jobs in support of the strategy to make travel affordable by reducing costs and improving turnround time (which in turn reduces cost). This is codified in procedures and guidelines but much depends on individual internalising of the strategy on a personal level. Pilots may be seen loading luggage when things are tight, or flight attendants helping to clean aircraft cabins, instead of sticking to a limited job description.

Certain limits are clearly understood, the best example in the aircraft industry being operating procedures and regulations. The combination of innovation with discipline may explain why Southwest has the most efficient company of its size in the industry (it has the lowest operating costs per passenger or per aircraft mile) and the best safety record.

There are simple but highly effective techniques used by experienced leaders to bring strategy alive, help others to remember vital points and find a connection with the details of the strategy:

Compensation

The most powerful way to bring strategy alive is through compensation. This is difficult – but works best at lower levels where there is an identifiable connection between action and reward. Continental Airlines dramatically improved customer satisfaction and on-time performance by giving flight crews bonuses tied to these performance indicators.

Similarly, sales people working on commission always understand the incentives that will help them earn more money.

Mnemonics

We often use memory aids – phrases or combinations of letters and numbers – to help remind us of something. The 'Five Rs', 'E3' and other executive mutterings mean nothing to most of us but can help explain a concept for employees. But advertising slogans – Volkswagen's 'Drivers wanted' or BMW's 'The ultimate driving machine' – do little to help employees to relate the strategy to their jobs.

The best candidates are sayings or mnemonics that highlight attributes such as quality, speed, cost, satisfaction and other things employees can affect directly. 'E3' reminds staff: 'Everyone knows the customer; everyone improves quality; and everyone sells'.

The intent is clear: to provide a service that will garner loyalty and encourage customers to buy again.

Storytelling

Oral history was a powerful part of all human societies before writing and printing developed and remained so for centuries afterwards. We remember stories that a parent told us as a child, often in a way that helped us learn an important lesson.

Corporate storytelling can clarify ideas and reinforce certain kinds of behaviour. It can deal with issues such as serving customers, intelligent risk-taking or looking for product opportunities.

The US pharmaceutical group Merck developed a drug to treat river blindness in Africa and South America – though it would have to be given away because sufferers could not afford to buy it. When recruiting, the company retells this story to describe its culture in a compelling and memorable way.

Making the strategy come alive is more difficult in complex businesses operating in several segments or industries but it generally starts with a statement of purpose. On its website, Unilever says: 'Our purpose in Unilever is to meet the everyday needs of people everywhere – to anticipate the aspirations of our consumers and customers and to respond creatively and competitively with branded products and services which raise the quality of life.'

Making this come alive for workers requires adaptation at lower levels and within segments but here playing off consumer aspirations and raising the quality of life are obvious choices.

In large organisations the statement of purpose sets a general context; beyond this, lower-level managers may have to provide more detailed aims for divisions or product groups to help them 'walk in the customers' shoes'.

The desire by individuals to feel valuable and make a contribution to a group is universal. Leaders throughout a company can improve their chances of achieving corporate aims, both for individual satisfaction and for the benefit of the business, by finding ways to bring the strategy alive in a personal way through easily understood examples, reminders and stories.

The writer is vice-dean for executive education at The Wharton School, University of Pennsylvania.

Q1 Select an organisation (perhaps the one you are working with on a consulting project) whose strategy you understand. How would you relate that strategy using (i) a mnemonic; (ii) storytelling? Prepare your response in the project log.

Q2 A client manager asks you to define the word 'strategy'. What definition would you offer?

Q3 A client manager suggests 'my organisation does not need a strategy'. What response would you make? (Hint: ask the client some questions first.)

15 Consulting project planning

The learning outcomes from this chapter are:

- to recognise the *key tasks* which contribute to the consulting project;
- to recognise how tasks might be *allocated* between team members;
- to develop a *plan* for the project with an allocated budget;
- to understand how *meetings* with the client can be made effective;
- to be able to *monitor* the project and its progression.

15.1 Individual roles for team members

The advantage of working in a team is that it allows individuals to specialise their contributions. Differentiating and co-ordinating activities is a way to make the team more effective. It also allows individuals to specialise in the way in which they want and to develop the skills they prefer to use.

Some of the types of role the consulting project will demand are as follows. However, one individual may take on a number of these roles in the consulting exercise.

A team co-ordinator and leader

The team co-ordinator is the individual who organises the team as a whole, who allocates tasks and ensures that deadlines and targets are met. In short, this person is the project leader. The leadership role will demand assessment and motivation of other team members.

A client contact

As the project progresses it will be important to keep in contact with the client. This requirement will be driven by a need to get information from the client. It will also act to keep the client informed and reassured that the project is progressing. It is better if the client gets to know a particular member of the team and knows that it is he or she whom they can contact. This enables a definite one-to-one relationship to be built. This relationship is the one around which the project rotates. It will be particularly valuable if there is a crisis in the project and objectives need to be renegotiated.

An information gatherer or researcher

The information gatherer is the person who identifies what information is needed for the project, or who receives information requests from other team members and then finds sources of that information. When secondary research cannot provide answers the information gatherer may undertake or initiate primary research.

An information analyst

The information analyst is that member of the team who takes information from the information gatherer and makes sense of it so that it can be used to support decision-making. The analysis may call upon formal techniques that demand numerical manipulation (for example, financial ratio analysis). The analyst can require the use of industry analysis methods (for example, those described by Professor Michael Porter in his 1985 book *Competitive Advantage)*. At other times, more intuitive techniques will be used such as mind mapping and brainstorming (discussed in Chapter 10). In these cases the information analyst may facilitate the analytical creativity of the consulting team as a whole.

A report writer

The final report is the physical manifestation of the project as a whole. It is the tangible thing the client is getting from the consulting team. The final report is important. It is not only a communication; it is a representation of the team as a whole. Modern word-processing technology allows the report to evolve. It is not necessary to write and rewrite drafts. A framework can be laid down early in the project and the details can be filled in as the project progresses. It is useful to assign responsibility for this to a particular team member. This person will have responsibility not only for producing the report but also for circulating interim drafts at intervals to get the opinion of other team members. This approach to developing the final report is expanded upon in Section 17.2.

A report presenter

The final report must be delivered to the client. A good report speaks for itself. However, it can be useful for a member of the team to talk the client through it and be available to answer any questions the client may have. The report may be supported with a formal presentation. If so, a member of the team will have to prepare a presentation and lead its delivery.

A team coach

Teams are made up of individuals. And individuals occasionally come into conflict with each other. Disagreements can arise over a wide variety of issues. They may relate to the definition of objects or the management of the project. Often a conflict can arise if more than one person sees himself or herself as the leader of the project. Personal issues outside the bounds of the project may complicate matters. Such conflicts are a normal part of team dynamics (and are discussed further in Section 20.4). However, such disputes need rapid resolution if the team is to work effectively. The team coach is the person who acts as an arbiter and helps reconcile conflicts between members. In a more general sense, the team coach will keep the whole team motivated and interested in the project, especially when the project is going through a difficult patch. Often, but not inevitably, the team coach will be the person who has taken on the leader's role.

There is a great degree of latitude in the way in which these tasks are distinguished, formalised and allocated. Some teams will be quite homogeneous, with all members engaging in all tasks and perhaps only occasionally dedicating specific types of task. Others will operate with a high degree of formality, even to the point of having individual job descriptions within the team. A number of factors drive specialisation. Some of the more important are the size of the team, the nature of the task the team is taking on, the expertise of team members, the longevity of the team, the team leader's style and external influences. These factors are explored in more depth in Section 20.2.

15.2 Setting a timetable

Objectives have little meaning unless it is known when they can be delivered. Setting a timetable for the project lets the client know when he or she can expect the outcomes to become available. It is also a way to set signposts so that it can be seen that the project is on track and to highlight when slippage is occurring. A timetable is the basis of effective time management (*see* Chapter 17). A good timetable also ensures that resources are used in an optimal way.

The level of detail in the timetable will reflect the complexity of the project. A simple project may need a list of only a few key events. An extensive project will require a detailed list of activities and their interconnections. At its simplest a timetable will be a list of important events and when they will be achieved. It is important to include things like an initial meeting with the client, the preparation of a formal proposal, a period for information gathering, analysis sessions with individuals and perhaps the team as a whole, regular contacts with the client and a period for preparing the final report.

15.3 Critical path analysis

Critical path analysis is a technique that has been developed to aid the management of complex projects. In essence, the technique involves identifying the critical path, the sequence of tasks that will define the schedule for the project as a whole. These tasks must be undertaken in order, and the time needed for undertaking them determines the rate at which the project progresses. Other tasks can be fitted around the critical path.

Two American industrialists, J.E. Kelly and M.R. Walker, developed the method to aid plant maintenance in the chemicals industry. Critical path analysis has found particular favour in the management of very complex, new product development programmes, designing a new aircraft for example. In such projects, a large number of tasks must be integrated if the project is to be achieved on time and on budget.

The method is quite straightforward. The individual tasks that make up the project are listed. The time needed to undertake the task (and, if appropriate, its cost) is then assigned. The way tasks connect to each other is analysed. Particularly important is recognising when one task cannot be undertaken until another has been completed. Many tasks will not have a unique time period/cost relationship. One can be played off against another. Many tasks can be done more quickly – the term is 'crashed' – if more is spent. The relationship between cost and time is called the time–cost curve. Computer software is available to help with critical path planning.

Most consulting projects will not have the level of complexity that demands use of sophisticated planning techniques. However, a simplified version of critical path analysis can help organise the project. Figure 15.1 shows how the stages of the consulting project described in Chapter 8 are organised into a critical path. The times shown are typical.

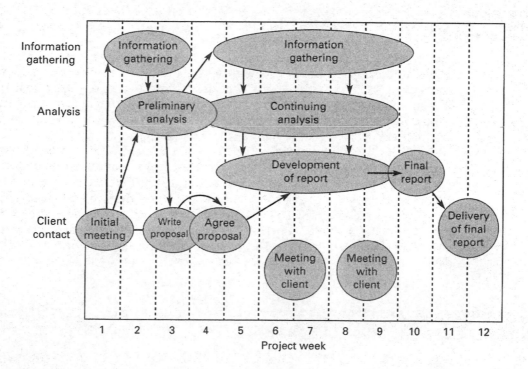

Figure 15.1 A simplified critical path analysis for a consulting project

15.4   Project budgeting

Most student consulting projects are undertaken for the experience they offer rather than as a way of generating funds. However, there will still be expenses. The client manager may make some money available to support the project, to pay for market research perhaps.

Being able to cost and budget the project is a useful skill. Even if it is not part of the student project, it is a transferable skill that will be useful in the future. Broadly, budgeting means assigning expenditure in two dimensions: *over time* and by *type of expenditure*. The timescale will depend on the length of the project. Typically, weeks or months are used as the basis. The type of expenditure will depend on the nature of the project. Some of the most common categories of expenditure on consulting projects are detailed in Table 15.1.

Table 15.1 A typical budget sheet for a consulting project

Expenditure category	Period 1	Period 2	....	Period N	Category total
Consultant's fees*					
Travel expenses					
Periodicals and reports					
Commissioned market research					
Telephone and postage					
Report preparation					
Period total					**Grand total**

* (Daily rates × number of days worked)

The budget has two parts. Expected expenditure is a forecast of what will be spent. This is money that must be reserved for the project. This is replaced by actual expenditure as the project progresses. Comparison can then be made. Actual expenditure is often different from what was budgeted. However, both under- and over-expenditure should be avoided. Over-expenditure means additional funds must be found while under-expenditure means money that could have been used elsewhere is tied up.

15.5   Organising meetings and reviews

Meetings are among the most common of business communication forums. The formality of a meeting with the client will depend on the situation, the relationship with the client, the objectives and significance of the meeting and those present.

Management Consultancy and Skills

Meetings are so pervasive as a form of organisational communication that the advantages of actively managing them can be overlooked. Meetings are resource intensive. They are time consuming and can be a distraction. But dividends are available if thought and preparation are put into setting up and running meetings properly. Some key considerations are as follows.

The meeting's objectives

Consider the objective of the meeting. What is it setting out to do? What will be achieved as a result of holding it? How do the objectives of the meeting fit with the objectives of the project as a whole? Are all present aware of the objectives? The project log is a good place to review these issues.

Is the meeting really necessary?

This is an obvious question but one which is well worth asking. Might a less disruptive and time-consuming form of communication be better? Being called to a meeting he or she does not feel to be necessary will not impress the client.

Consider who needs to be present at the meeting

Clearly, the members of the consulting team should usually be present at an important meeting. In principle, the client is free to invite whoever in their organisation should be present. In practice, however, they will often ask the advice of the consultant.

A balance needs to be struck. On the one hand, people are easily offended if they are not invited to meetings to which they feel they should have been invited. On the other hand, being asked to attend a meeting that is not relevant makes people feel that their time has been wasted. The solution is to advise the client to inform people about the meeting and explain its objectives. They can then ask those informed whether they would like to attend. There will be more commitment to making the meeting successful if everybody attending has requested to be present.

Plan ahead

Recognise that people are busy and diaries fill quickly. Try to give as much notice of the meeting as possible to give people a chance to plan their schedules.

Consider what information will be needed at the meeting

Inform people of the information they are expected to bring to the meeting. If information is to be shared and discussed at the meeting, prepare and copy it in advance. Consider the way the information might be presented to make it easier to understand and more likely to have an impact.

Prepare an agenda for the meeting

An agenda should detail the points that the meeting needs to discuss. It should be distributed in advance, along with the objectives of the meeting and indications of special information that will be required.

Make sure that the keys roles have been allocated for the meeting. These include:

1 a *chairman* who has overall responsibility for co-ordinating and guiding the meeting. This may or may not be the project leader;

2 an *opener* who has responsibility for opening the meeting and giving a short verbal presentation (which may be supported with visual stimuli) on what the objective of the meeting is and what the background issues are. This person is usually the chairperson but having the same person in both roles is certainly not compulsory;

3 someone to take the *minutes* of the meeting. Formal minutes detailing everything that has been said are rarely necessary unless the meeting is particularly formal. However, a short statement of the objectives of the meeting and details of the key action points decided upon (and who it has been agreed will follow them up) are useful. The minutes should be distributed to all who attend (plus other interested parties) as soon as possible after the meeting. Even if formal minutes are not required, the project log is a good place to keep personal notes on the meeting.

Plan the venue

Planning the venue is the responsibility of the consulting team if they are calling the meeting at their own venue. Make sure the room is adequate for all who wish to attend. Consider seating arrangements. Get into the habit of allocating places rather than just letting people sit where they want. If you know that two people are particularly likely to come into conflict, sit them next to one another rather than opposite one another. (It is much harder to argue with someone who is sitting next to you!)

Before the meeting starts ensure that any communication tools (overhead projectors, laptops, beamers, flip charts, etc.) are available, set up and working. Are people seated so they can see them properly?

Maintain focus on the key issues

Meetings are a great chance for people to get together and discuss the host of issues they have on their mind. It is easy for the original objective of the meeting to be lost and the conversation to be diverted into discussion of a variety of unrelated issues. It is the job of the chairman to maintain the focus of the meeting and ensure that it keeps to its objectives. Learn to recognise when productive discussion on one agenda point has come to an end. When this happens, close discussion on it with a summary of the key points raised and move on to the next point. It is useful to have an idea of the time available for each agenda point to keep the meeting on schedule. If the discussion has drifted on to an issue unrelated to the core business, a good way to redirect the discussion is to summarise the point being discussed and offer to take it to a separate forum. Get those involved in the discussion to agree to this. This simple device can prevent people feeling they have not been allowed to have their say.

Pre-agreement on particular contributions may also help keep the meeting on track. For example: 'Right, that brings us to the marketing issues. A, I think you had a number of points to make on that.'

Management Consultancy and Skills

129

Involve everybody

People vary greatly in their confidence. Some people are open and extrovert. They will contribute easily and with little prompting. Other people are more introvert. They will not feel comfortable about pushing in to make their contribution. This doesn't mean to say that they have nothing to say. Far from it! The quietest people often have the best ideas. Another important role for the chairperson is to ensure that space is created for everybody to contribute. Doing this involves two things – first, controlling the contribution of extroverts; second, encouraging the contribution of introverts.

These two things go hand in hand. If someone is dominating the debate, you cannot just tell that person to be quiet, not without creating a lot of ill feeling anyway! There are a number of useful devices for handling this, such as interrupting with, for example, 'That's actually a very interesting point – how does everybody else feel about this?' or 'Thanks for raising that, A. How will it affect you, B?' The point of these interventions is to move the conversation on while leaving the dominating speaker with the feeling that he or she has made a useful contribution.

Encouraging quiet people to speak is often just a case of redirecting the conversation towards them. For example, 'What's your opinion, A?' or 'How will that affect your approach, B?' If someone is particularly nervous about contributing in meetings it may help to discuss their contribution with them before the meeting and set aside a slot within the meeting for them to make it.

It is useful here to recognise how people have differentiated their tasks within the team. If an issue comes up which will benefit from the comments of one who has taken a particular role, use this to draw that person into the discussion.

15.6 Monitoring achievement

Good objectives have signposts attached. It is evident when they are achieved. The progression of the project towards its objectives should be monitored. Keep track of signposts and recognise when they are passed. It will be motivating to see the project progress in this way. If a signpost is missed, this should be a warning to get things moving.

A variety of time management techniques to help with monitoring the project are discussed in Chapter 17. A good place to review the achievement of objectives is in the project log. If the log is planned ahead, the points at which various stages of achievement are reached can be noted in advance.

Team discussion point

Read the following short case study.

The Manor House Restaurant is a small but well-regarded restaurant in the south-east of England. It has seating for 30 people and has four bedrooms. The restaurant's manager, Linda Morgan, has invited in a consulting team. The main issue, she explains, is that the restaurant is very busy at the weekend but is empty during the week. Profits and cash flow would be much better if people used the restaurant outside of weekends.

Linda has a 'database' of customers (a collection of visitors' books going back five years). She has asked the consulting team if they will go through the book to analyse how often people are using the restaurant. She wants regular customers to be identified. She plans to offer them a special rate if they will use the restaurant during the week.

After the meeting, the team agree that the project is not particularly exciting. (They were expecting something more challenging than just going through old visitors' books!)

How would you approach this situation? As a team, develop a strategy to negotiate with Linda and open up the project. You might consider the following:

■ What are Linda's desired outcomes?

■ How do these relate to the details of the project she has suggested?

■ Can the project be broadened in a way that will work for Linda and make it a more rewarding educational and managerial experience?

◆ Summary of key ideas

■ A few simple planning rules can make the consulting project more rewarding and more successful.

■ The consulting project will be managed around the key tasks of collecting information, performing analysis, communicating with the client and the overall co-ordination of the team.

■ The team can take on individual roles based on these key tasks.

Key reading

Cope, M. (2003) *The Seven Cs of Consulting: The Definite Guide to the Consulting Process*. Harlow, Essex: Financial Times Prentice Hall.

Porter, M.E. (1985) *Competitive Advantage: Creating and Sustaining Superior Performance*. New York: Free Press.

Schaffer, R. (2002) *High-Impact Consulting: How clients and consultants can work together to achieve extraordinary results*. Chichester, West Sussex: Jossey Bass Wiley.

How to link projects, planning and profits

By Carlos Cordon and Thomas Vollmann

13 August 2003

In the past decade project management has become a vital skill for managers. Organisations have shifted from being places where people have static roles and routine activities to places where work is increasingly organised into projects of varying size and duration.

Manufacturing companies such as Nokia create a stream of new products, each of which is run as a separate development project – and each of which needs to come in on time. When installing systems such as SAP or Siebel, software companies run the work as a project. Banks and finance companies also need project management to run any new product or service.

One reason for the rise of project management is mass customisation, a technique for producing many variations of a single product.

Hewlett-Packard, for instance, uses mass customisation to make printers with the right voltages and power supply fittings for all its world markets. This model makes it imperative for managers to have control; late projects mean higher costs and missed targets, which can damage a company.

In any business, managers hold a spectrum of views on projects: some think of a project as a list of hopes; others as a commitment to action. How can a company move closer to the latter?

The march of time

Most projects involve an implicit trade-off between time, cost and specifications. In the classic engineering-driven project, specifications tend to drive everything else, often resulting in overdesigned products that cost too much and appear too late in the marketplace. Current thinking teaches that time is the crucial factor in any of these trade-offs. Delays usually mean higher costs. In many companies costs at the earlier stages are now allowed to escalate as long as the timing of the project is not threatened.

A new design for a product may have three or four big problems, one of which is particularly thorny. In the past managers would leave the most intractable problem until last, hoping that a solution would reveal itself while they worked on the others. Now, companies try to eliminate the biggest uncertainties early. Te Strake, the Dutch engineering company, follows this approach. The company therefore finds out early if

projects are unfeasible. Reson, a Danish electronics company (see below), has a variant: it 'front-loads' its projects by assigning more staff and resources early on – rather than try to catch up at the end.

It is important to discern which factors may become critical during the project to eliminate unreliable elements. Eliyahu Goldratt, author of *The Critical Chain*, explains that activities vulnerable to change should receive extra resources to be completed earlier. Raymond Ford, vice-president of manufacturing at Harris, the US communications equipment maker, describes how the company used this approach to build a manufacturing plant for integrated circuits in record time.

Goldratt argues that adding time to project plans tends to ensure these plans will not be met. He points to the student syndrome: the idea that students always wait until the last minute to do their work. In a project, a delay in one activity will not necessarily be compensated for by an early finish in another. Managers should always try to estimate the most likely timing – not the worst-case scenario.

Project management software has now become a sector of the information technology industry in its own right: Microsoft has MS Project 2002 while Oracle offers its Enterprise Project Management modules. Some tools are undoubtedly useful. Yet it is all too easy for managers to come to rely on these tools: software may support managers but is not a substitute for analysis and leadership. Similarly, senior managers should not micromanage project leaders. The best strategy is to have a project leader sign up to a clear set of targets - and then give him or her maximum flexibility to get on with the project.

Clarify the scope

Time is not the only important factor in project management. If the scope of the project – the details of what it is supposed to achieve – is ill-defined, it will take longer and its aims may drift. At Reson, managers will not categorise a plan as a project until the assigned project leader is happy that its scope has been clearly defined. If someone is held accountable for the project, they should only accept the responsibility when they know precisely what they have to deliver. Put another way, It is extremely difficult to set

deadlines on projects where it isn't clear how the project will come to fruition.

In inventing a new cancer drug, for example, the timing is unpredictable as researchers have to explore an unknown number of blind alleys. Projects of this type should be dealt with using different standards and managed using statistical techniques based on probabilities of success.

If the scope changes, the timing will shift too. How should managers cope? Project scope is easiest to define for small sections within shorter time frames. For example, if it takes three years to implement a new computer system, the broader business requirements will change during that period. By breaking up big projects into small ones that can be operational within six months, the prospect of change becomes more palatable.

Projects at the core

Those who lead projects may be responsible for the main sources of growth for a business. Yet rewards for project managers have failed to keep pace with the growing importance of their work. In too many cases successful project management is seen only as a rite of passage – a way to get a 'real' job in the company. Companies need to look urgently at the way they evaluate, pay and recognise project teams.

For team members, the work needs to be seen as enjoyable and professionally appealing: as good for their company, good for the workers, personally rewarding and a source of learning and professional growth. Project managers need to establish a reward structure for their teams and celebrate successes with those who make the contributions.

Projects have a multitude of uses. They can lead to great improvements in performance, such as lean manufacturing, Six Sigma quality management and new computer systems. If projects are planned correctly, executed according to plan and carried out enthusiastically by a large segment of workers, a company can enhance its capacity for learning. This may well be the most important competency a company can have.

Carlos Cordon is professor of operation management at IMD, Switzerland. Thomas E. Vollmann is professor of manufacturing management at IMD, Switzerland. The ideas in this article are strongly influenced by the work of Eliyahu Goldratt.

Personal responsibility helps to shorten deadlines

Reson is a Danish company specialising in underwater acoustics and high-power ultrasonic devices. It changed its marketing approach in the late 1990s and began to focus on a different set of customers, for whom it needed to reduce its product development times from three years to about three months.

Managers take personal responsibility for a project, knowing they will be penalised if they do not meet their deadlines. In some cases they can be fired or not allowed to work as a project leader until taking additional training or working under another project leader. On the other hand, they have 'unlimited financial resources – and unlimited trust'. They can do whatever they feel is necessary as long as the time requirements are achieved. And since project managers are held personally responsible for the project, their goal is to be 95 per cent certain about the scope of the project before they commit to it.

Q1 What are the implications for eliminating uncertainties for the design and implementation of consulting projects?

Q2 Refer back to the consulting process (Chapter 4). What types of uncertainties present at each stage? How might these uncertainties be managed?

Q3 How would you design a consulting project to introduce project-based working in a client business? Consider objectives and process.

22 Presenting your ideas

Learning outcomes

The learning outcomes from this chapter are:

- to recognise the importance of delivering your findings to the client;
- to understand the means by which those findings can be delivered;
- to appreciate some rules which will make the communication of findings more effective.

22.1 Planning the communication

The communication of the findings of the consulting exercise to the client is an event of great importance. The client is likely to see this as what he or she has 'paid for'. If the consulting exercise was an information-gathering exercise then the communication is the means by which the information is delivered. If the project is offering advice on a business development strategy then the final communication is the means by which that advice is made known. Even if the consulting has taken a process approach and the outcomes delivered are a result of the consultant–client interaction, the final report provides a tangible 'capstone' to the project.

The consulting project will have generated a lot of information and ideas. The main challenge in producing the communication is organising that material so that the message you want to send is delivered in a coherent and convincing way.

Barbara Minto, a consultant for McKinsey & Company who went on to specialise in communication, describes one very effective approach in her book *The Pyramid Principle*. The basis is to organise ideas into a hierarchy (a pyramid) so that they are sorted and interrelated. Minto lays down three rules for connecting ideas:

1 Ideas at any level in the pyramid must be summaries of the ideas below them; conversely, ideas at any level may be expanded upon at a lower level.

2 Ideas in each grouping (pathway in the pyramid) must be ideas of the same kind – that is, they must relate in some way and can be grouped together.

3 Ideas in a grouping must be ordered according to some internal logic.

Minto's ideas apply to business communications in general. There are a number of ways in which they might be applied to the challenge of producing a consulting report. The following is my own approach. You may interpret directly Barbara Minto's ideas to devise your own. I use four levels. These are illustrated in Figure 22.1.

The 'big idea'

The 'big idea' is what the whole consulting exercise is about. It is the central theme that unifies the exercise. It should be related to the original aims and objectives of the project. So, the 'big idea' might be 'to expand the business' or 'to improve profit margins' or 'to enter an international market' and so on.

Means of achievement

How can the big idea be achieved? Expanding on this is where the consultant adds value. So, if the big idea is to expand the business, this level must expound on the options for expanding the business. It might include increasing market share in existing markets, developing new products or entering new markets. If the big idea is to increase profit margins, the means of achievement level might consider increasing prices, altering the portfolio mix or reducing costs. This level may also be used to close off options which it is felt will not deliver the big idea.

Logic

This third level connects the means of achievement to the big idea. It provides the explanation of why the big idea will be achieved by the means described in the second level. In some cases the logic will be 'obvious' (to you at least). In others it will rely on subtle interpretations. If in doubt, assume your audience would like to have the idea explained.

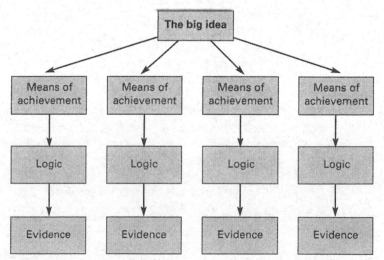

Figure 22.1 The pyramid of ideas for relating consulting findings

Management Consultancy and Skills

Evidence

This final level contains any evidence that is available to justify the logic. It might include internal data on sales or costs. It might be data obtained through market research on the market, its potential and the opportunity it presents. It can include discoveries made through creative sessions and explorations of the type reviewed in Chapter 10.

Any of these levels can be expanded into sublevels if this helps clarify communication of findings. The pyramid of ideas can be developed as a team exercise through a brainstorming session. An example is shown in Figure 22.2.

Don't forget, this expansion should be undertaken with a clear view of the objective of the communication. As discussed in Chapter 18, a communication objective relates to what you want the recipient to do, not just what you want him or her to know. Presumably, you will want the client to be impressed by your ideas, recognise their value to his or her business and make an effort to implement them. No good consultant would want less.

22.2 The consulting report

A report provides a tangible, accessible and permanent communication of the findings of the consulting exercise. It need not be a long document. In fact, it is a safe assumption that managers do not like to read long reports. What it should be is a succinct and impactful presentation of the opportunity you have discovered for the business. Remember your objectives: it should be a call to action.

The report may comprise the following sections.

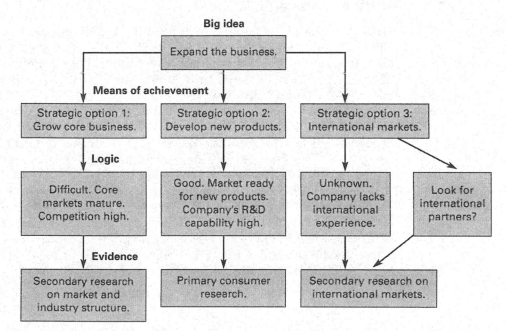

Figure 22.2 An application of the pyramid of ideas

Management Consultancy and Skills

Executive summary

This is a summary of the findings of the consulting project. But it must be more than *just* a summary. The executive summary is the gateway to the report. It must be short but inviting. A good rule is a one-page maximum. Use bullet points to isolate and summarise your ideas and recommendations. Use an active language style. Be positive. Talk about what the business might achieve if the ideas in the report are implemented.

Ask two questions about the executive summary. First, does it invite the reader in? On reading the executive summary will the reader be motivated to delve further into the report? Second, if the reader reads only the executive summary, what is the message he or she will get? Briefly, will the executive summary deliver your objectives for the communication? These two questions may seem contradictory but they are not. If the executive summary is both complete in itself and an invitation to go further it will have impact and set the scene for the expansion of the ideas it relates.

Introduction

The introduction should illuminate the context of the report. It should give any relevant information on the business and its situation. It should also specify the goals, objectives and outcomes that were agreed originally. The introduction will repeat much of the ground covered by the original project proposal. This proposal will provide a template for the introduction. The introduction might be used to give a flavour of what is to come: a further invitation to move into the body of the report.

Body of the report

This is the part of the report where you can expand on your ideas and develop your case. The body of the report can be given a suitable title. It may be broken down into subsections if appropriate. Don't forget, it is generally better to have a lot of short, well-defined and titled subsections than long sections. They make reading and later accessing easier.

The pyramid discussed in the previous section can be used to organise the material for the body of the report. It is better to work your way across the levels rather than down the groups. You don't need to provide logic and evidence upfront for every idea. Lay out the skeleton of your overall case first, then flesh out the details later. Be explicit. Tell the reader what your case will be and promise to support it later. Layer your ideas. The written page must be linear. But our thinking is not: it is hierarchical. Expand your themes in a hierarchical manner. Use internal references to signpost where your ideas are going. If the reader feels tempted to jump from one section to another, fine.

You may also want to use visual representations of ideas and information. Some techniques are discussed in Section 10.4. A picture really is worth a thousand words!

Summary and recommendations

Remember your objectives. You should close your report with a final call to action. A good way to do this is with a succinct summary of findings and the recommendations listed as bullet points. This format not only repeats the message but also makes the recommendations accessible.

We value originality. Some people feel uncomfortable with this approach to report writing. They feel that they are repeating themselves by saying the same thing in the executive summary, the body of the report and then again in the summary of recommendations. So what? It has been observed that a good business communication tells the reader what it will say, says it and then tells the reader what has been said! If the message is a good one, don't be afraid of getting it across.

Appendices

The trick with appendices is to be cynical. Assume they won't be read! They are a good place to put any information that you have used to make your case and that might be of interest to the reader in the future. If the information is valuable to your case then a summary of it (perhaps using a visual representation) should be in the body of the report.

Information that will be of use in the implementation of recommendations (say a list of potential customers) should not be hidden away in appendices, it should be highlighted and accessible in the body of the report.

Clearly, the report will speak for you. It will be a representation of your efforts. You should be proud of it. Make time for its planning and preparation. Check the copy and make sure that typographical, spelling and grammatical errors have been removed. Be warned. Many people find it difficult to check their own copy. It is better to have someone other than the report writer to do the copyediting.

Modern word-processing technology makes report writing easy. Sections can be added, revised and moved with ease. Spellcheckers take the strain out of copy checking. Impressive visuals can be edited in. A variety of graphics can be used to decorate the report. But ultimately, it is the substance of the report that matters. A simple, well-written, well-laid-out report relating ideas that will have a real impact on the performance of the business is much better than a report rich with graphics but lacking substance.

22.3 Formal presentations

A formal presentation is a very effective means of getting your message across. It allows the message to be fine-tuned using both verbal and visual communications, to get instant feedback from the client and to respond immediately to points and questions. Formal presentations are being used increasingly as a means of inter- and intra-organisational communication. The formal presentation is, however, a challenging mode of communication. To be effective it must be well organised and delivered with confidence. This confidence comes through preparation and practice.

It is worthwhile to take time to plan the visual aids to be used. The images need careful consideration if they are to have an impact. They can be relatively expensive and take time to produce and copy, so plan ahead. Some useful points to remember are as follows.

- Analyse the audience. What images will they find relevant and will have impact? What interpretative skills do they have?
- Don't make the images too complicated. Clear, simple images have much more impact.
- Consider the relationships you need to communicate. Use images that emphasise the relevant relationships.
- Don't forget you can use a sequence of images to build up ideas.
- Use the pyramid principle to organise your message.

The images in the presentation should be used to support the presentation. They are *aides-mémoire* for the presenter and add impact to what the presenter says.

There are a number of technologies for producing visual material. The oldest and simplest is just a pen and paper. With a little care and attention, quite professional diagrams and graphs can be produced. Word-processing and desktop publishing systems and drawing packages are readily available and with a little practice they can be used to produce sophisticated and professional visual material.

Colour is an effective stimulus in visual communication and can be used to differentiate relationships (say, by the use of different coloured lines on graphs). Primary colours have most impact. Desktop publishing packages usually have colour facilities. Colour is reproduced well on overhead acetates and in electronic presentations. Beware, however, if it is intended to photocopy the overheads for later distribution – colour information is lost in black and white copies. A good deal of information can still be represented in black and white by using broken and dotted lines and different cross-hatching styles for areas.

The most common devices for visuals are the overhead projector that uses A4-sized acetates and, more commonly now, laptops with electronic presentations, e.g. PowerPoint (these are better for large audiences and more formal presentations). The following are a few points for producing effective visual support of the presentation:

- Remember that the visual material is supporting the presentation not making it! Don't put text on the screen and read from it.
- Keep the images simple. They should add impact to the presentation, not distract from it.
- Put up bullet points to indicate to your audience the key issues you are identifying. These will also act as *aides-mémoire* if you are presenting without notes.
- Use lower-case text. Upper-case is austere and can be difficult to read.
- Use a pointer (either a traditional stick or one of the laser type).
- Consider your positioning relative to the projector. You wish to face the audience, not the screen, so position yourself so that you can see the screen with a slight turn of the head. Avoid blocking the audience's view and don't block the image by standing in the light path.

The audience may find it useful to retain copies of the slides you have used, so photocopies may be provided. You must decide whether you wish to give out the copies at the beginning or at the end of the presentation. Giving them out beforehand allows the audience to annotate them during the presentation. However, the audience will inevitably flip through them. They may feel that all they need is in the handouts and so they don't need to follow the presentation in detail. Also you will lose control of when the audience sees particular images for the first time. For these reasons the presentation may lose some of its impact if handouts are distributed first.

The formal presentation can be quite nerve-racking for the inexperienced, but planning, preparation and practice are great builders of confidence. The rules for a presentation are the same as for any other communication. Think about what you want to achieve from it. Be sure of what you want people to do as a result of the communication. Analyse the audience. Some simple rules for an effective presentation are as follows.

- Rehearse and practise the presentation. This is best done as a team. Not everybody need be involved in the actual delivery, but all can add to it.
- Use notes as *aides-mémoire* but try not to read from a script. It is better to consider the points you wish to make and learn them using the visual stimuli as a prompt.
- Time your presentation. Make sure it is the right length for the time available. Make mental notes of some time-points to enable you to time the presentation and make sure it is on track. Place a watch or clock where you can see it discreetly (say, beside the laptop). Avoid looking at a watch on your wrist. It sends a bad message to the audience.
- On the day, dress appropriately, but comfortably. You'll feel much more confident.
- Before the presentation check that the equipment (e.g. overhead projectors, laptops, beamers, microphones, etc.) is working. It is stressful to have to sort out equipment in front of the audience before the presentation can begin.
- Make sure that the slides you intend to use are in the right order.
- When making the presentation use confident body language: make open gestures and avoid the temptation to cross your arms in a protective gesture. Try to make eye contact with the audience. Smile!
- Pace your speech. Take regular deep breaths. This will help control nervousness.

Try not to be anxious about the presentation. The audience are not out to get you! They are interested in what you have to say. With a little practice effective presenting becomes second nature – then you can concentrate on what you want to say! Increasingly, being able to give an effective presentation is a key skill in the modern business world.

22.4 Making a case: persuading with information

Information is needed for making decisions but decisions are not made on the basis of information alone. How it is presented and the context in which it is presented is also important in influencing decision-making. In business,

Management Consultancy and Skills

information is usually presented with the intention of encouraging the recipient to take a particular course of action (the 'what do you want the audience to do as a result of receiving the information?' objective). Being influential with information is a matter not only of identifying that information which makes your case but also of delivering it sympathetically to the audience.

Information will be more influential if it:

- is relevant to the decisions the recipient needs to make;
- is pitched at the right level of understanding;
- is presented in a form which makes it easy to understand and digest;
- is supported by impactful visual stimuli;
- is placed in appropriate opinion and feeling contexts;
- is delivered in a situation of good rapport (*see* Section 19.1);
- is part of an interactive process where the recipient is encouraged and supported to explore the information;
- has key points signposted and highlighted.

Don't forget, if you need to organise the information before presenting it, use the pyramid principle described in Barbara Minto's book.

22.5 Answering questions and meeting objections in presentations

Formal presentations usually end with an invitation for questions to be asked. It is useful to develop some skills in dealing with the questions – and their close relative: objections.

After having invited questions, look around the audience for signs of someone wishing to ask one. As the presenter you are in control. Even after you have invited questions potential questioners may still be looking for a sign from you that they have a right to speak. Eye contact and a 'yes' will usually be sufficient to elicit the question.

When the questioner speaks, really listen to the question being asked. Use active listening (*see* Section 19.4). Consider the nature of the question being asked as well as the question itself. Is it a 'head' question, a rational seeking of further information, or a 'heart' question, a more emotionally rooted seeking of reassurance?

Some useful points to remember in answering questions are as follows.

- Summarise the question being asked before attempting an answer. This will ensure that you have understood the question and that the rest of the audience have understood it. It will also give you some thinking time.

- If the question is complex and, in fact, contains more than one question, break it down into individual questions. Indicate that you will answer each in turn.

- Answer the question to the best of your ability. You can do no more! If you do not have the necessary information to hand, say so. Take the questioner's details and offer to get back to him or her with the information. But don't forget to do so!

- After answering a question don't just move on to the next questioner. Close the answer by asking the questioner whether the answer is satisfactory: 'Is that OK?'; 'Does that answer your question?'; 'I hope that's a little clearer'; etc.

Objections are a little more difficult to deal with but there are a few good points to remember. Objections may be more heart than head. They may be individual or may summarise what might be the concerns of the entire audience. Meeting objections may require more than fighting fact with fact. If you come up against an objection, try the following.

- Start by recognising (and even welcoming) the objection: 'Thank you. I'm glad you raised that'; 'Right. I can understand your concerns there'; 'An interesting point. Let me see if I can deal with it.'

- Consider the speaker's feelings when meeting objections (even if he or she doesn't seem to be considering yours). If he or she is seeking reassurance rather than information, give reassurance.

- If the objection is clearly emotional or no answer is obvious, ask a question back. 'This is obviously a major concern for you. Why is that?'; 'Have you encountered this kind of problem before?'; etc. This will get the objector to explore his or her objection (forcing him or her to put it on a rational footing). It will also give you some thinking time!

It may sound difficult, but learn to regard objections as an opportunity to make positive points.

> **Team discussion point**
>
> Prepare a short formal presentation (of five minutes with one or two overheads) on the theme of what you feel you have gained from the consulting project experience in terms of learning outcomes, transferable skills and enhanced career prospects.
>
> Each member of the team should give this presentation and invite (positive) criticism from the other members of the team.

◆ Summary of key ideas

- The final communication of the consulting findings is the 'product' the client is 'paying for'.

- The communication may take the form of a report, a personal presentation or a combination of the two.

- The communication should be planned with the objective of positively influencing the client and getting him or her to implement the ideas presented.

- Using the pyramid principle, organise your message into four levels: the big idea, means of achievement, logic and evidence.

- The most important part of the report is the executive summary: this sells the report to the reader and invites him or her in.

- A presentation should be planned in advance. Impact will be gained if the presentation is pitched to the audience, their level of understanding and interests.

- Visual materials should support the presentation, have an impact and reinforce the key ideas.

Key reading

Bradbury, A. (2000) *Successful Presentation Skills* (2nd edn). London: Kogan Page.

DiResta, D. (1998) *Knockout Presentations*. Worcester, MA: Chandler House Press.

Hansen, M.T. and Haas, M.R. (2001) 'Competing for attention in knowledge markets: Electronic document dissemination in a management consulting company', *Administrative Science Quarterly*, Vol. 46, No. 1, pp. 1–17.

Minto, B. (1987) *The Pyramid Principle*. London: Pitman Publishing.

Weissman, J. (2003) *Presenting to Win: The Art of Telling Your Story*. New York: FT Prentice Hall.

Discussion point

Why it matters to measure what matters

By **Mike Garstka, Pierre Lavallee and Paul Smith**

16 September 2003

Too many telecom executives still believe that more information is always better. One telco chief executive recently ended up with no fewer than 6,000 distinct metrics he could use to diagnose the state of the business. While many metrics raised red flags, few told the chief executive who in his organisation was responsible and could fix the problem.

There's a better way. In our experience, management teams should concentrate on no more than 20 vital metrics, assessed weekly and compiled monthly, that fit on a single page. This exercise forces executives to allocate precious metrics, which in turn often serves to sharpen a company's strategic priorities: how many of the Vital 20 should focus on overall corporate performance versus individual business units? How much should they emphasise emerging businesses versus core cash generators?

Companies also need to ensure their metrics are leading indicators that illuminate meaningful trend lines rather than backward looking reports that show what happened last month. The Vital 20 should include operating measures that can point to root causes,

and avoid a bias toward financial metrics that usually identify symptoms. Finally, each metric should be linked to an owner accountable for explaining the right trends and correcting the wrong ones.

The information overload came about naturally enough. During the industry's rapid build-up, telecom executives felt pressure from investors to expand quickly into new business opportunities, from Internet retailing to wireless services. Indicators for different businesses proliferated; different parts of the business were measured differently. New measures were added and few were removed.

The sheer mass of information has its own consequences. The massive reports that make a thud on chief executive's desks around the globe every month don't synthesise the flood of information in a meaningful way, and so tend to get ignored. And the pain of producing such reports usually delays their compilation, meaning they are often out of date by the time they hit the desk.

The likelihood that measures will spur action diminishes when companies rely too much on financial metrics. At one telco,

more than 95 per cent of metrics looked backward, measuring things like profit per customer instead of analysing trends that influence investment decisions, like the number of high value customers acquired last month or the number of new corporate contracts closed. Capital expenditures and other cash outlays are important factors in a company's free cash flow – a current bellwether for telecom investors – but measuring returns on recently invested capital actually serves as a better predictor of profit.

Companies also tend to measure where information is easier to gather. Financial data is readily available and can be useful for understanding a company's state of health. But operating metrics can diagnose the causes of problems and help management prescribe a cure. Declining sales numbers, for instance, point to a problem, but what telco executives really need to know is revenue churn – specifically, how much revenue went 'out the door' with customers cancelling contracts. This tells managers where to start taking action.

To spur useful action, metrics must be both tied to an owner and consistent throughout the ranks. The few metrics that the CEO sees for the wireless business unit, for instance, should be the same key metrics at the top of the list for the head of the wireless business. It does little good for the CEO to fume about wireless churn among high-value corporate customers if the head of wireless tracks churn differently.

Focused measures helped Japan Telecom Holdings achieve an impressive earnings and cash flow turnaround at its fixed line subsidiary Japan Telecom. When Bill Morrow stepped in as president of the company in December 2001, it was heading for its worst reported financial performance, but there were few alarm bells.

Mr Morrow recently commented, 'Early warning indicators (EWIs) and key performance indicators (KPIs) were at the top of my list as we began building the turnaround plan.' An initial set of metrics was in place within weeks. Many metrics were structured to look forward on a run-rate basis and were monitored against Japan Telecom's targets. Over time, the results book evolved into a highly-focused, single-page summary starting with five key financial metrics-revenue, contribution margin, overhead costs, ebitda (earnings before interest, tax and depreciation) and cash flow. These cascaded into 16 metrics at the business unit level, supported by measures for major products, cost categories and operations. At a glance, this one-page summary allowed management to identify the root causes of trends, determine who was accountable and agree on actions in monthly operations reviews.

The results? For the fiscal year ended March 2003, revenue growth in the strategic core data business was up 25.6 per cent, despite an anaemic Japanese economy. Japan Telecom reduced costs by 14.8 per cent, and net income moved from a loss of $640m to a profit of $130m, boosting free cash flow just under a billion dollars. The turnaround positioned Japan Telecom Holding for the sale of its fixed line business to private equity firm Ripplewood, announced on 21 August. That move allows Japan Telecom and lead shareholder Vodafone to focus on and recapitalise their core J-Phone mobile business.

As Japan Telecom knows, what gets measured gets done. Focusing on the Vital 20 metrics will help telecom chief executives, and those in other industries, to tap the right metrics to make the right decisions – and act on them.

Mike Garstka is a vice-president in the Tokyo office of Bain & Company (http:// www.bain.com/bainweb/home.asp). Pierre Lavallee is a Bain vice-president in Toronto. Paul Smith is a Bain director in Boston.

'Why it matters to measure what matters' by Mike Garstka, Pierre Lavallée and Paul Smith of Bain & Company, from FT.com, The Financial Times Limited, 16 September 2003, © Bain & Company.

Q1 How would you present the key ideas in this article to a client? Detail the key points you would wish to make.

Q2 You have devised a complex measure of some aspect of a client business. This measure is informative, but quite technical. Your client is not familiar with this technical area. How would you go about explaining the use of this measure in a presentation?

Q3 How would you go about measuring the success and impact of a presentation?

Part 2

Developing Management Skills

Introduction

This book is designed to help to guide individuals in improving their own personal management competencies. It is a practical guide to effective managerial behaviour and not a discussion of how some prominent industrialist has turned round a specific organisation. Unlike many 'airport' guides to successful management it is based on sound research and is designed along accepted teaching principles.

Management into the twenty-first century

Managers need to apply certain competencies backed by developable skills to perform effectively in the changing world of organisations. These competencies are in addition to their own functional expertise, they are about people skills. As Meredeth Belbin, management guru, often says in his lectures: *You are hired for what you are and fired for who you are.* This book is about developing these skills, but before we begin we need to say something about the word 'competence', which has acquired an almost mythical status in the past decade and, of course, the changing world of organisations.

Competency

There are as many definitions of competency as there are consultants attempting to sell competency training.

At a workshop organised by the British Psychological Society in 1989, a group of six human resource specialists were asked to come up with an agreed definition of competency. The chair of the group opened his report to the plenary meeting with the words: *Before presenting my report from all six of us I have to tell you that there are five minority reports!* The laughter was from understanding, relief and sympathy.

We are going to take our definition from the Cannon Working Party Report: *Progress and Change, 1987–94* (1994):

> The term competency is taken to mean the ability to perform effectively functions associated with management in a work-related situation.

1

Table 0.1 Skills required in the millennium – Ashridge survey, quoted by Colin Coulson-Thomas

	Ranking (%)
Strategic thinking, e.g., longer, broader, perspective, anticipating	78
Responding to and managing change	75
An orientation towards total quality/customer satisfaction	67
Financial management, e.g., role and impact of key indicators	46
Facilitating others to contribute	44
Understanding the role of information and IT	42
Verbal communication, e.g., coherent, persuasive	38
Organisational sensitivity, e.g., cross-functional understanding	37
Risk assessment in decision making	35

Quoted by Watson from an Ashridge Management Research Group Questionnaire (1994)

James Watson, also reporting to the Cannon Working Party, quoted from earlier work by Constable that the number of managers (and here he was speaking of the UK alone) would shrink overall by the year 2000 from 2.5–3.0 million to 2–2.25 million. Watson lists the skills needed for this new brand of manager (see Table 0.1). Colin Coulson-Thomas (1992), in a then British Institute of Management survey, came to similar conclusions.

Allred *et al.* (1996) looked at the changes in organisations and their demands on managers. Their premise was that 'organisational structure dictates core managerial competencies'. They then list the fashionable organisational structures since the First World War to one they predict for the immediate future, giving the core managerial competencies required with each development:

1. The traditional military style organisation where technical and commercial competencies predominated.

2. The matrix organisation appearing in the late 1950s and early 1960s:

   In trying to keep clients satisfied by effectively managing multifunctional resources and meeting budgets, project and brand managers in matrix organisations developed and used many of the same general management skills exercised by division managers in a diversified firm. In the global matrix organisations that appeared in the 1970s, country managers played the project management role through interactions with global functional and product divisions, responding to local needs by drawing on the resources of company-wide units. Thus country managers tended to develop a complete repertoire of technical, commercial and self-governance competencies. (Allred *et al.*, 1996)

3. The current evolution – the networked firm.

   To become more competitive, organisations downsized, delayered and outsourced many functions during the 1980s. In addition to the technical and commercial and competencies of the previous organisations, they need a raft of communications, collaborative and conflict competencies with their associated management skills. They demanded the competencies of self-learning and development.

4. Future developments – the cellular organisation.

   Allred *et al.* (1996) foresee a developing organisation where hierarchy has no part and 'managers and leaders' have to survive in an organic 'pond'. Here the interpersonal skills discussed in this book will predominate and the technical competencies will largely be replaced by technologies.

Greg Boudreux (1997) helpfully distinguishes between competencies and skills – confirming the usage of our book – and lists the competencies needed in the millennium.

- Skills are specific job-related abilities that can be developed through training.
- Competencies, acquired by constant practice of the relevant skills, are the habit of doing or saying the right things at the right time.

This book will help you acquire, develop and hone skills – turning these into competencies has to be left to you, and time.

The skills of the new organisations

As Allred *et al.* (1996) have pointed out, the new organisations will call upon more and more interpersonal skills. These skills need to be discussed.

The skills are behavioural. They are not personal attributes or stylistic tendencies. They consist of an identifiable set of actions that individuals perform and that lead to certain outcomes. An important implication, therefore, is that individuals can learn to perform these actions and can improve their current level of performance. People with different styles and personalities may apply the skills differently, but there is a core set of observable attributes of effective skill performance that are common across a range of individual differences.

The skills seem, in several cases, to be contradictory or paradoxical. For example, they are neither all soft nor humanistic in orientation, nor all hard driving and directive. They are oriented neither towards teamwork and interpersonal relations nor towards the individualism of an entrepreneur exclusively. A variety of types of skills are present. This was also in the findings of the Ashridge Managerial Research Group (1994), as quoted in the Cannon Report (1994).

For example, Cameron and Tschirhart (1988) assessed the skill performance of over 500 mid-level and upper-middle managers in about 150 organisations. They used the 25 most frequently mentioned management skills taken from those in Tables 0.2 and 0.3 as well as from research by Ghiselli (1963), Livingston (1971), Miner (1973), Katz (1974), Mintzberg (1975), Flanders (1981) and Boyatzis (1982).

In an analysis of the data we found that the skills could be sorted into four main groups. The first group focused on participative and human relations skills (for example, constructive communication and team building), while the second group focused on just the opposite, that is, on competitiveness and control (for example,

Table 0.2   The most frequently discussed skills of effective managers

1. Verbal communication – including listening
2. Managing time and stress
3. Managing individual decisions
4. Recognising, defining and solving problems
5. Motivating and influencing others
6. Delegating
7. Setting goals and articulating a vision
8. Self-awareness
9. Team building
10. Managing conflict

assertiveness, power and influence skills). A third group focused on innovativeness and entrepreneurship (such as creative problem solving), while a fourth group emphasised quite the opposite type of skills, namely maintaining order and rationality (for example, managing time and rational decision making).

One conclusion from the study was that effective managers are required to demonstrate paradoxical skills – that is, the most effective managers can be both participative and hard driving, both nurturing and competitive. These people were able to be flexible and creative while also being controlled, stable and rational. The second characteristic associated with effective management, then, is the mastery of diverse and seemingly contradictory skills.

Third, these critical skills were interrelated and overlapping. No effective manager performed one skill or one set of skills independent of others. For example, in order to motivate others effectively, skills such as supportive communication, influence and delegation were also required. Effective managers, therefore, develop a constellation of skills that overlap and support one another and allow flexibility in managing diverse situations.

Improving management skills

Successful management is more than just following a cookbook list of sequential behaviours. Developing highly competent management skills is much more complicated than developing skills such as those associated with a trade (e.g., welding) or a sport (e.g., scoring goals). Management skills are:

- Linked to a more complex knowledge base than other types of skills.
- Inherently connected to interaction with other (frequently unpredictable) individuals.

A standardised approach to welding or scoring goals may be feasible, but no standardised approach to managing human beings is possible.

Management Consultancy and Skills

Table 0.3 Identifying critical management skills: a sample of studies

1 – Study 2 – Respondents 3 – Focus	Results	
1. **Prentice** (1984) 2. 230 executives in manufacturing, retail and service firms 3. Critical skills for managing organisations	• Listening • Communication • Leadership • Problem solving • Time management • Adaptability to change	• Interpersonal relations • Formal presentations • Stress management
1. **Margerison and Kakabadse** (1984) 2. 721 CEO's in US corporations 3. Most important things you've learned in order to be a CEO	• Communication • Managing people • Delegation • Patience • Respect • Control • Understanding people • Evaluating personnel • Tolerance • Team spirit	• Strategic planning • Decision making • Self-discipline • Analytical ability • Hard work • Flexibility • Financial management • Time management • Knowledge of the business • Clear thinking
1. **Margerison and Kakabadse** (1984) 2. 721 CEO's in US corporations 3. Key management skills to develop in others to help them become senior executives	• Human relations • Communication • Planning and goal setting • People management and leadership	• Decision making • Financial management • Entrepreneurial skills • Delegating • Broad experience • Teamwork
1. **Cameron** (1984) 2. 50 consultants, professors, management development experts and public administrators 3. Critical management skills needed by state government managers	• Managing conflict • Motivating others • Managing stress and time • Decision making • Delegation	• Leadership • Knowledge and experience
1. **Hunsicker** (1978) 2. 1,845 US Air Force officers 3. Skills that most contribute to successful management	• Communication • Human relations • General management ability • Technical competence	

Management Consultancy and Skills

Table 0.3   (Cont'd)

1 – Study 2 – Respondents 3 – Focus	Results	
1. **Luthans** *et al.* (1985) 2. 52 managers in 3 organisations 3. Participant observation of skills demonstrated by most effective managers versus least effective managers	• Managing conflict • Communicating with outsiders	• Decision making • Communicating with insiders • Developing subordinates • Processing paperwork • Planning and goal setting
1. **Benson** (1983) 2. A survey of 25 studies in business journals 3. A summary of the skills needed by students entering the profession	• Listening • Written communication • Oral communication • Motivating/persuading	• Interpersonal skills • Informational interviewing • Group problem solving
1. **Curtis** *et al.* (1989) 2. 428 members of the American Society of Personnel Administrators in the US 3. (a) Skills needed to obtain employment (b) Skills important for successful job performance (c) Skills needed to move up the organisation	(a) • Verbal communication • Listening • Enthusiasm • Written communications • Technical competence • Appearance (c) Ability to: • work well with others one-to-one • gather information and make a decision • work well in groups • listen and give counsel • give effective feedback • present a good image of the firm • use computers and business machines	(b) • Interpersonal skills • Verbal and written communication • Persistence/ determination • Enthusiasm • Technical competence (d) Knowledge of: • the job • management theory • finance • marketing • accounting

Management Consultancy and Skills

Skills have a potential for improvement through practice. Any approach to developing management skills, therefore, must involve practical applications. At the same time, practice without the necessary conceptual knowledge is sterile and ignores the need for flexibility and adaptation to different situations. Therefore, developing skill competency is inherently tied to both conceptual learning and behavioural practice.

The method we have found to be most successful in helping individuals develop management skills is based on social learning theory (Bandura, 1977a; Davis and Luthans, 1980). This approach marries rigorous conceptual knowledge with opportunities to practise and apply observable behaviours. Variations on this general approach have been used widely in on-the-job supervisory training programmes (Goldstein and Sorcher, 1974), as well as in allied professional education classrooms such as teacher development and social work (Rose *et al.*, 1977; Singleton *et al.*, 1980).

The original learning model consisted of four steps:

1. The presentation of behavioural principles or action guidelines, generally using traditional instruction methods.
2. Demonstration of the principles by means of cases, films, scripts or incidents.
3. Opportunities to practise the principles through role plays or exercises.
4. Feedback on performance from peers, instructors or experts.

Our own experience in teaching complex management skills has convinced us that three important modifications are necessary in order for this model to be most effective:

- The behavioural principles must be grounded in social science theory and in reliable research results and not the generalisations and panacea prescriptions that appear regularly in the popular management literature. To ensure the validity of the behavioural guidelines being prescribed, the learning approach must include scientifically based knowledge about the effects of the management principles being presented.

- Individuals must be aware of their current level of skill competency and be motivated to improve upon that level in order to benefit from the model. Most people receive very little feedback about their current level of skill competency. Most organisations provide some kind of annual or semi-annual evaluation (for example, exams in colleges or performance appraisal interviews in firms), but these evaluations are almost always infrequent and narrow in scope, and they fail to assess performance in the most critical skill areas. To help people to understand what skills to improve and why, therefore, a pre-assessment activity must be part of the model. In addition, most people find change rather uncomfortable and therefore avoid taking the risk to develop new behaviour patterns. A pre-assessment activity in the learning model helps to encourage these people to change by illuminating their strengths and weaknesses. Individuals then know where their own weaknesses lie and the areas that need to be improved. Pre-assessment activities generally take the form of self-evaluation instruments, case studies or problems that help to highlight personal strengths and weaknesses in a particular skill area.

Management Consultancy and Skills

Table 0.4 A system for developing management skills

Steps	Contents	Objectives
1. Skill pre-assessment	Survey instruments Role plays	Assess current level of skill competence and knowledge; create readiness to change
2. Skill learning	Written text Behavioural guidelines	Teach correct principles and present a rationale for behavioural guidelines
3. Skill analysis	Case studies	Provide examples of appropriate and inappropriate skills performance; analyse behavioural principles and the reason that they work
4. Skill practice	Exercises Simulations Role plays	Practise behavioural guidelines; adapt principles to personal style; receive feedback and assistance
5. Skill application	Assignments (behavioural and written)	Transfer classroom learning to real-life situations; foster ongoing personal development

- An application component is needed in the learning model. Most management skill training takes place in a classroom setting where feedback is immediate and it is relatively safe to try out new behaviours and make mistakes. Therefore, transferring learning to an actual job setting is often problematic. Application exercises help to apply classroom learning to examples from the real world of management. Application exercises often take the form of an outside-of-class intervention, or a consulting assignment, or a problem-centred intervention, which the student then analyses to determine its degree of success or failure.

In summary, evidence suggests that a five-step learning model is most effective for helping individuals develop management skills (see Cameron and Whetten, 1984). Such a model is outlined in Table 0.4.

- Step 1 involves the pre-assessment of current levels of skill competency and knowledge of the behavioural principles.
- Step 2 consists of the presentation of validated, scientifically based principles and guidelines for effective skill performance.
- Step 3 is an analysis step in which models or cases are made available in order to analyse behavioural principles in real organisational settings. This step also helps to demonstrate how the behavioural guidelines can be adapted to different personal styles and circumstances.

- Step 4 consists of practice exercises in which experimentation can occur and immediate feedback can be received in a relatively safe environment.
- Step 5 is the application of the skill to a real-life setting outside the classroom with follow-up analysis of the relative success of that application.

Research on the effectiveness of training programmes using this general learning model has shown that it produces results superior to those based on the traditional lecture and discussion approach (Moses and Ritchie, 1976; Burnaska, 1976; Smith, 1976; Latham and Saari, 1979; Porras and Anderson, 1981). In addition, evidence suggests that management skill training can have significant impact on the financial performance of a firm.

> The US Postal Service completed a study a few years ago in which 49 of the largest 100 post offices in America were evaluated. An important question in the study was, 'How can we make post offices more effective?' Productivity and service quality were both monitored over a five-year period. The two major factors that had impact on these effectiveness measures were:
>
> **1.** Degree of mechanisation (automation)
> **2.** Investment in training.
>
> Two kinds of training were provided:
>
> (a) maintenance training (training in operating and maintaining the equipment)
> (b) management training (training in developing management skills).
>
> The overall conclusion of the study was: 'Performance levels in these organisations vary systematically and predictably as training levels vary. The training/performance relationship is positive and statistically significant.' More specifically, the study found that:
>
> - providing management training was more important than providing maintenance training in accounting for improved productivity and service in the post offices;
> - both kinds of training were more important than having automated or up-to-date equipment in the post office (mechanisation);
> - low-tech offices outperformed high-technology offices when managers were provided with management skill training.
>
> In short, its five-year study convinced the US Postal Service that helping employees to develop management skills was the best way to improve organisational effectiveness.

Successful managers must be able to work effectively with people. Unfortunately, interpersonal and management skills have not always been a high priority for business school students and aspiring executives. In a survey of 110 Fortune 500 CEOs, 87 per cent were satisfied with the level of competence and analytic skills of business school graduates, 68 per cent were satisfied with conceptual skills of graduates, but only 43 per cent of the CEOs were satisfied with graduates' management skills, and only 28 per cent were satisfied with their interpersonal skills!

To assist you in improving your own management skills, this book emphasises practising management skills, rather than just reading about them. We have organised the book with this specific approach in mind.

Management Consultancy and Skills

157

Organisation of the book

This book focuses on the management skill areas that research has identified as most important. Part 1, comprising the first three chapters of the book, focuses on intrapersonal skills: developing self-awareness, managing stress, and effective problem solving – each skill overlapping with other skills. No skill stands alone. Part 2 concentrates on the interpersonal skills of management – constructive communication, effective motivation, and constructive conflict management – while Part 3 deals with the hard management skills of effective empowerment and delegation and the issues of teams, leaders and managers. These skill areas also overlap with managers having to rely on combinations of skills taken from all areas to function effectively. As one progresses from personal to interpersonal to group skills, the core competencies developed in the previous area help to form a foundation for successful performance of the new skill area.

The final parts of the book are supplements and appendices, one of which covers the scoring procedures for the exercises, etc., in the text.

The supplements are devoted to specific skill areas that we have found in practice to require special attention:

- Conducting meetings

- Making oral presentations

- Interviewing

- Management of information.

We make no apology for including a section on data management. As we produce this book we find that its references become out of date and any practising manager needs to be up to date. The new technologies that are clumped under the word 'Internet' allow managers to be up to date in a way that their predecessors were never able to envisage – unless they wished to become academics and forget their management duties entirely. Using these new resources involves a new set of skills that fit happily under our title – *Developing Management Skills for Europe*.

Each chapter is organised on the basis of a cyclic learning model that allows the reader a measure of control over his or her learning. The chapters begin with questionnaires that allow you, the reader and learner, to find out your current level of skills in the area to be covered. After completing the questionnaires you will be able to focus your attention on areas of personal competence as well as areas needing improvement in both knowledge and performance – develop your own learning objectives. The body of each chapter will bring the reader up to speed on current thinking in the area and quote key references for further study if required. In practice we find that we have two clusters of readers: students and working managers who wish to improve the skills they are already using and perhaps give legitimacy to practices they have developed for themselves. The references and further reading provide a good starting point for projects and examination assessment. The summaries at the end of each chapter list the key behavioural guidelines.

Since we believe that '*When all is said and done, more is said than done*', we now ask you to practise your newly considered skills, initially on graded case studies and finally on real-life assignments based at home and at work. The purpose of these assignments is to help you to transfer behavioural guidelines into everyday practice now or later. You may be asked to teach the skill to someone else, to consult with another manager to help to resolve a relevant problem, or to apply the skill in an organisation or your home life. Having finished each chapter we invite you to go back to the questionnaires and see how your answers and behavioural application may have changed.

Practice and application

The last section of each chapter (Skill Application) contains exercises for practice and application. As we have said before, we consider that improvement in management skills is primarily the responsibility of the learner. If the application of the principles covered in this book is not conscientiously applied within the real world, then little or nothing will have been achieved. Effective management is no different from effectiveness in most other human enterprises. It requires the same kind of skills to live a productive and successful life as it does to manage people effectively. That is why, even though some readers may have responsibility for others at work, and indeed may never become managers, they should neither dismiss these skills as irrelevant nor wait until they become managers before attempting to practise them.

The researchers Staw, Sandelands and Dutton claimed in 1981 that people under stress revert to a 'dominant response pattern' – that is, they rely on behaviour patterns that are most deeply ingrained and may not be the most appropriate in the exact, new and novel circumstances. For example, if a person who has been accustomed to responding to conflict aggressively, but who has recently begun practising a more constructive mode is faced with an intense, emotional confrontation, that person may begin by reacting supportively. But as pressure mounts, he or she is likely to revert to the more practised, combative style: *we do what we do because that is always what we have done – forget all these new fangled theories.* The only way of adopting appropriate actions is practice and it is never too early to begin that practice. Whatever stage of our careers we find ourselves in, we should practise and apply the skills we are about to learn even if it is in our friendships, student organisations, families or social groups. With conscientious practise, following the behavioural guidelines will become second nature.

People learn best that which affects them, and they feel affected by something if they see an immediate effect on their lives. The converse is also true – if you do not practise the skills we are about to work on together, they will not be available for later, and perhaps vital, applications. Think about learning an unfamiliar language – practise among those actually speaking it is much more effective than any amount of study in isolation. Application is a crucial component of the skill development process, but it generally takes extra effort and ingenuity to make application exercises effective and worth while. We would encourage you to put that extra effort.

We are not entirely writing for practising managers and would-be managers. It is intended to help people in general to improve the management of many aspects of their lives and relationships. In fact, John Holt (1964, p. 165) put it in a way we do not wish to improve on. He equated management skill to intelligence:

> When we talk about intelligence, we do not mean the ability to get a good score on a certain kind of test or even the ability to do well in school; these are at best only indicators of something larger, deeper and far more important. By intelligence we mean a style of life, a way of behaving in various situations. The true test of intelligence is not how much we know what to do, but how we behave when we don't know what to do.

Fostering this intelligence is the purpose of our book.

So let's begin. This time we will close our Introduction with our skill assessment questionnaire and this time the questionnaire will cover the contents of the whole book and not just a single chapter.

Personal assessment of management skills

The questionnaires are designed to let you, our readers, understand where you rate now and where you rate when you have finished the book, on the key skill areas we are about to cover. There are a series of statements of behaviour and you should rate how well this behaviour fits you now, not how you would like it to be or how you think we would like it to be. Some of the statements may well relate to activities of which you have no experience. If this is the case, think about them and try to answer honestly 'How I would if I were . . .'. A scoring key in Appendix 1 at the end of the book will help you generate an overall profile of your management skill strengths and weaknesses.

RATING SCALE

1 = strongly disagree   **2** = disagree   **3** = slightly disagree
4 = slightly agree   **5** = agree   **6** = strongly agree

	Assessment	
	Pre-	Post-
In regard to my level of self-knowledge		
1. I seek information about my strengths and weaknesses so that I can improve myself.	___	___
2. I am willing to share my beliefs and feelings to others so that I can improve myself.	___	___
3. I am fully aware of how I prefer to gather information and make decisions.	___	___
4. I understand how I cope with ambiguous and uncertain situations.	___	___
5. I have a well-developed set of personal standards and principles that guide my behaviour.	___	___

These issues will be discussed in Chapter 1: Developing Self-awareness

When faced with stressful or time-pressured situations

6. I use effective time-management methods such as keeping track of my time, making action lists and prioritising tasks.   _____ _____

7. I frequently check my priorities so that less important things don't drive out the more important.   _____ _____

8. I work to keep myself fit.   _____ _____

9. I maintain an open, trusting relationship with someone with whom I can share my frustrations.   _____ _____

10. I know and practise several temporary relaxation techniques such as deep breathing and muscle relaxation.   _____ _____

11. I strive to redefine problems as opportunities for improvement.   _____ _____

These and issues 12 and 13 will be discussed in Chapter 2: Managing Stress

When I delegate tasks to others

12. I specify the level of performance I expect and the degree of initiative the other person should assume.   _____ _____

13. I follow up and maintain accountability for delegated tasks on a regular basis.   _____ _____

When I approach a typical, routine problem

14. I always attempt to define problems clearly and explicitly.   _____ _____

15. I always generate more than one alternative solution to the problem.   _____ _____

16. I keep problem-solving steps distinct; that is, I make sure that the processes of formulating definitions, generating alternatives and finding solutions are separated.   _____ _____

When faced with a complex or difficult problem that does not have a straightforward solution

17. I try to be flexible in the way I approach the problem; I don't just rely on conventional wisdom or past practice.   _____ _____

18. I try to unfreeze my thinking by asking lots of questions around the issue.   _____ _____

19. I often use metaphors or analogies to help me see issues differently.   _____ _____

20. I strive to look at problems from different perspectives so as to generate multiple definitions.   _____ _____

21. I only evaluate potential solutions when I have completed a list of alternatives – however bizarre some of them may seem.   _____ _____

When trying to foster more creativity and innovation among those with whom I work

22. I make sure there are divergent points of view represented in every problem-solving group.   _____ _____

Management Consultancy and Skills

161

23. I try to acquire information from customers regarding their preferences and expectations.   ____ ____

24. I recognise that those who support ideas and those involved with the implementation need recognition along with the 'idea people'.   ____ ____

25. I encourage informed rule-breaking in pursuit of creative solutions.   ____ ____

Issues 14–25 will be discussed in Chapter 3: Effective Problem Solving

In situations where I have to provide negative feedback or offer corrective advice

26. When I counsel others I help them to their own solutions.   ____ ____

27. I know when it is correct to offer advice and direction and when it is not. ____ ____

28. I attempt to give feedback focused on tasks and not personalities.   ____ ____

29. My feedback is specific and to the point, rather than general or vague. ____ ____

30. When I have to give negative feedback I describe the events objectively, their consequences and my feelings about them.   ____ ____

31. I take responsibility for my statements and views by using 'I' statements and avoid attributing things to 'them'.   ____ ____

32. I convey flexibility and openness to conflicting opinions when presenting my point of view, even when I feel strongly about it.   ____ ____

33. I do not patronise those who happen to have less authority or knowledge. ____ ____

34. I attempt not to dominate conversations.   ____ ____

Issues 26–34 will be discussed in Chapter 4: Constructive Communication

When another person needs to be motivated

35. I always determine if a person has the necessary resources and support to succeed in a task.   ____ ____

36. I use a variety of rewards to reinforce exceptional performances.   ____ ____

37. I design task assignments to make them interesting and challenging.   ____ ____

38. I make sure to give timely and focused feedback.   ____ ____

39. I always help to establish performance goals that are challenging, specific and time-bound.   ____ ____

40. I regard getting rid of staff as a last resort, however poorly I judge their performance.   ____ ____

41. I maintain consistent feedback when I feel effort is below expectations and capabilities.   ____ ____

42. I make sure that people feel fairly and equitably treated.   ____ ____

43. I provide immediate and appropriate praise for effective effort.   ____ ____

Issues 35–43 will be covered in Chapter 5: Effective Motivation

When I see someone doing something that needs correcting

44. I avoid making personal accusations and attributing self-serving motives
    to the other person.   ____ ____

45. I accept the need for two-way communication by encouraging questions
    and the expression of alternative views.   ____ ____

46. I make a specific request, detailing what I see as preferred option.   ____ ____

When someone complains about something I've done

47. I show genuine concern and interest, even when I disagree.   ____ ____

48. I seek additional information by asking questions that provide specific and
    descriptive information.   ____ ____

49. I ask the other person to suggest more acceptable behaviours.   ____ ____

When two people are in conflict and I am the mediator

50. I do not take sides but remain neutral.   ____ ____

51. I help the parties generate multiple alternatives.   ____ ____

52. I help the parties find areas on which they agree.   ____ ____

Issues 44–52 are discussed in context in Chapter 6: Effective Conflict Management

Where I have an opportunity to empower others

53. I help people feel competent in their work by recognising and celebrating
    any small successes.   ____ ____

54. I provide regular feedback and needed support.   ____ ____

55. I try to provide all the information required to accomplish their tasks.   ____ ____

56. I am genuinely concerned for those I work with.   ____ ____

When delegating work to others

57. I specify clearly the results I desire.   ____ ____

58. I specify clearly the level of initiative I want others to take (e.g. wait for
    directions, do part of the task and then report, do the whole task and then
    report, etc.).   ____ ____

59. As far as possible, I let the people actually doing the work develop, with my
    assistance and understanding, how work will be done.   ____ ____

60. I avoid upward delegation by asking people to recommend solutions, rather
    than merely asking for advice or answers, when a problem is encountered.   ____ ____

Issues 53–60 will be covered in Chapter 7: Effective Empowerment and Delegation

When working in a team

61. I like to be comfortable with my co-workers, understand my function and role
    as well as making close contacts.   ____ ____

62. I accept responsibility and do not expect to be told everything. ____ ____

When leading a team

63. I specify why things need to be done and what needs to be done and work towards the team, taking responsibility for the actual task. ___ ___

64. I accept that teams and individuals need developing. ___ ___

65. I see my job as facilitating the work, in every respect, monitoring the output and communication to authority and other teams. ___ ___

66. I accept that I need to be flexible in my management and leadership style. ___ ___

67. As a leader I maintain my position by modelling the behaviour I need and not by exercising power. ___ ___

68. I see the role of team leader as a privilege and not a right. ___ ___

Issues 61–68 will be developed in Chapter 8: Teams, Leaders and Managers

When communicating or requiring information

69. I keep myself up to date with my own area of expertise. ___ ___

70. I read generally about management – maybe a book a month. ___ ___

71. I have access to the Internet. ___ ___

72. I use e-mail and similar means to communicate with people. ___ ___

73. I use the Internet as a source of information about my job, including the business of my customers, clients, etc. ___ ___

Issues 69–72 will be developed in Supplement D: Management of Information

---

 EXERCISE 0.1

WHAT DOES IT TAKE TO BE AN EFFECTIVE MANAGER?

The purpose of this exercise is to help you to find out for yourself the role of a manager and the skills required to perform that job successfully.

Your assignment is to interview at least three full-time managers using the questions we list as a starting point. Treat the interviews as confidential and do not allow your notes to identify individual managers. Tell the managers that no one will be able to identify them from their responses.

Your notes should be as detailed as possible so that you can reconstruct the interviews for use later – if you are a student, to your class. The notes should include each person's job title and a brief description of his or her organisation.

Discussion questions

1. What would be a typical day at work?
2. What are the most critical problems you face as a manager?
3. What are the most critical skills needed to be a successful manager in your area?

4. What are the major reasons that some managers are less successful than others?

5. What are the outstanding skills or abilities of other effective managers you have known?

6. If you had to train someone to replace you in your current job, what key abilities would you focus on?

On a scale of 1 (very rarely) to 5 (constantly), can you rate the extent to which you use the following skills or behaviours during your workday?

Managing personal stress	____	Managing time	____
Facilitating group decision making	____	Orchestrating change	____
Making private decisions	____	Appraising others, formally or informally	____
Recognising or defining problems	____	Goal setting	____
Using verbal communication skills	____	Listening and counselling	____
Delegating	____	Disciplining	____
Motivating others	____	Self-learning	____
Managing conflict	____	Team building	____
Interviewing	____	Problem solving	____
Negotiation	____	Conducting or attending meetings	____

EXERCISE **0.2**

USING YOUR MANAGEMENT SKILLS

Another way to assess your own strengths and weaknesses in management skills is to engage in an actual managerial work experience. Some companies in developing their managers use this process. Trainee managers of any seniority are sent into 'strange' departments inside their own organisation or outside into 'sister' organisations and given an actual project to complete. Such action learning, pioneered by Enid Mumford of Manchester Business School, is outside the scope of our book.

A further technique, taking less resources but with an action learning element, is the simulation or management 'game' – either indoors or on occasion out of doors. Since this is a book, we have to chose an even simpler course of action – we would like you to work on a case study from the point of view of a manager faced with the issues.

Complete the exercise and assignments and then compare your own decisions with those of other class mates. Ideally the discussions should then be taken to plenary with a tutor for further analysis and discussion.

If you have not been given a case study before we would suggest a way of proceeding. Read it all through quickly and then go through it again, highlighting the main points. Although we hate to say it, this case study, as all the other case studies we have met, is full of packing and finding the key points at the beginning helps a lot.

Management Consultancy and Skills

CASE STUDY **0.1**

THE THAMES PUMP & VALVE COMPANY

The Thames Pump & Valve Company, whose managing director is John Manners, is a subsidiary of Arnold Chemicals & Equipment Ltd. Its operations have been quite successful. Beginning with a capital investment of slightly less than £750,000 in 1947, its capital investment today is in excess of £500 million. Thames Pump & Valve own a newly constructed office building in Slough and a manufacturing and assembly plant, also in Slough. There are two sales outlets in the UK in Reading and one in Henley. The mainland Europe sales are through strategically placed agents.

The company, excluding top management, employs 60 engineers and 32 technicians, and about 1,000 people in the production. The production unit works two 38-hour shifts a week.

John Dunn is the production manager. All valves and pump assemblies and components are either manufactured or assembled in the production department according to detailed specifications. The specifications are distributed to various sites and locations according to set procedures or are stored in the company's warehouses in Reading and Henley. Centralised product and planning enables the company to maintain rigid production and quality controls over all units that become a part of completed products. In addition, carefully planned production and shipping schedules reduce the amount of time that completed units must be stored at production points. As a result, distribution costs are reduced and the company is better able to ensure that contracted completion dates are met.

The research and development division, currently under the direction of Tom Evans, has grown from two engineers to its present size of 30 engineers and 12 technicians and draftsmen. Partly because of the plant manager's intense interest, 10 per cent of the company's profits are allocated to research and development. The research division has developed, among other things, a less expensive and longer lasting rust inhibitor system, a rotary arc-welding unit for the plant and a new method for testing the strength and quality of welded unions. Also, the division was responsible for the design of expansion joints which are formed and assembled in the company's plant, ready for immediate installation at construction sites.

Bill Marshall is the financial controller and has approximately 15 people in the accounts department. Alan Cushwell's personnel department is also staffed by 15 people, while there is a total of 82 employees in the marketing department headed by James Barber.

John Manners, the managing director, suffered a severe heart attack on 12 April and died. It had been noticed that he appeared tired and overworked recently but nothing was done about it. His place has been taken by Richard West, transferred from Kent Pump & Valve, a slightly smaller subsidiary of the Arnold Group.

Assignment

Today is Sunday, 11 April 1999. Richard West has just come into the office, for the first time at 17.45 p.m. He must leave in time to catch the midnight plane for an important meeting in Cologne. He will not be back until next Monday, 20 April. His secretary is Doreen Powell, who was secretary to John Manners before he died.

Doreen Powell has left a number of letters in Richard West's in-tray (Items 0.1–0.11 below). You are to assume the role of Richard West and go through all the material, taking whatever action you deem appropriate for each item and prioritising your actions. Every action you wish to take should be written down, including memos to the secretary, memos to 'yourself' (Richard West), etc. Draft letters where appropriate, and write out any plans or agendas for meetings or conferences that you plan. These letters, memos, notes, etc., may be in 'rough draft' form.

---

10 April 1999

OFFICE MEMORANDUM
TO: Richard West
FROM: Doreen Powell
SUBJECT: SAM Presentation (See attached)

Mr West:

Just a note to let you know that Mr Manners did nothing towards developing the programme scheduled for 24 April, except to send the title to Mr Johnson via E-Mail. The title was announced to members some time ago. I don't think Mr Manners discussed the matter with any of the department heads.

Doreen

Item 0.1 A

THE SOCIETY FOR THE ADVANCEMENT OF MANAGEMENT
Berkshire Branch
PO Box 106
Windsor, Berks

1 April 1999

Mr John Manners
Managing Director
Thames Pump & Valve Ltd
Wokingham Road
Slough
Berks

Dear John

This is a reminder that we are counting on you and on the Thames Pump & Valve Company to provide us with the three-hour evening programme for our meeting on 24 April.

I know you and your team will provide a stimulating and worthwhile programme. The title of the programme you are to present, 'The Image of Today's Executive', sounds very interesting and already the dinner and programme is a 'sell out'. It means you can look forward to a full house on the night of your presentation.

Could you prepare a brief outline of the programme and text of any speeches that will be presented, indicating who will present them so we can go ahead with the programme and press releases?

We are all looking forward to seeing you on 24 April.

Best regards

Paul Johnson
Secretary, Berkshire Branch.

Item 0.1 B

PERSONAL

7 April 1999

OFFICE MEMORANDUM
TO: John Manners
FROM: Alan Cushwell, Industrial and Employee Relations
SUBJECT: Frank Munro

I have been told confidentially from an unimpeachable source that Frank Munro has been offered a job with N.C.A. and he is going to give a firm answer next week. I don't think anyone else knows this yet, I just stumbled onto the information. I understand that he has been offered more money than we can offer him now based on present wage and salary policy. As you know, Munro has only been with the company a short time and is already earning somewhat more than others at his level. This presents a problem which needs to be ironed out. I'm afraid I mentioned the possibility of just such an eventuality when you instituted the plan last November. Perhaps we need to reconsider some of the aspects of your plan before we make offers to June graduates.

I know that you and Tom Evans feel that Munro is one of the most valuable men in research and development. It's not certain that Munro will take the job but I thought I'd better give you advance warning in case he does leave us. Please let me know what action you are likely to take on this matter.

Alan Cushwell

Item 0.2

---

3 April 1999

OFFICE MEMORANDUM
TO: John Manners
FROM: Alan Cushwell, Industrial and Employee Relations
SUBJECT: Testing Programme

I feel it is essential that we institute a professional and systematic testing programme for recruiting secretarial and clerical personnel. The following are some suggested tests and other criteria we might want to consider. Do you have any suggestions for types of tests or other selection procedures which we might want to look at before we finalise the programme?
(1) Clerical Personnel:
   (a) Saville and Holdsworth's Aptitude Test (including measurements on spelling, arithmetic and general aptitude)
   (b) Mann-Watson Typing Test
   (c) Age to 40
(2) Secretarial Personnel:
   (a) Saville and Holdsworth's Aptitude Test
   (b) Mann-Watson Typing Test
   (c) Collins Shorthand Skill Inventory (via recording)
   (d) College diploma
   (e) Age to 40

Alan Cushwell

Item 0.3

Management Consultancy and Skills

7 April 1999

OFFICE MEMORANDUM
TO: John Manners
FROM: Bill Marshall, Finance
SUBJECT: Dismissal of Robert Roberts

This is a summary of my reasons for dismissing Robert Roberts. As you know, Mr Roberts was employed as an assistant credit controller on 4 March, 1997. For the two years he has been working with us on a full-time basis while attending the technical college at night. He has continually been a source of irritation to those who have been working closely with him. The main problem is that he often oversteps his authority. He has frequently been involved in controversies with the sales staff over problems which were not his concern. In general he did an adequate job on the work he was assigned but many of the accounts staff felt he wasn't putting enough effort into the job. He seemed to have a lot of free time which he spent in the canteen or gossiping with others in the department. The final straw came when he was told to pick up a cheque from Gavins, who have always been a good account in the past. He returned without the cheque, claiming that the amount owed was disputed. But in the meantime Gavins' boss George Thomas had been on the phone complaining about Roberts's attitude. He said Roberts was arrogant, off-hand and highly sarcastic about the outstanding debt, so much so that Gavins are now refusing to pay the invoice until we have formally apologised for Roberts's behaviour.

Bill

Item 0.4

3 April 1999

OFFICE MEMORANDUM
TO: John Manners
FROM: James Barber, Marketing
SUBJECT: Sales Promotion of Rust

As you know, we are moving into our campaign to push the new rust inhibitor. I would like to have your permission to set up a contest among our sales representatives with a trip to Hong Kong for the sales rep with the best sales figures in the next six-month period. I want to make the prize good enough to tempt the sales force to push this launch as hard as they can.

Jim

Item 0.5

8 April 1999

OFFICE MEMORANDUM
TO: John Manners
FROM: Alan Cushwell, Industrial and Employee Relations
SUBJECT: Employment of John Jones, Engineer

I would like to bring you up to date on my feelings concerning the engineer, John Jones, whom Evans wishes to employ. Evans is from Birmingham and I don't think that he fully understands the morale problems we would have if we recruited a black engineer who would have supervision over several white assistants. I realise that we are going to have to protect our interests in local authority contracts, but I think we can find a better way to do so than starting at this level. I would suggest that you talk with Evans about this problem and the possible complications that could arise.

Alan Cushwell

Item 0.6

3 April 1999

OFFICE MEMORANDUM
TO: John Manners
FROM: Bill Marshall, Finance
SUBJECT: Annual Budget Request

We are late in turning in our budget request to Arnold Chemical and Equipment Ltd for the next fiscal year since the report from R & D is still not in. All other department heads have turned in sound budgets which, if approved, should greatly facilitate the cutting of costs next year. Can you do something to speed up action?

Bill Marshall

Item 0.7

3 April 1999

OFFICE MEMORANDUM
TO: John Manners
FROM: Bill Marshall, Finance
SUBJECT: Coffee breaks

This morning I timed a number of people who took 40 minutes drinking their coffee during the mid-morning break. These people were mainly from the production and research department. I am able to control this in my department and I feel you should see that this matter is taken care of by the heads of the other departments. I estimate that the waste amounts to 125,000 man hours (in excess of £1 million) a year.

Bill Marshall

item 0.8

---

6 April 1999

OFFICE MEMORANDUM
TO: John Manners
FROM: Tom Evans, Research and Development
SUBJECT: Allocation for Research

This department has been successful in developing an efficient method for extracting certain basic compounds from slag and other similar by-products that are currently classified as waste by a large number of chemical plants within this area.

It is my recommendation that this company take every step necessary to commercially develop this extraction method. I have brought this matter to Bill Marshall's attention on two separate occasions, requesting that the necessary funds be allocated to fully develop this programme. He has advised me on both occasions that the funds could not possibly be made available within the next fiscal year. He has also indicated that we should reduce the emphasis on research in the chemical area, since this is an unnecessary duplication of functions within the Gateshead and Carlisle plants which the Arnold group own.

It is my opinion that Thames Pump & Valve Company should capitalise on its advantageous position now, before our competitors are able to perfect a similar method.

The above is for your consideration and recommendations.

Tom Evans

cc: Mr O J Thompson, Director
    Research & Development

Item 0.9

BRITISH FEDERATION OF FOUNDRY WORKERS
Erdington Road
Solihull
Near Birmingham

3 April 1999

Mr John Manners
Managing Director
Thames Pump & Valve Ltd
Wokingham Road
Slough
Berks

Dear Sir

On several occasions I have noticed that you and your staff have used your company newspaper as a vehicle for undermining the present union leadership.

In addition, a series of supervisory bulletins have been circulated that were designed to cause supervisory personnel to influence the thinking of union members in the forthcoming union elections. I am also aware of your 'support' for Brendan Sullivan and others who have been more than sympathetic towards company management.

As you know, such behaviour as I have described is in direct breach of Article 21 of our contract with the Arnold group. I am sure you are also aware of the potential damage that a charge of unfair management practices could have on future elections and negotiations.

I trust such action will not become necessary and that you will take steps to prevent any further discrimination against this union administration.

Yours sincerely

Humphrey Swindells
Branch secretary

cc: Mr A Cushwell

Item 0.10

7 April 1999

OFFICE MEMORANDUM
TO: John Manners
FROM: John Dunn, Production
SUBJECT: Quality Control

The Marketing Department has put pressure on us to increase production for the next two months so that promised deliveries can be made. At the present time we cannot increase production without taking some risks in terms of quality. The problem is that marketing does not check with us before committing us to specific delivery dates. This problem has come up before, but nothing has been done. Could we meet in the near future to discuss the situation?

John

Item 0.11

Developing Self-awareness

SKILL DEVELOPMENT OUTLINE

Skill Pre-assessment surveys

- Self-awareness
- Defining issues test
- Learning Style Indicator
- Cognitive style instrument
- Locus of control scale
- Tolerance or ambiguity scale
- Interpersonal orientations and needs (Firo-B)

Skill Learning material

- Key dimensions of self-awareness
- The sensitive line
- Cognitive styles
- Learning styles
- Personal values
- Ethical decision making

- Attitudes towards change
- Interpersonal needs
- Summary
- Behavioural guidelines

Skill Analysis case studies

- The Communist prison camp
- Decision dilemmas

Skill Practice exercises

- Improving self-analysis through self-disclosure
- Identifying aspects of personal culture

Skill Application activities

- Suggested assignments
- Application plan and evaluation

LEARNING OBJECTIVES

- Understanding of one's self as a starting point for working with others
- An ability to look at values and beliefs analytically

- Understanding the process of learning and the adaptation to change
- The acceptance of psychological needs as a prime source of motivation in management

30

Management Consultancy and Skills

INTRODUCTION

The starting point of this book is you. Our aim in this first chapter is to help you to develop a greater knowledge of yourself, so that when we begin to explore the skills of working with and managing other people, you understand something about our starting point.

> Two managers were working together on the design of a new working area. There was no argument about the specification to which they were working – the size of each employee's working area was tightly laid down, as was the lighting and ventilation plan. The desks and fittings would conform to company standards and the computer screens would conform to health and safety regulations.
>
> These things brought no problems. What did bring problems was finishing the project off with discretionary items – 'accessories'. One manager was keen on plants and the other on partitions – each saw the other's ideas as a waste of time. Discussion showed that they were 'coming from different directions'. One manager, brought up as an only child, attached great importance to privacy – he wanted the partitions. The other manager, brought up with a large number of siblings, liked the comfort of being able to see others about him, and preferred the plants. Once they accepted that what they wanted for others reflected what they wanted for themselves, a compromise was reached. The working area contained partitioned areas and open plant-ornamented areas and the people using the area were encouraged to choose where they wanted to work.

Some of the ways we will look at ourselves may need some defending, and you may feel that questioning values is a trifle intrusive. We can only say that the values we bring to the job are becoming increasingly important. In 1996 we took one week's newspapers and listed the cases of dysfunctional values operating in European business – frauds leading to corporate embarrassment of various degrees. One airline was being accused of tapping into a competitor's database and using the information to 'poach' passengers from a rival airline. An Italian computer company was being accused of using bribes to obtain contracts, and Europe's largest car manufacturer was alleged to be using industrial espionage in a way that would have made a writer of spy fiction blush. There were many other 'less important' cases. In 1998 these particular issues are still bringing problems to their 'originators'. Values are important.

Collins and Porras (1995) studied the habits of several exceptional companies and discovered a common feature. They all had clear core ideologies reflecting issues beyond being profitable and reflecting real values. It was these core ideologies that shaped management practice. However, we will begin with one of the most fundamental ways in which our behaviour is formed: how we take on and assimilate data.

31

Management Consultancy and Skills

177

Skill pre-assessment

SELF-AWARENESS

The first survey is designed to explore your view of yourself and how you can tailor your learning to your specific needs. When you have completed the survey, use the scoring key at the end of the book to identify the skills that are most important for you to master.

Step 1   For each statement circle a number on the rating scale in the Pre-assessment column. Your answers should reflect your attitudes and behaviour as they are now, not as you would like them to be. Be honest. When you have completed the survey, use the scoring key in Appendix 1 to identify the skill areas discussed that are most important for you to master. The process of improving these skill areas should help you with your learning objectives.

Step 2   When you have completed the chapter and the Skill Application assignments, record your responses in the Post-assessment column then use the scoring key in Appendix 1 to measure your progress. If your score remains low in specific skill areas, use the behavioural guidelines at the end of the Skill Learning section to guide your Application Planning.

RATING SCALE

1 = Strongly disagree	**2** = Disagree	**3** = Slightly disagree
4 = Slightly agree	**5** = Agree	**6** = Strongly agree

	Assessment	
	Pre-	Post-
1. I seek information about my strengths and weaknesses from others as a basis for self-improvement.	____	____
2. When I get negative feedback about myself, I do not get angry or defensive.	____	____
3. In order to improve, I am willing to share my beliefs and feelings with others.	____	____
4. I am very much aware of my personal style of gathering information and making decisions.	____	____
5. I am very much aware of my own interpersonal needs when it comes to forming relationships with other people.	____	____
6. I understand how I cope with situations that are ambiguous and uncertain.	____	____
7. I have a well-developed set of personal standards and principles that guide my behaviour.	____	____
8. I feel very much in charge of what happens to me, good and bad.	____	____
9. I seldom, if ever, feel angry, depressed, or anxious without knowing why.	____	____

10. I am conscious of the areas in which conflict and friction most frequently arise in my interactions with others.   ___ ___

11. I have a close relationship with at least one other person in whom I can share personal information and personal feelings.   ___ ___

SURVEY **1.2**

DEFINING ISSUES TEST

This second survey is designed to look at your approach to controversial social issues. Complete the survey by yourself before discussing it with others – the differences between your approach and that of others may be revealing. The survey seeks to investigate two points:

- In making a decision about these social problems, what are the most important questions one should ask oneself?
- On what principles would you want people to base the decisions?

You are presented with three problem stories. Following each problem story there are 12 statements (or questions). Read each story and rate each statement (question) in terms of its importance in making a decision. Take your top 4 and rank these from the most to the least crucial for making a quality decision. Some statements will raise important issues, but you should ask yourself: Are these relevant to the decision in hand? Some statements may sound impressive but are nonsensical while others are confused or confusing – these are 'of no importance' to you and rate a score of 0.

Use the following rating scale for your responses to the statements of questions:

4. Of great importance – something that is absolutely crucial.

3. Very important – something that one should clearly take notice of before making the decision.

2. Important – something that concerns you but will not sway the decision.

1. Of little importance.

0. Of no importance – a waste of time to consider, nonsense or confused.

The analysis of the scoring is given in Appendix 1.

The escaped prisoner

A man had been sentenced to prison for 10 years. After one year, however, he escaped from prison, moved to a new area, and adopted the name of Thompson. For eight years he worked hard, and gradually he saved enough money to buy his own business. He was fair to his customers and his staff, as well as being an active and worthwhile member of the community. Then one day, Mrs Jones, an old neighbour, recognised Thompson from an old newspaper photograph as a man who had escaped from prison eight years previously. Should Mrs Jones report Mr Thompson to the police and have him sent back to prison? (*Tick one.*)

____ Should report him
____ Can't decide
____ Should not report him.

Importance in Mrs Jones's decision (1 to 5)

1. Hasn't Mr Thompson proved that he is not really bad by being good for so long?   ____

2. Every time someone escapes punishment for a crime, doesn't that just encourage more crime?   ____

3. Wouldn't we be better off without prisons and the oppression of our legal systems?   ____

4. Has Mr Thompson really paid his debt to society?   ____

5. Would society be failing if it did not deliver what Mr Thompson should fairly expect?   ____

6. Leaving out the obvious fact that he has broken the rules, what benefit would prison be to someone who is evidently a good man?   ____

7. How could anyone be so cruel and heartless as to send Mr Thompson back to prison?   ____

8. Would it be fair to all the prisoners who had to serve their full sentences if Mr Thompson was let off?   ____

9. Was Mrs Jones a good friend of Mr Thompson?   ____

10. Wouldn't it be a citizen's duty to report an escaped criminal, regardless of the circumstances?   ____

11. How would the will of the people and the public good best be served?   ____

12. Would going to prison do any good for Mr Thompson or protect anybody?   ____

From the list of 12 questions, select the four most important and rank these from most to least important.

The doctor's dilemma

A woman had an incurable cancer and was told that she had a maximum of six months to live. She was in terrible pain and very weak, so weak that a medium dose of morphine would accelerate her death. She was delirious in her pain but, in her calm periods, she would ask the doctor to give her enough morphine to kill her. She argued that she had nothing to live for and that she was going to die in a few months anyway. What should the doctor do? (*Tick one.*)

____ He should give the overdose
____ Can't decide
____ Should not give the overdose.

Importance in the doctor's decision (1 to 5)

1. Whether the woman's family is in favour of giving her the overdose or not. ____

2. Does the doctor work to the same set of laws as everybody else if giving her an overdose would be the same as killing her? ____

3. Whether people would be much better off without society regimenting their lives and even their deaths. ____

4. Whether the doctor could make it appear like an accident. ____

5. Does the government have the right to force continued existence on those who don't want to live? ____

6. What is the value of death prior to society's perspective on personal values? ____

7. Whether the doctor has sympathy for the woman's suffering or cares more about what society might think. ____

8. Is helping to end another's life ever a responsible act of co-operation? ____

9. Whether only God should decide when a person's life should end. ____

10. What values the doctor has set for himself in his own personal code of behaviour. ____

11. Can society afford to let everybody end their lives when they want to? ____

12. Can society allow suicides or mercy killings and still protect the lives of individuals who want to live? ____

From the list of questions above, select the four most important and rank them from the most crucial to the least.

The newspaper

Frank wanted to produce a newspaper at his school to act as a platform on which he could express his views on a number of controversial issues. In particular, he wanted to speak out about waste, environmental pollution and also about the pettiness of some of the school's rules. He had been very proud of growing a pigtail but had been told to stay at home until he cut it off.

When he started his newspaper, he asked his headmaster for permission and the head responded very positively: he could produce his newspaper provided he sent in his articles for the head's approval before publication. Frank agreed and duly submitted the first two issues for approval, which was granted. The head had not expected Frank's newspaper to receive so much attention. Pupils were so excited by the paper that they began to organise protests against the 'petty rules' – 'petti-coat rules' as they had begun to call them. Several vocal parents phoned the head objecting to everything about the newspaper and insisting that it be banned. What should the head do? (*Choose one.*)

____ Should stop it
____ Can't decide
____ Should not stop it.

Importance in the head's decision (1 to 5)

1. Is the head more responsible to the pupils or to the parents? _____
2. Did the head give her word that the newspaper could be published for a long time, or did she just promise to approve the newspaper one issue at a time? _____
3. Would the pupils start protesting even more if the head stopped the newspaper? _____
4. When the good name of the school is threatened, does the head have the right to tell the pupils what to do? _____
5. Does the head have the freedom of speech to say 'no' in this case? _____
6. If the head stopped the newspaper, would she be preventing full discussion of important problems? _____
7. Would the head's order make Frank lose respect for her? _____
8. Was Frank really loyal to his school? _____
9. What effect would stopping the paper have on the pupils' education in critical thinking and judgements? _____
10. Was Frank in any way violating the rights of others in publishing his own opinions? _____
11. Should some angry parents be allowed to influence the head when she knows best what is going on in the school? _____
12. Was Frank using the newspaper to stir up hatred and discontent? _____

From the list of questions above, select the four most important, ranking them from most to least crucial.

Source: Rest (1979)

SURVEY **1.3**

LEARNING STYLE INDICATOR

We are presenting six sets of views on management. You have 10 points to distribute within each set. For instance, you could give all 10 points to one statement that you feel completely reflects your views, or perhaps distribute the 10 points more evenly. At the end of the exercise, you should have a total of 60 points in six batches of 10. There is no right or wrong view and the questions are intended to illustrate differences between effective managers in the field. If you have no managerial experience, try to see yourself as a manager and how you would feel about the various issues.

Score

1. My personal aim as a manager in an organisation is:

   a. To extend knowledge or understanding in my area _____
   b. To be useful _____
   c. To solve problems _____
   d. To keep the organisation on a moral basis. _____

2. I am proud of:

   a. My staff or peers as people   ____

   b. What we have/will have achieved   ____

   c. Our abilities to solve problems   ____

   d. My department or discipline.   ____

3. I feel we should be judged on:

   a. Our useful contacts   ____

   b. The stimulus provided to the organisation   ____

   c. Things that we have actually done which can be of use   ____

   d. Our reputation as a centre of excellence.   ____

4. I get my personal job rewards from:

   a. Working with difficult problems   ____

   b. Interacting with challenging people   ____

   c. The respect from others doing similar things   ____

   d. Sudden flashes of insight.   ____

5. I see my job as a people manager as:

   a. Making sure that 'good people' can be effective   ____

   b. Developing their analytical skills   ____

   c. Developing my people   ____

   d. Maintaining a 'tight ship'.   ____

6. I think the best reports I produce:

   a. Excite and stimulate my readers   ____

   b. Extend knowledge in some way   ____

   c. Clearly recommend courses of action   ____

   d. Present argued alternatives.   ____

When you have completed the form, score in the following way:

Section	Why?	What?	How?	If?
1	d.	a.	c.	b.
2	a.	d.	c.	b.
3	b.	d.	a.	c.
4	b.	c.	a.	d.
5	c.	b.	d.	a.
6	a.	b.	d.	c.
Total				

Source: From *The New Manager* (Woods, 1988)

SURVEY **1.4**

COGNITIVE STYLE INSTRUMENT

The purpose of the instrument is to look at the way you view the information you use in your work. There are no right or wrong answers, and one alternative is just as good as another. Try to indicate the ways you do, or would, respond, not the ways you think you should respond. For each scenario there are three pairs of alternatives. For each pair, tick the alternative that comes closest to the way you would work. Answer each item. If you are not sure, make your best guess. When you have finished answering all the questions, use the scoring key in Appendix 1 at the end of the book to see how you rate against other people.

Suppose you are a scientist whose job it is to gather information about the moons of Saturn. Which alternative would be more interesting to you?

1. a. How the moons are similar to one another ____
   b. How the moons differ from one another ____

2. a. How the whole system of moons operates ____
   b. The characteristics of each moon ____

3. a. How Saturn and its moons differ from Earth and its moon ____
   b. How Saturn and its moons are similar to Earth and its moon. ____

Suppose you are the chief executive of a company and have asked division heads to make presentations at the end of the year. Which of the following would be more appealing to you?

4. a. A presentation analysing the details of the data ____
   b. A presentation focused on the overall perspective ____

5. a. A presentation showing how the division contributed to the company as a whole ____
   b. A presentation showing the unique contributions of the division ____

6. a. Details of how the division performed ____
   b. General summaries of performance data. ____

Suppose you are visiting a country from Eastern Europe for the first time, and you are writing home about your trip. Which of the following would be most typical of the letter you would write?

7. a. A detailed description of people and events ____
   b. General impressions and feelings ____

8. a. A focus on similarities between our culture and theirs ____
   b. A focus on the uniqueness of their culture ____

9. a. Overall, general impressions of the experience ____
   b. Separate, unique impressions of parts of the experience. ____

Suppose you are attending a concert featuring a famous symphony orchestra. Which of the following would you be most likely to do?

10. a. Listen for the parts of individual instruments ____
    b. Listen for the harmony of all the instruments together ____

11. a. Pay attention to the overall mood associated with the music   _____
    b. Pay attention to the separate feelings associated with different parts of
       the music   _____

12. a. Focus on the overall style of the conductor   _____
    b. Focus on how the conductor interprets different parts of the score.   _____

**Suppose you are considering taking a job with a certain organisation. Which of the
following would you be more likely to do in deciding whether or not to take the job?**

13. a. Systematically collect information on the organisation   _____
    b. Rely on personal intuition or inspiration   _____

14. a. Consider primarily the fit between you and the job   _____
    b. Consider primarily the politics needed to succeed in the organisation   _____

15. a. Be methodical in collecting data and making a choice   _____
    b. Mainly consider personal instincts and gut feelings.   _____

**Suppose you inherit some money and decide to invest it. You learn of a new
high-technology firm that has just issued shares. Which of the following is
most likely to be true of your decision to purchase the firm's shares?**

16. a. You would invest on a hunch   _____
    b. You would invest only after a systematic investigation of the firm   _____

17. a. You would be somewhat impulsive in deciding to invest   _____
    b. You would follow a pre-set pattern in making your decision   _____

18. a. You could rationally justify your decision to invest in this firm and not in another   _____
    b. It would be difficult to rationally justify your decision to invest in this firm and
       not another.   _____

**Suppose you are being interviewed on TV, and you are asked the following questions.
Which alternative would you be most likely to select?**

19. How are you more likely to cook?

    a. With a recipe   _____
    b. Without a recipe.   _____

How would you predict the next winner of the European Football Cup?

20. a. After systematically researching the personnel and records of the teams   _____
    b. On a hunch or by intuition.   _____

Which games do you prefer?

21. a. Games of chance (like bingo)   _____
    b. Games of skill (like chess, draughts or Scrabble).   _____

**Suppose you are a manager and need to hire an executive assistant. Which of the
following would you be most likely to do in the process?**

22. a. Interview each applicant using a set outline of questions   _____
    b. Concentrate on your personal feelings and instincts about each applicant   _____

Management Consultancy and Skills

23. a. Consider primarily the personality fit between yourself and the candidates ____
    b. Consider the match between the precise job requirements and the candidates' capabilities ____
24. a. Rely on factual and historical data on each candidate in making a choice ____
    b. Rely on feelings and impressions in making a choice. ____

SURVEY 1.5

LOCUS OF CONTROL SCALE

This survey assesses your opinions about certain issues. Each item consists of a pair of alternatives marked 'a' or 'b'. Select (*tick*) the alternative with which you most agree, forcing the choice – do make a choice. Since this is an assessment of opinions, there are obviously no right or wrong answers. When you have finished each item, turn to the scoring key in Appendix 1 for instructions on how to tabulate the results and for comparison data.

This survey is similar to, but not exactly the same as, the original locus of control scale developed by Julian Rotter, and the comparison data provided in Appendix 1 is based on the original scale. No significant differences are expected.

1. a. Leaders are born, not made
   b. Leaders are made, not born ____
2. a. People often succeed because they are in the right place at the right time
   b. Success is most dependent on hard work and ability ____
3. a. When things go wrong in my life it is generally because I have made mistakes
   b. Misfortunes occur in my life regardless of what I do ____
4. a. Whether there is war or not depends on the actions of certain world leaders
   b. It is inevitable that the world will continue to experience wars ____
5. a. Good children are mainly the products of good parents
   b. Some children turn out bad no matter how their parents behave ____
6. a. My future success depends mainly on circumstances I cannot control
   b. I am in charge of myself – I am 'master of my fate' ____
7. a. History judges certain people to have been effective leaders mainly because circumstances made them visible and successful
   b. Effective leaders are those who have made decisions or have taken actions that resulted in significant contributions ____
8. a. To avoid punishing children is to guarantee that they will grow up irresponsible
   b. Spanking children is never appropriate ____
9. a. I often feel that I have little influence over the direction my life is taking
   b. It is unreasonable to believe that fate or luck plays a crucial part in how my life turns out ____
10. a. Some customers will never be satisfied no matter what you do
    b. You can satisfy customers by giving them what they want when they want it ____

11. a. Anyone can get good results at school if he or she works hard enough   ____
    b. Some people are never going to excel in school no matter how hard they try   ____

12. a. Good marriages result when both partners continually work on the relationship   ____
    b. Some marriages are going to fail because the partners are simply incompatible   ____

13. a. I am confident that I can improve my basic management skills through learning and practice   ____
    b. It is a waste of time to try to improve management skills in the classroom   ____

14. a. More management skill courses should be taught in business schools   ____
    b. Less emphasis should be put on skills in business schools   ____

15. a. When I think back to the good things that have happened to me, I believe they happened mainly because of something I did   ____
    b. The bad things that have happened in my life have mainly resulted from circumstances outside my control   ____

16. a. Many exams I took at school were unconnected to the material I had studied, so studying hard didn't help at all   ____
    b. When I prepared well for exams in school, I generally did quite well   ____

17. a. 'What the Stars Say' in the papers sometimes influences me   ____
    b. No matter what the stars say, I can determine my own destiny   ____

18. a. Government is so big and bureaucratic that it is very difficult for any one person to have any impact on what happens   ____
    b. Single individuals can have a real influence on politics if they will speak up and let their wishes be known   ____

19. a. People seek responsibility at work   ____
    b. People try to get away with doing as little as they can   ____

20. a. Most popular people have a special, inherent charisma that attracts people to them   ____
    b. People are popular because of the way they behave   ____

21. a. Things over which I have little control just seem to occur in my life   ____
    b. Most of the time I feel responsible for the outcomes I produce   ____

22. a. Managers who improve their personal competence will succeed more than those who do not   ____
    b. Management success has very little to do with the competencies possessed by individuals   ____

23. a. Teams that win championships in most sports are usually the teams that have the most luck   ____
    b. More often than not, the teams that win championships are those with the most talented players and those who train hardest. (Gary Player: 'The more I practice, the better my luck gets')   ____

24. a. Teamwork in business is a pre-requisite of success   ____
    b. Individual effort is the best hope of success   ____

25. a. Some workers are just lazy and can't be motivated to work harder no matter what you do ____
    b. If you are a skilful manager, you can motivate almost any worker to make an effort ____

26. a. Over all, people can improve their country's economic strength by their own actions ____
    b. The economic health of a country is largely out of the control of individuals ____

27. a. I am persuasive when I know I am right ____
    b. I can persuade most people even when I'm not sure that I'm right ____

28. a. I tend to plan ahead and generate steps to accomplish the goals I have set ____
    b. I seldom plan ahead because things generally sort themselves out ____

29. a. Some things are just meant to be ____
    b. We can change anything in our lives by hard work, persistence and ability ____

SURVEY **1.6**

TOLERANCE OF AMBIGUITY SCALE

Circle the number that best represents your agreement with each statement. The scoring key is given in Appendix 1.

1 = Strongly disagree   **2** = Moderately disagree   **3** = Slightly disagree
4 = Neither agree nor disagree   **5** = Slightly agree   **6** = Moderately agree
7 = Strongly agree

1. An expert who doesn't come up with a definite answer probably doesn't know too much.   1 2 3 4 5 6 7

2. I would like to live in a foreign country for a while.   1 2 3 4 5 6 7

3. There is really no such thing as a problem that can't be solved   1 2 3 4 5 6 7

4. People who fit their lives to a schedule probably miss most of the joy of living.   1 2 3 4 5 6 7

5. A good job is one where what is to be done and how it is to be done are always clear.   1 2 3 4 5 6 7

6. It is more fun to tackle a complicated problem than to solve a simple one.   1 2 3 4 5 6 7

7. In the long run it is possible to get more done by tackling small problems rather than large and complicated ones.   1 2 3 4 5 6 7

8. Often the most interesting and stimulating people are those who don't mind being different and original.   1 2 3 4 5 6 7

9. What we are used to is always preferable to what is unfamiliar.   1 2 3 4 5 6 7

10. People who insist upon a yes or no answer just don't know how complicated things really are.   1 2 3 4 5 6 7

11. A person who leads an even, regular life in which few surprises or unexpected happenings arise ought to be grateful.   1 2 3 4 5 6 7

12. Many of our most important decisions are based on insufficient information. 1 2 3 4 5 6 7

13. I like parties where I know most of the people more than ones where all or most of the people are complete strangers. 1 2 3 4 5 6 7

14. Teachers or supervisors who hand out vague assignments give one a chance to show initiative and originality. 1 2 3 4 5 6 7

15. The sooner we all acquire similar values and ideals the better. 1 2 3 4 5 6 7

16. A good teacher is one who makes you wonder about your way of looking at things. 1 2 3 4 5 6 7

Source: Budner (1962)

SURVEY **1.7**

INTERPERSONAL ORIENTATIONS AND NEEDS (FIRO-B)

The surveys up to this point can be taken as learning tools and not as the basis of any true analysis of either behaviour or personality. The next instrument we want you to complete is a fully validated test used in professional counselling. For each statement below, decide which of the following answers best applies to you. Circle the number of the answer at the right of the statement. When you have finished, turn to the scoring key in Appendix 1.

For the next group of statements, choose one of the following answers:
1 = Usually   **2** = Often   **3** = Sometimes   **4** = Occasionally
5 = Rarely   **6** = Never

1. I try to be with people. 1 2 3 4 5 6

2. I let other people decide what to do. 1 2 3 4 5 6

3. I join social groups. 1 2 3 4 5 6

4. I try to have close relationships with people. 1 2 3 4 5 6

5. I tend to join social organisations when I have an opportunity. 1 2 3 4 5 6

6. I let other people strongly influence my actions. 1 2 3 4 5 6

7. I try to be included in informal social activities. 1 2 3 4 5 6

8. I try to have close, personal relationships. 1 2 3 4 5 6

9. I try to include other people in my plans. 1 2 3 4 5 6

10. I let other people control my actions. 1 2 3 4 5 6

11. I try to have people around me. 1 2 3 4 5 6

12. I try to get close and personal with people. 1 2 3 4 5 6

13. When people are doing things together I tend to join them. 1 2 3 4 5 6

14. People easily lead me. 1 2 3 4 5 6

15. I try to avoid being alone. 1 2 3 4 5 6

16. I try to participate in group activities. 1 2 3 4 5 6

For each of the next group of statements, choose one of the following answers:
1 = Most people   **2** = Many people   **3** = Some people
4 = A few people   **5** = One or two people   **6** = Nobody

17. I try to be friendly to people.	1	2	3	4	5	6
18. I let other people decide what to do.	1	2	3	4	5	6
19. My personal relations with people are cool and distant.	1	2	3	4	5	6
20. I let other people take charge of things.	1	2	3	4	5	6
21. I try to have close relationships with people.	1	2	3	4	5	6
22. I let other people strongly influence my actions.	1	2	3	4	5	6
23. I try to get close and personal with people.	1	2	3	4	5	6
24. I let other people control my actions.	1	2	3	4	5	6
25. I act cool and distant with people.	1	2	3	4	5	6
26. People easily lead me.	1	2	3	4	5	6
27. I try to have close, personal relationships with people.	1	2	3	4	5	6

For each of the next group of statements, choose one of the following answers:
1 = Most people   **2** = Many people   **3** = Some people
4 = A few people   **5** = One or two people   **6** = Nobody

28. I like people to invite me to things.	1	2	3	4	5	6
29. I like people to act close and personal with me.	1	2	3	4	5	6
30. I try to influence strongly other people's actions.	1	2	3	4	5	6
31. I like people to invite me to join in their activities.	1	2	3	4	5	6
32. I like people to act close towards me.	1	2	3	4	5	6
33. I try to take charge of things when I am with people.	1	2	3	4	5	6
34. I like people to include me in their activities.	1	2	3	4	5	6
35. I like people to act cool and distant towards me.	1	2	3	4	5	6
36. I try to have other people do things the way I want them done.	1	2	3	4	5	6
37. I like people to ask me to participate in their discussions.	1	2	3	4	5	6
38. I like people to act friendly towards me.	1	2	3	4	5	6
39. I like people to invite me to participation in their activities.	1	2	3	4	5	6
40. I like people to act distant towards me.	1	2	3	4	5	6

For each of the next group of statements, choose one of the following answers:
1 = Usually   **2** = Often   **3** = Sometimes   **4** = Occasionally
5 = Rarely   **6** = Never

41. I try to be a dominant person when I am with people.	1	2	3	4	5	6
42. I like people to invite me to things.	1	2	3	4	5	6
43. I like people to act close towards me.	1	2	3	4	5	6
44. I try to have other people do things I want done.	1	2	3	4	5	6
45. I like people to invite me to join their activities.	1	2	3	4	5	6

46. I like people to act cool and distant towards me.   1 2 3 4 5 6

47. I try to influence strongly other people's actions.   1 2 3 4 5 6

48. I like people to include me in their activities.   1 2 3 4 5 6

49. I like people to act close and personal with me.   1 2 3 4 5 6

50. I try to take charge of things when I'm with people.   1 2 3 4 5 6

51. I like people to invite me to participate in their activities.   1 2 3 4 5 6

52. I like people to act distant towards me.   1 2 3 4 5 6

53. I try to have other people do things the way I want them done.   1 2 3 4 5 6

54. I take charge of things when I'm with people.   1 2 3 4 5 6

When you return to the surveys after reading the chapter you may find that some of your views and opinions have changed. We would hope for some changes but suspect that the Learning Style Inventory and Firo-B will remain relatively constant.

Skill Learning

Key dimensions of self-awareness

We need to understand ourselves before we can even consider understanding other people. In this we have many sources:

The ancient dictum 'know thyself' has been variously attributed to Plato, Pythagoras and Thales, and Socrates, quoted by Plutarch, noted that this inscription was carved on the Delphic Oracle – that mystical sanctuary where kings and generals sought advice on matters of greatest importance to them.

'It matters not what you are thought to be, but what you are', as Publilius Syrus proposed in 42 BC; or, as stated by Alfred Lord Tennyson, 'Self-reverence, self-knowledge, self-control, these three alone lead to sovereign power'; or as written by Shakespeare in Polonius's advice in Hamlet: 'to thine own self be true, and it must follow, as the night the day, thou canst not then be false to any man'.

As Messinger reminded us: 'He that would govern others must first master himself.' We consider that the setting of personal priorities and goals through self-awareness allows us to direct our own lives. It is the foundation stone upon which rests the practice of the skills we will discuss later.

Figure 1.1 illustrates our point that problems of dysfunctional stress may well have their roots in a lack of self-awareness – our priorities or goals have become out of balance. Increased self-awareness and a constant review of priorities are the keys. To know one's self is a necessary starting point for working with others, and many techniques have grown up to satisfy the demand for self-knowledge. We are not attempting to summarise or indeed criticise any of these techniques; rather, we will discuss the importance of self-awareness in managerial behaviour, and we introduce several self-assessment assignments which research has shown to relate to managerial success. We will attempt in our discussions to avoid 'common sense' generalisations and work from information validated by research.

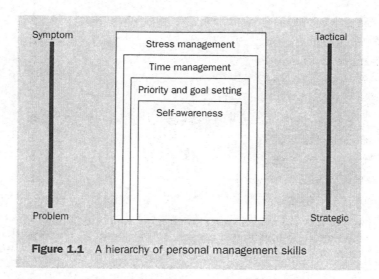

Figure 1.1 A hierarchy of personal management skills

The enigma of self-awareness

Erich Fromm (1939) was one of the first behavioural scientists to observe the close connection between one's self-concept and one's feelings about others: 'Hatred against oneself is inseparable from hatred against others.' Carl Rogers (1961) later proposed that self-awareness and self-acceptance are prerequisites for psychological health, personal growth, and the ability to know and accept others. Rogers further suggested that the basic human need is for self-regard, which he found, in his clinical cases, to be more powerful than physiological needs. Hayakawa (1962) has asserted that the first law of life is not self-preservation, but self-image-preservation.

'The self-concept,' he states, 'is the fundamental determinant of all our behaviour. Indeed, since it is an organisation of our past experiences and perceptions as well as our values and goals, it determines the character of the reality we see.' There is considerable empirical evidence that self-awareness and self-acceptance are strongly related to personal adjustment, interpersonal relationships and life success. Brouwer (1964) asserted:

> The function of self-examination is to lay the groundwork for insight, without which no growth can occur. Insight is the 'Oh, I see now' feeling which must consciously or unconsciously precede change in behaviour. Insights, real, genuine glimpses of ourselves as we really are, can be reached only with difficulty and sometimes with real psychic pain. They are, however, the building blocks of growth. Thus, self-examination is a preparation for insight, a groundbreaking for the seeds of self-understanding which gradually bloom into changed behaviour.

There is little question that the knowledge we possess about ourselves, which makes up our self-concept, is central to improving our management skills. We cannot improve ourselves or develop new capabilities unless and until we know what level of capability we currently possess. On the other hand, self-knowledge may inhibit personal improvement rather than facilitate it. The reason for this is that individuals frequently evade personal growth and new self-knowledge. They resist acquiring additional information in order to protect their self-esteem or self-respect. If they acquire new knowledge about themselves, there is always the possibility that it will be negative or that it will lead to feelings of inferiority, weakness or shame, so they avoid it. As Maslow (1962) notes,

> We tend to be afraid of any knowledge that would cause us to despise ourselves or to make us feel inferior, weak, worthless, evil, shameful. We protect our personally ideal image and ourselves by repression and similar defences. These are essentially techniques by which we avoid becoming conscious of unpleasantness or dangerous truths.

The implication is that personal growth is avoided for fear of finding out that we are not all that we would like to be. If there is a better way to be, the current state must therefore be inadequate or inferior. The realisation that one is not totally adequate or knowledgeable is difficult for many people to accept. This resistance is the 'denying of our best side, of our talents, of our finest impulses, of our highest potentialities, of our creativeness is the struggle against our own greatness' (Maslow, 1962). Freud (1956) asserted that to be completely honest with oneself is the best effort an individual can make, because complete honesty requires a continual search for more information about the self and a desire for self-improvement.

The sensitive line

Seeking knowledge of the self, therefore, seems to lead to an enigma. The very self-knowledge that must act as a starting point of self-growth may indeed prevent us from wanting to grow. We may well not wish to move forward because we fear the unknown.

How, then, can improvement be accomplished? How can management skills be developed if they are being resisted? The answer lies in understanding that there is a sensitive line beyond which all of us become defensive or protective when encountering information about ourselves that is inconsistent with our self-concept and we are under pressure to alter our behaviour. Most of us are regularly told things about ourselves that do not quite fit or are marginally inconsistent with our perceptions. For example, a friend might say, 'You look tired. Are you feeling well?' If you are feeling fine, the comment is inconsistent with how you feel about yourself at that time, but because the discrepancy is relatively minor, it would not be likely to offend or to evoke a strong defensive reaction, merely some sort of polite exchange. However, imagine a situation where you think that you are coping effectively with ageing relatives or tiresome children, and you hear a friend remark that 'you do not seem to be coping'. Most of us would find ourselves across the sensitive line and defending ourselves. The comment, if accepted, would mean a review of your perceptions and possibly a change of behaviour. Equally, having a colleague judge you incompetent as a manager may push you across your sensitive line if you think you are doing a good job, and even more so if the colleague is influential. Hayakawa (1962) stated the point differently, saying that 'the self-concept tends

to rigidify under threat', so that if an individual encounters discrepant information that is threatening, the current self-concept is reasserted with redoubled force.
Haney (1979) refers to a 'comfort zone' similar to a thermostat. When a situation
becomes too uncomfortable, protective measures are brought into play that bring
the situation back to normal. When marked discrepancies in the self-image are
experienced, either the validity of the information or its source is denied, or we
put in place other defensive mechanisms to ensure that the self-concept remains
stable.

How then, in the light of our innate defensiveness, can increased self-knowledge
and personal change ever occur? There are at least two answers.

Firstly, if the information about us can be checked, is predictable and control-
lable, then the sensitive line is less likely to be crossed than with information without those characteristics. Thus if:

- an individual can test the validity of the conflicting information and some
  objective standard exists

- the information is not unexpected or 'out of the blue' but is received at regular
  intervals and if there is some control over what, when and how much
  information is received, it is more likely to be heard and accepted.

We will deal in detail with these points in our chapters on effective communication
and constructive conflict management, when we discuss effective feedback.

We have attempted at the start of this chapter to allow you feedback from our
self-assessment surveys. Their reliability and validity have been established. Moreover, they have been found to be associated with managerial success. Therefore, in
your analysis of your scores, you can gain important insight that can prove helpful
to you.

A second answer to the problem of overcoming this resistance to self-
examination lies in the role other people can play in helping insight to occur. It is
almost impossible to increase skill in self-awareness without interacting with and
disclosing ourselves to others. Unless one is willing to open up to others, to discuss
aspects of the self that seem ambiguous or unknown, little growth can ever occur.
Self-disclosure, therefore, is a key to improvement in self-awareness and allows one
to move across the sensitive line.

Harris (1981) points out:

> In order to know oneself, no amount of introspection or self-examination will
> suffice. You can analyse yourself for weeks, or meditate for months, and you will
> not get an inch further any more than you can smell your own breath or laugh
> when you tickle yourself. You must first be open to the other person before you
> catch a glimmer of yourself. Our self-reflection in a mirror does not tell us what
> we are like; only our reflection in other people. We are essentially social creatures,
> and our personality resides in association, not in isolation.

The practice exercises at the end of this chapter will hopefully encourage you
to discuss your insights with someone else. For example, several studies have shown
that people who discuss personal matters are likely to be healthier and more socially acceptable than those who do not (Jourard, 1964). However, there is always the

caveat that self-disclosure is a game for two or more players – one who discloses and does not listen is known in technical terms as a bore.

The enigma of self-awareness can be managed, then, by exercising some control over when and what kind of information you receive about yourself, and by sharing with others your pursuit of self-understanding. The social support individuals receive from others during the process of self-disclosure is important, besides helping to increase feedback and self-awareness without crossing the sensitive line.

Important areas of self-awareness

In the remainder of this chapter we will focus on six major areas of self-awareness, found to be the key in developing successful management:

- Cognitive styles
- Learning styles
- Personal values
- Ethical decision making
- Attitudes towards change
- Interpersonal needs

Cognitive styles

The way in which we take on information and learn from it is a foundation of our behaviour. George Kelly, as described by Bannister and Fransella (1971), considered mankind as, in his metaphor, a scientist. In the Kelly model we are continually making decisions as we refine our universe. Thus when we are very young we may see our outside world as comfortable or uncomfortable. As we develop the construct of comfort is split into warm or cold and then warm is split again into inside and outside. We go on splitting our world into a massive decision tree. In practice, we have found Kelly's personal Construct Theory of less use in skill training than a series of concepts codified as Cognitive Style and Experiential Learning Theory. We will take cognitive styles first, accepting that there are many overlaps between the two.

We are all faced with an overwhelming amount of information, most of which, in order to preserve our sanity, survive or indeed do the jobs we are paid to do, we learn to ignore. No process for filtering the information is inherently good or inherently bad, and not everyone adopts an identifiable, consistent process that becomes part of his or her cognitive style. However, about 80 per cent of us do eventually develop, mostly unconsciously, a preferred process of handling information, and these make up our cognitive style.

The cognitive style instrument in the Pre-assessment section looks at the two core dimensions of the way we prefer to process information. The model upon which it is based is grounded in the work of Jung (1971). Figure 1.2 illustrates its dimensions. The vertical dimension has its poles Sensing and Intuition. Thus at its extremes one individual would physically collect information while another would rely on

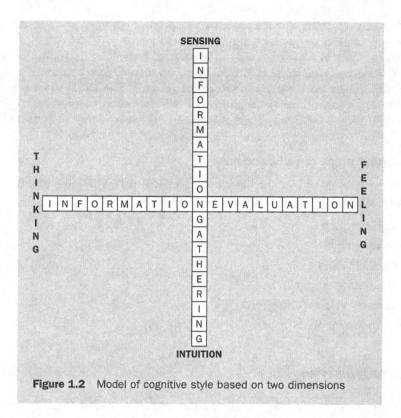

Figure 1.2   Model of cognitive style based on two dimensions

his or her intuition. In our example of the interview, one manager would check the information on the disc, go back to the candidate's application form and find out what he or she could about his present employer. The other would see the elements of the problem as a pattern and act accordingly.

The horizontal dimension is from Feeling to Thinking and is concerned with information processing. The manager on the Feeling pole would know what he or she was comfortable with while one on the Thinking pole would 'work it out'.

The various strategies we employ for internalising information lie within the vertical and horizontal axes.

Vertical axis

An **intuitive strategy** takes a holistic view and emphasises commonalities and generalisations – the perceived relationships among the elements of available data. Intuitive thinkers often have preconceived notions about what sort of information may be relevant, and they look at the information to find what is consistent with their preconceptions. They tend to be convergent thinkers in general opposed to the new.

The **sensing strategy** focuses on detail, or on the specific attributes of each element of data, rather than on relationships among the elements. Sensing thinkers are rational and have few preconceptions about what may be relevant, so they insist on a close and thorough examination of the information. They attach special importance to the unique attributes of various parts of the information they encounter, and tend to be the divergent thinkers (a term we will define in Chapter 3 when we discuss problem-solving strategies).

- An intuitive strategy focuses on the whole, a sensing strategy on the parts of the whole.

- An intuitive strategy looks for commonalities and overall categories, a sensing strategy for uniqueness, detail and exceptions to the general rule.

Horizontal axis

The horizontal axis, which is concerned with interpreting and judging information, has also two strategies.

A **thinking strategy** evaluates information using a systematic plan with specific sequential steps and logical progressions. Individuals who use a thinking style generally rely on objective data, problems are considered against known models. When managers with such a style defend their decisions they emphasise the methods and procedures they have used.

Vertinsky (1976) refers to people using the thinking strategy as 'members of a continuous culture', meaning that they operate consistently with existing patterns of thought.

A **feeling strategy** approaches a problem on the basis of 'gut feel', or an internal sense of how to respond. The problem is often defined and redefined, and approaches are tried on a trial-and-error basis rather than through a logical procedure. Feeling individuals prefer the subjective or impressionistic against the objective. They often cannot describe how they achieved their conclusions. They often use analogies and metaphors relating the problem to 'unrelated' past experiences. Vertinsky (1976) refers to these individuals as 'members of a discontinuous culture'.

Implications

These strategies have important implications for managerial behaviour, each having advantages and disadvantages. We do have to remember that very few individuals operate all the time on one of the poles of our figure. However, we can draw certain generalisations.

- **Sensing managers** find they cannot prioritise and have to give each detail attention. Thus in chaotic situations they are more likely to overload than intuitive managers, and tend to suffer from dysfunctional stress.

- **Intuitive managers**, because they focus on the relationships between elements, on the whole handle detail and confusion relatively easily. However, their stresses occur when either the information they attempt to collect is confused, or their preconceived patterns fail to work. Exceptions to the rule faze the intuitive manager where the sensing manager simply looks further into the detail.

Table 1.1   Characteristics of cognitive styles

INFORMATION GATHERING

Intuitive types	Sensing types
Like solving new problems.	Dislike new problems unless there are standard ways of dealing with them.
Dislike doing the same thing over and over again.	Like an established routine.
Enjoy learning a new skill more than using it.	Enjoy using skills already learned more than learning new ones.
Work in bursts of energy powered by enthusiasm, with slack periods in between.	Work more steadily with realistic idea of how long things will take.
Jump to conclusions frequently.	Must usually work all the way through to reach a conclusion.
Are patient with complicated situations.	Are impatient when the details are complicated.
Are impatient with routine details.	Are patient with routine details.
Follow inspirations good of bad.	Rarely trust inspirations, and don't usually feel too inspired.
Often tend to make errors of fact.	Seldom make errors of fact.
Dislike taking time for precision.	Tend to be good at precise work.

INFORMATION EVALUATION

Feeling types	Thinking types
Tend to be very aware of other people and their feelings.	Are relatively unemotional and uninterested in people's feelings.
Enjoy pleasing people even in unimportant things.	May hurt people's feelings without knowing.
Like harmony. Efficiency may be badly disturbed by office feuds.	Like analysis and putting things Into logical order. Can get along without harmony.
Often let decisions be influenced by their own or other people's personal likes and wishes.	Tend to decide impersonally, sometimes ignoring people's wishes.
Need occasional praise.	Need to be treated fairly.
Dislike telling people unpleasant things.	Are able to reprimand people or fire them when necessary.
Relate well to most people.	Tend to relate well only to other thinking types.
Tend to be sympathetic.	May seem hard-hearted.

- **Thinking managers** prefer issues where a structured approach is effective and find problems where a creative approach is needed or where there is no pool of relevant information. The reader may consider that most people problems fall into this category.

  > We were working with a chemist whose job was to design and mimic flavours and aromas. His instrument was an 'aroma organ' which brought together a vast array of elements at great precision into his potions. He saw the whole world on the basis of his 'aroma organ'. We might argue that he had elements of an intuitive manager, but since his work was based on logic and theory, we would see him as 'thinking'. Whatever his psychometric profile, he found the vagaries of handling people impossible – they never fitted patterns, never reacted according to plan and never came with complete information.

- **Feeling managers** have a tendency to try new approaches, to redefine problems, and to reinvent the solution without, at least first, using the tried and tested. This generally leads to inefficient problem solving or even solving the wrong problem. Thinking and intuitive managers do not justify such criticism – perhaps to a fault.

We find that individuals are inflexible in their approach to problems – preferring their own style, whatever the problem. For example, in one study, managers who were more thinking than feeling implemented more computer-based systems and rational procedures for decision making. Managers in another study defined identical problems differently, depending on their different cognitive styles. Another study found that differences in cognitive style led to significantly different decision-making processes in managers (see Henderson and Nutt, 1980; Mulkowsky and Freeman, 1980). Of course we find successful managers moving to work that welcomes their cognitive style – thinking people working in thinking jobs.

An understanding of one's own cognitive style can help managers in many ways – in learning new skills, in choosing the right career, and even in selecting the most effective team members for difficult jobs. Table 1.1 summarises some personal characteristics associated with each of these major cognitive patterns.

Learning styles

Students with different cognitive styles have also been found to approach learning differently and different kinds of educational experiences hold meaning for different types of people. For example, individuals who emphasise intuitive strategies tend to do better in conceptual courses and learn more easily through reading and through discussing general relationships. Exams with one right answer may be easier for them than for those who emphasise sensing. Individuals who emphasise sensing strategies tend to do better in factual courses or courses in which attention to detail and dissimilarity is important. Critical and analytical learning activities (e.g., debates) facilitate their learning, and exams emphasising implications and applications may be easiest for these individuals. Individuals who emphasise a thinking strategy do best in courses that take an orderly, step-by-step approach to

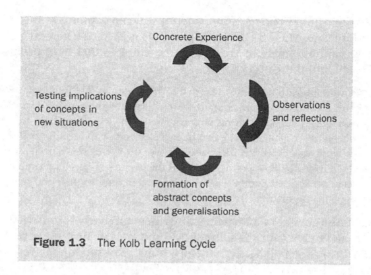

Figure 1.3 The Kolb Learning Cycle

the subject, courses in which what is learned builds on, and follows directly from, what was learned earlier (e.g., mathematics). On the other hand, feeling individuals do best in courses requiring creativity and idea generation. Learning activities in which the student must rely on a personal sense of what is appropriate (e.g., sculpting) are likely to be preferred by these individuals. Okanlawon (1989), using the Kolb Learning Style Inventory, an instrument similar to the Cognitive Style Instrument, went much further. Working with a large group of managers and students in Nigeria, his findings were that the teaching methods employed for effective learning had two dimensions – the learning style and the learning objective. He also found that the choice of method was much more critical for managers than for students. It is interesting to note that several workers, including Bernice McCarthy, have used the Kolb Inventory for career advice and for the design of teaching materials.

Kolb derives his work from many sources, but primarily the work of Jung and his ideas are introduced in this book by our first survey – the Kolb/McCarthy Learning Style Inventory. Kolb chooses to work from different axes from those used for the cognitive style (Figure 1.3) and makes the intuitive leap that they can be made into what he calls a Learning Cycle. (Note that the figure resembles a 'dartboard' with 5 rings. These rings represent the percentiles of individuals falling within each 'circle'. The percentiles were originally for a sample of 1933 individuals in the USA but Okanlawon confirmed the values for UK and Nigeria.)

Kenneth Raymont, following up the work of Reid, reviewed the current state of the debate on Kolb's work. Raymont, working with Bradford Management Centre MBA, found the concept useful but he concludes:

On first acquaintance, Kolb's Experiential Learning Theory appears as light on murky water. It purports to explain individual learning differences by a 'type' model and seemingly explains that because individuals view the same situation differently there is an inbuilt conflict mechanism in any group venture. Indeed, it was this very aspect that attracted the writer to it. Differences in opinion and modes of working were merely an expression of the respective individuals learning style.

Management Consultancy and Skills

200

Table 1.2 Summary of the various notations for learning styles

Quadrants	Kolb	Lewis and Margerison (1979)	Woods (1989)
1	Diverger	Imaginatives	WHY? people
2	Assimilator	Logic	WHAT? people
3	Converger	Practical	HOW? people
4	Accommodator	Enthusiast	IF? people

The simplicity of the theory with the equally simple method of measuring an individuals learning style from which their learning type can be determined appeared an all too easy solution to what are complex problems. It was the discovery of some minor flaws in Kolb's supporting evidence that led to this more in-depth study of the underlying structure of Kolb's model.

Much of the criticism of Kolb's tool is to be found in the work of Wilson (1986) who discussed the validity of the survey itself and Stumph and Freedman (1981) who took a more theoretical approach. Woods (1989) simplified the language and discussed areas as opposed to points. Table 1.2 summarises various notations.

Kolb's first premise is that learning is cyclic and in four steps, which can be shown as right-angled axes:

1. Concrete Experience, where we 'measure' the world about us with our senses.

2. Reflective Observation, where we think about and consider what we have observed.

3. Abstract Conceptualisation, where we pattern our thoughts ready for practical application.

4. Active Experimentation, where we 'try' to apply what we have observed, considered and patterned.

Kolb's second premise is that individuals whose main energy lies between the axes have certain characteristics, and he developed a tool – the Learning Style Index (LSI) – to codify this. The LSI classifies individuals who 'specialised' in particular ways of learning. The Kolb classification titles were:

1. Divergers, who preferred the segment of the cycle involved in moving from Concrete Experience to Reflective Observation.

2. Assimilators, preferring the segment moving from Reflective Observation to Abstract Conceptualisation.

3. Convergers, preferring the segment moving from Abstract Conceptualisation to Active Experimentation.

4. Accommodators, who preferred the final segment moving Active Experimentation to new Concrete Experience.

Bernice McCarthy (1987) in the USA and, later, Woods and Okanlawon (1991) in Nigeria and the UK used the concepts to consider the teaching process. Many trainers, often working from the CCDU unit of Leeds University Psychology Department, pushed the ideas further and took Kolb's second premise to consider management style. This work was summarised by Woods (1989) who also introduced a simplified nomenclature and the short survey we found at the beginning of the chapter. (The full survey is to be found in a technical manual due to David Kolb (1978).)

The Kolb patterns

- Indicate a process of learning – asking WHY? questions, WHAT? questions, HOW? questions and finally the consequential questions, the IF? questions, in sequence.

- Accept that these profiles can correspond to behavioural patterns. The reader may like to see how his or her interpretation of the first survey fits their own behaviour as generalised in Exercise 1.1.

EXERCISE **1.1**

GENERALISED BEHAVIOURS OF THE FOUR BASIC KOLB PATTERNS

Although most of us have strength in two or more quadrants, look back at the Learning Style Indicator at the beginning of the chapter and see if your largest quadrant is WHY?, WHAT?, HOW? or IF?

The WHY? quadrant

Those with a largest WHY? quadrant are **imaginatives** who think about personal experience.

The WHY? person:

- has a clear picture of a total situation
- uses imagination and fantasy
- works in bursts of energy
- is good at imagining himself or herself in new situations
- is unhurried, casual, friendly, avoids conflict
- uses insight.

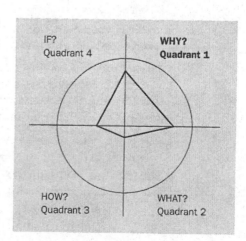

The WHY? manager:

- cannot be pushed until ready
- listens to others, shares ideas with a small number of people
- likes assurance from others, uses eyes and ears, listens, observes and asks questions
- attempts to develop his or her people.

These are the innovative learners and their strength is ideas. Their goal is self-fulfilment and bringing order to chaos. They are to be found fulfilled in careers spanning primary school teaching, counselling, the humanities, training forecasting and organisational development.

The WHAT? quadrant

Those with a predominance in the WHAT? quadrant are **logics** who think and theorise. They uses intuition plus thinking.

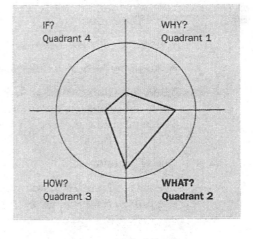

The WHAT? person:

- likes to place experience in a theoretical context
- is able to make new models mentally
- is a good synthesiser
- is precise, thorough and careful
- is organised and likes to follow a plan
- reacts slowly and wants facts
- calculates the probabilities.

The WHAT? manager:

- avoids becoming over-emotional
- analyses experiences often by writing them down
- looks for similar past experiences from which to extract learning.

These are the analytical learners. Their strength is the development of concepts and models and their goal is personal satisfaction and intellectual recognition. They are to be found in careers based on basic science, mathematics, economics, planning, etc.

The HOW? quadrant

Those with strength in the HOW? quadrant are the **practicals** who combine theory with doing things.

The HOW? person:

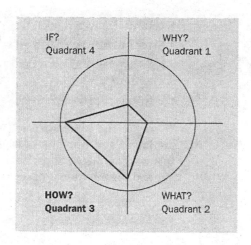

- applies ideas to solving problems
- makes theories useful
- has good detective skills
- enjoys the search and solve
- uses reason to meet goals
- likes to be in control of situations
- acts independently and then gets feedback.

The HOW? manager:

- uses factual data, books and theories

- learns by testing out new situations and assessing the results.

These are common-sense learners whose strength is the practical application of ideas and whose goal is to bring ideas into reality. People with such a profile are to be found in the engineering professions, physical science, nursing and technology.

The IF? quadrant

Strength in the IF? quadrant indicates the **enthusiast** who relies on his or her own intuition and experience.

The IF? person:

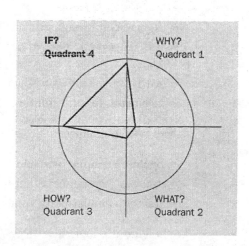

- enjoys new situations often rushing in
- operates on trial and error
- uses 'gut' reactions
- gets others opinions, feelings and information
- involves other people
- likes risks, change and excitement
- adapts well and revels in new situations.

The IF? manager:

- looks to the future and the untested
- can be impulsive

Management Consultancy and Skills

204

- relies heavily on a support network
- likes to discharge emotion.

These are the dynamic learners and their strengths and goals are concerned with getting things done. Likely careers for people with such a pattern would be marketing, sales, 'action-centred' management jobs.

Figure 8.11 in Chapter 8 indicates how the dominant area in the profiles can correspond to particular managerial styles and indicates how individuals will relate to work situations

> The career adviser of Manchester Grammar School ran a Kolb survey with school leavers. Three students indicated that they wanted to be vets – the three students had their main energy in quadrants 2, 3 and 4 respectively. Since career advice is not about what you do but about reflecting on consequences, the adviser took the three students separately. The student predominantly in quadrant 2 would see the job as one of research. Was he good enough for this career? The quadrant 3 student would be a practical animal worker. Did he have the aptitude and the finance to work in the field – a muddy field at that? The quadrant 4 person was concerned with the glamour, and before he had had time to be interviewed, had decided he wanted to be a jet pilot.

Our first two related issues have been concerned with the way we take in information – part of the picture. The next issue is how we filter the information – our value systems.

Personal values

Personal values are considered to be: 'the core of the dynamics of behaviour, and play so large a part in unifying personality' (Allport *et al.*, 1931). That is, all other attitudes, orientations and behaviours arise out of individuals' values. Two major types of value are considered: those that are concerned with meeting our objectives and those concerned with the objective itself – instrumental and terminal (Rokeach, 1973). We present research findings that relate personal development in these two types of value to successful managerial performance. The pre-assessment instrument designed to assess your values development is discussed, along with information concerning the scores of other groups of people to enable you to compare your scores with those of more and less successful managers.

Value development is connected to ethical decision making, and its implications are direct.

The second area of self-awareness is cognitive style, which refers to the manner in which individuals gather and process information. A discussion of the critical dimensions of cognitive style is presented, based on the pre-assessment instrument that you used to assess your own style. Empirical research linking cognitive style to managerial behaviour is discussed, and your scores are compared to other successful managers in a variety of organisations.

Third, a discussion of attitudes towards change focuses on the methods people use for coping with change in their environment.

All of us, but especially managers, are faced with increasingly fragmented, rapidly changing, chaotic conditions. It is important that you become aware of how you adapt to these conditions. We have considered two dimensions – the locus of control and tolerance of ambiguity – and how these two factors relate to effective management.

Finally, we have looked at the way we relate to others, and what we need from our relationships.

These four areas of self-awareness – values, cognitive style, adaptation to change, and interpersonal orientation – constitute the very core of the self-concept.

- Values define an individual's basic standards about what is good and bad, worth while and worthless, desirable and undesirable, true and false, moral and immoral.

- Cognitive style determines individual thought processes and perceptions. It determines not only what kind of information is received by an individual, but how that information is interpreted, judged and responded to.

- Attitudes towards change identifies the adaptability of individuals. It includes the extent to which individuals are tolerant of ambiguous, uncertain conditions, and the extent to which they are inclined to accept personal responsibility for the consequences that follow from their actions.

- Interpersonal orientation determines the behaviour patterns that are most likely to emerge in interactions with others. The extent to which an individual is open or closed, assertive or retiring, controlling or dependent, affectionate or aloof, depends to a large degree on interpersonal orientation.

Figure 1.4 summarises these four aspects of self-awareness. Of course we could have looked at other aspects of self-awareness – emotions, attitudes, temperament, personality and interests – but we consider that these are all related fundamentally to our four core concepts. What we value, how we feel about things, how we behave towards others, what we want to achieve, and what we are attracted to are all strongly influenced by our values, cognitive style, orientation towards change, and interpersonal style. These are among the most important building blocks upon which other aspects of the self emerge. On the other hand, if you want to do a more in-depth analysis of multiple aspects of self-awareness there are several psychometric tests currently available. The leading European exponents are Saville and Holdsworth Ltd, who have a wide range of occupational tests and personality surveys, and Belbin Associates. Both offer computerised systems and Belbin's Interplace system has the added advantage of using the views of observers as well as self-perception. Self-knowledge is a vital key to management success.

Values

Values are the foundation stones of our lives, shaped by our upbringing and education. (Carr and Haldane, 1993). They are the basis upon which attitudes and personal preferences are formed and form the basis for crucial decisions, life directions, and personal tastes. Much of what we are is a product of the basic values we have developed throughout our lives. Organisations have values, although they

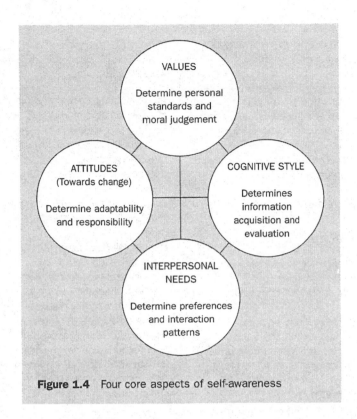

Figure 1.4 Four core aspects of self-awareness

are usually discussed as organisational culture. If individual values match organisational values, we are much more likely to be productive and satisfied workers within that organisation. The reverse is also true. Employees whose values differ from that of the organisation can be seen as 'difficult' or 'awkward'. Considerable problems arise when by design or accident individual or corporate values change. Equally unfortunate is the situation where individuals mis-read organisational values and find that their life work has been towards a personally unacceptable goal. Being aware of one's own priorities and values, therefore, is important if one expects to achieve compatibility at work and in a long-term career.

Simon (1974) and others have suggested that people sometimes lose touch with their own values, behaving in ways that are inconsistent with those values. That is, they pursue lower priorities at the expense of higher priorities, substituting goals with immediate payoffs for those with more long-term, central values. They may pursue an immediate reward or a temporary satisfaction, for example, in place of longer-term happiness and inner peace. The long-term effect of such a mismatch can be unsatisfactory for the organisation and the individual. On the whole, most people feel that they have quite a clear concept of their values, and because their values are seldom challenged they rarely review them. It is this lack of review that leads us to ignore our priorities and behave incongruously. We are inclined to reserve a review of our values to when we are threatened or are caught in a contradiction.

Table 1.3 The Rokeach value system

Terminal values	Instrumental values
A comfortable life (a prosperous life)	Ambitious (hard-working, aspiring)
An exciting life (a stimulating, active life)	Broadminded (open-minded)
A sense of accomplishment (lasting contribution)	Capable (competent, effective)
A world at peace (free of war and conflict)	Cheerful (light-hearted, joyful)
A world of beauty (beauty of nature and the arts)	Clean (neat, tidy)
Equality (brotherhood, equal opportunity for all)	Courageous (standing up for your beliefs)
Family security (taking care of loved ones)	Forgiving (willing to pardon others)
Freedom (independence, free choice)	Helpful (working for the welfare of others)
Happiness (contentedness)	Honest (sincere, truthful)
Inner harmony (freedom from inner conflict)	Imaginative (daring, creative)
Mature love (sexual and spiritual intimacy)	Independent (self-reliant, self-sufficient)
National security (protection from attack)	Intellectual (intelligent, reflective)
Pleasure (an enjoyable, leisurely life)	Logical (consistent, rational)
Salvation (saved, eternal life)	Loving (affectionate, tender)
Self-respect (self-esteem)	Obedient (dutiful, respectful)
Social recognition (respect, admiration)	Polite (courteous, well-mannered)
True friendship (close companionship)	Responsible (dependable, reliable)
Wisdom (a mature understanding of life)	Self-controlled (restrained, self-disciplined)

Rokeach (1973) claims that we all have the same small set of values, differing only in degree. For example, everyone values peace, but some make it a higher priority than others. Rokeach classifies the 'small set of values' we all choose from as being those about our goals – the 'ends' – and those about our way of achieving our goals – the 'means'. Some of us would believe, for instance, 'that the end justifies the means' while others would accept the Olympic motto that 'taking part is more important than winning'. Most of us would accept that there is some truth in both extremes. Rokeach called 'means'-orientated values *instrumental* and 'end'-orientated values *terminal*.

- Instrumental values relate to morality and competence. Violating moral values (e.g., behaving dishonestly) causes feelings of guilt, while violating competence values (e.g., behaving stupidly) brings about feelings of shame.
- Terminal values relate to the desired ends or goals for the individual and are fewer in number, according to Rokeach. Terminal values are either personal (e.g., peace of mind) or social (e.g., world peace).

Management Consultancy and Skills

Rokeach has found that when individuals become more concerned with one personal value, they increase the values of other personal values at the expense of social values, and vice versa. Thus, if one suddenly becomes particularly concerned with one's safety one is likely to find other personal goals, such as comfort, rising as well, whereas one's social concerns for fighting poverty and world peace will fall. Table 1.3 lists the 18 terminal values 'judged to represent the most important values in American society' (Rokeach, 1973).

Schmidt and Posner (1982) asked 1,460 American managers to rank the Rokeach's Terminal and Instrumental values for their importance in the workplace. 'Responsible' and 'honest' were by far the most desired value in employees (over 85 per cent of the managers selected them), followed by 'capable' (65 per cent), 'imaginative' (55 per cent) and 'logical' (49 per cent). 'Obedient', 'clean', 'polite' and 'forgiving' were the least important, being selected by fewer than 10 per cent of the managers. Different groups of people tend to differ in the values they hold. Cavanaugh (1980), also working in America, found that business school students and professors tend to rate ambition, capability, responsibility and freedom higher than the general population, and give lower concern for helpfulness to others, aesthetics and cultural values, and overcoming social injustice. Rokeach (1973), in America, compared highly successful, moderately successful, and unsuccessful managers. Highly successful managers gave significantly higher scores to values relating to economic (e.g., a comfortable life) and political values (e.g., social recognition) than less successful managers. Also in America, Clare and Sanford (1979) found that the instrumental value managers held highest for themselves was 'ambition', and their highest-held terminal value was a 'sense of accomplishment'.

In comparing the research findings from America we have two concerns. Firstly, that of taking a comparison of values across national boundaries and, secondly, the value of quoting population averages when individual differences are highly pronounced.

On the issue of national boundaries, a study of opinions organised in 1994 by *The Guardian* in the UK, *Asahi Shimun* in Japan, *Der Spiegel* in Germany and the *New York Times* brought to light some considerable differences between the UK, Japan, Germany and America. This discrepancy is illustrated in Table 1.4.

The reasons for the differences of opinions, and presumably the value systems upon which they are based, are certainly complex. Carr and Haldane (1993) cite one significant factor in the formation of values. It is concerned with education systems. These differ from country to country and within countries. European countries are inclined to train potential managers differently from those who are perceived to be potential 'shop floor workers'. This brings us onto our second concern about the direct use of research information. Individual differences can make nonsense out of average figures. (See Chapter 6 on the work of Galloway and motivation (1990).)

The reader will find it interesting to make a personal ranking of the two sets of values – as has been said many times before: If you do not know where you are going, you will end up somewhere else. What is rarely discussed are the values concerned with 'where you are going'. It is, in our opinion, valuable to review a personal value system when we are not under pressure.

Management Consultancy and Skills

Table 1.4 Percentage of respondents giving each reply to the question: 'What is the most serious problem facing the world in 1994?'

Problem	UK	Germany	Japan	US
Bosnia	0	10	8	0
Crime	7	0	0	17
Drugs	0	0	0	7
Economy	0	10	0	7
Ethnic strife	0	0	14	0
Famine	11	4	6	7
Morals	0	0	0	6
Pollution	12	11	10	0
Population	0	4	0	0
Poverty	11	0	0	0
Unemployment	6	0	0	0
War	23	40	13	8

Kohlberg (1969), Graves (1970) and Flower *et al.* (1975) all argue that the behaviour displayed by individuals (i.e., the means used to achieve their valued ends) is related to the maturity of their value system. People progress from one level of maturity to another, and, as they do, their value priorities change. Individuals who have progressed to more mature levels of values development possess a qualitatively different set of instrumental values than individuals who are at less mature levels. The maturity of value systems is therefore important if we are to relate value systems to managerial effectiveness. However, we could argue that the term 'maturity is value laden. Working with multi-ethnic groups, any codification has to be agreed and presented as culturally based.

Kohlberg's model is the best-known and most widely researched approach to the maturity of values. The model focuses on the kind of reasoning used to reach a decision about an issue that has value or moral connotations. The model consists of three major levels, each of which contains two stages. Table 1.5 summarises the characteristics of each stage. In brief, the stages are sequential (for example, a person cannot progress to stage 3 before passing through stage 2), and each stage represents a higher level of maturity.

The first level of maturity, the self-centred level, contains the first two stages of values development. Moral reasoning and instrumental values are based on personal needs or wants and on the consequences of an act. For example, something could be judged as right or good if it helped an individual to obtain a reward or avoid punishment and if the consequences were not negative for someone else. Stealing 50,000EUs is worse than stealing 500EUs in the self-centred level because the consequences are more negative for someone else.

The second level, or conformity level, contains stages 3 and 4. Moral reasoning is based on conforming to and upholding the conventions and expectations

Table 1.5 Kohlberg classification of moral judgement into levels and stages of development

Level	Basis of moral judgement	Stage of development
I	Moral value resides in external, quasi-physical happenings, in bad acts, or in quasi-physical needs, rather than in persons and standards.	1. Obedience and punishment orientation. Egocentric deference to superior power or prestige, or a trouble-avoiding set. Objective responsibility.
		2. Naively egotistic orientation. Right action is that instrumentally satisfying the self's needs and occasionally others'. Awareness of relativism of value to each actor's needs and perspectives. Naive egalitarianism and orientation to exchange and reciprocity.
II	Moral value resides in performing good or right roles, in maintaining the conventional order and the expectancies of others.	3. Good-boy orientation. Orientation to approval and to pleasing and helping others. Conformity to stereotypical images of majority or natural role behaviour, and judgement by intentions.
		4. Orientation to doing duty, 'showing respect for authority', and maintaining the social order for its own sake. Regard for earned expectations of others.
III	Moral value resides in conformity by the self to shared or shareable standards, rights or duties.	5. Contractual legalistic orientation. Recognition of an arbitrary element or starting point in rules or expectations for the sake of agreement. Duty defined in terms of contract, general avoidance of violation of the will or rights of others, and majority will and welfare.
		6. Conscience of principle orientation. Orientation not only to actually ordained social rules, but to principles of choice involving appeal to logical universality and consistency. Orientation to conscience as a directing agent and to mutual respect and trust.

Source: Kohlberg, 1969

Management Consultancy and Skills

211

of society. This level is sometimes referred to as the 'law and order' level because the emphasis is on conformity to laws and norms. Right and wrong are judged on the basis of whether or not behaviours conform to the rules of those in authority. Respect from others based on obedience is a prized outcome. Stealing 50,000EUs and stealing 500EUs are equally wrong at this level because both violate the law. Most adults in the Western culture function at this level of values maturity.

Third is the principled level. This contains the final two stages of maturity and represents the most mature level of moral reasoning and the most mature set of instrumental values. Right and wrong are judged on the basis of the internalised principles of the individual. That is, judgements are made on the basis of a set of principles that have been developed from individual experience. In the highest stage of maturity, this set of principles is comprehensive (it covers all contingencies), consistent (it is never violated) and universal (it does not change with the situation or circumstance). Thus, stealing 50,000EUs and stealing 500EUs are still judged to be wrong, but the basis for the judgement is not the violation of laws or rules, but the violation of a comprehensive, consistent, universal principle developed by the individuals. Few individuals, according to Kohlberg, reach this highest level of maturity. (Kohlberg uses the terms 'pre-conventional', 'conventional' and 'post-conventional' to describe the three levels. We have chosen instead to use terms that capture the dominant characteristics of each stage.)

Self-centred individuals view rules and laws as outside themselves, but they obey because, by doing so, they may be rewarded or at least avoid punishment. Conformist individuals view rules and laws as outside themselves, but they obey because they have learned and accepted those rules and laws. Principled individuals examine the rules and laws and develop a set of internal principles. If there is a choice to be made between obeying a rule or obeying a principle, they choose the principle. Internalised principles supersede rules and laws in principled individuals. Again reverting to our experience in working with multi-ethic groups we find that it is argued that retribution and conscience can be confused. The linear progression becomes a loop.

Kohlberg uses a story to explain the levels. We will do the same.

A child was dying of a rare disease, the treatment for which could only be obtained at a clinic in the United States. The child's case was publicised on a TV programme and a public subscription allowed the child to go for what was expected to be a complete course of treatment.

When the child first returned home she showed considerable improvement but then began to revert to her previous lethargic state. The American clinic was helpful and explained that they had always been aware that the child might have to return for further treatment – of course at extra cost.

The sick child's father, Heinz, went back to the TV company but found that they had lost interest. He made various attempts to borrow the money, and even to start an appeal on his own. He failed. He also failed to get the bank that employed him to provide him with a loan to be paid back out of his salary.

Heinz worked in the computer services department of the bank and was explaining the problem to a colleague over a coffee. The colleague was enthusiastic to help and explain a 'foolproof' scam which would use Heinz's access to the computer system and his special knowledge to 'generate' enough money to send his child to America. Heinz was well aware that what he would have to do was stealing.

Now answer the following questions:

	Yes	No
1. Would it be wrong for Heinz to steal from his employer?	——	——
2. Was the company right in refusing to give him a loan against his salary?	——	——
3. Did Heinz have an obligation to steal for his child?	——	——
4. If the sick child was not his favourite child, did he still have the same obligations to steal for her?	——	——
5. Suppose the child was that of his best friend and not his, should he steal?	——	——
6. Suppose the child was not close to Heinz personally. Should Heinz steal?	——	——
7. Suppose Heinz read in the paper about the child. Should he steal for her?	——	——
8. Would you steal to save your own life?	——	——
9. If he were caught, should he be sent to jail?	——	——

For individuals in the self-centred level of maturity, stealing might be justified because Heinz's child had instrumental value, she could give him pleasure and perhaps look after him in old age. A stranger, however, would not have the same instrumental value for Heinz, so it would be wrong to steal for a stranger. Individuals in the conformity level would base their judgements on the closeness of the relationship and on law and authority. Heinz has an obligation to steal for family members, according to this reasoning, but not for non-family members. The governing principle is always whether it is against the law (or society's expectations) or not. Principled individuals base their judgements on a set of universal, comprehensive and consistent principles. They may answer any question yes or no, but their reasoning will be based on their own internal principles, not on externally imposed standards or expectations. (For example, they might feel an obligation to steal for anyone because they value human life more than property.)

Research on Kohlberg's model of value development has revealed some interesting findings that have relevance to managerial behaviour. For example, moral judgement stories were administered to college pupils who had earlier participated in Milgram's (1963) obedience study. Under the guise of a reinforcement-learning experiment, Milgram's subjects had been directed to give increasingly intense shocks to a person who was observed to be in great pain. Of the respondents at the principled level (stages 5 and 6), 75 per cent refused to administer the shocks, while only 12.5 per cent of the respondents at the conformity level refused. Higher levels of values development were associated with more human behaviour towards other people. Haan *et al.* (1968) found that although both principled and self-centred individuals are inclined to join in massive social protests, self-centred individuals are motivated by the desire to better themselves individually, while principled individuals are motivated by justice and the rights of the larger community.

Becoming mature in value development requires that individuals develop a set of internalised principles by which they can govern their behaviour. The development of those principles is enhanced and value maturity is increased as value-based issues are confronted, discussed and thought about. Lickona (1976) notes that 'Simply increasing the amount of reciprocal communication that occurs among people is likely to enhance moral development.'

To help you to determine your own level of values maturity an instrument, developed by James Rest at the University of Minnesota's Moral Research Center, was included in the Pre-assessment section. It has been used extensively in research because it is easier to administer than Kohlberg's method for assessing maturity. According to Kohlberg (1976), 'Rest's approach does give a rough estimate of an individual's moral maturity level.' Rather than placing a person on one single level of values maturity, it identifies the stage that the person relies on most. That is, it assumes that individuals use more than one level of maturity (or set of instrumental values), but that one level generally predominates. By completing this instrument, therefore, you will identify your predominant level of value maturity. To determine your maturity level, refer to the self-scoring instructions in Appendix 1. An exercise in the Skill Practice section will help you develop or refine principles at stages 5 and 6.

Ethical decision making

In addition to its benefits for self-understanding, awareness of your own level of values maturity also has important practical implications for ethical decision making. Unfortunately, there have been several highly publicised examples of unethical dealings in recent years in Europe. The publisher Robert Maxwell was able to ransack millions of pounds from the unsuspecting pension funds of companies he had bought in a flurry of acquisitions. At least his mysterious death prevented him from being imprisoned; not so lucky were Ernest Saunders and Gerald Ronson who were jailed for their involvement in the attempt to inflate the value of Guinness shares during its take-over bid. The magnitude of the scandal at the Bank of Credit and Commerce International (BCCI) will perhaps never be rivalled, but hundreds of investors have been ruined in the process. British Airways has paid a high price for its 'dirty tricks' campaign against Virgin Airlines, while the defence electronics group Ferranti eventually collapsed when it became the victim of a million pound fraud. Volkswagen and GM have issues of industrial espionage at the highest level. There have also been widespread accusations that French and Spanish companies have contributed to political parties in exchange for public favours, and there has been a wholesale indictment of Italy's corrupt business and political class, particularly after the Olivetti scandal. Neil Hamilton in the UK, with his alleged corruption of the British parliament, may have brought a government down. A recent cartoon summarises this state of affairs. It showed a group of executives sitting at a conference table. The leader remarked: 'Of course honesty is one of the better policies.'

Corporate behaviour that exemplifies unethical decision making is not our concern here. What is more to the point is a study by the American Management Association that included 3,000 managers in the USA. It reported that most individual managers felt that they were under pressure to compromise personal standards to meet company goals (Cavanaugh, 1980). As an illustration, consider the following incident.

> You are interviewing for a senior position and the candidate in front of you satisfies every criterion – he is perfect. Having decided, without telling the candidate that he is 'in', you begin to close the interview. At this point he says:
>
> 'You know my present employer is of course a major rival – perhaps this disc will be of use.'
>
> The disc he explains contains details of all the accounts of his present employer. The information would be VERY valuable to your company. What do you do and why?

This sort of incident is common and is described by Kenneth Blanchard and Norman Peale (1988) who, in their excellent book on ethical management, go well beyond the scope of this book. Looking at Kohlberg's Stages of Development we imagine six ways of deciding what to do:

1. If I take them I will be caught – fired.
2. I might be caught but the advantages far outweigh/are less than the risks.
3. I would get my boss's approval/disapproval if I did.
4. It would be letting the side down/help us.
5. It would be illegal.
6. It's wrong.

Managers in the real world have to resolve the conflict between commercial short- and long-term gain and their own need to 'sleep at night' on a surprisingly regular basis (Hosmer, 1987). To do so we need to understand our own values, accepting that, in the short term, trade-offs are inevitable. The stress that these trade-off's produce and the way in which individuals can cope are discussed in the next chapter. It is a great advantage to the individual if he or she can call out an absolute set of values to guide.

Working with groups of different ethnic backgrounds, Islam provides such a set of principles – a 'joke' of Islam is that when oil comes up the well Allah goes down the hole.

For those less fortunate and not possessing a guiding faith we recommend three questions, due again to Blanchard and Peale (1988):

1. Is it legal? Will I be violating either civil law, company policy or 'standard' practice?
2. Is it balanced? Is it fair to all concerned in the short term as well as the long term? Does it promote win–win relationships?
3. How will it make me feel about myself? Will it make me feel proud? Would I feel good if my decision was published in a newspaper for my family to read?

Look at the example of the candidate who was willing to 'sell' his previous employer and ask the questions. The answers you come to will be about YOU and not about the theory we can cover.

In all we have reviewed it is inevitable now that we consider your ability to cope with change. The environment we all face continues to become more chaotic, more temporary, more complex, and more overloaded with information, and you need to survive and prosper. We all have an attitude to change.

Attitudes towards change

Almost no one disagrees with the prediction that change will increase. Toffler (1980) states it this way:

> A powerful tide is surging across much of the world today, creating a new, often bizarre, environment in which to work, play, marry, raise children or retire. In this bewildering context, businessmen swim against highly erratic economic currents; politicians see their ratings bob wildly up and down; universities, hospitals, and other institutions battle desperately against inflation. Value systems splinter and crash, while lifeboats of family, church and state are hurled madly about. Many observers have suggested that we are now entering a post-industrial environment, 'characterised by more and increasing information, more and increasing turbulence, and more and increasing complexity' (Huber, 1984).

These views were from the 1980s and things have accelerated since then – the ONLY certainty is change. We are called upon to make decisions much more quickly against a rising tide of information (Cameron and Ulrich, 1986); we are only human so more and more decisions are made on the basis of incomplete and ambiguous information (Simon, 1973). We all need increasingly to function in conditions of ambiguity and turbulence, and become hostages to our attitude to change.

The first step is to be aware of our own attitude to change. Again our approach is to look at the dimensions of the system – our orientation to change. We find two dimensions: *tolerance of ambiguity* and *locus of control*.

Tolerance of ambiguity

One's personal tolerance of ambiguity is a guide to how we will function in ambiguous, chaotic situations where the data may well be confused and 'too much' is happening. Regardless of one's cognitive style, people vary in their ability to cope. Individuals who have a high tolerance of ambiguity also tend to be those who are more cognitively complex. They tend to pay attention to more information, interpret more cues, and possess more patterning capability than less complex individuals.

> Perhaps the most ambiguous work situation known to human beings is code breaking. Various writers, and most excitingly Robert Harris in his novel, *Enigma*, describes the recruitment of code breakers working against the ever-changing flood of German messages in World War II. A crossword competition was set up and the winners were recruited.

Bieri and his co-workers (1966) found that cognitively complex and tolerant individuals were better communicators, and Schneier (1979) found that they were more sensitive to the critical characteristics of others when appraising their work. Haase *et al.* (1979) showed them to be more flexible under ambiguous and over-loaded conditions than less tolerant and less complex individuals. Managers with a high tolerance of ambiguity are more likely to be entrepreneurial in their actions (Schere, 1982), to screen out less information in a complex environment (Haase *et al.*, 1979) and to choose specialities in their occupations that involve less structured tasks (Budner, 1962). However, individuals who are more tolerant of ambiguity have more difficulty focusing on important details, are inclined to pay attention to a variety of items and may have somewhat less ability to concentrate without being distracted by interruptions. This said, a high tolerance of ambiguity is an advantage in our changing world.

In the Skill Pre-assessment section of this chapter, the Tolerance of Ambiguity Scale (Budner, 1962) should help you to assess the extent to which you have a tolerance for these kinds of complex situations.

In scoring the Tolerance of Ambiguity Scale (Appendix 1, page 611), we look at three different factors:

- The *novelty* score, which relates to the extent to which you are tolerant of new, unfamiliar information or situations.

- The *complexity* score, which indicates the extent to which you are tolerant of multiple, distinctive, or unrelated pieces of information.

- The *insolubility* score, which indicates the extent to which you are tolerant of problems that are very difficult to solve, where alternative solutions are not evident, information is unavailable, or the problem's components seem unrelated to each other.

In general, the more tolerant people are of novelty, complexity and insolubility, the more likely they are to succeed as managers in information-rich, ambiguous environments. They are less overwhelmed by these ambiguous circumstances. However, cognitive complexity and tolerance for ambiguity are not related to intelligence (Smith and Leach, 1972), and your score on the Tolerance of Ambiguity Scale is not an evaluation of how smart you are. Most importantly, individuals can learn to tolerate more complexity and more flexibility in their information-processing abilities. The first step is becoming aware of where you are now.

The Skill Analysis and Skill Practice sections of this chapter, together with our chapter on effective problem solving, should continue the process. Although intelligence and a tolerance of uncertainty are not linked, a second dimension of our attitudes to change – discussed here as 'locus of control' – is.

Locus of control

Locus of control refers to the attitude people have concerning the extent to which they are in control of their own destiny. When we take any action, some actions are rewarded and others penalised – we receive positive or negative feedback and this feedback reinforces our behaviour for the 'next time'. If we interpret the feedback as determined by, or contingent on, our actions, it is within our internal locus of control: *'I was the cause of the success or failure of the change.'*

If, however, we interpret the feedback as being determined by outside factors, we have something in an external locus of control: *'It was not my fault. I was rescued by . . .'*

Over time, people develop an overall view of where the reinforcement for their actions will come – internally or externally. Over 1,000 studies have been done using the Locus of Control Scale. Not surprisingly, the research suggests that, in American culture, internal locus of control is associated with the most successful managers (see Hendricks, 1985, and Spector, 1982, for reviews of the literature). Julian B. Rotter (1966), whose scale it was, summarised several studies and showed that people with an internal locus of control are more likely to:

- be attentive to aspects of the environment that provide useful information for the future;
- engage in actions to improve their environment;
- place greater emphasis on striving for achievement;
- be more inclined to develop their own skills;
- ask more questions;
- remember more information than people with an external locus of control (also see Seeman, 1982).

Elsewhere in the literature it is claimed that people with high internal locus of control are:

- more able to manage stress and outperform in stressful situations (Oakland, 1997; Anderson *et al.* 1977);
- less alienated from the work environment (Mitchell, 1975; Seeman, 1982; Wolf, 1972);
- more satisfied with their work (Organ and Greene, 1974; Pryer and Distefano, 1971);
- able to experience less job strain and more position mobility (promotions and job changes) than externals (Gennill and Heisler, 1972);
- more likely to act as leaders and be more effective in this role than those with a dominant external locus of control (Anderson and Schneider, 1978);
- likely to engage in more entrepreneurial activity (Durand and Shea, 1974);
- more active in managing their own careers (Hammer and Vardi, 1981), and had higher levels of job involvement than externals (Runyon, 1973).

In the leadership role, externally focused individuals tend to use coercion and threats, whereas internally focused leaders rely more on persuasion and expertise as a source of power (Goodstadt and Hjelle, 1973; Mitchell *et al.*, 1975) and are more able to use a participative management style, when relevant, than the externally focused manager (Runyon, 1973).

Management Consultancy and Skills

218

A study of locus of control among top executives found that the firms controlled by outside management were less likely to take risks. Sentient-controlled firms engaged in more innovative risky projects, took more leadership in the marketplace, had longer planning horizons, engaged more scanning of the environment, and demanded more highly developed technology (Miller *et al.*, 1982).

In summarising his conclusions about locus of control, McDonald (1970) stated that 'all research points to the same conclusion: "In the American culture, people are handicapped by external locus of control."'

An internal locus of control is not the panacea for all management problems and is not always a positive attribute. As leaders, those with an external locus of control are more inclined to define roles, clarify structures and show consideration. (Durand and Shea, 1974). Internally focused individuals are less likely to accept authority and provide unbiased feedback. (Cravens and Worchel, 1977). Internals also have more difficulty arriving at decisions when those decisions have serious consequences for someone else (Wheeler and Davis, 1979).

The dominant locus of control can shift over time, particularly as roles change at work (Harvey, 1971). Rothenberg in 1980 gave comfort to those with a dominant high external locus of control – they can get to the top.

People who look at change as inevitable and as an opportunity to grasp, perceiving themselves as masters of their own fate, are more likely to be effective managers in most circumstances in our culture.

Using the Locus of Control Scale at the beginning of the chapter will give you a view of your own internal/external locus ratio. Remember that whatever the value is, you can be a successful manager in the right setting, and you can alter the ratio when you like.

Summary

Two key attitudes towards change – tolerance of ambiguity and locus of control – have been found to be associated with performance in management roles. Knowing your scores on these two factors can help you capitalise on your strengths and enhance your potential. While substantial research exists associating some positive managerial behaviours with internal locus of control and tolerance of ambiguity, possessing these orientations is neither an assurance of success as a manager nor a solution to the problems that managers face. By knowing your scores, however, you will be able to choose situations in which you will more likely feel comfortable, perform effectively, and understand the point of view of those whose perspective differs from yours. Self-understanding is a prerequisite to self-improvement and change.

Interpersonal needs

Sayles (1964) suggests that management involves virtually constant contact with people, and individuals who do not enjoy such contact are likely to be ineffective, frustrated and dissatisfied. Enjoying contact with others is about satisfying certain fundamental needs and this is the fourth critical area of self-awareness we will be discussing. Although all of us need to relate to others, the quantity and quality of the relationships vary from individual to individual. Some of us require the constant buzz of the herd while others prefer the company of a few chosen friends with whom they can relate closely. Some of us need both. Some of us need to have clarity in our relationships, knowing who is in charge and who is the follower, while others prefer equality. The further complication is what we say we want for ourselves and what we want from others.

Schutz (1958) proposed a validated method of quantifying interpersonal needs. The basic assumption behind Schutz's model is that people need people and that all of us seek to establish compatible relationships with other individuals in their social interactions. He goes further in stating that three interpersonal needs must be satisfied if the individual is to function effectively and avoid unsatisfactory relationships. It is the process of striving to achieve a personal balance of these needs that determines much of our behaviour towards others.

The first interpersonal need is for inclusion. We all, at some level, need to maintain a relationship with other people, to be included in their activities, and to include them in our own activities. The personal balance is between identifying with a group and wanting to be alone. It is a trade-off between tendencies towards extroversion and introversion. We differ in the strength of their relative needs: (1) the need to include others, or expressed inclusion, and (2) the need to be included by others, or wanted inclusion.

A second interpersonal need is for control. This is the need to maintain a satisfactory balance of power and influence in relationships. We all need, in some measure, to be masters of our own fate, to exert control, direct, or structure other people while at the same time being independent of them. We also have a need to be controlled, directed, or structured by others but at the same time to maintain freedom and discretion. Essentially, this is a trade-off between authoritarianism and dependency. Individual differences arise, therefore, in the need to control others, or expressed control, and the need to be controlled by others, or wanted control.

A third need is the need for affection, or the need to form close personal relationships with others. This need is not restricted to physical affection or romantic relationships but includes needs for warmth, intimacy and love without overtones. We all need, to some measure, close personal relationships with other people, but there is a personal balance between what we see as welcome and smothering. We all need, in some measure, to have others show warmth and affection to us, while maintaining a chosen degree of distance. This is a trade-off between high affiliative needs and high independence needs. Individuals therefore vary in their needs for expressing affection towards other people and for wanting affection to be expressed towards them.

The three interpersonal needs thus have two aspects: a desire to express the need and a desire to receive the needed behaviour from others. These three needs determine an individual's interpersonal orientation. That is, individuals differ uniquely in their needs and thus their behaviours to achieve their needs.

In the Skill Pre-assessment section we provided the instrument Schutz developed to assess inclusion, control and affection needs. Ideally you should compute your score before continuing the chapter. This way you will be able to personalise the discussion. The process of answering the 54 questions and their analysis may take about 20 minutes, but it is time well spent. The template for the analysis is at the end of the book. Use the analysis instructions at the end of the book to fill in the matrix.

	INCLUSION *The need to join and belong*	CONTROL *The need for role and control*	AFFECTION *The need for individual relationships*
Expressed			
Wanted			

First, add all the figures together and come up with a grand total. The maximum points possible in each cell are 9 and with six cells we have a maximum of 54. Scores above 35 are regarded as high. If you have a high score you are best suited to a job with a high people content. Scores from 34 to 15 are regarded as average – you like contact with people, but can work effectively without such contact. Scores below 14 are regarded as low and indicate that human contact is not your primary objective at work – the task is of primary importance to you. Adding along the rows we find out more.

Score – *row total*	*Inclusion*	*Control*	*Affection*
High: 12–18	You need the 'buzz' of people around you – you need to be associated with teams or groups	You like to know where you are – clarity of position/ role and structure is needed for you to be effective	You like the company of intimates and probably, if your inclusion and control scores are only medium, you prefer to deal with your staff on a one-to-one basis
Average: 6–11	You are ambivalent about working in teams or groups	Although you probably prefer clarity in your role, it is not essential	You probably prefer the company of a select few, but it is not essential
Low: 0–5	You prefer your own company or that of a few friends	You are happy to function in situations of uncertainty	You may well be unhappy or embarrassed in stressed, intimate situations

We can get an even better focus by looking at the content of individual cells in the matrix. We are looking here at the difference between the expressed needs and the wanted needs – what you say you want from others and what you actually want – for each cell, 6–9 is high, 3–5 is medium and 0–2 is low.

	Inclusion	Control	Affection
High top/high bottom	Clear and expressed wish to be 'in the action'	A wish to control in a tightly controlled environment	A high and clearly expressed need for individual contacts
High top/ medium bottom	High express wish to 'be in the action' but in fact a rather ambivalent attitude when it comes time to join in	A strong wish to control with perhaps some reluctance to accept authority or procedures	A high and clearly expressed wish for intimate human contact which may on occasion be one-way
High top/ low bottom	A high expressed wish to be included as a social necessity but not as a genuine need	A wish to control but remain independent	A perhaps dangerous demand for intimacy that will not be reciprocated
Medium top/ high bottom	Some reluctance to ask to be included in things – but want to be involved	Control can be taken but regretfully	Some shyness to express real feeling
Medium top/ medium bottom	Genuine ambivalence to groups teams and their membership	Control and structures are not the major factor but accepted – weak or strong	A straightforward relationship is preferred – privacy or intimacy is acceptable
Medium top/ low bottom	Lack of clarity of messages – do you want to be involved or not – you do not!	Perhaps unassertive, wish for structures but a reluctance to accept it from others	A lack of clarity of signals – do you wish intimacy and trust – you do not!
Low top/ high bottom	A lonely position where it is difficult not to watch others from afar and hope to be invited in	A wish for other things, events of people to dominate or set rules	A shy position that once breached is inclined to surprise, if not frighten others by its intensity
Low top/ medium bottom	An only partially expressed hope to be 'let in'	Control, order and certainty are not major issues	A partially expressed hope to share with individuals
Low top/ low bottom	No need to have to face others or join in	Control, order and certainty mean very little indeed	What you see is what you get – an expressed and real need for privacy

The issue we need to pursue is the interaction between individuals, as the following story exemplifies:

Stuart Blyth was becoming exasperated. He had only been at Vulcan Computers for three months and already he was finding Helen impossible to work with. 'I've got enough problems without her rambling memos,' he muttered to his secretary. Stuart's predecessor, Duncan Johnson, had appreciated being kept in constant touch with developments by Helen. 'I really look forward to reading your personal memos,' he used to say at their weekly meetings. 'They keep me in touch with the pulse of the company.' That was why Helen was completely mystified by Stuart's reaction. Hadn't he said he wanted to be informed about staff changes when he joined the company? And now after three months he had finally snapped and had thrown back her latest memo: 'Don't keep sending me these boring reports. I haven't got time to read all this stuff – just tell me.'

Source: Thomas and Woods (1994)

The clue to the boss's personal orientation lies in the last line of the case study – 'just tell me'. Stuart probably had a high need for affection – one-to-one contact. By reporting in written format, Helen was not giving Stuart what he needed. Helen, by recognising her boss's orientation, could have saved herself a great deal of grief.

Managers with high inclusion needs will prefer to use group meetings to give information and may well find themselves damaged when they have to act in a way that alienates them from their working team.

Sam was the manager of a distribution depot and enjoyed his regular 'Saturday night out with the boys'. The company was running into financial problems and was laying off staff. During one fateful Saturday evening he was asked whether he would sack any of the team. He replied that he could never do that and he would fight for them 'come hell or high water'.

The next Monday he received orders to make 25 per cent of his team redundant. He did the job but it was made very clear to him that he would not be welcome for the next Saturday night out.

We met him in a counselling session where he was suffering from depression. His Firo-B score for inclusion was 8/7 and 'belonging' to the team was very important to him.

Managers with high affection needs may find it difficult to discipline subordinates with whom they wish to retain one-to-one relationships. Managers with a high expressed control need and a low wanted control may well find themselves in conflict with their own boss. Manager's with the reverse low expressed control and high wanted control may well be seen as unsure and lacking determination.

Individuals who have high expressed scores and low wanted scores are called 'controllers' by Ryan (1970) because they want to express but are unwilling to accept in return. The reverse pattern, high wanted scores and low expressed scores, is called a 'passive' pattern by Ryan because these individuals want to receive but are unwilling to initiate any interaction.

Knowing your interpersonal orientation, then, can be an important factor in your managerial success. Not only does it enhance good interpersonal relations by helping you diagnose potential areas of incompatibility, but it helps you generate alternatives for behaviour when you attempt to solve interpersonal difficulties. For example, some problems can be solved simply by increasing inclusion activities, by allowing someone else to express a little more control, or by redefining an issue as an affection problem instead of a control problem.

Management Consultancy and Skills

SUMMARY

Modern organisations have begun more and more to discover the power of developing self-awareness among their managers. Managers have completed instruments designed to increase self-awareness in such companies as Barclays Bank, British Gas, ICI, KLM UK, Marks and Spencer, Nissan UK, Peugeot, Unilever and Volvo.

An awareness of how individuals differ in their value priorities and values maturity, cognitive style, orientation towards change and, for example, after requiring his top 100 managers to undergo self-awareness training, the president of the computer reservations company of Hilton Hotels and Budget Rent-a-Car stated:

> We had some real morale problems. I realised I had a mixed bag of people reporting to me and that this training could help us better understand each other and also understand how we make decisions. We wouldn't have made it through [a recent company crisis] without self-awareness training.
>
> *Source*: Moore (1987)

Not only does self-awareness training assist individuals in their ability to understand, and thereby manage, themselves, but it also is important in helping individuals develop understanding of the differences in others. Most people will regularly encounter individuals who possess a different style, a different set of values and a different perspective from their own. Most workforces are becoming more, not less, diverse.

Self-awareness training, as discussed in this chapter, therefore, can be a valuable tool in helping individuals develop empathy and in understanding the expanding diversity they will face in work and school settings. The relationship between the four critical areas of self-awareness and these management outcomes is summarised in Figure 1.5.

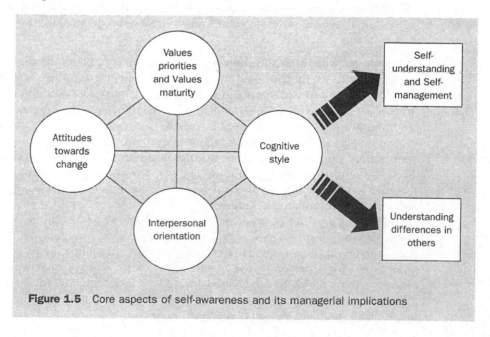

Figure 1.5 Core aspects of self-awareness and its managerial implications

Management Consultancy and Skills

Most of the following chapters relate to skills in interpersonal or group interaction, but successful skill development in those areas will occur only if individuals have a firm foundation in self-awareness. In fact, there is an interesting paradox in human behaviour: we can know others only by knowing ourselves, but we can know ourselves only by knowing others. Our knowledge of others, and therefore our ability to manage or interact successfully with them, comes from relating what we see in them to our own experience. If we are not self-aware, we have no basis for knowing certain things about others. Self-recognition leads to recognition and understanding of others. As Harris (1981) puts it: Nothing is really personal that is not first interpersonal, beginning with the infant's shock of separation from the umbilical cord. What we know about ourselves comes only from the outside, and is interpreted by the kind of experiences we have had; and what we know about others comes only from analogy with our own network of feelings.

Behavioural guidelines

The guidelines will help you develop your self-awareness:

1. Identify your sensitive line. Determine what information about yourself you are most likely to defend against.

2. Identify a comprehensive, consistent and universal set of principles on which you will base your behaviour. Identify the most important terminal and instrumental values that guide your decisions.

3. Expand your cognitive style, your tolerance of ambiguity, and your internal locus of control by increasing your exposure to new information and engaging in activities different from those you are used to. Seek ways to expand and broaden yourself.

4. Compute incompatibility scores with those you regularly interact with and identify areas in which potential incompatibilities may arise. Apply principles of constructive communication (Chapter 4) and constructive conflict management (Chapter 7) when disagreements arise.

5. Engage in honest self-disclosure with someone who is close to you and accepting of you. Investigate aspects of yourself that you are not sure of.

6. Keep a diary, and make time regularly to engage in self-analysis. Balance life's activities with some time for self-renewal.

Skill Analysis

CASE STUDY **1.1**

COMMUNIST PRISON CAMP

To find examples of a more intensive destruction of identification with family and reference groups and the destruction of social role and self-image, we must turn to the experiences of civilian political prisoners interned in Chinese communist prisons.

In such prisons the total regimen, consisting of physical privation, prolonged interrogation, total isolation from former relationships and sources of information, detailed regimentation of all daily activities, and deliberate humiliation and degradation, was geared to producing a complete confession of alleged crimes and the assumption of a penitent role preceding the adoption of a communist frame of reference. The prisoner was not informed of his crimes, nor was he permitted to evade the issue by making up a false confession. Instead, what the prisoner learned he must do was re-evaluate his past from the point of view of the communists and recognise that most of his former attitudes and behaviour were actually criminal. For example, a priest who had dispensed food to needy peasants in his mission church had to recognise that he was actually a tool of imperialism and was using his missionary activities as cover for exploitation of the peasants. Even worse, he may have had to recognise that he had used food as blackmail to accomplish his aims.

The key technique used by the communists to produce social alienation to a degree sufficient to allow such redefinition and revaluation to occur was to put the prisoner into a cell with four or more other prisoners who were somewhat more advanced in their 'thought reform' than he. Such a cell usually had one leader who was responsible to the prison authorities, and the progress of the whole cell was made contingent upon the progress of the 'least reformed' member. This condition meant, in practice, that four or more cell members devoted all their energies to getting their 'least reformed' member to recognise the truth about himself and to confess. To accomplish this they typically swore at, harangued, beat, denounced, humiliated, reviled and brutalised their victim 24 hours a day, sometimes for weeks or months on end. If the authorities felt that the prisoner was basically unco-operative, they manacled his hands behind his back and chained his ankles, which made him completely dependent on his cell mates for the fulfilment of his basic needs.

It was this reduction to an animal-like existence in front of other humans, which, I believe, constituted the ultimate humiliation, and led most reliably to the destruction of the prisoner's image of himself. Even in his own eyes he became something which was not worthy of the regard of his fellow man.

If, to avoid complete physical and personal destruction, the prisoner began to confess in the manner desired of him, he was usually forced to prove his sincerity by making irrevocable behavioural commitments, such as denouncing and implicating his friends and relatives in his own newly recognised crimes. Once he had done this he became further alienated from his former self, even in his own eyes, and could seek security only in a new identity and new social relationships.

Aiding this process of confessing was the fact that the crimes gave the prisoner something concrete to which to attach the free-floating guilt which the accusing environment and his own humiliation usually stimulated.

A good example was the plight of the sick and wounded prisoners of war who, because of their physical confinement, were unable to escape from continual conflict with their interrogator or instructor, and who therefore often ended up forming a close relationship with him. Chinese communist instructors often encouraged prisoners to take long walks or have informal talks with them and offered as incentives cigarettes, tea and other rewards. If the prisoner was willing to cooperate and become a 'progressive', he could join with other 'progressives' in an active group life.

Within the political prison, the group cell not only provided the forces towards alienation but also offered the road to a 'new self'. Not only were there available among the fellow prisoners individuals with whom the prisoner could identify because of their shared plight, but once he showed any tendency to seek a new identity by truly trying to re-evaluate his past, he received again a whole range of rewards, of which perhaps the most important was the interpersonal information that he was again a person worthy of respect and regard.

Source: Schein (1960)

Discussion questions

1. To what extent is the self-concept a product of situational factors or inherited factors?

2. What is the relationship between self-knowledge and social pressure?

3. Is self-awareness constant, or do people become more and less self-aware over time?

4. What mechanisms could have been used by prisoners of war to resist the destruction of their self-concepts?

5. What could have been done to facilitate the reform of the self-concepts of prisoners?

6. What can be done to enhance a positive self-concept?

CASE STUDY **1.2**

DECISION DILEMMAS

For each of the five scenarios below, select the choice you would make if you were in the situation.

1. A young manager in a high technology firm was offered a position by the firm's chief competitor for almost double her salary. Her firm sought to prevent her from changing jobs, arguing that her knowledge of certain specialised manufacturing processes would give the competitor an unfair advantage. Since she had acquired that knowledge through special training and unique opportunities in her current position, the firm argued that it was unethical for her to accept the competitor's offer. What should the young manager do?

Accept the offer/Reject the offer

Management Consultancy and Skills

2. A consumer organisation conducted a survey to determine whether Bene beer was really more 'thirst quenching' than any other beer. After testing a number of other popular beers, each beer brand received approximately the same number of votes for quenching thirsts. The consumer group proposed that Bene should no longer advertise its product as being 'more thirst quenching' than its rivals. The company indicated that its own tests showed different results, and that the image of the beer was the important factor, not the test results. Should the advertisements cease or not?

Cease to advertise/Continue to advertise

3. After several profitable years, the Joe Jameson Organic Vitamin Company was made available for sale. Joe's film and TV appearances prevented him from keeping control of a large company, and it became apparent that, if present trends continued, the company would either have to expand substantially or lose a large share of the market. Several firms were interested in purchasing the company for the asking price, but one firm was particularly aggressive. It sponsored several parties and receptions in Joe's honour, a 35-foot yacht was made available for his use during the summer, and several gifts arrived during the holidays for family members. His wife questioned the propriety of these activities. Was it appropriate for him to accept the gifts? Should he sell to that firm?

Proper to accept/Not proper to accept
Should not sell/Should sell

4. Keith Waller was a successful athletics coach who had helped produce several international sprinters and long-distance runners. He was very vocal about the need to clean up the sport, and in particular about drug taking. He had heard rumours that some members of his athletics club had taken performance-enhancing drugs, but after confronting those he thought were involved he was satisfied with their assurances that the rumours were unfounded. At the beginning of the next track season he received conclusive evidence that seven club members had in fact taken drugs. What should Keith do?

Report them to the National Athletics Body/
Suspend them for part of the season/Warn them but do nothing

5. Roger's company had been battered by competition from Asian firms. Not only were their products selling for less money, but the quality was substantially higher. By investing in some high-technology equipment, and by fostering better union–management relations, Roger was relatively certain that the quality gap could be overcome. But his overhead rate was more than 40 per cent above the competitor firms. He thought that the most efficient way to lower costs would be to close one of his older sites, lay off the employees, and increase production in the newer plants. He knew just which plant to close. Unfortunately, the community depended on this factory as its major employer and had recently invested a great deal of money for road repair and street light construction around the site. Many of the workforce were older people who

had lived in the area most of their lives. It was unlikely that they could obtain alternative employment in the same area. Should Roger close the plant or not?

Close the plant/Do not close

Discussion questions

Form a small group and discuss the following questions regarding the previous five scenarios:

1. Why did you make the choices you did in each case? Justify each answer.
2. What principles or basic values for decision making did you use in each case?
3. What additional information would you need in order to be certain about your choices?
4. What circumstances might arise to make you change your mind about your decision? Could there be a different answer to each case in a different circumstance?
5. What do your answers tell you about your own values, cognitive style, attitude towards change and interpersonal orientation?

Skill Practice

EXERCISE **1.2**

IMPROVING SELF-AWARENESS THROUGH SELF-DISCLOSURE

In the nineteenth century the concept of 'looking-glass self' was developed to describe the process used by people to develop self-awareness. It means simply that other people serve as a 'looking-glass' for each of us. They reflect our actions and behaviours. In turn, we form our opinions of ourselves as a result of observing and interpreting this 'mirroring'. The best way to form accurate self-perceptions, there-fore, is to share with others our thoughts, attitudes, feelings, actions and plans. This exercise helps you do that by asking you to analyse your own styles and inclina-tions and then share and discuss them with others. They may provide insights that you hadn't thought of.

Assignment

In a group of two or three, share your scores on the Skill Pre-assessment instruments with the others. Determine what similarities and differences exist among you. Do systematic ethnic or gender differences exist? Now complete the 11 statements listed below and say them out loud. Each person should complete each statement, but take turns at going first. The purpose of completing the statements aloud is to help you articulate aspects of your self-awareness and to receive reactions to them from others.

1. In taking the instruments, I was surprised by . . .
2. Some of my dominant characteristics captured by the instruments are . . .
3. Among my greatest strengths are . . .
4. Among my greatest weaknesses are . . .
5. The time I felt most successful was . . .
6. The time I felt least competent was . . .
7. My three highest priorities in life are . . .
8. The way in which I differ most from other people is . . .
9. I get along best with people who . . .
10. The best analogy that captures how I think of myself is . . .
11. From what you've said, I have noticed that you . . .

EXERCISE **1.3**

IDENTIFYING ASPECTS OF PERSONAL CULTURE

Not only do our experiences and interactions affect our self-concept, but each person enters this world with certain inclinations and talents, sometimes called 'temperament' by psychologists. This temperament may be developed both socially by our close family interactions and as a result of genetic factors.

This exercise helps you identify and analyse the major family influences that may have had an important impact on your values, attitudes, styles and personality. Not only is each person's physiology different, but each person's family culture is different as well. This exercise can help you highlight important aspects of your family culture.

Assignment

The outcome of this exercise will be a written autobiography. In order to help you prepare such a document, the following four steps should be completed. Use the results to construct an autobiography.

Step 1 On the chart in Figure 1.6, plot the points in each area of self-awareness that correspond to where you would ideally like to have scored. The vertical axis in the figure ranges from Very Satisfied to Very Dissatisfied. Your plots will represent your level of satisfaction with the scores you received on each instrument. For example, if you are satisfied with the score on the Defining Issues Test, make a mark near the top for 1. If you are dissatisfied with your score on Firo-B, make a mark near the bottom on 5. Connect each point so you have a 'self-awareness satisfaction profile'.

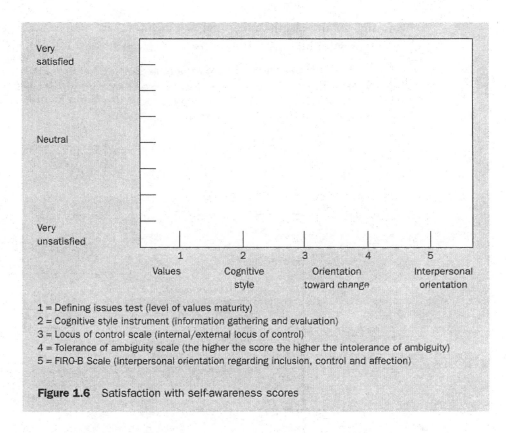

1 = Defining issues test (level of values maturity)
2 = Cognitive style instrument (information gathering and evaluation)
3 = Locus of control scale (internal/external locus of control)
4 = Tolerance of ambiguity scale (the higher the score the higher the intolerance of ambiguity)
5 = FIRO-B Scale (interpersonal orientation regarding inclusion, control and affection)

Figure 1.6   Satisfaction with self-awareness scores

Step 2   On the chart in Figure 1.7, draw your lifeline, plotting the major activities and events of your life. The vertical axis represents the importance or significance of events in terms of their impact on who you are today and how you think. The horizontal axis represents time in years.

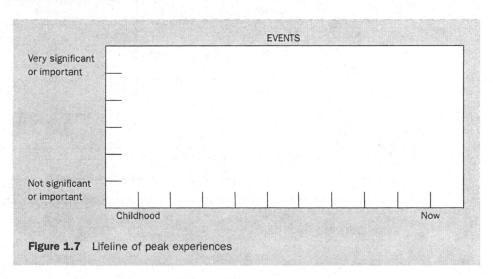

Figure 1.7   Lifeline of peak experiences

Management Consultancy and Skills

Your line should identify times that had major impact on forming your values, styles and orientations. Label each of these 'peak' experiences on your lifeline.

Step 3   On the chart in Figure 1.8, complete as much of your family tree as you can. Below each name, identify the major traits you associate with the person and the major way in which the person influenced your life. Then identify the way in which your family differs from other families you know.

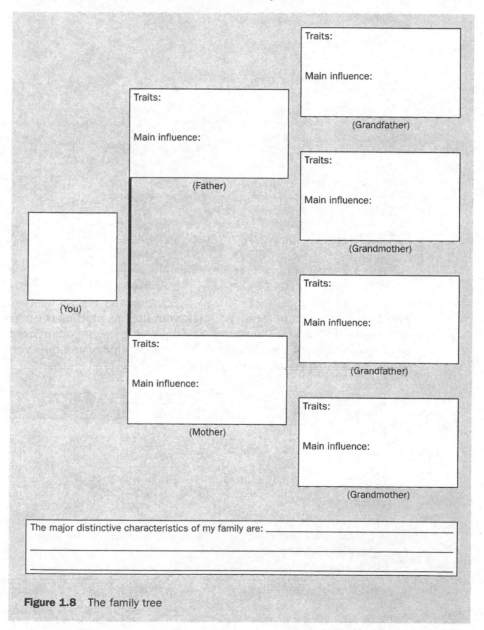

Figure 1.8   The family tree

Step 4 Now combine all the information you have generated in steps 1, 2 and 3 and write an autobiography, essentially an answer to the question, 'Who am I?' Include in your autobiography your answers to the following five questions. Your analysis should include more than just the answers to these questions, but be sure to include them.

1. How would you describe your personal style?

2. What are your main strengths and weaknesses?

3. What behavioural principles lie at the centre of your life?

4. What do you want to achieve in the next five years?

5. What legacy do you want to leave with your life?

Skill Application

ACTIVITY **1.1**

SUGGESTED ASSIGNMENTS

1. Keep a diary for at least the remainder of this course. Record significant discoveries, insights, learning and personal recollections, not just daily activities. Write in your diary at least twice a week. Give yourself some feedback.

2. Write down the comprehensive, consistent and universal principles that guide your behaviour in all circumstances and that you will rarely violate.

3. After completing these personal assessment instruments and discussing their implications with someone else, write a statement or an essay responding to the following four questions:

   • Who am I?
   • What are my main strengths and weaknesses?
   • What do I want to achieve in my life?
   • What legacy do I want to leave?

4. Spend an evening with a close friend or relative discussing your values, cognitive style, attitude towards change and interpersonal orientation. You may want to have that person complete the instruments, giving his or her impressions of you, so you can compare and contrast your scores. Discuss implications for your future and for your relationship.

5. Teach someone else the value of self-awareness in managerial success, and explain the relevance of values maturity, cognitive style, attitudes towards change and interpersonal orientation. Describe the experience in your journal (see 2 above).

Management Consultancy and Skills

ACTIVITY **1.2**

APPLICATION PLAN AND EVALUATION

The intent of this exercise is to help you apply your skills in a real-life, out-of-class setting. Now that you have become familiar with the behavioural guidelines that form the basis of effective skill performance, you will improve the most by trying out those guidelines in an everyday context. The trouble is, unlike a classroom activity in which feedback is immediate and others can assist you with their evaluations, this skill application activity is one you must accomplish and evaluate on your own. There are two parts to this activity. Part 1 helps prepare you to apply the skill. Part 2 helps you evaluate and improve on your experience. Be sure to actually write down answers to each item. Don't short-circuit the process by skipping steps.

Part 1: Plan

1. Write down the two or three aspects of this skill that are most important to you. These may be areas of weakness, areas you most want to improve, or areas that are most salient to a problem you face currently. Identify the specific aspects of this skill that you want to apply.

2. Now identify the setting or the situation in which you will apply this skill. Establish a plan for performance by actually writing down the situation. Who else will be involved? When will you do it? Where will it be done?

3. Identify the specific behaviours you will engage in to apply this skill. Convert the theory into practice.

4. What are the indicators of successful performance? How will you know you have succeeded in being effective? What will indicate that you have performed competently?

Part 2: Evaluation

5. After you have completed your implementation, record the results. What happened? How successful were you? What was the effect on others?

6. How can you improve? What modifications can you make next time? What will you do differently in a similar situation in the future?

7. Looking back on your whole skill practice and application experience, what have you learned? What has been surprising? In what ways might this experience help you in the long term?

Further reading

Institute of Management Foundation (1998) *Test your management skills: the management self-assessment test on disk*. Oxford: Butterworth–Heinemann. (Diskette)

Management Consultancy and Skills

Norton, R. and Burt, V. (1997) *Practical self-development*. London: Institute of Management Foundation.

Palmer, S. (1998) *People and self management*. Oxford: Butterworth-Heinemann.

Pedler, M. Burgoyne, J. and Boydell, T. (1994) *A manager's guide to self-development*, 3rd edn. Maidenhead: McGraw-Hill.

Scutt, C.N. (1997) *Personal effectiveness*. Oxford: Butterworth-Heinemann.

Management Consultancy and Skills

235

Managing Stress

SKILL DEVELOPMENT OUTLINE

Skill Pre-assessment surveys
- Stress management
- Time management
- Type A personality inventory
- Social Readjustment Rating Scale (SRRS)-Life Change Units (LCU)

Skill Learning material
- Stress at work
- Stress for individuals
- Stressors
- Eliminating stressors
- Developing resilience
- Temporary stress-reduction techniques
- Summary
- Behavioural guidelines

Skill Analysis cases
- The day at the beach
- The case of the missing time

Skill Practice exercises
- The small-wins strategy

Skill Application activities
- Life-balance analysis
- Deep relaxation
- Monitoring and managing Time
- Personal stressors
- Teaching others
- Implement techniques
- Application plan and evaluation

LEARNING OBJECTIVES

To increase proficiency in:
- eliminating stressors
- developing resilience
- coping with temporary stress

90

Stress, like change, is an ever-present and growing element in our lives, as students and as managers. Unfortunately many books on stress tend to deal with the clinical aspects – they are not designed for 'well people'. In this book we hope to strike a balance. We accept that stress is a part of all our working lives and that without stress not only would things be intolerably dull for most of us, but also very few things would be done. Tolerable levels of stress are the winding mechanism of our world. As individuals we develop strategies to deal with accustomed levels of stress. We have simple techniques for dealing with temporary surges and stronger techniques for negotiating our way out of uncomfortable but predictable pressures. We can 'stand on the shoulders' of those before us and learn from their skills and application. However, we also need to recognise that prolonged and personally intolerable levels of stress can lead to serious illness, although we have, as a right, the alternative of engineering our lives so that this does not occur. This book does not suggest that we all take up farming in one of the remote places of the world, but that there are easily acquired skills that will make our lives easier, and more personally fulfilling and fruitful, without financial penalty. The skills we will discuss will assist us in our studies and make us more efficient and effective in our jobs. By learning about stress in what we feel is a stress-free way, we will not only help ourselves but also those around us. Stress is a contagious disease. Therefore, we are offering a diagnosis, a prognosis and helpful advice towards a cure, all of which you can practise in the safety of these pages before trying them out in what you may find to be an unforgiving world.

Skill Pre-assessment

We will begin with a number of surveys designed to:

- explore your own responses to situations you may find stressful
- look at the techniques you use to manage your own time
- help you to establish a personality *type*
- consider the factors that others find stressful and introduce you to methods of coping.

As with the rest of the book, we would like you to complete the questionnaires before starting the chapter. We feel the process will set the agenda for what is to follow. The first questionnaire is designed for acting managers but may well provide you, if you are a student, with insights of the managerial world. After completing the chapter, the readers should be able to relate what they have read, and hopefully discussed, to their own world and set about personal action planning.

91

SURVEY **2.1**

STRESS MANAGEMENT

Step 1 For each statement circle a number on the rating scale in the Pre-assessment column on the left. Your answers should reflect your attitudes and behaviour as they are **now**, not as you would like them to be. Be honest. When you have completed the survey, use the scoring key in Appendix 1 to identify the skill areas discussed that are most important for you to master. The process of improving these skill areas should help you with your learning objectives.

Step 2 When you have completed the chapter and the Skill Application assignments, review your responses in the right-hand Post-assessment column to measure your progress. If your score remains low in specific skill areas, use the behavioural guidelines at the end of the Skill Learning section to guide your Application Planning.

RATING SCALE

1 = Strongly disagree   **2** = Disagree   **3** = Slightly disagree
4 = Slightly agree   **5** = Agree   **6** = Strongly agree

	Assessment	
	Pre-	Post-
When faced with stressful or time-pressured situations		
1. I make lists, set priorities, use time diaries to manage my time well.	___	___
2. I maintain a programme of regular exercise for fitness.	___	___
3. I maintain trusting relationships with those with whom I can share my frustrations.	___	___
4. I practice relaxation techniques such as deep breathing and muscle relaxation.	___	___
5. I make sure that less important things don't drive out the more important.	___	___
6. I maintain balance in my life by pursuing interests outside of work.	___	___
7. I have a good relationship with someone who serves as mentor or adviser.	___	___
8. I use other people appropriately to complete what has to be done.	___	___
9. I encourage people who come to me with problems or concerns to consider solutions, not just questions.	___	___
10. I strive to redefine problems as opportunities for improvement.	___	___
When I get others to do things for me		
11. I check they have the means and authority to do what needs to be done.	___	___
12. I specify clearly what I want achieved and how much they can do without referring it back to me.	___	___
13. I delegate effectively passing on information and providing resources.	___	___

14. When I delegate I explain exactly what is required.   ____   ____

15. I monitor and maintain accountability for delegated tasks on a regular basis   ____   ____

SURVEY **2.2**

TIME MANAGEMENT

Students and practising managers need to manage their time. The first section of the questionnaire is universal but the second section, although it may provide insights for students, is designed specifically for working managers.

In responding to the statements, circle the number that indicates the frequency with which you do each activity. Assess your behaviour as it is, not as you would like it to be. How useful this questionnaire will be depends on your ability to assess your own behaviour.

Turn to Appendix 1 to find the scoring key and an interpretation of your scores.

RATING SCALE

0 = Never   **1** = Seldom   **2** = Sometimes   **3** = Usually   **4** = Always

---

Section I

1. I read selectively, skimming until I find what is important, then highlighting it.   0 1 2 3 4

2. I make a list of tasks to accomplish each day.   0 1 2 3 4

3. I keep everything in its proper place at work.   0 1 2 3 4

4. I prioritise the tasks I have to do according to their importance and urgency.   0 1 2 3 4

5. I concentrate on one major task at a time, but do multiple trivial tasks together.   0 1 2 3 4

6. I make a list of short five- or ten-minute tasks to do.   0 1 2 3 4

7. I divide large projects into smaller, separate stages.   0 1 2 3 4

8. I identify the 20 per cent of my tasks that will produce 80 per cent of the results.   0 1 2 3 4

9. I do the most important tasks at my best time during the day.   0 1 2 3 4

10. I arrange to have some time during each day when I can work uninterrupted.   0 1 2 3 4

11. I don't procrastinate. I do today what needs to be done.   0 1 2 3 4

12. I keep track of the use of my time with devices such as a time log.   0 1 2 3 4

13. I set deadlines for myself.   0 1 2 3 4

14. I do something productive whenever I am waiting.   0 1 2 3 4

15. I try to confine my fire-fighting to one set time during the day.   0 1 2 3 4

16. I set myself targets to finish at least one thing every day.   0 1 2 3 4

17. I set some time during the day for personal time – thinking, planning, exercise.   0   1   2   3   4
18. I confine my time for 'worrying' to one particular time during the day.   0   1   2   3   4
19. I have clearly defined long-term objectives towards which I work.   0   1   2   3   4
20. I always seek to find ways to use my time more efficiently.   0   1   2   3   4

Section II: for working managers

1. I hold routine meetings at the end of the day.   0   1   2   3   4
2. I hold all short meetings informally – sitting or standing appropriately.   0   1   2   3   4
3. I set a time limit at the outset of each meeting.   0   1   2   3   4
4. I cancel scheduled meetings that are not necessary.   0   1   2   3   4
5. I have a written agenda circulated before each meeting.   0   1   2   3   4
6. I stick to the agenda so that all understand their required actions for each item.   0   1   2   3   4
7. I ensure that someone takes minutes and watches the time.   0   1   2   3   4
8. I start all meetings on time wherever possible.   0   1   2   3   4
9. I prepare prompt action minutes of meetings and follow them through.   0   1   2   3   4
10. When people come with problems I listen and ask them to suggest solutions.   0   1   2   3   4
11. I meet visitors in the doorway.   0   1   2   3   4
12. I go to subordinates' offices when feasible so that I can control when I leave.   0   1   2   3   4
13. I leave at least one-fourth of my day free from meetings and appointments.   0   1   2   3   4
14. I have someone else who can answer my calls and greet visitors where possible.   0   1   2   3   4
15. I have one place where I can work without being interrupted.   0   1   2   3   4
16. I process all the papers I receive – action or ignore – nothing is 'held'.   0   1   2   3   4
17. I keep my workplace clear of everything except the things I am working on.   0   1   2   3   4
18. I work to delegate tasks where others have the background and skills to assist.   0   1   2   3   4
19. I define the freedom of initiative others have when I delegate a task.   0   1   2   3   4
20. I am happy to let others take the credit for tasks they accomplish.   0   1   2   3   4

SURVEY **2.3**

TYPE A PERSONALITY INVENTORY

Rate the extent to which each of the following statements is typical of you most of the time. Focus on your general way of behaving and feeling. There are no right or wrong answers. When you have finished, turn to the scoring key in Appendix 1 to interpret your scores.

Management Consultancy and Skills

RATING SCALE

The statement is:
1, not typical of me;   **2**, somewhat typical of me;   **3**, typical of me

1. My greatest satisfaction comes from doing things better than others.   ____
2. I tend to bring the theme of a conversation around to things I'm interested in.   ____
3. In conversations, I use strong movements to emphasise my points.   ____
4. I move, walk and eat rapidly.   ____
5. I feel as though I can accomplish more than others.   ____
6. I feel guilty when I relax or do nothing for several hours or days.   ____
7. It doesn't take much to get me to argue.   ____
8. I feel impatient with the rate at which most events take place.   ____
9. Having more than others is important to me.   ____
10. One aspect of my life (e.g. work, family care, school, etc.) dominates all others.   ____
11. I frequently regret not being able to control my temper.   ____
12. I find myself hurrying others in conversation and even finishing their sentences for them.   ____
13. People who avoid competition have low self-confidence.   ____
14. To do something well you have to concentrate and screen out all distractions.   ____
15. I feel others' mistakes and errors cause me needless aggravation.   ____
16. I find it intolerable to watch others perform tasks I know I can do faster.   ____
17. Getting ahead in my job is a major personal goal.   ____
18. I simply don't have enough time to lead a well-balanced life.   ____
19. I take out my frustration with my own imperfections on others.   ____
20. I frequently try to do two or more things simultaneously.   ____
21. When I encounter a competitive person, I feel a need to challenge him or her.   ____
22. I tend to fill up my spare time with thoughts and activities related to my work.   ____
23. I am frequently upset by the unfairness of life.   ____
24. I find it anguishing to wait in line.   ____

Source: Adapted from Friedman and Rosenman (1974)

SURVEY **2.4**

SOCIAL READJUSTMENT RATING SCALE (SRRS) – LIFE CHANGE UNITS (LCU)

Consider this table and answer the questions that follow.

Management Consultancy and Skills

Life event	Rank '65	LCU '65	Rank '95	LCU '95
Death of spouse	1	100	1	119
Divorce	2	73	2	98
Marital separation from mate	3	65	4	79
Detention in jail or other institution	4	63	7	75
Death of a close family member	5	63	3	92
Major personal injury or illness	6	53	6	77
Marriage	7	50	19	50
Losing your job	8	47	5	79
Marital reconciliation with partner	9	45	13	57
Retirement from work	10	45	16	54
Major change in the health or behaviour of a family member	11	44	14	56
Pregnancy	12	40	9	66
Sexual difficulties	13	39	21	45
Gaining a new family member	14	39	12	57
Major business readjustment	15	39	10	62
Major change in financial state	16	38	15	56
Death of a close friend	17	37	8	70
Change to a different type of work	18	36	17	51
Change in form or number of arguments with spouse	19	35	18	51
Taking out a mortgage or loan for a major purchase	20	31	23	44
Foreclosure on a mortgage or loan	21	30	11	61
Major change in responsibilities at work	22	29	24	43
Son or daughter leaving home	23	29	22	44
Trouble with in-laws	24	29	28	38
Outstanding personal achievement	25	28	29	37
Spouse beginning or ceasing work outside the home	26	26	20	46
Beginning or ending formal education	27	26	27	38
Major change in living conditions	28	25	25	42
Change in personal habits	29	24	36	27
Trouble with the boss	30	23	33	29
Major change in working hours or conditions	31	20	30	36
Moving home	32	20	26	41
Change to a new college, school, university	33	20	31	35
Major change in usual type and/or amount of recreation	34	19	34	29
Major change in outside activities – church, etc.	35	19	42	22
Major change in social activities	36	18	38	27
Taking out a mortgage or loan for a lesser purchase	37	17	35	28
Major change in sleeping habits	38	16	40	26
Major change in number of family get-togethers	39	15	39	26
Major change in eating habits	40	15	37	27
Holiday	41	13	41	25
Christmas	42	12	32	30
Minor violations of the law	43	11	43	22
Grand Mean LCU values (for all events)		**34**		**49**

Sources: Miller *et al.* (1997); Holmes and Rahe (1967)

Management Consultancy and Skills

EXERCISE BASED ON THE SRRS
SOURCES OF PERSONAL STRESS

1. Identify the factors that produced the most stress for you over the past few years. Consider whether there is a pattern?

2. Accepting that the relative value of the stressors given in the above table are based on work in the USA in 1965 and then 20 years later using samples of some 400 people, compare how seriously your 'life events' affected you on the same scale of 1 to 100. Thus 'major personal injury or illness' is sixth with a relative value as a stressor of 77 (53 in 1965) and in your view 'Personal injury' would only have an impact of say 30 – What helped you cope?

List the factors that give you most stress and keep these in your mind as you complete the chapter.

Skill Learning

Stress at work

The prevalence of stress

The problems currently associated with stress at work appear to be particularly acute and are becoming worse in Europe and the USA. Miller and Rahr (1997), working in the USA, found the top 43 stressors were now 45 per cent more stressful than they were in 1965. We will discuss the pattern of change later. Stress is not an issue for individuals in the abstract, the effects of stress are important commercially. Charlesworth (1997), working specifically with managers the Institute of Management, conducted a survey of 1,100 managers and showed that 270,000 people take time off every day through work-related stress at a total cost to the economy of £7 billion. He found that 85 per cent of the respondents reported increased workloads and 50 per cent agreed that they had a 'great increase in workload since 1994'. The Samaritans, a charity in the UK dealing with individuals considering suicide, showed stress as having more sinister consequences. This was confirmed by a study for the British Heart Foundation which has estimated that coronary heart disease costs £200 per employee per year and that some coronary heart disease can be attributable to stress. Davidson and Sutherland (1993), however, suggest an indirect linkage. Common behavioural responses to stress, such as cigarette smoking, poor dietary habits, physical inactivity and/or escapist drinking, are all risk factors for cardiovascular disease. Thus, as a consequence, stress may be both directly and indirectly implicated as a causal factor in the aetiology of heart disease.

The financial cost of stress to industry

The costs of work-related stress, however, extend beyond coronary heart disease. Kearns (1986) comments that 60 per cent of absence from work is caused by stress-related

Management Consultancy and Skills

243

illness, while Gill (1987) reports that approximately 100 million working days are lost each year because people cannot face going to work. Additionally, Cooper *et al.* (1988) note that there is mounting evidence to suggest that days lost in British Industry due to mental and stress-related causes are on the increase. This view is further endorsed by a recent estimate completed by Summers (1990) for the Confederation of British Industry, which showed the annual cost of stress-related absenteeism in labour turnover to be around £1.5 billion. A further factor is the growing movement to litigation. Ian Campbell (1995) details recent successful compensation claims over work-related stress. His advice is that companies would be wise to introduce risk management programmes to avoid such claims in the future. He sees the programmes as having the direct effect of avoiding litigation and also of combating lost productivity.

The cost to individuals

The personal costs of job-related stress can be very high. This example is adapted from an Associated Press article.

> Patrick was an ambulance attendant and the job was getting to him. He was becoming too involved in the continuous insights into personal tragedy and the personal alienation caused by the shift pattern. His marriage was in trouble and his only child was having respiratory problems that could well involve an operation. He was drinking too much. One night it all blew up.
>
> On the way to pick up his ambulance a new manager called him over and told him that his cab was dirty and he should have it cleaned before meeting the public. Patrick dumped his frustrations and had to be restrained from hitting the 'new broom'.
>
> His mildest comment was: 'If you came out and did the job instead of sitting at a desk you would not worry about ashtrays.' The manager was left forming a report that Patrick thought might well lose him his job. He desperately needed the money.
>
> It was Patrick's turn to ride in the back while his partner drove. Their first call was for a man whose leg had been cut off by a train. His screaming and agony were horrifying, but the second call was worse. It was a child beating. As the attendant treated the youngster's bruised body and snapped bones, he thought of his own child. His fury grew.
>
> Immediately after leaving the child at the hospital, the attendants were sent out to help a heart attack victim seen lying in a street. When they arrived, however, they found not a cardiac patient but a drunk who had passed out. As they lifted the man into the ambulance, their frustration and anger came to a head. They decided to give the drunk a ride he would remember.
>
> The ambulance vaulted over railroad tracks at high speed. The driver took the corners as fast as he could, flinging the drunk from side to side in the back. To the attendants, it was a joke.
>
> Suddenly, the drunk began having a real heart attack. The attendant in the back leaned over the drunk and started shouting. 'Die, you fool!' he yelled. 'Die!' He watched as the drunk shuddered. He watched as the drunk died. By the time they

reached the hospital, they had their stories straight. Dead on arrival, they said. Nothing they could do.

Patrick talked about that night in a counselling session on 'professional burnout' – a growing problem in high-stress jobs.

As this story illustrates, stress can produce totally dysfunctional outcomes – a man in this case was killed. Less dramatically, the personal outcomes can range from the inability to concentrate, through anxiety and depression, stomach disorders and heart disease. Overall we have a loss of personal resilience to disease of all types. For organisations, consequences range from absenteeism and job dissatisfaction, to high accident and turnover rates.

The role of management

A 25-year study of employee surveys revealed that incompetent management is the largest cause of workplace stress. In three out of the four surveys employees put their relationships with their immediate supervisors as the worst aspect of the job. Research shows that stress not only affects the physical well-being of workers but also produces less visible (though equally detrimental) consequences in the workplace. Thus dysfunctionally stressed managers tend to:

- perceive information selectively and see only that which confirms their previous biases
- become very intolerant of ambiguity and demanding of right answers
- consider only a single approach to a problem
- overestimate how fast time is passing (hence, they always feel rushed)
- adopt a short-term perspective or crisis mentality and cease to consider long-term implications
- have less ability to make fine distinctions in problems, so that complexity and nuances are missed
- consult and listen to others less
- rely on old habits to cope with current situations
- have less ability to generate creative thoughts and unique solutions to problems

Sources: Staw *et al.* (1981); Weick (1984)

Stress affects employees in a personally negative way and reduces the effective behaviour – listening, making good decisions, solving problems effectively, planning, and generating new ideas. Developing the skill of managing stress therefore can have significant advantages to all concerned. The ability to deal appropriately with stress not only enhances individual self-development, but can also have an enormous financial impact on entire organisations.

Unfortunately, most of the scientific literature on stress focuses on its consequences. Too little examines how to cope effectively with stress and even less addresses how to prevent stress. We begin our discussion by presenting a framework for understanding stress and learning how to cope with it. Here we will explain the major types of stressors faced by managers, the primary reactions to stress and the reasons some people experience more negative reactions than others. In the last section, we will present principles for managing and adapting to stress, along with specific examples and behavioural guidelines.

Stress for individuals

One way to understand the dynamics of stress is to think of it as the product of a 'force field' (Lewin, 1951). Kurt Lewin suggested that all individuals and organisations exist in an environment filled with reinforcing or opposing forces (i.e., stresses). These forces act to stimulate or inhibit the performance desired by the individual. Figure 2.1 indicates this – a person's level of performance in organisation results with stress from factors that may either complement or contradict one another. Certain forces drive or motivate changes in behaviour, while other forces restrain or block those changes.

According to Lewin's theory, the forces affecting individuals are normally balanced in the force field. The strength of the driving forces is exactly matched by the strength of the restraining forces. (In the figure, longer arrows indicate stronger forces.) Performance changes when the forces become out of balance. If the driving forces become stronger than the restraining forces, or more numerous or enduring, then change occurs. Conversely, if restraining forces become stronger or more numerous than driving forces, change occurs in the opposite direction. Feelings of stress are a product of a combination of stressors from inside ourselves or from our immediate environment. These stressors are the driving forces in our model; they exert pressure on the individuals to change their existing levels of performance – physiologically, psychologically and interpersonally. Unrestrained, those forces can lead to pathological results (e.g., anxiety, heart disease and mental breakdown). However, most people have developed a certain resilience, or restraining forces, to counteract the stressors thus inhibiting their pathological effects. These restraining forces include behaviour patterns, psychological characteristics and supportive

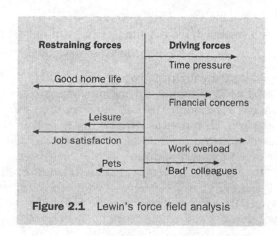

Figure 2.1 Lewin's force field analysis

social relationships. Strong restraining forces lead to low heart rates, good interpersonal relationships, emotional stability and effective stress management. Without the restraining forces, which have to be developed by individuals over time, the stressors reign.

Of course, stress produces positive as well as negative effects. In the absence of any stress, people feel completely bored and lack any inclination to act. Even when high levels of stress are experienced, equilibrium can be restored quickly if sufficient resilience is present. In the case of the ambulance driver, for example, multiple stressors overpowered the available restraining forces and burnout occurred. Before such an extreme state is reached, however, individuals typically progress through three stages of reactions: an alarm stage, a resistance stage, and an exhaustion stage.

Reactions and defence mechanisms

We all have our own first sign of being under stress – a first sign may be prickly heat in the legs, or a sudden wish to go to the toilet or perhaps a dryness of the mouth. As functioning adults we recognise these first signs and ignore them at our peril. We accept the first alarm sign as a notice of anxiety or fear, recognising that some stressor is perceived by us as a threat, or by sorrow or depression if the stressor is perceived as a loss. A feeling of shock or confusion may result if the stressor is particularly acute. Physiologically, the individual's energy resources are mobilised and heart rate, blood pressure and alertness increase – hence the prickly heat from our flooded capillaries or the dryness of the mouth. The reactions are largely self-correcting if the stressor is of brief duration, but if the stressor continues we move into a resistance stage, in which defence mechanisms predominate and the body begins to store up excess energy. In the veldt of our ancestors we were preparing for 'fight or flight', but in the office, these responses are seldom appropriate; however, our bodies do not know this.

Five types of defence mechanism are typical of most people who experience extended levels of stress.

1. Aggressive – the stressor is attacked directly. It may also involve violence against oneself, other people or even objects (e.g., kicking the table).
2. Regression – the adoption of patterns of response that were successful earlier, perhaps in childhood (childish behaviours such as sulking).
3. Denial – forgetting, avoiding or redefining the stressor.
4. Escape – in physical or psychological form including an escape to fantasy.

   > We were working with a manager whose company was taken over by a larger group and whose job was definitely at risk. He chose to take a three-week holiday in India until the 'noise' subsided. His defence mechanism was successful and against all the odds he resumed his job as Personnel Director – now of the extended group.

5. Fixation – a response repeated of its effectiveness – repeatedly redialling a phone number or rechecking that we have 'all the notes'.

If our defence mechanisms work to reduce such symptoms as high blood pressure, anxiety or other disorders the only signs of prolonged stress need be

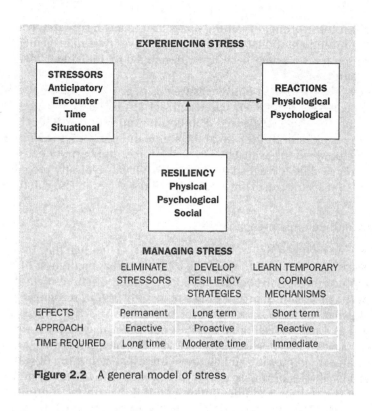

Figure 2.2   A general model of stress

an increase in apparent defensiveness. However, if the pressures overwhelm our defences, our available energy is exhausted and the body may well be defeated.

While each reaction stage may be experienced as being uncomfortable, the exhaustion stage is the most dangerous. When stressors overpower or outlast the resilient capacity of individuals, or their ability to defend against them, negative personal and organisational consequences may well occur. The consequences may be physiological (heart disease, ulcers), psychological (severe depression) or inter-personally (hostility).

Figure 2.2 identifies the major categories of stressors (driving forces) managers experience, as well as the major attributes of resilience (restraining forces) that inhibit the negative aspects of stress.

Coping with stress

Individuals vary in the extent to which they are affected by stress. Some people are what Eliot and Breo (1984) labelled 'hot reactors', meaning they have a predisposition to experience extremely negative reactions to stress. For others, stress has less serious consequences. Think in terms of some athletes who perform at their peak in 'the big game' while others are crushed. Managers are no different.

Our physical condition, personality characteristics and social support mechanisms work with us producing resiliency or the capacity to cope effectively with stress. In

Table 2.1 Coping strategies

Approach	Short term	Medium term	Long term
	Immediate	Delayed	Considered
	Reactive	Proactive	Proactive – eliminate
	Example – relaxation	Examples – job	the stressor
	techniques	redesign, life style	Example – divorce,
		changes. . . .	quitting job . . .

effect, resiliency serves as a form of inoculation against the effects of stress. It eliminates exhaustion. One classification of those most liable to 'suffer' from dysfunctional stress reaction is the Type A Personality Inventory, the interpretation of which is given in the 'scoring key' at the end of the book.

An effective way of coping with stress can be seen through a hierarchy of strategies for personal stress management, the most effective being those concerned with managing stress.

The most obvious way to manage stress is to eliminate or minimise the stressors by simply eliminating the situations that cause them – the proactive strategy (Weick, 1979). In practice few of us have complete control over our environment or circumstances and elimination or avoidance is more easily said than done in the short or medium term. Imagine a broker on the floor of the stockmarket – the job is *about* stress and he or she can always leave if the pressure does not suit. A second approach that the broker will certainly adopt to survive, and retain the job, is to try to increase his or her personal resiliency – the proactive strategy (Table 2.1). He or she may develop ways of releasing tensions in sport, take up yoga or reduce weight. Both these strategies take time and a reactive short-term may well be the best way to handle the immediate issues. Reactive strategies such as controlled breathing can be applied on the spot as temporary remedies against the ill effects of stress when the first warning signs are recognised. Relaxation techniques are covered later in the chapter. Most people do rely first on temporary reactive methods to cope with stress because these actions can be implemented immediately. But reactive strategies also have to be repeated whenever stressors are encountered because their effects are short-lived. The unwise broker may adopt dysfunctional short-term strategies such as excessive alcohol intake, heavy smoking, sleeping pills or letting off steam through anger. All these can become habit-forming and harmful in themselves. We need to put medium-term strategies into place whenever we realise that the stressors that get to us are persistent. It takes more time and effort to develop proactive resiliency strategies, but although the payoff is delayed the effects are more long-lasting. The best and most permanent strategies are those that eliminate stressors altogether. They require the longest time to implement and may involve complex arrangements but since the stress is purged, the payoff is enduring. It is our choice whether we, as the stockbroker, wish to continue with the material rewards of weathering stress or live longer. It is no surprise that many

Management Consultancy and Skills

trading floor workers plan for an early retirement. Death is God's way of saying slow down!

Stressors

In the next section we will work through the three components of the stress model shown in Figure 2.2.

Classification of stressors

Time stressors generally result from having too much to do in too little time, or the exact opposite. These are the most common and most pervasive sources of stress faced by managers in corporations (Mintzberg, 1973; Carlson, 1951; Sayles, 1964).

> In the story of the ambulance drivers presented earlier, time stressors were evidenced by the driver's work overload – the drivers felt compelled to accomplish a large number of tasks in a short time, but were not in control of the time available.
>
> Our culture seems obsessed with time and appears to grow more time conscious every year. The bleeping wrist watch alarms may have been replaced by the mobile phones, but the purpose is the same – to make use of our every moment, as if there is some great time diary in the sky. This constant concern with time is a significant source of stress. A variety of researchers, for example, have studied the relationships between being expected to take on an increasing range of potentially conflicting, ambiguous responsibilities and chronic time pressures, against the psychological and physiological dysfunctions (French and Caplan, 1972). The researchers found significant relationships between the presence of time stressors and job dissatisfaction, tension, perceived threat, heart rate, cholesterol levels, skin resistance and other factors.

The presence of temporary time stressors, however, may serve as motivators for getting work done; some individuals accomplish much more when faced with an immediate deadline than when left to work at their own pace. Against this, a constant state of time pressure – having too much to do and not enough time to do it – is usually harmful.

Encounter stressors

Encounter stressors are caused by flawed interpersonal interactions. Quarrels debilitate, be they with friends, flatmates, or one's spouse. Trying to work with an employee or supervisor with whom there has been an interpersonal conflict, or trying to accomplish a task in a group that is divided by lack of trust and cohesion, is often unproductive and usually stressful.

> For Patrick the ambulance man, the encounter stressor that 'wound him up' was the meeting with the new manager. His cab was dirty and in other circumstances he would have acknowledged the fault and the manager's right to comment. This particular night the incident was one factor that led to manslaughter.

Encounter stressors arise from three types of conflicts:

- Role conflicts, in which roles performed by group members are incompatible
- Issue conflicts, in which disagreement exists over how to define or solve a problem
- Interaction conflicts, in which individuals fail to get along well because of mutual antagonism (Hamner and Organ, 1978).

In our own research we have found that encounter stressors in organisations can reduce both work satisfaction and actual productivity (Cameron, Kim and Whetten, 1987 a & b). Other workers have found encounter stressors to be at the very heart of most organisational dysfunction (Likert, 1967), most frequently affecting managers with responsibility for people rather than for equipment. The highest levels of encounter stress exist among managers who interact frequently with other people and have responsibility for individuals in the workplace (French and Caplan, 1972). Mishra (1993), reviewer of literature on interpersonal trust, showed that a lack of trust among individuals not only blocks effective communication, information sharing, decision competence and problem-solving capabilities, but also results in high levels of personal stress. In a United States survey of workers, encounter stressors were cited as a major cause of burnout. When workers were reported as feeling not free to interact socially, experiencing workplace conflict, not being able to talk openly to managers, feeling unsupported by fellow employees, being stifled by red tape, and not feeling recognised, burnout was significantly higher than when those encounter stressors were not present. Of the ten most significant stressors associated with burnout, seven dealt with encounter stressors. The other three were situational stressors, to which we turn next.

Situational stressors

Situational stressors arise from the environment in which a person lives or from individual circumstances. One of the most common forms of situational stress is a poor working environment. For the ambulance drivers, for example, this would include continual crises, long hours and isolation from colleagues.

One of the most well-researched links between situational stressors and negative consequences involves rapid change, particularly the effects of changes in life events (Wolff *et al.*, 1950; Holmes and Rahe, 1970; Miller and Rahe, 1997). The Social Readjustment Rating Scale (SRRS) was introduced in 1967 to track the number of changes some 427 individuals had experienced over the past 12 months. Since changes in some events were thought to be more stressful than others, a scaling method was used to assign weights to each life event. Numerous studies among a variety of cultures, age groups and occupations have confirmed the relative weightings in the 1967 instrument (see Rahe *et al.*, 1980) which generally hold true regardless of culture, age or occupation. You completed this instrument in the Pre-assessment section and may like to look at your own rating now.

Statistical relationships between the amount of life-event change and physical illness and injury have been found consistently among managers (Kobasa, 1979), sports figures (Holmes and Masuda, 1974), naval personnel (Rahe, 1974), and the general population (Jenkins, 1976). For example, scores of 150 points or below result in a probability of less than 37 per cent that a serious illness will occur in the next year, but the probability increases to about 50 per cent with scores of 151–300. Those who score over 300 on the SRRS have an 80 per cent chance of serious illness (Holmes and Rahe, 1967).

Holmes and Holmes (1970) studied the extent to which daily health changes occurred as a result of life-event changes. Rather than focusing on major illness or injuries, they recorded minor symptoms such as headache, nausea, fever, backache, eyestrain, etc., over 1,300 work days. The results revealed high correlations between scores in life-event changes and the chronic presence of these symptoms. As we have pointed out earlier, a 45 per cent increase the mean value of the intensity of the events has been recorded over a 30-year period. The change of the ranking of the events may show specific changes in American society based on and not be reflected in European culture. We must caution, of course, that a high score on the SRRS does not necessarily mean that an individual is going to become ill or be injured – they are average values. A variety of coping skills and personal characteristics, to be discussed later, may counteract those tendencies. The point to be made here is that situational stressors are important factors to consider in learning to manage stress skilfully. For example, we were using the SRRS with a group of Hungarian managers, one of whom was an interpreter. She reported that in one year of her life she had a score of over 300. Wanting to talk, she explained that she had been released from Auschwitz, got married and had her first child – all in one year. In 1995 she still looked remarkably well for her years.

Anticipatory stressors

Anticipatory stressors arise from disagreeable events that we feel could occur – unpleasant things that have not yet happened, but might happen. Stress results from the anticipation or fear of the event.

Patrick, the Ambulance man, was concerned for his child and what might happen 'if she needed an operation', the boss's report and losing his job plus the consequences of having no money and the possibility of being found out about the drunk. Anticipatory stressors were probably the focus of his counselling sessions. We have met many people like Patrick in our work and getting them to face 'the worst scenario' is a great challenge.

Anticipatory stressors can be used for manipulation. Schein (1960) reported that dramatic behavioural and psychological changes occurred in American prisoners in the Korean War. He identified anticipatory stressors (e.g., threat of severe punishment) as major contributors to psychological and physiological pathology among the prisoners.

Anticipatory stressors need not be highly unpleasant or severe, however, to produce stress. For example, Schachter (1959), Milgram (1963) and others induced high levels of stress by telling individuals that they would experience a loud noise or a mild shock, or that someone else might become uncomfortable because of their actions. Fear of failure or fear of embarrassment in front of peers is a common anticipatory stressor. The middle-age anxieties about retirement and losing vitality have been identified by Levinson (1978), Hall (1976) and others as common stressors.

Table 2.2 Management strategies for eliminating stressors

Type of stressor	Elimination strategy
Time	Time Management Delegation
Encounter	Delegation Interpersonal competence
Situational	Work re-design
Anticipatory	Prioritising Planning

Eliminating stressors

Because eliminating stressors is a permanent stress-reduction strategy, it is by far the most desirable. It would be impossible, and perhaps not even an advantage, for individuals to eliminate all the stressors they encounter, but they can effectively eliminate those that are harmful. One way is to 'evolve' the environment rather than merely 'reacting' to it (Weick, 1979). Accepting that we can take control of the world around us and not merely accept 'the slings and arrows' passively, is a release in itself which leads to the elimination of the stressors. By working to create more favourable environmental circumstances we can rationally and systematically eliminate stressors.

Table 2.2 outlines several ways in which the four kinds of stressor can be eliminated.

Eliminating time stressors

Time stressors are often the greatest sources of stress for managers. Research by Mintzberg (1973) and Kotter (1987) showed, for example, that managers experience frequent interruptions (over 50 per cent of their activities last nine minutes or less); they seldom engage in long-range planning but allow fragmentation, brevity and variety to characterise their time use. On the average, no manager works more than 20 minutes without interruption, and most of a manager's time is controlled by the most tiresome, persistent and energetic people (Carlson, 1951). Junior managers can be in a worse position. Guest (1956) found that industrial foremen engage in between 237 and 1,073 separate incidents a day with no real breaks.

Effective time management can enable managers to gain control over their time and to organise their fragmented, chaotic environment.

Two different sets of skills are important for managing time effectively and for eliminating time stressors. The first focuses on efficiently using time on a daily basis while the second focuses on effectively using time over the long-term. Because the effectiveness approach to time management serves as the foundation for the efficiency approach, we will explain it first. We will then review the tools and techniques for achieving efficiency in time use.

Time management

Overload and lack of control are the greatest sources of time stress for most of us – managers or not. Somehow, no matter how much time is available, it seems to get filled up and squeezed out. Probably the most commonly prescribed solutions for attacking problems of time stress are to use diaries and planners, to generate 'to-do' lists, and to learn to say 'no'. But although almost everyone has tried such tactics, nearly all of us still claim to be under enormous time stress. This is not to say that diaries, lists and saying 'no' are not useful, but they do not eliminate the cause, they only reduce the symptoms. To reduce time stressors we must learn to be more effective and this means we:

- spend more time on important matters, not just urgent matters
- distinguish clearly between what they view as important versus what they view as urgent
- focus on outputs rather than processes
- stop feeling guilty when we say 'no'.

The 'time management matrix' (Figure 2.3) is the key to improved effectiveness (Covey, 1988). Key activities are categorised on a scale of Importance and Urgency. Important activities are those that produce a valued output or achieve a worthwhile purpose. Urgent activities are those that demand immediate attention.

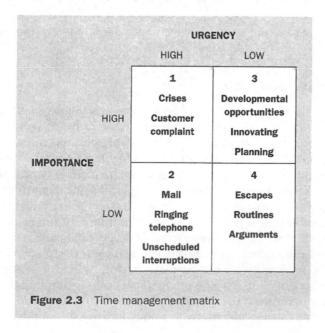

Figure 2.3 Time management matrix

They are associated with a need expressed by someone else, or they relate to an uncomfortable problem or situation that requires a solution as soon as possible.

Activities such as handling employee crises or customer complaints are both *urgent* and *important*. A ringing telephone, the arrival of the post or unscheduled interruptions might be examples of *urgent but potentially unimportant* activities. *Important but non-urgent* activities include developmental opportunities, innovating, planning and so on.

Unimportant and *non-urgent* activities are escapes and routines that people may pursue but which produce little valuable payoff – for example, computer games, small talk, daydreaming, shuffling paper and arguing.

Activities in the *important/urgent* quadrant (Cell 1) usually dominate the lives of managers. They are seen as activities that demand immediate attention. Attending a meeting, responding to a call or request, interacting with a customer, or completing a report might all legitimately be defined as important/urgent activities. The trouble with spending all one's time on activities in this quadrant, however, is that they all require the manager to *react*. Someone else usually controls them, and they may or may not lead to a result the manager wants to achieve.

The problem is even worse in the *unimportant/urgent* quadrant (Cell 2). Demands by others that may meet their needs but that serve only as deflections or interruptions to the manager's agenda only escalate time stressors. Because we may not achieve results that are meaningful, purposeful and valued – important to us – the stressors persist, we experience overload and a lack of control. Being purely reactive is not a solution to anything.

If the time stressors persist we generally try to escape into *unimportant/non-urgent* activities (Cell 4). We seek to escape by attempting to shut out the world or put everything on hold. Stress may be temporarily relieved but no long-term solutions are implemented, so time stress comes back with perhaps more urgency. One can spend 95 per cent of life in reactive battles with crises and 5 per cent in relieving tensions that could well be avoided in the first place.

A better alternative is to focus on activities in the *important/non-urgent* quadrant (Cell 3). These activities might be labelled *opportunities* instead of *problems*. They are oriented towards accomplishing high priority results. They prevent problems from occurring, or build systems that eliminate problems rather than just coping with them. Preparation, preventive maintenance, planning, building resiliency and organising are all activities that are crucial for long-term success. Cyert and March (1963) discuss this use of 'slack resources' as a preferred way of dealing with all organisational change. Handy uses a metaphor we will use several times in the book – 'Drinking in Davy's Bar' – once we have settled down to handling the situation, we have progressed beyond the point when we can tackle the underlying problems. *Important/non-urgent* activities should be the number one priority on the time management agenda. By making certain that these kinds of activities get priority, the urgent problems being encountered can be reduced. Time stressors can be eliminated.

One of the most difficult yet crucially important decisions one must make in managing time effectively is determining what is important and what is urgent. There are no automatic rules of thumb that divide all activities, demands or opportunities

Management Consultancy and Skills

into those neat categories. Problems don't come with categorising labels attached, it's a very personal classification – one secure individual's 'non-urgent' may be another's perceived key to survival in the corporate jungle. We categorise our own activities.

> We advised a harassed chief executive to change her habits and move away from the precedent of her predecessor. Instead of leaving her appointments diary in the control of her secretary, she should spend her first moments in the office deciding what activities were her priority and allocating specific blocks of time accordingly. Only after she had made these decisions should she make the diary available to her secretary to schedule other appointments.

We still need to answer the 'How?' question – How can people make certain that they focus on activities that are important, not just urgent? The answer is to identify clear and specific personal priorities. It is important for people to be aware of their own core values and to establish a set of basic principles to guide their behaviour. In order to determine what is important in time management, those core values, basic principles and personal priorities must be clearly identified. Otherwise, individuals are at the mercy of the unremitting demands that others place upon them. 'If you don't know where you are going, you will finish somewhere else.'
Answer the following questions:

1. What do I stand for? What am I willing to die (or live) for?

2. What do I care passionately about?

3. What legacy would I like to leave? How would I like to be remembered?

4. If I could persuade everyone to follow a few basic principles, what would they be?

5. What do I want to have accomplished twenty years from now?

From these questions you can create a *personal* mission statement – an expression of what is truly important to you. With this statement you can be proactive in determining what is important to you.

> Two people aged 26 and 56 wrote their Mission Statements. The 26-year-old was concerned with learning new skills so that in four years time he and his partner could set up a business on their own. The 56-year-old was concerned with her grandchildren, and passing her skills and the progress she had made in the organisation on to a new generation of managers.

Basing time management on core principles to judge the importance of activities is also the key to being able to say 'no' without feeling guilty. When you have decided what it is that you care about passionately, what it is you most want to accomplish and what legacy you want to leave, you can more easily say 'no' to activities that don't fit these principles – provided you have time. This is why it is easier to say 'no' to *important/non-urgent* activities (Cell 3) because you have time. Unfortunately, against time pressures, we allow our goal setting to be completely reactive and pragmatic, fumbling ourselves into more stress.

Understanding, communicating and acting upon our core principle does not mean that we have to weigh and decide instantly on every action. To act in a proactive way we need to be in sympathy with the ethics of our organisation – our mission statement must match that of our employees or we have endemic personal stress. There are times when we decide that external pressures mean that we 'go with the flow', but it is our choice. Blanchard and Peale (1990) list five principles for what they term ethical power:

1. *Purpose*. The mission of our organisation is communicated from the top. Our organisation is guided by the values, hopes, and a vision that helps us to determine what is acceptable and unacceptable behaviour.
2. *Pride*. We feel proud of ourselves and of our organisation. We know that when we feel this way, we can resist temptations to behave unethically.
3. *Patience*. We believe that holding to our ethical values will lead us to success in the long term. This involves maintaining a balance between obtaining results and caring how we achieve these results.
4. *Persistence*. We have a commitment to live by ethical principles. We are committed to our commitment. We make sure our actions are consistent with our purpose.
5. *Perspective*. Our managers and employees take time to pause and reflect, take stock of where we are, evaluate where we are going and determine how we are going to get there.

Effectiveness in time management then means that you accomplish what you want to accomplish with your time. How you achieve those accomplishments relates to efficiency of time use, to which we now turn.

Pitfalls in time management

In addition to structuring our time in line with our core principles and those of the organisation we also need to think of our actual use of time. Table 2.3 lists common ways of wasting time.

Being aware of the pitfalls is often enough to reduce the stressors that following them generates. For example, if we do things that are planned before things that are unplanned, some important tasks may never get done unless they are consciously scheduled. Because many people have a tendency to do things that are urgent before things that are important, they may find themselves saying 'no' to important things in order to attend to urgent things, thereby perpetuating feelings of overload. If we do the things that are easiest before the things that are difficult, our time may be taken up dealing with mundane and easy-to-resolve issues while difficult but important problems go unresolved.

Time is such a universal stressor that time management is hugely important. The Time Management Survey at the beginning of the chapter is designed to highlight your own competencies in the area. The first section of the survey applies to everyone in his or her daily life. The second section is most applicable to individuals who have managed or worked in an organisation. The key to scoring is at the end of the book and will show you how well you manage your time. The questionnaire is derived from our Rules of Time Management. It should also be pointed out that no individual can or should implement all of these time management techniques at

Table 2.3 Potential time-management pitfalls

- We do what we like to do before we do what we don't like to do.
- We do the things we know how to do faster than the things we do not know how to do.
- We do the things that are easiest before things that are difficult.
- We do things that require a little time before things that require a lot of time.
- We do things for which the resources are available.
- We do things that are scheduled (for example, meetings) before non-scheduled things.
- We sometimes do things that are planned before things that are unplanned.
- We respond to demands from others before demands from ourselves.
- We do things that are urgent before things that are important.
- We readily respond to crises and emergencies.
- We do interesting things before uninteresting things.
- We do things that advance our personal objectives or that are politically expedient.
- We wait until a deadline before we really get moving.
- We do things that provide the most immediate closure.
- We respond on the basis of who wants it.
- We respond on this basis of the consequences to us of doing or not doing something.
- We tackle small jobs before large jobs.
- We work on things in the order of arrival.
- We work on the basis of the squeaky-wheel principle (the squeaky wheel gets the grease).
- We work on the basis of consequences to the group.

once. The amount of time spent trying to implement all the techniques would be so overwhelming that time stressors would only increase. Therefore, it is best to incorporate a few of these techniques at a time into everyday life. Implement first those hints that will lead to the most improvement in your use of time. Saving just 10 per cent more time, or using an extra 30 minutes a day more wisely, can produce astounding results over months and years. Effective time management not only helps a person to accomplish more in a typical work day, but also helps eliminate feelings of stress and overload.

The rules of effective time management

The first 20 rules are applicable to everyone; the second set relate more directly to managers and the management role.

Rule 1: Read selectively   Most of us have too much to read, ranging from unsolicited trash mail to vital instructions. Except when you read for relaxation or pleasure, most reading should be done the way you read a newspaper; skim most of it, but stop to read what seems most important. Even the most important articles don't need a thorough reading, since important points are generally at the beginnings of paragraphs or sections. Furthermore, if you underline or highlight what you find important, you can review it quickly when you need to.

Rule 2: Make a list of things to perform each day   This is a common-sense rule which implies that you need to do some advance planning each day and not rely solely on your memory. (It also implies that you should have only one list, not multiple lists on multiple scraps of paper.)

Rule 3: Have a place for everything and keep everything is its place   Letting things get out of place robs you of time in two ways: you need more time to find something when you need it, and you are tempted to interrupt the task you are doing to do something else. For example, if material for several projects is scattered on top of your desk, you will be continually tempted to switch from one project to another as you shift your eyes or move the papers.

Rule 4: Prioritise your tasks   Each day you should focus first on important tasks, then deal with urgent tasks. During the Second World War, with an overwhelming number of tasks to perform, General Eisenhower successfully managed his time by following Rule 4 strictly. He focused his attention rigorously on important matters that only he could resolve, while leaving urgent, but less important matters to be dealt with by subordinates.

Rule 5: Do one important thing at a time but several trivial things simultaneously   You can accomplish a lot by doing more than one thing at a time when tasks are routine, trivial or require little thought. This rule allows managers to get rid of multiple trivial tasks in less time – e.g., sign letters while talking on the phone.

Rule 6: Make a list of some five- or ten-minute discretionary tasks   This helps to use the small bits of time almost everyone has during his or her day (waiting for something to begin, between meetings or events, talking on the telephone, etc.). Beware, however, of spending all your time doing these small discretionary tasks while letting high-priority items go unattended.

Rule 7: Divide up large projects   This helps you avoid feeling overwhelmed by large, important, urgent tasks. Feeling that a task is too big to accomplish contributes to a feeling of overload and leads to procrastination.

Rule 8: Determine the critical 20 per cent of your tasks   Pareto's law states that 20 per cent of the tasks produce 80 per cent of the results. Therefore, it is important to analyse which tasks make up the most important 20 per cent and spend the bulk of your time on those.

Rule 9: Save your best time for important matters   Time spent on trivial tasks should not be your 'best time'. Do routine work when your energy level is low, your mind is not sharp or you aren't on top of things. Reserve your quality time for accomplishing the most important and urgent tasks. As Carlson (1951) pointed out, managers are often like puppets whose strings are being pulled by a crowd of unknown and unorganised people. Don't let others interrupt your best time with unwanted demands. Control your own time.

Management Consultancy and Skills

Table 2.4   The divisions of priority

1. Importance	**3. Delegation**
(a) Very important – a must	(a) I am the only one who can do it
(b) Important – should be done	(b) It can be delegated but requires
(c) Not so important but it would be	some authority, training or
nice if it were done	instruction
(d) Unimportant – no real point in it	(c) Virtually anyone could do it
anyway when you think	**4. Interactions**
2. Urgency	(a) I must see these people every day
(a) Very urgent – must be done NOW	(b) I need to see these people
(b) Urgent – should be done soon	frequently
(c) Not urgent – should be fitted in	(c) I should see them sometime
sometime	(d) I do not NEED to see these people
(d) Time is not a factor	at all

Rule 10: Reserve some time during the day when others don't have access to you   Use this time to accomplish *important/non-urgent* tasks, or spend it just thinking. This might be the time before others in the household get up, after everyone else is in bed or at a location where no one else comes. The point is to avoid being in the line of fire all day, every day, without personal control over your time.

Rule 11: Don't put things off   If you do certain tasks promptly, they will require less time and effort than if you procrastinate. Of course, you must guard against spending all your time on trivial, immediate concerns that crowd out more important tasks. The line between procrastination and time wasting is a fine one.

Rule 12: Keep track of how you use your time   This is one of the best time-management strategies. It is impossible to improve your management of time or decrease time stressors unless you know how you spend your time. You should keep time logs in short enough intervals to capture the essential activities. We suggest that units of 30 minutes provide a balance between accuracy and feasibility and that you keep the time log for at least two weeks. Table 2.4 should be used to classify your activities and eliminate obvious slack.

Rule 13: Set deadlines   This helps improve your efficient use of time. Work always expands to fill the time available, so if you don't specify a termination time, tasks tend to continue longer than necessary.

Rule 14: Do something productive while waiting for other jobs   Up to 20 per cent of your time is likely to be spent in waiting. Use this time for reading, planning, preparing, rehearsing, reviewing, outlining or doing other things that help you to accomplish your work.

Rule 15: Do quality work at one set time during the day   Because it is natural to let simple tasks drive out difficult tasks, specify a certain period of time to do quality work which fits your own personal 'clock'. Many people do their best work in the morning – if this is you, don't waste the mornings on trivia.

Rule 16: Finish at least one thing every day – set realisable targets Reaching the end of a day with nothing completely finished, however small, serves to increase a sense of overload and time stress. Finishing a task is a reward in itself.

Rule 17: Schedule personal time You need some time when no interruptions will occur, when you can get off the 'fast track' and be alone. This time should be used to plan, prioritise, take stock, pray, meditate or just relax. Among other advantages, personal time also helps you to maintain self-awareness.

Rule 18: Don't worry about anything on a continuing basis – if it is a continuing concern FIX IT!

> A remote village had the problem of a dog who had fallen down the well and contaminated the water. The village elders consulted the Zen priest who advise them to draw seven buckets of water before drinking again. They drew seven times seven and still the water was foul. They went back to the priest who delayed answering and then said: *Of course you have removed the dog!*

Very often we prefer to worry and go over the same thing time and time again when it is quite obvious what we need to do. Pointless worry stops us focusing on essentials.

Rule 19: Have long-term objectives Know what you need to achieve and do not sabotage your real aims with expediency.

Rule 20: Be on the alert for ways to improve your management of time

The next set of rules cover the major managerial activities. As managers report that approximately 70 per cent of their time is spent in meetings (Mintzberg, 1973; Cooper and Davidson, 1982), rules relating to meetings are given pride of place.

Rule 21: Hold routine meetings at the end of the day Energy and creativity levels are highest early in the day and shouldn't be wasted on trivial matters. Furthermore, close of the day meetings are inclined to be shorter and set their own priorities.

Rule 22: Hold short meetings standing up This guarantees that meetings will be kept short. Getting comfortable helps to prolong meetings.

Rule 23: Set a time limit This establishes an expectation of when the meeting should end and creates pressure to conform to a time boundary. Set such limits at the beginning of every meeting and appointment.

> An idea used by one organisation to make their meetings more efficient was to specify times and purposes for each item in a pre-published agenda. Thus you would book 10 minute slots and specify whether you wanted to pass information, make a decision or solve a problem. The discipline of the time/purpose agenda for a few meetings carried forward even when the rules were relaxed.

Rule 24: Cancel meetings when they are not needed The occasional cancellation makes the meetings that are held more productive and more time efficient.

Management Consultancy and Skills

Rule 25: Have agendas; stick to them; and keep action minutes with timing and accountability These rules help people to prepare for a meeting, stick to the subject and remain work oriented. Many things will be handled outside of meetings if they have to appear on a formal agenda to be discussed. Managers can set a verbal agenda at the beginning of even impromptu meetings. Keeping action minutes ensures that assignments are not forgotten, that follow-up and accountability occur, and that everyone is clear about responsibilities.

Rule 26: Start meetings on time This shows commitment – people who arrive on time should be rewarded, not asked to wait for laggards.

Rule 27: Prepare minutes promptly and follow them up This practice keeps items from appearing again in a meeting without having been resolved. It also creates the expectation that most work should be done outside the meeting. Commitments and expectations made public through minutes are more likely to be fulfilled.

Rule 28: Present and demand solutions, not problems

> Winston Churchill working with a committee on the issues of landing the major Allied forces on open beaches in July 1945 instructed: *'I want solutions not problems – the problems speak loudly enough for themselves.'*

Meetings can easily become forums for upward delegation and the hedging of responsibility. Problem setters are often better positioned to present solutions than the less initiated. Only when the obvious is ruled out do we need 'creative' solutions. Meetings are often to communicate proposed actions so that their wider implications can be understood by all the stakeholders.

Rule 29: Meet visitors in your doorway It is easier to keep a meeting short if you are standing in the doorway rather than sitting in your office.

Rule 30: Hold meetings in the appropriate place Often the appropriate place is the home territory of the key stakeholder. Such appropriately placed meetings can call upon extra data and unplanned 'witnesses' without formality and delay. This rule does not apply if the manager's travelling time is impracticable or where the 'home territory' cannot be protected from dysfunctional interruptions.

> We were called upon to comment on the appraisal systems of Bass Taverns. Managers used the public houses of the landlords during opening hours as sites for formal annual assessments and were finding difficulties. The idea might have been good, but in practice the interviews were interrupted. Bringing the landlords to the head office had the double benefit of uninterrupted work and of convincing the landlords that they were valued and that the process of appraisal was meaningful.

Rule 31: Use technology Telephone technology allows the re-routing of calls, conferencing systems exist, and e-mail is common place. Meetings may not be the best way of disseminating data – fax and the simple office memo are less glamorous but may fit the need more efficiently than face to face.

Rule 32: Have a place to work uninterrupted Not all of us have a 'protected' workplace but we do not have to meet in a formal office. Lawns or even canteens can allow us more confidentiality on occasion. Think always of the purpose of the meeting and the state of mind you want and expect from those present.

> Working for what became Birds Eye Walls, we had a spell in fish processing. The manager's office was halfway down the fish filleting lines, which in the 1970s was a very tough place. Anyone 'called' to the office had to face some hundred filleters who chose to humble the visitor by banging their knives on the stainless steel belts. Most visitors were severely shaken if not stirred by the time they got to the manager's office.

Rule 33: Do something definite with every piece of paperwork you handle   Either bin it or action it; never shuffle it.

Rule 34: Keep the working space clear   Those who know at least two of the authors will laugh at this rule, as our working spaces are piled high; however, it is a good rule. A hint is also to use staples and not paper clips – paper clips seem to take great delight in losing their charges and gaining sheets from other documents. However, remember that 'reorganising the paper work' is a great time-wasting game.

Rule 35: Time taken to delegate is never wasted   Delegation is such a key management skill as to merit part of its own chapter.

Remember that these rules of thumb for managing time are a means to an end, not the end itself. If the implementation of rules creates more stress rather than less, the rules should not be applied. However, research has indicated that managers who use these kinds of techniques have better control of their time, accomplish more, have better relations with subordinates and eliminate many of the time stressors that most managers ordinarily encounter. Therefore, you will find that as you select a few of these hints to apply in your own life, the efficiency of your time use will improve and your time stress will decrease.

Most time-management techniques involve single individuals changing their own work habits or behaviours by themselves. However, effective time management must often take into account the behaviour and needs of others – my time management without understanding its impact on the time management of others may well be dysfunctional. Really effective time management may require all one's management skills, and we still have encounter stressors to deal with.

Eliminating encounter stressors

Unsatisfactory personal relationships are significant stressors. Encounter stressors result directly from abrasive, non-fulfilling relationships. Even though work is going smoothly, when encounter stress is present, everything else seems wrong.

Collaboration

One important factor that helps to eliminate encounter stress is membership in a stable, closely knit group or community. Our evidence is based on anthropologists' studies of particular communities. Thirty years ago Dr Stewart Wolf found that the residents of Roseto, Pennsylvania, were completely free from heart disease and other stress-related illness. He suspected that their protection sprang from the town's uncommon social cohesion and stability.

> The town's population consisted entirely of descendants of Italians who had moved there 100 years ago from Roseto, Italy. Few married outside the community; the firstborn was always named after a grandparent; conspicuous consumption and displays of superiority were avoided; and social support among community members was a way of life.

Wolf predicted that residents would begin to display the same level of stress-related illness as the rest of the country if the modern world intruded. It did, and they did. By the mid-1970s, residents in Roseto had exotic cars, mansion-style homes, mixed marriages, new names, competition with one another and a rate of coronary disease the same as in any other town (Farnham, 1991). They had ceased to be a cohesive, collaborative clan and instead had become a community of selfishness. Self-centredness, it was discovered, was dangerous to health.

The most important psychological discovery resulting from the Vietnam and Persian Gulf wars was the strength associated with the small, primary work group. In Vietnam, unlike with Desert Storm, strong primary groups of soldiers who stayed together over time were not formed. The constant injection of new personnel into squadrons, and the constant transfer of soldiers from one location to another made soldiers feel isolated, without loyalty and vulnerable to stress-related illness. In the Gulf War, by contrast, soldiers were kept in the same unit throughout the campaign, brought home together and given lots of time to debrief together after the battle (Farnham, 1991). Professional debriefing and the use of a closely knit group to provide interpretation and social support was found to be the most powerful deterrent to post-battle trauma: Post-Traumatic Stress Disorder (PSMS). Woods and Whitehead (1993) give three examples of social support:

- the restoration of civilian morale in Darmstadt, Germany, after one of the most intensive aerial bombardments in the Second World War
- the recovery after the flooding and destruction of Les Salles in southern France
- the acceptance of the horrors of the Bradford Football Stadium fire where 55 people were burnt to death in the sight of their friends.

In all these cases the support of tight-knit communities aided recovery.

Collaborative or even clan-like relationships are a powerful deterrent to encounter stress. One way of developing this kind of relationship is by applying a concept introduced by Covey (1989) in describing habits of highly effective people. Covey used the metaphor of an emotional bank account to describe the trust or feeling of security that one person has towards another. This approach has been seen by many as being manipulative in a very obvious way, but the point is made. Covey, controversially, regards the more 'deposits' made in an emotional bank account, the stronger and more resilient the relationship becomes. He quoted going to a ball game with his son as an example – apparently Covey is indifferent to ball games. Conversely, too many 'withdrawals' from the account weakens relationships by destroying trust, security and confidence. 'Deposits' are made through treating people with kindness, courtesy, honesty and consistency. The emotional bank account grows when people feel they are receiving love, respect and caring. 'Withdrawals' are made by not keeping promises, not listening, not clarifying expectations or allowing choice – cashing in on the relationship. Relationships, according to Covey, are ruined because the account becomes overdrawn, but the mechanistic model is widely challenged.

The common-sense prescription, therefore, is to base relationships with others on mutual trust, respect, honesty and kindness. Collaborative, cohesive communities are, in the end, a product of the one-on-one relationships that people develop with each other. As Dag Hammarskjöld, former Secretary General of the United Nations, stated: 'It is more noble to give yourself completely to one individual than to labour diligently for the salvation of the masses.' Feeling trusted, respected and loved is, in the end, what each of us desires as individuals. We want to experience those feelings personally, not just as a member of a group.

Interpersonal competence

In addition to one-on-one relationship building, a second major category of encounter stress eliminators is developing *interpersonal competence*. We are discussing competencies to:

- resolve conflict
- build and manage high-performing teams
- conduct efficient meetings
- coach and counsel employees
- provide positive and constructive negative feedback
- influence
- motivate, energise and empower themselves and others.

These seven elements of interpersonal competence in a manager are about support. A survey of workers found that employees who rated their manager as supportive and interpersonally competent had lower rates of burnout, lower stress levels, lower incidence of stress-related illness, higher productivity, more loyalty to their organisations, and more efficiency in work than employees with non-supportive and interpersonally incompetent managers.

Eliminating situational stressors

Job redesign

A medium-term strategy is to redesign the work process. We have to accept that many of us report feeling stress because it seems fashionable to be stressed. 'I'm busier than you are' is a common game many of us enjoy playing. We discuss the problems of repeated reorganisations; the vulnerability of our jobs; traffic delays; and the lack of discipline in others, all in terms of our personal stresses. The whole issue is serious since the time lost through stress-related illness and its medical treatment costs twice as much as industrial injuries (Farnham, 1991). The costs are rising. A significant source of stress, as we all 'know', arises from our 'situation'.

For decades, researchers in the area of occupational health have examined the relationship between job strain and stress-related behavioural, psychological and physiological outcomes. Studies have focused on various components of job strain, including the level of task demand (e.g., the pressure to work quickly or excessively), the level of individual control (e.g., the freedom to vary the work pace), and the level of intellectual challenge (e.g., the extent to which work is interesting).

The kind of stress experienced by individuals will vary according to their culture. In a study by Cary Cooper *et al.* (1988) of nearly 1,000 senior top level executives in 10 countries it was found that each country presents its own idiosyncratic work pressures. Cooper also looked specifically at the stresses of women managers.

US executives perceived their greatest source of pressure at work to be 'the lack of power and influence', 'incompetent bosses' and 'beliefs conflicting with those of the organisation'. However, Japanese executives rated 'keeping up with new technology' as their major source of strain and job dissatisfaction, while Swedish executives cited stresses involving encroachment of work upon their private lives. German complaints were more specific; they complained of 'time pressures' and 'working with inadequately trained subordinates'.

Other research in this area, however, has challenged the common myth that job strain occurs most frequently in the executive suite (Hingley and Cooper, 1986). In a General Household Survey 1974–75, the frequency of deaths due to major causes increases as we move from professional and white collar jobs down to the unskilled. This applies both to stress-related illness and to other illness such as pneumonia and prostrate cancer. In the UK, blue-collar workers consult their doctors more often and have more days off than white-collar workers. Professional males average 12 days off per year, while unskilled manual workers average around 20 days. An explanation for this could well be that low-discretion, low-interest jobs with high demand produce at least as much stress as high-profile work. This is borne out by research. A review of this research suggests that the single most important contributor to stress is lack of freedom (Adler, 1989).

Studies throughout the Goddard Space Flight Centre showed that staff with higher discretionary decision-making power experience less from all four of the stressor classifications – time, situational, encounter and anticipatory (French and Caplan, 1972).

Cecilia Macdonald (1996) considers that managers need to manage their own stress and then 'get creative about managing the stress of their employees'. She sees the reactive policy of 'waiting for their annual vacation as being unhelpful. Positive measures are needed. Her recommendations include a 'small wins strategy' and a short time for reflection at the end of the day. Siobahn Butler (1996) explains that the stress issues of the company Cable Midlands in the UK provide enough concern for the HR department to offer stress management courses which include clinical hypnosis and aromatherapy. Sara Zeff Gerber (1996) sees an impending disaster in the growth of chronically stressed employees throughout US industry and proposes even more drastic remedies. The examples we have quoted are simply examples drawn from one year – 1997. The concerns over stress are not new but the present interest is now overwhelming.

The urgency of the problem makes us hesitate slightly to quote a key response from the 1970s. Hackman and his colleague (1975) proposed a model of job re-design that has proved effective in reducing stress and in increasing satisfaction and productivity. Hackman recommended the following policy:

1. Combine tasks   When individuals are able to work on a whole project and per-form a variety of related tasks (e.g., programming all components of a computer software package), rather than being restricted to working on a single repetitive task or sub-component of a larger task, they are more satisfied and committed. In such cases, they are able to use more skills and feel a certain pride of ownership in their job.

2. Form identifiable work units   When tasks are combined people feel more integ-rated, and the strain associated with repetitive work is diminished. Productivity often improves even further when groups combine and co-ordinate their tasks, making their own decisions on how to complete their work. This formation of nat-ural work units has received a great deal of attention in Japanese auto plants in America and the UK as workers have combined in teams to assemble an entire car from start to finish, rather than do separate tasks on an assembly line. Workers learn one another's jobs, rotate assignments and experience a sense of completion in their work. The process reduces work-related stress dramatically.

3. Establish customer relationships   One of the most enjoyable parts of a job is see-ing the consequences of one's labour. In most organisations, producers are buffered from consumers by intermediaries, such as customer relations departments and sales personnel. The process of allowing producers to obtain first-hand unfiltered contact with customers and understand the problems, needs and expectations, is not only efficient and motivating, it also reduces situational stress.

4. Increase decision-making authority   Decisions being made at the appropriate level is again both efficient, motivating and helps to reduce stress of all concerned. It allows individuals to feel that they are valued and in control of what we will call later their 'Circle of Concern'.

> Zenica, a producer of fine chemicals in Huddersfield, Yorkshire, began their empowerment programme by creating legends. One such legend took place in a working store room which the Change Manager found in partial darkness. The rea-son for the room being in darkness was a single electric bulb that had failed. The manager asked the operators why it had not be replaced and was told that a light bulb had been requisitioned but the supervisor required for the authorisation was off sick. The manager asked how much the bulb would cost in the local supermarket and was told about 60p. He fished the money out of his pocket and told the oper-ator to buy one.

The issue is about the role of management in the new world – the subject of the last chapter. New managers should understand 'why' things are to be done, explain 'what' needs to be done and allow maximum participation in 'how' things are done

– consulting and monitoring the processes on a continuous basis. Cameron *et al.* (1990) found a significant decrease in experienced stress in firms that were downsizing when workers were given authority to make decisions about how and when they did the extra work required of them.

5. Provide feedback – listen and communicate   At its simplest we need to be told how our efforts fit into the grand scheme.

> A Central Office of Information (COI) film made in Britain during the Second World War described a strike in a factory making luxury sheepskin gloves during the Battle of Britain. The women operators wanted to 'do something for the war effort and not make luxury items'. The Ministry of Aircraft Production – for whom the factory was supplying the goods – brought a wounded fighter pilot to meet the operators and show how the gloves contributed to his performance in an unheated cabin of a Spitfire warplane. The strike vanished.

Knowing your place in the 'grand scheme' is not enough – we need to know what is expected of us and how we are judged. The effective manager needs to communicate expectations clearly, giving timely and accurate feedback, these expectations need to include quality standards and achievements. Firms that allow the workers who assemble a product to test its quality, instead of shipping it off to a separate quality assurance group, find that quality increases substantially and that conflicts between production and quality control personnel are eliminated.

These practices are used widely today in all types of organisations, such as Volvo, Saab and Philips Industries. They have all undertaken extended projects of job redesign. Philips have pursued a programme of work structuring. Job enrichment and job enlargement have been attempted and greater opportunities for worker participation have been provided.

Eliminating anticipatory stressors

While redesigning work can help structure an environment where stressors are minimised, it is much more difficult to eliminate entirely the anticipatory stressors experienced by individuals. Stress associated with anticipating an event is more a product of psychological anxiety than current work circumstances. To eliminate anticipatory stressors requires a change in thought processes, priorities and plans. As we have said earlier, it is important to establish clear personal priorities – identifying long-term goals and hence what cannot be compromised or sacrificed. A personal mission statement acts as a map or guide. It makes clear where you will eventually end up, and fear of the unknown – another way of defining anticipatory stress – is thus eliminated.

Goal setting

Establishing short-term plans helps eliminate anticipatory stressors by focusing attention on immediate goal accomplishment instead of a fearful future. Short-term planning, however, implies more than just specifying a desired outcome. Several action

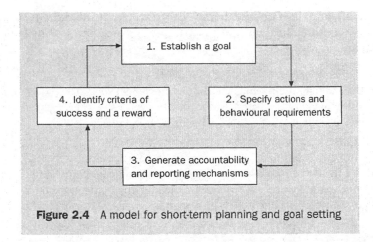

Figure 2.4 A model for short-term planning and goal setting

steps are needed if short-term plans are to be achieved. The model (Figure 2.4) illustrates the four-step process associated with successful short-term planning.

Step 1 Identify the desired goal. Most goal-setting, performance appraisal or management-by-objectives (MBO) programmes specify that step, but most also stop at that point. Unfortunately, the first step alone is not likely to lead to goal achievement or stress elimination. Merely establishing a goal, while helpful, is not sufficient.

Step 2 Identify, as specifically as possible, the tactics necessary to achieve the goal. The more difficult the goal is to accomplish, the more rigorous should be the tactic setting.

> A friend approached one of us with a problem. She was a single woman about 25 years old who had a high degree of anticipatory stress because of her size. She weighed well over 300 pounds and seemed to be unable to lose any of it. She was concerned both from the health and the social consequences of her size. She set a goal, or short-term plan, to lose 100 pounds in the next 10 months. As counsellors we saw this as a distant goal and asked her to list a dozen or so specific actions that would help her to reach that goal. Her list included: never eat alone, never carry any small change (in order to avoid the impulse buying of chocolates), exercise with friends each evening in a gym, get up 7:00 a.m., eat a controlled breakfast with a friend, cut back on television and so reduce the temptation to eat snacks and finally go to bed by 10:30 p.m. These were her tactics, and were in no way influenced by us. The tactics were rigid, but the goal was so difficult that they were necessary to ensure progress. Success came with a weight loss of 100 pounds within the 10 months. She was happy.

Step 3 Establish accountability and reporting mechanisms. The principle at the centre of this step is to make it more difficult to stay the same than to change. We do this by involving others in ensuring that we stick to the plan, establishing a social support network to obtain encouragement from others, and instituting penalties for not doing so. In addition to announcing her goal to her workmates and friends, our slimmer arranged to take up private medical treatment if she did not succeed. The treatment was both unpleasant and costly, but was a great motivating factor to success by cheaper means.

> In our change programmes we insist that participants complete a formal contract of what they are going to achieve and how they will achieve it. The contract has to be countersigned by a witness and is filed by us for the record. The contract is sent to the individuals after a specified period for comment.

Step 4 Establish an evaluation and reward system. What evidence will there be that the goal has been accomplished? In the case of losing weight, it's easily established – the scales rule OK. In softer goals – improving management skills, developing more patience, establishing more effective leadership – the criteria of success are not so easily identified. That is why this step is crucial. 'I know it when I see it' is not good enough. Our objectives must be SMART (Table 2.5): **S**pecific, **M**easurable, **A**greed, **R**ealistic and **T**imed. For our slimmer, the specific goal was to lose weight 100 pounds and this was agreed by her, her doctor and her friends. The weight loss was realistic, whereas 200 pounds would not have been, and the time scale was 'by Christmas' – ten months away. The key is making the goal specific and the purpose is to eliminate anticipatory stress by establishing a focus and direction for activity. The anxiety associated with uncertainty and potentially negative events is dissipated when mental and physical energy are concentrated on purposeful activity.

Small wins

Turning the vague goal to a series of specific goals can be described as a small wins strategy.

> We were working with a manager whose job was to make the public transport system of Miscolc, Hungary, into an effective system based on UK lines. Her problems were aged buses, demotivated staff, lack of any form of financial support, hostility of the public, political blindness. There was no possibility of **achieving** effectiveness in one stage – in fact we identified six stages for success. At each stage there was an assessible victory and no step blinded us to the next of the total objective.

By 'small wins' we mean a tiny but definite change made in a desired direction. One begins each step by changing something that is relatively easy to change. Then another 'change' is added, and so on. Each individual success may be relatively modest when considered in isolation, but the small gains mount up and show measurable progress. The progress we see helps to convince us, as well as others, of our ability to accomplish our objective. The fear associated with anticipatory change is eliminated as we build self-confidence through small wins. We also gain the support of others as they see that things are happening.

In the case of our overweight friend, one key was to begin changing what she could change, a little at a time. Tackling the loss of 100 pounds all at once would have been too overwhelming a task. But she could change the time she shopped, the time she went to bed and what she ate for breakfast. Each successful change generated more and more momentum that, when combined together, led to the

Table 2.5   The SMART system

Action	Goal			Reader's goal
	Improve management skills	Become more patient	Becoming a better leader	
Specific	Learn and practise running meetings	Learn and listen more effectively	Give instructions on a particular project to a particular subordinate	
Measurable	Reduce the business carried forward to the next meeting to two items	Get a friend to watch you in an interview – aim to speak not more than 30% of the time	Reduce the number of times he or she needs to return to you for clarification to once a week	
Agreed	Check with those attending the meeting	Check out with a friend that 30% sounds right – you are now at 80%	Explain the goal to the subordinate	
Realistic	Reduction to two items is fine – no carry forward would be unrealistic	30% is realistic from what you have read	Now we have continuous seeking of clarification – old habits die hard – once a week allows some latitude	
Timed	Our next meeting is on Friday – the plan will start then and be in action by Friday week	The next difficult meeting you will work from 80% to 60% and then by meeting three you will achieve the 30%	This is a real project with real time scales. At the end of its run – 3 months – you will have success	

larger change that she desired. Her ultimate success was a product of multiple small wins.

Similarly, Weick (1993) has described Poland's peaceful transition from a communistic command economy to a capitalistic free-enterprise economy as a product of small wins. Not only is Poland now one of the most thriving economies in eastern Europe, but it made the change to free enterprise without a single shot being fired, a single strike being called or a single political upheaval. One reason for this is that long before the Berlin Wall fell, small groups of volunteers in Poland began to change the way they lived.

Poles adopted a theme that went something like this: If you value freedom, then behave freely; if you value honesty, then speak honestly; if you desire change, then

Management Consultancy and Skills

change what you can. Polish citizens organised volunteer groups to help at local hospitals, assist the less fortunate and clean up the parks. They behaved in a way that was outside the control of the central government, but reflected their free choice. Their changes were not on a large enough scale to attract attention and official opposition from the central government, but their actions nevertheless reflected their determination to behave in a free, self-determining way. They controlled what they could control, namely, their own voluntary service. These voluntary service groups spread throughout Poland; thus, when the transition from communism to capitalism occurred, a large number of people in Poland had already got used to behaving in a way consistent with self-determination. Many of these people simply stepped into positions where independent-minded managers were needed. The transition was smooth because of the multiple small wins that had previously spread throughout the country relatively unnoticed.

In summary, the rules for instituting a small wins strategy are simple:

- Identify your area of concern.
- Identify your ultimate goal.
- Look for realistic steps towards your goal.
- Take one step at a time – rewarding each step as you make it.
- Consolidate your successes and move on.

Anticipatory stressors are eliminated because the fearful unknown is replaced by a focus on immediate successes. The alternative strategy is to prepare for the worst and feel good when it does not happen.

> Douglas Construction, a Midlands-based construction company, was being acquired by Tilbury. Tilbury was an unknown to the Douglas managers who feared redundancy. What was the worst that could happen? They were all fired and lost their pension rights. OK, prepare for that but remember that Tilbury has paid a lot for Douglas. Why? The obvious answer is the skills of the Douglas managers. They are the assets that Tilbury has bought – exploit this opportunity.

Developing resilience

Some stress cannot be eliminated. People vary widely in their ability to cope with stress: some individuals seem to crumble under pressure, while others appear to thrive. Resilience is associated with balancing the various aspects of one's life.

The pie chart (Figure 2.5) represents resilience development. Each wedge in the figure identifies an important aspect of life that must be developed in order to achieve resilience. The most resilient individuals are those who have achieved life balance. If the centre of the figure represents the zero point of resilience development and the outside edge of the figure represents maximum development, shading in a portion of the area in each wedge would represent the amount of development achieved in each area. Individuals who are best able to cope with stress would shade in a majority of each wedge, indicating that they have not only spent time

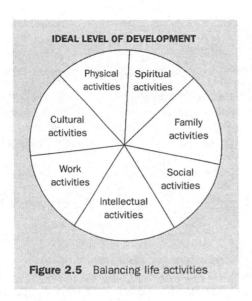

IDEAL LEVEL OF DEVELOPMENT

Figure 2.5 Balancing life activities

developing a variety of aspects of their lives, but also that the overall pattern is relatively balanced. A lopsided pattern is as non-adaptive as minimally shaded areas.

- Generally, when people are feeling stress in one area of life, such as work, they respond by devoting more time and attention to work. While this is a natural reaction, it is counterproductive for several reasons. Firstly, the more that individuals concentrate exclusively on work, the more restricted and less creative they become. As we shall see in the discussion of creativity in a later chapter, breakthroughs in problem solving come from using analogies and metaphors gathered from unrelated activities. That is why several major corporations send senior managers on high adventure wilderness retreats (Scully, 1989); invite actors to perform plays before the executive committee; require volunteer community service; or encourage their managers to engage in completely unrelated activities outside of work (*Business Week*, 30 Sept. 1985, pp. 80–4).

- Secondly, refreshed and relaxed minds think better. A bank executive commented recently during an executive development workshop that he had gradually become convinced of the merits of taking the weekend off from work. He finds that he gets twice as much accomplished on Monday as his colleagues who have been in their offices all weekend.

- Thirdly, the cost of stress-related illness decreases markedly when employees are able to receive support from occupational health services. People need to be able to obtain unbiased advice, within their place of work on stress-related problems (Woods and Whitehead, 1993).

- Well-developed individuals, who give time and attention to cultural, physical, spiritual, family, social and intellectual activities in addition to work, are more productive and less stressed than those who are workaholics.

Management Consultancy and Skills

Table 2.6   Resilience: moderating the effects of stress

Physiological resilience	Psychological resilience	Social resilience

• Cardiovascular conditioning
• Proper diet
	• Balanced lifestyle
	• Hardy personality
	  – High internal control
	  – Strong personal commitment
	  – Love of challenge
	• Small-wins strategy
	• Deep-relaxation techniques
		• Supportive social relations
		• Mentors
		• Teamwork

In this section, therefore, we concentrate on three common areas of resilience development for managers: physical resilience, psychological resilience and social resilience. Development in each of these areas requires initiative on the part of the individual and takes a moderate amount of time to achieve. These are not activities that can be accomplished by lunchtime or the weekend. Rather, achieving life balance and resilience requires ongoing initiative and continuous effort. Components of resilience are summarised in Table 2.6.

Physiological resilience

One of the most crucial aspects of resilience development involves one's physical condition, because physical condition significantly affects the ability to cope with stress. Two aspects of physical condition combine to determine physical resilience: cardiovascular conditioning and dietary control.

Cardiovascular conditioning

Henry Ford is reputed to have stated: 'Exercise is bunk. If you are healthy, you don't need it. If you are sick, you shouldn't take it.' Fortunately, European business has not taken Ford's advice; thousands of major corporations now have in-house fitness facilities. An emphasis on physical conditioning in business has resulted partly from overwhelming evidence that individuals in good physical condition are better able to cope with stressors than those in poor physical condition. Table 2.7 illustrates the benefits of regular physical exercise.

Marks & Spencer, well known for its work in this area, is one of the founder members of the Wellness Forum. One of the examples of care they give their employees is the provision of oral cancer screening. As a result of its Live for Life programme, Johnson & Johnson lowered absenteeism and sickness cost to produce a saving of about £160 per employee in 1982. Prudential Life Insurance found a 46 per cent reduction in major medical expenses over five years resulting from a workplace fitness programme. The advantages of physical conditioning, both for individuals and for companies, are irrefutable.

Table 2.7 Confirmed benefits of regular vigorous exercise

- Blood pressure is lowered.
- Resting heart rate is lowered; the heart is better able to distribute blood where needed under stress.
- Cardiac output is increased; the heart is better able to distribute blood where needed under stress.
- Number of red blood cells is increased; more oxygen can be carried per quart of blood.
- Elasticity of arteries is increased.
- Triglyceride level is lowered.

- Blood cholesterol level is decreased. High-density cholesterol, which is more protective of blood vessels than low-density cholesterol, is proportionately increased.
- Adrenal secretions in response to emotional stress are lowered.
- Lactic acid is more efficiently eliminated from the muscles. (This has been associated with decreased fatigue and tension.)
- Fibrin, a protein that aids in the formation of blood clots, is decreased.
- Additional routes of blood supply are built up in the heart.

Source: Goldberg (1976)

Psychological resilience

Three primary purposes exist for a regular exercise programme: maintaining optimal weight, increasing psychological well-being and improving the cardiovascular system. One indirect cause of stress is the sedentary lifestyle adopted by many individuals. An office worker burns up only about 1,200 calories during an eight-hour day. That is fewer calories than are contained in the typical office worker's lunch. It is little wonder that many people are overweight. The resulting excessive strain on both the heart and the self-image makes overweight individuals more vulnerable to stress (Wolman, 1982).

An advantage of regular physical exercise is that it improves mental as well as physical outlook. It increases self-esteem and gives individuals the energy to be more alert and attentive throughout the day. Episodes of depression are far less frequent. Exercise fosters the necessary energy to cope with the stresses of both unexpected events and dull routine. Physically active individuals are less prone to anxiety, have less illness and fewer days off work (Griest *et al.*, 1979). Researchers have found a chemical basis for the psychological benefit of exercise: the brain releases endorphins (similar to morphine) during periods of intense physical activity. This substance numbs pain and produces a feeling of well-being, sometimes referred to as joggers' high – a euphoric, relaxed feeling reported by long-distance runners.

Another vital benefit of exercise is a strengthened cardiovascular system (Greenberg, 1987). The best results come from aerobic exercises that do not require more oxygen than a person can take in comfortably (as compared with all-out sprinting or long-distance swimming). This type of exercise includes brisk walking, jogging, riding a bicycle or climbing stairs. However, the cardiovascular system is improved by exercise only when the following two conditions are met:

1. The target heart rate is sustained throughout the exercise. This rate is 60–80 per cent of the heart's maximum. To work your target rate, subtract your age in years from 220, then take 60–80 per cent of that number. You should begin your exercise programme at the 60 per cent level and gradually increase to the 80 per cent rate. To check your heart rate during your exercise, periodically monitor your heartbeat for six seconds and multiply by 10.

2. The exercise should be for 20–30 minutes, three or four time a week. Since cardiovascular endurance decreases after 48 hours, it is important to exercise at least every other day.

Dietary control

The adage 'You are what you eat' is sobering, especially given the fact that Americans, who are often seen as trend-setters, have developed some bad eating habits. Annually they consume approximately 100 pounds of refined sugar, 125 pounds of fat, 36 gallons of carbonated beverages, and 25 times more salt than the human body requires (Perl, 1980). Europeans, however, do seem to be eating a more healthy diet and government programmes throughout the EC are encouraging this. After years of attack by health professionals, magazines, newspapers, books and TV programmes, old eating habits are finally being swept away. It is now clearly understood that a good diet is linked to good health. A healthy diet need not be hard work, and a few simple changes can soon put you on the right road:

- Eat plenty of fresh fruit and vegetables.
- Cut down on your sugar by opting for unsweetened fruit juices or low calorie soft drinks and eating less sugary foods such as cakes, puddings, sweets and biscuits.
- Limit the quantity of salt you take by using less in cooking and at the table and by eating fresh fruit instead of salty crisps and nuts – which are also high in fat.

Source: The Flora Project for Heart Disease Prevention

Hardiness

In their book, *The Hardy Executive*, Maddi and Kobasa (1984) described three elements that characterise a hardy, or highly stress-resistant, personality. Hardiness results from feeling:

- in control of one's life, rather than powerless to shape external events
- committed to and involved in what one is doing, rather than alienated from one's work and other individuals
- challenged by new experiences rather than viewing change as a threat to security and comfort.

According to these authors, hardy individuals tend to interpret stressful situations positively and optimistically, responding to stress constructively. As a result, their incidence of illness and emotional dysfunction under stressful conditions is considerably below the norm.

Three concepts – control, commitment and challenge – are central to the development of a variety of management skills, and are crucial for mitigating the harmful effects of stress (Kobasa, 1982).

Individuals with a high degree of **internal control** feel that they are in charge of their own destinies. They take responsibility for their actions and feel they can neutralise negative external forces. They generally believe that stressors are the result of their personal choices rather than uncontrollable, capricious or even malicious external forces. The belief that one can influence the course of events is central to developing high self-esteem. Self-esteem, in turn, engenders self-confidence and the optimistic view that bad situations can be improved and problems overcome. Confidence in one's own efficacy produces low fear of failure, high expectations, willingness to take risks and persistence under adversity (Mednick, 1982; Anderson, 1977; Ivancevich and Matteson, 1980), all of which contribute to resilience under stress.

Commitment implies both selection and dedication. Hardy individuals not only feel that they choose what they do, but they also strongly believe in the importance of what they do. This commitment is both internal (that is, applied to one's own activities) and external (that is, applied to a larger community). The feeling of being responsible to others is an important buffer against stress (Antonovsky, 1979). Whereas self-esteem and a sense of purpose help to provide a psychological support system for coping with stressful events, an individual's belief that others are counting on him or her to succeed, and that he or she belongs to a larger community, fosters psychological resilience during stressful periods. Feeling part of a group, cared about and trusted by others engenders norms of co-operation and commitment, and encourages constructive responses to stress.

Hardy people also welcome **challenge**. They believe that change, rather than stability, is the normal and preferred mode of life. Therefore, much of the disruption associated with a stressful life event is interpreted as an opportunity for personal growth rather than as a threat to security. This mode of thinking is consistent with the Chinese word for crisis, which has two meanings: 'threat' and 'opportunity'. Individuals who seek challenges search for new and interesting experiences and accept stress as a necessary step towards learning. Because these individuals prefer change to stability, they tend to have high tolerance for ambiguity and high resilience under stress (Ivancevich and Matteson, 1980; Maddi and Kobasa, 1984). The three characteristics of hardy personalities – control, commitment and challenge – have been found to be among the most powerful ways of reducing the dysfunctional consequences of stress. By contrast, a different complex of personality attributes, the so-called 'Type A Syndrome', is associated with reduced hardiness and higher levels of psychological stress.

Type A personality

A second important aspect of psychological resilience relates to a personality pattern that many of us develop as we enter the competitive worlds of advanced

Table 2.8   Characteristics of the Type A personality

- Signs of personal tension, such as a clenched jaw, tight muscles, tics.
- Personal commitment to having, rather than being.
- Unawareness of the broader environment. Ignorance of elements outside the immediate task.
- Strong need to be an expert on a subject; otherwise, lack of involvement.
- Compulsion to compete with other Type A's rather than understanding and co-operate with them.
- Speech characterised by explosive accentuation, acceleration of the last few words of a sentence, impatience when interrupted.
- Chronic sense of being in a hurry.
- Polyphasic thoughts and actions, that is, a tendency to do several things simultaneously.
- Impatience with the normal pace of events. Tendency to finish others' sentences.
- Doing everything rapidly.
- Feelings of guilt when relaxing.
- Tendency to evaluate all activities in terms of measurable results.
- Belief that Type A attributes are what lead to success.
- Frequent knee-jiggling or finger-tapping.
- Determination to win every game, even when playing with those who are less skilled or experienced.

education and management. By far the most well-known connection between personality and resilience relates to a combination of attributes known as the Type A personality. For at least three decades scientists have been aware of a link between certain personality attributes and stress-related behavioural, psychological and physiological problems such as anxiety, deteriorating relationships and heart disease (Friedman and Rosenman, 1959). Table 2.8 summarises the primary attributes of Type A personalities that have emerged from the research.

The manner in which Friedman and Rosenman, both cardiologists, discovered the link between personality and heart disease is intriguing. Observing that their waiting room was becoming a bit shabby, they decided to have their chairs re-upholstered. The decorator pointed out that only the front edges of the chairs were worn. The doctors suddenly realised that their patients seemed to be 'on edge', literally sitting on the edges of their seats, prepared for action.

Following up their observations with intensive interviews, they noted that during interviews many of their patients showed signs of impatience and hostility such as fidgeting, eye-blinking, grimaces, rapid or explosive speech, interrupting, and filling in incomplete sentences during a pause. The opposite personality types – which they labelled Type B – appeared more relaxed, patient and able to listen without interrupting. Over 15 per cent of Friedman and Rosenman's Type A patients had had heart attacks, compared to 7 per cent of Type B patients. Subsequent research has found that, in America, about 70 per cent of men and 50 per cent of women exhibit Type A personality traits, such as extreme competitiveness, strong desires for achievement, haste, impatience, restlessness, hyper-alertness, explosive speech, tenseness of facial muscles, free-floating hostility and so on. Rosenman suggested that anger, impatience and competitiveness were the most debilitating factors in the Type A personality; others have proposed hostility (Greenberg, 1987) and some have blamed a feeling of urgency that keeps adrenaline constantly flowing (Kobasa, 1979). Regardless of the key ingredient, the Type A personality is certain to have a disastrous effect on well-being.

In the most extensive study of personality effects on heart disease ever conducted, an eight-year survey of 3,400 men found that Type A individuals in the 39–49 age group had approximately 6.5 times the likelihood of heart disease as Type Bs. Even when factors such as cigarette smoking, parental medical history, blood pressure and cholesterol levels were taken into account, the Type A personality still accounted for two to three times greater likelihood of heart disease. This research concluded that personality is a better predictor than physiology of cardiovascular illness (Friedman and Rosenman, 1974). Ironically, subsequent research has also found that whereas Type A personalities are more prone to experience heart attacks, they are also more likely to recover from them. Janice Ho (1995) working in Singapore, would add to this finding. Her Type A *reported* more stress but the Type B were not physiologically less healthy. Her sample from three sectors – service, financial and banking – quoted time, encounter and situational stressors but seemed well versed in coping mechanisms.

Most Type A individuals believe that it is their Type A personality that has led to their success. Many are unwilling to give up that orientation because hard-driving, intense, persistent action is generally admired and valued among managers. This has often been associated with the traditional male management role, but it has also been connected to the disproportionately high incidence of heart disease among men. In fact, Goldberg (1976) and Jourard (1964) initially linked Type A personality characteristics to certain sex-linked behaviour patterns. Specifically, males or females that follow the stereotypic views of appropriate male behaviour were found to be more likely to experience stress-related illness. They tended to equate low self-disclosure, low emotional involvement, low display of feelings, high defensiveness and high insensitivity to the acquisition of power and control – the presumed prerequisites for success. These were so typical of male behaviour in the workplace that they became known as the 'lethal aspects of the male role' (Jourard, 1964). As more women began to enter the workforce, this same pattern became less and less gender-linked. Many women also behaved as if acceptance in the workplace required 'acting as masculine', i.e., as their male counterparts. As a result, the gap between stress-related illness among professional men and women has narrowed. In recent years, female stress-related illness (e.g., heart attacks, suicides, and migraine headaches) has actually surpassed those of males in some professions. This trend is not only tragic but ironic, because corporations are spending huge amounts each year on training workshops designed to encourage their managers to become more sensitive, understanding and supportive. The folly of the Type A approach to management is illustrated in the following Zen story.

> Matajura wanted to become a great swordsman, but his father said he wasn't quick enough and could never learn. So Matajura went to the famous dueller, Banzo, and asked to become his pupil. 'How long will it take me to become a master?' he

asked. 'Suppose I become your servant, and spend every minute with you; how long?'

'Ten years.' said Banzo.

'My father is getting old. Before ten years have passed, I will have to return home to take care of him. Suppose I work twice as hard; how long will it take me?'

'Thirty years.' said Banzo.

'How is that?' asked Matajura. 'First you say ten years. Then when I offer to work twice as hard, you say it will take three times as long. Let me make myself clear: I will work unceasingly; no hardship will be too much. How long will it take?'

'Seventy years,' said Banzo. 'A pupil in such a hurry learns slowly.'

This Type A sense of urgency, of thinking that any obstacle can be overcome by working harder and longer, works against the ability to develop psychological hardiness. When stressors are encountered, arousal levels increase, and the tendency is to combat them by increasing arousal levels or effort even further. But at high arousal levels, coping responses become more primitive (Staw *et al.*, 1981). Patterns of response that were learned most recently are the first ones to disappear, which means that the responses that are most finely tuned to the current stressful situation are the first ones to go. The ability to distinguish among fine-grained stimuli actually deteriorates, so the extra energy expended by individuals trying to cope becomes less and less effective. Weick (1984) pointed out that highly stressed people consequently find it difficult to learn new responses, to brainstorm, to concentrate, to resist relying on old non-adaptive behaviour patterns, to perform complex responses, to delegate and to avoid the vicious spiral of escalating arousal. Resilience deteriorates.

The small-wins strategy

An effective antidote to this Type A escalation problem is working for 'small wins', as discussed earlier. When individuals work for small wins, they consciously remain sensitive to their small successes – and celebrate them – while coping with a major stressor.

A hypothetical example introduced by Kuhn and Beam (1982, pp. 249–50) illustrates the power of small wins:

> Your task is to count out a thousand sheets of paper while you are subject to periodic interruptions. Each interruption causes you to lose track of the count and forces you to start over. If you count the thousand as a single sequence, then an interruption could cause you to lose count of as many as 999. If the sheets are put into stacks of 100, however, and each stack remains undisturbed by interruptions, then the worst possible count loss from interruption is 108. That number represents the recounting of nine stacks of 100 each plus 99 single sheets. Further, if sheets are first put into stacks of 10, which are then joined into stacks of 100, the worst possible loss from interruption would be 27. That number represents nine stacks of 100 plus nine stacks of 10 plus nine single sheets. With this system there is far less recounting time, but the chances of completing the count are vastly higher.

When individuals work for a small, concrete outcome, giving them a chance to enjoy visible success, there is a sense of heightened confidence, excitement and optimism. They then want to go for another 'small win'. When one solution has been identified, the next solvable problem often becomes more visible. Additional resources also tend to flow towards winners, so the probability of additional success increases.

Research clearly demonstrates that a small-wins strategy is superior to a strategy of trying to cope with stressors in large chunks. For example, successive small requests are more likely to be approved and achieve compliance than one large request (Freedman and Fraser, 1966). Positions advocated within the latitude of acceptance (i.e., that are only slightly different from current positions) modify opinions more than does advocacy of a position that exceeds those limits (i.e., large differences exist between current and proposed positions). People whose positions are close to one's own tend to be the targets of the most intensive persuasion attempts, while those whose positions are farther away are dismissed, isolated or derogated.

Cognitive therapy is most successful when the patient is persuaded to do just one thing differently that changes his or her pattern of coping up to that point. Learning tends to occur in small increments rather than in large, all-or-nothing chunks. Retention of learning is better when individuals are in an emotional state similar to the one in which they learned the original material. Over 75 per cent of the changes and improvements in both individuals and reorganisations over time can be accounted for by minor improvements, not major alterations (Hollander, 1965). The point is that the incremental approach used in a small-wins strategy is the most basic and the one most compatible with human preferences for learning, perception, motivation and change (Weick, 1984). What does this have to do with hardiness and resilience? A small-wins strategy both engenders hardiness and helps overcome the Type A personality syndrome, which is basically a winner-takes-all approach to stress. You may recall that hardiness is composed of control, commitment and challenge. The deliberate cultivation of a strategy of small wins helps to produce precisely those psychological states. Small wins reinforce the perception that individuals can influence what happens to them and it helps motivate further action by building on the confidence of past successes and produces changes of manageable size that serve as incentives to learn and seek new opportunities (Weick, 1984, p. 46).

Deep-relaxation strategies

A further medium-term strategy is the practice of deep relaxation (Curtis and Detert, 1981; Greenberg, 1987; Davis et al., 1980). Deep-relaxation techniques differ from temporary, short-term relaxation techniques, which we will discuss later. Deep relaxation, like physical exercise, takes time to develop because its benefits cannot be achieved quickly, but it serves to engender resilience towards stress. Deep-relaxation techniques include meditation, yoga, autogenic training or self-hypnosis, biofeedback, and so on. Considerable evidence exists that individuals who practise such techniques regularly are able to condition their bodies to inhibit the negative effects of stress (Cooper and Aygen, 1979; Stone and Deleo, 1976; Orme-Johnson, 1973; Beary and Benson, 1977; Benson, 1975). Most of these deep-relaxation techniques must be practised over a period of time in order to develop fully, but they are not difficult to learn. Most deep-relaxation techniques require the following conditions:

1. *A quiet environment* in which external distractions are minimised.

2. *A comfortable position* so that muscular effort is minimised.

3. *A mental focus.* Transcendental meditation (TM) advocates recommend concentrating on one word, phrase or object. Benson (1975) suggests the word 'one'. Others suggest picturing a plain vase. The ancient Chinese used a carved jade object that resembled a mountain, sitting on a desktop. The purpose of focusing on a word or object is to rid the mind of all other thoughts.

4. *Controlled breathing*, i.e., deliberate breathing, with pauses between breaths. Thoughts are focused on rhythmic breathing, which helps to clear the mind and aids concentration.

5. *A passive attitude*, so that if other thoughts enter the mind they are ignored.

6. *Focused bodily changes.* While meditation uses the mind to relax the body, autogenic training used bodily sensations of heaviness and warmth to change the psychological state. Feelings of warmth and heaviness are induced in different parts of the body which, in turn, create deep relaxation (Luthe, 1962; Kamiya, 1978).

7. *Repetition.* Because physiological and psychological results depend on consistent practice, the best results occur when such techniques are practised from 20 to 30 minutes each day. (The Skill Practice section (page 149) contains an example of a deep-relaxation exercise.)

Social resilience

The third factor moderating the harmful effects of stress and contributing to resilience involves developing close social relationships. Individuals who are embedded in supportive social networks are less likely to experience stress and are better equipped to cope with its consequences (Beehr, 1976). Supportive social relations provide opportunities to share one's frustrations and disappointments, to receive suggestions and encouragement, and to experience emotional bonding. Such supportive interactions provide the empathy and bolstering required to cope with stressful events. They are formed most easily among individuals who share close emotional ties (e.g., family members) or common experiences (e.g., co-workers). Dramatic evidence for the value of social support systems during periods of high stress comes from the experiences of soldiers captured during the Second World War and the Korean and Vietnam wars. When it was possible for prisoners to form permanent, interacting groups, they maintained better health and morale and were able to resist their captors more effectively than when they were isolated or when groups were unstable. Indeed, the well-documented technique used by the Chinese during the Korean War for breaking down soldiers' resistance to their indoctrination efforts involved weakening group solidarity through planting seeds of mistrust and doubt about members' loyalty. Apart from personal friendships or family relations, two types of social support systems can be formed as part of a manager's job. One is a mentor relationship; the other is a task team. Most individuals, with the possible exception of the most senior managers, can profit from a mentoring relationship. The research is clear that career success, work satisfaction and resilience to stress are enhanced by a mentoring relationship (Hall, 1976; Kram, 1985). Individuals need someone else in the organisation who can provide a role model, from whom they can learn, and from whom they can receive personal attention and a reinforcement of self worth, especially in uncertain, crucial and stressful situations.

Many organisations formally prescribe a mentoring system by assigning a senior manager to shepherd a younger manager when he or she enters the organisation. With rare exceptions, when the contact is one-way, from the top down, these relationships do not work out (Kram, 1985). The junior manager must actively seek and foster the mentoring relationship as well. The junior manager can do this, not by demonstrating over-dependence or over-adaptation, but by expressing a desire to use the senior person as a mentor and then by making certain that the relationship does not become a one-way street. The subordinate can pass along important information and resources to the potential mentor, while both will share in working out solutions to problems. That way, the mentoring relationship becomes mutually satisfying and beneficial for both parties, and resilience to stress is enhanced because of the commitment, trust and co-operation that begin to characterise the relationship. A mentor's guidance can both help to avoid stressful situations and provide support for coping with them.

Smoothly functioning work teams also enhance social resilience. The social value of working on a team has been well-documented in the research (Dyer, 1981). The more cohesive the team, the more support it provides its members. Members of highly cohesive teams communicate with one another more frequently and positively, and report higher satisfaction, lower stress and higher performance levels than do individuals who do not feel as though they are part of a work team (Shaw, 1976).

The value of work teams has also been amply demonstrated in practice.

> In the Fremont, California, plant of General Motors a dramatic change occurred when US workers came under Japanese management. In just one year, marked improvements in productivity, morale and quality occurred, due in a large part to the use of effective work teams. Relationships were formed based not only on friendship, but on a common commitment to solving work-related problems and to generating ideas for improvement. Teams met regularly during work hours to discuss ideas for improvement and to co-ordinate and resolve issues.

Similar dynamics have been fostered in many of the successful companies in Europe. Changes at British Aerospace have been attributed largely to the effective use of work teams. The marked improvements that occur in individual satisfaction and lowered stress levels suggest that the model should be followed wherever it is appropriate. The idea would be that the team, rather than independent individuals, becomes the standard unit for working.

Temporary stress-reduction techniques

So far we have emphasised eliminating sources of stress and developing resilience to stress as the most desirable stress management strategies. However, even in practical circumstances it may be impossible to eliminate all stressors, and individuals must use temporary reactive mechanisms in order to maintain more equilibrium. Although increased resilience can buffer the harmful effects of stress, people must sometimes take immediate action in the short term to cope with stress. Implementing short-term strategies reduces stress temporarily so that longer-term stress elimination or resilience strategies can be incorporated. Short-term strategies are largely reactive and must be repeated whenever stressors are encountered because, unlike other strategies, their effects are temporary. On the other hand, they are especially useful for the immediate calming feelings of anxiety or apprehension. Individuals can use them when they are asked a question they cannot answer, when they become embarrassed by an unexpected event, when they are faced with a presentation or an important meeting, or almost any time they are suddenly stressed and must respond in a short period of time. Five of the best-known and easiest to learn techniques are briefly described below. The first two are physiological; the last three are psychological.

Muscle relaxation

Muscle relaxation involves easing the tension in successive muscle groups. Each muscle group is tightened for five or ten seconds, then completely relaxed. Starting with the feet and progressing to the calves, thighs, stomach, and on to the neck and face, one can relieve tension throughout the entire body. All parts of the body can be included in the exercise. One variation is to roll the head around on the neck several times, shrug the shoulders or stretch the arms up towards the ceiling for five to ten seconds, then release the position and relax the muscles. The result is a state of temporary relaxation that helps eliminate tension and refocus energy.

The Management Training Centre of Unilever UK Holdings in Port Sunlight, UK, was well known for promoting a particular technique of relaxation at meetings. Individuals, feeling under stress, were encouraged to push hard on the underside of the table with their little fingers. The legend was that after several years and several generations of managers had been training in this technique, the table spontaneously levitated at a Unilever Board meeting. After this incident, the legend goes, training in the technique was stopped. In fact the trainers moved on.

Deep breathing

A variation of muscle relaxation involves deep breathing. You take several successive, slow, deep breaths, holding them for five seconds and exhaling completely. You should focus on breathing itself, so that the mind becomes cleared for a brief time while the body relaxes. After each deep breath, muscles in the body should consciously be relaxed.

Imagery and fantasy

A third technique uses imagery and fantasy to eliminate stress temporarily by changing the focus of one's thoughts. Imagery involves visualising an event, using 'mind pictures'. In addition to visualisation, however, imagery also can include re-collections of sounds, smells and textures. The mind focuses on pleasant experiences from the past (e.g., a fishing trip, family holiday, visit with relatives, a day at the beach) that can be recalled vividly. Fantasies, on the other hand, are not past memories but make-believe events or images. It is especially well known, for example, that children often construct imaginary friends, make-believe occurrences or special wishes that are comforting to them when they encounter stress. Adults also use daydreams or other fantasy experiences to get them through stressful situations. The purpose of this technique is to relieve anxiety or pressure temporarily by focusing on something pleasant so that other more productive stress-reducing strategies can be developed for the longer term.

Rehearsal

The fourth technique is called rehearsal. Using this technique, people work them-selves through potentially stressful situations, trying out different scenarios and alternative reactions. Appropriate reactions are rehearsed, either in a safe environ-ment before stress occurs, or 'off-line', in private, in the midst of a stressful situ-ation. Removing oneself temporarily from a stressful circumstance and working through dialogue or reactions, as though rehearsing for a play, can help an indi-vidual to regain control and reduce the immediacy of the stressor.

Reframing

The last strategy, reframing, involves temporarily reducing stress by optimistically redefining a situation as manageable. Although reframing is difficult in the midst of a stressful situation, it can be developed using cues:

'I understand this situation.'
'I've solved similar problems before.'
'Other people are available to help me get through this situation.'
'Others have faced similar situations and made it through.'
'In the long run, this really isn't so critical.'
'I can learn something from this situation.'
'There are several good alternatives available to me.'

Each of these statements can assist an individual to reframe a situation in order to develop long-term proactive or evolutionary strategies.

SUMMARY

We have shown that four kinds of stressor – time, encounter, situational and anti-cipatory – can cause negative physiological, psychological and social reactions in individuals and that these reactions have adverse effects on organisations. Individuals adopt short-, medium- and long-term strategies to cope. The medium-term strategy is to eliminate the stress through time management, delegation, collaboration, interpersonal competence, work redesign, prioritising, goal setting and small-wins strategies. Failing this, removing oneself from the situation is a drastic but permanent solution. This is the long-term strategy.

Resistance to stress can be increased by improving one's personal resilience. Physiological resilience is strengthened through increased cardiovascular conditioning and improved diet. Psychological resilience and hardiness are improved by practising small-wins strategies and deep relaxation. Social resilience is improved by learning to work with others and fostering teamwork. However, when circumstances make it impossible to apply longer-term strategies for reducing stress, short-term relaxation techniques can temporarily alleviate the symptoms of stress.

Behavioural guidelines

Cynthia Berryman-Fink and Charles Fink (1996) suggest a series of tips for managing personal stress – practising relaxation techniques, developing an exercise programme, practising healthy eating, socialising outside work, developing social support and practising time management. We would agree, adding a clarification of personal goals and the longer-term solutions of work redesign even to the point of leaving.

1. Use effective time management practices. Make sure that you use time effectively as well as efficiently by generating your own personal mission statement. Make sure that low-priority tasks do not drive out time to work on high-priority activities.

2. Make better use of your time by using the guidelines in the Time Management Survey on page 93.

3. Build collaborative relationships with individuals based on mutual trust, respect, honesty and kindness. Make 'deposits' into the 'emotional bank accounts' of other people. Form close, stable communities among those with whom you work.

4. Consciously work to improve your interpersonal competency by learning and practising the principles discussed in other chapters of this book.

5. Redesign your work to increase its skill variety, importance, task clarity, autonomy and feedback. Make the work itself stress-reducing rather than stress-inducing.

6. Reaffirm priorities and short-term plans that provide direction and focus to activities. Give important activities priority over urgent ones.

7. Increase your general resilience by leading a balanced life and consciously developing yourself in physical, intellectual, cultural, social, family, and spiritual areas, as well as in your work.

8. Increase your physical resilience by engaging in a regular programme of exercise and proper eating.

9. Increase your psychological resilience and hardiness by implementing a small-wins strategy. Identify and celebrate the small successes that you and others achieve.

10. Learn at least one deep-relaxation technique and practise it regularly.

11. Increase social resilience by forming an open, trusting, sharing relationship with at least one other person. Facilitate a mentoring relationship with someone who can confirm your worth as a person and provide support during periods of stress.

12. Establish a teamwork relationship with those with whom you work or study by identifying shared tasks and structuring co-ordinated action among team members.

13. Learn at least two short-term relaxation techniques and practise them consistently.

Skill Analysis

CASE STUDY **2.1**

THE DAY AT THE BEACH

Not long ago I came to one of those bleak periods that many of us encounter from time to time, a sudden drastic dip in the graph of living when everything goes stale and flat, energy wanes, enthusiasm dies. The effect on my work was frightening. Every morning I would clench my teeth and mutter: 'Today life will take on some of its old meaning. You've got to break through this thing. You've got to!'

But the barren days went by, and the paralysis grew worse. The time came when I knew I had to have help. The man I turned to was a doctor. Not a psychiatrist, just a doctor. He was older than I, and under his surface gruffness lay great wisdom and compassion. 'I don't know what's wrong,' I told him miserably, 'but I just seem to have come to a dead end. Can you help me?'

'I don't know,' he said slowly. He made a tent of his fingers and gazed at me thoughtfully for a long while. Then, abruptly, he asked, 'Where were you happiest as a child?'

'As a child?' I echoed. 'Why, at the beach, I suppose. We had a summer cottage there. We all loved it.'

He looked out of the window and watched the October leaves wafting down. 'Are you capable of following instructions for a single day?' 'I think so,' I said, ready to try anything. 'All right. Here's what I want you to do.'

I was living in The Hague at the time and he told me to drive down to a quieter part of the local beach by myself the following morning, arriving not later than nine o'clock. I could take some lunch; but I was not to read, write, listen to the radio or talk to anyone. 'In addition,' he said, 'I'll give you a prescription to be taken every three hours.'

He tore off four prescription blanks, wrote a few words on each, folded them, numbered them and handed them to me.

Management Consultancy and Skills

'Take these at nine, twelve, three and six.'

'Are you serious?' I asked. He gave a short bark of laughter. 'You won't think I'm joking when you get my bill!'

The next morning, with little faith, I drove to the beach. It was lonely. A north-easter was blowing; the sea looked grey and angry. I sat in the car, the whole day stretching emptily before me. Then I took out the first of the folded slips of paper. On it was written: LISTEN CAREFULLY.

I stared at the two words. 'Why,' I thought, 'the man must be mad.' He had ruled out music, news programmes and human conversation. What else was there?

I raised my head and I did listen. There were no sounds but the steady roar of the sea, the creaking cry of a gull, the drone of some aircraft high overhead. All these sounds were familiar. I got out of the car. A gust of wind slammed the door with a sudden clap of sound.

'Was I supposed to listen carefully to things like that?' I asked myself.

I looked out over the deserted beach, it was winter and not a very nice day. Here the sea bellowed so loudly that all other sounds were lost. And yet, I thought sud-denly, there must be sounds beneath sounds – the soft rasp of drifting sand, the tiny wind whisperings in the dune grasses – if the listener got close enough to hear them. On an impulse I ducked down and, feeling fairly ridiculous, thrust my head into a clump of seaweed. Here I made a discovery: If you listen intently, there is a frac-tional moment in which everything seems to pause. In that instant of stillness, the racing thoughts halt. For a moment, when you truly listen for something outside yourself, you have to silence the clamorous voices within. The mind rests.

I went back to the car and slid behind the wheel. LISTEN CAREFULLY. As I lis-tened again to the deep growl of the sea, I found myself thinking about the white-fanged fury of its storms. I thought of the lessons it had taught us as children. A certain amount of patience: you can't hurry the tides. A great deal of respect: the sea does not suffer fools gladly. An awareness of the vast and mysterious interde-pendence of things: wind and tide and current, calm and squall and hurricane, all combining to determine the paths of the birds above and the fish below. And the cleanness of it all, with every beach swept twice a day by the great broom of the sea.

Sitting there, I realised I was thinking of things bigger than myself – and there was relief in that. Even so, the morning passed slowly. The habit of hurling myself at a problem was so strong that I felt lost without it. Once, when I was wistfully eye-ing the car radio, a phrase from Carlyle jumped into my head: *Silence is the element in which great things fashion themselves.*

By noon the wind had polished the clouds out of the sky, and the sea had a hard, polished and merry sparkle.

I unfolded the second 'prescription.' Again I sat there, half amused and half exas-perated. Three words this time: TRY REACHING BACK.

Back to what? To the past, obviously. But why, when all my worries concerned the present or the future?

I left the car and started tramping back to the foreshore. The doctor had sent me to the beach because it was a place of happy memories. Maybe that was what I was to reach for: the wealth of happiness that lay half-forgotten behind me. I decided to experiment: to work on these vague impressions as a painter would, retouching the colours, strengthening the outlines. I would choose specific incidents and recapture as many details as possible. I would visualise people complete with dress and gestures. I would listen carefully for the exact sound of their voices, the echo of their laughter.

The tide was going out now, but there was still thunder in the surf. So I chose to go back 20 years to the last fishing trip I made with my younger brother. (He died in the Battle of the Atlantic in the Second World War and his body was never recovered.) I found that if I closed my eyes and really tried, I could see him with amazing vividness. I could even see the humour and eagerness in his eyes that far-off morning.

I could see it all: the ivory scimitar of beach where we were fishing; the skies smeared with sunrise; the great rollers creaming in, stately and slow. I could feel the backwash swirl warm around my knees, see the sudden arc of my brother's rod as he struck a fish, hear his exultant yell. Piece by piece I rebuilt it, clear and unchanged under the transparent varnish of time. Then it was gone.

I sat up slowly. TRY REACHING BACK. Happy people were usually assured, confident people. If, then, you deliberately reached back and touched happiness, might there not be released little flashes of power, tiny sources of strength?

This second period of the day went more quickly, people appeared and seemingly resented each other, keeping in little knots of privacy. As the sun began its long slant down the sky, my mind ranged eagerly through the past, reliving some episodes, uncovering others that had been almost completely forgotten. For example, when I was around 13 and my brother 10, Father had promised to take us to the circus. But at lunch there was a phone call: some urgent business required his attention. We braced ourselves for disappointment. Then we heard him say, 'No, I won't be down. It'll have to wait.' When he came back to the table, Mother smiled. 'The circus keeps coming back, you know, she said.' 'I know,' said Father, 'but childhood doesn't.' Across all the years I remembered this and knew from the sudden glow of warmth that no kindness is ever wasted or ever completely lost.

By three o'clock the tide was out and the sound of the waves was only a rhythmic whisper, like a giant breathing. I stayed in my sandy nest, feeling relaxed and content, and a little complacent. The doctor's prescriptions, I thought, were easy to take. But I was not prepared for the next one. This time the three words were not a gentle suggestion. They sounded more like a command. RE-EXAMINE YOUR MOTIVES.

My first reaction was purely defensive. 'There's nothing wrong with my motives,' I said to myself. 'I want to be successful – who doesn't? I want to have a certain amount of recognition – but so does everybody. I want more security than I've got – and why not?'

'Maybe', said a small voice somewhere inside my head, 'those motives aren't good enough. Maybe that's the reason the wheels have stopped going around.' I picked up a handful of sand and let it stream between my fingers. In the past, whenever my work went well, there had always been something spontaneous about it, something uncontrived, something free. Lately it had been calculated, competent and dead.

Why? Because I had been looking past the job itself to the rewards I hoped it would bring. The work had ceased to be an end in itself, it had become merely a means to make money, to pay bills. The sense of giving something, of helping people, of making a contribution, had been lost in a frantic clutch at security. In a flash of certainty, I saw that if one's motives are wrong, nothing can be right. It makes no difference whether you are a postman, a hairdresser, an insurance salesman, a housewife . . . As long as you feel you are serving others, you do the job well. When you are concerned only with helping yourself, you do it less well. That is a law as inexorable as gravity. For a long time I sat there. Far out on the bar I heard the murmur of the surf change to a hollow roar as the tide turned. Behind me the spears of light were almost horizontal.

My time at the beach had almost run out, and I felt a grudging admiration for the doctor and the 'prescriptions' he had so casually and cunningly devised. I saw, now, that in them was a therapeutic progression that might well be of value to anyone facing any difficulty.

Listen carefully: To calm a frantic mind, slow it down, shift the focus from inner problems to outer things.

Try reaching back: Since the human mind can hold only one idea at a time, you blot out present worry when you touch the happiness of the past.

Re-examine your motives: This was the hard core of the 'treatment', this challenge to reappraise, to bring one's motives into alignment with one's capabilities and conscience. But the mind must be clear and receptive to do this – hence the six hours of quiet that went before.

The western sky was a blaze of crimson as I took out the last slip of paper. Six words this time. I walked slowly along the beach. A few yards below the high-water mark I stopped and read the words again: WRITE YOUR TROUBLES ON THE SAND. I let the paper blow away, reached down and picked up a fragment of shell. Kneeling there under the vault of the sky, I wrote several words on the sand, one above the other. Then I walked away, and I did not look back. I had written my troubles on the sand. And the tide was coming in.

Source: Adapted from *The Day at the Beach*, by Arthur Gordon. (© 1959 by Arthur Gordon. First published in *Reader's Digest*. Reprinted by permission of the author. All rights reserved.)

Discussion questions

1. What is effective about these strategies for coping with stress? Why did they work? Upon what principles are they based?

2. Which of these techniques can be used on a temporary basis without going to 'the beach'?

3. Are these prescriptions effective coping strategies or merely escapes?

4. What other prescriptions could the author take besides the four mentioned here? Generate your own list.

5. What do these prescriptions have to do with the model of stress management presented in this chapter?

CASE STUDY **2.2**

THE CASE OF THE MISSING TIME

At approximately 07.30 on Tuesday, 17 June 1997, Chris Craig, a senior production manager in Norris Printing Ltd, set off to drive to work. It was a beautiful day and the journey to the factory took about 20 minutes, giving Chris an opportunity to think about plant problems without interruption.

The Norris Company owned and operated three factories and had a Europe-wide reputation for quality colour printing. Three hundred and fifty people worked for the company, about half working in Chris's Belgium plant which also housed the company's headquarters.

Chris was in fine spirits as he relaxed behind the wheel. Various thoughts occurred to him, and he said to himself, 'This is going to be the day to really get things done.'

He began to run through the day's work, first one project, then another, trying to establish priorities. After a few minutes he decided that progressing with the new system of production control was probably the most important, certainly the most urgent of his jobs for the day. He frowned for a moment as he remembered that on Friday the general manager had casually asked him if he had given the project any further thought.

Chris realised that he had not been giving it much thought lately. He had been meaning to get to work on this idea for over three months, but something else always seemed to crop up. 'I haven't had much time to sit down and really work it out,' he said to himself.

'I'd better get going and sort this one out today.' With that he began to break down the objectives, procedures and installation steps of the project. He grinned as he reviewed the principles involved and calculated roughly the anticipated savings. 'It's about time,' he told himself, 'this idea should have been followed up long ago.' Chris remembered that he had first thought of the production control system nearly 18 months ago, just before leaving the Norris factory in Spain. He had spoken to his boss, Jim Quince, manager of the Spanish factory about it then, and both agreed that it was worth looking into.

The idea was temporarily shelved when he was transferred to the Belgium plant a month later. Then he started to think through a procedure for simpler transport of dies to and from the Spanish plant. Visualising the notes on his desk, he thought about the inventory analysis he needed to identify and eliminate some of the slow-moving stock items, the packing controls that needed revision, and the need to design a new special-order form. He also decided that this was the day to settle on a job printer to do the simple outside printing of office forms. There were a few other projects he couldn't remember, but he could tend to them after lunch, if not before.

When he entered the plant Chris knew something was wrong as he met Albert Marsden, the stockroom foreman, who appeared troubled.

'A great morning, Albert,' Chris greeted him cheerfully.

'Not so good, Chris; the new man isn't in this morning.'

'Did he phone in – let you know why?' asked Chris.

'No, nothing,' replied Marsden. Chris shared Albert's concern. He knew that 'the new man' had been taken on to deal with a major problem in the warehouse. Without him, and particularly without him at no notice, the whole of the new automated stock delivery system could and probably would grind to a halt.

'OK, we have a problem, ask Personnel to call him and see if he intends to come in.' Albert Marsden hesitated for a moment before replying, 'Okay, Chris, but can you find me a man with real computer skills? – you know the problem as well as I do.'

'OK, Albert, I'll call you in half an hour with something, even if I have to do it myself.'

Making a mental note of the situation, Chris headed for his office. He greeted the group of workers huddled around Marie Heinlinne, the office manager, who was discussing the day's work schedule with them. As the meeting broke up, Marie picked up a few samples from the pallet, showed them to Chris, and asked if they should be sent out as they were or whether it would be necessary to inspect all of them. Before he could answer, Marie went on to ask if he could suggest another operator for the sealing machine to replace the regular operator, who was absent. She also told him that George, the industrial engineer, had called and was waiting to hear from Chris. After telling Marie to send the samples as they were, he made a note of the need for a sealer operator for the office and then called George. He agreed to go to George's office before lunch and started on his routine morning tour of the factory. He asked each team leader the types and volumes of orders they were running, the number of people present, how the schedules were coming along, and the orders to be run next. He helped the folding-room team leader find temporary storage space for consolidating a consignment; discussed quality control with a press operator who had been producing work off specification; arranged to transfer four people temporarily to different departments, including one for Albert from accounts who 'was not frightened of computers'; and talked to the shipping foreman about collecting some urgent ink supplies and the special deliveries of the day. As he continued through the factory, he saw to it that reserve stock was moved out of the forward stock area, talked to another pressman about his holiday, had a 'heart-to-heart' talk with a press assistant who seemed to need frequent reassurance, and approved two type changes and one colour change with three press operators and their team leader.

Returning to his office, Chris reviewed the production reports on the larger orders against his initial estimates and found that the plant was running behind schedule. He called in the folding-room team leader and together they went over the production schedule in detail, making several changes. During this discussion, the composing-room foreman stopped in to note several type changes, and the routing foreman telephoned for approval of a revised printing schedule. The stockroom team leader called twice, first to inform him that two standard, fast moving stock items were dangerously low, later to advise him that the paper stock for the urgent Pitman's job had finally arrived. Chris made the necessary calls to inform those concerned. He then began to put delivery dates on important and difficult enquiries received from customers and salesmen – Marie handled the routine enquiries. While he was doing this he was interrupted twice, once by a sales rep to ask for a better delivery date than originally scheduled, and once by the personnel director asking him to set a time when he could hold an initial training and induction interview with a new employee. After sorting the customer and salesmen enquiries, Chris headed for his morning conference in the executive offices. At this meeting he answered the sales director's questions in connection with some problem orders, complaints, and the status of large-volume orders and potential new orders. He then met the general manager to discuss a few ticklish policy matters and to answer questions on several specific production and personnel problems. Before leaving the executive offices, he stopped at the office of the secretary–treasurer to enquire about delivery of cartons, paper and boxes, and to place a new order for paper.

On the way back to his own office, Chris conferred with George about the two current engineering projects that had been discussed earlier. When he reached his desk, he looked at his watch. He had five minutes before lunch – enough to make a few notes of the details he needed to check in order to answer difficult questions raised by the sales manager that morning.

After a lunch of sandwiches grabbed from the canteen, Chris started again. He began by checking the previous day's production reports, did some rescheduling to get out urgent orders, placed appropriate delivery dates on new orders and enquiries received that morning, and helped a team leader with a personal problem. He spent about 20 minutes on the phone going over routine problems with the Spanish factory.

By mid-afternoon Chris had made another tour of the site, after which he met with the personnel director to review a touchy personal problem raised by one of the clerical employees, the holiday schedules submitted by his foremen, and the pending job-evaluation programme. Following this meeting, Chris hurried back to his office to complete the special statistical report for U.W.C., one of Norris's best customers. As he finished the report, he discovered that it was 18.10 and he was the only one left in the office. Chris was tired. He put on his coat and headed for his car; on the way he was stopped by two team leaders from the incoming night shift with urgent issues needing decisions.

With both eyes on the traffic, Chris reviewed the day he had just completed. 'Busy?' he asked himself. 'Too busy – but did I actually DO anything? There was the usual routine, the same as any other day. The factory kept going and I think it must have been a good production day. Any creative or special project work done?' Chris grimaced as he reluctantly answered, 'No'. Feeling guilty, he probed further. 'Am I a senior manager – a true executive? I'm paid like one, respected like one, and have a responsible assignment with the necessary authority to carry it out. Yet an executive should be able to think strategically and creatively and not just firefight. An executive needs time for thinking. Today was typical and I did little, if any, creative work. The projects that I planned in the morning have not moved an inch. What's more, I have no guarantee that tomorrow or the next day will be any different. This is the real problem.' Chris continued talking silently to himself. 'Taking work home? Yes, occasionally, it's expected but I've been doing too much lately. I owe my wife and family some of my time. After all, they are the people for whom I'm really working. If I am forced to spend much more time away from them, am I being fair to them or myself. What about work with the Scouts? Should I stop it? It takes up a lot of my time, but I feel I owe other people some time, and I feel that I am making a valuable contribution. When do I have time for a game of squash or even a quiet drink with my friends these days? Maybe I'm just making excuses because I don't plan my time better, but I don't think so. I've already analysed my way of working and I think I plan and delegate pretty well. Do I need an assistant? Possibly, but that's a long-term project and I don't believe I could justify the additional overhead expenditure. Anyway, I doubt whether it would solve the problem.'

All the way home he was concerned with the problem – even as he pulled into the drive. His thoughts were interrupted as he saw his son running towards the car, 'Mummy, Daddy's home.'

Discussion questions

1. Which of Chris's personal characteristics inhibit his effective management of time?
2. What are his organisational problems?
3. What principles of time and stress management are violated in this case?
4. If you were hired as a consultant to Chris, what would you advise him to do?

Skill Practice

EXERCISE **2.1**

THE SMALL-WINS STRATEGY

An ancient Chinese proverb states that long journeys are always made up of small steps. In Japan, the feeling of obligation to make small, incremental improvements in one's work is known as *Kaizen*. In this chapter the notion of small wins was explained as a way to break up large problems and identify small successes in coping with them. Each of these approaches represents the same basic philosophy – to recognise incremental successes – and each helps an individual to build up psychological resilience to stress.

Answer the following questions. An example is given to help clarify each question, but your response need not relate to the example.

1. What major stressor do you currently face? What creates anxiety or discomfort for you? (For example, 'I have too much to do.')
2. What are the major components of the situation? Divide the major problem into smaller parts or sub-problems. (For example, 'I have said "yes" to too many things. I have deadlines approaching. I don't have all the resources I need to complete all my commitments right now.')

Management Consultancy and Skills

3. What are the sub-components of each of those sub-problems? Divide them into yet smaller parts. (For example, 'I have the following deadlines approaching: a report due, a large amount of reading to do, a family obligation, an important presentation, a need to spend some personal time with someone I care about, a committee meeting that requires preparation.')

4. What actions can I take that will affect any of these sub-components? (For example, 'I can engage the person I care about in helping me prepare for the presentation. I can write a shorter report than I originally intended. I can carry the reading material with me wherever I go.')

5. What actions have I taken in the past that have helped me to cope successfully with similar stressful circumstances? (For example, 'I have found someone else to share some of my tasks. I have got some reading done while waiting/travelling/eating. I have prepared only key elements for the committee meeting.')

6. What small thing should I feel good about as I think about how I have coped or will cope with this major stressor? (For example, 'I have accomplished a lot under pressure in the past. I have been able to use what I had time to prepare to its best advantage.')

Repeat this process each time you face major stressors. The six specific questions may not be as important to you as:

- Breaking the problem down into parts and then breaking those parts down again.
- Identifying alternative actions that you have previously found successful in coping with components of the stressor.

Skill Application

ACTIVITY **2.1**

LIFE-BALANCE ANALYSIS

The prescription to maintain a balanced life seems to contain a paradox:

> *It makes sense that life should have variety and that each of us should develop multiple aspects of ourselves. Narrowness and rigidity are not highly valued by anyone.*

However, the demands of work, school, or family, for example, can be so overwhelming that we don't have time to do much except respond to those demands. Work could take all of one's time. So could school. So could family. The temptation for most of us, then, is to focus on only a few areas of our lives that place a great deal of pressure on us, and leave the other areas undeveloped. Use Figure 2.5 (Balancing Life Activities) to complete this exercise. In responding to the four items in the exercise, think of the amount of time you spend in each area, the amount of experience and development you have had in the past in each area, and the extent to which development in each area is important to you.

Management Consultancy and Skills

1. In Figure 2.5 (Balancing Life Activities), shade in the portion of each section that represents the extent to which that aspect of your life has been developed. How satisfied are you that each aspect is adequately cultivated?

2. Now write down at least one thing that you can start doing to improve your development in the areas that need it. (For example, you might do more outside reading to develop culturally, invite a foreign visitor to your home to develop socially, go to Church regularly to develop spiritually, and so on.)

3. Because the intent of this exercise is not to add more pressure and stress to your life but to increase your resilience through life balance, identify the things you will stop doing that will make it possible to achieve a better life balance.

4. To make this a practise exercise and not just a planning exercise, do something today from your list for items 2 and 3 above. Write down specifically what you will do and when. Don't let the rest of the week go by without implementing something you've written.

ACTIVITY **2.2**

DEEP RELAXATION

To engage in deep relaxation, you need to reserve time that can be spent concentrating on relaxing. By focusing your mind, you can positively affect both your mental and physical states. This exercise describes one technique that is easily learned and practised. The particular technique we are presenting combines key elements of several well-known formulas. It is recommended that this technique be practised for 20 minutes a day, three times a week (Robinson, 1985; Davis *et al.*, 1980). Reserve at least 30 minutes to engage in this exercise for the first time. Find a quiet spot with your partner or a friend, and have that person read the instructions below. When you have finished, switch roles. Since you will practise this exercise later in a different setting, you may want to make a tape recording of these instructions.

Step 1   Assume a comfortable position. You may want to lie down. Loosen any tight clothing. Close your eyes and be quiet.

Step 2   Assume a passive attitude. Focus on your body and on relaxing specific muscles. Make your mind a blank – thinking of a colour such as grey often helps.

Step 3   Tense and relax each of your muscle groups for five to ten seconds, in the following order:

• *Forehead*   Wrinkle your forehead. Try to make your eyebrows touch your hairline for five seconds, then relax.

• *Eyes and nose*   Close your eyes as tightly as you can for five seconds, then relax.

• *Lips, cheeks and jaw*   Draw the corners of your mouth back and grimace for five seconds, then relax.

• *Hands*   Extend your arms in front of you. Clench your fists tightly for five seconds, then relax.

- *Forearms* Extend your arms out against an invisible wall and push forward for five seconds, then relax.
- *Upper arms* Bend your elbows and tense your biceps for five seconds, then relax.
- *Shoulders* Shrug your shoulders up to your ears for five seconds, then relax.
- *Back* Arch your back off the floor for five seconds, then relax.
- *Stomach* Tighten your stomach muscles by lifting your legs off the ground about two inches for five seconds, then relax.
- *Hips and buttocks* Tighten your hip and buttock muscles for five seconds, then relax.
- *Thighs* Tighten your thigh muscles by pressing your legs together as tightly as you can for five seconds, then relax.
- *Feet* Bend your ankles towards your body as far as you can for five seconds, then point your toes for five seconds, then relax.
- *Toes* Curl your toes as tightly as you can for five seconds, then relax.

Step 4 Focus on any muscles that are still tense. Repeat the exercise for that muscle group three or four times until it relaxes.

Step 5 Now focus on your breathing. Do not alter it artificially, but focus on taking long, slow breaths. Concentrate exclusively on the rhythm of your breathing until you have taken at least 45 breaths.

Step 6 Now focus on the heaviness and warmth of your body. Let all the energy in your body seep away. Let go of your normal tendency to control your body and mobilise it towards activity.

Step 7 With your body completely relaxed, relax your mind. Picture a plain object such as a glass ball, an empty white vase, the moon, or some favourite thing. Don't analyse it; don't examine it; just picture it. Concentrate fully on the object for at least three minutes without letting any other thoughts enter your mind. Begin now.

Step 8 Now open your eyes, slowly get up, and return to your hectic, stressful, anxiety ridden, Type A environment better prepared to cope with it effectively.

ACTIVITY **2.3**

MONITORING AND MANAGING TIME

Managers and business school students very often identify time management as their most pressing problem. They feel overwhelmed at times with the feeling of not having achieved those things that they know they could have achieved. Even when extremely busy, people experience less dysfunctional stress if they feel they are in control of their time and, in particular, in control of their ability to take time out. It is the existence of time that is under your control, which includes time out – discretionary time, that is the key to effective time management. This next activity should help you identify and better manage your discretionary time.

Management Consultancy and Skills

The exercise, in one form or another, is a key element in most time-management programmes. It takes one week to complete and requires you to keep a time diary for the whole period. Complete the following five steps, then use your partner or a friend to get feedback and ideas for improving and refining your plans.

Step 1 Beginning tomorrow, keep a time diary for a whole week. Record how you spend each 30 minutes in the next seven 24-hour periods, using the following format in a notebook you can carry with you.

Time	*Required/discretionary activity*	*Productive/unproductive*
09.00–09.30		
09.30–10.00		
10.00–10.30		
. . .		

Step 2 Under the heading 'Required/discretionary activity,' write whether someone required the time spent in each 30-minute block (R) or it was actually discretionary (D).

Step 3 Under the heading 'Productive/unproductive', and beside only the discretionary time blocks, rate the extent to which you used each one productively; that is, whether or not it led to improvements of some kind. Use the following scale for your rating: **4**, used productively; **3** used somewhat productively; **2**, used somewhat unproductively; **1**, used unproductively.

Step 4 Draw a plan to increase your weekly discretionary time. (The Time Management Survey earlier in the chapter may help.) Write down the things you will implement.

Step 5 How can you use your discretionary time more productively, especially any blocks of time you rated 1 or 2 in Step 3. What will you do to make sure the time you control is used for more long-term benefit? What will you stop doing that impedes your effective use of time?

ACTIVITY **2.4**

PERSONAL STRESSORS

Do a systematic analysis of the stressors you face in your job/college/family and social life – using our classification – Time, Encounter, Situational, Anticipatory. Identify strategies to eliminate or sharply reduce them. Record this analysis in your notebook.

ACTIVITY **2.5**

TEACHING OTHERS

Find someone you know well who is experiencing a great deal of stress. Teach him or her how to manage that stress better by applying the concepts, principles, techniques and exercises in this chapter. Describe what you taught and record the results in your notebook.

ACTIVITY **2.6**

IMPLEMENT TECHNIQUES

1. Implement at least three of the time-management techniques suggested in the Time Management Survey or elsewhere that you are not currently using but think you might find helpful. In your time diary, keep track of the amount of time these techniques save you over a one-month period. Be sure to use that extra time productively.

2. With a colleague or fellow student, identify ways in which your work can be redesigned to reduce stress and increase productivity.

3. Write a personal mission statement. Specify precisely your core principles; those things you consider to be central to your life and your sense of self-worth; and the legacy you want to leave. Identify at least one action you can take in order to accomplish your mission statement. Begin working on it today.

4. Establish a short-term goal or plan that you wish to accomplish this year. Make it compatible with the top priorities in your life. Specify the steps, the reporting and accounting mechanisms, and the criteria of success and rewards.

5. Share this plan with others you know so that you have an incentive to pursue it even after you finish this assignment.

6. Have a physical examination, then outline and implement a regular physical fitness and diet programme. Even if it is just regular walking, do some kind of physical exercise at least three times a week. Preferably, institute a regular, vigorous cardiovascular fitness programme. Record your progress in your diary.

7. Pick at least one long-term deep-relaxation technique. Learn it and practise it on a regular basis. Record your progress in your diary.

8. Establish a mentoring relationship with someone with whom you work or go to college. Your mentor may be a tutor, a senior manager, or someone who has been around longer than you have. Make certain that the relationship is reciprocal and that it will help you to cope with the stresses you face at work or college.

ACTIVITY **2.7**

APPLICATION PLAN AND EVALUATION

This activity is designed to help you apply your time-management skills to real life. Unlike a 'training' activity, in which feedback is immediate and others can assist you with their evaluations, this skill application activity is one you must accomplish and evaluate on your own. There are two parts to this activity.

Part 1 helps to prepare you to apply the skill. Part 2 helps you to evaluate and improve on your experience. Be sure to write down answers to each item. Don't short-circuit the process by skipping steps.

Part 1: Plan

1. Write down the two or three aspects of this skill that are most important to you. These may be areas of weakness, areas you most want to improve, or areas that are most salient to a problem you are currently facing. Identify the specific aspects of this skill that you want to apply.

2. Now identify the setting or the situation in which you will apply this skill. Establish a plan for performance by actually writing down a description of the situation. Who else will be involved? When will you do it? Where will it be done?

3. Identify the specific behaviours you will engage in to apply this skill.

4. What are the indicators of successful performance? How will you know you have been effective? What will indicate that you have performed competently?

Part 2: Evaluation

5. After you have completed your implementation, record the results. What happened? How successful were you? What was the effect on others?

6. How can you improve? What modifications can you make next time? What will you do differently in a similar situation in the future?

7. Looking back on your whole skill practice and application experience, what have you learned? What has been surprising? In what ways might this experience help you in the long term?

Further reading

Brewer, K.C. (1997) *Managing stress.* Aldershot: Gower.

Cooper, C. and Ferrario, M. (1997) *The essence of stress management.* London: Prentice Hall.

Cooper, C. and Lewis, S. (1998) *Balancing your career, family and life.* London: Kogan Page.

Handy, C. (1995) *Beyond certainty: the changing worlds of organisations.* London: Hutchinson.

Haynes, M.E. (1996) *Make every minute count: how to manage your time effectively,* 2nd edn. London: Kogan Page.

Management Consultancy and Skills

Effective Problem Solving

SKILL DEVELOPMENT OUTLINE

Skill Pre-assessment surveys

- Problem solving, creativity and innovation
- How creative are you?
- Innovative Attitude Scale

Skill Learning material

- Problem solving, creativity and innovation
- Steps in rational problem solving
- A basis for all problem solving
- Limitations of the rational problem-solving model
- Impediments to creative problem solving
- Problems requiring a creative Input
- Conceptual blocks
- Review of conceptual blocks
- Conceptual blockbusting

- Stages in creative thought
- Methods for improving problem definition
- Generate more alternatives
- Hints for applying problem-solving techniques
- Summary
- Behavioural guidelines

Skill Analysis case

- The Sony Walkman

Skill Practice exercise

- Applying conceptual blockbusting

Skill Application activities

- Suggested further assignments
- Application plan and evaluation

LEARNING OBJECTIVES

- To allow individuals to assess their existing problem-solving skills and give them a chance to improve them.
- To provide a framework for rational problem solving and see where this framework falls down.

- To look at the blocks to creativity and how to reduce them.
- To understand how creativity can be fostered and managed in organisations.

156

INTRODUCTION

The words 'problem solving' are jargon, but they have become so much part of the language of managers that it is easy to forget that they imply a special meaning only to be understood by their select band. Problem solving, in the managerial context, implies a logical process which is called upon when something out of the routine occurs or when something out of the routine is needed. Handling the non-routine can be a problem in anyone's language – a challenge. The concept of 'problem solving' may well not be new to you, but, as with other parts of the book, we will discuss common sense that is not commonly applied. Let's look at a very ordinary way of handling the routine.

Every time we are faced with any form of new activity we need to be motivated – we need to be impressed by WHY things need to change. Then we need to understand WHAT has to be changed, have a practical assessment of HOW it can be changed. We then explore the consequences, IF – and if the consequences are acceptable or inevitable we proceed.

Suppose that we were told to travel to Munich to deliver some drawings to our agent tomorrow. The journey is routine and part of our job. We accept the WHYs without question – this is our job and the boss knows what he or she is doing. The WHATs are also obvious and, provided there are no politics involved, accepted without question – we will take the drawings, a clean set of underwear and revise our knowledge on the project so that we can answer questions. The fact that we need to revise our knowledge probably rules out driving to Munich and we will either go by train or plane – these are our HOWs. We may choose the train to give us more time and the consequences, our IFs, seem fine. The work in the office can be either delegated or postponed but a snag arises. Suppose just before we set out a very near and dear relative is taken ill and needs our support for the time we are to be away. This is a problem, and we will go round the cycle again, beginning with questioning the WHY. The original issue implied that we should go to Munich now with the drawings – but we now need to start asking questions.

- Do we have to be *with* the drawings?
- Could anyone else take them?
- Are *all* the drawings and instructions needed tomorrow? What is so important about tomorrow?
- Is the time so important? Could there be a delay while we sorted out day care?

Suppose in our new set of WHY questions we find that the agent could start work on some limited instructions with the ability to contact us. The drawings could be delayed because he has a lot of pre-work before the detail is required. Workings from this point our new WHATs would be to get instructions out immediately, being available for questioning, getting the drawings out as soon as possible but delaying our visit.

The HOWs would be about faxing the basic instructions and being available on an e-mail address. A commercial courier could send the drawings and we could

Management Consultancy and Skills

follow at the end of the month when the agent was ready with the really deep questions.

The IFs may well be acceptable to us, the company and the agent but they need to be reviewed in the light of the present situation and previous experience.

Unfortunately, this common-sense and logical approach is rarely used rigorously although it may seem intuitive. To stick to it in simple cases we need constant encouragement, but in complex cases we need some form of detailed procedure that all the stakeholders can accept, understand and follow. There is also the point that common sense and logic will not answer all problem issues. Sometimes we need to take a lateral view and provide a creative solution. Our chapter will close with the commonly acknowledged blocks to logical and creative thinking in the real world.

Skill Pre-assessment

SURVEY **3.1**

PROBLEM SOLVING, CREATIVITY AND INNOVATION

Step 1 Before you start the chapter, please respond to the following statements by writing a number from the rating scale below in the left-hand column (Pre-assessment). The questions do prompt towards best practice but your answers should reflect your attitudes and behaviour as they are now, not as you would like them to be. Be honest. This instrument is designed to help you to discover your level of competency in problem solving and creativity so that you can tailor your learning to your specific needs. When you have completed the survey, use the scoring key at the end of the book to identify the skills that are most important for you to master.

Step 2 After you have completed the chapter, cover up your first set of answers and respond to the same statements again, this time in the right-hand column (Post-assessment). When you have completed the survey, go back to the scoring key to measure your progress. If your score remains low in specific skill areas, use the behavioural guidelines at the end of the Skill Learning section to guide your further practice.

RATING SCALE

1 = Strongly disagree   **2** = Disagree   **3** = Slightly disagree
4 = Slightly agree   **5** = Agree   **6** = Strongly agree

	Assessment	
	Pre-	Post-
When I approach a typical, routine problem		
1. I always define clearly and explicitly what the problem is.	____	____
2. I always generate more than one alternative solution to the problem.	____	____

3. I evaluate the alternative solutions based on both long- and short-term consequences. ____ ____

4. I define the problem before solving it, thus avoiding imposing my predetermined solutions. ____ ____

5. I keep problem-solving steps distinct, separating definitions, alternatives and solutions. ____ ____

When faced with a complex or difficult problem that does not have a straightforward solution

6. I try to define the problem in several different ways. ____ ____

7. I try to be flexible in the way I approach the problem, not relying on past concepts or practice. ____ ____

8. I look for patterns or common elements in different aspects of the problem. ____ ____

9. I try to unfreeze my thinking by asking lots of questions about the nature of the problem. ____ ____

10. I try to apply both logic and intuition to the problem. ____ ____

11. I frequently use metaphors or analogies to help me look more widely at a problem. ____ ____

12. I strive to look at problems from different perspectives so as to generate multiple definitions. ____ ____

13. I list the alternatives before evaluating any of them. ____ ____

14. I often break the problem down into smaller components and analyse each one separately. ____ ____

15. I strive to generate multiple creative solutions to problems. ____ ____

When trying to foster more creativity and innovation among those with whom I work

16. I help others to work on their ideas outside the constraints of normal procedures. ____ ____

17. I make sure there are divergent points of view represented in every problem-solving group. ____ ____

18. I can produce wild ideas to help stimulate people to find new ways of approaching problems. ____ ____

19. I try to acquire information from customers regarding their preferences and expectations. ____ ____

20. I do involve outsiders – customers or recognised experts – in problem-solving discussions. ____ ____

21. I acknowledge not only the ideas of people but also supporters, providers and implementers. ____ ____

22. I encourage informed rule-breaking in pursuit of creative solutions. ____ ____

SURVEY **3.2**

HOW CREATIVE ARE YOU?

The following questionnaire is based on the personality traits, attitudes, values, motivations and interests of known 'high creatives' and asks you to rate yourself against them. Be as frank as possible.

RATING SCALE

For each statement, write in the appropriate letter:
A = agree   **B** = undecided or do not know   **C** = disagree
The scoring key is at the end of the book (see Appendix 1).

---

1. I am usually certain that following the correct procedure will solve the problem. ____
2. It is a waste of time to ask questions if I have no hope of obtaining answers. ____
3. I concentrate harder than most people on whatever interests me. ____
4. I feel that a logical step-by-step method is best for solving problems. ____
5. In groups I occasionally voice opinions that seem to turn some people off. ____
6. I am concerned about what others think of me. ____
7. It is better to do what I believe is right than to try to win the approval of others. ____
8. People who seem uncertain about things lose my respect. ____
9. More than most, I need the things I take part in to be interesting and exciting. ____
10. I know how to keep my inner impulses in check. ____
11. I am able to stick with difficult problems over extended periods of time. ____
12. On occasion I get overly enthusiastic. ____
13. I often get my best ideas when doing nothing in particular. ____
14. For solving problems I rely on hunches and the feeling of 'rightness' or 'wrongness'. ____
15. When problem solving, I work faster when analysing the problem and slower when synthesising the information I have gathered. ____
16. I sometimes enjoy breaking the rules and doing what I am not supposed to do. ____
17. I like hobbies that involve collecting things. ____
18. Daydreaming has provided the impetus for many of my better projects. ____
19. I like people who are objective and rational. ____
20. In choosing a different job for me, I would rather be a doctor than an explorer. ____
21. I can get on better with people from the same social and business class. ____
22. I have a high degree of aesthetic sensitivity. ____
23. I am driven to achieve high status and power in life. ____
24. I like people who are sure of their conclusions. ____
25. Inspiration has nothing to do with the successful solution of problems. ____

26. In an argument, my greatest pleasure would be for the person who disagrees with me to become a friend, even at the price of sacrificing my point of view.   ____

27. I am much more interested in having new ideas than in selling them to others.   ____

28. I would enjoy spending an entire day alone, just thinking.   ____

29. I tend to avoid situations in which I might feel inferior.   ____

30. In evaluating information, the source is more important to me than the content.   ____

31. I resent things being uncertain and unpredictable.   ____

32. I like people who follow the rule, 'business before pleasure'.   ____

33. Self-respect is much more important than the respect of others.   ____

34. I feel that people who strive for perfection are unwise.   ____

35. I prefer to work with others in a team effort rather than solo.   ____

35. I like work in which I must influence others.   ____

37. Many of my problems cannot be resolved in terms of a good or bad solution.   ____

38. It is important for me to have a place for everything and everything in its place.   ____

39. Writers who use strange and unusual words merely want to show off.   ____

Below is a list of terms that describe people. Highlight the 10 words that best characterise you.

alert	observant	self-confident	tactful	retiring
energetic	dedicated	factual	self-demanding	flexible
formal	unemotional	open-minded	cautious	efficient
curious	fashionable	well-liked	absent-minded	egotistical
persuasive	forward looking	involved	inhibited	poised
informal	modest	thorough	habit-bound	independent
stern	good-natured	impulsive	enthusiastic	acquisitive
practical	understanding	sociable	polished	helpful
realistic	determined	persevering	courageous	perceptive
restless	looking	dynamic	resourceful	predictable
organised	clear-thinking	original	innovative	quick

Source: Eugene Raudsepp (1981)

SURVEY **3.3**

INNOVATIVE ATTITUDE SCALE

Please indicate how far each of the following statements are true of either your actual behaviour or your intentions at work. Use the rating scale for your responses.

RATING SCALE

1 = Almost never true   **2** = Seldom true   **3** = N/A
4 = Often true   **5** = Almost always true

Use the scoring key in Appendix 1 to interpret your answers.

Management Consultancy and Skills

1. I discuss my progress and opportunities with my supervisor or boss. ____
2. I try new ideas and approaches to problems. ____
3. I take things or situations apart to find out how they work. ____
4. I welcome uncertainty and unusual circumstances related to my tasks. ____
5. I attempt to negotiate the conditions under which I work. ____
6. I can be counted on to find a new use for existing methods or equipment. ____
7. In my team, I will be the first, or nearly the first, to try out a new idea or method. ____
8. I like the opportunity to bring new information to my team from outside. ____
9. I demonstrate originality. ____
10. I will work on a problem that has caused others great difficulty. ____
11. I provide an important role in developing a new solution. ____
12. I will provide well-researched proposals of ideas to my work group. ____
13. I develop contacts with outside experts. ____
14. I will use influence to take on the parts of group projects I most enjoy. ____
15. I make time to pursue my own pet ideas or projects. ____
16. I set aside time and energies for the pursuit of risky ideas or projects. ____
17. I accept that rules may have to be broken to reach ideal solutions. ____
18. I speak out in group meetings. ____
19. I like working with others to solve complex problems. ____
20. I see myself as sometimes providing light relief to others. ____

Source: Ettlie and O'Keefe (1982)

Skill Learning

Problem solving, creativity and innovation

If there were no problems in organisations, there would be no need for managers, or putting it another way, no incompetent problem-solver succeeds as a manager.

Effective managers are able to solve problems both rationally and creatively, even though different skills are required. Thamia and Woods (1984), reviewing 146 problem-solving sessions in a R&D department of Unilever, found that problem-solving techniques were used throughout the development process, and that a range of techniques, both creative and rational, were applied with varying degrees of success. Of the projects tackled over a three-year period, 32 per cent were rational systems and 68 per cent were termed 'creative' systems. The success rate judged on an assessment by senior management some 10 years later was approximately 60 per cent for creative problem solving and about 80 per cent for rational systems. Geshka (1978), working with German industrial firms, gave figures for success of creative techniques of between 24 and 50 per cent.

Table 3.1 Stages in the innovation process and problem solving technique employed

Stage	No of sessions (total 146)	% of total sessions
Conception	42	29
Product/Process specification	12	8
Process engineer specification	19	13
Engineering/Production specification	32	22
Exploitation	12	18
Contingency planning	7	5
Clerical back-up	11	8
Completed commercial exploitation	11	8

Source: Thamia and Woods (1984)

Table 3.1 gives the split of the usage of techniques, both creative and rational, for the various stages of the development process.

In practice most managers begin the process of problem solving with rational systems and only move reluctantly towards the creative mode. (The Thamia and Woods data is obviously biased in its estimate of creative to rational problem solving since much of the rational problem solving occurred informally and is never recorded.) In spite of the reluctance on the part of many managers to think creatively, the ability to solve problems in the creative mode separates the sheep from the goats, career successes from career failures and achievers from derailed executives. It can also produce a dramatic impact on organisational effectiveness.

Therefore, the aim of this chapter is to harness the problem-solving skills of individuals. This process is not an isolated exercise but part of the effective manager's portfolio. We see training and skill development in this area as a very large contribution towards the development of a learning organisation. The advancement of specific techniques, of which there are many (Thamia and Woods recorded 15 distinct types in their study) will be left to more specialised texts (Twiss, 1980; Buzan, 1974; Rickards, 1974, 1988).

Steps in rational problem solving

Most people, including managers, don't like problems. Problems are time-consuming and stressful. In fact, most people try to get rid of problems as soon as they can. Their natural tendency is to select the first reasonable solution that comes to mind (March and Simon, 1958), but these are rarely the best solutions. In the West, as opposed to within the Pacific Basin, we often try to implement the marginally acceptable or satisfactory solution, as opposed to the optimal or ideal solution.

One of the objectives of the Bradford University MBA programme is to allow the delegates to explore cultural differences. Since the programme has delegates from all over the world, this is a unique opportunity for future managers in a global economy. Particular learning is when a multi-ethnic group engages in problem solving. On one occasion a Japanese student was reduced to total impotence in a group of two Latins and two Brits. In the feedback he explained what had happened. In his culture the solutions would have been fought out until an agreed compromise had been reached and then there would have been full commitment of all the team for implementation. The process of compromise might have taken a very long time. The Latins and Brits competed for their solution and the 'owner' of the 'winning' solution attempted to lead the group towards implementation. It was the implementation that took the long time and full commitment by all the members of the group was poor.

Some observers see the consensus mode of problem solving as a major factor in the growth of the Japanese economy. At the time of writing the success of the Japanese economy is in question.

A basis for all problem solving

The model shown in Figure 3.1 is due to David Kolb and has already been discussed in Chapter 1. Adapting the model to problem solving helps us to understand that problem solving can be divided into four phases and that these form a cycle. The phases should ideally be distinct and in sequence:

- Exploring and developing our motivation for solving the problem and that of the 'problem owner' – should that be different – asking WHY questions.
- Deciding WHAT needs to be done to satisfy the WHY issues.
- Seeking practical solutions to the specific WHAT issues – the HOW's.
- Looking at the consequences of the practical steps we have chosen (the HOW's) and reviewing our actions.

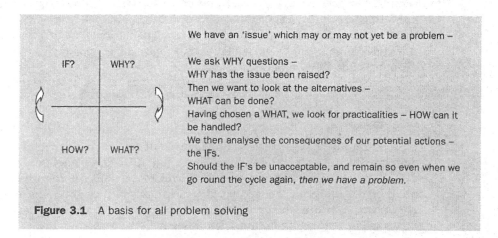

We have an 'issue' which may or may not yet be a problem –

We ask WHY questions –
WHY has the issue been raised?
Then we want to look at the alternatives –
WHAT can be done?
Having chosen a WHAT, we look for practicalities – HOW can it be handled?
We then analyse the consequences of our potential actions – the IFs.
Should the IF's be unacceptable, and remain so even when we go round the cycle again, *then we have a problem*.

Figure 3.1 A basis for all problem solving

Management Consultancy and Skills

- If the consequences are acceptable, adopting the 'solution'; should they be unacceptable, returning to the WHY phase and finding new objectives and actions.

> A management exercise we use to demonstrate the Kolb Cycle consists of asking a group to imagine that they are the Board of a subsidiary company. The Board receive a memo from head office instructing them to close the factory, sell the land as real estate and move the rump to another country with a very tight time scale. Ideally they should question the memo, to the extent of checking its factual content and then decide what needs to be done. They should then look at the practicalities of the proposals and only then look at the consequences.

> Most groups, with or without a Chair, confuse all the stages and maintain no pattern. Thus the opening remark of one participant was to worry about his children's schooling after the move – a very assumptive consequence.

Kolb further points out that managers often prefer to approach problems from one or two of the phases, basically ignoring the others. Thus some managers will persist in reviewing the purpose and asking WHY questions well after the group has moved on to solutions and practicalities. More commonly managers will be bored by the analysis stages and want to get on with practicalities. Even more 'difficult' managers will, as in our example, assume everything and move on to consequences. The job of the Chair is to make sure that this does not happen:

> *If we do not know where we are going, we will finish up somewhere else.*

A detailed model of rational problem solving – a modified Kepner Tregoe approach

The relatively informal and basically intuitive Kolb process may fail for three reasons. The first is that however many times we move through the cycle, the consequences of the actions we propose may not be acceptable. In this case we need to move to the creative processes we will describe later. The second reason is that the complexity of the issues is such that the informal approach gets bogged down. The information necessary for the decision making is not readily available or significant stakeholders cannot be brought together easily. The third and often related issue is that the matter is so important that nothing can be left to chance. We need a formalised approach that acts as a driving agenda.

The constructs behind the system are that individuals work within a personal 'area of concern'. Inside the 'area of concern' they are empowered to act, but that there is always an individual or group with a higher level 'area of concern'. Within our own 'area of concern' we must achieve the achievable. Things we feel are necessary to implement chosen solutions outside our own 'area of concern' need to be passed to this higher level.

The system we are proposing is due to Kepner and Tregoe (1965) and consists of an enlargement and formalisation of the basic model we have already discussed. Its formalisation does, in our opinion, fit the real world of complexity and politics, and is summarised and compared with the basic model.

Kolb phase	Step	Questions	Issues
WHY?	1. The problem as given		Problems as given are invariably 'wrong' containing implied solutions and misunderstandings.
WHAT?	2. Define the constraints	• What is our 'area of concern' in relation to the problem issue? • Who is the 'client' – who will decide whether we have a 'solution'? • What is our time scale and cost bracket? • What environment does our 'solution' face? • Who will implement the solution? • What are the 'legal' constraints?	• We define a 'cage' within which the potential solution or solutions will operate. • In looking at time and cost we often split potential solutions into short, medium and long term. • It can be argued that 'too much' problem analysis limits creativity – the analysis may be 'stored' to prevent this.
HOW?	3. Redefine the problem	• We need a consensus redefinition – recommended 200 words maximum. • If the problem 'splits' – short, medium and long term – take one at a time.	• Although a general consensus is desirable, agreement by the 'client' is essential. • The 'client' should be consulted at all times in this stage.
	4. Quantify the objectives – what MUST be achieved and what we would LIKE to achieve	• The objectives should be SMART: – **S**pecific in time, cost, quality, quantity – **M**easurable – **A**greed – **R**ealistic – **T**imed • The first step is to consider, and if necessary eliminate, the obvious. After this other perspectives need to be considered.	• In practice the client will probably have set the problem because he or she does not exactly understand it. • Often at this stage the problem 'vanishes' to the blindingly obvious. • **If the obvious should work – move to Stage 7.** • The 'stakeholders' very often have a solution that politically it has been impossible to table in acceptable form.

Management Consultancy and Skills

Kolb phase	Step	Questions	Issues
	5. Generate alternatives	• Collect alternatives without criticism and *within reason*, without reference to the constraints. • Take the stakeholders' views first. • Avoid any evaluation.	• Concurrent evaluation often means that the first reasonable solution 'wins'. • Evaluation often involves control issues.
IF?	6. Balance alternatives against the objectives	• Consider all the alternatives against the MUST achieve objectives. • A paper exercise where logic rules. • Distinguish between short- medium- and long-term objectives. • Alternatives meeting MUST objectives are 'traded' against the LIKE objectives.	• Alternatives failing the MUST test may have germs of ideas and be used to produce composite solutions. • This can be a lengthy process and often new or revised objectives 'appear'. • The process is often politically sensitive.
	7. Make a tentative decision	• Do not expect that any solution will 'work'. • Consult all the stakeholders. • Brief the 'Implementor' on the system and the checklists to be used.	• This stage is still relatively cheap – we need to make sure nobody can ever say – 'Well I could have told you, it went wrong last time.'
	8. Conduct a Potential Problem Analysis on the decision	• Consult ALL the stakeholders and relevant experience. • Seek out all potential problems and seek potential solutions. • Design contingency plans for potential problems outside our 'area of concern'. • Refer all likely contingencies to the client. • Accepting the review may mean changing the tentative decision.	
	9. Proceed and put contingency plan into action	• Plan in appropriate detail, resource and monitor.	• This is the expensive bit!

Management Consultancy and Skills

The total system looks and is, in its way, cumbersome. It is, however, common sense. We are suggesting that the process is always followed, each step being completed before the next is begun. Our only proviso is that the relative weight of the steps may vary and there are times when gambling on a quick decision is vital – however, this situation is MUCH rarer than we normally find argued.

> Thamia and Woods (1984) showed that an unfortunate history of failed projects had encouraged the use of the system – in fact the ruling from the Head of the Laboratory was that 'the system does not have to be followed but if the project fails and the system has not been followed then . . .'. The payoff was immediate, transparent and provided legitimacy for the other 'creativity tools' implemented at the same time.

Step 1   The problem as given

Problem issues are very often defined in terms of the symptoms and usually with implied solutions:

> Mary seems to have an attitude problem, she is always late – sort it out.
>
> The pallets in No 2 building are always falling over, see if you can get the packing more even.
>
> We are losing market share – see what the competitors are doing.

> Consultants were asked to look into labour turnover in an animal-testing unit in a large laboratory. The concern was that the percentage of people leaving far exceeded the laboratory average. Looking closer at the figures the consultants found that like was not being compared with like – labour turnover figures being used were for the whole laboratory whose average age was 37 with 15 per cent women in the population. Taking the animal handlers in isolation, the average age was 23 with 100 per cent women. Taking a similarly composed sample in other industries, the turnover was below average.

Step 2   Define the Constraints

Any potential solution has to operate with a cage – a cage of constraints. The cage has six walls – the client, cost, time, environment, staff and a strange concept we will call 'legal'. Let's take them one at a time using Mary's lateness as a vehicle. Who is the client, or putting it more simply, who has the problem? If Mary is the 'client' then we need to find out why she is late and solutions may range from buying her an alarm clock that works to social support. If the manager is the client then stopping Mary's lateness by any means, including sacking her, are potential solutions. However, in the real world – OUR MANAGER IS THE CLIENT. He or she operates in a higher level 'circle of concern'. This means that any proposed solution has to be approved implicitly or explicitly by him or her. He or she may be a control freak who watches every clock and every chart, a socially aware 'people person' or a professional in-between. Suppose he or she is the professional and in this case our proposed solutions need to fit the professional model or they will not be accepted.

Cost and time are our next constraints. Mary's lateness is costing £200 per incident in lost production, as the line cannot operate until she is in position. Mary is, however, a very skilled operative and replacing her would be costly – in time and cash. We do not want to lose her in the short or medium term.

The environment on the line is good. Years of good employee relationships have meant that everyone is positive and wants the company to succeed. Mary is a key worker and greatly liked by her co-workers. Her co-workers – the staff in our model – do not now have the skills to replace her.

Legally we could sack Mary since the plant is not unionised, but custom and practice – a very important issue in the constraint we have loosely called 'legal' – dictates that this would be unwise.

A map is of no use unless you know where you are. Solving a problem without understanding what it is you have to solve is worse than useless, but is unfortunately a common practice.

Step 3   Redefine the problem

Here we are looking at a 200 word maximum statement of what we see is the problem and we submit this to the client – our manager – for comment before we proceed.

In the long term the issue is that a single operative has skills which are not shared by any other employee. In the short term, the single operative – Mary Wellingborough – is arriving late on four or five mornings a month, costing up to £1,000 in lost production each month. In the immediate term the problem is to stop or significantly reduce this loss in production without alienating the rest of the work force, who are sympathetic to Mary. In the long term the issue is to avoid being in this position again.

Step 4   Quantify the objectives

In our experience the balancing of resources employed against potential gain is something we all need to consider.

> A number of engineers were asked to look at alternative feeding systems for fish farming. When the constraints were considered, the problem evaporated. It was necessary that one operator inspected each of the fish cages every day using a small boat. In addition, as safety regulations dictated that the operator needed a companion in case of trouble, it was fairly obvious that the companion might as well be feeding the fish as doing nothing.

If we go back to Mary – the problem is 'worth' £1,000 a month. However, the risk of alienating the line – and with possible industrial action by the others – is worth much more than this, about £60,000 a month. We will attempt the short-term solution.

The criteria against which the solutions we propose will be judged could be – and this has to be agreed with the client:

- We are talking about the short term.

- MUST be capable of implementation within 1 month – LIKE to achieve by next week.

- MUST not cost more that £1,000 a month – LIKE to be lost in 'management time'.
- MUST not disrupt the line or endanger industrial action.
- MUST not make a long-term solution – deskilling, succession training – more difficult.

These are strategic objectives that will not mean much to Mary. If we accept them we can chunk down the objectives to:

- How to get Mary in on time.
- How to get the line running if Mary is late.
- How to replace Mary.

What often happens is that we work on mixed objectives – in logical, and indeed creative, problem solving we need to hone in on one chosen objective at a time. Let us suppose we choose to 'get Mary in on time'.

Step 5 Generate alternatives

The generation of alternatives requires postponing the selection of one solution until several alternatives have been proposed. Deferring judgement, as Gordon (1961) would put it, is an essential step in any form of effective problem solving. Maier (1970) found that the quality of the final solution can be significantly enhanced by considering multiple alternatives. Judgement and evaluation, therefore, must be postponed so the first acceptable solution suggested isn't the one that is immediately selected. As Broadwell (1972, p. 121) noted:

> The problem with evaluating an alternative solution too early is that we may rule out some good ideas by just not getting around to thinking about them. We hit on an idea that sounds good and we go with it, thereby never even thinking of alternatives that may be better in the long run. As many alternatives as possible should be generated before evaluating any of them – poor alternatives often lead to good ones and without them quality solutions can often be missed.

With logical decision making the 'solutions' come from linear thinking; however, creative solutions can 'appear'. Creative solutions are invariably out of the mindset of at least some of the stakeholders and are subject to conceptual blocks that we will consider later in the chapter. Good alternative-generation should:

1. Work with the relevant stakeholders.
2. List all alternatives to be proposed before evaluation is allowed.
3. Allow as diverse a group as possible to contribute.
4. Create an atmosphere during the process which is positive. Angry or bitter people are unlikely to contribute much more than their discontent and may do actual harm by being given a platform.
5. Generate alternatives which cover both short- and long-term potential 'solutions' – the evaluation stage may well rule out ideas that do not meet the needs of the 'client', but the generation stage is not the right place to make such a judgement.

6. Create alternatives which are allowed to build upon one another – bad ideas may become good ideas if combined with, or modified by, other ideas.

7. Ensure that the agenda is adhered to and that alternatives are confined to potential solutions of the problem in hand. It is often interesting to go down new pathways, but this should be avoided if it does not relate to the current problem.

The issue is one of credibility. In our experience very few organisations, with the notable exception of advertising agencies, find the process of problem solving – and, in particular, problem solving involving people from all over and even outside the organisation – a natural activity. The presentation of half-baked, subversive or irrelevant ideas to managers not involved in the seductive process of idea generation can be a very dangerous activity, and can seriously damage people's career prospects.

Taking us back to Mary and the problem of getting her to work on time, the only relevant stakeholders are Mary and, if appropriate, a 'witness' to see fair play. Later we may choose to bring in her supervisor to consider possible solutions, but at present the group is very select. The first issue is to transfer the problem to Joe – to get her to understand the WHY of the issue:

- I have a problem in that your coming in late is delaying the start of the line; this cannot go on.
- Could we talk about why you have been so often late recently?

Then the WHAT:

- WHAT can WE do about it?

Unless we establish the problem as shared, there is no chance of Joe coming up with alternative solutions.

Step 6   *Balance alternatives against the objectives*

The evaluation and selection step involves careful weighing up of the advantages and disadvantages of the proposed alternatives before making a final selection. In selecting the best alternative, skilled problem solvers make sure that the alternatives are judged in terms of the extent to which:

- They meet the standards set for the 'solution' to the problem. Certain objectives are MUST while others are merely advantages.
- They fit within the organisational constraints (e.g., it is consistent with policies, norms and budget limitations).
- All the individuals involved will accept, and are happy to work with, the alternative suggested.
- Implementation of the alternative is likely.
- They will solve the problem without causing other unanticipated problems.

Care is taken not to short-circuit these considerations by choosing the most conspicuous alternative without considering others. March and Simon (1958, p. 141) point out:

> Most human decision-making, whether individual or organisational, is concerned with the discovery and selection of satisfactory alternatives; only in exceptional cases is it concerned with the discovery and selection of optimal alternatives. To optimise requires processes several orders of magnitude more complex than those required to satisfy. An example is the difference between searching a haystack to find the sharpest needle in it and searching the haystack to find a needle sharp enough to sew with.

Given the natural tendency to select the first satisfactory solution proposed, the evaluation and selection step must not be underrated.

1. The evaluation of alternatives should be systematic and rigorous. There are, however, exceptions:

> We were asked to consider how to promote a food product, which in this case was a factory-produced and very ordinary sausage. About 10 minutes into the discussion someone suggested that the sausages should be promoted along with the inevitable mustard to be found on the British sausage-eater's plate. The client, the brand manager for the sausage product, leapt to his feet and rang up a friend in Colman's Mustard and arranged a deal. The session finished in disarray but a placard promoting the sausage AND the mustard appeared on billboards within weeks.

If the client is satisfied, it is pointless to demand a structured approach to assessing ALL the ideas.

2. Alternatives should always be evaluated in terms of the goals of the organisation and the individuals involved. The implementation of ideas needs both the support of the organisation and of the key individuals concerned.

> We were asked to evaluate a concept for making quality envelopes for the domestic market in a continuous process from a single strip of paper, the standard method being 'old fashioned'. The idea was fine and it met the criteria for new ideas laid out by the organisation. However, nobody in the organisation was happy enough with the idea to put his or her career on the line to implement it. The idea was dropped.

3. Alternatives are evaluated in terms of their effects in the wider world – the 'legal' aspect of the constraints in Stage 2.

> The Shell Company in 1995 evaluated various alternatives for the disposal of a redundant oil rig in the Atlantic. Logically, disposal at sea was the obvious choice – provided one did not predict the way in which environmentalists could exploit the issue to bring publicity against industrial pollution. However, Greenpeace chose to fight the decision and won, so that a precedent of what they saw as bad practice was not established and the company had to back down from their 'logical' decision.

Step 7   Make a tentative decision

From Stage 6 we are likely to have an objective that stands out. Often it will be an amalgam of several ideas, thus Mary may be having trouble with one of her children and getting her to school cannot be left to the eldest. She may see that getting a neighbour to help is a possibility but that a little preparation the previous evening plus phoning in on difficult days could reduce the problem.

The tentative alternative chosen must be stated explicitly with the reasoning behind the decision, including the case for and against both the chosen route and the non-recommended alternatives. We now try to find fault with the tentative decision – with a group of the stakeholders where necessary. In Mary's case we would suggest that her line supervisor would compose the 'group'. We may decide that the tentative solution is worth further discussion, but if we were not satisfied we would return to select a different 'solution' or go back to the problem definition stage.

Step 8   Conduct a Potential Problem Analysis on the decision

Woods and Davies (1973) proposed a formal system between the assessment and implementation stages of structured problem solving. They suggested that a delegated team had a 'Circle of Concern' within which they were empowered to take all necessary actions for success. However, certain things were beyond the mandate of the team or individual and required higher authority. These they termed 'contingency actions'.

In the methodology they proposed, a 'Potential Problem Analysis' session would be conducted before the implementation stage (Stage 9) in which all likely snags would be considered and solutions proposed. Residual problems, the problems likely to involve contingency work, would be listed at this point and referred to the problem owner for him or her to review what should be done, and indeed whether a complete rethink would be necessary.

In the 1970s, many food companies were considering alternative processes for making animal-protein substitutes from various plant products. One source of such protein was derived from various pulses. Unfortunately several pulses, in the uncooked or semi-cooked state, contained a toxin which inhibits the human digestive system. The detoxification of the pulse material needed to be at the boiling point of water to be effective.

During a Potential Problem Analysis session with the team responsible for the implementation, it was pointed out that the factory designated for the production of the product was likely to be at a height well above sea level and that open cooking might not detoxify the beans. The contingency plan would be to cook the beans in pressure vessels. Due consideration of the cost of the implementation of such pressure cooking led to a complete re-evaluation and abandonment of the process.

Thamia and Woods (1984) found seven examples of such contingency planning work in their studies.

With Mary, the issues within our own 'Circle of Concern' include informing the necessary people of our arrangements. We need to make sure that Mary's phone call will be taken and acted up, agree what she needs to do in preparation the previous evening, making sure there is a supervisor available and, of course, monitoring and reviewing. However, we are establishing a precedent and this needs to be discussed with, in this case – the Personnel Department.

Stage 9 Proceed and put contingency plan into action

Implementation of any solution requires sensitivity to possible resistance from those who will be affected by it. Almost any change engenders some resistance. Therefore, the best problem solvers are careful to select a strategy that maximises the probability that the solution will be accepted and fully implemented. This may involve 'selling' the solution to others or involving others in the implementation of the solution. Tannenbaum and Schmidt (1958) and Vroom and Yetton (1973) provide guidelines for managers to determine which of these implementation behaviours is most appropriate in which circumstances. Generally speaking, participation by others in the implementation of a solution will increase its acceptance and decrease its resistance.

Effective implementation also requires some follow-up to check on implementation, prevent negative side-effects and ensure a solution of the problem. Follow-up not only helps to ensure effective implementation, but serves as a feedback function as well as providing information that can be used to improve future problem solving. Drucker (1974, p. 480) explained:

> A feedback has to be built into the decision to provide continuous testing of the expectations that underlie the decision, against actual events. Few decisions work out the way they are intended to. Even the best decision usually runs into snags, unexpected obstacles and all kinds of surprises. Even the most effective decision eventually becomes obsolete. Unless there is feedback from the results of the decision, it is unlikely to produce the desired results.

Effective implementation and follow-up should include some of the following attributes:

1. Implementation occurs at the right time and in the proper sequence.
2. The implementation process includes opportunities for feedback. We need to be able to communicate how well the selected solution works.
3. Implementation is supported by the whole 'team', all of which should have been involved wherever and whenever possible in the process.
4. A system for monitoring the implementation process is set up with short-, medium- and long-term goals clearly laid out.
5. Evaluation of success is based on problem-solution, not on side-benefits. Although the solution may provide some positive outcomes, unless it solves the problem being considered, it is unsuccessful.
6. Contingency planning.

Limitations of the rational problem-solving model

Most experienced problem solvers are familiar with these steps in rational problem solving, which are based on empirical research results and sound rationale (Kepner and Tregoe 1965; Maier, 1970; Huber, 1980; Elbing, 1978; Filley *et al.*, 1976). Unfortunately, managers do not always practise them: the demands of the job often pressure managers into circumventing some of these steps, thus problem solving suffers as a result. When these steps are followed, however, effective problem solving is markedly enhanced.

The research by Thamia and Woods records an incident where a senior manager in the multi-national they studied had been 'taught' the Kepner and Tregoe method on a course finishing on a Friday. On the next Monday he was in a senior management meeting where he proposed to use the technique to help to make a significant decision. He was told: 'I know you have been on a course, but we simply do not have time for all that clap trap – what does everyone think we should do?' On the other hand, simply learning about and practising the steps of problem definition, generating alternatives, evaluation and selection and implementation and follow up, does not guarantee success. There are two principle reasons for this.

Firstly, these problem-solving steps are useful mainly when the problems faced are straightforward, when alternatives are readily available, when relevant information is present, and when a clear standard exists against which to judge the correctness of a solution. Thompson and Tuden (1959) call problems with these characteristics 'computational problems', for which the main tasks are to gather information, generate alternatives and make an informed choice. The trouble is, many managerial problems are not of this type. Definitions, information, alternatives and standards are seldom unambiguous or readily available, so knowing the steps in problem solving and being able to follow them are not the same thing. Table 3.2 presents the internal and external constraints which make it difficult to follow any strict model.

A second reason why the rational problem-solving model is not always effective for managers concerns the nature of the problem itself. The problem may not be amenable to a systematic or rational analysis. In fact, for some problems, a rational problem-solving approach may not lead to an effective solution. Sufficient and accurate information may not be available, outcomes may not be predictable or the method of implementation may not be evident. In order to solve such problems, a new way of thinking may be required, multiple or conflicting definitions might be needed and alternatives never before considered may have to be generated; in short, creative problem solving must be used.

Impediments to creative problem solving

One of the ways we survive in an increasingly complex world is to create patterns, classifications, bundles of what we see, feel and hear around us. Once we have established a pattern we make generalities and assumptions about things within the pattern – 'People in organisations are inclined to . . .', 'He is German and we all know that Germans are good engineers . . .'. From our experience and 'learning' the classifications are convenient and help us survive without having to think about everything at every level. It is these very patterns, we will call them conceptual blocks, that we need to break down in creative problem solving, and the process makes us uncomfortable and vulnerable. The more we become experts or specialists, the more the patterns become unquestioned.

Table 3.2 Some constraints on the rational problem-solving model

Steps	Constraints
1. Define the problem	• There is seldom consensus as to the definition of the problem. • There is often uncertainty as to whose definition will be accepted. • Problems are usually defined in terms of the solutions already possessed.
2. Generate alternative solutions	• Solution alternatives are usually evaluated one at a time as they are proposed. • Usually, few of the possible alternatives are known. • The first acceptable solution is usually accepted. • Alternatives are based on what was successful in the past.
3. Evaluate and select an alternative	• Limited information about each alternative is usually available. • Search for information occurs close to home – in easily accessible places. • The type of information available is constrained by importance – primacy versus recency, extremity versus centrality, expected versus surprising, and correlation versus causation. • Gathering information on each alternative is costly. • The best alternative is not always known. • Satisfactory solutions, not optimal ones, are usually accepted. • Solutions are often selected by oversight or default. • Solutions are often implemented before the problem is defined.
4. Implement and follow up on the solution	• Acceptance by others of the solution is not always forthcoming. • Resistance to change is a universal phenomenon. • It is not always clear what part of the solution should be monitored or measured in follow-up. • Political and organisational processes must be managed in any implementation effort. • It may take a long time to implement a solution.

Place half-a-dozen bees and the same number of flies in a bottle, and lay it on its side, with its base to the window. The bees will persist, attempting to find a way through the glass of the base until they drop. The flies, moving at random, will soon find the neck of the bottle and escape. The bees' superior intelligence is the cause of their undoing. They appear to have learnt from past experience that the exit of EVERY prison is towards the brightest light, and they act accordingly. They persist on previous learning to their own destruction accepting that there is one right answer to escaping from confinement. In their persistence they ignore the new factor of the transparent barrier since they have no previous knowledge or experience of it and they do not have the adaptability to handle the new information. The less intelligent flies, with no such learning ability, ignore the call of the light and move at random until, suddenly, they are free. There is no one right answer because circumstances are always different.

We have a paradox which we need to understand when we develop creative problem solving as a skill. On the one hand, more education and experience may inhibit creative problem solving and reinforce conceptual blocks but expertise is necessary for evaluation and implementation. As bees, individuals may not find solutions because the problem requires less 'educated' or more seemingly playful approaches, so it is with people. As several researchers have found, training can significantly enhance creative problem-solving abilities and managerial effectiveness (Barron, 1963; Taylor and Barron, 1963; Torrance, 1965).

Creative thinking involves three stages:

1. The destruction of the set patterns in our thought.
2. An uncomfortable stage of insecurity while we establish new patterns.
3. The re-establishment of new patterns.

Allen (1974) defined conceptual blocks as 'mental obstacles that constrain the way the problem is defined and limit the number of alternative solutions thought to be relevant', but as we have said – we need them and therefore would advocate a temporary lifting.

Thus, for example, most of us do not think about the mechanisms involved in switching on an electric light every time we enter a room. If we are an electrician we may need to think about a fairly complex device connected by wires embedded in the plaster leading to a local distribution box, which is itself connected to . . . No, if we are to remain sane, we segment our recall and simply turn on the light. Yet all of this information is available and is held by your brain. What we have done is to group the complexities into patterns and set them aside, noticing only the deviations from the patterns when events lead us to question 'conventional wisdom'. The process of grouping and setting aside is the origin of our conceptual blocks.

Paradoxically a logical problem is an acceleration of the process of group and setting aside – we choose a pattern of actions and put other actions aside 'if needed'. Formal education, except for the very talented, is about accepting patterns so that further patterns can be learnt – so is the job experience that we all value. It has been estimated that most adults over 40 display less than 2 per cent of the creative problem-solving ability of a child under 5. Formal education is teaching about grouping information and how to present the grouping to the satisfaction of all-knowing examiners, and is based on 'right answers', analytic rules and thinking boundaries. Experience in a job teaches proper ways of doing things, specialised knowledge and rigid expectation of appropriate actions. Individuals lose the ability to experiment, improvise or take mental detours. Again, it is about grouping information to survive. John Gardner (1965, p. 21) identifies the paradox when he says:

> All too often we are giving our young people cut flowers when we should be teaching them to grow plants. We are stuffing their heads with the products of earlier innovation rather than teaching them to innovate. We think of the mind as a storehouse to be filled when we should be thinking of it as an instrument to be used.

Thus training in creative thinking is often a process of unlearning, and is more difficult for some people than others. It does, however, work. Parnes (1962), for example, found that training in thinking increased the number of good ideas produced in problem solving by 125 per cent. Bower (1965) recorded numerous examples of organisations that increased profitability and efficiency through training in the improvement of thinking skills. Increasingly organisations send their managers to creativity workshops in order to improve their creative-thinking abilities.

> Potters-Ballotini, an American-owned company operating in the UK, had two factories turning glass waste into beads – the size of the beads ranged from almost dust for glitter in Christmas Cards to quite large marbles used to de-burr stone and metals.
>
> The company's top six managers sat down together for a creative problem-solving session. No idea for a new use of the beads was rejected and some 100 ideas were collected. One idea – that of incorporating the beads into a reflective paint for road marking – won through and has provided the company with an obvious and visible success ever since.

Problems requiring a creative input

Some problems require creative rather than rational solutions. These are problems for which no acceptable alternative seems to be available, all reasonable solutions seem to be blocked or no obvious best answer is accessible. Handy (1994) tells the following story:

> I was travelling in Ireland and looking for a particular place in the Wicklow hills. I stopped to ask a local who gave me accurate directions involving going up a steep hill until I got to Dave's Bar: *'When you get to the bar, you have passed it.'*

DeBono (1971) gives a similar analogy of passing a turning and explains that creative thinking is like the reverse gear on a car. 'You do not need it all the time, but when you do, you better be able to use it.' Cyert and March (1963), and developed by Probst and Buchel (1997), discuss the concept of 'slack'. The time to be creative is not when you are against the wall but you have spare capacity.

Something happens that makes a rational approach ineffective – we find ourselves in a useless Dave's Bar or in a cul-de-sac – we need to move into a creative problem-solving mode and this can happen at all levels of the organisation. To illustrate creative problem solving we will use two examples – the invention of the microwave cooker for Raytheon, and Post-It Notes for 3M.

PERCY SPENCER AND THE MAGNETRON

During the Second World War, Sir John Randall and Harry Boot, working on improving radar for the British Admiralty, developed a device they called the Cavity Magnetron. Radar systems using the Cavity Magnetron allowed aeroplanes to 'see' the surface of the earth and the sea. Apart from improving the offensive nature of the bomber, the device made it possible to detect and destroy submarines on the surface at great distances and was significant in winning what was called the Battle of the Atlantic. The original development, one of the closest secrets of the Second World War, was completed for £200 on a laboratory bench, but when Sir John Cockcroft took it across the Atlantic in 1940, it was considered to be one of the most valuable cargoes ever to sail.

Raytheon was one of several US firms invited to produce magnetrons for the Second World War. The workings of a magnetron were not well understood, even by sophisticated physicists, and among the firms that made them few understood what made the device work. A magnetron was tested, in those early days, by holding a neon tube next to it. If the neon tube got bright enough, the magnetron tube passed the test. In the process of conducting the test, the hands of the scientist holding the neon tube got warm. It was this phenomenon that led to a major creative breakthrough that eventually transformed lifestyles throughout the world.

At the end of the war, the market for radar essentially dried up and most firms stopped producing magnetrons. In Raytheon, however, a scientist named Percy Spencer had been experimenting with magnetrons, trying to think of alternative uses for the devices. He was convinced that magnetrons could be used to cook food by using the heat produced in the neon tube. The problem was, Raytheon was in the defence business – cooking devices seemed odd and out of place. Spencer was convinced that Raytheon should continue to produce magnetrons, even though production costs were prohibitively high. But Raytheon had lost money on the devices, and now there was no available market for magnetrons. The consumer product Spencer had in mind did not fit within the bounds of Raytheon's business. As it turned out, Percy Spencer's solution to Raytheon's problem produced the microwave oven and a revolution in cooking methods.

SPENCE SILVER AND THE GLUE THAT DID NOT STICK

Spence Silver was assigned to work on a temporary project team within the 3M company searching for new adhesives. Silver obtained some material from AMD, Inc., which had potential for a new polymer-based adhesive. He described one of his experiments in this way: 'In the course of this exploration, I tried an experiment with one of the monomers in which I wanted to see what would happen if I put a lot of it into the reaction mixture. Before, we had used amounts that would correspond to conventional wisdom' (Nayak & Ketteringham, 1986). The result was a substance that failed all the conventional 3M tests for adhesives. It didn't stick. It preferred its own molecules to the molecules of any other substance. It was more cohesive than adhesive. It hung around without making a commitment – it was a 'now-it-works, now-it-doesn't' kind of glue.

For five years Silver went from department to department within the company trying to find someone interested in using his newly found substance in a product. Silver had found a solution; he just couldn't find a problem to solve with it. Predictably, 3M showed little interest. The company's mission was to make adhesives that adhered ever more tightly. The ultimate adhesive was one that formed an unbreakable bond, not one that formed a temporary bond. After four years the task force was disbanded and the team members assigned to other projects. But Silver was still convinced that his substance was good for something. He just didn't know what. As it turned out, Silver's solution has become the prototype for innovation in American firms and has spawned a half-billion dollars in annual revenues for 3M in a unique product called Post-It Notes.

The two case studies – the Magnetron and Post-It Notes – are examples of how solving a problem in a unique way can lead to phenomenal business success. Both examples show how conceptual blocks needed to be overcome.

Conceptual blocks

Table 3.3 summarises four types of conceptual blocks that inhibit creative problem solving. Each is discussed and illustrated below with problems or exercises. We encourage you to complete the exercises and solve the problems as you read the book because doing so will help you become aware of your own conceptual blocks. Later we shall discuss in more detail how you can overcome them.

Table 3.3 Conceptual blocks that inhibit creative problem solving

1. *Consistency*	
Vertical thinking	Defining a problem in only one way without considering alternative views.
One thinking language	Not using more than one language to define and assess the problem.
2. *Commitment*	
Stereotyping based on past experience	Present problems are seen only as the variations of past problems.
Ignoring commonalities	Failing to perceive commonalities among elements that initially appear to be different.
3. *Compression*	
Distinguishing figure from ground	Not filtering out irrelevant information or finding needed information.
Artificial constraints	Defining the boundaries of a problem too narrowly.
4. *Complacency*	
Non-inquisitiveness	Not asking questions.
Non-thinking	A bias towards activity in place of mental work.

Consistency

Consistency involves an individual becoming wedded to one way of looking at a problem or to one approach of defining, describing or solving it. Consistency is a valued attribute for most of us, most of the time. We like to appear at least moderately consistent in our approach to life, and consistency is often associated with maturity, honesty and even intelligence. We judge lack of consistency as untrustworthy, peculiar or erratic. Several prominent psychologists theorise, in fact, that a need for consistency is the primary motivator of human behaviour (Festinger, 1957; Heider, 1946; Newcomb, 1954). Many psychological studies have shown that once individuals take a stand or employ a particular approach to a problem, they are highly likely to pursue that same course without deviation in the future (see Cialdini, 1988, for multiple examples).

While consistency is a virtue when we are pursuing the correct course of action, it can be a fault when we are not and an alternative action would be better. Digging a different hole may well be better than digging the same hole deeper, faster or more cheaply. We can describe the block of consistency in terms of two ways of thinking – 'vertical' thinking and thinking confined to one 'language'. We will now explain these two terms.

Vertical thinking

The terms 'vertical thinking', and its converse, 'lateral thinking', were coined by Edward De Bono (1968). In vertical thinking, a problem is defined in a single way and that definition is then pursued without deviation until a solution is reached – no alternative definitions are considered. All information gathered and all alternatives generated are consistent with the original definition. In a search for oil, for example, vertical thinkers determine a spot for the hole and drill the hole deeper and deeper hoping to strike oil. Instead of drilling one hole deeper and deeper, lateral thinkers would drill a number of holes in different places in search of oil, or even drill somewhere else.

The vertical-thinking conceptual block arises from not being able to view the problem from multiple perspectives. Returning to our hole metaphor, we see that we are getting less and less advantage from the hole we have begun and stand aside to think that new holes, or even a tunnel, might be preferred. When faced with a problem, lateral thinkers generate alternative ways of viewing a problem and produce multiple definitions.

> Mechanical cod fish processing in Britain and Germany had been developed from the highly skilled craftsmanship of the fish filleter. The filleter had to prepare neat fillets to be attractive for sale from fishmongers' slabs. As more and more cod fish were sent directly to factories to be made into frozen shaped fish pieces, the craftsmanship of the filleter was mechanised and refined. Nobody asked: 'Why do we need perfect fillets when there is no fishmongers' slab to exhibit them?'
>
> Once the question had been asked, Nordsee in Germany and the Unilever company, Birds Eye, in the UK, came up with a range of new processes where the fish went directly into the process with no intermediate step of the perfect fillet.

What has happened is that the problem solver has changed the definition of the problem from 'How do you improve processing of fish fillets?' to 'How do you get whole fish in a form acceptable to a processing plant?'.

Plenty of examples exist of creative solutions that have occurred because an individual refused to get stuck with a single problem definition. Alexander Graham Bell was trying to devise a hearing aid when he shifted definitions and invented the phonograph. Colonel Sanders was trying to sell his recipe to restaurants when he shifted definitions and developed his Kentucky Fried Chicken business. Karl Jansky was studying telephone static when he shifted definitions, discovered radio waves from the Milky Way galaxy, and developed the science of radio astronomy.

In our first case study above, Percy Spencer shifted the definition of the problem from 'How do you save our military radar business at the end of the war?' to 'How do you find other applications for the magnetron?'. Other problem definitions followed, such as 'How do you make magnetrons cheaper?', 'How do you mass-produce magnetrons?', 'How do you convince someone besides the military to buy magnetrons?', 'How do you enter a consumer products market?', 'How do you make microwave ovens practical and safe?', and so on. Each new problem definition led to new ways of thinking about the problem, new alternative approaches, and eventually, to a new microwave oven industry. In the second case study, Spence Silver at 3M also needed to change problem definitions. He began with 'How can I get an adhesive that has a stronger bond?', but switched to 'How can I find an application for an adhesive that doesn't stick?'. Eventually, other problem definitions followed:

- 'How can we get this new glue to stick to one surface but not another (e.g., to note-paper but not normal paper)?'
- 'How can we replace staples, drawing pins and paper clips in the workplace?'
- 'How can we manufacture and package a product that uses non-adhesive glue?'
- 'How can we get anyone to pay $1.00 for a pad of scrap paper?'

And so on.

Shifting definitions is not easy, of course, because it is not normal behaviour. It requires that individuals deflect their tendencies towards constancy. Later we will discuss some hints and tools that can help overcome the constancy block while avoiding the negative consequences of being inconsistent.

A single thinking language

A second manifestation of the constancy block is the use of only one thinking language. Most people faced with a problem attempt to express it in words – spoken or written. The problem is that words almost always carry images with them.

Working with training groups in Unilever, Mike Woods and George Davies used to say that they were wishing to design a new garden 'truck' – a wheelbarrow. They would then ask the group members to describe what he or she saw when the word wheelbarrow was mentioned. Almost always, under questioning, the participant would be able to describe the wheelbarrow in detail; its colour, age, scars

Management Consultancy and Skills

and even where it was – 'propped up against the wall of a garden shed'. The word 'wheelbarrow' produced a complete image, so any new design of the wheelbarrow needed to compete against that total image before it was accepted as a viable concept. Thus, if a new concept for a garden 'truck' was called a wheelbarrow and it would not park easily against a particular garden shed, it might well be rejected.

To confirm this, the groups were presented with a new concept 'wheelbarrow' and asked to write down the first comment that came into their heads. Eighty per cent of the comments were negative – comments related to the fact that the word 'wheelbarrow' conjured up the image of a very detailed status quo to be challenged by the concept.

Rational problem solving reinforces the use of words and the subsequent dangers. Some writers, in fact, have argued that thinking cannot even occur without words (Vygotsky, 1962). However, other thought languages are available, such as non-verbal or symbolic languages (e.g., mathematics), sensory imagery (e.g., smelling or tactile sensation), feelings and emotions (e.g., happiness, fear or anger), and visual imagery (e.g., mental pictures). The more languages available to problem solvers, the better and more creative will be their solutions. As Koestler (1967) puts it, '[Verbal] language can become a screen which stands between the thinker and reality. This is the reason that true creativity often starts where [verbal] language ends.' Percy Spencer at Raytheon is a prime example of a visual thinker:

> One day, while Spencer was lunching with Dr Ivan Getting and several other Raytheon scientists, a mathematical question arose. Several men, in a familiar reflex, pulled out their slide rules, but before any could complete the equation, Spencer gave the answer. Dr Getting was astonished. 'How did you do that?' he asked. Spencer replied that he had learnt cube roots and squares by using blocks as a boy. Since then he had retained the visualisation. (Scott, 1974, p. 287)

The microwave oven not only depended on Spencer's command of multiple thinking languages, but it would never have got off the ground without a critical incident that illustrates the power of visual thinking. By 1965, Raytheon was just about to give up on any consumer application of the magnetron when a meeting was held with George Foerstner, the president of the recently acquired Amana Refrigeration Company. In the meeting, costs, applications, manufacturing obstacles and so on were discussed. Foerstner galvanised the entire microwave oven effort with the following statement, as reported by a Raytheon vice president.

> George says, 'It's no problem. It's about the same size as an air conditioner. It weighs about the same. It should sell for the same. So we'll price it at $499.' Now you think that's silly, but you stop and think about it. Here's a man who really didn't understand the technologies. But there is about the same amount of copper involved, the same amount of steel as an air conditioner. And these are basic raw materials. It didn't make a lot of difference how you fitted them together to make them work. They're both boxes; they're both made out of sheet metal; and they both require some sort of trim. (Nayak and Ketteringham, 1986, p. 181)

In short sentences Foerstner had taken one of the most complicated military secrets of the Second World War and translated it into something no more complex than a room air conditioner. He had painted a picture of an application that no one else had been able to capture by describing a magnetron visually, as a familiar object, not as a set of calculations, formulas or blueprints.

A similar occurrence in the Post-It Note chronology also led to a breakthrough. Spence Silver had been trying for years to get someone in 3M to adopt his un-sticky glue. Art Fry, another scientist with 3M, had heard Silver's presentations before. One day while singing in Church, Fry was fumbling around with the slips of paper that marked the various hymns in his book. Suddenly, a visual image popped into his mind.

> 'I thought, gee! If I had a little adhesive on these bookmarks, that would be just the ticket. So I decided to check into that idea the next week at work. What I had in mind was Silver's adhesive. . . . I knew I had a much bigger discovery than that. I also now realised that the primary application for Silver's adhesive was not to put it on a fixed surface like the bulletin boards. That was a secondary application. The primary application concerned paper to paper. I realised that immediately.' (Nayak and Ketteringham, 1986, pp. 63–4)

Years of verbal descriptions had not led to any application for Silver's glue. Tactile thinking (handling the glue) had also failed. However, thinking about the product in visual terms, as applied to what Fry initially called 'a better bookmark', led to the breakthrough.

> This emphasis on using alternative thinking languages, especially visual thinking, is now becoming the new frontier in scientific research. With the advent of super-computers, scientists are more and more working with pictures and simulated images rather than with numerical data. 'Scientists who are using the new computer graphics say that by viewing images instead of numbers, a fundamental change in the way researchers think and work is occurring. People have a lot easier time getting an intuition from pictures than they do from numbers and tables of formulas. In most physics experiments, the answer used to be a number or a string of numbers. In the last few years the answer has increasingly become a picture.' (Markoff, 1988, p. D3)

To illustrate the differences among thinking languages, consider the following two simple problems.

1. Below is the Roman numeral 9. By adding only a single line, turn it into a 6. Look at page 623 to see how the problem is solved.

IX

2. Look at the configuration of seven match sticks in Figure 3.2 By moving only one matchstick, make the figure into a true equality (i.e., the value on one side equals the value on the other side).

Before looking up the answer on page 623, try to define the problems differently, and try to use different thinking languages. How many answers can you find?

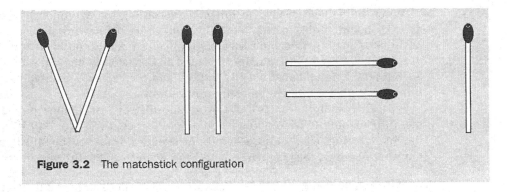

Figure 3.2 The matchstick configuration

Commitment

Commitment can also serve as a conceptual block to creative problem solving.

> Many local government-owned housing estates throughout Europe suffer from neglect and vandalism. A process whereby the houses are sold to the tenants is increasing – the political issues are not our concern. The concern is that many of the problems of disrepair vanish with ownership. Where previously the local government official was blamed for not repairing the gutter or painting the window and nothing was done, now with ownership the ladders appear and the paint pots are emptied. Commitment by ownership works.

A host of other studies have demonstrated the same phenomenon. However, commitment is not always a positive effect, it may well be its own conceptual block.

Stereotyping based on past experience – defending the status quo

March and Simon (1958) point out that a major obstacle to innovative problem solving is that individuals tend to define present problems in terms of problems they have faced in the past. Current problems are usually seen as variations on some past situation, so the alternatives proposed to solve the current problem are ones that have proved to be successful in the past. Both problem definition and proposed solution are therefore restricted by past experience. This restriction is referred to as 'perceptual stereotyping' (Allen, 1974). That is, certain preconceptions formed on the basis of past experience determine how an individual defines a situation. With perceptual stereotyping the new is compared with the established and dismissed accordingly.

> Working with a group developing new ready meals, we were testing various concepts including roast beef and Yorkshire pudding. The sample group showed a great divergence in acceptance of the concept, some members rejecting the concept completely. Further discussion with the people who were particularly dismissive found that these individuals had recently been in military service and 'roast beef and Yorkshire pudding' consisted of very thin over-cooked meat and biscuit-consistency Yorkshire pudding. The very words 'roast beef and Yorkshire pudding' conjured up a very unhappy experience in their lives and they reacted accordingly.

When individuals receive an initial cue regarding the definition of a problem, all subsequent problems may be framed in terms of that initial cue. There are advantages in this, perceptual stereotyping helps organise problems on the basis of a limited amount of data, and the need to consciously analyse every problem encountered is eliminated. On the other hand, perceptual stereotyping prevents individuals from viewing a problem in novel ways.

Both the creation of microwave ovens and that of Post-It Notes provide examples of overcoming stereotyping based on past experiences. Scott (1974) described the first meeting of Sir John Cockcroft, the technical leader of the British radar system that invented the magnetron, and Percy Spencer of Raytheon as follows:

> Cockcroft liked Spencer at once. He showed him the magnetron and the American regarded it thoughtfully. He asked questions – very intelligent ones – about how it was produced and the British scientist answered at length. Later Spencer wrote, 'The technique of making these tubes, as described to us, was awkward and impractical.' Awkward and impractical! Nobody else dared draw such a judgement about a product of undoubted scientific brilliance, produced and displayed by the leaders of British science.

Cockcroft saw the magnetron as university developed scientific equipment and had allowed its development as a war weapon to move linearly from this image of men and women in white coats supported by lab technicians. Spencer worked without this image and saw the magnetron as a commercial development issue – no white coats or subservient technicians.

Similarly, Spence Silver at 3M described his invention in terms of breaking stereotypes based on past experience.

> The key to the Post-It adhesive was doing the experiment. If I had sat down and factored it out beforehand, and thought about it, I wouldn't have done the experiment. If I had really seriously cracked the books and gone through the literature, I would have stopped. The literature was full of examples that said you can't do this. (Nayak and Ketteringham, 1986, p. 57)

This is not to say that one should avoid learning from past experience or that failing to learn the mistakes of history does not doom us to repeat them. Rather, it is to say that commitment to a course of action based on past experience can inhibit viewing problems in new ways, and it can even inhibit us from being able to solve some problems at all.

In Figure 3.3 there are four volumes of Shakespeare on the shelf. The pages of each volume are exactly two inches thick and the covers are each one-sixth of an inch thick. A bookworm started eating at page 1 of Volume I and ate straight through to the last page of Volume IV. What is the distance the worm covered? (The answer can be found in Appendix 1, page 624.) Solving this problem is relatively simple, but it requires that you overcome a stereotyping block to get the correct answer. (A clue – one of your authors finds the problem virtually impossible unless we can work with real books – we need to touch and try before we can come to an answer. However, we gave it to a 12-year-old on a rainy day on holiday and he came up with the correct answer within seconds.)

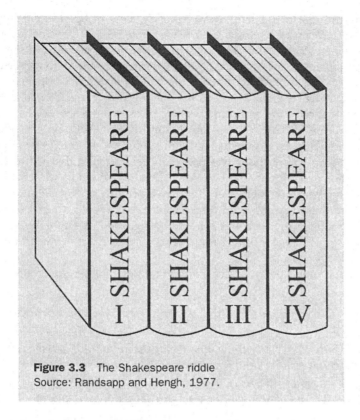

Figure 3.3 The Shakespeare riddle
Source: Randsapp and Hengh, 1977.

Ignoring commonalities

A second manifestation of the commitment block is the failure to identify similarities among seemingly disparate pieces of data. This is among the most commonly identified blocks to creativity. It means that a person becomes committed to a particular point of view, to the fact that elements are different, and becomes unable to make connections, identify themes or perceive commonalties.

The ability to find one definition or solution for two seemingly dissimilar problems is a characteristic of creative individuals (Dellas and Gaier, 1970; Steiner, 1978). The inability to do this can overload a problem solver by requiring that every problem encountered be solved individually. The discovery of penicillin by Sir Alexander Fleming resulted from his seeing a common theme among seemingly unrelated events. Fleming was working with some cultures of staphylococci that had accidentally become contaminated. The contamination, a growth of fungi and isolated clusters of dead staphylococci, led Fleming to see a relationship no one else had ever seen previously and thus to discover a wonder drug (Beveridge, 1960). The famous chemist Friedrich Kekule saw a relationship between his dream of a snake swallowing its own tail and the chemical structure of organic compounds. This creative insight led him to the discovery that organic compounds such as benzene have closed rings rather than open structures (Koestler, 1967).

For Percy Spencer at Raytheon, seeing a connection between the heat of a neon tube and the heat required for cooking food was the creative connection that led to his breakthrough in the microwave industry. One of Spencer's colleagues re-called: 'In the process of testing a bulb [with a magnetron] your hands got hot. I don't know when Percy really came up with the thought of microwave ovens, but he knew at that time – and that was 1942. He remarked frequently that this would be a good device for cooking food.' Another colleague described Spencer this way: 'The way Percy Spencer's mind worked is an interesting thing. He had a mind that allowed him to hold an extraordinary array of associations on phenomena and relate them to one another' (Nayak and Ketteringham, 1986, pp. 184, 205). Sim-ilarly, the connection Art Fry made between a glue that wouldn't stick tightly and marking hymns in a choir book was the final breakthrough that led to the devel-opment of the revolutionary Post-It Note business. Working with inventors we have found that many of them seem to carry a number of 'key solutions' in their minds, continuously searching for 'lock problems'. They do not tell others when the key fails to open the lock – this is the background of Tudor Rickards (1988) and his Puxxels. He sees a positive way of increasing inventiveness in deliberately listing the 'lock problems'.

To test your own ability to see commonalities, answer the following three questions:

1. What are some common terms that apply to both water and finance?

2. What is humorous about the following story? *Descartes, the philosopher, walked into a university class. Recognising him, the instructor asked if he would like to lecture. Descartes replied, 'I think not', and promptly disappeared.*

3. What does the single piece of wood look like that will pass through each hole in the transparent block in Figure 3.4, but that will touch all sides as it passes through?

Our answers are in Appendix 1, page 624.

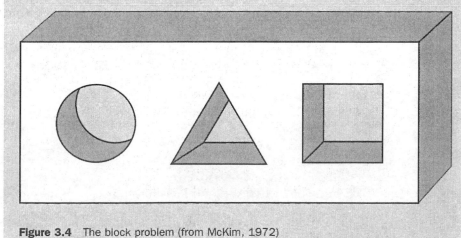

Figure 3.4 The block problem (from McKim, 1972)

Management Consultancy and Skills

Compression

Conceptual blocks also occur as a result of compression of ideas – looking too narrowly at a problem, screening out too much relevant data, or making assumptions that inhibit problem-solution, are common examples.

Artificial constraints

Sometimes people place boundaries around problems, or constrain their approach to them, in such a way that the problems become impossible to solve. Such constraints arise from hidden assumptions people make about problems they encounter. People assume that some problem definitions or alternative solutions are out of bounds – somehow cheating, and they ignore them. For an illustration of this conceptual block, look at Figure 3.5. Without lifting your pencil from the paper, draw four straight lines that pass through all nine dots. Complete the task before reading further.

By thinking of the figure as more constrained than it actually is, the problem becomes impossible to solve. To solve the problem we have to MOVE OUTSIDE THE SQUARE, which could be called 'cheating'! The assumption we make is that we have to 'join the dots' *without* moving outside the square. See Figure 3.6 for the basic solution.

Now 'cheat' some more – move further out on the assumptions that you have set for yourself when you saw the problem – join the dots with three lines and try it with one line. Can you determine how to put a single straight line through all nine dots without lifting your pencil from the paper? (Some rather exotic answers are given on page 624.)

Artificially constraining problems means simply that the problem-definition and the possible alternatives are limited more than the problem requires. Creative problem solving requires that individuals become adept at recognising their hidden assumptions and expanding the alternatives they consider – or, using the metaphor, MOVING OUTSIDE THE SQUARE.

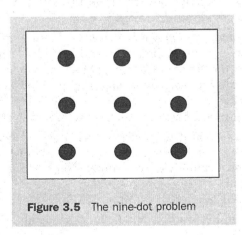

Figure 3.5   The nine-dot problem

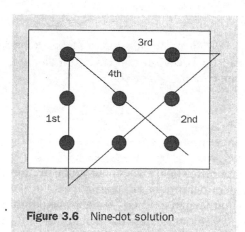

Figure 3.6   Nine-dot solution

A British-based textile company found itself faced with very strong opposition from the Far East and reduced sales. The large sales force was spurred on to work much harder and make more visits, but the situation only got worse and profitability fell still further. 'Moving outside the square' with the management team, the problem was was found to be that marginal sales to an increased number of customers was actually costing the company money. In the rush for sales at any price the sales staff were offering a diversity of products that made the manufacturing division operate at a loss. *The solution was not more visits but less*. Marginal customers were gently recommended to shop with competitors, and focused meetings with valued volume customers were set up.

Edward De Bono (1971) explains a technique for 'moving outside the square' and looking at the constraints that define a problem. He sees the constraints around a situation as being defined by five factors:

1. *The dominant idea*   This organises the approach to a problem and may be stated explicitly or merely implied. It may well be coached in language such as, 'we are a manufacturing company', 'we are responsible for the well-being of the neighbourhood and are responsible citizens'.

2. *Tethering factors*   'The dominant idea may be a powerful organisational idea, but the tethering factor may be a small, almost insignificant idea.' An example could be that the CEO is on the Board of Governors of a local school and is expected to award the prizes every year. Any change in policy towards local employment could well embarrass the relationship. We may well wish to consider the priorities of running a business against this 'tethering factor'.

3. *Polarising factors*   Polarising factors are constraints disguised as 'either, or'. An organisation could be either a manufacturer or an importer of finished goods. Polarising factors dismiss the possibility of the halfway house – for instance 'a part-finished goods assembler'.

4. *Boundaries*   Boundaries are the framework within which the problem is supposed to be considered. In the example of a fictitious company, we may

think of these in terms of the position of the shareholders of the bank – 'we have to live within the constraints set by the bank', 'the shareholders have bought into a UK-based company'. The statement may be true but check it!

5. *Assumptions* Boundaries are the limits of the ideas and assumptions are the building blocks that created the boundaries. We assume that the bank is not open to negotiation and that the shareholders will not be open to reasoned argument.

Using a non-judgemental questioning of the five factors we can redesign the problem creatively and have a chance of reaching new solutions.

De Bono concludes that it is never possible to examine all the constraints, but that in setting them out to look for them logically, one becomes aware of the cage within which one is operating. Thus it is possible to consider whether this particular cage is relevant for the present time and place.

The Ford Motor Company EQUIP programme for training and developing engineers in Europe insists that assumptions are recorded and shared before meetings. The agenda of the meeting is circulated in advance and nothing is discussed before the sharing is completed. Thus, they might be discussing safety bags in small cars and the pooled assumptions might include:

- Too bulky for the current small cars range.
- European drivers would not want it.
- Difficult to make reliable at a price.

Any of the assumptions if not tabled BEFORE the discussion could well encourage the individual holding the assumption to act negatively or even sabotage the discussion. Tabled, they can be seen for what they are – assumptions capable of challenge.

Seeing the wood from the trees

Questioning constraints in the way that De Bono suggests will not always lead to solutions. Sometimes it is the lack of clear constraints that prevents clear thought. Problems almost never come clearly specified, so problem-solvers must determine what the real problem is. They must filter out inaccurate, misleading or irrelevant information in order to define the problem and to generate appropriate alternative solutions. The inability to separate the important from the unimportant – to appropriately compress problems – serves as a conceptual block because it exaggerates the complexity of the problem and inhibits a simple definition.

We expect the past to help us to predict the future – which may be true but is by no means always true.

You have tossed a coin three times and each time it has come down heads. What are the odds of it coming down heads on the fourth throw? The answer is 50:50, all other things being equal, but somehow we expect it to come down heads again.

Past history and past experience MAY help, but they are only one way to consider a new problem.

Management Consultancy and Skills

An example of using past history was given by a well-known weather forecaster when he was asked how he could improve the quality of his forecasts. He explained that if he said that the weather would be much the same as yesterday, his forecasts would be more accurate that those derived by detailed analysis.

The compression block – seeing the wood from the trees, and artificially constraining problems – were important factors in the microwave oven and the Post-It Note breakthroughs. George Foerstner's contribution to the development and manufacture of the microwave oven was directly a product of his ability to compress the problem – that is, to separate out all the irrelevant complexity that constrained others. Whereas the magnetron was a device so complicated that few people understood it, Foerstner focused on its basic raw materials, its size and its functionality. By comparing it to an air conditioner, he eliminated much of the complexity and mystery, and, as described by two analysts, 'he had seen what all the researchers had failed to see, and they knew he was right' (Nayak and Ketteringham, 1986, p. 181).

On the other hand, Spence Silver had to add complexity, to overcome compression, in order to find an application for his product. Because the glue had failed every traditional 3M test for adhesives, it was categorised as a useless configuration of chemicals. The potential for the product was artificially constrained by traditional assumptions about adhesives – more stickiness, stronger bonding – until Art Fry visualised some unconventional applications – a better bookmark, a bulletin board, a notepad, and, paradoxically, a replacement for 3M's main product, tape.

The issue of seeing the wood from the trees – refusing to accept the constraints implied by the question and the questioner – is an art and is the art practised by all good consultants.

Complacency

This occurs because of fear, ignorance, insecurity, or just plain mental laziness. Two especially prevalent examples of the complacency block are a lack of questioning and a bias against thinking.

Non-inquisitiveness

Sometimes the inability to solve problems results from a reticence to ask questions, to obtain information or to search for data. Individuals are often reluctant to admit that things are not clear or that they do not see the reason why particular assumptions are being made. We have a fear of looking stupid, naive or ignorant, and asking questions puts us at risk of exposing our ignorance. Others may also feel threatened by our questions and react with hostility or even ridicule. Comments such as 'If you had been here at the beginning of the project . . .', and 'Surely everyone knows that . . .', can be damaging remarks.

Creative problem solving is inherently risky because it potentially involves interpersonal conflict. In addition, it is also risky because it is fraught with mistakes. As Linus Pauling, the Nobel laureate, said, 'If you want to have a good idea, have a lot of ideas, because most of them will be bad ones.' Most of us are not rewarded for bad ideas. To illustrate, answer the following questions for yourself:

1. How many times in the last month have you tried something for which the probability of success was less than 50 per cent?
2. When was the last time you asked three 'why' questions in a row?

Children begin by asking WHY questions, but most are trained by the age of 10 to accept the status quo. The key to creativity is accepting the naivety of a child and building in the experience of an adult to provide the WHAT's and the HOW's.

> We were once asked to look at the future of food processing and chose to work with a small panel of 6- to 9-year-olds. The kids were all from middle-class families, most being concerned with the client company in some way. The first question we asked was – 'Does food go bad?' The answer was a resounding NO, but under pressure they admitted that milk occasionally 'went off' – 'and Daddy makes it into cream cheese, but Mummy throws it away when he is not looking'.
>
> We then went on to ask why we put things into tins – baked beans, for instance. 'Because if we didn't they would run all over the shelf', was the answer that came back. We persisted. 'Does meat go bad?', 'No', 'No never, we have some pigs behind our house running about and they don't go bad.'
>
> Very easy to laugh but the questions for us, after the children had left, were 'Why does meat on the hoof not go bad?' and 'Is life used as a method of preserving food anywhere in the world?' The answer to the last question is yes; many hot countries sell live animals in the market place for slaughter directly before preparation. The more adult question moves on to, 'What is different about life from death?' – a question we were not able to answer ourselves so we called in an expert enzymologist to help us. He explained that one way of looking at life and death is a battle fought by the enzymes of vitality and decay, with the decay processes winning once the brain ceases to referee the battle on the side of life. He explained that enzymes were used to 'tenderise' or accelerate the 'rotting' of meat by injection into live animals prior to slaughter and that there was no reason why they should not be used for the opposite purpose. We had a new line of research.

David Feldman (1988) lists more than 100 questions designed to shake complacency. For example:

- Why are people immune to their own body odour?
- Why are there twenty-one guns in a twenty-one-gun salute?
- What happens to the tread that wears off tyres?
- Why doesn't sugar spoil or get mouldy?
- Why doesn't a two-by-four measure two inches by four inches?
- Why doesn't postage-stamp glue have flavouring?
- Why is the telephone keypad arranged differently from that of a calculator?
- How do people who throw their hats in the air find them later?
- Why is Jack the nickname for John?
- How do they print 'M&M' on M&M sweets?

Management Consultancy and Skills

Tudor Rickards (1988) suggests that you should go about your work with a notebook and write down the things that annoy you, but about which you are too busy to do anything at the time. He suggests that you call them Puxxles. John Oakland (1994), working from the concept of Total Quality Management, calls these problem items 'Snags' and advises managers to create a Snag list. The point of Puxxles and Snags is that by giving time and importance to the process of asking WHY we provide opportunities for innovation.

> In a session on Puxxles in the University of Miskolc in Hungary in 1993, a group run by Mike Woods came up with five 'problems' in the spectacles that many of us wear. Why do:
>
> * the screws holding the frames come out?
> * the lenses fall out?
> * the lenses get scratched?
> * long-sighted people always lose them?
> * they become a danger when they break?
>
> These problems were converted in statements beginning with the words 'How to . . .': 'How to stop the screws falling out.' 'How to avoid having any screws to fall out.' These reframed questions can be seen as an opportunity to develop a design that has hardly changed since the days of Samuel Pepys in the seventeenth century.

Most of us are a little too complacent to even ask such questions, let alone to find out the answers! We often stop being inquisitive as we get older because we learn that it is good to be intelligent and being intelligent is interpreted as already knowing the answers (instead of asking good questions). Consequently, we learn less well at 35 than at 5; we take fewer risks; we avoid asking why; and we function in the world without trying to understand it. Creative problem solvers, on the other hand, are frequently engaged in inquisitive and experimental behaviour. Spence Silver at 3M described his attitude about the complacency block this way:

> 'People like myself get excited about looking for new properties in materials. I find that very satisfying, to perturb the structure slightly and just see what happens. I have a hard time talking people into doing that – people who are more highly trained. It's been my experience that people are reluctant just to try, to experiment – just to see what will happen.' (Nayak and Ketteringham, 1986, p. 58)

Bias against thinking

A second demonstration of the complacency block is in an inclination to avoid doing mental work. This block, like most of the others, is a mixture of cultural and personal bias. For example, assume that you passed by your assistant's office one day and noticed that she was leaning back in a chair, staring out the window. A half-hour later, as you passed by again, her position was the same. What would be your conclusion? Most of us would assume that no work was being done. We would assume that unless we saw action, our assistant was not being productive. However, she may well be THINKING.

When was the last time you heard someone say, 'I'm sorry. I can't go to the football (concert, dance, party or cinema) because I have to think?' or 'I'll do the dishes tonight. I know you need to catch up on your thinking?' The fact that these statements sound humorous illustrates the bias most people develop towards action rather than thought, or against putting their feet up, rocking back in their chair, looking off into space and engaging in solitary mental activity. This does not mean daydreaming or fantasising, but *thinking*.

There is a particular conceptual block in our culture against the kind of thinking that uses the right hemisphere of the brain. Left-hemisphere thinking, for most people, is concerned with logical, analytic, linear or sequential tasks. Thinking using the left hemisphere is apt to be organised planned and precise, for example, language and mathematics are left-hemisphere activities.

Right-hemisphere thinking, on the other hand, is concerned with intuition, synthesis, playfulness and qualitative judgement. It tends to be more spontaneous, imaginative and emotional than left-hemisphere thinking. The emphasis in most formal education is towards left-hemisphere thought development. Problem solving on the basis of reason, logic and utility is generally rewarded, while problem solving based on sentiment, intuition or pleasure is frequently considered tenuous and inferior.

A number of researchers have found that the most creative problem solvers are ambidextrous in their thinking; that is, they can use both left- and right-hemisphere thinking and easily switch from one to the other (Bruner, 1966; Hermann, 1981; Martindale, 1975). Creative ideas arise most frequently in the right hemisphere but must be processed and interpreted by the left, so creative problem solvers use both hemispheres equally well.

Try the exercise in Table 3.4, the idea of which came from von Oech (1986), and was developed by the authors of the work on Neuro Linguistic Programming

Table 3.4 Exercise in ambidextrous thinking

List 1	List 2	List 3	List 4
Decline	Sunset	Warmth	Explosion
Very	Cow	Sadness	Bell
Ambiguous	Red	Hugging	Piano
Resources	Brick	Burnt toast	Bugle
Term	Monkey	Daydream	Click
Conceptual	Castle	Handshake	Grunt
About	Pencil	Cut grass	Guitar
Appendix	Computer	Perfume	Rifle shot
Determine	Cheeseboard	Bonfire	Applause
Forget	Ship	Fur	Beethoven's 5th
Quantify	Tree	Slime	Referee's whistle
Survey	Rabbit	Toffee	Stamping feet

by Bandler and Grindler (1979). It illustrates this ambidextrous principle. There are four lists of words. Take a minute to memorise the first list. Then, on a piece of paper write down as many as you can remember. Now memorise the words in each of the other three lists, one at a time taking a minute for each, writing down as many as you can remember.

Most people will have a preferred list but few are most effective on the first list. The second list contains words that relate to visual perceptions, the third list relates to what Grindler and Bandler call 'kinesthetic' sensations, and the fourth list relates to the auditory senses. Your preference relates to the way in which you prefer to perceive your universe. Thus, some people visualise and 'see' things in context (List 2). Others need to 'feel' their way round a problem (List 3), while still others, those who remembered most from List 4, like to attach sounds to what they learn or remember.

All but the first list combine right-brain activity as well as left-brain activity. People can draw mental pictures, feel and sense or hear at the same time as attempting the cold process of intellectualisation. Fantasy is possible.

Allowing fantasy, the connection of the left and right brain, using visual, sensing and auditory communications allows us to remember more and, in the context of this book, to be more creative. We will discuss how we encourage fantasy later.

Review of conceptual blocks

So far we have suggested that certain conceptual blocks prevent individuals from solving problems creatively. These blocks, summarised in Table 3.3, narrow the scope of problem definition, limit the consideration of alternative solutions and constrain the selection of an optimal solution. Unfortunately, many of these conceptual blocks are unconscious, and it is only by being confronted with unsolvable problems because of conceptual blocks, that individuals become aware that they exist. We have attempted to make you aware of your own conceptual blocks by asking you to solve problems that require you to overcome these mental barriers. These conceptual blocks, of course, are not all bad; not all problems can be addressed by creative problem solving. But research has shown that individuals who have developed creative problem-solving skills are far more effective with problems that are complex and that require a search for alternative solutions, than others who are conceptually blocked (Dauw, 1976; Basadur, 1979; Guilford, 1962; Steiner, 1978).

In the next section we provide some techniques and tools that overcome these blocks and help improve creative problem-solving skills. In the last section we discuss how creativity and innovation can be fostered in others.

Conceptual blockbusting

Conceptual blocks cannot be overcome all at once because most blocks are a product of years of habit-forming thought processes. Overcoming them requires practice in thinking in different ways over a long period of time. You will not become a skilled creative problem solver, of course, just by reading this book. On the other hand, by becoming aware of your conceptual blocks and practising the following techniques, you can enhance your creative problem-solving skills.

Stages in creative thought

A first step in overcoming conceptual blocks is simply to recognise that creative problem solving is a skill that can be developed. Being a creative problem solver is not a quality that some people have and some don't. As Dauw (1976, p. 19) has noted:

> Research results [show] . . . that nurturing creativity is not a question of increasing one's ability to score high on an IQ test, but a matter of improving one's mental attitudes and habits and cultivating creative skills that have lain dormant since childhood.

Haefele (1962) reviewed the literature and found agreement that creative problem solving involves four stages: preparation, incubation, illumination and verification.

- The *preparation* stage includes gathering data, defining the problem, generating alternatives and consciously examining all available information.

- The *incubation* stage involves mostly unconscious mental activity in which the mind combines unrelated thoughts in the pursuit of a solution. Conscious effort is not involved.

- *Illumination*, the third stage, occurs when an insight is recognised and a creative solution is articulated.

- *Verification* is the final stage, which involves evaluating the creative solution relative to some standard of acceptability.

The primary difference between skilful creative problem solving and rational problem solving is in how the preparation stage is approached. Creative problem solvers are more flexible and fluent in data gathering, problem definition, alternative generation and examination of options. In fact, it is in this stage that training in creative problem solving can significantly improve effectiveness (Allen, 1974; Basadur, 1979; McKim, 1972) because the other three steps are not amenable to conscious mental work. We will therefore limit our discussion to improving functioning in this first stage.

Two types of techniques help the preparation stage. One type helps individuals to think about and define the problem more effectively; the other helps individuals to gather information and generate more alternative solutions to the problem.

One major difference between effective, creative problem solvers and other people is that creative problem solvers are less constrained. They allow themselves to be more flexible in the definitions they impose on problems and the number of solutions they identify. They develop a large repertoire of approaches to problem solving. In short, they do what Karl Weick (1979, p. 261) prescribes for unblocking decision making – they generate more conceptual options. As Interaction Associates (1971, p. 15) explained:

Flexibility in thinking is critical to good problem solving. A problem solver should be able to conceptually dance around the problem like a good boxer, jabbing and poking, without getting caught in one place or 'fixated'. At any given moment, a good problem solver should be able to apply a large number of strategies [for generating alternative definitions and solutions].

Moreover, a good problem solver is a person who has developed, through his understanding of strategies and experiences in problem solving, a sense of appropriateness of what is likely to be the most useful strategy at any particular time.

Anyone visiting a library or bookshop will find that the number of books claiming to enhance creative problem solving is enormous. Therefore, in the next section we present just a few tools and hints that we have found to be especially effective and relatively simple for executives and students of business to apply. Whereas some of them may seem a little game-like or playful, that is precisely what they are supposed to be – they are designed to unfreeze you and make you more like the child, asking WHY questions without fear of seeming naive.

Methods for improving problem definition

Problem definition is probably the most critical step in creative problem solving. Once a problem is defined appropriately, solutions often come easily. However, Campbell (1952), Medawar (1967) and Schumacher (1977) point out that individuals tend to define problems in terms with which they are familiar. Medawar (1967, Introduction) notes: 'Good scientists study the most important problems they think they can solve.' When a problem is faced that is strange or does not appear to have a solution (what Schumacher calls 'divergent problems'), the problem either remains undefined or is redefined in terms of something familiar. Unfortunately, new problems may not be the same as old problems, so relying on past definitions may lead to solving the wrong problem.

Birds Eye, part of the Unilever group in the UK, was considering a new product – pineapple fritters – based on fruit jelly. The pineapple jelly was cut into finger-shaped pieces and was to be battered ready for frying by the consumer. The initial pilot plant to make the product was developed from a redundant conveyor system that had been used to make fish fingers – a similarly SHAPED product produced by the company in vast quantities but made from hard frozen fish.

The modified fish finger equipment produced a sticky and ungovernable mess when used with the fruit jelly 'fingers'. Quite suddenly someone asked: 'Why do we expect fruit jelly slices to behave the same way as rigid fingers of fish?' Once asked, the answer was obvious. Once the conceptual block was broken the whole concept of making the fruit jelly product was reviewed and the final product was manufactured in a machine derived from the confectionery industry, not the technology of frozen fish.

Applying some hints for creative problem-definition can help individuals to see problems in alternative ways so their definitions are not so narrowly constrained. Three such hints for improving and expanding a definition are discussed below.

Make the strange familiar and the familiar strange

Synectics is a well-known technique for improving creative problem solving (Gordon, 1961). The goal of *Synectics* is to help you put something you don't know in terms of something you do know, and vice versa. By analysing what you know and applying it to what you don't know, new insights and perspectives can be developed.

It works like this. First you form a definition of a problem (make the strange familiar). Then you try to make that definition out-of-focus, distorted or transposed in some way (make the familiar strange). Use analogies and metaphors to create this distortion. Then you postpone the original definition of the problem while you analyse the analogy or metaphor. You impose the analysis on the original problem to see what new insights you can uncover.

For example, suppose you have defined a problem as low morale among members of your team. You may form an analogy or metaphor by answering questions such as the following about the problem:

- What does this remind me of?
- What does this make me feel like?
- What is this similar to?
- What isn't this similar to?

> In the days before the banning of CFCs a group was asked to consider 'How to avoid offensive odours in the John' – it was an American group who preferred the word 'John' to the more European WC.
>
> A member of the group suggested that holding down smells reminded him of smog, and they were caused by meteorological inversions. The problem was then, 'How to cause a meteorological inversion in a lavatory bowl'. The group member promptly left for his own laboratory and returned with a long graduated cylinder – added lemon oil and sprayed a neat CFC aerosol in at the top. The inversion of temperature stopped any odour of the lemon oil.
>
> The company sponsoring the 'session' – Glamorene of the States – launched the product named 'Before' within weeks of the concept, only to be stopped by Ozone Layer protection concerns.

Metaphors and analogies are immensely useful and often give us new insights. By analysing the metaphor or analogy, we identify attributes of the problem that were not evident before. Gordon (1961) provides a list of 'worlds' from which analogies can be drawn.

> The Trustee Saving Bank in the UK was concerned with the problem of direct mail going to customers who had already been refused the bank's credit facilities. Using the world of sport – football – the concept of 'own goals' appeared. Own goals are often scored by the most effective players in defence and are reduced by a continual dialogue between the goalkeeper and his players. The fruitful discussion that followed on what such a continual dialogue would look like in the bank led to a 'solution' to the problem.

The ideas of Gordon are not new. William Harvey used the pump analogy to the heart, which allowed him new insights into the body's circulation system. Niels Bohr compared the atom to the solar system and supplanted Rutherford's 'raisin pudding' model of matter. Creativity consultant Roger von Oech (1986) helped to turn around a struggling computer company by applying a restaurant analogy to the company's operations. By analysing the problems of a restaurant – 'safe' environment – the management of the computer company were able to highlight the problems of their own company by comparison. Major contributions in the field of organisational behaviour have occurred by applying analogies to other types of organisation, such as machines, cybernetic or open systems, force fields, clans and so on. Probably the most effective analogies (called parables) were used by Jesus to teach principles that otherwise were difficult for individuals to grasp, given their culture and heritage.

Some hints to keep in mind when constructing analogies are:

1. Include action or motion in the analogy (for example, driving a car, cooking a meal, attending a funeral).

2. Include things that can be visualised or pictured in the analogy (for example, stars, football games, crowded shopping malls).

3. Pick familiar events or situations (for example, families, kissing, bedtime).

4. Try to relate things that are not obviously similar (for example, saying an organisation is like a crowd is not nearly so rich a simile as saying an organisation is like a psychic prison or a poker game).

Synectics recommends four styles of analogy:

- *Personal*, where individuals try to identify themselves as the problem: 'If I were the problem, how would I feel, what would I like, what could satisfy me?'

  Technicians and scientists developing a machine to automate bacteriological testing – the Colworth 2000 – worked in the final stages of the design by 'becoming the machine'.

- *Direct*, where individuals apply facts, technology and common experience to the problem (e.g., Brunel solved the problem of underwater construction by watching a shipworm tunnelling into a tube). Often the analogies are from the living world and are then called bionic analogies.

  A design for a floor-cleaning mop was based on the way in which a cat's tongue works.

- *Symbolic*, where symbols or images are imposed on the problem (e.g., modelling the problem mathematically or diagramming the logic flow).

- *Fantasy*, where individuals ask the question: 'In my wildest dreams, how would I wish the problem to be resolved?' We might say, for example: 'I wish all employees could work with no supervision.'

Elaborate on the definition

There are a variety of ways to enlarge, alter or replace a problem definition once it has been specified. One way is to force yourself to generate at least two alternative

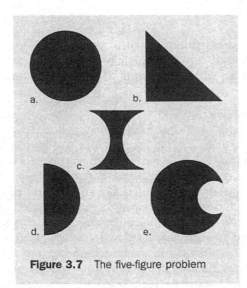

Figure 3.7 The five-figure problem

hypotheses for every problem definition. That is, specify at least two plausible definitions of the problem in addition to the one originally accepted. Think in plural terms rather than in singular terms. Instead of asking 'What is the problem?', 'What is the meaning of this?', 'What is the result?', ask questions like, 'What are the problems?', 'What are the meanings of this?', 'What are the results?'. As an example, look at Figure 3.7. Which shape is the odd-one out?

Most people select (b) because it is the only figure that is all straight lines, and they are, of course, correct. Others may pick (a) as it is the only figure with a continuous line and no points of discontinuity; they are also correct. The choice of (c) as the only figure with two straight and two curved lines; (d) as the only figure with one curved and one straight line, or (e) as the only figure that is non-symmetrical or partial, are ALL correct choices. The point is, there can often be more than one problem definition, more than one right answer and more than one perspective from which to view a problem.

Another way to elaborate definitions is to use a question checklist:

1. Is there anything else?

2. Is the reverse true?

3. Is there a more general problem?

4. Can it be stated differently?

5. Who sees it differently?

6. What past experience is this like?

As an exercise, take a minute now to think of a problem you are currently experiencing. Write it down so that it is formally specified. Now manipulate that definition by answering each of the six questions in the checklist. If you can't think of a problem, try the exercise with this one: 'I am not as effective as I would like to be.'

Reverse the definition

A third tool for improving and expanding problem definition is to reverse the definition of the problem – that is, turn the problem upside down, inside out or back to front. Reverse the way in which you think of the problem. For example, consider the following fable:

> Many years ago, a small businessman found himself with a large debt to a creditor. The creditor, rumoured to have been associated with organised crime, became adamant that repayment be made by a deadline that was impossible for the businessman to meet. Business was not good and the businessman could not even keep up the interest payments, let alone the loan principal. The creditor, however, had become attracted to the businessman's daughter and, in his conniving ways, decided he would rather have the girl than the small, failing business. The daughter, however, was repulsed by such a suggestion and resisted all his advances.
>
> The creditor was a gambling man and always enjoyed the thrill of a contest. He decided to propose a game to the businessman and his daughter that would decide her fate and that of the business. He indicated that he would put a white pebble and a black pebble into a bag and then have the young woman pick out a pebble. If she chose the black pebble, she would become his wife and the businessman's debt would be considered paid in full. If she chose the white pebble, she could stay with her father and the debt would be cancelled. If she refused to participate in the game, the entire balance would be made due by the end of the month.
>
> Reluctantly, the businessman agreed to the creditor's proposal. They met on the pebble-strewn path of a local park to conduct this game of chance. As they chatted, the creditor stooped down, picked up two pebbles and put them into a bag. The young woman, sharp-eyed with fright, noticed that the creditor had put two black pebbles in the bag. He held up the bag and asked the young woman to select the pebble that would decide her fate and that of her father's business.
>
> (Based upon De Bono, 1968)

Accepting that the story is a fable from a world before 'political correctness' had been invented, what would you advise the girl to do? A common approach is to maintain a constant definition of the problem and try to manipulate the circumstances. Most individuals suggest one of these alternatives:

1. The young woman should accuse the creditor of cheating. The negative consequence of this is that she risks antagonising the man and her father losing his business.

2. The young woman should try to change the rules of the contest. However, she should accept that the creditor is no fool and he is unlikely to make life more difficult for himself when he sees himself in a powerful position.

3. The young woman should try to cheat by picking up a white pebble from the ground. This is perfectly possible if the young woman is a practised conjuror but risky otherwise.

4. She should sacrifice herself and then try to get out of the marriage later.

All the suggestions maintain a single definition of the problem. Each assumes that the solution to the problem is associated with the pebble that the girl selects. If the problem is reversed, other answers normally not considered become evident. That is, the pebble remaining in the bag could also determine her fate:

> In the fable, the girl selects a pebble from the bag, but then quickly drops it to the ground on the pebble-strewn path. She exclaims, 'Oh, how clumsy of me. But never mind the one I chose will be obvious. All you have to do is look in the bag and see the colour of the one left.' By reversing the definition, she changed a situation with zero probability of success to a situation with 100 per cent probability of success.

This reversal is similar to what Rothenberg (1979) refers to as 'Janusian thinking'. Janus was the Roman god with two faces that looked in opposite directions. Janusian thinking means thinking contradictory thoughts at the same time – that is, conceiving two opposing ideas to be true concurrently. Rothenberg claimed, after studying 54 highly creative artists and scientists (e.g., Nobel Prize winners), that most major scientific breakthroughs and artistic masterpieces are products of Janusian thinking. Creative people who actively formulate antithetical ideas and then resolve them produce the most valuable contributions to the scientific and artistic worlds. Quantum leaps in knowledge often occur:

An example is Einstein's account (1919, p. 1) of 'having the happiest thought of my life'. He developed the concept that, for an observer in free fall from the roof of a house, there exists during his fall, no gravitational field in his immediate vicinity. If the observer releases any objects, they will remain, relative to him, in a state of rest. 'The [falling] observer is therefore justified in considering his state as one of rest.' Einstein concluded, in other words, that two seemingly contradictory states could be present simultaneously: motion and rest. This realisation lead to the development of his revolutionary general theory of relativity.

In another study, Rothenberg (1979) gave individuals a stimulus word and asked them to respond with the words that first came to mind. He found that highly creative students, Nobel scientists and prize-winning artists responded with antonyms significantly more often than did individuals with average creativity. Rothenberg argued, from these results, that creative people think in terms of opposites more often than do other people.

For our purposes, the whole point is to reverse or contradict the currently accepted definition in order to expand the number of perspectives considered. For instance, a problem might be that morale is too high instead of (or in addition to) too low in our team, or that employees need less motivation instead of more motivation to increase productivity. Opposites and backward looks often enhance creativity.

The techniques for improving creative problem definition are summarised below:

1. Make the strange familiar and the familiar strange.
2. Elaborate on the definition.
3. Reverse the definition.

Their purpose is not to help you generate alternative definitions just for the sake of alternatives, but to broaden your perspectives, to help you to overcome conceptual blocks and to produce more high-quality, relevant and 'simple' solutions.

Generate more alternatives

We began by pointing out that unskilled problem definition often contains an implied solution – how to stop Mary coming in late (March and Simon, 1958). This process reduces the scope of the problem solving unless we take time to redefine the initial problem. Guilford (1962) asserted that effective creative problem solvers were both fluent – able to produce a large number of ideas in a given length of time – and flexible – able to provide a diversity of ideas.

Brainstorming (Osborn, 1953) is perhaps the most widely used technique to promote both fluency and flexibility and operates under five rules:

1. Quantity and not quality.

2. Defer judgement.

3. Encourage wild ideas.

   The problem given to a team was to remove the bones from cooked chickens efficiently and quickly. The existing commercial equipment had been studied and an 'anatomical' report on chicken prepared. However, one jokey solution appeared – the chicken should be 'blown up' using an explosive charge placed in its body cavity: 'that would certainly take all the flesh off the bones'. The idea of blowing up the chicken, taken first as a joke, led to the use of rubber bags on stems inserted into the chickens and inflated so that the chickens could be held.

4. Build on ideas.

   In the chicken project, it was found that people who worked on taking the flesh off cooked chickens, found that they were slippery to handle. The rubber bag on a stem formed a sort of shoemaker's last that got over what proved to be the major problem. Logical processes allowed a creative and way-out solution to be implemented.

5. If a group is used – use as wide a range of experience as possible.

   A problem of handling frozen fish blocks at speed brought in 'experts' in guns ('How are bullets dispensed at speed?', paper ('How do photocopiers feed at speed?') and, quite accidentally, a player of arcade games. The solution that was adopted was similar to that used for a table ice hockey game where air reduced the friction of the puck.

Brainstorming techniques are best used in a group setting so individuals can stimulate ideas from each other. Maier (1967) showed that generating alternatives in a group setting produces more and better ideas than can be produced alone. The very quantity and rate of production of ideas – 100 ideas in a 30-minute session would be normal – means that people are unable to screen their own or other people's ideas to their own conceptual blocks.

In a brainstorming session one member of the group acts as a facilitator, recording the ideas – preferably numbered and on a flipchart. In no circumstances must the facilitator contribute to idea generation; his or her job is that of a scribe, a servant of the group who is allowed to clarify but not to modify.

A brainstorming session often works in spurts of creativity. In the first stage, fairly mundane ideas appear – often ideas that are already in the minds of the individuals in the group. There is often then a surge of ideas, building on the previous batch; the surge then stops but can be revived by the facilitator asking for votes on the 'worst idea' yet. By discussing what is positive on the bad idea a new surge of ideas often occurs.

The best way to get a feel for the power of brainstorming groups is to participate in one. Spend at least 20 minutes in a small group, brainstorming ideas.

> List as many uses as possible of a table-tennis ball. Give a token prize for the worst idea. As a variation you can table the worst idea and see if anyone can build on it so as to make it feasible and thus lose its status for the prize.

Examples of lists we have generated on training courses include: a bob for a fishing line, Christmas decoration, a toy for a cat, gear-lever knob, part of a molecular structure model, wind gauge when hung from a string, head of a puppet and a miniature football. Your list may well be much longer.

Sometimes brainstorming in a group is not possible or is too costly in terms of the number of people involved and the time required. Managers pursuing a hectic organisational life may feel that brainstorming is a waste of time and outside the organisational culture. This is a great pity, but even the process of individuals sitting together in relaxed circumstances jotting down ideas on a flipchart is better than nothing. Liam Hudson (1966) showed that even the most professed 'non-creatives' could produce quantities of ideas by being set the problem in rather manipulative terms. He asked his 'non-creatives' to pretend that they were brainstorming in the role of, say, the marketing manager who they regarded as a waste of time. His non-creatives produced some very sick ideas, but they were flexible and fecund.

Tony Buzan (1974) introduced the concept of 'mind mapping', a technique that has been developed considerably with the introduction of Total Quality Management systems. John Oakland (1994) cites a variation of brainstorming – the use of the cause and effect analysis. The technique was developed by Sumitomo Electric and is known as CEDAC – a cause and effect diagram with the addition of cards.

The concept of the cause and effect diagram is due to Ishikawa and provides a logical and acceptable way of structuring ideas from a brainstorming session devoted to solving a problem. Suppose we have a problem concerned with quality. The causes of the quality problem are grouped on the spines of a 'fishbone' classified as procedures, equipment and plant, materials, information and people. The effect side of the diagram is a quantified description of a problem with an agreed and quantified target. The cause side of the diagram uses two different coloured cards for writing FACTS and IDEAS. FACTS are placed on the left of the diagram and IDEAS on the right, each card being initialled by the individual owning it.

The cause and effect diagram systems have one considerable advantage over the brainstorming approaches from which they were built – they are seen to be practical and sensible. Many of the more esoteric systems, and in particular synectics, although very effective in practice, are difficult to justify in a hard-nosed environment.

Build on the current alternatives

One useful technique for building on the alternatives that comes from simple brainstorming is the technique of *subdivision*. This simply means dividing a problem into smaller parts. March and Simon (1958, p. 193) suggest that *subdivision* improves problem solving by increasing the speed with which alternatives can be generated and selected. They explain that:

> The mode of subdivision has an influence on the extent to which planning can proceed simultaneously on several aspects of the problem. The more detailed the factorisation of the problem, the more simultaneous activity is possible, the greater the speed of problem solving.

To see how subdivision helps to develop more alternatives and speeds the process of problem solving, go back to your list of ideas. Decide on the properties of the table tennis ball – weight, colour, texture, shape, porosity, strength, hardness chemical properties and conduction potential. This is one side of a matrix. The other side is a field of use – domestic, leisure, industrial, agricultural, transport, etc. Fit your existing ideas into the matrix and find new ideas for the empty squares:

- Shape/domestic – cut in half and used as a pastry cutter.
- Weight/agricultural – marking the surface of a liquid slurry tank.
- Chemical/property – a valve designed to fail when the gases overheat.
- Strength/transport – a collision damper.

The technique is also known as morphology and claims to have given rise to the Wankel engine. It is useful, when working for an industrial client, to use a matrix of the attributes and of the divisions of the organisation – industrial, domestic, medical, etc.

> Divide Figure 3.8 into exactly four pieces equal in size, shape and area. Try to do it in a minute or less. The problem is easy if you use subdivision. It is more difficult if you don't. One possible answer is given on page 625.

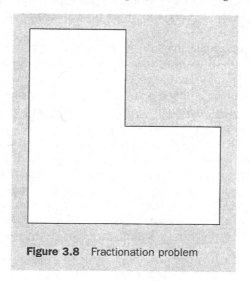

Figure 3.8   Fractionation problem

Combine unrelated attributes

A third technique focuses on helping problem solvers to expand alternatives by forcing the integration of seemingly unrelated elements. Dellas and Gaier (1970) have shown that an ability to see common relationships among disparate factors is a characteristic of creative people. A 'relational algorithm' was devised by Crovitz *et al.* (1970) to help us all share the process.

Suppose you are faced with the following problem: Customers are dissatisfied with our service. The two major elements in this problem are *customers* and *service*. They are connected by the phrase 'are dissatisfied with'. With the relational algorithm technique, the relational words in the problem statement are removed and replaced with other relational words to see if new ideas for alternative solutions can be identified. For example, consider the following connections where new relational words are used:

- Customers among service (e.g., customers interact with service personnel).
- Customers as service (e.g., customers deliver service to other customers).
- Customers and service (e.g., customers and service personnel work together).
- Customers for service (e.g., customer focus groups help improve our service).
- Service near customers (e.g., change the location of the service).
- Service before customers (e.g., prepare service before the customer arrives).
- Service through customers (e.g., use customers to provide additional service).
- Service when customers (e.g., provide timely service).

Looking at the strange connections and keeping an open mind, it is easy to become excited by the new ways of thinking they expose.

Hints for applying problem-solving techniques

Thamia and Woods (1984) found that a very large number of techniques were used during the three years of their study in one major organisation. The reasons for this were significant:

- A series of failures in innovation had been highlighted by a top management report: 'A major cause of failure had been the hardening of research effort on a limited range of solutions too early in projects.'

This had led to:

- The perceived need for creativity and the pressure for novel solutions came from the top management.
- Rational and creative problem solving were seen as activities in their own right with procedures for booking time spent in sessions employing the techniques.
- A core of two people was set up to provide 'hand-holding support' for groups and individuals requiring help in solving problems.

- Rarely was a 'pure' technique applied – only the key process of analysis, synthesis, collation and judgement was maintained and disciplines of brainstorming were imposed throughout.

We all have enormous creative potential, but the stresses and pressures of daily life, coupled with the inertia of conceptual habits, tend to submerge that potential. By following our hints, this potential can be unlocked.

1. Give yourself some relaxation time. The more intense your work, the more your need for complete breaks. Break out of your routine sometimes. This frees up your mind and gives room for new thoughts.

2. Find physical space where you can think. It should be a place where interruptions are eliminated, at least for a time. Reserve your best time for thinking and don't be made to feel guilty for not being 'active and doing something' – you are.

3. Talk to other people about ideas. Isolation produces far fewer ideas than does conversation. Make a list of people who stimulate you to think. Spend some time with them.

4. Ask other people for their ideas about your problems. Find out what others think about them. Don't be embarrassed to share your problems, but don't become dependent on others to solve them for you.

5. Read widely. Read at least one thing regularly that is outside your field of expertise. Keep track of new thoughts from your reading.

6. Protect yourself from idea-killers. Don't spend time with 'black hole people', people who absorb all of your energy and light but give nothing in return. Don't spend more time than you must on patent searches in your own area. Don't let yourself or others negatively evaluate your ideas too soon.

Figure 3.9 summarises the two problem-solving processes – rational and creative – and the factors you should consider when determining how to approach each type of problem.

- When you encounter a problem that is straightforward – that is, outcomes are predictable, sufficient information is available, and the way to achieve the end is clear – then the rational process is most appropriate.

- If the problem is not straightforward and, in particular, when rational processes have a history of failure – the creative problem-solving techniques are probably most appropriate.

Fostering innovation

The successful manager may or may not be creative but he or she must be able to unlock the creative potential of others. Fostering innovation and creativity among those with whom you work is at least as great a challenge as increasing your own creativity.

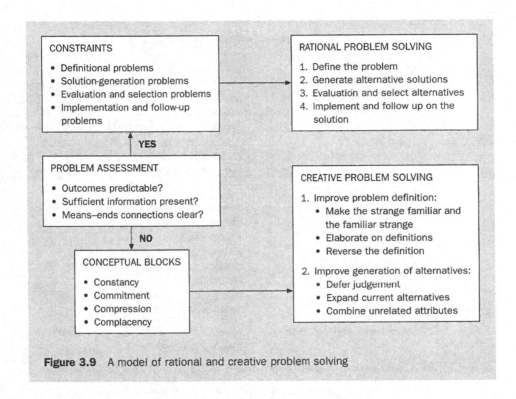

Figure 3.9   A model of rational and creative problem solving

Management principles for innovation

Neither Percy Spencer nor Spence Silver could have succeeded in their creative ideas had they not had managerial support, and an organisation that fostered innovation. The macro-organisational issues associated with innovation, e.g., organisation design, strategic orientation and human resource systems are covered well elsewhere (Galbraith, 1982; Kanter, 1983; McMillan, 1985; Tichy, 1983; Amabile, 1988). Here we will focus on the managerial level and what individual managers can do to foster **innovative thinking**. Table 3.5 presents the three management principles required.

Pull people apart – put people together

Percy Spencer's magnetron project was a consumer product hidden away from Raytheon's main-line business of missiles and other defence contract work. Spence Silver's new glue resulted when a polymer adhesive task force was separated from 3M's normal activities. Apple and IBM used task forces to develop products novel to them. Many new ideas come from individuals being given some time and resources and allowed to work apart from the normal activities of the organisation. 3M gives its staff 'skunk time' periods which are not formally accounted for and should be reserved for 'wild ideas' and 'personal projects' which just might work. Establishing nursery slopes, practice fields or sandlots is as good a way to develop

Management Consultancy and Skills

Table 3.5 Three principles for fostering innovative thinking

Principle	Examples
1. Pull people apart – put people together	Let individuals work alone as well as with teams and task forces Encourage minority reports and legitimise devil's advocate roles Encourage heterogeneous membership in teams Separate competing groups or subgroups Trust good people
2. Monitor and prod	Talk to customers Identify customer expectations both in advance and after the sale Hold people accountable Balance responsibility with authority Be interested Use a 'sharp' prod Never accept second best
3. Reward multiple roles	Accept and encourage the Idea Champion Sponsor and mentor Orchestrator and facilitator Rule breaker

new skills in business as it has proved to be in athletics. Because most businesses are designed to produce the 10,000th part correctly or to service the 10,000th customer efficiently, they do not function very well at producing a novel first part. That is why pulling people apart is often necessary to foster innovation and creativity:

> Data General divided their development effort for the new Eagle mini-computers into two competing groups on two separate sites. The 'high-status' site was beaten by the 'low-status' site.

However, in the real world of complexity, teams are almost always more productive than individuals. The lone inventor occurs but almost always in such an unplanned way as to make planning for it absurd. Teams do, however, need to be planned. Nemeth (1986) found that creativity increased markedly when minority influences were present in the team, for example, when devil's advocate roles were legitimised, a formal minority report was always included in final recommendations, and individuals assigned to work on a team had divergent backgrounds or views:

> Those exposed to minority views are stimulated to attend to more aspects of the situation, they think in more divergent ways and they are more likely to detect novel solutions or to come to new decisions. (Nemeth, 1986, p. 25)

Management Consultancy and Skills

Belbin, in his work with team role, showed that the presence of what he call a Plant in an otherwise dull group stimulated effective performance. Nemeth further found that positive benefits occur in groups even when the divergent or minority views are wrong. Similarly, Janis (1971) found that narrow-minded 'groupthink' was best overcome by establishing competing groups working on the same problem, participation in groups by outsiders, assigning a role of critical evaluator in the group, having groups made up of cross-functional participants, and so on. The most productive groups are those that are characterised by fluid roles, lots of interaction among members and flat power structures.

The point is that innovative thinking can be fostered when individuals are placed in teams and when they are at least temporarily separated from the normal pressures of organisational life. Those teams, however, are most effective at generating innovative ideas when they are characterised by attributes of minority influence, competition, heterogeneity and interaction. You can help foster innovation among people you manage, therefore, by letting people have their own space as well as putting people together in temporary teams.

Monitor and prod

Neither Percy Spencer nor Spence Silver were allowed to work on their projects with no accountability. Both men eventually had to report on the way they used their 'skunk time' and the freedom they were allowed was related to trust. They were, with some limits, allowed appropriate company materials and resources to work on them. We will discuss the concept of FRAME where individuals are given total freedom within absolute boundaries in our chapters on motivation and empowerment and delegation (Chapters 5 and 7).

Holding people accountable for outcomes, in fact, is an important motivator for improved performance. Data General made it clear to their two leaders for the Eagle project that their jobs were on the line.

> Two innovators in the entertainment industry captured this principle with these remarks: 'The ultimate inspiration is the deadline. That's when you have to do what needs to be done. The fact that twice a year the creative talent of this country is working until midnight to get something ready for a trade show is very good for the economy. Without this kind of pressure, things would turn to mashed potatoes.' (von Oech, 1986, p. 119)

In addition to accountability, innovative thinking is stimulated by what Gene Goodson at Johnson Controls called 'sharp-pointed prods':

> After taking over the automotive group at that company, Goodson found that he could stimulate creative problem solving by issuing certain mandates that demanded innovative thinking. One such mandate was: 'There will be no more forklift trucks allowed in any of our plants.' At first hearing, that mandate sounds absolutely outrageous. Think about it. You have a plant with tens of thousands of square feet of floor space. The loading docks are on one side of the building, and many tons of heavy metal raw materials are unloaded weekly and moved from the loading docks to workstations throughout the entire factory. The only way it

can be done is with forklifts. Eliminating forklift trucks would ruin the plant, right? Wrong. This sharp-pointed prod simply demanded that individuals working in the plant find ways to move the work stations closer to the raw materials, to move the unloading of the raw materials closer to the workstations or to change the size and amounts of material being unloaded. The innovations that resulted from eliminating forklifts saved the company millions of dollars in materials handling and wasted time, dramatically improved quality, productivity and efficiency, and made it possible for Johnson Controls to capture business from their Japanese competitors.

In our work as consultants we have found examples of managers who have heard of 'sharp-pointed prods' in some guise or other and applied them insensitively: *'Apply a prod and watch the eyes and keep watching the eyes. Always keep in mind why you are applying them and remember a prod that stays irritating can cause an infection.'*

One of the best methods for generating useful prods is to monitor customer preferences, expectations and judgements on a regular basis. Creative ideas often come directly or indirectly from customers. Everyone should be in regular contact with their own customers, internal and external, formally and informally, asking questions and monitoring performance.

We all have customers, whether we are students in college, members of a family, players on a rugby team, or whatever. Customers are simply those for whom we are trying to produce something or whom we serve. Students, for example, can count on their tutors, their fellow classmates and their potential employers as customers whom they serve. *A priori* and *post hoc* monitoring of their expectations and evaluations helps to foster new ideas and can be done by personal contact, follow-up calls, surveys, customer complaint cards and suggestion systems, whatever is appropriate.

Innovative thinking is best fostered by holding people accountable for having new ideas and by stimulating them with periodic prods:

> There is a story of a manager who delegated a subordinate to tackle a very difficult problem. The man wrote a report giving a solution. The manager rejected the report and said that the solution was not good enough. The man tried again, and again was rejected. Finally the man, close to resigning, handed in his third report. 'Good,' said his manager, 'I will read this report and we will take action on it.'

Reward multiple roles

The success of the sticky yellow notes at 3M is more than a story of the creativity of Spence Silver. In fact, without a number of people playing multiple roles, the glue would probably still be on a shelf somewhere. Instead, it provides a good illustration of the necessity of multiple roles in innovation and the importance of recognising and rewarding them. The four crucial roles in the innovative process are:

- The *champion* who owns and may have come up with the innovative problem solution.
- The *sponsor* or *mentor* who helps provide the resources, environment, and encouragement for the idea champion to work on the idea.

Several studies, notably Project SAPPHO developed by Andrew Robertson in his book *Lessons of Failure*, showed that the mentor had to be at the appropriate level in the organisation – not too lowly and not too senior. Lowly mentors did not have organisational 'clout' but too senior mentors were inclined to be too inaccessible for the informal contacts necessary to understand the gravity of problems and too involved in strategic success to accept failure.

- The *orchestrator* or *facilitator* who brings together cross-functional groups and necessary political support to facilitate implementation of the creative idea.

- The *rule breaker* who is able to go beyond organisational boundaries and barriers to ensure the success of the innovation.

Each of these roles is present in most important innovations in organisations, and they are illustrated by the Post-It Note case study below:

1. Spence Silver, by experimenting with chemical configurations that the academic literature indicated wouldn't work, invented a glue that wouldn't stick. He stuck with it, however, and spent years giving presentations to any audience at 3M that would listen, trying to pawn it off on some division that could find a practical application for it. The trouble was, no one else got stuck on it.

2. Henry Courtney and Roger Merrill developed a coating substance that allowed the glue to stick to one surface but not to others. This made it possible to produce a permanently temporary glue – that is, one that would peel off easily when pulled but would otherwise hang on for ever.

3. Art Fry found the problem that fitted Spence Silver's solution. He found application for the glue as a better 'bookmark' and as a note pad. The trouble was, no equipment existed at 3M to coat only a part of a piece of paper with the glue. Fry, therefore, carried 3M equipment and tools home to his own basement, where he designed and made his own machine to manufacture the forerunner of Post-It Notes. Because the working machine became too large to get out of his basement, he blasted a hole in the wall to get the equipment back to 3M. He then brought together engineers, designers, production managers and machinists to demonstrate the prototype machine and generate enthusiasm to make the product.

4. Geoffrey Nicholson and Joseph Ramsey began marketing the product inside 3M. They also submitted the product to the standard 3M market tests. The trouble was, the product failed miserably. No one wanted to pay $1.00 for a notepad. However, they broke 3M rules by personally visiting test market sites and giving away free samples. Only then did the consuming public become addicted to the product.

Spence Silver was both a rule breaker and an idea champion. Art Fry was also an idea champion, but more importantly he orchestrated the coming-together of the various groups needed to get the innovation off the ground. Henry Courtney and Roger Merrill helped to sponsor Silver's innovation by providing him with the coating substance that would allow his idea to work. Geoff Nicholson and

Joe Ramsey were both rule breakers and sponsors in their bid to get the product accepted by the public. In each case, not only did all these people play unique roles, but they did so with tremendous enthusiasm and zeal. They were both confident of their ideas and willing to put their time and resources on the line as advocates. They fostered support among a variety of constituencies both within their own areas of expertise as well as among outside groups. Most organisations are inclined to give in to those who are sure of themselves, persistent in their efforts and persuasiveness enough to make converts of others.

Not everyone can be an idea champion. But when managers also reward and recognise those who sponsor and orchestrate the ideas of others, innovative thinking increases in organisations. Teams form, supporters replace competitors and creativity thrives. Facilitating multiple role development is the job of the innovative manager. The converse is also true as the following example shows:

> A major multinational working from the UK was looking to diversify, and one idea that came forward was to use the Dolby sound system for a new generation of hearing aids. The idea, although exciting, had several 'issues' that needed to be settled before the project went forward.
>
> The senior manager in charge of the project asked one question: 'Who would like to run with the idea and to head a venture company to sell it?' Nobody wanted to stake their reputation on the idea so it was quietly killed in spite of the apparent general enthusiasm of the team.

SUMMARY

It is no accident that many of the techniques and studies described in this book date from the late 1970s and early 1980s. This was the period when the West began to stock-take and realise that it no longer had a monopoly of invention. The situation was highlighted in the UK by the Finneston Report (1980). Monty Finneston produced a well-argued case that not only had the UK declined as 'the workshop of the world', but that unless major effort was redirected into the engineering wealth-creation industries, the decline would accelerate. A key statistic was that whereas in the late 1970s UK, Sweden, France and the USA had between 1.3 per cent (France) and 1.7 per cent (UK) of the population as graduate engineers, Japan had 4.2 per cent (Germany was at 2.3 per cent.)

Engineering graduate numbers are obviously not the whole story, but the Finneston Report and the climate that commissioned it stirred activity in the West that has not faded. Innovation, and not just innovation in engineering, is the key to the survival of our economies. Innovation and problem solving, as treated in this book, are keystones to innovation.

We have shown that a well-developed model exists for solving problems. It consists of four separate and sequential stages: defining the problem; generating alternative solutions; evaluating and selecting a solution; implementing it and following it up. This model, however, is mainly useful for solving straightforward problems. Many problems faced by managers are not of this type and frequently they are called on to exercise creative problem-solving skills. That is, they must broaden their perspective of the problem and develop alternative solutions that are not immediately obvious.

Management Consultancy and Skills

We have also discussed and illustrated eight major conceptual blocks that inhibit most people's creative problem-solving abilities. Conceptual blocks are mental obstacles that artificially constrain problem definition and solution, and keep most people from being effective creative problem solvers. The four major conceptual blocks were summarised in Table 3.3 (page 180).

Overcoming these conceptual blocks is a matter of skill development and practice in thinking, not a matter of innate ability. Everyone can become a skilled creative problem solver with practice. Becoming aware of these thinking inhibitors helps individuals to overcome them. We also discussed three major principles for improving creative problem definition and three major principles for improving the creative generation of alternative solutions. Certain techniques were described that can help to implement these six principles.

We concluded by offering some hints about how to foster creativity and innovative thinking among other people. Becoming an effective problem solver yourself is important, but effective managers can also enhance this activity among their subordinates, peers and superiors.

Behavioural guidelines

1. Follow the four-step procedure outlined in Table 3.2 when solving straightforward problems. Keep the steps separate and do not take shortcuts.

2. When approaching a difficult problem, try to overcome your conceptual blocks by consciously doing the following mental activities:
   - Use lateral thinking in addition to vertical thinking.
   - Use several thought languages instead of just one.
   - Challenge stereotypes based on past experiences.
   - Identify underlying themes and commonalities in seemingly unrelated factors.
   - Ignore the superfluous and collect missing information when studying the problem.
   - Avoid artificially constraining problem boundaries.
   - Ignore reticence to be inquisitive.

3. When defining a problem, make the strange familiar and the familiar strange by using metaphor and analogy, first to focus and then to distort and refocus the definition.

4. Elaborate the problem definitions by developing at least two alternative and perhaps opposite definitions.

5. Reverse the problem definition by beginning with the end result and working backwards.

6. In generating potential solutions, defer judging any until the list is seen to be complete.

7. Use the four rules of brainstorming:
   - Do not evaluate.
   - Encourage wild ideas.
   - Encourage quantity.
   - Build on other people's ideas.

Management Consultancy and Skills

8. Expand the list of current alternative solutions by subdividing the problem along an attribute/usage matrix.

9. Increase the number of possible solutions by combining unrelated problem attributes.

10. Foster innovative thinking among those with whom you work by doing the following:

   - Find a 'safe place' to experiment and try out ideas.
   - Put people holding different perspectives in teams to work on problems.
   - Hold people accountable for innovation.
   - Use sharp-pointed prods to stimulate new thinking.
   - Recognise, reward, and encourage people in the roles of idea champion, sponsor, orchestrator and rule breaker.

Skill Analysis

CASE STUDY **3.1**

THE SONY WALKMAN

They had been disappointed at first, but it wasn't something that was going to keep them awake at nights. Mitsuro Ida and a group of electronics engineers in Sony Corporation's Tape Recorder Division in Tokyo had tried to redesign a small, portable tape recorder, called 'Pressman', so that it gave out stereophonic sounds. A year earlier, Ida and his group had been responsible for inventing the first Pressman, a wonderfully compact machine – ideal for use by journalists – which had sold very well.

But the sound in that tape machine was monaural. The next challenge for Sony's tape recorder engineers was to make a portable machine just as small, but with stereophonic sound. The very first stereo Pressman they made, in the last few months of 1978, didn't succeed. When Ida and his colleagues got the stereo circuits into the Pressman chassis (5.25 inches by 3.46 inches, and only 1.14 inches deep), they didn't have any space left to fit in the recording mechanism. They had made a stereophonic tape recorder that couldn't record anything. Ida regarded this as a good first try but a useless product. But he didn't throw it away. The stereo Pressman was a nice little machine. So the engineers found a few favourite music cassettes and played them while they worked.

After Ida and his fellow designers had turned their non-recording tape recorder into background music, they didn't entirely ignore it. They had frequent discussions about how to fit the stereo function and the recording mechanism into that overly small space. It was not an easy problem to solve, and because of that it was all the more fascinating and attractive to Ida and his group of inveterate problem solvers. Their focus on the problem of the stereo Pressman blinded them to the solution that was already in their hands, accepting that it was a solution to a different problem.

'And then one day,' said Takichi Tezuka, manager of product planning for the Tape Recorder Division, 'into our room came Mr Ibuka, our honorary chairman. He just popped into the room, saw us listening to this and thought it was very interesting.'

It is the province of honorary chairmen everywhere, because their status is almost invariably ceremonial, to potter about the plant looking in on this group and that group, nodding over the latest incomprehensible gadget. To this mundane task, Masaru Ibuka brought an undiminished intelligence and an active imagination. When he entered the Tape Recorder Division and saw Ida's incomplete tape recorder, he admired the quality of its stereophonic sound. He also remembered an entirely unrelated project going on elsewhere in the building, where an engineer named Yoshiyuki Kamon was working to develop lightweight portable headphones.

'What if you combined them?' asked Ibuka. 'At the very least,' he said, 'the headphones would use battery power much more efficiently than stereo speakers. Reduce power requirements and you can reduce battery consumption.' But another idea began to form in his mind. If you added the headphones, wouldn't you dramatically increase the quality of what the listener hears? Could you leave out the recorder entirely and make a successful product that just plays music? In the world of tape recorders, Ibuka's thought was heresy. He was mixing up functions. Headphones traditionally were supposed to extend the usefulness of tape recorders, not be essential to their success. This idea was so well established that if Ibuka had not made an association between a defective tape recorder design and the unfinished headphone design, Walkman may well have remained a little byway in musical history. Design groups within Sony tend to be very close-knit and remain focused on short-term task completion. Even when they weren't busy, there was no reason for tape recorder people ever to communicate with headphone people. They had nothing to do with each other. Tezuka, the man who later was described as the secretariat of the Walkman project, said, 'No one dreamed that a headphone would ever come in a package with a tape recorder. We're not very interested in what they do in the Headphone Division.'

But, even without this insularity, there was no guarantee that someone else at Sony would have made the connection that Ibuka made. To people today, the relationship between a cassette player and a set of headphones is self-evident. But to people at Sony, and at virtually every consumer electronics company, that connection was invisible in 1978.

Ibuka got a predictable response from the researchers in the electronics lab and from others in the Tape Recorder and Headphone divisions. They were painfully polite but non-committal. Ibuka might be right that the headphones would improve Pressman's efficiency, but nobody could guess how much of an improvement that would be. No one wanted to tell Ibuka that the idea of removing the speaker in favour of headphones was crazy. But it was! What if the owner of the device wanted to play back a tape so that more than one person could listen?

When Ibuka ventured further into illogic by suggesting a playback machine with no speaker and no recorder, he lost everybody. Who would want to buy such a thing? Who in Sony Corporation would support even ten minutes of development on such a hare-brained scheme?

Management Consultancy and Skills

In a way, they were right and Ibuka was wrong. This was an idea that violated most industries' well-established criteria for judging the natural increments of product development. It makes sense that a new product prototype should be better than the previous generation of product. Ida's non-recording prototype seemed worse. The idea had no support from the people who eventually would be responsible for funding its development, carrying out the research and trying to sell it to a consumer market. The idea should have been killed.

For Honorary Chairman Ibuka, the handwriting was on the wall. Even though he was a revered man at Sony, he had no authority to order such a project undertaken against the wishes of the division's leaders. It was clear that the only way to sell a bad idea to a group of cautious, reasonable businessmen was to find an ally. So, in his enthusiasm, he went straight to the office of his partner and friend, Akio Morita.

Source: Nayak and Ketteringham, (1986)

Discussion questions

1. What principles of rational problem solving and creative problem solving were used in this case?

2. How was innovative thinking fostered within Sony by top managers?

3. What roles were played by the various characters in the case that led to the success of the Walkman?

4. If you were a consultant to Sony, what would you advise to help foster this kind of innovation more frequently and more broadly throughout the company?

Skill Practice

EXERCISE **3.1**

APPLYING CONCEPTUAL BLOCKBUSTING

Creative problem solving is most applicable to problems that have no obvious solutions. Most problems people face can be solved relatively easily with a systematic analysis of alternatives. But other problems are ambiguous enough that obvious alternatives are not workable, and they require non-traditional approaches to find reasonable alternatives. This following assignment is one such problem. It is real, not fictitious, and it probably characterises your own college, university or public library. Apply the principles of creative problem solving in the book to suggest some realistic, cost-effective and creative solutions to this problem. Don't stop at the first solutions that come to mind, because there are no obvious right answers.

Assignment

Small groups should be formed to engage in the following problem-solving exercise. Each group should generate solutions to the case. The case is factual, not fictitious. Try to be as creative in your solutions as possible. The creativity of those solutions should be judged by an independent observer, and the best group's solution should be given recognition.

In defining and solving the problems, use the basic steps used in the Kepner and Tregoe system (*loc. cit.*), Table 3.2 and creative techniques to generate alternatives. Do not skip steps.

- Write down the problem.
- Consider the constraints and, in particular, determine who the client is. Make sure that all group members agree.
- Redefine the problem in not more than 200 words.
- Decide on the objectives that any potential solutions should satisfy.
- Propose some alternative solutions to the problem. Write these down and be prepared to report them to the larger group. All small groups should report their top three alternatives to the large group. The top three are the ones that most group members agree would produce the best solution to the problem.
- In your small group, generate at least five plausible alternative definitions of the problem. Use any of the techniques for expanding problem definition discussed in the text. Each problem statement should differ from the others in its definition, not just in its attributions or causes, of the problem.
- After the group has agreed on the wording of the five different statements, identify at least 10 new alternatives for solving the problems you identified. Your group should have identified some new alternatives, as well as more alternatives than you did initially.
- Report to the large group the three alternatives that your small group judges to be the most creative.

An observer should provide feedback on the extent to which each group member applied these principles effectively, using the Observer's Feedback Form found in the scoring key at the end of this book. Take one potential solution and decide what could go wrong, how this issue could be solved and whether you would need to review your recommendations.

The problem: The bleak future of knowledge

Libraries throughout the world are charged with the responsibility of preserving the accumulated wisdom of the past and gathering information in the present. They serve as sources of information and resources, alternate schools, and places of exploration and discovery. No one would question the value of libraries to societies and cultures throughout the world. The materials housed there are the very foundation of civilisation. But consider the following problems.

Hundreds of thousands of books are in such advanced states of decay that when they are touched they fall to powder. Whereas parchments seem to survive better when they are handled, and books printed before 1830 on rag paper stay flexible and tough, books printed since the mid-nineteenth century on wood-pulp paper are being steadily eaten away by natural acids. The new British Library has a backlog of 1.6 million urgent cases requiring treatment. At the newly constructed (but not yet opened) Bibliotheque Nationale in France, more than 600,000 books require treatment immediately. At the Library of Congress in the States, about 77,000 books out of the stock of 13 million enter the endangered category every year. Fairly soon, about 40 per cent of the books in the biggest research collections in America will be too fragile to handle. An example of the scale of the problem comes from the Library of Congress which estimates that it will take 25 years to work through the backlog of cases, even if the cost of $200 a volume can be met. The obvious solution of converting to CD ROM or microfiche is not only more costly but subject to its own form of 'decay' – no 'permanent' form is yet available.

Budgets are tight throughout the world and it is doubtful that book preservation will receive high funding priority in the near future.

Source: The Economist, 23 December 1989

Skill Application

ACTIVITY **3.1**

SUGGESTED FURTHER ASSIGNMENTS

1. Teach someone else to solve problems creatively and record your experiences in your diary.

2. Think of a problem that is important to you now and has no obvious solution. Use the principles and techniques discussed in the book and work out a satisfactory creative solution. Take your time and do not expect immediate results. Record any results in your diary.

3. Help to direct a group (your family, classmates, sports team) in a creative problem-solving exercise using the relevant techniques of the book. Issues could include arranging a social, raising funds, increasing membership or fixing a programme of activities. Record how it went in your diary.

4. Write a letter to a person in authority – MP, Managing Director, Senior Police Officer – about some difficult problem in his or her authority. Make the issue something about which you have both knowledge and concern and include within your letter possible solutions. Record how you arrived at these possible solutions as well as the solutions themselves.

ACTIVITY **3.2**

APPLICATION PLAN AND EVALUATION

This exercise is designed to help you apply your skill in a real life setting. There are two parts in the activity: Part 1 will help the preparation, and Part 2 will help you to evaluate and improve on the experience. Do not miss out the steps and be sure to complete each item.

Part 1: Plan

1. Write down the two or three aspects of a skill that is most important to you. This may be an area of weakness, an area you most want to improve or an area that is most salient to a problem that you face now. Identify the specific aspects of this skill that you want to apply.

2. Now identify the setting or the situation in which you wish to apply this skill. Establish a plan for the performance by actually writing down the situation. Who else is involved? When will you do it? Where will it be done?

3. Identify the specific behaviours you will engage to apply the skill. Put these behaviours into detailed actions.

4. How will you judge success?

Part 2: Evaluation

5. After you have completed your implementation, record the results. What happened? How successful were you? What was the effect on others?

6. How can you improve? What modifications would you make for next time?

7. Looking back on your experience, what have you learnt? What has been surprising? In what ways might the experience help you in the long term?

Further reading

Johnson, G. (1997) *Monkey business: why the way you manage is a million years out of date.* Aldershot: Gower.

Malone, S.A. (1997) *Mind skills for managers.* Aldershot: Gower.

Murdock, A. and Scutt, C.N. (1997) *Personal effectiveness*, 2nd edn. Oxford: Butterworth-Heinemann.

Pearce, S. and Cameron, S. (1997) *Against the grain: developing your own management ideas.* Oxford: Butterworth-Heinemann.

Management Consultancy and Skills

Constructive Communication

SKILL DEVELOPMENT OUTLINE

Skill Pre-assessment surveys

- Communicating constructively
- Communication styles

Skill Learning material

- The importance of effective communication
- Focus on accuracy
- Constructive communication
- Coaching, counselling and consulting
- Setting objectives
- Defensive and patronising behaviours
- Summary
- Behavioural guidelines

Skills Analysis cases

- Find someone else
- Rejected plans

Skill Practice exercises

- Vulcan Computers
- Brown vs Thomas

Skill Application activities

- Suggested further assignments
- Application plan and evaluation

LEARNING OBJECTIVES

- To introduce the concept of choice in personal communication between immediate gain and long-term advantage.

- To develop techniques what we will call 'constructive communication' – communication between individuals where relationships are fostered and developed.

- An understanding of the processes that lead us to dysfunctional responses – aggressiveness and defensiveness.

- To understand where counselling and coaching are required.

- Develop the various roles in any conflict situation including that of the mediator.

224

INTRODUCTION

Not all communication is constructive or needs to be. Constructive communication is a two-way process – the speaker is also the listener and the listener can become the speaker. There is also a hidden agenda bringing in medium-term as well as immediate goals – it is preparing for the next communication, and the next. Non-constructive, directive communication has its place. There are times when the job to be done is so confining that there is no time, need or latitude for the communicator to accept feedback, worry about feelings or tomorrow. If a child is about to put its hand in a fire or a walker is about to fall down a hole, that is such a time. The crew of a sinking ship are unlikely to want the opportunity for discussion when the captain is ordering the lifeboats to be manned. However, directive communication can be totally ineffective.

> A long time ago Mike Woods, one of our authors, was in his pram, his mother was notified that the postman had been unable to deliver any post to their house 'due to their dangerous dog'. She duly attended an interview with a very pompous head postmaster who talked down to her explaining that the refusal by the postman to deliver mail, and run the risk of being bitten by the Woods' household pet, was entirely in the Woods' interest.
>
> 'If the postman is bitten, you may well have to pay significant damages.'
>
> He drooled on, not allowing Mrs Woods any comment. Finally, Mrs Woods had her chance. 'I agree with everything that you say, but there is just one thing that worries me. We don't have a dog.'

The story illustrates the breaking of virtually all of the 10 commandments of effective communication that we will develop in this chapter.

The spoken and sometimes written word is obviously one of the tools we use in communication, but we have seen previously that words in themselves conjure up images well beyond their literal meaning. Beyond words there lies a complexity of non-verbal signals and clues. Who we are or are perceived to be, how we dress, how we gesture in a myriad of complexities that, unless we understand them, stand between us and clear unequivocal communication.

(It may be useful, if the subject of human communication is new to you, to watch your favourite soap opera on TV. For the first half watch it as you would normally and for the second half, turn the sound off and watch only the gestures. The question is, how much did you miss when you could not hear the words? The answer may surprise you. Good television and good radio – and indeed quality face-to-face communication and e-mail or audio-only telephone 'conversations' – are different media.)

225

Skill Pre-assessment

SURVEY **4.1**

COMMUNICATING CONSTRUCTIVELY

Step 1 Before you read the material in this book, please respond to the following statements by writing a number from the rating scale below in the left-hand column (Pre-assessment). Your answers should reflect your attitudes and behaviour as they are now, not as you would like them to be. Be honest. The instrument is designed to help discover your level of competency in communicating constructively, so you can tailor your learning to your specific needs. The scoring key, which will help you to identify the areas of the book most important to you, is in Appendix 1.

Step 2 After you have completed the reading and the exercises in this book, and as many of the Skill Application assignments as possible, cover up your first set of answers. Then respond to the same statements again, this time in the right-hand column (Post-assessment). When you have completed the survey, check out your scores using the scoring key in Appendix 1. If your score remains low in specific skill areas, use the behavioural guidelines at the end of the Skill Learning section (page 260) to guide further practice.

RATING SCALE

1 = Strongly disagree   **2** = Disagree   **3** = Slightly disagree
4 = Slightly agree   **5** = Agree   **6** = Strongly agree

	Assessment	
	Pre-	Post-

There are times when all of us feel that others are not doing the things that we feel are correct in these situations, and when we feel it is necessary to do something:

1. I understand clearly when it is appropriate to offer advice and direction to others and when it is not. ____ ____

2. I help others recognise and define their own problems when I counsel them. ____ ____

3. I am completely honest in the feedback that I give to others, even when it is negative. ____ ____

4. I always give feedback that is focused on the problem and its solution, not on the characteristics of the person. ____ ____

5. I always explain the reason for my giving negative feedback with an explanation of what I perceive as having been done wrongly. ____ ____

6. When I correct someone's behaviour, our relationship is almost always strengthened. ____ ____

Management Consultancy and Skills

7. I am descriptive in giving negative feedback to others. That is, I objectively describe the event, its consequences and my feelings about it.   ____ ____

8. I always suggest some specific alternatives to those whose behaviour I am trying to correct.   ____ ____

9. I make sure to reinforce other people's sense of self-worth and self-esteem in my communication with them.   ____ ____

10. I convey genuine interest in the other person's point of view, even when I disagree with it.   ____ ____

11. I don't talk down to those who have less power or less information than I do.   ____ ____

12. I convey a sense of flexibility and openness to new information when presenting my point of view, even when I feel strongly about it.   ____ ____

13. I strive to identify some area of agreement in a discussion with someone who has a different point of view.   ____ ____

14. My feedback is always specific and to the point, rather than general or vague.   ____ ____

15. I don't dominate conversations with others.   ____ ____

16. I take responsibility for my statements and point of view by using, for example, 'I have decided' instead of acting as an agent and saying 'they have decided'.   ____ ____

17. When discussing someone's concerns, I use responses that indicate understanding rather than advice.   ____ ____

18. When asking questions of others in order to better understand their viewpoint, I generally ask WHAT questions instead of WHY questions.   ____ ____

19. I hold regular, private, one-to-one meetings with people I work with and/or live with.   ____ ____

20. I am clear about when I should coach someone and when I should provide counselling instead.   ____ ____

SURVEY **4.2**

COMMUNICATION STYLES

In this questionnaire some managerial experience is assumed. If you do not have such experience, use your imagination.

The questionnaire is divided into two parts. In Part 1, four people complain about problems they face in their jobs. Following each complaint are five possible responses. Rank three of the responses you would be most likely to make in reverse order, with 3 being your first choice, 2 being your second choice and 1 being your third choice. Part 2 describes a particular situation. Several pairs of statements follow. Place a tick next to the one statement in each pair that you would be most likely to use in responding to the given situation. The scoring key for this questionnaire can be found in Appendix 1.

Management Consultancy and Skills

Part 1

1. *I've been in this job for six months and I hardly know anyone at all in the company. I just can't seem to make friends or be accepted by other people. Most people are extremely busy and don't take time to socialise. I feel isolated and excluded from what's going on.*

   a. Don't be concerned about not making friends so soon. Things will get better the longer you're with the company.

   b. When you first meet people, what do you say? Are you the one to be friendly first? ____

   c. Because company employees are so busy, probably no one has time to get close socially. You shouldn't expect too much. ____

   d. So you're feeling that people haven't accepted you in the company? ____

   e. It's not as serious as you may feel. When I first joined the company it took me more than six months to get settled in, I still don't know everyone. ____

2. *I can't stand my boss. He is the most autocratic, demanding person you can imagine. I've never worked around anyone who cared less for his employees than he does. His complete insensitivity and lack of humanity have made this place miserable.*

   a. You sound as if you're having difficulty dealing with rigid control and authority. ____

   b. I know how you feel because last year we had a woman in our department who would drive anybody round the bend. She was the ultimate domineering boss. ____

   c. You're going to have problems unless you work this out. I think you should go to him and tell him how you feel. ____

   d. You really are having a hard time adjusting to your boss, aren't you? ____

   e. Why is it you feel so strongly about him? ____

3. *What I want to know is, how was I passed over for Mac's job? I felt I was perfect for the job – I have the experience and the seniority – now you bring in someone from outside. Where do I go from here?*

   a. What was it that made you think the supervisor's job was yours, George? Are you aware of what it needed and what kind of person we were looking for? ____

   b. Don't be discouraged, George. Your work is good, and if you're patient I'm sure other chances will come along. I'll try to help you be ready next time. ____

   c. I think you have the wrong impression about this, George. The criteria were very clear for the job and we simply needed a fresh mind. ____

   d. In other words, George, you're puzzled about where you stand with the company. ____

   e. Are you interpreting this set-back as a challenge to your technical competence? ____

4. *Excuse me Paul, what's the idea of not approving my request for an update for our PC systems? We really need it. The ones we are using are not downward compatible with the systems in accounts and we have to do some jobs with paper and pencil. We are very busy as you know and this puts us back. Please don't come up with the tight resources argument – you know new equipment has been in the budget for at least two years.*

   a. You sound really upset about not getting your request approved, Susan. ____

   b. Why do you need a new system – surely when problem issues occur you can borrow a compatible machine? ____

   c. You know Susan, several other departments have the same problem. A new
      system for you would get them all on my back and we don't have the time or
      money for training, let alone new systems. _____

   d. I know you're upset, Susan. Believe me you have to be patient and leave it to
      me. I have changes in the pipeline. _____

   e. I'm sorry, Susan, but it's true that resources are really tight. That's why we turned
      you down, so you're just going to have to make do. _____

Part 2

You are the manager of Carole Thompson, a 58-year-old supervisor with 21 years' service with the company. Carole retires in two years' time but her performance is sliding, she will not take on any extra work and the work she does do is often found to be lacking. Her attitude towards customers is often brusque and she shows a lack of sensitivity to her shop-floor staff. Her attitude to customers is particularly worrying since the company survives in this harsh world though its reputation for customer service.

Carole has done nothing that would merit a disciplinary interview, but you feel that unless her performance improves, it may lead to one. You are having your monthly one-on-one meeting with her in your office. Which of the statements in each pair is nearest to what you would say?

1. a. I've received complaints from some of your customers that you are not being
      sufficiently sympathetic to complaints and requests. _____
   b. You don't seem to be motivated to do a good job anymore, Carole. _____

2. a. I know that you've always done a good job, but there's just one small thing I want
      to raise with you about a customer complaint – probably not too serious. _____
   b. I have some concerns about several aspects of your performance on the job and I'd
      like to discuss them with you. _____

3. a. I've had one of your people seeing me about you criticising him in public and I am
      worried. I would like you to go to him direct and sort things out – then let me know
      what you have agreed. _____
   b. You know, of course, that you're wrong to have criticised your subordinate's work in
      public. That's a sure way to create antagonism and lower morale. _____

4. a. I would like to see the following changes in your performance: (1) . . . , (2) . . .
      and (3) . . . _____
   b. I have some ideas for helping you to improve; but first, what do you suggest? _____

5. a. I must tell you that I'm disappointed in your performance. _____
   b. Several of our employees seem to be unhappy with how you've been performing
      lately. _____

Skill Learning

The importance of effective communication

Effective communication is a key competence of management and its demonstration may range from giving effective orders to delivering formal speeches at dinners. The dominant skill required in all these activities is effective face-to-face, one-to-one communication. In a study of 88 organisations, both from the public and private sectors, Crocker (1978) found that, of 31 skills assessed, interpersonal constructive communication skills were rated as the most important. Thorton (1966) summarised a variety of survey results by stating, 'A manager's number-one problem can be summed up in one word: communication.' This is hardly surprising since some 80 per cent of all managers' time is spent on verbal communication.

In a study of major manufacturing organisations undergoing large-scale changes, Cameron (1988) asked two key questions:

1. What is your major problem in trying to get organisational changes implemented?
2. What is the key factor that explains your past success in effectively managing organisational change?

To both questions a large majority of managers gave the same answer – communication. Unfortunately most of us see ourselves as good communicators and that the problems are caused by other people. Haney (1979) reported on a survey of more than 8,000 people in universities, businesses, military units, government and hospitals, in which virtually everyone felt that he or she was communicating at least as well as, and in many cases better than, almost everyone else in the organisation. Most people readily admit that their organisation is fraught with faulty communication, but it is almost always other people who are responsible. Thus we are not ready to accept the necessity let alone the responsibility of improving our own skill level.

Focus on accuracy

Much of the writing on interpersonal communication focuses on the accuracy of the information being communicated, and emphasises that the communication skill which needs the greatest improvement is the ability to transmit clear, precise messages. Inaccurate communication can have humorous as well as serious results.

A motorist in a veteran car was stopped by the police for a roadside check. Everything seemed fine. The officers decided to test the brakes.

'Right, we would like you to drive at about 30 mph in front of our police car and when you hear the sound of our horn, make an emergency stop. Give the brakes everything they have got – OK?'

The driver did all that was asked of him but unfortunately at 30 mph the traffic began to pile up and one impatient driver of a sports car who was forced to overtake vented his anger by shaking his fist and sounding his horn. The old car, the brakes of which were in fact very good, stopped immediately and the police car banged straight into him.

Source: A student legend of the 1950s used by Richard Gordon in his book, *Doctor in the House*.

A woman of 35 came in one day to tell me that she wanted a baby but had been told that she had a certain type of heart disease that, while it might not interfere with a normal life, would be dangerous if she ever had a baby. From her description, I thought at once of mitral stenosis. This condition is characterised by a rather distinctive rumbling murmur near the apex of the heart and especially by a peculiar vibration felt by the examining finger on the patient's chest. The vibration is known as the 'thrill' of mitral stenosis. When this woman had undressed and was lying on my table in her dressing gown, my stethoscope quickly found the heart sounds I had expected.

Dictating to my nurse, I described them carefully. I put my stethoscope aside and felt intently for the typical vibration which may be found in a small and variable area of the left chest. I closed my eyes for better concentration and felt long and carefully for the tremor. I did not find it, and with my hand still on the woman's bare breast, lifting it upward and out of the way, I finally turned to the nurse and said: 'No thrill.' The patient's eyes flashed, and with venom in her voice she said, 'Well, what a shame – may be just as well you didn't. That isn't what I came for.' My nurse almost choked, and my explanation still seems a nightmare of futile words. (Loomis, 1939)

Pizza Hut, in their point of sale advertisements. Include the words: 'Order by phone – if not collected in 20 minutes – £1 off.' Perhaps they meant: 'Order by phone – if not ready for collecting in 20 minutes we will charge you £1 less than our quoted prices.'

Attempts to improve the communications of an organisation often centre on improving the *mechanics*: networked phones, fax systems, e-mail, answering machines and desk publishing. Sophisticated information-based technology has made major strides in enhancing both the speed and accuracy of communication. There is a snag, however, about any mechanical information processing, and a statement Josiah Stamp made over 80 years ago illustrates this point:

The government is very keen on amassing statistics. They collect them, add them, raise them to the nth power, take the cube root and prepare wonderful diagrams. But you must never forget that every one of these figures comes in the first instance from the village watchman, who just puts down what he pleases.

Stamp might well have said 'garbage in garbage out'.

However, irrespective of the availability of sophisticated information technologies and systems, individuals still communicate much as they always did. They can be ineffectively abrasive, insensitive and plain misguided.

In my own office we used to abide by the rule of NEVER posting a rude letter to anyone the day of writing. Read it the next morning and then post it or bin it. E-mail has changed all that – e-mail allows instant misunderstanding that may take years to correct.

Group communications – team briefings, company newsletters, etc. – have also received much attention, but interpersonal aspects of communication have been largely ignored. People still become offended at one another, make insulting statements and communicate clumsily. The interpersonal aspects of communication involve the nature of the relationship between the communicators. The effect of who says what to whom, what is said, why it is said, and how it is said on the relationship between people has important implications for the effectiveness of the

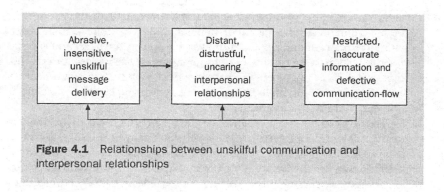

Figure 4.1   Relationships between unskilful communication and interpersonal relationships

communication, aside from the accuracy of the statement. The interaction between the message, the messenger and a backlog of suppositions and preconceptions about the messenger and his or her role – collectively called the *shadow* – is discussed by Woods and Whitehead (1993). Ineffective communication may lead individuals to dislike each other, be offended by each other, lose confidence in each other, refuse to listen to each other and disagree with each other. These interpersonal problems, in turn, generally lead to restricted communication flow, inaccurate messages and misinterpretations of meanings. Figure 4.1 summarises this process.

To illustrate, consider the following situation.

> Alan is in a team conceived to overcome a quality problem in the final assembly of video players. After Alan's carefully prepared presentation to the management meeting, John raises his hand. 'In my opinion, this is a naive approach to solving our quality problems. It's not as easy as Alan seems to realise. I don't think we should waste our time by pursuing his plan any further.'

John's opinion may be justified, but the manner in which he delivers the message will probably eliminate any hope of its being dealt with objectively. Instead, Alan will probably hear 'You're naïve' as 'You're stupid and incompetent'. Expectedly, Alan's response would be either defensive or hostile. Future communications between Alan and John would probably have been jeopardised and future communication between the two will probably be minimal. Issues of the quality improvement suggested will be marginalised.

Constructive communication

Communication is always about achieving a purpose. It is a process towards a task. At its simplest, we want a job done, so the communication needs to include WHY?, WHAT?, HOW? and IF?.

> Imagine we are visitors in a factory and we notice that a drum of material labelled as 'flammable' is leaking in front of the hut that we are to occupy to complete our report. We regard the situation as urgent and speak to a forklift truck driver who is passing.

WHY? That drum is leaking and could cause a hazard.
WHAT? It is only the one drum – it should be moved to within a bund.
HOW? Could you move it for me with your truck?
IF? I will notify security of what is happening and your manager. OK?

Not much thought in our example of developing a sustained relationship with the forklift operator – just getting a dangerous situation resolved.

Constructive communication is about thinking about the individual and the future *as well as the task*. With constructive communication not only is a message delivered accurately, but the relationship between the two communicating parties is supported, even enhanced, by the interchange. The goal of constructive communication is not merely to be liked by other people or to be judged to be a nice person. It is not merely to produce social acceptance but has positive value in organisations. Researchers have found, for example, that organisations that encourage constructive communications enjoy higher productivity, faster problem solving, improved quality and reduced unproductive conflict, compared with groups and organisations where the communications style is less positive. Moreover, delivering world-class customer service is almost impossible without using constructive communication. Effective customer service requires constructive communication skills. Therefore, not only must managers be competent in using this kind of communication, but they must also help their subordinates to develop this competence.

Good employee relations are an essential for any effective organisation (Ouchi, 1981; Peters, 1987). Working with 40 major organisations in America, Hanson (1986) found that, over a five-year period, employee relations was by far the most significant factor in their success – more important than the four next most powerful variables (market share, capital availability, firm size and sales growth rate) combined. Techniques that foster good employee relations are not simply a 'feel good factor' that can be abandoned under pressure – they make sound business sense. There is, however, a strong proviso – some organisational cultures do not accept the concepts of constructive communication.

A very simple test is recommended. Imagine your boss has asked you to prepare a detailed report on a particular part of your department's work to the Board. One of your subordinates has the skills, knowledge and aptitude for writing the report and you do not. He or she writes the report, which, on your restricted expertise, seems excellent. In your opinion would the organisation expect you to:

(1) take the report and present it to the Board?
(2) take your subordinate with you to the Board and endorse his or her presentation?
(3) sit back while the report is presented?
(4) allow the subordinate to present the report, your own presence being irrelevant?

If you feel that (1) or (2) would be 'the way things are done' in your organisation, you may find the whole idea of constructive communication a dangerous concept to pursue. The culture of such organisations is echoed by the phrase:

They are paid to do the job – what else do they want?

Coaching, counselling and consulting

Ross (1986) sees coaching, counselling and consulting as essential managerial activities and Hersey and Blanchard (1986) can be interpreted as seeing management of subordinates towards empowerment and delegation, as a sequence of steps using the activities in turn.

Step 1   We have individuals or groups who do not know what is required of them. The manager needs to be clear in explaining *why* the job needs to be done and *what* needs to be done – he or she is the only person who can impart this information and needs to TELL it to the others by setting clear objectives. The telling may be dressed up as selling but telling it remains – the manager is in authority.

The manager has high task concern and low individual concern. We need then to move progressively to Step 2.

Step 2   The task is clear but the means of doing it need to be clarified – the problem being that every one needs to be able to do the jobs allocated to them. This means *coaching* and the manager remains with a high task concern but now has a high concern for individuals. The penalty for the manager if he or she does not make sure that individuals can actually do, and feel confident in, their allocated jobs can be very severe.

> A chicken-processing plant in the north of England decided to move to the first phase of automation. The new equipment, as subsequent interviews showed, frightened a key supervisor, who saw as his skill as that of controlling 200 women working in quite stressed conditions. The managers, to whom the change was very elementary, dismissed the man's fear and gave him no training or coaching to face his new environment – 'he will soon get a hand on it or he can go'. The strike he organised subsequently closed the factory.

Step 3   When people know why they are doing the task, what their role is, and are competent and confident in it – the constructive manager allows them to detail how they do it. If this step is not reached the manager must continually *consult* his or her staff on 'the detail' and give *counselling* where the new roles do not 'fit' individuals in spite of the coaching. Without such consultation the task will drift. We will return to this point later when we discuss motivation, delegation and empowerment.

At this step the manager in consulting is less concerned with the task and remains with a high concern for individuals.

Step 4   As people take over the task, they begin to know more about how they will do it than the manager who, basically needs to trust them – the process of true *delegation* is happening. He or she must extend the role to outside communications and monitor the work that is done to ensure that it meets the standards and constraints that are laid down. The managerial job is now low in involvement with the task but needs maintain relationships.

The ineffective manager

The ineffective manager moves from TELLING to DELEGATING without passing through the two high relationship stages without using the principle skills of constructive feedback – coaching, counselling and consulting.

- The clarity of the progression is not always obvious in the real world. Coaching and counselling may be needed at any time in management – if only because employees lose motivation or the skills base towards the task changes. Thus, tasks do not *stay* delegated and the effective manager needs to able to act appropriately all the time.
- The progression from TELLING to DELEGATING is not inevitable. The manager may simply not have the time to coach, counsel and consult, the task may be unclear or the organisation may not ALLOW the manager to delegate.

Coaching, counselling and consulting are essential for the maintenance of relationships and are especially important for:

1. Facilitation – equipping the person for the job and finding training needs.
2. Dealing with inappropriate behaviour or attitudes.
3. Developing working procedures for the mutual benefit of the individual and all others concerned.
4. Appraising and rewarding good performance.
5. Correcting poor performance.
6. Developing standards and targets.

This chapter will discuss the first three roles and the final three will be covered in the chapter on motivation.

Setting objectives

The first question we always need to answer is: What are our objectives in each case?

If you do not know where you are going, you will certainly end up somewhere else.

As a manager, faulty human communication can have serious consequences.

Mary managed a floor of telephone salespeople in a major financial institution. One of her subordinates, Harry, was noted for leaving early and putting work onto other people. On the afternoon in question she was talking with her floor supervisor when she noticed that Harry was putting on his coat and leaving. Confirming on her watch that Harry should still be at his station she called out across the floor:
'Where are you going?'
'Out!'
Mary ran after Harry and narrowly missed hitting the door as Harry slammed it behind him. Mary's loss of face was never retrieved and she had to move jobs.

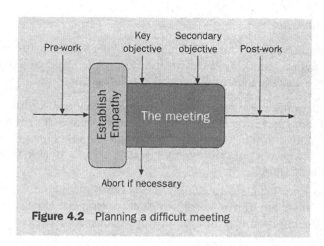

Figure 4.2 Planning a difficult meeting

The actual contact time for a potentially difficult meeting is a dangerous time and one for which a skilled manager plans. Figure 4.2 summarises the planning process.

Imagine that Mary had managed the encounter effectively. Firstly, the open office situation was NOT the time or the place for a difficult meeting. At the most, in hindsight she should have expressed non-verbal disapproval and left Harry's grand gesture unchallenged. Again, with hindsight, calling the supervisor over to her office, collecting 'records' and instructing that Harry should report directly to her in the morning would have been good. This was her pre-work.

Mary would see her key objective as establishing her authority over Harry. If Harry remained truculent, she would simply stop the meeting and take further action – action that Harry would not like. If Harry accepted her authority, Mary could go on to detail the office rules and close by setting up procedures to make sure that Harry observed them. There is one factor from our diagram that we have not mentioned: 'establish empathy'. We will discuss this later in our 10 Commandments of supporting communications. Summarising: in any potentially difficult meeting we need to plan and establish:

Pre-work	What do you need to do BEFORE the meeting?
Key objective	What do you HAVE to achieve at the meeting?
Second objective	What would you LIKE to get from the meeting?
Post-work	What needs to be done AFTER the meeting?

As managers we need to defuse problem situations and at the same time develop relationships with our subordinates that will hold us in good stead for the next time.

Read the following case studies and consider your key objectives, visualising how you would achieve them:

Tim Nelson – Regional Sales

Your firm makes and sells components for the aerospace industry and Tim Nelson is a newly appointed regional sales manager, promoted from 'the ranks'. Tim reports directly to you and his sales results are consistently below those met by other regions. In addition to his poor performance, his monthly reports are almost always late. In honesty, you have allowed the situation to drift and have not devoted sufficient time to Tim's induction to his new and challenging job.

You make an appointment to meet him in his office to discuss the latest sales figures but he is out of his office. His assistant tells you that one of Tim's team leaders has complained of general slackness in the group – lateness and extended coffee breaks. At this moment Tim is giving the group a piece of his mind and reminding them of what is required of them in sales results. You wait for 15 minutes until he returns.

Betty Mason – MBA

Betty Mason came highly recommended when she joined your financial planning group some months ago. However, she seems to be trying to enhance her own reputation at the expense of others. You have heard increasing complaints lately that Betty is arrogant, self-promotional and openly critical of other group members' work. In your first conversation with her about her performance she denied that there was a problem. She said that, if anything, she was having a positive impact on the group by raising its standards. You arrange another meeting with Betty after the latest set of complaints from her colleagues.

Coaching and counselling issues

A wise manager thinks initially about coaching – checking whether people can *do* the tasks assigned, before he or she moves to counselling. Counselling – checking on the complexities surrounding motivation, attitudes and other 'soft' issues – is always more uncertain in its outcomes.

Returning to our case studies, Tim's manager has the overall objective of improving the unit's output. Tim, as far as his manager can see, is keen, highly motivated and personable. These are the reasons why he was promoted in the first place. The question is whether he has the tools or skills of his new trade – has he been trained in management skills or even company procedures, formal or informal? Does he know the importance and expected content and form of the monthly reports? Does he know company disciplinary procedures? These are about coaching. Using the Hersey and Blanchard model, we have a high task and a high relationship concern – the manager needs to maintain a strong concern for the task while helping the subordinate. Repeating ourselves, we would always recommend tackling the coaching issues first, and, should the problem remain, look at the more tortuous issues of motivation and attitudes. So we plan our meeting with Tim:

- *Pre-work*   What preparation has Tim had for promotion? Has he been on any training courses? Are there any special issues in his sales region? Are there any 'markers' that Tim is in serious trouble – excessive labour turnover for instance?

- *Key objective*   We believe he is a potentially good worker who needs help. We need to identify what help is needed.

- *Second objective*   To develop agreed procedures for training and information flow so that Tim can progress and develop.

- *Post-work*   Monitor that what has been agreed on for implementation.

Management Consultancy and Skills

Betty's manager has a completely different issue. Betty most certainly has the training and knowledge to perform satisfactorily but things are still going wrong. Even accepting Betty's qualifications, an aware manager would check out that she has the *correct* skills and understanding to perform the job – for our case study we will assume she has. This takes us to a counselling issue and we need to under- stand why 'things are going wrong', assuming nothing.

Counselling issues are about the person doing the task, their suitability, motiva- tion and aptitudes. Belbin has a sound bite: 'We get our jobs for *what* we are and we get fired for *who* we are.' Counselling is about *who* we are.

The manager's starting point is his or her overall objective. Betty is presenting a serious challenge to the efficient running of the unit and this must be corrected. Should she not respond constructively, she will have to go. As a manager there is only a certain amount of quality time available, and although employee relations are a significant part of your job, they are rarely factors upon which YOU are judged. Betty, in the Hersey and Blanchard model, seems to have the task skills to do the job, but the way she is doing it is giving difficulty – the manager needs to keep a low concern for the task and a high concern for relationships.

The goal is to help Betty to recognise that a problem exists and that she is the only person who can solve it. Coaching applies to ability problems, and the man- ager's approach is: 'I can help you do this better.' Counselling applies to attitude problems, and the manager's approach is: 'I can help you to recognise that a problem exists. It gives me a problem because . . . and you have a problem because my problem needs to be resolved.'

- *Pre-work*   We would suspect the meeting could well become acrimonious so we need to prepare ourselves, perhaps reading the chapter on stress could help. We need to be clear on the organisation's disciplinary procedures and our own authority. We would also need, as in the Tim case study, to check on our facts for ourselves. Second-hand reports of a personal nature are often biased.

- *Key objective*   We must get Betty to recognise that *she* has a problem to handle. If she refuses to accept that there is any problem we should be prepared to close the meeting and reconsider our actions.

- *Second objective*   If Betty accepts a need for her to change, we agree some goals – for example, we could recommend the small-wins strategy discussed in the chapter on stress.

- *Post-work*   Monitoring the results of the agreed action, with the option of being flexible in our response if things do not go the way we want.

Many problems involve both coaching and counselling. Frequently managers have to give direction and advice (coaching), as well as help to facilitate understand- ing and willingness to change (counselling), but the two approaches must be kept apart.

'Right, we both agree that a few days in despatch will help you to understand some of the problems they have with order changes Tim. I'll see that that happens. You have to let me know how it goes. Now there is another issue, but let's have a cof- fee first.' Pause for refreshment and preferably some change of seating – possibly to an informal layout. 'Now, something else is giving me a problem. You know I am also responsible for expenses and recently some of your people have been using what at best could be called imagination. You simply have to get them under control.'

This works, but the reverse order undoes the good work. Suppose we have the following dialogue with Betty:

> Thanks for helping me. Let's confirm what we have agreed. You do accept that the atmosphere in your group is less than useful and that some of it may be due to the way the others perceive you. I do not accept that is jealousy but the fact that you are more highly qualified than even some of the Board may be an issue and certainly you telling Harry just that was, in both our views, a mistake. I agree that I have not given you a detailed enough set of targets, and we will fix that. You will 'take it back a little' – your words, and maybe cut down the 'power dressing' – your words, again. I think 'being aware of the way others see you', my words, will help. OK? (*Pause for some movement to a more formal seating arrangement.*) Now there is just one more thing. I intend to send you on a basic finance course. I don't know what they taught you on that MBA but your book-keeping is appalling.'

Betty's response is likely to be explosive and in management speak, will move to defensiveness, aggression or a total resistance to change.

Summarising

Tim Nelson knows that a problem exists but he doesn't know how to resolve it. Coaching is needed, not problem recognition. Should you find yourself doing both coaching and counselling in the same interview, we suggest that you adopt some token way of underlining your changing role in the meeting. For instance, should the meeting with Tim go drastically wrong and he begins to attack you and the organisation, it may well be useful to stand up, go over to a window and sit down again in a different chair. People need to know whether they are talking to a coach, an expert, or a counsellor who may seem to be a friend but in this context is a potential threat.

If we accept that the purpose of constructive communication is to produce empowered subordinates, the strategy must be to relinquish as much control as possible to the subordinate.

The questions that remain, however, are: How do I effectively coach or counsel another person? What are the behavioural guidelines that help me perform effectively in this situation? Coaching and counselling both rely on the same set of key constructive communication principles.

Defensive and patronising behaviours

If the principles of constructive communication are not followed when coaching, counselling or consulting subordinates, two major problems result (Gibb, 1961; Sieburg, 1978) and are summarised in Table 4.1.

Table 4.1 Constructive communication helps to overcome defensive behaviour in others and patronising behaviour in ourselves

Defensive behaviour	Patronising behaviour
• One individual feels threatened or attacked as a result of the communication. • Self-protection becomes paramount. • Energy is spent on constructing a defence rather than on listening. • Aggression, anger, competitiveness, and/or avoidance are common reactions.	• One individual feels incompetent, unworthy or insignificant as a result of the communication. • Attempts to re-establish self-worth take precedence. • Energy is spent trying to portray self-importance rather than on listening. • Showing off, self-centred behaviour, withdrawal, and/or loss of motivation are common reactions.

Think of constructive communication as a process that occurs when people establish empathy – neither is superior nor inferior to the other as human beings and each respect the other's position. If either party feels that he or she is being placed in a situation where it is necessary to admit inferiority or indeed superiority to satisfy the other, constructive communication will be disrupted. The most obvious form of such positioning is direct persecution:

'You are inadequate in your job' or 'Your whole attitude is wrong', either of which 'demands' a response of 'Sorry'.

The recipient may say 'Sorry' backed with some mumbling that he or she is lucky to be alive on the planet and working for such a good boss, but is more likely to come back aggressively or defensively:

- 'If you were a better boss and gave me reasonably clear objectives.'
- 'Who are you to say that, you are always on the golf course when things happen.'
- 'I do my best with in a difficult situation. My spouse has been taken into hospital and . . .'

None of the three styles of response – craw eating, aggression or defensiveness – is useful. The recipient has turned inwards and is not listening to the intended message.

A less obvious way of tilting the level playing field of communication is patronising behaviour:

- 'It's quite a difficult problem Tim. Let me explain it in your language and give me feedback if I am going too fast.'
- 'Of course Betty, you are a new manager who will, when you have my experience, understand these things.'

Management Consultancy and Skills

Table 4.2   10 Commandments of constructive communication
1. Know where you are going – establish a key objective and plan.
2. Play the ball and not the player – your objective and style it must be related to the job and remain strictly professional.
3. Be prepared to be honest and dismiss any personal or hidden agenda.
4. Chose and appropriate time and place and be willing to postpone or move if necessary.
5. Find common ground and use this as a starting point for the communication.
6. Establish empathy – match the pace of your 'client', neither rushing nor delaying.
7. Be prepared to discuss the specific and never make global criticism.
8. Listen and never judge.
9. There must always be benefits for all parties – never play 'I win, you lose'.
10. Always remember that you can MAKE anyone do anything – ONCE.

Such a flawed attempt to communicate, what may well be a difficult problem, will get the recipients thinking – *Who does he think he is?* – rather than listening.

A version of patronising behaviour, which demands the opposite response, is flattery: 'This is your sort of area Betty with your MBA. You see I came up in the University of Life and don't know these things.' Betty or indeed any sensible recipient of flattery is so puzzled at what is the 'required' response as to be incapable of listening to the substance of the communication or indeed relating to the messenger for quite some time.

Accordingly we have 10 Commandments, or principles, of constructive communication (Table 4.2).

1. Know where you are going – classify your objectives and plan but, ~~'keep it simple'~~

The planning process was summarised in Figure 4.1. We would see the very act of thinking of a difficult communications 'event' in a logical way as being half way to making it successful, as Eisenhower, Supreme Commander Allied Forces Europe in the Second World War, is quoted as saying: 'Planning is everything, plans are nothing.' In the event, good management is about controlling chaos, and being prepared helps immeasurably. We have used the concept of 'Keeping it Simple' and perhaps we should have added – 'Keep it Modest'.

2. Play the ball and not the player – constructive communication is about problems and not personalities

Any communication that concentrates on the negative characteristics of the individual can be interpreted as saying that the person is inadequate. Since we can at least attempt to change what we do, but cannot begin to change what we are, there is nothing we can do about personally directed criticism. The relationship fails and

Management Consultancy and Skills

the problems are not solved. Personal criticism is often used to try to persuade the other individual that 'this is how you should feel' or 'this is the kind of person you are': 'You are an incompetent manager, a lazy worker or an insensitive colleague.'

Most of us have learnt to accept ourselves as we are and when we are TOLD otherwise we devote our mental effort to defending, justifying or blaming. Any form of praise that is not tied into actual accomplishments or behaviour that we recognise will confuse us. The key is adding agreed and possible behavioural change to the communication. Always begin by describing the behaviour and how it effects you, the speaker:

> 'Betty, I have a department to keep happy and some things that I have observed you doing are not helpful. Firstly, the fact that you have been late on three occasions this week and that you are a manager, makes it impossible for me to tighten up on the others.'

Provided that you have your facts right, this is unarguable, but *'Betty, you are undisciplined'* is likely to start a row. Imputing motives to an individual is also 'playing the person and not the ball: *'I suppose you think that coming in when you want implies your seniority'* is equally dysfunctional. Remember the 'ball' you wish to play.

Our communication should also be linked to accepted standards or expectations rather than to personal opinions. Personal opinions are more likely to be interpreted as 'playing the person' and arouse defensiveness than statements where the behaviour is compared to an accepted standard. For example, the statement *'The way you dress is not appropriate'*, is an expression of a personal opinion and will probably create resistance, especially if the listener does not feel that the communicator's opinions are any more legitimate than his or her own. On the other hand, 'Your dress is not in keeping with the company dress code', or 'Everyone is expected to wear a tie to work', may sound stuffy but have that have legitimacy. Provided that the standards to which the messenger refers are accepted by the recipient, we have constructive communication. It is possible, but still slightly dangerous, to express personal opinions or feelings about the behaviour or attitudes of others, as long as they are 'owned' – 'I *feel unhappy about the way you dress in the office'*.

3. Be prepared to be honest and express personal feelings, dismissing any personal or hidden agenda

Rogers (1961), Dyer (1972) and others argue that the best interpersonal communications, and the best relationships, are based on congruence – that is, matching the communication, verbally and non-verbally, exactly to what the individual is thinking and feeling. Two kinds of incongruence are possible. One is a mismatch between what one is experiencing and what one is aware of. For example, an individual may not even be aware that he or she is experiencing anger towards another person or generating such anger, regardless of what an independent observer may feel. A second kind of incongruence, and the one more closely related to constructive communication, is a mismatch between what one feels and what one communicates, thus genuine compassion may come over as patronising behaviour.

Heather and Woods (1991), in their summary article on Neuro Linguistic Programming (NLP), describe an exercise where a volunteer from a training group is asked to think first of an individual he or she likes and then of an other individual he or she dislikes. In the process of 'fixing' the liked and disliked individuals the rest of the class observe the volunteer very carefully. The volunteer is then asked to choose at random one or other of the individuals and fix his or her thoughts on that individual. The observers have to 'guess' whether the individual now being concentrated upon is liked or disliked. The observers then have to give reasons for their choice.

A wide range of 'clues' are noted by the observers – twitching, tightening of the muscles about the mouth, crinkling about the eyes, foot movements. Using their observations, the analyses are very usually correct and almost always made with certainty.

The point of the exercise is that it is very difficult to hide one's feelings – others are continuously using a finely tuned 'computer' analysis of our smallest non-verbal signals, and believe in the analysis, whether it is consciously surfaced or not. We also believe our own judgement against what can be rising evidence. Put at its crudest – if we don't like people, it shows, however much we dress it up. For this reason alone it is better to be honest and straightforward in our communications. Genuine, honest statements are always better than artificial or dishonest statements. Managers who hold back their true feelings or opinions, or who don't express what is really on their minds, create the impression that a hidden agenda exists. Subordinates sense that there is something else which has not been said. Therefore, they trust the communicator less and focus on trying to work out what the hidden message is, not on listening or trying to improve. False impressions and miscommunication result.

Rogers (1961) suggests that congruence in communication lies at the heart of a general law of interpersonal relationships. The greater the congruence of experience and awareness with the communication, the more at ease we will be. The reverse is also true – a lack of congruence leads to distrust and a dysfunctional communication.

As we attempt to achieve congruence we must realise that the immediate surfacing of personal emotions may well be counterproductive. The time and place for anger or tears may not be on the shop floor in front of the night shift. We must always be aware of context. However, in general, where the communications issues are very difficult, error on the side of congruence – an indication of feelings in a controlled manner works, the emphasis is on the word controlled. Take, for example, an interview with a subordinate who is performing below his or her ability and displays a nonchalant attitude when given hints that the whole team is being affected. What could the superior say that would strengthen the relationship with the subordinate and still resolve the problem? How can one express honest feelings and opinions and still remain problem-focused, not person-focused? How can one be completely honest without offending another person? Does it matter that the other person is offended? Being aware of the issue is half the answer.

4. Choose an appropriate time and place and be willing to postpone or move if necessary

A very elementary aspect of congruence is 'choosing the right time and place' for a communication and abandoning the communication if the time and place become unsuitable.

> We were told of a case where an employee had just received a very worrying report from his doctor and was attempting to tell his manager that he had to take time off for an operation. The manager, who was under time pressures, heard but did not listen to the employee's concerns and continued with what was a very minor disciplinary matter. The relationship between the employee and the manager was permanently scarred and later the employee had no recollection of the focus of the 'minor disciplinary matter'. The manager remained unaware of the employee's issue – 'There is none so deaf as those that do not want to listen.' (English proverb).

There is a time and a place for everything and constructive communication needs to be part of the general flow and not something that stands out. The flow is not even when:

- The contributions are not balanced or relevant to the subject matter. This can happen when one person dominates and takes significantly more 'air time' than his or her contribution merits or constantly interrupts.

- There are extended pauses. When speakers pause for long periods in the middle of their speeches or when there are long pauses before responses, the communication becomes disjointed. Pauses do not necessarily equate to complete silences – umm's and aah's or repetitions can equally sabotage constructive communication.

- There are unilateral shifts in the topics being discussed. Sieburg (1969) found that more than 25 per cent of the statements made in small-group discussions failed to refer to or even acknowledge previous speakers or their statements.

Constructive communication requires discipline in all three areas.

It is perfectly possible to train individuals to improve their ability to maintain and not impede the flow of communications with others.

> We were working with a group who were becoming impatient with one of their members who boorishly dominated all the conversations, breaking all three of our principles. He consented to write down his statements before opening his mouth. He then, if he still wanted to speak, had to relate his interjection to what the previous person had said – proving it by a summary. The process was painful for him, but in a final statement he said that he had found, over the two days, that much of what he thought was vital was indeed being expressed by others. As an aside, the discipline at the workshop was relaxed during coffee breaks, where he talked incessantly.

Figure 4.3 illustrates that a continuum may exist for conjunctive statements.

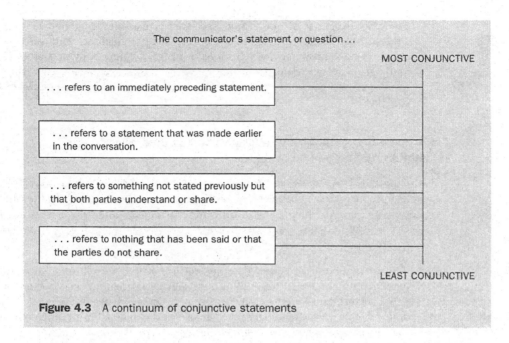

Figure 4.3 A continuum of conjunctive statements

The principle whereby we move communications along a progression, building from previous statements and opinions, is important throughout a conversation, but vitally important when we begin a communication where no formal precedents have been established.

5. Establish common ground

Always check the basic facts before any form of professional communication. Is it the right person I have before me? Has the person been told anything in advance? Is he or she aware of what is going to be discussed? Think in terms of a lecturer meeting a class for the first time and beginning a new subject.

> 'My objective for today is to get you to be able to make a presentation with Power Point. Now we need to find out something about your needs. How many of you have already used Power Point? Good. Now, I imagine one or two of you may not be too certain of even using Windows – fine that's three of you. OK, but can I take it that all of you have actually used a PC? Fine. So let's bore the 'experts' by starting from using Windows, right at the beginning. When you switch the screen on . . .'

Without establishing common ground the communicator is wasting everyone's time. If Tim did not share his manager's unspoken desire to do well for himself and his firm, then the interview would be pointless. So it is with Betty, she needed to do better or lose her job and both she and her manager accept this. If Tim was into sabotage and Betty had a private income or had an exciting job offer from another company, then the manager's job would be much more difficult, if not impossible.

The chief executive of one of our associated universities circulated all staff with a beautifully crafted article about the University's finances. The article would certainly have answered the questions of his own ruling body and probably the bank. It answered none of the questions his staff were concerned with: What resources can I call upon next year? Where are the cuts going to be felt? Am I still in a job?

6. Establish empathy – match the pace of your 'client', neither rushing nor delaying

In Figure 4.1 we showed an overlapping area before the key objective which we called 'Empathy'. Empathy is a strange unquantifiable property in constructive communications, which cover a multitude of defects and allows a successful process. If individuals are comfortable with each other, then constructive communication 'happens'.

Phil was a technician turned sales person responsible for selling a range of products to industrial customers. As a new and inexperienced sales person he was either accompanied or given 'safe' customers. On this occasion the 'safe' customer rang through to the regional sales manager and explained in no uncertain terms that *'If you send that young man to me again, you can forget my custom.'*

The manager put Phil into a series of role plays with mock customers and watched the tapes. The first role play was excellent – the 'customer' was a busy buyer for a supermarket chain who had 'spared' Phil a few minutes. Phil got down to work immediately – the samples and the patter perfectly presented. Even watching it you became out of breath. In the second role play the buyer had his feet on the desk and was playing with a cup of coffee. Phil was offered a cup but declined. The buyer then asked Phil about the traffic but Phil was not to be drawn – out came the samples and on went the pressured patter. Discussing things afterwards Phil admitted that the 'safe' customer seemed to want to talk but that, it being the end of the day, Phil wanted to get home: *'I don't have time for all that social chit chat – it's a job.'*

The point of the story is that *'all that social chit chat'*, for someone who is relaxing after a hard day, is an indication of the pace the customer wants to conduct the interview. If the customer is standing up, answering telephone calls, breathing rapidly, talking in short bursts – then he or she is indicating that he or she wants to take the communication at a rapid pace. Reading the signals provided allows us to judge the pace at which we conduct the encounter. Heather and Woods (1991) regard the balancing of pace in communications as the first and most basic means of establishing empathy. Using the language of NLP they go further and explain how, by mirroring body postures and even styles of language, empathy can be further enhanced and the barriers to constructive communication further lowered.

7. Be specific and never global in any criticism

In general, the more specific a statement is, the more useful it is. For example, the statement, 'You're a poor time manager' is too general to be useful, whereas 'I am concerned that you appear to have spent an hour scheduling meetings today when that could have been done by your assistant' provides specific information that can serve as a basis for behavioural change. Specific statements avoid extremes and absolutes. Think about hearing these statements and see how you would feel:

- 'You never ask for my advice.'
- 'You have no consideration for others' feelings.'
- 'Your work is always inadequate.'
- 'Can't you ever come in on time?'

We suggest in all these cases that the obvious response is negative and is likely to block any future understanding – they are not a route to constructive communication.

Another poor route to communications failure is the 'either–or' statement:

- 'You either do what I say or I will be forced to get rid of you.'
- 'Do you want to do a good job or not?'

The uselessness of polarised statements lies in their denial of any alternatives, and possible responses are severely limited. About the only response to such statements is to contradict or deny it, and this simply leads to defensiveness and arguments. A statement in 1931 by Adolf Hitler illustrates the point: 'Everyone in Germany is a National Socialist – the few outside the party are either lunatics or idiots.' The non-global specific statement allows the smooth flow of the communication process to continue:

A: You made that decision yesterday without asking for my advice.
B: That is right, I did. Normally I do like to get your opinion, but on this occasion there wasn't time.

A: The tone of the memo you have just sent on the loss of the Smithson order will offend Finance unnecessarily.
B: Yes I regret that now. I unfortunately am inclined to put pen to paper without thinking out the consequences.

A: It's difficult to hear in this lecture room.
B: That may be true and perhaps we need to use a hotel for the next big presentation.

As these examples point out, the use of qualifier words such as 'normally', 'inclined', 'may' and 'perhaps' help to link the reply to a specific incident.

Specific statements may not be useful if they focus on things over which another person has no control. 'I hate it when it rains', for example, may relieve some personal frustration, but the referent of the statement is something about which little can be done. The communication is not very useful. Similarly, communicating the message (even implicitly) 'I don't like people of your background' or 'Your personality bothers me' only prove frustrating for the interacting individuals. Such statements are usually interpreted as personal attacks. Specific communication is useful to the extent that it focuses on an identifiable problem or behaviour about which something can be done (e.g., 'It bothers me that you checked up on me four times today').

Management Consultancy and Skills

8. Listen and never judge – communication is not a one-way street

Constructive communication is owned, not disowned. Taking responsibility for one's statements, acknowledging that the source of the ideas is oneself and not another person or group is owning communication. Using first-person words, such as 'I', 'me', 'mine', indicates owning communication. Disowning communication is suggested by use of third-person or first-person-plural words – 'We think', 'The Management Committee has decided' or 'They said'. In disowning the comments the communicator avoids taking responsibility for the message and conveys the message that he or she is aloof or uncaring for the receiver, or is not confident enough in the ideas expressed to take responsibility for them.

Glasser (1965) based his approach to therapy on the concept of responsibility for, or owning, communication and behaviour. According to Glasser, individuals are mentally healthy if they accept responsibility for their statements and behaviours. They are ill if they avoid taking responsibility. According to this theory, taking responsibility for one's communication builds self-confidence and a sense of self-worth in the communicator. It also builds confidence in the receiver of the communication by confirming that he or she is valued.

One result of disowning communication is that the listener is never sure whose point of view the message represents and is apt to misinterpret it: 'How can I respond if I don't know to whom I am responding?' Moreover, an implicit message associated with disowned communication is, 'I want to keep distance between you and me'. The speaker communicates as a representative rather than as a person, or as a message-conveyer rather than as an interested individual. Owning communication, on the other hand, indicates a willingness to invest oneself in the relationship and to act as a colleague or helper. The danger of owning the communication is that we can feel that we can become a judge. We forget that communication is a two-way street.

'Judge not or you will be judged' – our owned constructive communication must contain a description of the behaviour being discussed and not, at this point, be evaluative. Evaluative communication generally makes the other person feel under attack and respond defensively. If this does not matter and the actions demanded are immediate, evaluative communication is fine:

> 'Don't do that, you are not qualified to wire the machine safely – get an electrician and have it wired properly and get it cleared for safety.'

So the man about to be a danger to himself and anyone else who uses the equipment, has had his pride hurt. There may be an argument, bad feelings, exchanging blame and a weakening of the interpersonal relationship result, but nobody will get killed.

The tendency to evaluate others is strongest when the issue is charged with emotion or when a person feels threatened. When people have strong feelings about an issue or experience anxiety as a result of a situation, they have a tendency to make negative evaluations of others' behaviour. Sometimes they try to resolve their own feelings or reduce their own anxiety by placing a label on others: 'You are bad, and that implies I am good. Therefore, I feel better.' At other times they may have such

Table 4.3   Descriptive communication

Step 1
- Describe as objectively as possible the event, behaviour or circumstance.
- Avoid accusations.
- Present data or evidence, if needed.

Step 2
- Describe your own reactions to or feelings about the event, behaviour or circumstance.
- Describe the objective consequences that have resulted, or will likely result.
- Focus on the behaviour and on your own reaction, not on the other individual or his or her personal attributes.

Step 3
Suggest a more acceptable alternative.

strong feelings that they want to punish the other person for violating their expectations or standards.

The problem with this approach is that evaluative communication is likely to be self-perpetuating. Placing a label on another individual generally leads that person to respond by placing a label on you, which makes you defensive in return. The accuracy of the communication as well as the strength of the relationship deteriorates.

An alternative to evaluation is the use of descriptive communication. Because is it difficult to avoid evaluating other people without some alternative strategy, the use of descriptive communication helps to eliminate the tendency to evaluate or to perpetuate a defensive interaction. Descriptive communication involves three steps, as summarised in Table 4.3.

The first stage of descriptive communication is to describe, as objectively as possible, the event that occurred or the behaviour that needs to be modified. The description should contain the elements of the behaviour that can be related to accepted standards and are observable or observed. Subjective impressions or attributions to the motives of another person are not helpful in describing the event. The description 'You have finished fewer projects this month than anyone else in the unit' can be confirmed and relates strictly to the behaviour and to an objective standard, not to the motives or personal characteristics of the subordinate. Put as bluntly as in our example, the subordinate may still feel threatened, but over his or her job performance and not about him or her as a person. 'You are not up to the job' will produce quite different feelings. Describing a behaviour, as opposed to evaluating a behaviour, is relatively neutral.

The second stage is to focus on the reactions or consequences of the behaviour: 'I am unhappy that your performance will demotivate the whole team and will certainly reduce the group bonus.' By owning the feelings we reduce the chances of the person retreating into his or her shell, thinking only of defence and not of solving the problem.

Thirdly, we need to move on to a mutually acceptable 'solution'. It is important that the 'solution' is actionable. We have a paraplegic friend who at a job interview was told: *'You would have been ideal for this job except that you don't have legs.'* Brutality will get you nowhere.

The actionable solution can be presented on a scale of directness: 'This is what I want you to do' or 'I have a few ideas but would like to hear your ideas first', or preferably 'You see our problem. How do you think we should approach it?' The three approaches allow the person to save face (Goffman, 1955) and feel valued (Sieburg, 1978) by separating the individual from the behaviour. If self-esteem is preserved, the behaviour stands a good chance of being modified and the relationship with the boss improved. Our emphasis has moved from establishing who is right and who is wrong to a positive search for a solution. Blanchard and Johnson (1983), in their series of influential management monographs, suggest certain very firm guidelines for giving negative criticism:

- Warn the person involved before the meeting and have the meeting as soon as possible.
- Be specific about your criticism – detail the behaviour.
- Express your feelings in no uncertain terms – anger, sorrow, shame, disappointment.
- Allow your feelings to register with the other person.
- Outline what they have to do.
- Re-establish the relationship – it is the behaviour that is wrong not the person concerned.
- Close the meeting and the subject once and for all.

The whole interview should take less than one minute. Blanchard and Johnson regard this 'One Minute Manager' approach as suitable for most managerial communications, and certainly, with appropriate modifications, for giving praise.

Descriptive communication does require common ground to be established before it works. Thus if our subordinate does not share our objectives and values, or perhaps dislikes the rest of the team, then we will not have constructive communication and perhaps a row.

Effective managers never abandon the three steps. They simply switch the focus, chunking down or up to find common ground.

- 'I am surprised to hear that you do not think the work worth while. Obviously this needs to be discussed. Could we meet next week to go though your ideas?' (Chunking up)
- 'This is the first time I have heard the team bonus criticised. I would like to have your views. Could you give me a few points on paper for next week and we can discuss them?' (Chunking down)

McGregor (1960) would say that our assumption that most people are professionals who wish to do and be seen to do a good job as corresponding to Theory Y as opposed to Theory X. In Theory X employees are 'only doing it for the money, cannot be trusted and need a sharp stick to get them off their backsides'. It is our assumption that, given positive support, most people want to do better, to perform successfully and to be respected. To us, constructive communication is one aspect of that positive support.

It is important to keep in mind, however, that the steps of descriptive communication do not imply that one person should do all the changing. Constructive communication is not a one-way street and should break the stereotypical roles where management is about telling and subordinates are about complying.

'I have discussed what you said about the lack of direction in the unit with the Management Committee and we are forced to agree. What we propose is that we have a weekend off site and bring the whole team together. The Committee will attend on Sunday morning and listen. It's a real opportunity.'

We always have to be willing to move off our prepared agenda and listen. Looking back on Figure 4.1, this is what we showed as 'abort if necessary' – we stop in our tracks and listen, not necessarily only to our 'client'.

As Maier *et al.* (1973) stated: 'In any conversation, the person who talks the most is the one who learns the least about the other person. The good supervisor therefore must become a good listener.'

In a survey of personnel directors in 300 businesses and industries, conducted to determine the skills that are most important in becoming a manager, Crocker (1978) reported that effective listening was ranked highest. Despite its importance in managerial success, however, and despite the fact that most people spend at least 45 per cent of their communication time listening, most people have underdeveloped listening skills. Tests have shown, for example, that individuals are usually about 25 per cent effective in listening (Huseman *et al.*, 1976) – that is, they listen to and understand only about a quarter, on average, of what is being communicated. Even when asked to rate the extent to which they are skilled listeners, 85 per cent of all individuals rate themselves as average or worse. Only 5 per cent rate themselves as highly skilled (Steil, 1980). It is particularly unfortunate that listening skills are poorest when people interact with those closest to them, such as family members and colleagues.

When individuals are preoccupied with meeting their own needs (e.g., saving face, persuading someone else, winning a point, avoiding getting involved), when they have already made a judgement, or when they hold negative attitudes towards the communicator or the message, they can't listen effectively. Because a person listens at the rate of 500 words a minute but speaks at a normal rate of only 125 to 250 words a minute, the listener's mind can dwell on other things half the time. Therefore, being a good listener is neither easy nor automatic. It requires developing the ability to hear and understand the message sent by another person, while at the same time helping to strengthen the relationship between the interacting parties.

Rogers and Farson (1976) suggest that this kind of listening conveys the idea that 'I'm interested in you as a person, and I think what you feel is important. I respect your thoughts, and even if I don't agree with them, I know they are valid for you. I feel sure you have a contribution to make. I think you're worth listening to, and I want you to know that I'm the kind of person you can talk to.'

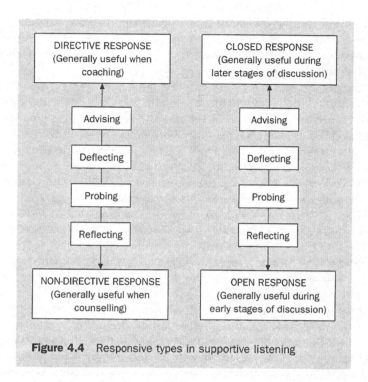

Figure 4.4 Responsive types in supportive listening

People do not know they are being listened to unless the listener makes some type of response; however, we would not suggest learning 'appropriate' responses, but we should be aware of our effect on others. Sophisticated non-verbal indicators of listening can include obscuring one's own mouth, nodding, echoing the end phrase of the other's sentence and a gaze which includes the mouth of the other person. Constructive listening is best learnt by watching competent managers at work.

We can, however, school ourselves in the verbal tools of response types. Figure 4.4 lists four major response types and arranges them on a continuum from most directive and closed to the most non-directive or open. Closed responses eliminate discussion of topics and provide direction to individuals. They represent methods by which the listener can control the topic of conversation. Open responses, on the other hand, allow the communicator, not the listener, to control the topic of conversation. Each of these response types has certain advantages and disadvantages, and none is appropriate at all times in all circumstances.

Most people get into the habit of relying heavily on one or two response types, and they use them regardless of the circumstances. Moreover, most people have been found to rely first and foremost on evaluative or judgemental responses (Rogers, 1961). That is, when they encounter another person's statements, most people tend to agree or disagree, pass judgement, or immediately form a personal opinion about the legitimacy or veracity of the statement. On average, only about 80 per cent of most people's responses have been found to be evaluative. Constructive listening, however, avoids evaluation and judgement as a first response. Instead, it relies on flexibility in response types and the appropriate match of responses to circumstances. Here are the four response types indicating active listening:

- Advising
- Deflecting
- Probing
- Reflecting

Advising

The advising response provides direction, evaluation, personal opinion or instruction. Advising responses place the 'listening manager' firmly in control. The advantages of an advising response are that it helps the communicator to understand something that may have been unclear before, it helps to identify a solution to a problem, and it can provide clarity about how the communicator should feel or act in the future. It is most appropriate when the listener has expertise that the communicator doesn't possess or when the communicator is in need of direction. This is a case where listening also does much of the talking and is not a difficult response for many people. The mouth takes over from the ears very quickly.

One problem with advising is that it can produce dependence. Individuals get used to having someone else generate the answers, directions or clarification. They are not permitted to work out the issues and the solutions for themselves. Rogers (1961) found that most people, even when they seem to be asking for advice, mainly desire understanding and acceptance, not advice. They want the listener to share in the communication, but not take charge of it. When we take on the role of adviser we concentrate more on the legitimacy of the advice or on the generation of alternatives and solutions than on simply listening attentively. We are often impatient and base our advice on our own experience rather than developing an understanding of the world of our 'client'. The final problem arises from the state of mind of the person asking for the advice. Quite often people ask for advice to demonstrate that the situation is impossible and that they have tried everything possible. They may want the adviser to admit his or her own incompetence, but more often they want their own inability shared. In either case the interview can close with a very sour note. Overall the disadvantages of advising are such that we would NOT recommend it as a first response.

> One concept that we find useful is that of seeing yourself as working with your ears – listening and not participating except to encourage and collate; working with your hands – showing others how to do things by example; and working with your mouth – advising. All need to be used appropriately. Sticking to one channel – ears, hands or mouth – all the time can be very ineffectual.

Responses that allow communicators to have control over the topics of conversation, that show understanding and acceptance, and that encourage self-reliance on the part of communicators have their place. In addition, the advice that is given should be connected to an accepted standard. 'You are expected to conform to the standards of dress on every day but Friday' or 'I am sorry but your behaviour is not acceptable'. An accepted standard means that communicators and listeners both acknowledge that the advice will lead to a desired outcome and that it is inherently good, right or appropriate. When this is impossible, the advice should be communicated as the listener's opinion or feeling, and as only one option (i.e., with flexibility), not as the only option. This permits communicators to accept or reject the advice without feeling that the adviser is being invalidated or rejected if the advice is not accepted.

Deflecting

A deflecting response switches the focus from the communicator's problem to one selected by the listener. It simply means that the listener changes the subject. Listeners may substitute their own experience for that of the communicator:

'Let me tell you something similar that happened to me.'

They may introduce an entirely new topic:

'That reminds me of [something else].'

The listener may think the current problem is unclear to the communicator and the use of examples or analogies will help. Or the listener may feel that the communicator needs to be reassured that others have experienced the same problem and that support and understanding are available.

Deflecting responses are most appropriate when a comparison or reassurance is needed. They can provide empathy and support by communicating the message:

'I can recognise what you are saying.'

They can also convey assurance:

'That's OK. These things happen.'

The disadvantages of deflecting responses, however, are that they can imply that the communicator's message is not important or that the experience of the listener is more significant than that of the communicator. It may produce competitiveness or feelings of being up-staged by the listener.

> In the earlier days of one of the authors, he was a caver on an international expedition. The expedition doctor had a simple way of avoiding any action whatsoever. Any complaint was greeted by the response: 'Yes that is terrible – I have exactly the same symptom.' The doctor was not well respected but the 'malingering' was negligible.

Deflecting responses are most effective when they are clearly connected to what the communicator just said, when the listener's response leads directly back to the communicator's concerns, and when the reason for the deflection is made clear. That is, deflecting can produce desirable outcomes in coaching and counselling if the communicator feels supported and understood, not invalidated, by the change in topic focus.

Probing

A probing response clarifies what has been said about a topic relevant to the interview. The intention makes clear what is being said and to progress the conversation towards a useful conclusion – it is neutral and implies no comment on what is being proposed. Probing questions help the listener adopt the communicator's frame of reference so that in coaching situations suggestions can be specific (not general) and in counselling situations statements can be descriptive (not evaluative).

Probing questions can sometimes have the unwelcome effect of switching the focus of attention from the communicator's statement to the reasons behind it. The question 'Why do you think that?' might force the communicator to justify a feeling or a perception rather than just report it and lose the direction of the remarks. Probing should be honest and not used to fog the communicator's presentation.

Two important points should be kept in mind to make probing more effective. One is that 'why' questions are seldom as effective as 'What' questions. 'Why' questions are inclined to lead to hostility of 'rabbit holes' where speculation overtakes real insights. For example, the question, 'Why do you feel that way?' can lead to statements such as 'Because my id is not sufficiently controlled by my ego' or 'Because my father was an alcoholic and my mother beat me – so what?' My professional problem is that production is down and in all honesty half-baked psychological analysis is not my job. 'What happened?' pushes us back to what earns both of us our daily bread.

A second hint is to tailor the probes to fit the situation. When the communicator's statement does not contain enough information or part of the message is not understood, check it out: 'Can you tell me more about that?' When the message is not clear or is ambiguous, clarify: 'What do you mean by that?' A repetition probe should be used when the communicator is avoiding a topic or hasn't answered a previous question: 'I am sorry but I still don't understand – where were you when the explosion occurred?' A reflective probe is most effective when the communicator is being encouraged to keep pursuing the same topic in greater depth.

Reflecting

A reflecting response mirrors the message that was heard, communicates understanding and encourages further development of the statement. Reflecting involves paraphrasing and clarifying the message and is not just a parrot-like mimicry of what has been said. It contributes to understanding and the acceptance of what is being said while allowing communicators to pursue topics of their choice. Rogers (1961), Benjamin (1969), Athos and Gabarro (1978) and others argue that this response should be used most of the time in coaching and counselling since it leads to the most clear communication and the most constructive relationships.

A potential disadvantage of reflective responses is that communicators can get the opposite impression to the one intended. That is, they can get the feeling that they are not being understood or listened to carefully. If they keep hearing reflections of what they just said, their response might begin to be:

'I just said that. Aren't you listening to me?'

A 'health warning' – Reflective responses can be perceived as a technique, as a superficial response lacking integrity.

9. There must be benefits for all parties – never play 'I win, you lose'

Constructive communication must never 'put people down'. Even descriptive communication can still be destructive. Barnlund (1968) observed:

> People do not take time, do not listen, do not try to understand, but interrupt, anticipate, criticise or disregard what is said; in their own remarks they are frequently vague, inconsistent, verbose, insincere or dogmatic. As a result, people often conclude conversations feeling more inadequate, more misunderstood and more alienated than when they started.

The key in our experience is to treat people as adults, unless you have very strong evidence that this is not so, and to act naturally.

> A personnel manager of a large company was well known as a dour Scot – he never joked and was known in the department as 'an ill wind that brings nobody any good'. He was, however, efficient and respected. He was sent on a course on constructive communication and returned with the objective of empowering the staff.
>
> One of his first gross failures was with a senior and highly effective, personal assistant to a colleague. He started the phone conversation by asking whether she wanted the good news or the bad news first. The bemused lady, who did not know about the training course, asked for the bad news and was told that she had sent a memo out with a typographical error. He then went on to the good news that was that she had been regraded and would receive a substantial pay increase. She only heard the bad news and was in tears to her manager because she thought she had been sacked.

Communication that is invalidating arouses negative feelings about self-worth, identity and relatedness to others. It denies the presence, uniqueness or importance of other individuals. Especially important are communications that invalidate people by conveying superiority, rigidity and indifference (Sieburg, 1978; Galbraith, 1975; Gibb, 1961). Communication that is based on assumptions of grade or seniority gives the impression that the communicator is informed while others are ignorant, adequate while others are inadequate, competent while others are incompetent, or powerful while others are impotent. It creates a barrier between the communicator and those to whom the message is sent.

Communication based on a feeling of superiority can take the form of putdowns, in which others are made to look bad so that the communicator looks good. Or it can take the form of 'one-upmanship', in which the communicator tries to elevate himself or herself in the esteem of others. We can, consciously or unconsciously put others down by various means:

1. We can use jargon, acronyms, or words in such a way as to exclude others or create barriers in communication. Doctors, lawyers, government employees and many other professionals are well known for their use of jargon or

acronyms to exclude others, or to elevate themselves rather than to clarify a message. Speaking a foreign language in the presence of people who don't understand it also creates the impression of superiority. In most circumstances, using words or language that a listener can't understand is simply bad manners.

2. We can be rigid and show that we do not listen. The communication is portrayed as absolute, unequivocal or unquestionable. No other opinion or point of view could possibly be considered. Individuals who communicate in dogmatic, 'know-it-all' ways often do so in order to minimise the contributions of others or to invalidate their perspectives. It is possible to communicate rigidity, however, in ways other than just being dogmatic. Rigidity is communicated, for example, by:

   - never expressing agreement with anyone else, or when agreement is expressed expressing it in terms of 'they agree with me', not 'I agree with them'
   - reinterpreting all other viewpoints to conform to one's own
   - never saying, 'I don't know', but having an answer for everything
   - not expressing openness to others' opinions or information
   - using evaluative and invalidating statements, instead of communicating understanding and validation for others
   - appearing unwilling to tolerate criticism or alternative points of view
   - reducing complex issues to simplistic definitions
   - using all-encompassing and over-generalised statements (that is, communicating the message that everything worth while that can be said about the subject has just been said)
   - merging definitions of problems with solutions so that alternatives are not considered
   - placing exclamation points after statements, creating the impression that the statement is final, complete or unqualified.

We can indicate our indifference by a variety of ways – silence, by making no verbal response, avoiding eye contact or any facial expression, by interrupting the other person frequently, or by doing unrelated activities. Indifference, however conveyed, indicates a lack of respect of the other and is hostile.

Sieburg (1978) discusses a further way in which we can 'put people down' – being impervious to arguments. We can show this by saying:

'You shouldn't feel that way' – who are you to know?
'You don't understand' – who has the duty to explain?
'Your opinion is uninformed' – who appointed me anyway?

In all these put downs we are expected to say sorry – perhaps for using the resources of the planet. Although most of us have non-OK days, hopefully most of us like feeling good about ourselves. People 'demanding' grovelling from their sub-ordinates collect subordinates willing to grovel. This is not a good idea.

Invalidation is even more destructive in coaching and counselling than criticism or disagreement, because criticism and disagreement validate the other person by recognising that what was said or done is worthy of correction, response or at least notice (Jacobs, 1973). As William James (1965) stated, 'No more fiendish punishment could be devised, even were such a thing physically possible, than that one could be turned loose in a society and remain absolutely unnoticed by all the members thereof.'

We abandoned an exercise to demonstrate this point when it proved too effective. In the exercise, five volunteers are assembled from a group of managers in a training course. The first in the group is praised for being him/herself – 'It's great to have a really positive person in a group – now sit down.' The second is praised for completing a trivial act well – clapping in tune. The third is given a further trivial task – clapping to the rhythm of a nursery rhyme – and is admonished for not being very good at the task. The fourth person is dismissed personally – 'Why you volunteered is beyond me; you are the sort of person who learns nothing from management courses.'

When the four are seated, at various levels of discontent, the tutor resumed the session, leaving the fifth standing. After a few minutes a range of things may have happened. The ignored fifth person may have become hostile, crept back to his or her seat, or simply stayed looking awkward.

We then debrief the five people. The one who was really hurt was not the one who was told off – the one who was ignored feels the worst. On one occasion, the man felt so bad about being left and ignored that we abandoned the use of the demonstration on all subsequent courses. He was HURT.

The obverse of invalidation communication helps people to feel recognised, understood, accepted and valued. Validating communication is not based on hierarchy and is flexible. It is also a two-way process.

Where coaches or counsellors are senior to those being counselled it is easy for subordinates to feel invalidated. They do have less organisational power and information than their manager. Constructive communicators, however, help subordinates to feel that they have a stake in identifying problems and resolving them 'together'. They treat subordinates as worth while, competent and insightful, and emphasise joint problem solving rather than project a superior position with a tacit acceptance that the roles are different and will stay that way. The point is that being a senior is a privilege with responsibilities and not some God-given right. There is, however, always a question of trust and confidentiality. Imagine the following situation.

You are Harry's manager and are counselling him over lateness. Your key objective in the session is to stop lateness becoming endemic in your section and Harry becoming a role model for the others. Your secondary objective is to get Harry in work on time and, failing this, to begin disciplinary action. You have done your pre-work. During the interview, which you have explained to Harry is confidential and 'between equals', Harry admits that he is involved in serious crime – unrelated to his work with you. What do you do?

The manager's dilemma, which is based on an actual incident, is real and is based on a misconception. We glibly use the word counselling in a managerial context – working with individuals in a work situation so that the work may be performed more effectively – and think of counselling in a social services context. In the social service context the counsellor is, or should be independent and should be, or is, working purely in the interest of the client. They have points in common but diverge greatly in many situations.

1. The manager owes his or her loyalty to the organisation responsible for his or her wages. His or her loyalty to the 'client' is, in all but unusual cases, not part of the job. The social worker/counsellor has a divided loyalty to the organisation and to the 'client'. Few would argue that in all but extreme cases, the client comes first.

2. The manager's circle of concern is the job for which he or she is paid. Very clearly, if matters come to light that are not effecting the 'job' in any way, they are not the manager's concern. An example of the legal aspect of this is the case when an employee is *suspected* of a criminal activity such as theft, at work. The manager can suspend the employee on suspicion but is highly discouraged in investigating the 'crime'. His or her job is progressing the interests of the organisation and not becoming a policeman.

Returning to Harry, a manager is NEVER wise to say 'And I promise this will go no further'. If something is discovered during managerial counselling that is against the interests of the organisation, then the manager's duty is to pass on the information. Things are said in confidentiality and there can be confusion. Good managers maintain a level of professionalism that allows their subordinates to 'understand'. In situations such as the Harry issue they learnt to say such things as: *Listen Harry, this is not something that you should be telling me.*

Listening always means keeping an open mind and having genuine humility. As Bertrand Russell stated: 'One's certainty varies inversely with one's knowledge.' Disraeli noted that 'To be conscious that you are ignorant is a first great step towards knowledge.' We might say that only an expert is aware that there is more to learn.

A witness being sworn in at a trial, as reported by Haney (1979), put it beautifully:

Court Clerk: Do you swear to tell the truth, the whole truth, and nothing but the truth, so help you God?
Witness: Look, if I knew the truth, the whole truth, and nothing but the truth, I would be God!

10. Always remember that you can MAKE anyone do anything ONCE

Managerial power has some of the properties of potential energy – if you use it you lose it.

We were working with a major supermarket chain and one manager in particular, whose style was similar to that of Genghis Khan. Watching him move round the shelves was a revelation. There were sudden rumours that 'Ted was about' and people would become intensely busy. When he passed out of sight, everyone stopped working and gossiped. It was a very inefficient supermarket.

Pushing people unwillingly, however the communication is perfected, does not bring long-term success.

SUMMARY

Although the technical processes of communications in organisations have been greatly improved within and between organisations, the problems of interpersonal communications have hardly changed. A major reason for these problems is that the kind of communication used does not support a positive interpersonal relationship. Instead, it frequently engenders distrust, hostility, defensiveness, and feelings of incompetence and low self-esteem.

Most people have little trouble in giving good news – it is giving bad news that creates problems. Often when we intend to give actionable feedback, we simply generate hostility. Commenting on poor performance, saying 'no' to a proposal or request, resolving a difference of opinion between two subordinates, correcting problem behaviours, receiving criticism from others, or facing other negative interactions, are areas in which we can run into trouble. We often also fail in the key tasks of coaching and counselling subordinates. Handling these situations in a way that fosters interpersonal growth and a strengthening of relationships is one mark of an effective manager.

In this chapter we have pointed out that communication works best with greater clarity and understanding when the other person feels accepted, valued and supported. We pointed out that artificiality of any kind will be noticed and that the manager must always concentrate on the professional rather than the personal message. The principles we have discussed are important tools in helping to improve your communication competence.

Behavioural guidelines

The following behavioural guidelines will help you practise constructive communication:

1. Differentiate between coaching situations, where advice and direction are required, and counselling situations where the relative roles are much more equal, and understanding and consulting is needed.

2. Keep to the task or the problem – describe behaviours or events and not personalities.

3. Be honest – communicate using true feelings without acting them out in destructive ways.

4. Use descriptive, not evaluative statements: describe objectively what occurred; describe your reactions to the event and its objective consequences; and suggest an alternative that is acceptable to you.

5. Show that you value the other person and communicate that the relationship is important to you. Listen and be prepared to be flexible, revising your approach with what you hear. Encourage dialogue, identifying areas of

agreement or positive characteristics before working through areas of disagreement or negative factors.

6. Use specific statements rather than global statements. Allow yourself the use of words that do not reflect absolutes; practise being flexible. Focus on the things that can be controlled – 'You are too tall' is hardly a criticism that others can act upon.

7. Use statements that flow smoothly from what was said previously; don't dominate the conversation; don't cause long pauses; and acknowledge what was said before.

8. Own your statements: use personal words ('I') rather than impersonal words ('they').

9. Demonstrate constructive listening: use a variety of responses to others' statements depending on whether you are coaching or counselling someone else, but with a bias towards reflecting responses.

Skill Analysis

CASE STUDY **4.1**

FIND SOMEONE ELSE

Ron Davis, the relatively new general manager of the machine tooling group at Parker Manufacturing, was visiting one of the factories. He arranged a meeting with Mike Leonard, a plant manager who reported to him.

Ron: Mike, I've arranged this meeting with you because I've been reviewing performance data and I wanted to give you some feedback. I know we haven't talked face-to-face before, but I think it's time we review how you're doing. I'm afraid that some of the things I have to say are not very favourable.

Mike: Well, since you're the new boss, I'll just have to listen. I've had meetings like this before with new people who come onto my site and think they know what's going on.

Ron: Look, Mike, I want this to be a two-way interchange. I'm not here to read an edict to you, and I'm not here to tell you how to do your job. There are just some areas for improvement I want to review.

Mike: Fine. I've heard that before. But you called the meeting. Fire away.

Ron: Well, Mike, there are several things you need to hear. One is what I noticed during the site tour. I think you're too familiar with some of your female personnel. You know, one of them might take offence and get you involved in a sexual harassment charge.

Mike: Oh, come on. You haven't been around this factory before, and you don't know the informal, friendly relationships we have. The office staff and the women on the floor are flattered by a little attention now and then.

Ron: That may be so, but you need to be more careful. You may not be sensitive to what's really going on with them. And that raises another thing I noticed – the appearance of your shop floor. You know how important it is in Parker to have a neat and clean shop floor. As I walked through this morning, I noticed that it wasn't as orderly and neat as I would like to see it. Having things in disarray reflects poorly on you, Mike.

Mike: My site is as neat as any other in Parkers. You may have seen a few tools out of place because someone was just using them, but we take a lot of pride in our neatness. I don't see how you can say that things are in disarray. You've got no experience around here, so who are you to judge?

Ron: Well, I'm glad you're sensitive to the neatness issue. I just think you need to pay attention to it, that's all. But regarding neatness, I notice that you don't dress like a factory manager. I think you're creating a sub-standard impression by not wearing a tie, for example. Such casual dress can be used as an excuse for workers to come to work in really grubby attire. That may not be safe.

Mike: Look, I don't agree with making a big separation between the managers and the employees. By dressing like people out on the shop floor, I think we eliminate a lot of barriers. Besides, I don't have the money to buy clothes that might get oil on them every day. You seem to be nit-picking.

Ron: I don't want to nit-pick, Mike. But I do feel strongly about the issues I've mentioned. There are some other things, though, that need to get corrected. One is the appearance of the reports you send into head office. There are often mistakes, misspellings, and, I suspect, some wrong numbers. I wonder if you are paying attention to these reports. You seem to be reviewing them superficially.

Mike: If there is one thing we have too much of, it's reports. I could spend three-quarters of my time filling out report forms and generating data for some accountant in head office. We have reports coming out of our ears. Why don't you give us a chance to get our work done and eliminate all this paperwork?

Ron: You know as well as I do, Mike, that we need to carefully monitor our productivity, quality and costs. You just need to be more aware of your responsibility.

Mike: Fine. I'm not going to fight about that. It's a losing battle for me. No one on the top floor will ever reduce their demand for reports. But, listen, Ron, I also have one question for you.

Ron: What's that?

Mike: Why don't you go find somebody else to pick on? I need to get back to work.

Discussion questions

1. What principles of constructive communication and constructive listening are violated in this case?

2. How could the interaction have been changed to produce a better outcome?

3. Categorise each of the statements by naming the rule of constructive communication that is either illustrated or violated.

4. What should Ron do in his follow-up meeting with Mike?

CASE STUDY **4.2**

REJECTED PLANS

The following dialogue occurred between two employees in a large firm. The conversation illustrates several characteristics of constructive communication.

Helen: How did your meeting go with Mr Peters yesterday?

David: Not so well.

Helen: It looks as if you're pretty upset about it.

David: Yes, I am. It was a totally frustrating experience. Let's just say I would like to forget the whole thing.

Helen: Things can't have gone as well as you had hoped.

David: You can say that again. That man was impossible. I thought the plans I submitted were very clear and well thought out. Then he rejected the entire package.

Helen: You mean he didn't accept any of them?

David: Correct.

Helen: I've seen your work before, David. You've always done a first-rate job. I can't see why Mr Peters rejected your plans. What did he say about them?

David: He said they were unrealistic and too difficult to implement, and . . .

Helen: Really?

David: Yes, and then he said that I felt he was attacking me personally. But, on the other hand, I guess I was angry because I thought my plans were very good, and you know, I paid close attention to every detail in those plans.

Helen: I'm certain that you did.

David: It just annoys me.

Helen: I'm sure it does. I would be upset, too.

David: Peters must have something against me.

Helen: After all the effort you put into those plans, you still couldn't work out whether Mr Peters was rejecting you or your plans. Is that right?

David: Yes. How could you tell?

Helen: I can really understand your confusion and uncertainty when you felt Mr Peters' actions were unreasonable.

David: I just don't understand why he did what he did.

Helen: Right. If he said your plans were unrealistic, what does that mean? I mean, how can you deal with a rationale like that? It's just too general – meaningless, even. Did he mention anything specific? Did you ask him to point out some problems or explain the reasons for his rejection more clearly?

David: Good point, but I was so disappointed at the rejection that I just wasn't concentrating. You know what I mean?

Helen: Yes. It's such a demoralising experience. You have so much invested personally that you try to save what little self-respect is left.

David: That's right. I just wanted to get out of there before I said something I would be sorry for.

Helen: Yet, in the back of your mind, you probably thought that Mr Peters wouldn't risk the company's future just because he didn't like you personally. But then,

Management Consultancy and Skills

407

well – the plans were good! It's hard to deal with that contradiction on the spot, isn't it?

David: Exactly. I knew I should have pushed him for more information, but I just stood there like a dummy. But, what can I do about it now? It's spilt milk.

Helen: I don't think it's a total loss, David. I mean, from what you have told me – what he said and what you said – I don't think a conclusion can be reached. Perhaps he doesn't understand the plans, or perhaps it was just his off day. Who knows, it could be a lot of things. What would you think about pinning Mr Peters down by asking for his objections, point by point? Do you think it would help to talk to him again?

David: Well, I would certainly know a lot more than I know now. As it is, I wouldn't know where to begin revising or modifying the plans. And you're right, I really don't know what Peters thinks about my work or me. Sometimes I just react and interpret with little or no evidence.

Helen: Perhaps another meeting would be a good thing, then.

David: Well, I suppose I'd better get off my high horse and arrange an appointment with him for next week. I am curious to find out what the problem is with the plans, or me. (*Pause*) Thanks Helen, for helping me sort this out.

Discussion questions

1. Categorise each statement in the case according to the communication characteristic or the type of response. For example, the first statement by David is obviously not congruent, but the second is much more so.

2. Which statements in the conversation were most helpful? Which do you think would produce defensiveness or close off the conversation?

3. What are the potential disadvantages of giving outright advice for solving David's problem? Why doesn't Helen just tell David what he ought to do? Is it incongruent to ask David what he thinks is the best solution?

Skill Practice

EXERCISE **4.1**

VULCAN COMPUTERS

The role of manager encompasses not only one-to-one coaching and counselling with an employee, but it also frequently entails helping other people to understand coaching and counselling principles for themselves. Sometimes it means refereeing interactions and, by example, helping other people to learn about the correct principles of constructive communication. This is part of the task in this exercise. In a group setting, coaching and counselling become more difficult because multiple messages, driven by multiple motives, all interact. Skilled constructive communicators, however, help each group member to feel supported and understood in the interaction, even though the solution to the issue is not always the one he or she would have preferred.

Assignment

In this exercise you should apply the principles of constructive communication. First, form into groups of four people. Next, read the case and assign the following roles in your group: Mike, Sheila, John and an observer. Assume that a meeting is being held with Mike, Sheila and John immediately after the end of the incidents in the following case. Play the roles you have been assigned and try to resolve the problems. The observer should provide feedback to the three players at the end of the exercise. (An Observer's Feedback Form, to assist the observer in providing feedback, can be found in the scoring key in Appendix 1, page 626).

Vulcan Computers is a medium-sized computer hardware manufacturer based in the south-east of England. The parts are part-made in Taiwan and finished and assembled in the English factory, which is also the company's research and engineering centre.

The process design group consists of eight male engineers and their supervisor, Mike Coombes. They have worked well together for a number of years, and good relationships have developed among all the members. When the workload began to increase, Mike recruited a new design engineer, Sheila Williams, who recently received a first-class honours degree in engineering at Durham University. Her first assignment is to join a project team which is working on Vulcan's computer notebook. The three other members of the team are John Smith (aged 38, 15 years with the company), Philip Jones (aged 40, 10 years with the company) and Kevin Robson (aged 32, 8 years with the company).

As a new Vulcan employee, Sheila is fired with enthusiasm. She finds the work challenging as it offers her the opportunity to apply much of the knowledge she has gained at University. Although she is friendly with the rest of the project team, Sheila doesn't socialise much with them at work and doesn't join them for their traditional Friday night get-together at the Red Lion.

Sheila takes her work seriously and she regularly works after hours. Because of her persistence, coupled with her more recent education, she regularly finishes her portion of the various project stages several days ahead of her colleagues. She finds this irritating as it means that she is constantly having to ask Mike Coombes for additional work to keep her busy until the rest of the team has caught up with her. Initially she offered to help John, Philip and Kevin with their assignments, but each time she was abruptly turned down.

About five months after Sheila had joined the design group, John asked to see Mike about a problem the group was having. Their conversation went as follows:

Mike: What's the problem, John?

John: Look Mike, I don't want to waste your time, but some of the other design engineers want me to discuss Sheila with you. She is irritating everyone with her know-it-all, pompous attitude. She's just not the kind of person we want to work with.

Mike: I can't understand that, John. She's an excellent worker, and her design work is always well done and usually flawless. She's doing everything the company wants her to do.

John: The company never asked her to disrupt the morale of the group or to tell us how to do our work. The animosity in our group could eventually result in lower-quality work from the whole unit.

Mike: I'll tell you what I'll do. Sheila has a meeting with me next week to discuss her six-month performance. I'll keep your thoughts in mind, but I can't promise an improvement in what you and the others believe is a pompous attitude.

John: Immediate improvement in her behaviour is not the problem, it's her coaching others when she has no right to. She publicly shows others what to do. You'd think she was lecturing an advanced class in design with all her high-powered, useless equations and formulas. If she keeps this up there's going to be some real trouble.

Mike could not ignore John's views. A week later he called Sheila into his office for her first six-month appraisal. Part of the conversation went as follows:

Mike: There is one other aspect I'd like to discuss with you. As I've explained there's no problem with your technical performance but there are some questions about your relationships with the other workers.

Sheila: I don't understand – what questions are you talking about?

Mike: Well, to be quite frank, certain members of the design group have complained about your apparent know-it-all-attitude and the manner in which you try to tell them how to do their jobs. You're going to have to be patient with them and not publicly call them out about their performance. This is a good group of engineers, and their work over the years has been more than acceptable. I don't want any problems that will cause the group to produce less effectively.

Sheila: Let me make a few comments. First of all, I have never publicly criticised their performance to them or to you. Initially, when I finished ahead of them, I offered to help them with their work but was bluntly told to mind my own business. I took the hint and concentrated only on my part of the work. What you don't understand is that after five months of working in this group I have come to the conclusion that these engineers are working as slowly as they possibly can – they're ripping off the company. They're setting a work pace much slower than they are capable of. They're more interested in the music from Sam's radio, the local soccer team and going to the Red Lion. I'm sorry, but this is just not the way I was brought up or trained. And finally, they've never looked on me as a qualified engineer, but as a woman who has broken their professional barrier.

Source: Revised from a case-study by Szilagyi and Wallace (1983)

EXERCISE **4.2**

BROWN VS THOMAS

Effective one-to-one coaching and counselling are skills that are required in many settings in life, not just in management. It is hard to imagine anyone who would not benefit from training in constructive communication. Because there are so many aspects of constructive communication, however, it is sometimes difficult to remember all of them. That is why practice with observation and feedback is so important. These attributes of constructive communication can become a natural part of your interaction approach as you conscientiously practise and receive feedback from a colleague.

Assignment

In the following exercise, one individual should study the role of Harriet Brown, another the role of Judy Thomas. To make the role play realistic, do not read each other's role descriptions. When you have finished reading, role play a meeting between Harriet Brown and Judy Thomas. A third person should serve as the observer. (An Observer's Feedback Form, to assist the observer in providing feedback, can be found in the scoring key in Appendix 1, page 626.)

Harriet Brown, Department Head

You are Harriet Brown, head of a bank's operations department. You have only been in the organisation for two years and have been quickly promoted. You enjoy working for this bank. It has a high reputation and is acknowledged for its commitment to management development and training programmes – the bank pays for all external courses. Each employee is given an opportunity for a personal management interview each month, and these sessions are usually extremely productive.

One of the department members, Judy Thomas, has been in this department for 19 years, 15 of them in the same job. She is reasonably good at what she does, and she is always punctual and efficient. She tends to get to work earlier than most employees in order to read the *Financial Times* and trade magazines. You can almost set your watch by the time Judy has her coffee breaks and by the time she phones her daughter every afternoon.

Your view is that although Judy is a good worker she lacks imagination and initiative. This has been indicated by her lack of merit increases over the last five years and by the fact that she has had the same job for 15 years. She's content to do just what is assigned, nothing more. Your predecessor must have given hints to Judy that she might be in line for a promotion, however, because Judy has raised this with you more than once. Because she has been in her job so long, she is at the top of her pay range, and without a promotion, she cannot receive a salary adjustment above the basic cost-of-living increase.

The one thing Judy does beyond the basic minimum job requirements is to help to train young people who come into the department. She is very patient and methodical with them, and she seems to take pride in helping them to learn. She has not been hesitant to point out this contribution to you. Unfortunately, this activity does not qualify Judy for a promotion, nor could she be transferred into the training and development department. Once you suggested that she take a few courses at the local college, paid for by the bank, but she simply said that she was too old to go back to school. You think that she might be intimidated because she didn't go to college.

As much as you would like to promote Judy, there just doesn't seem to be any way to do that in good conscience. You have tried putting additional work under her control, but she seems to be slowing down in her productivity rather than speeding up. The work needs to be done, and expanding her role just puts you behind schedule.

This impending interview is probably your best chance to talk openly with Judy about her performance and her potential. You certainly don't want to lose her as an employee, but there is not going to be a change in job assignment for a long time unless she changes her performance dramatically.

Judy Thomas, Department Member

You are a member of a bank's operations department. You have been with the bank for 19 years, 15 of them in the same job. You enjoy working for the bank because of its friendly atmosphere, and the job is fairly secure. However, lately you have become more dissatisfied as you've seen person after person come into the bank and get promoted ahead of you. Your own boss, Harriet Brown, is almost 20 years your junior. Another woman who joined the bank at the same time as you is now a senior manager at head office. You cannot understand why you've been neglected. You are efficient and accurate in your work, you have a near-perfect attendance record and you consider yourself to be a good employee. You have gone out of your way on many occasions to help to train and orient young people who are just joining the bank. Several of them have written letters later telling you how important your help was in getting them promoted. A lot of good that does you!

The only explanation you can think of is that there is a bias against you because you haven't been to college or university. On the other hand, others have moved up without a degree. You have not taken advantage of any college courses paid for by the bank. The last thing you want after a long day's work is another three hours in a lecture room. Anyway, you only see your family in the evenings, and you don't want to take time away from them. It doesn't take a college degree to do your job anyway.

Your monthly personal management interview is coming up with your department head, Harriet Brown, and you've decided that the time has come to get a few answers. Several things need explaining. Not only have you not been promoted, but you haven't even received a merit increase for five years. You're not getting any credit for the extra contributions you make with new employees, nor for your steady, reliable work. Could anyone blame you for being a little bitter?

Skill Application

ACTIVITY **4.1**

SUGGESTED FURTHER ASSIGNMENTS

1. Tape-record an interview with someone such as a co-worker, friend or spouse. Focus on the issues or challenges faced right now by that other person. Try to assume the role of coach or counsellor. Categorise your statements in the interview on the basis of the constructive communication principles in this book. (The Rejected Plans case (Case Study 4.2) provides an example of such an interview.)

2. Teach someone you know the concepts of constructive communication and constructive listening. Provide your own explanations and illustrations so that the person understands what you are talking about. Describe your experience in your work book.

3. Think of an interpersonal problem you share with someone, such as a flatmate, parent, friend or instructor. Discuss the problem with that person, using constructive communication. Write about the experience in as much detail as possible. Concentrate on the extent to which you and the other person used the eight principles of constructive communication. Record and describe areas in which you need to improve.

4. Write two mini case studies. One should recount an effective coaching or counselling situation. The other should recount an ineffective coaching or counselling situation. The cases should be based on a real event either in your own personal experience or in the experience of someone you know well. Use all the principles of constructive communication and listening in your cases.

ACTIVITY **4.2**

APPLICATION PLAN AND EVALUATION

Part 1: Plan

1. Write down the two or three aspects of this skill that are most important to you. These may be areas of weakness, areas you most want to improve or areas that are most salient to a problem you face currently. Identify the specific aspects of this skill that you want to apply.

2. Now identify the setting or the situation in which you will apply this skill. Establish a plan for performance by actually writing down the situation. Who else will be involved? When will you do it? Where will it be done?

3. Identify the specific behaviours you will engage in to apply this skill. Try it.

4. What are the indicators of successful performance? How will you know you have succeeded in being effective? What will indicate that you have performed competently?

Part 2: Evaluation

5. After you have completed your implementation, record the results. What happened? How successful were you? What was the effect on others?

6. How can you improve? What modifications can you make next time? What will you do differently in a similar situation in the future?

7. Looking back on your whole skill practice and application experience, what have you learned? What has been surprising? In what ways might this experience help you in the long term?

Further reading

Adair, J. (1997) *Effective communication*. London: Pan.

Baguley, P. (1994) *Effective communication for modern business*. London: McGraw-Hill.

Bishop, S. and Taylor, D. (1998) *44 activities for interpersonal skills training*. Aldershot: Gower.

Ludlow, R. and Panton, F. (1992) *The essence of effective communication*. London: Prentice Hall.

MacLennan, N. (1998) *Counselling for managers*. Aldershot: Gower.

Scholes, E. (ed.) (1997) *Gower handbook of internal communication*. Aldershot: Gower.

Constructive Conflict Management

SKILL DEVELOPMENT OUTLINE

Skill Pre-assessment surveys

- Managing interpersonal conflict
- Strategies for handling conflict

Skill Learning material

- Management conflict
- Personal beliefs that fog one's appropriate actions
- Interpersonal conflict
- Responses to conflict
- Negotiation strategies
- Selecting the appropriate approach
- Resolving confrontations using the collaborative approach
- Summary
- Behavioural guidelines

Skill Analysis case

- Health Provisions Limited

Skill Practice exercises

- Argyll Steakhouse
- Avocado Computers
- Phelan Ltd
- Where's my speech?
- Can Harry fit in?
- Meeting at Hartford Manufacturing Co.

Skill Application activities

- Suggested further assignments
- Application plan and evaluation

LEARNING OBJECTIVES

To enable individuals to:

- understand and recognise the sources of conflict – productive and dysfunctional
- select the most appropriate responses to conflict
- manage interpersonal confrontations in any of the roles – initiator, respondent or mediator

330

If the word 'conflict' conjures up for you the image of two prize fighters battling it out to the death, this chapter may well come as a surprise.

> The Human Resource Director of a national charity asked us to work with his Executive Board. The Board consisted of six full-time directors and six lay members – the 'wise and the good'. The full-time directors worked well together but when the full Board of 12 met, lay and full-time members, nothing happened. The HRM Director put it very simply: 'We are all too nice. Nobody challenges anything, we discuss minutiae and skate round any discussion of principle. The lay members were called in to challenge principles. They don't even complain if the coffee is cold. When the full meeting is over, we send them packing and breathe a sign of relief, get on with our work and hope that the next month's full Board meeting gets cancelled.'

Without constructive conflict 'nothing happens', but there are limits:

> We were called to work with the Board of the UK subsidiary of a German manufacturer. The managing director's problem was dysfunctional conflict – also leading to nothing getting done. During our work with him – what trainers call 'team-building exercises' – we met the conflict head-on. The outsiders' impression was, in lay terms, that they hated each other. One director had left immediately before our work with them and another resigned during the team-building exercise itself. Later, but not much later, another director resigned and the CEO was faced with the problem, in this case welcome, of building a new team virtually from scratch.

This book is about the middle way – the situation where people are able to speak their minds, with due concern for others, and trust others to be honest with them and thus live and work more effectively.

Managing interpersonal conflict is about maintaining the middle way and is a major management skill that will bring together many of the skills discussed elsewhere in the book.

Skill Pre-assessment

SURVEY **6.1**

MANAGING INTERPERSONAL CONFLICT

Please complete the assessment as we explained at the beginning of Chapter 1.

RATING SCALE

1 = Strongly disagree   **2** = Disagree   **3** = Slightly disagree
4 = Slightly agree   **5** = Agree   **6** = Strongly agree

331

	Assessment	
	Pre-	Post-

On a personal level when I am working with others, and I feel that things are not going as they should be and I need to take a hand

1. I avoid making personal accusations and attributing self-serving motives to the other person. ____ ____

2. When stating my concerns, I present them as my problems. ____ ____

3. I describe the problem concisely in terms of the behaviour that occurred, its consequences, and my feelings about it. ____ ____

4. I specify my expectations and the standards that have not been achieved. ____ ____

5. I make a specific request, detailing a more acceptable option. ____ ____

6. I stay with my point of view until it is understood by the others. ____ ____

7. I encourage a dialogue by getting others to discuss their perspectives. ____ ____

8. When there are several concerns, I approach the issues one at a time, starting with the most straightforward and progressing to the more complex. ____ ____

When someone complains about something I've done

9. I look for our common areas of agreement. ____ ____

10. I show genuine concern and interest, even when I disagree. ____ ____

11. I avoid justifying my actions and becoming defensive. ____ ____

12. I seek additional information by asking questions that provide specific, descriptive information. ____ ____

13. I focus on one issue at a time. ____ ____

14. I find some aspects of the complaint with which I can agree. ____ ____

15. I ask the other person to suggest more acceptable behaviours. ____ ____

16. I strive to reach agreement on a remedial plan of action. ____ ____

When I find myself in the position of a mediator between two other people in dysfunctional conflict

17. I acknowledge that conflict exists and treat it as serious and important. ____ ____

18. I help create an agenda for the problem-solving meeting by identifying the issues to be discussed one at a time. ____ ____

19. I do not take sides but remain neutral. ____ ____

20. I help focus the discussion on the impact of the conflict on work performance. ____ ____

21. I keep the interaction focused on problems rather than on personalities. ____ ____

22. I make certain that neither party dominates the conversation. ____ ____

23. I help the parties generate multiple alternatives. ____ ____

24. I help the parties find areas on which they agree. ____ ____

SURVEY **6.2**

STRATEGIES FOR HANDLING CONFLICT

Indicate how often you use each of the following by circling the appropriate number. After you have completed the survey, use the scoring key in Appendix 1 at the end of the book to tabulate your results. Information on these five strategies is shown in Table 6.2 in the Skill Learning section.

RATING SCALE

1 = Never   **2** = Seldom   **3** = Sometimes   **4** = Usually   **5** = Always

1. I will stick with my position whatever.	1 2 3 4 5
2. I try to put the needs of others above mine.	1 2 3 4 5
3. I try to arrive at a compromise both parties can accept.	1 2 3 4 5
4. I try not to get involved in conflicts.	1 2 3 4 5
5. I strive to investigate issues, jointly and properly.	1 2 3 4 5
6. I try to find fault in the other person's position.	1 2 3 4 5
7. I strive to foster harmony.	1 2 3 4 5
8. I negotiate to get a portion of what I propose.	1 2 3 4 5
9. I avoid open discussions of controversial subjects.	1 2 3 4 5
10. I share information openly with others in resolving disagreements.	1 2 3 4 5
11. I enjoy winning an argument.	1 2 3 4 5
12. I go along with the suggestions of others.	1 2 3 4 5
13. I look for a middle ground to resolve disagreements.	1 2 3 4 5
14. I keep my true feelings to myself to avoid hard feelings.	1 2 3 4 5
15. I encourage the open sharing of concerns and issues.	1 2 3 4 5
16. I am reluctant to admit I am wrong.	1 2 3 4 5
17. I try to help others avoid losing face in a disagreement.	1 2 3 4 5
18. I stress the advantages of give and take.	1 2 3 4 5
19. I encourage others to take the lead in resolving controversy.	1 2 3 4 5
20. I state my position as only one point of view.	1 2 3 4 5

Skill Learning

Management conflict

Anthony Barnett (1998), discussing the world's biggest industrial merger to date – that of BP and Amoco – writes of a meeting between Brown and Fuller of BP and Amoco respectively:

This was the evening of the breakthrough (Saturday, 1 July 1998) – the carve up of key responsibilities of the top 22 executives. Messing with corporate egos is one of the thorniest problems in any merger and can scupper the best deals.

A less recent article in *Business Week* (1981) states that:

Some half to two-thirds of all company mergers fail. Why? One major reason is that key executives in the merging firms can't agree on their respective roles, status and 'perks'. Tensions are compounded by disagreements over which procedures to use and whose 'corporate culture' will dominate. The inability or lack of willingness to resolve these conflicts can unravel an otherwise attractive business marriage.

Paradoxically John Argenti (1976) claims that one of the leading causes of business failure among major companies is too much agreement among top management. They have similar training and experience, and this leads them to view conditions in the same way and to pursue similar goals. Boards of Directors failing to play an aggressive overview role compound this problem. They avoid conflict with the internal management team, who appear unified on key issues and very confident of their positions.

The Honda/Rover/BMW negotiations of 1994 showed issues of mishandling friendship as well as conflict that led to very personal 'pique'.

Mr Bernd Pischetsrieder, chairman of the BMW management board, is to meet Mr Nobuhiko Kawamoto, chief executive of Honda in Tokyo, next week in a first round of talks aimed at maintaining the alliance between the Japanese car maker and Rover.

BMW stunned Honda on Monday with its £800m take-over from British Aerospace of an 80 per cent stake in the UK car maker. Honda still holds the remaining 20 per cent of the equity in Rover and Land Rover vehicle operations. Mr Pischetsrieder is anxious to maintain Honda as a partner for Rover in vehicle production and development, at least in the medium term.

Honda and Rover have forged a close relationship in the past 14 years, and Mr Kawamoto was quick to express dismay at the entry of BMW as the majority owner of Rover. He said that the BMW take-over 'negated' the long-term efforts of Honda and Rover to establish a firm future for Rover as 'a British company with its own brand identity'.

Honda's resentment at the way that British Aerospace engineered the BMW take-over of Rover was also highlighted when Mr Andrew Jones, the company's UK plant manager, admitted the company was shocked by the deal.

Source: Financial Times, 2 February 1994

Constructive interpersonal conflict, correctly used, is an essential part of organisational life. Organisations in which there is little disagreement generally fail in competitive environments. Members are either so homogeneous that they are ill equipped to adapt to change, or so complacent that they see no need to change or improve. Conflict is the life-blood of vibrant, progressive, stimulating organisations. It sparks creativity, stimulates innovation and encourages personal improvement (Robbins, 1978; King, 1981; Thomas, 1977; Wanous and Youtz, 1986).

Management Consultancy and Skills

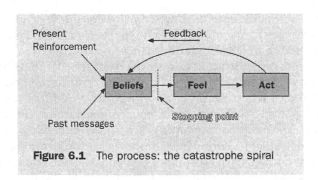

Figure 6.1 The process: the catastrophe spiral

This view is clearly in line with the management philosophy of Andrew Grove, President of INTEL:

> Many managers seem to think it is impossible to tackle anything or anyone head-on, even in business. By contrast, we at INTEL believe that it is the essence of corporate health to bring a problem out into the open as soon as possible, even if this entails a confrontation. Dealing with conflicts lies at the heart of managing any business. As a result, confrontation of issues about which there is disagreement can be avoided only at the manager's peril. Workplace politicking grows quietly in the dark, like mushrooms; neither can stand the light of day.
>
> *Source*: *Fortune*, 23 July 1984, p. 74

Appropriate conflict, neither too much nor too little, can be beneficial. Hambrick *et al.* (1998) in their collection of papers, *Navigating Change*, repeatedly allude to the importance of conflict in corporate governance – keeping companies on the road in the face of forceful individuals in authority. As these and other authors point out, conflict is a question of personal preference. Some people have a very low tolerance for disagreement while others seem to like to fly into the face of the tiger at the slightest provocation. The preference probably arises from family background, cultural values or personality characteristics, but is certainly reinforced by current experience.

Figure 6.1 illustrates the process. Past experience, confirmed by recent but perhaps irrelevant recent experiences, makes us believe that conflict is necessary or should be avoided. This is a knee jerk response NOT founded on a logical assessment of the detail of the present. We therefore feel either aggressive or passive, and act accordingly without review. If we act aggressively then others respond accordingly, and a new 'present' experience reinforces our decision to 'go for conflict' and a catastrophe spiral begins, ending dysfunctionally. Conversely, if 'knee jerk' turns into passivity, a spiral begins that results in our interests being crushed into the grass. The secret is to review our process before we feel either aggressive or passive and decide on appropriate action, which may or may not involve conflict.

While most writers would agree that some conflict is both inevitable and necessary in effective organisations, Abraham Maslow (1965) has observed a high degree of ambivalence regarding the value of conflict. Maslow notes that, intellectually, managers appreciate the value of conflict and competition. They agree it is a necessary ingredient of the free-enterprise system. However, their actions demonstrate a personal preference for avoiding conflicts whenever possible. Belbin (1981) emphasises the importance in teams of both balance and constructive conflict.

In Belbin's early work he constructed teams from managers attending a training programme on the basis of their IQs, and got the teams to perform competitive exercises. The teams with the highest IQs performed irregularly both from the point of view of conflict and results. The lowest IQ teams performed dully – little conflict and mediocre results. The addition or planting of a 'sparky' individual to the dull group caused both conflict and a considerable improvement in performance.

This tension between intellectual acceptance of a principle and emotional rejection of its enactment was more systematically studied in Boulding's (1964) classic study of decision making.

> Several groups of managers were formed to solve a complex problem. They were told a panel of experts would judge their performance in terms of the quantity and quality of solutions generated. The groups were identical in size and composition, with the exception that half of them included a 'mole'. Before the experiment began, the researcher instructed this person to play the role of 'devil's advocate'. This person was to challenge the group's conclusions, forcing the others to examine critically their assumptions and the logic of their arguments. At the end of the problem-solving period, the recommendations made by both sets of groups were compared. The groups with the devil's advocates had performed significantly better on the task. They had generated more alternatives and their proposals were judged as superior. After a short break, the groups were reassembled and told that they would be performing a similar task during the next session. However, before they began discussing the next problem, they were given permission to eliminate one member. In every group containing a 'mole', he or she was the one asked to leave. The fact that every high-performance group expelled their unique competitive advantage because that member made others feel uncomfortable demonstrates a widely shared reaction to conflict: 'I know it has positive outcomes for the performance of the organisation as a whole, but I don't like how it makes me feel personally.'

We believe that much of the ambivalence towards conflict stems from a lack of understanding of the causes of conflict, the variety of modes for managing it effectively, and from a lack of confidence in one's personal skills for handling the tense, emotionally charged environment typical of most interpersonal confrontations. It is natural for an untrained or inexperienced person to avoid threatening situations, and it is generally acknowledged that conflict represents the most severe test of a manager's interpersonal skills. The task of the effective manager, therefore, is to maintain an optimal level of conflict, while keeping conflicts focused on productive purposes (Robbins, 1974; Kelly, 1970; Thomas, 1976).

The balance requires that managers must be able to:

- recognise their own beliefs that may lead them to inappropriate action;
- diagnose the causes of conflict;
- decide upon their achievable objectives;
- settle upon a strategy to handle the conflict so that the objective is achieved (which normally will include making sure that the long-term relationships between the disputants is not damaged).

Personal beliefs that fog one's appropriate action

The concept is that the messages we have picked up from the past confuse us when we are attempting to handle current situations. Woods (1989) coined the name 'Mind Music' for these messages, his point being that the messages play in our heads when we 'think' we recognise a present situation that we can relate to something in our past experience. The confusion is enough to make us act inappropriately, and very often as others we respected from our past might have handled it. These messages we rationalise as our personal beliefs. Used appropriately, they are a bequest from the significant people of the past to guide us through our lives – used inappropriately, they lead us into the catastrophe spiral. Albert Ellis is quoted as saying that 99 per cent of the world's ills are founded in four beliefs:

- A cosmic order of things.
- A fundamental acceptance of hierarchy.
- Others.
- Self.

Cosmic order

The belief here is about absolute patterns, which at its strongest was described in *Einstein* by Stephen Hawking (1989). Einstein had the fundamental belief that 'God did not play dice' and that in his search for the laws of the universe he was looking at absolutes and not for probabilities. In Hawking's view, this delayed the advance of physics by many years. Cosmic beliefs lead us to think that in all our works, and we are somehow protected or somehow fated. Managers express this form of belief in phrases such as: 'It will be alright on the night' – blocking the need for detailed preparation; 'This sort of thing simply cannot happen' – blocking change; and 'It will never work' – blocking everything. With such messages in our heads we feel that conflict with the status quo is best avoided.

Hierarchy

The belief in hierarchy leads us to think that position determines the person. Thus, if people hold senior positions they are superior in *everything* and should not be challenged. It also leads us to think that there is an absolute man-made order. We hear managers with this belief system saying such things as '. . . they are bosses and they know best – they are on the shop floor and know nothing', and feeling in their hearts that '. . . there is small print under the small print of their contracts'. Conflicts with organisational structures should be avoided.

Others

The belief in others is a belief that because we behave in a particular way, others should have similar behaviour, beliefs and values. Those who do not behave in this way are somehow *wrong* as people. The Mind Music is concerned with messages such as: ' "Good" workers follow my example, believe in what I believe in and value what I value. Others should *understand* me and what I want done.'

We were called into a medium-sized business which had been rescued by a management buy-out from a multinational. After about a year and half of success they had a walkout by the finance department. Listening to the story, we understood why. The directors owned the business and had got used to using 'midnight oil equity' – they all worked 80 plus hours a week and were proud of their success. As the emergency had faded the necessity for the long hours had faded, but the habit had remained.

A junior member of the finance team had approached the finance director, who was drinking coffee, at 18.30 and asked whether it was OK for him to go home. He had recently become a father and wanted to bathe his son for the first time. The conversation went something like this:

A: *Why cannot you have the same dedication to work as the other directors and me?*
B: *It's not my problem that you are not organised. I have a home to go too.*
A: *Look, if you want to stay home, you only have to say the word.*

It got worse and the rest of the team supported the young man.

In the example, the finance director considered that others, her staff, should behave as she did. Her reactions to a reasonable request were dismissed because of the Mind Music in her head. She felt that the member of staff was somehow culpable because he did not conform to the same standards and values she had adopted and left unreviewed.

By following the Mind Music that others must behave in a proscribed way we inevitably fall into dysfunctional conflict.

Self

Beliefs in 'self' are concerned with reaching the targets set by people, probably well meaning, in the past. Parents and guardians set us objectives – *Do better than your father, pass exams, have a 'good' marriage, provide grandchildren*, etc. The snag is that having been given these objectives we believe that, to be a successful human being, we have to achieve them and not to achieve them is failure on the highest level – failure as a human being. Failures do not challenge assertively, and when they do challenge it is often at the wrong time or in the wrong place. Stewart and Joines (1987) describe a development of the Ellis codification which they term 'Drivers', and those wishing to pursue the area of beliefs are advised to look at their work.

Interpersonal conflict

The labelling of our workers and colleagues through our own belief systems does lead to serious interpersonal confrontations. We label others as 'trouble makers' or 'lazy' simply because they do not fit *our* patterns. Schmidt and Tannenbaum (1965) and Hines (1980) showed that unfortunate attitudes only account for a small percentage of organisational conflicts ('labelling'). We referred, in Chapter 4, to the

Table 6.1 Sources of conflict	
Sources of conflict	*Focus of conflict*
Personal differences	Perceptions and expectations
Information deficiency	Misinformation and misrepresentation
Role incompatibility	Goals and responsibilities
Environmental stress	Resource scarcity and uncertainty

problems of constructive communication when we have a set image of those with whom we chose to communicate.

This proposition is supported by research on performance appraisals (Latham and Wexley, 1981). It has been shown that managers generally attribute poor performance to personal deficiencies in workers (e.g., laziness, lack of skill, lack of motivation). However, when workers are asked the causes of their poor performance, they generally explain it in terms of problems in their environment (e.g., insufficient supplies, unco-operative co-workers). While some face-saving is obviously involved here, the line of research suggests that managers need to guard against the reflexive tendency to assume that bad behaviours imply bad people. In fact, the aggressive or harsh behaviours sometimes observed in interpersonal confrontations often reflect the frustrations of people who have good intentions but are unskilled in handling intense, emotional experiences.

On this basis we would propose four explanations for interpersonal conflict in Table 6.1, and not include 'attitudes' in these four. Our four categorisations are:

• Personal differences

• Information deficiency

• Role incompatibility

• Environmental stress.

Personal differences

Individuals bring different attitudes to their roles in organisations. Their values and needs have been shaped by different socialisation processes, depending on their cultural and family traditions, level of education, breadth of experience, etc. As a result, their interpretations of events, and their expectations about relationships with others in the organisation, will vary considerably. Conflicts stemming from incompatible personal values and needs are some of the most difficult to resolve. They often become highly emotional and take on moral overtones. A disagreement about who is factually correct easily turns into a bitter argument over who is morally *right*.

The following situation occurred in a major American company between a 63-year-old white executive vice-president and a 35-year-old black member of the corporate legal department who had been very active in the civil-rights movement during the 1960s. They disagreed vehemently over whether the company should accept a very attractive offer from the South African government to build a manufacturing facility. The vice-president felt the company had a responsibility to its stockholders to pursue every legal opportunity to increase profits. In contrast, the lawyer felt that collaborating with the South African government was tantamount to condoning apartheid.

Information deficiency

Conflicts can arise from deficiencies in the organisation's information system. An important message may not be received, a boss's instructions may be misinterpreted, or decision makers may arrive at different conclusions because they used different databases. A conflict based on misinformation or misunderstanding tends to be factual, in the sense that clarifying previous messages or obtaining additional information generally resolves the dispute. This might entail rewording the boss's instructions, reconciling contradictory sources of data, or redistributing copies of misplaced messages. This type of conflict is very common in organisations, but it is also easy to resolve. Because value systems are not being challenged, these confrontations tend to be less emotional. Once the breakdown in the information system is repaired, the disputants are generally able to resolve their disagreement with a minimum of resentment.

Role incompatibility

The complexity inherent in most organisations tends to produce conflict between members whose tasks are interdependent, but whose roles are incompatible. This type of conflict is exemplified by the classic goal conflicts between line and staff, production and sales, marketing and research and development (R&D). Each unit has different responsibilities in the organisation and, as a result, each places different priorities on organisational goals (e.g., customer satisfaction, product quality, production efficiency, compliance with European Union directives). It is also typical of firms whose multiple product lines compete for scarce resources.

> In the early days at Apple Computer, the Apple II division accounted for a large part of the company's revenue. It viewed the newly-created Macintosh division as an unwise speculative venture. The natural rivalry was made worse when a champion of Macintosh referred to the Apple II team as 'the dull and boring product division'. Since this type of conflict stems from the fundamental incompatibility of the job responsibilities of the disputants, it can often be resolved only through the mediation of a common superior.
>
> *Source*: Summarised from Sculley and Byrne (1989)

Conflicts arising from role incompatibility interact with personal differences and the way individuals seek power and influence. Personal differences may well lie dormant until individuals are forced to work together with unclear organisational boundaries. Members may also perceive that their assigned roles are incompatible because they are operating from different bases of information. They communicate with different sets of people, are tied into different reporting systems and receive instructions from different bosses.

Environmental stress

Conflicts stemming from personal differences and role incompatibilities are greatly exacerbated by a stressful environment. For example, when an organisation is forced to operate on an austere budget, its members are more likely to become embroiled in disputes over territorial claims and resource requests. Scarcity tends to lower trust, increase awareness of sexual, racial and class differences and reduce participation in decision making. These are ideal conditions for incubating interpersonal conflict (Cameron and Whetten, 1987).

> When a large bank announced major staff reductions, the threat to employees' security was so severe that it disrupted long-term, close working relationships. Even friendships were not immune to the effects of the stress induced by the enforced changes. Long-standing golf partnerships and car pools were disbanded because the tension among members was so high.

A second environmental condition that fosters conflict is uncertainty. When individuals find it difficult to predict what is going to happen to them from month to month, they become very anxious and prone to conflict. This type of conflict, arising from frustration, often stems from rapid, repeated change. If the way jobs are allocated, management philosophy, accounting procedures and lines of authority are changed frequently, members find it difficult to cope with the resulting stress. Sharp, bitter conflicts can easily erupt over seemingly trivial problems. This type of conflict is generally very intense, but dissipates quickly once a change becomes a routine and individuals' stress levels are lowered.

> When a major pet-food manufacturer announced that one-third of its managers would have to support a new third shift, the feared disruption of personal and family routines prompted many managers to consider resigning. In addition, the uncertainty of who was going to be required to work at night was so great that posturing and infighting disrupted even routine management work.

The issues often come to the fore when management decides that change is needed. Marks and Spencer has been a paragon of the well-managed store group and in the 1980s was judged by its own management as risking smugness. They decided, as an experiment, to introduce a group of highly motivated and brilliant young graduates to 'stir things up'. The outsiders were given a vague brief and appointed to various stores throughout the country.

> A fairly typical story was of a newcomer who set up an in-store promotion to sell some slow-moving goods. He found, after he had invested a great deal of time and effort in providing point-of-sale publicity, that the whole concept was against Marks and Spencer's philosophy and was 'asked' to stop.

The newcomers went two ways – they either left or they became so completely enveloped in the 'M&S' culture as to be barriers to change in themselves.

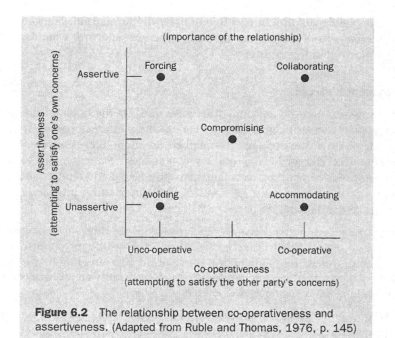

Figure 6.2 The relationship between co-operativeness and assertiveness. (Adapted from Ruble and Thomas, 1976, p. 145)

Responses to conflict

Now that we have examined the typical causes of conflict, we will discuss common responses. Figure 6.2 shows that conflict falls into five categories

- Forcing
- Accommodating
- Avoiding
- Compromising
- Collaborating

(Filley, 1975, 1978; Robbins, 1974). Each category can be organised along two dimensions, as shown in the figure. The five approaches to conflict reflect different degrees of co-operation and assertiveness. The co-operation dimension reflects the importance of the between-individual's relationship, whereas the assertiveness dimension reflects individuals' attempts to satisfy their own concerns.

The forcing response (assertive, unco-operative)

The forcing response involves an attempt to satisfy one's own needs at the expense of the other person's. This can be done by using formal authority, physical threats, manipulation, or simply by ignoring the claims of the other party. The blatant use of the authority of one's office: 'I'm the boss, so we'll do it my way', or manipulation 'I think you will find that to get on here you will need to do it my way', is a reflection of egoistic leadership style. Manipulative leaders often appear to be democratic by proposing that conflicting proposals be referred to a committee for further investigation. However, they make sure that the composition of the committee reflects their interests and preferences, so that what appears to be a selection based on merit is actually an authoritarian act. A related ploy used by some managers is to ignore a proposal that threatens their personal interests. If the originator enquires about the receipt of his or her memo, the manager pleads ignorance, blames the new secretary, and then suggests that the proposal be redrafted. After several of these encounters, subordinates generally get the message that the boss isn't interested in their ideas. The repeated use of the forcing approach is that it breeds hostility and resentment. While observers may intellectually admire authoritarian or manipulative leaders because they appear to accomplish a great deal, these management styles generally produce a backlash in the long run as people become unwilling to absorb the emotional cost. We discussed this point in the last of the 10 Commandments of Effective Communication.

The accommodating approach (co-operative, unassertive)

The accommodating approach is the obverse of the forcing approach, in that we may satisfy the other party while missing on our own concerns. As James Thurber said: 'One might as well fall flat on one's face as lean too far backwards.' An example of the accommodating approach would be a board of directors neglecting their responsibilities in favour of accommodating the wishes of their employees – a strategy which generally results in a lose–lose situation. The problem of a habitual use of the accommodating approach is that friendly relationships are temporarily preserved at the expense of tackling real issues.

During the early 1980s the boom in R&D expenditure was halted and subjected to critical appraisal in many organisations. Prior to this, R&D managers were typically R&D scientists and engineers who had been promoted, sometimes simply because of seniority. In one laboratory such appointment procedures had been accepted for years and management was entirely by accommodation. Unfortunately when belts had to be tightened and disciplines had to be imposed there was no history or any other approach to accommodation. Management had to say 'no' to requests but staff had never heard 'no' before and simply did not accept it. The subsequent dysfunctional conflicts incapacitated the laboratory for some three months.

The avoiding response (unco-operative, unassertive)

Avoidance neglects the interests of both parties by side-stepping the conflict or postponing a solution. The avoiding response is often the response of managers who are emotionally ill-prepared to cope with the stress associated with confrontations. It might also reflect recognition that a relationship is not strong enough to absorb the fall-out of an intense conflict. The repeated use of this approach causes considerable frustration for others because issues never seem to get resolved, tough problems are avoided because of their high potential for conflict, and the subordinates engaging in conflict are reprimanded for undermining the harmony of the work group. Sensing a leadership vacuum, people from all directions rush to fill it, creating considerable confusion and animosity in the process.

The compromising response

The compromising response is the intermediate between assertiveness and co-operation. A compromise is an attempt to obtain partial satisfaction for both parties, in the sense that both receive the proverbial 'half a loaf'. Both parties are asked to make sacrifices to obtain a common gain. While this approach has considerable practical appeal to managers, its indiscriminate use is counter-productive. If subordinates are continually told to 'split the difference', they may conclude that their managers are more interested in resolving disputes than in solving problems. This creates a climate of expediency that encourages game playing, such as asking for twice as much as you need.

We see a common mistake in management as trying to appear fair to both parties by compromising on competing corporate policies and practices – from Green issues to redundancy. When decisions are made on the basis of 'spreading the pain' rather than on the basis of merit, then harmony takes priority over value. Ironically, actions taken in the name of 'keeping peace' often end up being so illogical and impractical that the final showdown is often unyieldingly bitter. On a national scale it is the subject of bitter civil wars – on the corporate scale these are not unknown.

Collaboration (co-operative, assertive)

The collaborative approach is attempts to fully address the concerns of everyone and is often called the 'problem-solving' approach. The approach is objective as opposed to process driven, and it attempts to bring conflicts to conclusions that are satisfactory to both parties rather than to find fault or assign blame. In this way both parties can feel that they have 'won', and indeed this is the only win–win strategy. The avoiding mode results in a lose–lose outcome and the compromising, accommodating and forcing modes all represent win–lose outcomes. We will show later that the collaboration approach is not appropriate for all situations, but when appropriate, it is the most satisfactory. Constructive communication can be maintained without losing control of the situation, it encourages individuals to focus their disputes on problems and issues rather than on personalities, and it encourages empowerment.

A comparison of the five conflict management approaches is shown in Table 6.2.

Negotiation strategies

Savage *et al.* (1989) and Smith (1987) have drawn attention to the similarity of conflict management and negotiation practice. We find that negotiation strategies are commonly divided into two types: integrative and distributive. The negotiators

Table 6.2   A comparison of five conflict-management approaches

Approach	Objective	Your posture	Supporting rationale	Likely outcome
1. Forcing	Get your way.	'I know what's right. Don't question my judgement or authority.'	It is better to risk causing a few hard feelings than to abandon the issue.	You feel vindicated, but the other party feels defeated and possibly humiliated.
2. Avoiding	Avoid having to deal with conflict.	'I'm neutral on that issue. Let me think about it. That's someone else's problem.'	Disagreements are inherently bad because they create tension.	Interpersonal problems don't get resolved, causing long-term frustration manifested in a variety of ways.
3. Compromising	Reach an agreement quickly.	'Let's search for a solution we can both live with so we can get on with our work.'	Prolonged conflicts distract people from their work and cause bitter feelings.	Participants go for the expedient, rather than effective, solutions.
4. Accommodating	Don't upset the other person.	'How can I help you feel good about this? My position isn't so important that it is worth risking bad feelings between us.'	Maintaining harmonious relationships should be our top priority.	The other person is likely to take advantage.
5. Collaborating	Solve the problem together.	'This is my position, what is yours? I'm committed to finding the best possible solution. What do the facts suggest?'	Each position is important though not necessarily equally valid. Emphasis should be placed on the quality of the outcome and the fairness of the decision-making process.	The problem is most likely to be resolved. Also, both parties are committed to the solution and satisfied that they have been treated fairly.

Table 6.3 Comparison between negotiation and conflict-management strategies

Negotiation strategies	Distributive	Integrative
Conflict-management strategies	Compromising Forcing Accommodating Avoiding	Collaborating

using a distributive strategy start on the basis of a 'fixed size cake' whereas those using an integrative approach look for ways of expanding 'the cake' by collaboration. The distributive negotiators adopt an adversarial stance, assuming that for someone to gain, someone has to lose. The integrators, by adopting a 'problem-solving' approach, attempt to obtain a 'win–win' outcome. They are interested in finding the best solution rather than forcing a choice (Fisher and Brown, 1988; Bazerman, 1986; Pruitt, 1983).

Table 6.3 shows that four of the five conflict management strategies involve one or both parties sacrificing something in order to resolve the conflict. Compromising, forcing, accommodating and avoiding are distributive solutions. Compromise occurs when both parties make sacrifices in order to find common ground. Compromisers are generally more interested in finding an expedient solution than they are in finding an integrative solution. Forcing and accommodating demand that one party gives up its position in order for the conflict to be resolved. When parties to a conflict avoid resolution, they do so because they assume that the costs of resolving the conflict are so high that they are better off not even attempting resolution. The 'fixed cake' still exists, but the individuals involved view attempts to divide it as threatening, and so they avoid decisions regarding the allocation process altogether.

In Chapter 3 we explained that the adversarial strategies seem ingrained in western culture as opposed to that in Japan. Many people approach conflicts from the construct of W.C. Field's 'never give a sucker an even break' and actually use conflict to prove virility, with little thought of the short-term let alone the long-term consequences. We see effective negotiators as gladiators in spite of the growing evidence that 'macho' negotiation is generally ineffective and frequently counterproductive. There are times when each of the forms of conflict management are effective, but generally the integrative approach is recommended. Northcraft and Neale (1990) laid down a plan for effective integrative negotiation and these closely parallel the system shown in Table 3.2 of our chapter on effective problem solving, and the rules under which it operates are similar to those described in the chapter on constructive communication.

1. *Establish mutually agreed objectives – common goals.* In order to foster a climate of collaboration, both parties need to focus on what they have in common. Focusing on their shared goals – increased productivity, lower costs, reduced design time or improved relations between departments – allows everyone to

see that there can be a solution. Sometimes chunking up or down on the initial goal best sets the goals:

- *We want an improved remuneration package.*
- *UP – Basically we both want this company to survive. Right, let's start from there.*
- *How do we get more cash to distribute?*
- *DOWN – Right, let's get down to detail . . .*

2. *Play the ball and not the person.* We do, however, have to agree on a mutually acceptable ball first. Then we can see the other party as the advocate of a point of view, rather than as a rival – 'I find that an unreasonable request' rather than 'You are an unreasonable person.'

3. *Focus on interests, not positions.* Positions are demands the negotiator makes. Interests are the reasons behind the demands. Experience shows that it is easier to establish agreement on interests, given that they tend to be broader and multi-faceted. Recalling the discussion on creative problem solving, this step involves redefining and broadening the problem to make it more tractable. An integrative comment would be: 'Help me to understand where you are coming from.'

4. *Look for creative options.* Although it is true that some negotiations may necessarily be distributive, it is a mistake for negotiators to automatically adopt a win–lose posture. There are often alternatives that are valued by one party and cost the other party very little.

> Amex were designing a flatter organisation and reducing the number of grades from 15 to 5. Obviously this meant, in a very status conscious staff, some sadness. The creative solution was to split the five grades into classes – Gold, Silver and Bronze. The integrative negotiator would say something like: *Now that we better understand each other's concerns and needs, let's brainstorm ways of satisfying both of us without adding significantly to overheads.*

5. *Use objective criteria.* No matter how much we attempt to be integrative, there are bound to be some incompatible interests. Rather than seizing on these as opportunities for testing wills, it is far more productive to determine what makes most sense. This shift in thinking from 'getting what I want' to deciding 'what makes most sense' fosters an open, reasonable attitude. It encourages parties to avoid over-confidence or over-commitment to their initial position.

6. *Define success in terms of gains, not losses.* If a manager seeks a 10 per cent salary rise and receives only 6 per cent, that outcome can be viewed as either a 6 per cent improvement or as a 40 per cent shortfall. The first interpretation focuses on gains, the second on losses – in this case, unrealised expectations. The outcome is the same, but the manager's satisfaction with it varies substantially. It is important to recognise that our satisfaction with an outcome is affected by the standards we use to judge it. Recognising this, the integrative negotiator sets reasonable standards by which to judge the value of proposed solutions. The integrative approach to assessing proposals is: *Does this outcome constitute a meaningful improvement in current conditions?*

Management Consultancy and Skills

What happens if you are trying to collaborate and the other party is using combative, high-pressure negotiation tactics? Should you simply persist, hoping the other party will eventually follow suit, while at the same time risking the other party taking advantage of your non-combative posture? Or should you risk the possibility that you will eventually become so frustrated that you'll join the fraças?

In essence, the guidelines suggest shifting the focus of the discussion from 'content' to 'process'. By presenting your frustration, you are able to draw attention to the unsatisfactory negotiation process. In the course of a conversation of this type, the other party's underlying reasons for using a particular negotiation style often surface. We find time pressures, lack of trust, or unrealistic expectations and working on these we can build a more collaborative mode of interaction – 'How can we work together to resolve our concerns about how we work together so that we can both get something out of this?'

Selecting the appropriate approach

The presentation of alternative approaches inevitably leads to the question, 'Which of the five is best?', and for this we have no answer. The collaborative approach is probably the safest, but all the approaches can be appropriate, given the 'players' and the situation. However, we have preferred styles based on the value we place on conflict and our personality profile – we have a choice of three according to Cummings *et al.* (1971) and Porter (1973). The language they use might be criticised as jargon, but the concept is sound.

- *Altruistic-nurturing* personalities seek gratification through promoting harmony with others and enhancing their welfare, with little concern for being rewarded in return. This personality type is characterised by trust, optimism, idealism and loyalty.

- *Assertive-directing* personalities seek gratification through self-assertion and directing the activities of others with a clear sense of having earned rewards. Individuals with this personality characteristic tend to be self-confident, enterprising and persuasive.

- *Analytic-autonomising* personalities seek gratification through the achievement of self-sufficiency, self-reliance and logical orderliness. This personality type is cautious, practical, methodical and principled.

When altruistic-nurturing individuals encounter conflict, they tend to press for harmony by accommodating the demands of the other party. In contrast, the assertive-directing personality tends to challenge the opposition by using the forcing approach. The analysing-autonomising personality becomes very cautious when encountering conflict. Initially an attempt is made to rationally resolve the problem. However, if the conflict becomes very intense, this individual will withdraw and break contact.

While there appears to be a strong link between dominant personality characteristics and preferred modes of handling conflict, research on leadership styles has demonstrated that the most effective managers use a variety of styles (Schriesheim

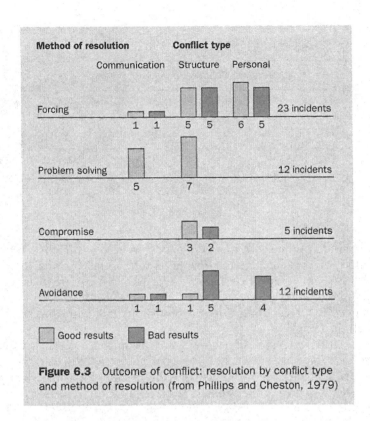

Figure 6.3 Outcome of conflict: resolution by conflict type and method of resolution (from Phillips and Cheston, 1979)

and Von Glinow, 1977), tailoring their response to the demands of the situation. This general principle has been borne out in research on conflict-management.

In one study, 25 executives were asked to describe two conflict situations – one with bad results and one with good (Phillips and Cheston, 1979). These incidents were then categorised in terms of the conflict-management approach used. As shown in Figure 6.3, there were 23 incidents of forcing, 12 incidents of problem solving, 5 incidents of compromise and 12 incidents of avoidance. Admittedly, this was a very small sample of managers, but the fact that there were almost twice as many incidents of forcing as problem solving, and nearly five times as many as compromising, is noteworthy. It is also interesting that the executives indicated that forcing and compromising were equally as likely to produce good as bad results, whereas problem solving was always linked with positive outcomes, and avoidance generally led to negative results.

It is striking that, despite the fact that forcing was as likely to produce bad as good results, it was by far the most commonly used conflict-management mode. Since this approach is clearly not superior in terms of results, one wonders why these senior executives reported a propensity for using it.

A likely answer is expediency. Evidence for this supposition is provided by a study of the preferred influence strategies of over 300 managers in three countries (Kipnis and Schmidt, 1983). The study reports that when subordinates refuse or

Management Consultancy and Skills

Table 6.4 Matching the conflict-management approach with the situation

Situational considerations	Conflict-management approach				
	Forcing	Accommodating	Compromising	Collaborating	Avoiding
Issue importance	High	Low	Med	High	Low
Relationship importance	Low	High	Med	High	Low
Relative power	High	Low	Equal-High	Low-High	Equal-High
Time constraints	Med-High	Med-High	Low	Low	Med-High

appear reluctant to comply with a request, managers become directive. When resistance in subordinates is encountered, managers tend to fall back on their superior power and insist on compliance. So pervasive was this pattern that Kipnis and Schmidt proposed an 'Iron Law of Power': 'The greater discrepancy in power between influence and target, the greater the probability that more directive influence strategies will be used.'

A second striking feature of Figure 6.3 is that some conflict-management approaches were never used for certain types of issues. In particular, the managers did not report a single case of problem solving or compromising when personal problems were the source of the conflict. These approaches were used primarily for managing conflicts involving incompatible goals and conflicting reward systems between departments. Two conclusions can be drawn from this study:

1. No one approach is most effective for managing every type of conflict.

2. Managers are more effective in dealing with conflicts if they feel comfortable using a variety of approaches.

If these conclusions are correct, to progress we need to look at where each of the techniques are most effective. Only then can we fit the style to the situation. The situational factors are summarised in Table 6.4.

The **forcing** approach is most appropriate when a conflict of values or perspectives is involved and it is necessary to defend the 'correct' position; when hierarchical control must be maintained and when being respected is more important than being liked, or when time pressures are over-riding. An example of such a situation might be when a subordinate needs to follow safety procedures.

The **accommodating** approach is most appropriate when keeping good working relationships outweighs all other considerations. Such a situation can happen anywhere, but is more common where the power does or could rest with the other party – a client, a colleague from another unit or a powerful boss. Time is also a consideration. Accommodation becomes especially appropriate when the issues are not vital to your interests and the problem must be resolved quickly.

Compromise is most appropriate when the issue is only moderately important, there are no obvious or simple solutions, and both parties have a strong interest in different facets of the problem. Time must not be a pressure. A classic case where compromise is essential would be a negotiation to avoid an industrial conflict. Experience shows that compromises are most appropriate when both parties have equal power and wish to maintain good long-term relationship. When either of these is not the case the issue may be one of damage limitation and not of conflict management.

The **collaborating** approach is most appropriate when the issues are critical, maintaining an ongoing supportive relationship between peers is important, and time constraints are not pressing. Although collaboration can be effective where there is a discrepancy of real or perceived power between the groups or individuals, it is most often employed when peers are involved. Here collaboration is more appropriate than either forcing or accommodation.

The **avoidance** approach is most appropriate when one's stake in an issue is not high and there is no strong interpersonal reason for getting involved, regardless of whether the conflict involves a superior, subordinate or peer. Severe time constraints can bring in avoidance by default, however much one might prefer to use compromise and collaboration.

Resolving confrontations using the collaborative approach

Part of the skill of effective conflict management is choosing an appropriate approach based on a thoughtful assessment of the situation. Characteristics of unsuccessful conflict managers are their habitual reliance on one or two strategies regardless of changing circumstances. For these managers the preferred strategies rarely include collaboration.

The study by Kipnis and Schmidt (1983), discussed earlier, found that although most managers appeared to support the collaborative approach in principle, they often took a directive approach under pressure. The reason for this may be that the collaborative approach to conflict management is the most difficult to implement successfully, requiring much more skill than the other systems. It is, for example, a fairly simple matter for managers to either give in or impose their will, but resolving differences in a truly collaborative manner is a very complicated and taxing process. Thus unskilled or highly pressured managers often take the path of least resistance and opt for more comfortable and familiar ground. Another explanation for the retreat from the collaborative approach may involve the issues of Mind Music we mentioned earlier. If we have a fundamental belief in hierarchy, then if the person of 'lower status' continues to wriggle when we are being 'reasonable', we listen to the messages in our head telling us that that person SHOULD respect our authority and and we should move over to asserting that authority.

The collaborative approach needs enhanced skills and practice.

While the general negotiation strategies and conflict management are similar in concept, they diverge when we deal with specific cases. This is probably because the nature of the issues is generally different. There are obvious overlaps, but negotiations tend to focus on substantive issues – the responsibility for the distribution of a new product – while interpersonal conflicts are more likely to be triggered by issues rooted in emotion, such as career failures, expenses or even sexual harassment. Because of this, interpersonal conflicts do not often lend themselves easily to collaborative solutions, even when collaboration is likely to be the most effective approach. To treat confrontations, often involving complaints and criticisms, we need a step-by-step approach similar to that covered in our chapter on problem solving. There are four stages:

1. Problem identification
2. Solution generation
3. Action plan formulation and agreement
4. Implementation and follow-up.

In real conflicts the first two stages – **problem identification** and **alternative generation** – are the most critical steps as well as the most difficult to manage effectively, in spite of being the only ones that can be controlled. If you get them wrong, everything goes wrong. When you initiate a complaint, you can control how you state it and whether you request a change in behaviour, but you cannot control whether the other party agrees to change or, having agreed, actually undertakes a follow-up. This is where we are subjected to our own Mind Music. We will, therefore, focus primarily on phases one and two during our skill training. Also in the early phases of a confrontation, the parties concerned often come from completely different spaces. And thus we need to look at the roles of each participant individually.

Virtually every confrontation involves two principal participants whom we shall term the **initiator** and the **respondent** – the individual with the issue and the person required to handle it. For example, a subordinate might complain about not being given a fair share of the opportunities to work overtime (the initiator); or the head of production (the initiator) might complain to the head of sales (the respondent) about frequent changes in order specifications.

Such a confrontation represents a greater challenge for respondents because they basically have responsibility for transforming a complaint into a problem-solving discussion. The transformation requires considerable patience and self-confidence, particularly when the initiator is unskilled. In such circumstances the unskilled initiator will generally begin the discussion by blaming the respondent for the problem, and should the respondent also be unskilled he or she will adopt a defensive position and probably look for an opportunity to come back aggressively.

If these lose–lose dynamics persist, a third party, whom we shall term the **mediator**, is needed to cool down the initiator and the respondent, to re-establish constructive communication and help the parties reconcile their differences. The presence of a mediator takes some of the pressure off the respondent because an impartial referee provides assistance in moving the confrontation through the problem-solving phases.

Below, we present guidelines for each of three roles – initiator, respondent and mediator – guidelines which those in the other two roles do not follow.

The initiator

Maintain personal ownership of the problem

It is important to recognise that your emotions and feelings are your problem and not the other person's. The first step in addressing this concern is acknowledging accountability for your feelings. Suppose someone enters your office with a smelly cigar without asking if it is all right to smoke. The fact that your office is going to stink for the rest of the day may infuriate you, but the odour does not present a problem for your smoking guest. One way to determine ownership of a problem is to identify whose needs are not being met. In this case, your need for a clean working environment is not being met, so the smelly office is your problem. Own your problem and, should it be wise to do so, explain your problem to the smoker. If the smoker happens to be your senior and is well known for his or her inability to take the mildest criticism, then we may decide that tolerating a smelly office and holding one's peace is the wisest action. Always remember the old riddle:

> *'What do you call a mad terrorist with a gun?'*
> *'Sir.'*

The advantage of acknowledging ownership of a problem when registering a complaint is that it reduces defensiveness (Adler, 1977). In order for you to get a problem solved, the respondent must not feel threatened by your initial statement of the problem. By beginning the conversation with a request that the respondent help solve your problem, you immediately establish a problem-solving atmosphere. For example, you might say, 'Mary, have you a few minutes? I have a problem I need to discuss with you.'

Describe your problem

The key is to reduce your concern to a few words, describing what has happened, the consequences and your feelings. A useful model for remembering how to state your problem effectively has been prescribed by Gordon (1970): 'I have a problem. When you do X, Y results, and I feel Z.' While we don't suggest using set formulas, we find that knowing they exist allows us confidence to build our own.

1. Describe the specific **behaviours** (X) that present a problem for you. This will help you to avoid what may be an automatic response to your feeling upset and avoid being evaluative: 'Your behaviour is bad' leads to trouble, but if we are specific the 'accused' has an opportunity to take actions other than defence. Your subordinate may have missed an important deadline – tell that person, detailing the circumstances. Another department may have missed giving you relevant information – tell them, explaining the information you needed.

2. Outline the specific, **observable consequences** (Y) of what you have detailed. Simply telling others that their actions are causing you problems

is often sufficient stimulus for change. In fast-paced work environments, people generally become insensitive to the impact of their actions. They don't intend to cause offence but become so busy meeting deadlines associated with 'getting the product out the door' that they don't notice subtle negative feedback from others. When this occurs, bringing to the attention of others the consequences of their behaviours will often prompt them to change.

Unfortunately, sometimes problems can't be resolved this simply. At times offenders are aware of the negative consequences of their behaviours and yet persist in them. In such cases, this approach is still useful in stimulating a rational discussion because it is non-threatening. Possibly the respondents' behaviours are constrained by the expectations of their boss or by the fact that the department is currently understaffed. Respondents may not be able to change these constraints, but this approach will encourage them to discuss them with you so that you can work on the problem together.

3. Describe the **feelings** (Z) you experience as a result of the problem. It is important that the respondent understands that his or her behaviour is not just inconvenient but is important to YOU. You need to explain how it is affecting you personally by engendering feelings of frustration, anger and insecurity. Explain how these feelings are interfering with what you see as your job. The named behaviour is – making it more difficult for you to concentrate, to satisfy customer demands, to be supportive of your boss, to work up to the 100 per cent you know is necessary.

Use the three-step model as a guide rather than as a formula, and do not use the same words every time. For example, it would get pretty monotonous if everyone in a work group initiated a discussion about an interpersonal issue with the words 'I have a problem'. Examples in Adler (1977) illustrate the process:

'I have to tell you that I get upset [feelings] when you make jokes about my bad memory in front of other people [behaviour]. In fact, I get so angry that I find myself bringing up your faults to get even [consequences].'

'I have a problem. When you say you'll be here for our date at six and don't show up until after seven [behaviour], the dinner gets ruined, we're late for the show we planned to see [consequences], and I feel hurt because it seems like I'm just not that important to you [feelings].'

'The employees want to let management know that we've been having a hard time lately with the short notice you've been giving when you need us to work overtime [behaviour]. That probably explains some of the grumbling and lack of co-operation you've mentioned [consequences]. Anyhow, we wanted to make it clear that this policy has really got a lot of the workers feeling pretty resentful [feeling].'

In presenting your problem, avoid the pitfalls of making accusations, drawing inferences about motivations or intentions, or attributing the respondent's undesirable behaviour to personal inadequacies. Statements such as 'You are always interrupting me', 'You haven't been fair to me since the day I disagreed with you in the board meeting', or 'You never have time to listen to our problems and suggestions because you manage your time so poorly', are good at starting rows but less effective for initiating rational problem solving.

Another key to reducing defensiveness is to delay proposing a solution until both parties agree on the nature of the problem. When you become so upset with someone's behaviour that you feel it is necessary to initiate a complaint, it is often because the person has not met the criteria you have laid down for that individual. For example, you might feel that your subordinate has failed to complete a project on time. Consequently, you might begin the interview by assuming that the subordinate was aware of your time scale. If he or she is not aware of that time scale and was working to another set of priorities, we will have a potentially dysfunctional conflict. Check on common ground: 'Were you aware that the whole project has to be completed by next week and that we are waiting on your parts before we complete?' Establish common ground first. If the respondent was unaware of the deadlines or the importance of his or her contribution, then you are the one who has slipped up. In this case any recriminations will lead at best to defensiveness.

Besides creating defensiveness, the principal disadvantage to initiating problem solving with a suggested remedy without establishing common ground, is that it doesn't work. Before completing the problem-articulation phase, you have immediately jumped to the solution-generation phase, based on the assumption that you know all the reasons for, and constraints on, the other person's behaviour.

Persist until understood

There are times when the other person will not clearly receive or acknowledge even the most effectively expressed message. Suppose, for instance, that you share the following problem with a co-worker (Adler, 1977):

> 'I've been bothered by something lately and I would like to discuss it with you. To be honest, I'm uncomfortable [feeling] when you use so much bad language [behaviour]. I don't mind an occasional "damn" or "hell", but the f-word is difficult for me to accept. Lately I've found myself avoiding you [consequences], and that's no good either, so I wanted to let you know how I feel.'

When you share your feelings in this non-evaluative way, it is likely that the other person will understand your position and possibly try to change behaviour to suit your needs. On the other hand, there are a number of less satisfying responses that could be made to your comment:

- Defending, rationalising and counter-attacking: *'Listen, these days everyone talks that way. And besides, you've got your faults, too, you know!'*

- Failing to understand how serious the problem is to you: *'Yes, I suppose I do swear a lot. I'll have to work on that some day.'*

- Totally misunderstanding: *'Listen, if you're still angry about my forgetting to tell you about that meeting the other day, you can be sure that I'm really sorry. I won't do it again.'*

- Showing discomfort and seeking to change the subject: *'Speaking of avoiding, have you seen Chris lately? I wonder if anything is wrong with him?'*

When we receive an unsolicited response it is quite likely that our Mind Music will be triggered, and to return to constructive communication we need to buy time. Think of your mind as a computer and the Mind Music as a series of unstructured programmes that take up our available RAM. When such an event happens, we need to switch off and reboot. So it is with us when the Mind Music appears, such thoughts as – *I'm his boss, he ought to agree. Look I'm being reasonable and nice, he ought to respond* – trigger us back to being directive. We have to buy time to restore our constructive communication processes.

The ideal response to buy us thinking time is the same for all these responses – acknowledge what the respondent says and return to your own bottom line, as often as is required. Thus, in the response that indicates misunderstanding: *The issue of the meeting is not the point. What is the point is that your use of the f-word is not acceptable.*

The respondent may continue to wriggle and change approach: *Everyone uses the occasional four-letter word*, but the reply is the same: *Other people's behaviour is not the point, your use of the f-word is not acceptable.*

To avoid introducing new concerns or shifting from a descriptive to an evaluative mode, keep in mind the 'X, Y, Z' formula for feedback. Persistence is most effective when it consists of 'variations on a theme', rather than 'variation in themes'. Woods (1989) describes the methodology as a combination of two techniques – Broken Record and Fielding. With Broken Record we define our bottom line, 'using the f-word is unacceptable', and repeat it calmly, whatever the other person says, until he or she hears our determination. We do not have to answer questions or defend our position.

Broken Record alone will win us no friends and is not part of constructive communication, so we add a second technique – Fielding. With Fielding we acknowledge what the other person says and accept that he or she has a right to that opinion, using some of his or her own words. We then return to the Broken Record theme.

The process continues until the respondent acknowledges our position.

Encourage two-way discussion

It is important that you establish a climate for rational problem solving by inviting the other person to express opinions and ask questions. Often there is a very simple explanation for another's behaviour, perhaps a radically different view of the problem. The sooner this information is introduced into the conversation, the sooner the issue is likely to be resolved. As a rule of thumb, the longer the opening statement of the initiator, the longer it will take the two parties to work through their problem. The reason for this is that the more lengthy the statement of the problem, the more likely it is to encourage a defensive reaction. The longer we talk, the more worked-up we get, and the more likely we are to violate the principles of constructive communication. Long statements can be seen as threatening and encourage a rebuttal or counter-attack. People simply turn off, and a collaborative approach is usually discarded in favour of the accommodation or forcing strategies, depending on the circumstances. When this occurs, it is unlikely that the actors will be able to reach a mutually satisfactory solution to their problem without third-party intervention. Keep it simple and keep it short. Only make one point and make sure that it is the best point. Here again we return to negotiation strategy – do not produce a range of arguments, the respondent will simply dispose of the weakest and ignore the strongest. Start and continue with your bottom line, only moving on when you know you have been heard. If and when the two-way communication occurs – listen.

Manage the agenda: approach multiple or complex problems incrementally

Your opening statement should only contain one point. This should be the essential point that must be resolved or your meeting is a failure. Thus swearing may only be one issue that is causing you concern – the respondent's dress may cause you lesser concern and the time he or she spends in the doorway smoking might also be a subject of discussion. Leave them and focus on what is, for you, the most important issue. The other issues may be taken up later, but not until he or she has accepted your primary issue as being important.

Focus on commonalities as the basis for requesting a change

Once the problem is clearly understood, the discussion should shift to the solution-generation phase of the problem-solving process. Most of us share some goals (personal and organisational), believe in many of the same fundamental principles of management, and operate under similar constraints. The most straightforward approach to changing another's offensive behaviour is making a request. The legitimacy of a request will be enhanced if it is linked to common interests. These might include shared values such as treating co-workers fairly and following through on commitments, or shared constraints such as getting reports in on time and operating within budgetary restrictions. This approach is particularly effective when the parties have had difficulty getting along in the past. In these situations, pointing out how a change in the respondent's behaviour would positively affect your shared fate will reduce defensiveness:

> 'Jane, we are not talking about a big deal. You are the most influential member of the accounts department and simply by abiding by the Flexi-Time rules, you will allow us to keep the system that has advantages for all of us.'

The respondent

Now we shall examine the problem-identification phase from the viewpoint of the person who is supposedly the source of the problem – the respondent, or 'the accused'. In a work setting, this could be a manager who is making unrealistic demands, a new employee who has ignored safety regulations or a co-worker who is claiming credit for your ideas. The overall strategy is to listen before responding. The tactics for doing this are shown in the following guidelines.

Management Consultancy and Skills

Establish a climate for joint problem solving

When a person complains to you, you should not treat that complaint lightly. While this sounds self-evident, it is often difficult to focus your attention on some-one else's problems when you are in the middle of writing an important project report or concerned about preparing for a meeting scheduled to begin in a few minutes. Also it is often wise to come prepared for a difficult meeting, and preparation may well necessitate your buying time. Therefore, unless the other person's emotional condition means that you need to take immediate action, it is usually fine to agree a time for another meeting after you have understood the issue to be discussed.

In most cases, the initiator will be expecting you to set the tone for the meeting. The tones to be avoided are over-reaction or defensiveness. Even if you disagree with the complaint and feel it has no foundation, you need to respond empathetically to the initiator's statement of the problem. The initiator MAY not have expressed the criticism correctly.

Most of us have had experience in not satisfying our bosses in the presentation of a written report. What frequently happens is that when we present a report, the grammar and even the spelling are criticised, but we would be unwise to leave it there. In experience many people find it easier to criticise the detail rather than explain their real complaint – i.e., that the report is inadequate in some much more radical way. It is the job of the respondent to tease out the 'real' criticism without dismissing the detailed complaints.

Learning from criticism is best done by conveying an attitude of interest and recep-tivity through your posture, tone of voice and facial expressions. One of the most difficult aspects of establishing the proper climate for your discussion is responding appropriately to the emotions of the initiator. Sometimes you may need to let a per-son blow off steam before trying to address the substance of a specific complaint. In some cases the therapeutic effect of being able to express negative emotions to the boss will be enough to satisfy a subordinate. This occurs frequently in high-pressure jobs where tempers flare easily as a result of the intense stress.

However, an emotional outburst can be very detrimental to problem solving. If an employee begins verbally attacking you or someone else, and it is apparent that the individual is more interested in getting even than in solving an interpersonal problem, you may need to interrupt and interject some ground rules for collabor-ative problem solving. By explaining calmly to the other person that you are will-ing to discuss a genuine problem but that you will not tolerate personal attacks or making scape-goats, you can quickly determine the true intentions of the initiator. In most instances he or she will apologise, emulate your emotional tone and begin formulating a useful statement of the problem.

Learning from criticism

Mike Woods (1989) calls the most effect techniques for learning from criticism Appropriate Assertion and Constructive Enquiry. Appropriate Assertion is designed to take the sting and negative emotion from a criticism by assertively affirming that you either agree or disagree with the comments:

'You are late with the training programme'
'That is correct, the training programme has been delayed'

– and then stop. If, however, the programme has not been delayed:

'That is completely untrue – the training programme is on schedule'

– and then stop.

The clarity and the uncompromising nature of the response disarms most people who have the intention of (persecuting) you. Once you have 'disarmed' the initiator you can move on to the next phase of learning from the criticism. The process of 'disarming' certainly includes removing the emotional element from the criticism. An adage that may be of use is: 'It is no use pouring the cold water of logic onto the hot coals of emotion.'

Learning from criticism involves rational problem solving on the part of the initiator and the respondent. Untrained initiators will typically present complaints that are both very general and highly evaluative. They will make generalisations from a few specific incidents about your motives and your personal strengths and weaknesses. If you are going to transform a personal complaint into a joint problem, you must redirect the conversation from general and evaluative accusations to descriptions of specific behaviours.

To do this, ask for details about specific actions that are forming the basis for the evaluation. You might find it useful to phrase your questions so that they reflect the 'X, Y, Z' model described previously: 'Can you give me a specific example of my behaviour that concerns you?', 'When I did that, what were the specific consequences for your work?', 'How did you feel when that happened?' When a complaint is both serious and complex, it is especially critical for you to understand it completely. In these situations, check your level of understanding by summarising the initiator's main points and asking if your summary is correct. Mike Woods, in the jargon of assertiveness training, calls this Constructive Enquiry.

Sometimes it is useful to ask for additional complaints: 'Are there any other problems in our relationship you'd like to discuss?' If the initiator is just in a griping mood, this is not a good time to probe further; you don't want to encourage this type of behaviour. But if the person is seriously concerned about improving your relationship, your discussion to this point has been helpful and you suspect that the initiator is holding back and not talking about the really serious issues, you should probe deeper. Often people begin by complaining about a minor problem to 'test the water'. If you lose your temper, the conversation finishes and the really critical issues aren't discussed. However, if you are responsive to a frank discussion about problems, the more serious issues are likely to surface.

Agree with some aspect of the complaint

Appropriate Assertion involves a clear acceptance or denial of the truth of criticism, unfortunately things are seldom black and white. There is an element of truth in many harsh criticisms, but this is difficult to accept. Acceptance may well fuel the complaining behaviour, so we need a further formula. In practice, this step is probably the best test of whether the respondent is committed to using the collaborative approach to conflict management rather than the avoiding, forcing or accommodating approaches. People who use the forcing mode will grit their teeth while listening to the initiator, just waiting to find a flaw they can use to launch a counter-attack. Or they will simply respond, 'I'm sorry, but that's just the way I am. You'll simply have to get used to it.' Accommodators will apologise profusely and ask for forgiveness. People who avoid conflicts will acknowledge and agree with the initiator's concerns, but only in a superficial manner because their only concern is how to end the awkward conversation as quickly as possible.

In contrast, collaborators will demonstrate their concerns for both co-operation and assertiveness by looking for points in the initiator's presentation with which they can genuinely agree. Even in the most blatantly malicious and hostile verbal assault (which may be more a reflection of the initiator's insecurity than evidence of your inadequacies), there is generally a grain of truth.

A few years ago a junior member in a business school who was being reviewed for promotion received a very unfair appraisal from one of his senior colleagues. Since the junior member knew that the critic was going through a personal crisis, he could have dismissed this criticism as irrelevant and insignificant. However, one particular phrase, 'You are stuck on a narrow line of research', kept coming back to his mind. There was something there that couldn't be ignored. As a result of turning what was otherwise a very vindictive remark into something personally useful, he accepted the partial truth of the remark and acted accordingly, changing his career path. Furthermore, by publicly giving the senior colleague credit for the suggestion, he substantially strengthened the interpersonal relationship.

There are a number of ways you can agree with part of a message without accepting it in full (Adler, 1977). You can find an element of truth and accept it: '*I accept that I may be seen to be pursuing a narrow line of research and I thank you for bringing it to my attention.*' (Accepting that this person may observe my behaviour in a certain way but NOT accepting that this was my intention or indeed that the remark is true.)

We may then move on and request further information and guidance: '*As I was unaware of the potential problem, perhaps you could help me by suggesting how I could be seen to broaden my approach.*'

Again, do not be stuck in a formal set of words: '*Well, I can see how you would think that. I have known people who have deliberately shirked their responsibilities.*' Or, you can agree with the person's feelings: '*It is obvious that our earlier discussion greatly upset you.*'

You are not agreeing with the initiator's conclusions or evaluations but accepting that the initiator has a right to his or her views. You will be seen to be listening, attempting to understand and foster a problem solving, rather than argumentative, discussion and this in itself will assist in developing a supportive environment. Generally, initiators prepare for a complaint session by mentally cataloguing all the evidence supporting their point of view. Once the discussion begins, they introduce as much evidence as necessary to make their argument convincing; that is, they keep arguing until you agree. The more evidence that is introduced, the broader the argument becomes and the more difficult it is to begin investigating solutions.

Ask for suggestions of acceptable alternatives

Once you are certain that you fully understand the initiator's complaint, proceed with the next aspect of constructive enquiry – look for possible solutions with the initiator. Mutual problem solving is an important transition in the discussion. Attention moves from negative historical aspects to positive and future concerns. It also tells the initiator that you are concerned with his or her opinions – a key element in the joint problem-solving process. Some managers listen patiently to a subordinate's complaint, express appreciation for the feedback, say they will rectify the problem, and then close the discussion. This leaves the initiator guessing about the outcome of the meeting. Will you take the complaint seriously? Will you really change? If so, will the change resolve the problem? It is important to eliminate this ambiguity by agreeing on a plan of action. If the problem is particularly serious or complex, it is useful to write down specific agreements, including assignments and deadlines, as well as providing for a follow-up meeting to check progress.

The mediator

Frequently it is necessary for a third party to intervene in a dispute (Walton, 1969). While this may occur for a variety of reasons, we will assume in this discussion that the mediator has been invited to help the initiator and respondent resolve their differences. We will further assume that the mediator is senior and concerned with both the initiator and the respondent, though this assumption is not necessary to discuss the process.

> A hair stylist in a beauty salon complained to the manager about the way the receptionist was favouring other beauticians who had been there longer. This allegation violated the manager's policy of allocating walk-in business strictly on the basis of beautician availability. The manager investigated the complaint and discovered considerable animosity between these two employees. The stylist felt the receptionist was keeping sloppy records, while the receptionist blamed the stylist for forgetting to hand in her slip when she finished with a customer. The problems between these two appeared serious enough to the participants and broad enough in scope that the manager called both parties into her office to help them resolve their differences.

Ten guidelines, due to William Morris and Marshall Sashkin (1976), which are intended to help mediators avoid the common pitfalls associated with this role, are presented in Table 6.5.

It is vital that the mediator takes the problems between conflicting parties seriously. If they feel they have a serious problem, the mediator should not belittle its significance. Remarks such as '*I'm surprised that two intelligent people like you*

Table 6.5 Ten ways to FAIL as a mediator

1. After you have listened to the argument for a short time, begin to non-verbally communicate your discomfort with the discussion (e.g., sit back, begin to fidget).
2. Take sides and communicate your agreement with **one** of the parties (e.g., through facial expressions, posture, chair position, reinforcing comments).
3. Say that you shouldn't be talking about this kind of thing at work or where others can overhear.
4. Discourage the expression of emotion. Suggest that the discussion would be better held later after both parties have cooled off.
5. Suggest that both parties are wrong. Point out the problems with both points of view.
6. Suggest part-way through the discussion that possibly you aren't the person who should be helping solve this problem.
7. See if you can get both parties to attack you.
8. Minimise the seriousness of the problem.
9. Change the subject (e.g., ask for advice to help you solve one of your problems).
10. Express displeasure that the two parties are experiencing conflict (e.g., imply that it might undermine the solidarity of the work group).

Source: Adapted from Morris and Sashkin (1976)

have not been able to work out your disagreement. We have more important things to do here than get all worked up over such petty issues', will make both parties defensive and interfere with any serious problem-solving efforts. While you might wish that your subordinates could have worked out their disagreement without bothering you, this is not the time to lecture them on self-reliance or inducing guilt that 'they are being emotional'.

One early decision a mediator has to make is whether to convene a joint problem-solving session or to first meet with the parties separately. The diagnostic questions shown in Table 6.6 should help you to weigh up the advantages and dis-advantages of each approach.

The overall methodology for the mediator

What is the current position of the disputants?

- Are they both aware a problem exists?
- Do they agree on the definition of the problem?
- Are they equally motivated to work on solving the problem?

The nearer the answer YES is to all three of the questions, the more likely are things to be resolved. If the answer to any of the three questions is NO, then the mediator should work towards some agreement through one-on-one meetings before bringing the disputants together.

Table 6.6   Choosing a format for mediating conflicts

Factors	Hold joint meeting	Hold separate meetings
Awareness and motivation		
• Both parties are aware of the problem	Yes	No
• They are equally motivated to resolve the problem	Yes	No
• They accept your legitimacy as a mediator	Yes	No
Nature of the relationship		
• The parties hold equal status	Yes	No
• They work together regularly	Yes	No
• They have a good overall relationship	Yes	No
Nature of the problem		
• This is an isolated (not a recurring) problem	Yes	No
• The complaint is substantive in nature and easily verified	Yes	No
• The parties agree on the root causes of the problem	Yes	No
• The parties share common values and work priorities	Yes	No

What is the current relationship between the disputants?

- Does their work require them to interact frequently?
- Is a good working relationship critical for their individual job performance?
- What has their relationship been like in the past?
- What is the difference in their formal status in the organisation?

As we discussed earlier, joint problem-solving sessions are most productive between individuals of equal status who are required to work together regularly. This does not mean that joint meetings should not be held between a supervisor and a subordinate, only that greater care needs to be taken in preparing for such a meeting. Specifically, if a department head becomes involved in a dispute between a worker and a supervisor, the department head should make sure that the worker does not feel that this meeting will serve as an excuse for two managers to gang up on a subordinate.

Separate fact-finding meetings with the disputants before a joint meeting are particularly useful when the parties have a history of recurring disputes, especially if these disputes should have been resolved without a mediator. Such a history often suggests a lack of conflict management or problem-solving skills on the part of the disputants, or it might stem from a broader set of issues that are beyond their control. In these situations, individual coaching sessions before a joint meeting will increase your understanding of the root causes and improve the individuals' abilities to resolve their differences. Following up these private meetings with a joint problem-solving session, in which the mediator coaches the disputants through the process for resolving their conflicts, can be a positive learning experience.

What is the nature of the problem?

Is the complaint substantive in nature and easily verifiable? If the problem stems from conflicting role responsibilities and the actions of both parties in question are common knowledge, then a joint problem-solving session can begin on a common information and experimental basis. In contrast, if the complaint stems from differences in managerial style, values, personality characteristics, etc., bringing the parties together immediately following a complaint may seriously undermine the problem-solving process. Complaints that are likely to be interpreted as threats to the self-image of one or both parties (Who am I?, What do I stand for?) warrant considerable individual discussion before a joint meeting is called. To avoid individuals feeling as though they are being ambushed in a meeting, you should discuss serious personal complaints with them ahead of time, in private.

In seeking out the perspective of both parties, maintain a neutral posture regarding the disputants, if not the issues. Effective mediation requires impartiality. If a mediator shows strong personal bias in favour of one party in a joint problem-solving session, the other party may simply get up and walk out. However, this type of personal bias is more likely to creep out in private conversations with the disputants. Statements like, 'I can't believe he really did that!' and 'Everyone seems to be having trouble working with Andrew these days', imply that the mediator is taking sides, and any attempt to appear impartial in a joint meeting will seem like mere window dressing to appease the other party. No matter how well intentioned or justified these comments might be, they destroy the credibility of the mediator in the long run. In contrast, the effective mediator respects both parties' points of view and makes sure that both perspectives are expressed adequately.

Occasionally, it is not possible to be impartial on the issues. One person may have violated company policy, engaged in unethical competition with a colleague or broken a personal agreement. In these cases the challenge of the mediator is to separate the offence from the offender. If a person is clearly in the wrong, the inappropriate behaviour needs to be corrected, but in such a way that the individual doesn't feel his or her image and working relationships have been permanently marred. This can be done most effectively when correction occurs in private.

Manage the discussion to ensure fairness

Keep the discussion confined to the issues in hand and do not allow them to stray on to criticism of personalities. The mediator must maintain the role of the problem solver and not the referee. This is not to say that strong emotional statements don't have their place. People often associate effective problem solving with a calm, highly rational discussion of the issues and associate a personality attack with a highly emotional outburst. However, it is important not to confuse affect and effect. Placid, cerebral discussions often don't solve problems, and impassioned statements don't have to be insulting. The critical point about conflict management is that it should be centred on the issues and the consequences of continued conflict on performance. Even when behaviour offensive to one of the parties obviously stems from a personality quirk, the discussion of the problem should be limited to the behaviour. As we stated earlier, attributions about motives or generalisations about specific events or personal proclivities distract participants from the problem solving process. It is important that the mediator establishes and maintains these ground rules.

It is also important for a mediator to ensure that neither party dominates the discussion. A relatively even balance in the level of inputs improves the quality of the final outcome. It also increases the likelihood that both parties will accept the final decision, because there is a high correlation between feelings about the problem-solving process and attitudes about the final solution. If one party tends to dominate a discussion, the mediator can help balance the exchange by asking the less talkative individual direct questions: 'Now that we have heard Bill's view of that incident, how do you see it?', 'That's an important point, Malcolm, so let's make sure Brian agrees. How do you feel, Brian?'

Facilitate exploration of solutions rather than judge responsibility for the problem

When the parties must work closely, and have a history of chronic interpersonal problems, it is often more important to teach problem-solving skills than to resolve a specific dispute. This is done best when the mediator adopts the posture of facilitator. The role of judge is to render a verdict regarding a problem in the past, not to teach people how to solve their problems in the future. While some disputes obviously involve right and wrong actions, most interpersonal problems stem from differences in perspective. In these situations it is important that the mediator avoids being seduced into delivering a verdict by comments like, 'Well, you're the boss, tell us which one of us is right', or more subtly, 'I wonder if I did what was right?' The problem with a mediator's assuming the role of judge is that it sets in motion processes that are antithetical to effective interpersonal – problem solving. The parties focus on persuading the mediator of their innocence and the other party's guilt rather than striving to improve their working relationship with the assistance of the mediator. The disputants work to establish facts about what happened in the past rather than to reach an agreement about what ought to happen in the future. Consequently, a key aspect of effective mediation is helping the disputants to explore multiple alternatives in a non-judgemental manner.

Explore options by focusing on interests, not positions

Conflict resolution is often hampered by the perception that where there are incompatible positions there are irreconcilable differences. As noted in the negotiation section, mediation of such conflicts can best be accomplished by examining the interests (goals and concerns) behind the positions. It is these interests that form the driving force behind the positions, and it is these interests that are ultimately what people want satisfied.

It is the job of the mediator to discover where interests meet and where they conflict. Interests tend not to be stated, often because they are unclear to the participants. In order to flesh out each party's interests, ask 'Why' questions: 'Why have they taken this position?', 'Why does this matter to them?' Understand that there is probably no single, or simple, answer to these questions. For example, each side may represent a number of constituents, each with a special interest.

After each side has articulated its underlying interests, help the parties identify areas of agreement and reconcilability. It is common for participants in an intense conflict to feel that they are on opposite sides of all issues – that they have little in common. Helping them recognise that there are areas of agreement and reconcilability often represents a major turning point in resolving long-standing feuds.

Make sure that all parties fully understand and support the agreed solution and that follow-up procedures have been established

Before concluding this discussion of conflict-management principles, it is important to briefly mention the last two phases of the problem-solving process: agreement on an action plan and follow-up. These will be discussed within the context of the mediator's role, but they are equally applicable to the other roles.

A common mistake of ineffective mediators is terminating the discussion prematurely. They feel that once the problem has been solved in principle, the disputants can be left to work out the details on their own. Or, they assume that because one of the parties has recommended a solution that appears very reasonable and workable, the second disputant will be willing to implement it. It is very important that when serving as a mediator you insist on a specific plan of action that both parties are willing to implement. If you suspect any hesitancy on the part of either disputant, this needs to be explored explicitly: 'Susan, I sense that you are somewhat less enthusiastic than Jane about this plan. Is there something that bothers you?' When you are confident that both parties support the plan, you should check to make sure that they are aware of their respective responsibilities and then propose a mechanism for monitoring progress. You might schedule another formal meeting, or you might pop into the offices of the individuals to get a progress report.

SUMMARY

In western culture conflict brings out a number of negative constructs and we place a high value on getting along with people – *good managers do not make waves*. For this reason many people feel uncomfortable in conflict situations. Conflict correctly handled can be highly productive and this chapter has attempted to show how this correct handling can be achieved. A summary model of conflict management is shown in Figure 6.4.

There are basically five approaches to handling conflict:

- Forcing
- Accommodating

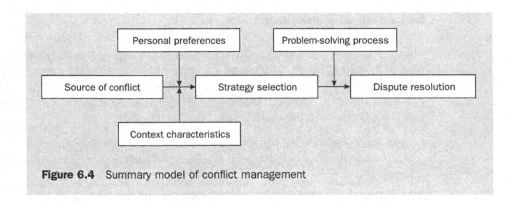

Figure 6.4 Summary model of conflict management

- Avoiding
- Compromising
- Collaborating

The model contains three phases: diagnosing the sources of conflict, selecting the appropriate conflict management strategy and using specific problem-solving techniques to resolve interpersonal disputes effectively. The first two phases comprise the diagnostic and analytical aspects of conflict management. We need to understand the causes of the conflict and hence how to respond. The third phase focuses on the behavioural component of conflict management. We have argued that conflict plays an important role in effective organisations. The operational component of this model focuses on successful resolution of specific disputes and not on eliminating, or preventing, all conflict.

Conflict can be produced by a variety of circumstances: irreconcilable personal differences, discrepancies in information, role incompatibilities and environmentally induced stress. These causes, and the resulting conflicts, differ in both frequency and intensity. For example, information-based conflicts occur frequently but are easily resolved because the disputants have low personal stakes in the outcome. In contrast, conflicts grounded in differences of perceptions and expectations are generally very intense and difficult to diffuse.

There is no best way to handle all conflicts. Instead, in choosing a response mode, managers should consider the quality and duration of the ongoing relationship between the actors, the nature and seriousness of their problem, as well as their personal preferences. Successful strategies need to be set into the context of the overall situation and the overall attitudes, philosophy and personality of the implementers.

The collaborative approach, like the integrative negotiation strategy, generally produces the highest-quality solutions and has the least detrimental effect on relationships. When it is used effectively, all parties tend to be satisfied with the outcome. The impositions of authority, withdrawal, splitting the difference or giving in, are easy options. The recommended option – the problem-solving collaborative approach – requires real skills, which are the basis of our behavioural guidelines.

Management Consultancy and Skills

453

Behavioural guidelines

Effective conflict management involves both analytical and behavioural elements. First, it is important to understand the true causes of a conflict and to select the appropriate conflict-management, or negotiation, approach. Second, it is necessary to implement the approach effectively. The behavioural guidelines for the diagnostic aspects of conflict management include the following:

- Collect information on the sources of conflict. Identify the source by examining the focus of the dispute. The four sources (and their respective focus) are:

  1. Personal differences (perception and expectations)
  2. Information deficiency (misinformation and misinterpretation)
  3. Role incompatibility (goals and responsibilities)
  4. Environmental stress (resource scarcity and uncertainty).

- Use the collaborative approach for managing conflict, including integrative negotiation tactics, unless specific conditions dictate the use of an alternative approach.

- Use the forcing approach only when: the issue is extremely important to you; a close, ongoing relationship is not necessary; you have much more power than the other person; there is a high sense of urgency.

- Use the accommodating approach only when: the issue is not important to you; a close, ongoing relationship is critical; you have no other option (low power); time is not a factor.

- Use the compromising approach only when the issue is very complex and of moderate importance to both parties (and the parties feel strongly about different aspects of the issues); the relationship is of moderate importance; the parties have relatively equal power; time constraints are low.

- Use the avoiding approach only when: the issue is not important to you; the relationship is not critical; your relative power is equal to high; time is not a factor.

The behavioural guidelines for effectively implementing the collaborative (problem-solving) approach to conflict management are summarised below. These are organised according to three roles. Guidelines for the problem-identification and solution-generation phases of the problem-solving process are specified for each role. Guidelines for the action plan and follow-up phases are the same for all three roles.

The first party: the initiator

Problem identification

1. Describe your problem briefly and clearly in terms of behaviours, consequences and feelings. ('When you do X, Y happens and I feel Z.')

- Maintain personal ownership of the problem.
- Use a specific incident to illustrate the expectations or standards violated.
- Stick to the facts, avoid drawing evaluative conclusions and attributing motives to the respondent.

2. Persist until understood and encourage two-way discussion.

- Restate your concerns or give additional examples.
- Avoid introducing additional issues or letting your frustration sour your emotional tone.
- Invite the respondent to ask questions and express another perspective.

3. Manage the agenda carefully.

- Approach multiple problems incrementally – proceeding from simple to complex, easy to hard, concrete to abstract.
- Conversely, don't become fixated on one issue. If you reach an impasse, expand the discussion to increase the likelihood of an integrative outcome.

Solution generation

4. Make a request.

- Focus on those things you have in common (principles, goals, constraints) as the basis for recommending preferred alternatives.

The second party: the respondent or 'accused'

Problem identification

1. Establish a climate for joint problem solving.

- Show genuine concern and interest; respond empathetically, even if you disagree with the complaint.
- Respond appropriately to the initiator's emotions; if necessary, allow the person to 'let off steam' before addressing the complaint.

2. Seek additional information about the problem.

- Ask questions that channel the initiator's statements from general to specific and from evaluative to descriptive.

3. Agree with some aspect of the complaint.

- Signal your willingness to consider making changes by agreeing with facts, perceptions, feelings or principles.

Solution generation

4. Ask for recommendations.

- To avoid debating the merits of a single suggestion, brainstorm multiple alternatives.

The mediator

Problem identification

1. Acknowledge that a conflict exists.
   - Select the most appropriate setting (one-to-one conference vs group meeting) for coaching and fact-finding.
   - Propose a problem-solving approach for resolving the dispute.

2. Maintain a neutral posture.
   - Assume the role of facilitator, not judge. Do not belittle the problem or berate the disputants for their inability to resolve their differences.
   - Be impartial towards the disputants and the issues (as long as policy has not been violated). If correction is necessary, do it in private.

3. Manage the discussion to ensure fairness.
   - Focus discussion on the conflict impact on performance and the detrimental effect of a continued conflict.
   - Keep the discussion issue-oriented, not personality-oriented.
   - Do not allow one party to dominate the discussion; ask directed questions to maintain a balance.

Solution generation

4. Explore options by focusing on the interests behind stated positions.
   - Explore the 'whys' behind disputants' arguments/claims.
   - Help disputants see commonalities among their goals, values and principles.
   - Use commonalities to generate multiple alternatives.
   - Maintain a non-judgemental manner.

Action plan and follow-up for all roles

1. Ensure that all parties support the agreed plan.
   - Verify understanding of, and commitment to, specific actions.

2. Establish a mechanism for follow-up.
   - Create benchmarks for measuring progress and ensuring accountability.
   - Encourage flexibility in adjusting the plan to meet emerging circumstances.

Skill Analysis

CASE STUDY **6.1**

HEALTH PROVISIONS LIMITED

Health Provisions Limited (HPL) provided one of the first private health-care schemes to the British market. The founders had all worked in the National Health

Service in some capacity and retained a conservative philosophy to the business, putting patient care very high on their list of priorities. Their main business was providing employee cover for blue-chip companies, and they kept out of the more competitive direct-consumer-marketing approach of the growing number of rivals. Until very recently they felt secure and in a good position to handle further changes in the economic and political environment.

Carolyn Richardson was one of the founders of HPL and is highly respected in the profession. The other partners, comfortable with Carolyn's conservative, yet flexible nature, elected her to the position of the first managing director. After that, Carolyn became known as 'the great equaliser'. She worked hard to make sure that all the partners were included in decisions and that strong relations were maintained. Her management philosophy was built on the concept of trust and loyalty – loyalty to the organisation, loyalty to its members, loyalty to friends and, most of all, loyalty to the clients.

As the total market grew, various overseas-funded health-care groups began to encroach on HPL's client base and its growth increasingly failed to keep pace with those of its rivals. As a result, Carolyn has reluctantly begun to consider the merits of more aggressive promotion and moving into direct selling.

One evening Carolyn talked about her concern with her bridge partner and life-long friend, Susan Ross, who owned a private hospital developed in conjunction with HPL. Everyone respected Susan for her knowledge, work rate and uncanny ability to predict trends. Susan knew what to do and when to do it, and her present preoccupation was modifying her hospital group for long-term mental-health patients.

When Susan heard Carolyn's concerns and need for an aggressive approach, she suggested to her friend that what HPL needed was some fresh blood, someone who could infuse enthusiasm into the organisation. She suggested a friend, Mark Western, who had worked in health-care in Canada and 'was good at sorting things out – if a bit abrasive'.

Carolyn suggested the idea of employing Mark at the next staff meeting, but it was met with caution and scepticism. 'Yes, he's had a brilliant career on paper,' said one senior partner, 'but he's never stayed in one place long enough to really finish what he has started. Look at his CV. During the past seven years, he's been with four different organisations.'

'That's true,' said Carolyn, 'but his references are really good. In fact, he's been described as a rising star, aggressive and productive. He's just what we need to help us explore new opportunities.' Throughout the discussion, Carolyn defended Mark's record and pointed to his impressive performance. She deflected concerns about his reputation by saying that he had been recommended by a loyal and trusted friend. Eventually, the other partners agreed, albeit reluctantly, to recruit Mark. When Carolyn offered Mark the job, he was promised the freedom to work out his own ideas.

Mark worked hard, regaining corporate clients and developing telephone-selling techniques for smaller companies and individuals. He set HLP on the road to recovery and was liked by many of the junior staff as a breath of fresh air. He was open to new ideas and was exciting to work with. His abrasive manner

Management Consultancy and Skills

confused and annoyed the other partners who thought Mark was attempting to move things too quickly. It was not uncommon for sharp disagreements to erupt in staff meetings but Carolyn tried to smooth ruffled feathers and maintain a productive atmosphere.

Mark seemed oblivious to all the turmoil he was causing. He was optimistic about potential growth opportunities. His main idea was similar to Susan Ross's – he thought that the group should go into long-term care of the mentally ill. The generous government grants now available should be used. His attitude was that – 'If we don't, the others will steal a march on us and we will be stuck doing what we do now for ever with smaller and smaller margins.'

Months passed and dissension among the managers grew. Mark's frustration over the lack of support among the senior partners began to undermine the day-to-day operations of HPL. He began to criticise his detractors in discussions with younger HPL employees. In addition, he moved staff away from the core business into his own, and as yet unproven, scheme.

Amid a rapidly spreading undercurrent of tension, one of the founding partners, Neville Watson, approached Carolyn one day: 'Carolyn, I speak for most of the senior staff when I say we are very troubled by Mark's approach. We've expressed ourselves well enough for Mark to understand, but his actions defy everything we've said. He's a catastrophe just waiting to happen.'

'You are right, Neville,' replied Carolyn. 'I'm troubled, too. We have an opportunity to attract new business with some of Mark's new ideas. And the younger staff love working on his projects. But he has stirred up a lot of turmoil'.

Neville agreed. 'The real issue is that HPL is no longer presenting a unified image. Mark is wilfully defying the stated objectives of our organisation. And some of our oldest clients don't like that. There is real concern for the sort of patients Mark's ideas will produce. They just won't mix with our existing people.'

'That's true, Neville. However, some of the clients think he is a breath of fresh air, and he does have a reputation for being right.'

'Come on, Carolyn. You and I both know that we must not risk our reputation and our core business in this way. Mark must be made to understand that or go. I'm sorry, I don't like speaking this way but the other partners agree.'

Carolyn realised that she faced the most difficult challenge of her career. She felt a strong personal investment in helping Mark to succeed, having personally recruited him and been his ally in the early days. Carolyn was also haunted by her promise to Mark that he would have the freedom and flexibility to perform as he pleased. However, this flexibility had clearly caused problems.

Reluctantly, Carolyn called Mark in for a meeting, hoping to find some basis for compromise.

Carolyn: I gather you know the kinds of concerns the senior partners have expressed regarding your approach.

Mark: I suppose you've talked with Neville. Well, we did have a small disagreement earlier this week.

Carolyn: The way Neville tells it, you're moving staff about without any form of discussion and the core business is suffering – he has tried to discuss it with you and you simply ignored him and went ahead. He is a senior partner and he calls it dangerous insubordination.

Mark: Well, it's just like Watson to see progressive change as an attempt to take away his power.

Carolyn: It's not quite that simple, Mark. When we founded HPL, we all agreed that a conservative stance was best. And right now, with the economic indicators looking soft, many experts agree that it may still be the best alternative.

Mark: Carolyn, what are you going to rely on – predictions or performance? Old views need to be challenged and ultimately discarded. How else are we going to progress and keep up with our competitors?

Carolyn: I agree we need to change, Mark, but gradually. Your ideas are good, but you have to have patience. You also have to take the people that matter with you. It's the way you try and do things. You make people defensive.

Mark: You're telling me. And at this rate, it doesn't make much difference which direction we're heading.

Carolyn: Come on, Mark, you are making things very difficult for yourself and me. They do have a point in saying that the presence of long-term mental patients will antagonise our existing clients. The sums sound fine, but you have to convince everyone – work with them and not against them – you could be wrong. The way ahead is likely to be a compromise and, the way we are going now, compromise seems a million miles off.

Mark's emotions betray his impatience with the pace of the organisation and he becomes agitated.

Mark: I've admired your enthusiasm and I value your advice but I honestly think you're kidding yourself. You seem to think you can get things done without ruffling a few feathers. Are you interested in appearance or substance? If you want appearance, then hire a good PR person. If you want substance, then back me up.

Carolyn: Mark, it simply isn't that easy. I'm not HPL, I'm simply its caretaker. You know we make decisions around here by consensus; that's the backbone of this organisation. To move ahead, the confidence of the others has to be won, especially that of the partners. Frankly your attitude is one of the main problems.

Mark: You promised me flexibility and autonomy. I'm not getting that any more, Carolyn. All I'm getting is grief.

Carolyn: That may be true. But your whole approach . . .

Mark: Oh, yes, I thought you would get onto that. The sports car, the bachelor lifestyle, the messy office. But, again, that's appearance, Carolyn, not substance. Performance is what counts. That's what got me this far. You know I could walk out of here and sell my ideas to any other group – and for more money.

Carolyn: Wow, slow down.

Mark: Do you honestly believe this can be salvaged? I don't think so. Maybe it's time for me to move on. Isn't that why you called me in here anyway?

Carolyn, feeling uncomfortable, breaks eye contact and shifts her gaze to the London skyline. After a long pause, she continues, still gazing out of the window.

Management Consultancy and Skills

Carolyn: I don't know, Mark. I feel I've failed. My grand experiment in change has polarised the office; we've a war out there. On one hand, you really have done a good job here. HPL will no doubt lose a good part of its customer base if you leave. You have created a good atmosphere in your department – with customers and staff. If you go we will lose all that, and the chance to change.

Mark: It's just like you Carolyn to take this problem personally. You take everything personally. Even when I beat you at squash. Your heart's in the right place but you just can't ever seem to go for the jugular. You know and I know that HPL needs change. But it doesn't appear to be ready for it yet. And I'm certainly not willing to move slowly.

Carolyn: Yes. Perhaps. It's just hard to give up . . . [long pause]. OK, forget it.

Mark: Fine.

Discussion questions

1. What are the sources of conflict in this case?

2. What approaches to conflict management are used by the people in this situation? How effective was each approach?

3. Based on the behavioural guidelines for the collaborative approach, how could Carolyn have managed this conflict more effectively?

Skill Practice

Not all conflicts are alike, therefore they should not all be managed in exactly the same way. Effective managers are not only able to assess the true cause(s) of conflict, but they are also able to match the type of conflict with the appropriate management strategy. For each of the following brief scenarios, select the most appropriate conflict-management strategy. Refer to Table 6.4 (page 350) to help you to match situational factors with the strategies:

- Forcing
- Accommodating
- Compromising
- Collaborating
- Avoiding.

EXERCISE **6.1**

ARGYLL STEAKHOUSE

You have decided to take your family out to the local steak house, Argyll Steakhouse, for dinner to celebrate your son's birthday. You are a single parent, so getting home from work in time to prepare a nice dinner is very difficult. On entering the restaurant, you ask the waiter to seat you in the non-smoking section because your daughter, Sheila, is allergic to tobacco smoke. On your way to your seat, you notice that the restaurant seems crowded for a Monday night.

After you and your children are seated and have placed your orders, your conversation turns to the family plans for the approaching Christmas holidays. Suddenly you notice that your daughter is sneezing and her eyes are beginning to water. You look around and see a lively group of businessmen seated at the table behind you, all of whom are smoking. Your impression is that they are celebrating a special occasion. Looking back at Sheila, you realise that something has got to be done quickly. You ask your son to take Sheila outside while you go and find the waiter.

Selection

1. The salient situational factors are:_____

2. The most appropriate conflict-management strategy is:_____

Please refer to the scoring key in Appendix 1 for an example of how this particular scenario could be tabled.

EXERCISE **6.2**

AVOCADO COMPUTERS

Your name is Bran Greenway. When the head of Avocado Computers ran into production problems with its new automated production line, you were lured from Western Computers – a competitor. It meant a significant increase in pay and the opportunity to manage a state-of-the-art production plant. What's more, there were very few other female production managers in the region. You've been in the post for a year, and it's been exciting to see your staff start working together as a team to solve problems, improve quality and finally get the plant up to capacity. In general, Robert, the owner, has also been a plus. He is energetic, fair and a proven industry leader. You feel fortunate to be in a coveted position, in a 'star' firm, in a growth industry.

However, there is one distraction that annoys you. Robert has an obsession with cleanliness, order and appearance. He wants all the robots painted the same colour, the components within the computer laid out perfectly on a grid, the workers wearing clean overalls and the floor 'clean enough to eat off'. You are worried by this compulsion. 'It might impress potential clients when they tour the production facility, but is it all that important? After all, who's ever going to look at the inside of their computer? Why should customers care about the colour of the robot that built their computers? And who, for heaven's sake, would ever want to have a picnic in a factory?'

Today is your first yearly performance appraisal interview with Robert. In preparation for the meeting, he has sent you a memo outlining 'Areas of strength' and 'Areas of concern'. You look with pride at the number of items listed in the first column. It's obvious that Robert likes your work. But you are a bit annoyed at the single item of concern: 'Needs to maintain a cleaner facility, including employee appearance'. You mull this 'demerit' over in your mind, wrestling with how to respond in your interview.

Selection

1. The salient situational factors are: _____
2. The most appropriate conflict-management strategy is: _____

EXERCISE **6.3**

PHELAN LTD

You are Philip Jameson, the head of sales for an office products firm, Phelan Ltd. Your sales personnel sell primarily to small businesses in Scotland. Phelan's performance is about average for this rapidly growing market. The firms new president, James Owen, is putting a lot of pressure on you to increase sales. You feel that a major obstacle is the firm's policy on extending credit. Celia, the head of the credit office, insists that all new customers fill out an extensive credit application. Credit risks must be low; credit terms and collection procedures are tough. You can appreciate her point of view, but you feel it is unrealistic. Your competitors already are much more lenient in their credit examinations, they extend credit to higher risks, their credit terms are more favourable, and they are less aggressive in collecting overdue payments. Your sales personnel frequently complain that they aren't playing on a 'level playing field' with their competitors. When you brought this concern to James, he said he wanted you and Celia to work things out. His instructions didn't give many clues to his priorities on this matter. You realise the need to increase sales, but the small business failure rate is alarming, so you want to be careful that you don't make bad credit decisions.

You decide it's time to have a serious discussion with Cclia. A lot is at stake.

Selection

1. The salient situational factors are: _____
2. The most appropriate conflict-management strategy is: _____

Management Consultancy and Skills

Exercises in resolving interpersonal disputes

The heart of conflict – management is resolving intense, emotionally charged confrontations. We have extensively discussed guidelines for utilising the collaborative (problem-solving) approach to conflict management in these situations. Assuming that the collaborative approach is appropriate for a particular situation, an initiator, a respondent or a mediator can use the general guidelines.

The following three situations involve interpersonal conflict and disagreement. The instructions at the beginning of each exercise will explain the situation. The wording of the assignment refers to work in large or medium-sized groups.

EXERCISE **6.4**

WHERE'S MY SPEECH?

- Divide the main group into subgroups of three.
- Choose two members who will take the roles of Janet as the initiator and Sarah as the respondent – making sure that each does not read the other's brief. The third member of the group acts initially as an observer working the Observer's Feedback Form to be found in Appendix 1.
- Run the role play for not more than 15 minutes and at the end allow the observer to give feedback for a similar time.

If the role play has not reached a satisfactory resolution:

- Continue the role play from the point previously reached, using the observer as mediator.
- Discuss what has happened using the Observer's Feedback Form.
- Discuss where in Beacon Lights organisation a mediator might be found and the consequences of failing to find one in time.
- Present to the whole group: (1) What went well in your role plays. (2) What went badly. (3) The key learning points for you.

Brief for Janet, director of personnel, Beacon Lights

You have been director of personnel for Beacon Lights for 10 years. Just when you thought you had everything under control, disaster struck. You have just heard that a former employee is suing the company for unfair dismissal, the sales director was forced to resign last month because of the company's poor performance, and your secretary just died of a heart attack.

You have been asked to give a speech at a seminar on a new productivity programme your company has pioneered, and you are looking forward to getting away from the office for a few days to catch your breath. You dictated your speech to your new secretary, Sarah, a couple of days ago so that she would have plenty of time to get it typed and reproduced.

This morning you have come into the office to proof-read and rehearse your speech before catching the midday train, and you are shocked to find a sick note from your secretary. You rush over to her desk and frantically begin searching for your speech notes. You find them mixed up with some material for the quarterly report that should have been completed two weeks ago, a stack of overdue correspondence and two days' unopened post. As you dial your secretary's home phone number, you realise that you are perspiring heavily and your face is flushed. This is the biggest disaster you can remember happening in years.

Brief for Sarah, secretary

You hear the phone ring, and it is all you can do to get out of bed and limp into the kitchen to answer it. You feel dreadful. Last night, you slipped on your son's skateboard in the drive and sprained your knee. You can hardly move today and the pain is excruciating. You are also reluctant to answer the phone because you know it is probably your boss, Janet, who will be moaning about your work rate. You realise you deserve some of the blame, but it isn't all your fault. Since you began working for Janet a month ago, you have asked several times for a thorough job description. You find you don't really understand either Janet's priorities or your specific responsibilities. You are replacing a woman who died suddenly after working for Janet for 10 years. You have found working with Janet extremely frustrating. She has been too busy to train you properly and she assumes that you know as much about the job as your predecessor. This is particularly a problem since you haven't worked as a secretary for three years and you feel that your skills are a bit rusty.

Janet's speech is a good example of the difficulties you have experienced. She gave you the notes a couple of days ago and said it was urgent, but that was on top of a quarterly report that was already overdue, a backlog of correspondence, filing and more. You have never compiled a report like this before, and every time you asked Janet a question she said she'd discuss it with you later and promptly ran off to another meeting. When you requested that you be given additional help to catch up on the overdue work, Janet said the company couldn't afford it because of poor sales. This annoyed you because you know you are being paid far less than your predecessor. You knew Janet faced some urgent deadlines, so you had planned to return to the office last night to type her speech and try to complete the report, but two hours in the waiting room at the hospital put an end to that plan. You tried calling Janet to explain the problem only to find out that her home number is ex-directory.

You sit down, prop up your leg and wince with pain as you pick up the phone.

EXERCISE **6.5**

CAN HARRY FIT IN?

- Divide the main group into subgroups of three.
- Choose two members who will take the roles of Harry as the initiator and Margaret as the respondent – making sure that each does not read the other's

brief. The third member of the group acts initially as an observer working the Observer's Feedback Form to be found in Appendix 1.

- Run the role play for not more than 15 minutes and then allow the observer to give feedback for a similar time.

If the role play has not reached a satisfactory resolution:

- Continue the role play from the point previously reached, using the observer as mediator.
- Discuss what has happened using the Observer's Feedback Form.
- Discuss where in the auditing team a mediator could be found and the consequences of not finding such a person.
- Present to the whole group: (1) What went well in your role plays. (2) What went badly. (3) The key learning points for you.

Brief for Margaret, office manager

You are the manager of an auditing team sent to Bangkok, Thailand, to represent a major international accounting firm with headquarters in Zurich, Switzerland. You and Harry, one of your auditors, were sent to Bangkok. Harry is seven years older than you and has been with the firm five years longer. Your relationship has become strained since you were recently appointed office manager. You feel you were given the post because you have established an excellent working relationship with the Thai staff as well as a broad range of international clients. But Harry has told other members of the staff that your promotion simply reflects the firm's heavy emphasis on 'Yes' people. He has tried to isolate you from the all-male accounting staff by focusing discussions on to sports, local night-spots, etc.

You are sitting in your office reading some complicated new reporting procedures which have just arrived from head office. Your concentration is suddenly interrupted by a loud knock on your door. Without waiting for an invitation to enter, Harry bursts into your office. He is obviously very upset, and you already know why he is in such a nasty mood. You recently posted the audit assignments for next month, and you scheduled Harry for a job you knew he wouldn't like. Harry is one of your senior auditors and the company norm is that choice assignments go with seniority. This particular job will require him to spend two weeks away from Bangkok in a remote town, working with a company with notoriously messy records.

Unfortunately, you have had to assign several of these less desirable audits to Harry recently because you are short of personnel. But that's not the only reason. You have received a number of complaints from the junior staff (all Thais) that Harry treats them in a condescending manner. They feel he is always looking for an opportunity to boss them around, as if he were their supervisor instead of an experienced, supportive mentor. As a result, your whole operation works more smoothly when you can send Harry out of town on a solo project for several days. It keeps him from coming into your office and telling you how to do your job, and the morale of the rest of the auditing staff is significantly higher. Harry slams the door and proceeds to express his anger over this assignment.

Brief for Harry, senior auditor

You are really fed up! Margaret is deliberately trying to undermine your status in the office. She knows that the company tradition is that senior auditors get the better jobs. And this isn't the first time this has happened. Since her promotion she has tried to keep you out of the office as much as possible. It's as if she doesn't want her rival for leadership of the office around. When you were asked to go to Bangkok, you assumed that you would be made the office manager because of your seniority in the firm. You are certain that the decision to pick Margaret is yet another indication of positive discrimination against white males.

In staff meetings, Margaret has talked about the need to be sensitive to the feelings of the office staff as well as the clients in this multi-cultural setting. She's got a nerve to be preaching about sensitivity! 'What about my feelings, for heaven's sake?' you wonder. This is nothing more than a straightforward power play. She is probably feeling insecure about being the only female accountant in the office and being promoted over someone with more experience. 'Sending me out of town,' you decide, 'is a clear case of out of sight, out of mind.'

Well, it's not going to happen that easily. You are not going to roll over and let her treat you unfairly. It's time for a showdown. If she doesn't agree to change this assignment and apologise for the way she's been treating you, you're going to register a formal complaint with her boss in Zurich. You are prepared to submit your resignation if the situation doesn't improve.

EXERCISE **6.6**

MEETING AT HARTFORD MANUFACTURING CO.

- Divide into subgroups of five.
- Choose one observer and four people to play the main characters – Peter Smith, Richard Hootten, Barbara Price and Christopher Jones. The person playing the role of Peter Smith, and nobody else, should read the letters shown as Exhibits 6.1, 6.2 and 6.3 – although he may choose to share them during the meeting. No characters should read other people's roles.
- The observer should watch the meeting using the Observer's Feedback Form found in Appendix 1.
- Run the role play for not more than 30 minutes and allow the observer to give feedback using the Observer's Feedback Form for a similar time.

If the role play has not reached a satisfactory resolution:

- Continue the role play from the point previously reached, using the observer as mediator.
- Discuss what has happened and present to the whole group: (1) What went well. (2) What went badly. (3) Key learning points.

T.J. WRIGHT
Chartered Accountants
Chorley Road
Birmingham

10 February 1999
Mr Peter Smith
Managing Director
Hartford Manufacturing Company
Chorley Industrial Estate
Birmingham

Dear Mr Smith

As you requested last month, we have now completed our audit of Hartford Manufacturing Company. We find accounting procedures and fiscal control to be very satisfactory. A more detailed report of these matters is attached. However, we did discover during our perusal of company records that the production department has consistently incurred cost overruns during the past two quarters. Cost per unit of production is approximately 5 per cent over budget. While this is not a serious problem given the financial solvency of your company, we thought it wise to bring it to your attention.

Yours sincerely

Trevor J Wright

Exhibit 6.1

The company

Hartford Manufacturing Company is the largest subsidiary of Riding Industries. Since its formation in 1918, Hartford Manufacturing has become an industrial leader in the UK. Its sales currently average approximately £25 million a year, with an annual growth of approximately six per cent. There are over 850 employees in production, sales and marketing, accounting, engineering and management.

Peter Smith has been managing director for two years and is well respected by his subordinates. He has the reputation of being firm but fair. Peter's training in college was in engineering, so he is technically minded, and he frequently likes to walk around the production area to see for himself how things are going. He has also been known to roll up his sleeves and help work on a problem on the shop floor. He is not opposed to rubbing shoulders with even the lowest-level employees. On the other hand, he tries to run a tight company. He holds high expectations for performance, especially from those in managerial positions.

Richard Hooton is the director of production at Hartford Manufacturing. He has been with the company since he was 19. He has worked himself up through the ranks and now at the age of 54 he is the oldest manager. Hooton has his own ideas of how things should be run in production and he is reluctant to tolerate any intervention from anyone, even Peter Smith. Because he has been with the company so

BAILDON INDUSTRIES
New Hall Way
Bradford
West Yorkshire

Mr Peter Smith   8 February 1999
Managing Director
Hartford Manufacturing Company
Chorley Industrial Estate
Birmingham

Dear Mr Smith

We have been purchasing your products since 1975 and we have been very satisfied with our
relations with your sales personnel.

Unfortunately this is no longer the case. Your sales representative for the Bradford area, Sam
Sneddon, has looked like and smelled like he was under the influence of alcohol on the last
three occasions he has appeared on our premises. Not only that, but our last order was
mistakenly recorded, so we received the wrong quantity of products.

I'm sure you don't make it a practice to put your company's reputation in the hands of someone
like Sam Sneddon, so I suggest you get someone else to cover this area. We cannot tolerate,
and I am sure that other companies in the Bradford area cannot tolerate, this kind of relationship
to continue. While we judge your products to be excellent, we will be forced to find other sources
if some action is not taken.

Yours sincerely

David Stokoe
Purchasing Manager

Exhibit 6.2

long, he feels he knows it better than anyone else, and he believes he has had a
hand in making it the success that it is. His main goal is to keep production running smoothly and efficiently.

Barbara Price is the director of sales and marketing. She joined the company
about 18 months ago after completing her MBA at Keele. She previously held the
position of assistant manager of marketing at Riding Industries. Price is a very conscientious employee and is anxious to make a name for herself. Her major objective, which she has never hesitated to make public, is to be a general manager one
day. Sales at Hartford Manufacturing have increased in the past year to near-record
levels under her guidance.

Christopher Jones is the regional sales manager for the Yorkshire region. He
reports directly to Barbara Price. The Yorkshire region represents the largest market
for Hartford Manufacturing, and Jones is considered to be the most competent
salesperson in the company. He has built personal relationships with several major
clients in his region, and it appears that some sales occur as much because of
Christopher Jones as because of the products of Hartford Manufacturing. Jones has
been with the company 12 years, all of them in sales.

Management Consultancy and Skills

HARTFORD MANUFACTURING COMPANY
CHORLEY INDUSTRIAL ESTATE
BIRMINGHAM
A subsidiary of Riding Industries

Memorandum
TO: Peter Smith, Managing Director
FROM: Barbara Price, Sales and Marketing Director
DATE: 11 February 1999

Mr Smith:

In response to your concerns, we have instituted several incentive programmes among our sales force to increase sales during these traditionally slow months. We have set up competition among regions with the sales people in the top region being recognised in the company newsletter and presented with engraved plaques. We have introduced a 'holiday in America' award for the top salesperson in the company and we have instituted cash bonuses for any salesperson who gets a new customer order. However, these incentives have now been operating for a month and sales haven't increased at all. In fact, in two regions they have decreased by an average of 5 per cent.

What do you suggest now? We have promised that these incentives will continue to run for the rest of this quarter, but they seem to be doing no good. Not only that, but we cannot afford to provide the incentives within our current budget, and unless sales increase, we will be in the red. **Regretfully, I recommend dropping the programme.**

Exhibit 6.3

This is Friday afternoon and tomorrow Peter Smith leaves for Copenhagen to attend an important meeting with potential overseas investors. He will be gone for two weeks. Before he leaves, there are several items in his in-tray that must receive attention. He calls a meeting with Richard Hooton and Barbara Price in his office. Just before the meeting begins, Christopher Jones calls and asks if he may join the meeting for a few minutes since he is at head office and has something important to discuss. It involves both Peter Smith and Richard Hooton. Smith gives permission for him to join the meeting as there may not be another chance to meet Jones before the trip. The meeting convenes with Smith, Hooton, Price and Jones all in the room.

Brief for Peter Smith, managing director

Three letters arrived today and you judge them to be sufficiently important to require your attention before you leave on your trip (see Exhibits 6.1, 6.2, and 6.3). Each letter represents a problem that requires immediate action, and you need commitments from key staff members to resolve these problems. You are concerned about this meeting, because these individuals don't work as well together as you'd like.

For example, Richard Hooton tends to be very difficult to pin down. He always seems suspicious of the motives of others and has a reputation for not making tough decisions. You sometimes wonder how a person could become the head of production in a major manufacturing firm by avoiding controversial issues and blaming others for the results.

In contrast, Barbara Price is very straightforward. You always know exactly where she stands. The problem is that sometimes she doesn't take enough time to study a problem before making a decision. She tends to be impulsive and anxious to make a decision, whether it's the right one or not. Her general approach to resolving disagreements between departments is to seek expedient compromises. You are particularly disturbed by her approach to the sales-incentive problem. You felt strongly that something needed to be done to increase sales during the winter months. You reluctantly agreed to the incentive programme because you didn't want to dampen her initiative. But you aren't convinced this is the right answer, because frankly, you're not sure what the real problem is, yet!

Christopher Jones is an aggressive sales manager. He is hard driving and sometimes ruffles the feathers of other members of staff with his uncompromising 'black-and-white' style. He is also fiercely loyal to his sales staff, so you're certain that he'll take the complaint about Sam Sneddon personally.

In contrast to the styles of your colleagues, you have tried to utilise an integrative approach to problem solving, focusing on the facts, treating everyone's input equally, and keeping conversations about controversial topics problem-focused. One of your goals since taking over this position two years ago is to foster a team approach within your staff.

(*Note: For more information about how you might approach the issues raised by Exhibits 6.1, 6.2 and 6.3 in your staff meeting, review the collaborating approach in Table 6.2 as well as the mediator's behavioural guidelines at the end of the Skill Learning section.*)

Brief to Richard Hooton, director of production

The backbone of Hartford Manufacturing is production. You have watched the company grow from a small, struggling factory to a thriving business, built on outstanding production processes. Your own reputation among those who know manufacturing is a good one, and you are confident that you have been a major factor in the success of Hartford Manufacturing. You have turned down several job offers over the years because you feel loyal to the company, but sometimes the younger employees don't seem to afford you the respect that you think you deserve.

The only time you have major problems in production is when the young know-it-alls fresh from college have come in and tried to change things. With their scientific management concepts and fuzzy-headed human relations training, they have more often made a mess of things. The best production methods have been practised for years in the company, and you have yet to see anyone who could improve on your system.

On the other hand, you have respect for Peter Smith as the managing director. He has lots of experience and the right kind of training, and he is also involved in the production side of the organisation. He has often given you good advice but he usually lets you do what you feel is best and he rarely dictates specific methods for doing things.

Your general approach to problems is to avoid controversy. You feel uncomfortable when production is made the scapegoat for problems in the company. Just because this is a manufacturing business, it seems as if everyone tries to pin the blame for problems on the production department. You've felt for years that the firm was getting away from what it does best – mass-producing a few standard products. Instead, the trend has been for marketing and sales to push for more and more products, shorter lead times, and greater customisation capability. These actions have increased costs and caused incredible production delays as well as higher reject rates.

(*Note*: *During the impending meeting, you should adopt the avoidance approach shown in Table 6.2. Defend your territory, place blame on others, defer taking a stand and avoid taking responsibility for making a controversial decision.*)

Brief for Barbara Price, director of sales and marketing

You are anxious to impress Peter Smith because you have your eye on a position in the parent company, Riding Industries, that is opening up at the end of the year. It would mean a promotion for you. A positive recommendation from Peter Smith would carry a lot of weight in the selection process. Given that both Hartford Manufacturing and Riding Industries are largely male dominated, you are pleased with your career progress so far, and you are hoping to keep it up.

One current concern is the suggestion of Peter Smith some time ago that you look into the problem of slow sales during the winter months. You implemented an incentive plan that was highly recommended by an industry analyst at a recent trade conference. It consists of three separate incentive programmes:

1. Competition among regions in which the salesperson in the top region would have his or her picture in the company newsletter and receive engraved plaques.
2. A holiday in America for the top salesperson in the company.
3. Cash bonuses for salespeople who obtained new customer orders.

The trouble is, these incentives haven't worked. Not only have sales not increased for the company as a whole, but two of the regions are down by an average of 5 per cent. You have told the salesforce that the incentives will continue in this quarter, but if sales don't improve your budget will be in the red. There is no budget for the prizes, since you expected the increased sales to more than offset the cost of the incentives. Obviously this was a bad idea that is not working, and it should be dropped immediately. You are a bit embarrassed about this aborted project. But it is better to cut your losses and try something else rather than support an obvious loser.

In general, you are very confident and self-assured. You feel that the best way to get work done is through negotiation and compromise. What's important is making a decision quickly and efficiently. Maybe everyone doesn't get exactly what they want, but at least they can get on with their work. There are no absolutes in this business, but you feel that the management process is being bogged down with 'paralysis by analysis'. You are impatient over delays caused by intensive studies and investigations of detail. You agree with Peter Smith: action is the hallmark of successful managers.

(Note: During this meeting, use the compromise approach shown in Table 6.2. Do whatever is necessary to help the group make a quick decision to enable you to get on with the pressing demands of your work.)

Brief for Christopher Jones, regional sales manager

You don't go to company headquarters very often because your customer contacts take up most of your time. You regularly work 50 to 60 hours a week and you are proud of the job you do. You also feel a special obligation to your customers to provide them with the best product available in the most timely fashion. This sense of obligation comes not only from your commitment to the company but also from your personal relationships with many of the customers.

Recently, you have been receiving more and more complaints about late deliveries. The time lag between ordering and delivery is increasing, and some customers have been greatly inconvenienced by the delays. You have sent a formal enquiry to production to find out what the problem is. They replied that they are producing as efficiently as possible and they see nothing wrong with past practices. The assistant to Richard Hooton even suggested that this was just another example of the salesforce's unrealistic expectations.

Not only will sales be negatively affected if these delays continue, but your reputation with your customers will be damaged. You have promised them that the problem will be quickly solved and that products will begin arriving on time. Since Richard Hooton is such a rigid person, however, you are almost certain that it will do no good to talk to him. His subordinate probably got his negative attitude from Hooton.

In general, Hooton is a 1960s production worker who is being pulled by the rest of the firm into the new age of the 1990s. Competition is different, technology is different and management is different. You need shorter lead times, a wider range of products and the capacity to do some customised work. Admittedly, this makes production's work harder, but other firms are providing these services with the use of just-in-time management processes, robots, etc. But Hooton is reluctant to change.

Instead of getting down to the real problems, head office, in their typical high-handed fashion, announced an incentives plan. This implies that the problem is in the field, not the factory. It made some of your people angry to think they were being pressed to increase their efforts when they weren't receiving the back-up support they required. They liked the prizes, but the way the plan was presented made them feel as if they weren't working hard enough. This isn't the first time you have questioned the judgement of Barbara, your boss. She certainly is intelligent and hard-working, but she doesn't seem very interested in what's going on out in the field. Furthermore, she doesn't seem very receptive to 'bad news' about sales and customer complaints.

(Note: During this meeting, use the forcing approach to conflict management and negotiations shown in Table 6.2. However, don't overplay your part – you are the senior regional sales manager and if Barbara continues to move up quickly in the organisation, you may be in line for her position.)

Management Consultancy and Skills

Skill Application

Assignment 1

Select a specific conflict with which you are very familiar. Using the framework for identifying the sources of a conflict, discussed in this book, analyse this situation carefully. It might be useful to compare your perceptions of the situation with those of informed observers. What type of conflict is this? Why did it occur? Why is it continuing? Next, using the guidelines for selecting an appropriate conflict-management strategy, identify the general approach that would be most appropriate for this situation. Consider both the personal preferences of the parties involved and the relevant situational factors. Is this the approach that the parties have been using? If not, attempt to introduce a different perspective into the relationship and explain why you feel it would be more productive. If the parties have been using this approach, discuss with them why it has not been successful thus far. Share information on specific behavioural guidelines (or negotiation tactics) that might increase the effectiveness of their efforts.

Assignment 2

Identify a situation where another individual is doing something that needs to be corrected. Using the respondent's guidelines for collaborative problem solving, construct a plan for discussing your concerns with this person. Include specific language designed to assertively state your case without causing a defensive reaction. Role play this interaction with a friend and incorporate any suggestions for improvement. Make your presentation to the individual and report on your results. What was the reaction? Were you successful in balancing assertiveness with support and responsibility? Based on this experience, identify other situations that you feel need to be changed and follow a similar procedure.

Assignment 3

Act as a mediator between two individuals or groups. Using the guidelines for implementing the collaborative approach to mediation, outline a plan of action prior to your intervention. Consider whether initial private meetings are appropriate. Report on the situation and your plan. How did you feel? What specific actions worked well? What was the outcome? What should you have done differently? Based on this experience, revise your plan for use in related situations.

Assignment 4

Identify a difficult situation involving negotiations. This might involve transactions at work, at home or in the community. Review the guidelines for integrative bargaining and identify the specific tactics you plan to use. Write down specific questions and responses to likely initiatives from the other party. In particular, anticipate how you might handle the possibility of the other party's utilising a distributive negotiation strategy. Schedule a negotiation meeting with the party involved and implement your plan. Following the session, debrief the experience with a co-worker or friend. What did you learn? How successful were you? What would you do differently? Based on this experience, modify your plan and prepare to implement it in related situations.

ACTIVITY **6.2**

APPLICATION PLAN AND EVALUATION

The objective of this exercise is to help you apply your skills in a real-life setting. Now that you have become familiar with the behavioural guidelines that form the basis of effective skill performance, you will improve the most by trying out those guidelines in an everyday context. The trouble is, unlike a classroom activity in which feedback is immediate and others can assist you with their evaluations, this skill application activity is one you must accomplish and evaluate on your own. There are two parts to this activity. Part 1 helps to prepare you to apply the skill. Part 2 helps you to evaluate and improve on your experience. Be sure to actually write down answers to each item. Don't short-circuit the process by skipping steps.

Part 1: Plan

1. Write down the two or three aspects of this skill that are most important to you. These may be areas of weakness, areas you most want to improve or areas that are most salient to a problem you face currently. Identify the specific aspects of this skill that you want to apply.

2. Now identify the setting or situation in which you will apply this skill. Establish a plan for performance by actually writing down the situation. Who else will be involved? When will you do it? Where will it be done?

3. What specific behaviours will you engage in to apply this skill? Practise them.

4. What are the indicators of successful performance? How will you know you have succeeded in being effective? What will indicate that you have performed competently?

Part 2: Evaluation

5. After you have completed your implementation, record the results. What happened? How successful were you? What was the effect on others?

6. How can you improve? What modifications can you make next time? What will you do differently in a similar situation in the future?

7. Looking back on your whole skill practice and application experience, what have you learned? What has been surprising? In what ways might this experience help you in the long term?

Further reading

Arnold, J.D. (1993) *When the sparks fly: resolving conflicts in your organization.* London: McGraw-Hill.

Eunson, B. (1998) *Dealing with conflict.* Chichester: Wiley.

Fritchie, R. and Leary, M. (1998) *Resolving conflicts in organizations: a practical guide for managers.* London: Lemos & Crane.

Hiltrop, J.M. and Udall, S. (1995) *The essence of negotiation.* London: Prentice Hall.

Teams, Leaders and Managers

LEARNING OBJECTIVES

To allow individuals to:

- understand how the work of the manager and leader is changing and why
- understand the present emphasis on team working

- understand how teams develop and to work with this process effectively

- choose an appropriate form of leadership for the spectrum of working situations

---

INTRODUCTION

This last chapter involves the application of all the skills we have discussed in the previous chapters. Managing and leading real people and real teams is an unforgiving process and one where we can very rarely say – 'Sorry about that, I'll come in again and start all over.' One can almost say that it is a case of doing so much right that you are forgiven for rare and inevitable lapses of judgement. With this in mind we could summarise our whole book by saying that it is about 'showing how to engage the brain before putting the mouth into gear', and this is never more true than in the final chapter.

In the 'good old days' of management, if they ever existed, there was a general acceptance of certain truths, divine and man-made order, and the wise manager slipped into this flow and made it work for him or her. From where I am sitting, this general acceptance of certain truths can no longer be assumed and the manager or leader survives, and hopefully prospers, on his or her own merits. How and when the change happened is not the concern of this book – it probably has happened in history but was not chronicled in a way to help us directly. It pays to see the threats as challenges leading to opportunities. However, one of your authors is always mindful of the Chinese Curse: 'May you live in interesting times.' If this is true, then we are all well cursed.

Skill Pre-assessment

SURVEY **8.1**

TEAM DEVELOPMENT BEHAVIOUR

Step 1 Before you read the material in this chapter, please respond to the following statements by writing a number, from the rating scale, in the column headed Pre-assessment. Your answers should reflect your attitudes and behaviour as they are now, not as you would like them to be. Be honest. This instrument is designed to help you to discover your level of competence in building effective teams so that you can tailor your learning to your specific needs. When you have completed the survey, use the scoring key in Appendix 1 to identify the skill areas discussed in this chapter that are most important for you to master.

Step 2 After you have completed the reading and exercises in this chapter and, ideally, as many of the Skill Application assignments as you can, cover up your first set of answers. Then respond to the same statements again, this time in the Post-assessment column. When you have completed the survey, use the scoring key in Appendix 1 to measure your progress. If your score remains low in specific skill areas, use the behavioural guidelines at the end of the Skill Learning section to guide further learning.

RATING SCALE

1 = Strongly disagree   **2** = Slightly disagree   **3** = Agree
4 = Slightly Agree   **5** = Agree   **6** = Strongly agree

	Assessment	
	Pre-	Post-
When attempting to build and lead an effective team:		
1. I know the stages teams go through as they develop.	____	____
2. When a team first forms, I make certain that all team members are introduced to one another.	____	____
3. When the team first comes together, I provide direction, answer team members' questions, and clarify goals, expectations, and outline working procedures.	____	____
4. I help team members to establish a mutual foundation of trust.		
5. I ensure that standards of excellence – not mediocrity or mere acceptability – characterise the team's work.	____	____
6. I provide quality feedback for team members' performance.	____	____
7. I encourage team members to balance individual autonomy with interdependence.	____	____
8. I help team members to become at least as committed to the success of the team as to their own personal success.	____	____
9. I help members to learn to play roles that assist the team in accomplishing its tasks as well as building strong interpersonal relationships.	____	____
10. I express a clear, exciting, passionate vision of what the team can achieve.	____	____
11. I help team members to become committed to the team vision.	____	____
12. I encourage a philosophy in the team where individual success is the success of the entire team.	____	____
13. I help the team to avoid 'group think' or making the group's survival more important than accomplishing its goal.	____	____
14. I use formal procedures to help the group to become faster, more efficient, and more productive, and to prevent errors.	____	____
15. I encourage team members to represent the team's vision, goals, and accomplishments outside the team.	____	____
16. I understand, use and develop the team's core competence.	____	____

17. I encourage the team to achieve dramatic breakthrough innovations as well as small continuous improvements.   ____ ____

18. I help the team to work towards preventing mistakes, not just correcting them later.   ____ ____

When preparing for and conducting team meetings:

19. I make certain that the purpose of a meeting is clear.   ____ ____

20. I ensure that the proper number and mix of people are invited to attend.   ____ ____

21. I prepare an agenda for every meeting.   ____ ____

22. I distribute the meeting agenda in advance, follow up after the meeting with action minutes, and make sure that the agreed actions are completed.   ____ ____

23. I have a clear idea of the stages an effective meeting should pass through, from start to finish.   ____ ____

24. I manage difficult team members effectively through supportive communication, collaborative conflict management, and empowerment.   ____ ____

SURVEY **8.2**

DIAGNOSING THE NEED FOR TEAM DEVELOPMENT

Teamwork has been found to have a dramatic effect on organisational performance. Some managers have credited teams with helping them to achieve incredible results. On the other hand, teams do not work all the time in all organisations. Therefore, managers must decide when teams should be organised. To determine the extent to which teams should be built in your organisation, complete the following survey.

Think of an organisation you know well and answer the questions with that organisation in mind. Circle the number on the right that you consider to be most appropriate.

RATING SCALE

1 = No evidence   **2** = Very little evidence   **3** = Some evidence
4 = A fair amount of evidence   **5** = Lots of evidence

---

1. Production or output has declined or is lower than desired.   **1 2 3 4 5**

2. Complaints, grievances, or low morale are present or increasing.   **1 2 3 4 5**

3. Conflicts or hostility between members is present or increasing.   **1 2 3 4 5**

4. Some people are confused about assignments, or their relationships with other people.   **1 2 3 4 5**

5. There is a lack of clear goals and lack of commitment to those that there are.   1 2 3 4 5

6. We see apathy or lack of interest and involvement by members.   1 2 3 4 5

7. There is insufficient innovation, risk taking, imagination, or initiative.   1 2 3 4 5

8. Ineffective and inefficient meetings are common.   1 2 3 4 5

9. Working relationships across levels and units are unsatisfactory.   1 2 3 4 5

10. Lack of co-ordination among functions is apparent.   1 2 3 4 5

11. Communications are poor; people do not listen, information is not shared and people are afraid to speak up.   1 2 3 4 5

12. There is a lack of trust between group and hierarchical leaders.   1 2 3 4 5

13. Decisions are made that some members do not understand, or do not agree with.   1 2 3 4 5

14. People feel that good work is not rewarded or that rewards are unfairly administered.   1 2 3 4 5

15. People are not encouraged to work together for the good of the organisation.   1 2 3 4 5

16. Customers and suppliers are not part of organisational decision making.   1 2 3 4 5

17. People work too slowly and there is too much redundancy in the work being done.   1 2 3 4 5

18. Issues and challenges that require the input of more than one person are being faced.   1 2 3 4 5

19. People must co-ordinate their activities in order for the work to be accomplished.   1 2 3 4 5

20. Difficult challenges that no single person can resolve or diagnose are being faced.   1 2 3 4 5

Source: Adapted from Dyer (1987)

SURVEY **8.3**

360° FEEDBACK QUESTIONNAIRE

This instrument is designed to let you see how others see you and how their view may differ from your own. We suggest that you photocopy the form and hand it out to between 5 and 8 people who work with you – members of your team, a boss or tutor and subordinates, where relevant. Complete Column 1 on your own form and ask each of your colleagues to complete column 2. Collect the forms and summarise the information on a blank form. Allow your 'observers' the option of remaining anonymous.

Look at the 'Areas for improvement' column and, in particular, where your own views differ from those of others. **Do Not** repeat the exercise immediately. Make your action plans, wait at least six months before repeating the exercise and, if possible, take different observers.

	Positive attribute (1)	Areas for improvement (2)	Not relevant (3)	No opinion (4)

Instructing and controlling

- Gives clear instructions
- Sets clear standards and challenging targets
- Listens to feedback
- Respected
- Loyal and reliable

Coaching

- Understanding and watchful
- Coaches skilfully
- Accepts the limits of his/her expertise

Consulting

- Builds a climate of trust
- Is willing to share views
- Makes time and is available
- Seeks and actions feedback
- Willing to learn

Delegating

- Values different approaches
- Plays to the strengths of others
- Delegates unselfishly
- Praises success appropriately
- Energises and motivates
- Matches authority with responsibility
- Delegates cleanly

Monitoring

- Remains appropriately in control
- Accepts appropriate responsibility
- Is respected up, across and below
- Maintains declared standards
- Vigilant but not smothering

Management Consultancy and Skills

481

	Positive attribute (1)	Areas for improvement (2)	Not relevant (3)	No opinion (4)

Communicating

- Good relations up, across and below
- Maintains links with other groups
- Is effective in 1 : 1 communication
- Is effective in group communication
- Runs effective meetings

Facilitating

- Encourages teamwork
- Anticipates the resource demands
- Able to stand in when necessary
- Loyal and dependable

Leadership

- Transmits sense of vision
- Maintains strategic direction
- Able to accept feedback and act flexibly
- Challenging
- Can enable others
- Models good attitudes and behaviours
- Tough in the face of opposition

Skill Learning

Developing teams and teamwork

Near the home of one of our authors, scores of Canada geese spend the winter. They fly over the house to the natural pond nearby almost every morning. What is distinctive about these flights is that the geese always fly in a V pattern. The reason for this pattern is that the flapping wings of the geese in front create an up draft for the geese that follow. This V pattern increases the range of the geese collectively by 71 per cent compared to flying alone. On long flights, after the lead goose has flown at the front of the V for some time, it drops back to take a place in the V where the flying is easier. Another goose then takes over the lead position, where the flying is most strenuous. If a goose begins to fly out of formation, it is not long before it returns to the V because of the resistance it experiences when not supported by the other geese's wing flapping.

Another noticeable feature of these geese is the loud honking that occurs when they fly. Canada geese never fly quietly, and one can always tell when they are in the air because of the noise. There is a reason for the honking; it occurs among geese in the rear of the formation in order to encourage the lead goose. The leader doesn't honk – just those who are supporting and urging it on.

If a goose becomes ill, or falls out of formation, two geese break ranks and follow the wounded or ill goose to the ground. There they remain, nurturing their companion, until it is either well enough to return to the flock or dies.

This remarkable phenomenon serves as an apt metaphor for our chapter on teamwork and leadership. The lessons garnered from the flying V formation help to highlight important attributes of effective teams and skilful teamwork. For example:

- Effective teams have interdependent members. Like geese, the productivity and efficiency of an entire unit is determined by the co-ordinated, interactive efforts of all its members.
- Effective teams help members to work together more efficiently.
- Like geese, effective teams outperform even the best individual's performance.
- Effective teams function so well that they create their own magnetism.
- Like geese, team members desire to affiliate with a team because of the advantages they receive from membership.
- Effective teams do not always have the same leader. Like geese, leadership responsibility often rotates and is shared broadly in skilfully controlled teams.
- In effective teams, members care for and nurture one another.
- No member is devalued or unappreciated.
- Each member is treated as an integral part of the team.
- In effective teams, members cheer for and bolster the leader, and vice versa.
- Mutual encouragement is given and received by each member.
- In effective teams, there is a high level of trust among members.
- Members are interested in others' success as well as their own.

Because any metaphor can be carried to extremes, we don't wish to overemphasise the similarities between Canada geese and work teams. But several points, which are the focus of this chapter, are among the important attributes of teams. Learning how to foster effective team processes, team roles, leadership, and positive relationships among team members are among the most important teambuilding skills discussed in this chapter. Our intent is to help you to improve your skill in managing teams, both as a leader and as a team member.

There are two sets of words of warning: one concerned with individuals and the other concerned with the process of moving towards teamworking in itself.

All this talk about teams and team membership is not good news for all of us, but there is a hope. Not all of us enjoy working in teams and indeed need to have a group around us to be effective. Look back at your FIRO-B scores in the first chapter and consider your *inclusion* needs. Those of you with very low scores in the Wanted Inclusion box – less than 3, say – really prefer to work alone. There is hope,

Management Consultancy and Skills

however. Forget the geese and think of a football team. To belong to a team and to work for a team does not mean you have to work AS a team. In a football team the mid-field players and the defenders must work as a team – a sub-team of the whole. However, the goalkeeper and the strikers are individuals in most of the teams at least one of your authors watches at great cost. The goalkeeper and the strikers have a special licence to be individuals – their record is for everyone to see in the record books. So it is for us. If we choose to work as specialists in a team, we had better be good specialists and not expect the special care of the injured team player. When we look at the new organisational structures proposed by Handy (1993) and Semler (1993), among others you will see that the team members who do not like being team players are well considered. Handy calls these portfolio people.

Our second consideration is concerned with the rush towards teamworking. Unfortunately the majority of restructurings fail. Rossiter (1995), working on a sample of small and medium-sized businesses in the north of the UK, confirmed the generally discussed 70 per cent failure rate. Moving towards teamworking is one process in restructuring. Although restructuring and the management of change are not the subject of this book, the discussion is relevant. In our opinion, borne out by Probst and Buchel (1997), there are two fundamental reasons for the failure of restructuring: the first is an insistence towards inappropriate teamworking and the second is timing.

We leave the restructuring until it's too late. Organisations with slack, undertaking change before they have fire-fighting problems, have a better chance of success. Handy (1994) uses the metaphor of Davy's Bar. He asks directions to a particular farm in Wicklow and is told how to find Davy's Bar. He is then told that when you have got to the Bar, you have passed the turning for the farm. Many organisations, in Handy's metaphor, are actually drinking in the Bar before they think they need to restructure. Reflect on the management arrogance we discussed in the interpretation of the Hawthorne Experiment. Managers still, in our observation as consultants, discount the wisdom of the shop floor. They bring teamworking as a 'new idea', ignoring the teams that already exist.

> AE Goetz, a major manufacturer of motor components, decided on teamworking. The issue was that these were 'new teams'. The workers already considered that they worked in teams – in a structure not dissimilar to those of the Hawthorne factory. There was considerable resentment over what was seen as the imposition of 'synthetic' teams.
>
> The Royal Mail move to teamwork has also been handicapped by a lack of understand of existing delivery teams.

In the beginning

Whether one is a manager, a subordinate, a student, or a homemaker, it is almost impossible to avoid being a member of a team. Teams are everywhere and therefore our discussions will centre on, but not be confined to, the workplace.

Biologists and anthropologists would claim that teamwork in human nature was greatly encouraged by the necessity of hunting on the savannah (Johnston, 1997). However, more mundanely the *Wall Street Journal* reports the first work team ever formed in organisation was established in Filene's department store in Boston in 1898. This innovation was slow to catch on, however, because the Industrial Revolution emphasised work processes and production techniques predicated on individualised tasks and specialised roles. Mass production focused the principles of scientific management and the 'one-person/one-job' philosophy. Frederick Taylor (1911), was the guru of such a philosophy. Bernard Burnes (1996) in his admirable book Managing Change quotes Taylor as he explains one of the roots of scientific management:

> The managers assume . . . the burden of gathering together all the traditional knowledge which has in the past been possessed by the workmen and then of classifying and reducing this knowledge to rules, laws and formula . . .

Taylor (1911) again lays down his principles by writing: 'All possible brainpower should be removed from the shop (floor) and centred in the planning (department).'

Taylor, who is widely accredited with the development of our mass production based society, feared, along with his contemporaries, organised labour and teams, which represented a local manifestation of workers wanting to determine how they performed tasks, were regarded as the enemy. The reader may like to look back at the original interpretation of the Hawthorne Experiment in our chapter on Motivation to see how this view lasted.

> The empire that became the Anglo-Dutch combine Unilever, was initially dependent of whale oil for its staples – margarine and soap. Initially whaling was regarded a highly skilled trade controlled by teams of highly prized and highly paid Norwegians, but William Hesketh Lever – later Lord Leverhulme – was unhappy with this arrangement and set about deskilling the process using locally recruited landlubbers from the area near his factories in Merseyside.

This was only one example. An inevitable consequence of scientific management was the encouragement of hierarchical or 'military model' organisations. In this chapter we will use the alternative title – the command and control organisation. In these organisations, everyone, except the mythical top, has someone to detail his or her job for them.

The death of the command and control organisation

In the world of the military

In the 1914–18 war much of French and British tactics were determined by the principle that people could not be trusted and provided the stereotype military model of organisations which had hardly changed from Roman days. However, the German Army was already questioning the system:

> In the final German attack in France for World War 1, Hauptmann Geyer virtually invented the concept of shock troops. His men were given a direction of attack and 'were told to move as fast and as deep as they could into the British lines without regard to what was happening on the flanks'. They were allowed in fact,

Management Consultancy and Skills

485

for what was probably the most disciplined army in the world, to become a self-directed team. They were given careful briefing but were allowed to decide for themselves how their orders were carried out. Successful fighting men had been doing this since the beginning of recorded time, but now they were fully equipped and trained to do so. (From Middlebrook, 1983)

Again in warfare:

Major John Howard commanded D Company of the Oxfordshire and Buckinghamshire Light Infantry to capture a key bridge in the first operation of the battle for Normandy on June 6th 1944 using the same 'loose–tight' command approach of Geyer.

He had to capture the bridge at Benouville and 'hold until relieved'. The army recognised that detailed instructions were impossible and that only empowered and highly trained troops could deal with the inevitable chaos of battle.

When the operation was successfully completed the 'team' or what was left of them, was broken up and sent to standard regiments. Elite forces are probably best as temporary arrangements. (From Ambrose, 1985)

More recently, pressure from the enquiry over a major aircrash in Tenerife led to an 'official' change in management style in the world's airways. A loaded KLM Boeing 747 collided with an American 747 on the runway. At the enquiry the voice recorder on the KLM machine revealed that the co-pilot had attempted to get the very experienced and authoritarian pilot to reverse his intention to take off in spite of not having full clearance. The pilot appeared to have ignored the warning and the crash, at the time of writing, was the most costly ever recorded, directly related to 'management style'. After the crash, airlines adopted a more teamworking approach and the authoritarian managerial style was actively discouraged. As one senior member of cabin crew said – 'It used to be just coffee and whitener. Now they actually tell you what is happening and why.'

The pressures for the rethinking of the military, strictly hierarchical, command and control organisation were a general acceptance of the reality of war. Generals, however well briefed, cannot know exactly what happens when a battle begins – things happen too quickly and the smoke and noise make monitoring from anyone other than those involved impossible. Inspirational leadership, clear briefing, careful training, detailed consultation and relevant equipment are the best that authority can provide. The people on the ground *have* to be left to get on with it. The choice against a strict command structure and for a measure of empowerment has become more imperative as battlefield skills become more specific and the necessity for rapid response, more demanding.

In the later 1980s Mike Angus, then chairman of Unilever, made a speech where he chided his fellow industrialists for maintaining the military model in their organisations, when it had been abandoned by the military for decades. Pressures on industry exactly parallel those that led to a review of the command and control model by the very organisations who created it.

The military metaphor we have chosen stands.

Management Consultancy and Skills

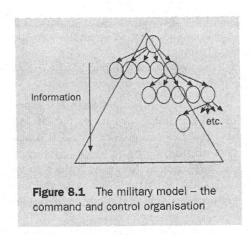

Figure 8.1 The military model – the command and control organisation

The new world of commerce, public service and industry

The traditional hierarchical organisation as laid down by Taylor and his supporters was top down – orders came as successive waves through a layered structure (Figure 8.1). Leadership came from the top and managers were there to see that orders were carried out. The number of employees largely determined the number of layers in an organisation. An arbitrary rule set the number of subordinates that could reasonably report to one manager as being five, so the number of layers was set accordingly. The overall philosophy of the system was that 'people could not be trusted' – extreme Theory X as we discussed in the chapter on motivation. It was also supported by a number of assumptions.

Omniscience of the top

First and foremost, since orders come from the top, we have to assume that the 'top' either knows everything necessary to run the business or can find out in time to make 'good' decisions and 'good' orders.

> There are stories about William Hesketh Lever when he was in total control of the vast soap works of his own building in Port Sunlight, Merseyside. Every day he would arrive on his horse, dismount and be met by his first line management. They would hurry like a cloud behind him waiting for him to stop at 'their' area of responsibility and be issued with their orders for the day: make more Lifebuoy, close line 2 . . .

More recently we were visiting a plastics reclaimer – a factory making millions of plastic refuse bags from low-grade polythene.

> The chairman and owner was explaining to us how he was empowering his staff and now left all the day-to-day running of the factory to his son and some very responsible divisional managers he had just hired. At this point, one of the new responsible managers knocked at the walnut door and was allowed in. The chairman was presented with a black polythene disposal bag: 'It doesn't seem right to me. Should I close the line?'

Management Consultancy and Skills

The chairman excused himself, blew into the bag so as to make it a balloon, tied its neck, placed it on his imperial chair, jumped up and landed hard on the bag. It deflated feebly. 'Yes, close the line.'

The 'empowered' manager bowed slightly, turned and left the room. He presumably closed the line.

The world of most organisations is more complicated than two types of soap for a new marketplace or one line of polythene bags for local councils. Such 'simple' environments are rare and in most parts of our chaotic world it is absolutely impossible for the 'top' to know everything he (or she) needs to know. The job of manager is to understand, analyse and convert his or her orders to the subset of orders required by direct subordinates so that they can in turn pass them down. The job is not only impossible – it is counter-productive in our changing world.

Chinese Whispers

The childhood game of Chinese Whispers, often played in the adult parties of our youth when nobody had anything else to do, involves passing a message along a line of people allowing no feedback. After four or five people, the message becomes hopelessly distorted.

> There is a legend, again of war, where a divisional commander sent the message down the line through a series of runners: 'Send reinforcements, I'm going to advance.' The message received at headquarters was: 'Send three and four pence, I'm going to a dance.'

The currency, well before decimalisation, let alone the EU, tells the age of the joke. Hunter (1957) details more scientific evidence of the Chinese Whisper phenomenon in descriptions of the Bartlett experiments in 1932. All but the simplest messages distort as they are passed 'down the line'. To pass messages down the line the context, made relevant to each recipient, needs to be understood and feedback is essential: *Sorry, do you actually mean . . . ?*

Feedback and the 'specialist'

We assume that true feedback is not necessary. Local feedback for reaffirming the accuracy of messages can occur in the command and control organisation but it seldom is more than local – the 'old man' rarely hears it from anyone other than his immediate deputies.

However, there has emerged a strange individual in the organisation who has specialised knowledge. He or she is the expert.

> The first that one of your authors saw the effect was when he was working for British Coal in the 1960s. The organisation was attempting to develop a number of open fire products and one promising alternative was the very rapid heating of coal dust in a device looking like a vast Dyson vacuum cleaner. The device was in a very early state of development and the scientist in charge, Stuart Troughton, was pressured to take on a 100-fold scale up. He refused, saying that the state of knowledge would not justify the risk. He was right.

Management Consultancy and Skills

In our organisations we now have people who *know*. They are computer specialists who *know* that particular systems are not stable enough to be allowed into the hands of customers, and marketing specialists who *know* that the sampling procedures *possible* in the time given will be biased. Senior management and strategic thinkers had better hear local experts and the command and control organisation has no way of hearing them since **the communication channels are down from the top, rarely two-way and never down up**. In the language of the book, command and control organisations do not support constructive communications.

People do what they are told

Maybe they did, in the years gone by or, in restricted places in the world, they may still do. Maybe leaders and managers supported by power, unemployment and a rigid social order can expect blind obedience, but now it is safer to assume no such thing. Our example of the scientist Stuart Troughton indicates that often it is just as well that people question instructions in a world of complexity. However the command and control organisation assumes that they do obey and, if they fail to obey, simply applies more pressure – including the summary courts martial.

> Working in countries outside Europe, and in particular Asia and the Middle East, the transition from the command and control assumptions is accelerating but by no means as complete as it is in Europe.
>
> One personnel manager for a company in Dubai, UAE, explained that the problems we have just discussed simply did not happen with the workforce at his command. *If they fail me in any way, their work permits are revoked and without work permits, they are deported.*

Organisational responses to the death of the command and control organisation

Coulson-Thomas and Coe (1991) conducted a survey for the then British Institute of Management (BIM) on the ways in which companies and organisations could better face the changing world (see Table 8.1). The survey showed that 86 per cent of the sample, taken from the membership of the BIM, regarded teamworking as a response to the changing world. In addition, the next two responses – flatter and more responsive organisations – can also be related to teamworking. This and other surveys indicated a fundamental questioning of current organisations and the leadership/management styles they had followed since the beginning of the Industrial Revolution.

The movement towards teams is not only concerned explicitly but also implicitly in all but the last factor. We will discuss teams specifically in the next sections of the chapter. Here we will discuss what companies actually do and how this further emphasises the team approach. To help us continue, Table 8.2 list some of the concepts that managers apply to the teamworking approach.

- **Teamworking**, and in particular the cross-functional team. Here individuals from a range of disciplines are taken, on a permanent or temporary basis, from

Table 8.1 Coulson-Thomas's survey of BIM membership

British Institute of Management survey – what respondents felt needed to be done to face the new business environment	Percentage regarding this factor as 'very important'
More work should be undertaken in teams	86
Creating a slimmer and flatter organisation	81
Creating a more responsive organisation	79
Procedures and permanency should give way to flexible and temporary arrangements	79
Functions should become more interdependent	76
Organisations should become more interdependent	67

Table 8.2 Essential associated concepts

- A **self-directed team** in which a group handles its own work structuring.
- A policy of **single customer contact**: organising teams around projects focused to the customer.
- **Multiskilling**: reducing the number of 'crafts' employed in an activity by deskilling and training within a working team.
- **Problem categorising**: accepting that many issues can be handled within a team and that only a few require specialist action.
- **Categorising decisions**: accepting the principle that decisions should be made at the lowest point – by working teams if possible.
- **'Annualising' or 'stacking'** working hours: accepting that when people are not required they are not around, but that they are available when needed. Work is done where, when and by whom it is appropriate.

the silos of their functional departments – finance, marketing, etc. – and formed into project or customer-based teams. The results have been mixed in that few organisations have appreciated the cultural changes involved. Where such projects have worked – Kodak and Rover, for example – the response has been very positive. The problems seem to arise when strong teams are developed with loyalties to themselves and particular customers, but the appraisal and reward systems continue to be supported by the function units – i.e., people are still rewarded for applying their professional skills and not for their personal contribution to team effort. We recognise the accountant, the chemist and the production specialist, but seldom the 'team player'.

- **Multiskilling** has followed in the wake of deskilling and the dying out of the apprentice system. Again the cultural changes needed to accept such changes have often been underestimated.

Management Consultancy and Skills

- **Problem and decision categorising**, although obvious in concept, involve a major training initiative on the part of the organisation. The current jargon states that the organisation needs to transform itself into a learning organisation – everyone, on a continuous basis, needs to extend his or her understanding of the skills necessary to perform the whole job. Handy (1997) discussed this as the Law of Subsidiarity – A higher-order body should not assume responsibilities that could and should be exercised by a lower-order body. He goes on to say that taking over another's responsibilities is wrong because it ultimately deskills them.

- **Annualising hours** – accepting that there is such a thing as a working year – is perhaps the most contentious of the new mechanisms.

We discussed some of these issues on the chapter on motivation. Correctly introduced they do motivate staff but, in the case of the changes, took Zeneca 18 months of hard bargaining.

Downsizing and flatter organisations

With the tactical techniques, real attempts have been made to turn organisations away from the hierarchies so suited to the command and control organisation. We will discuss two such concepts. The Shamrock Organisation of Charles Handy (1993) and the Three-Ring Circus of Ricardo Semler (1993).

In the shamrock organisation (Figure 8.2) we have three categories:

1. Core personnel who maintain the strategy and core activities of the organisation.
2. Contracted staff who perform the core activities of the organisation.
3. Out-sourcing – contracted outside organisations to perform 'support' activities, such as canteen, maintenance, training, wage rose, etc.

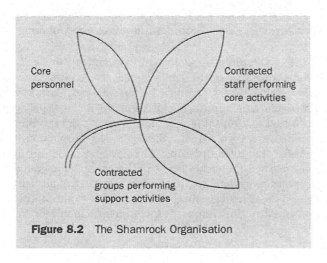

Figure 8.2   The Shamrock Organisation

Management Consultancy and Skills

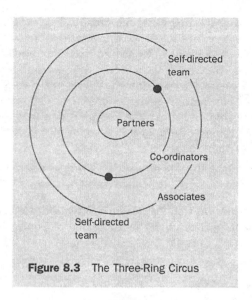

Figure 8.3   The Three-Ring Circus

In the 'Three-Ring Circus' organisation (Figure 8.3) we have reduced the hierarchy to three layers and Semler found it convenient to draw these layers in a circular representation:

1. Partners who are responsible for the direction of the company.
2. Co-ordinators (often called team leaders) who are responsible for steering teams of associates working on specific projects – usually identified around a customer.
3. Associates who, in self-directed teams, perform the actual project work of the organisation.

Very few companies have fully adopted either of the two new models, but many have taken steps towards the leaner, flatter and more directed organisation:

> Charles Walls (1997), a medium-sized marketing company in Leeds, UK, has adopted many of the principles of the Semler model. The co-ordinators are however called 'coaches' who assist the various self-directed teams. The coaches retain their functional roles and also monitor the performance of the teams using internal and customer-based auditing. The self-directed teams are customer focused and elect their leaders on a regular basis. The leaders have no authority beyond their personal presence but guide the teams. The CEO, the coaches and the team members with their elected leaders are the only 'layers' in the organisation. For internal purposes job titles beyond the three layers have been abolished. (They are retained or developed for customer convenience, as the CEO puts it.) Pay is tightly related to team performance. The company is still in transition but the current news is favourable.

The growth of team culture

It is important for the reader not to see the historical description of the development of teams as an inevitable evolution. There has been a general progression, but, as we will detail later, the stage of development needs to fit the organisation and its environment. From the 1898 experiments of Filene's department store in Boston, there was a gap in the development of recognised and formalised teamworking, although it obviously occurred naturally in millions of small organisations. In the 1920s, small-scale efforts were made to form **problem-solving** teams in some companies. These teams consisted of 5 to 12 workers who met for an hour or two each week to discuss ways to make improvements or solve problems in their company. By the time the 1987 General Accounting Office (GAO) study was conducted, 70 per cent of 476 large companies surveyed had installed these types of teams (although less than half the workforce actually participated in the teams). The widely publicised Japanese **quality circles** of the 1970s and 1980s present a variation on this type of team. Problem-solving teams have no power to implement decisions or changes; they simply meet to discuss issues and make recommendations to upper management.

In the early and middle 1980s special-purpose teams emerged in which members help to redesign work processes, introduce new technology, resolve labour and management differences, link with suppliers or customers, or co-ordinate across functional boundaries. These teams have power to take action and initiate changes in organisations as a result of delegated assignments from the top. They not only recommend, but also implement. Such teams are currently spreading in many industries, mainly among lower-level employees and especially in firms faced with the need to improve efficiency, competitiveness, and responsiveness. Poza and Markus (1980) demonstrated that a team approach to restructuring resulting in a lower head count, reduced absentee levels, reduced turnover and increased productivity in an automotive plant in Kentucky. Japanese transplants have been particularly effective in their use of teamworking – Wickens (1987) and Susman (1990) record the details for the UK and US respectively.

Table 8.3 list some 'early adopters' of teamworking principles among US companies.

Teams and teamwork are much more typical of manufacturing firms than of service firms, since relatively few service organisations have established work teams as yet (Hoerr, 1989).

The 1990s have witnessed the emergence of a new form of work team, **self-managing** teams. This type of team is still relatively rare and represents the most advanced form of teamwork. Self-managing teams plan and schedule their own work processes, hire and train team members, praise and reward their team's performance, and manage their own leadership. Team members learn all the tasks necessary for a particular process, product or service, and members rotate from job to job. Each team member can substitute for another member in case of absence or special demand. As summarised in Table 8.4, self-managing teams maintain all the responsibilities within the team that are normally spread across multiple

Table 8.3 Early examples of US companies using teamworking principles

Company	When started
Boeing	1987
Caterpillar	1986
Champion International	1985
Cummins Engine	1973
Digital Equipment	1982
Ford	1982
General Electric	1985
General Motors	1975
LTV Steel	1985
Procter and Gamble	1962
A.O. Smith	1987
Tektronix	1983

Source: *Business Week*, 'The payoff from teamwork,' July 10, 1989, p. 58

Table 8.4 The claimed advantages of self-managed teams

Self-managed teams:
- plan, control, and improve their own work processes
- share leadership and management functions
- set their own goals
- inspect their own work
- create their own schedules
- review their own performance
- prepare their own budgets
- co-ordinate with other units
- order their own supplies
- Manage their own inventories
- negotiate and contract with suppliers
- acquire training when needed
- hire their own replacements
- discipline their own members
- take responsibility for rewarding and recognising members
- are led by coaching and facilitating rather than controlling and directing
- reward based on team not individual performance
- rely on fewer management layers and fewer functions to accomplish work
- encourage individual member initiative and accountability
- **require a special type of leadership if they are not to become a danger to the organisation**

Management Consultancy and Skills

hierarchical levels and functions. In contrast to problem-solving or special-purpose teams, members of self-managing teams work together on an ongoing basis, not just as a temporary assignment. By 1991, surveys of more than 500 organisations by two consulting firms, Wyatt and DDI, found that about 27 per cent of organisations had begun using self-directed work teams (Moskal, 1991; Wellins *et al.*, 1991). A 1993 survey of 1,293 US organisations by the American Society for Quality Control (ASQC) and the Gallup Organisation found that over 80 per cent of respondents reported some form of teamwork activity, mainly problem-solving teams. Typically, two or more teams were found per company, but almost all teams were of recent origin, the median life span being only five years. Two-thirds of full-time employees indicated that they participate in teams, and 84 per cent participate in more than one team (ASQC, 1993).

The advantages of teams

Teams have captured the attention of modern managers because of increasing amounts of data that show improvements in productivity, quality, and morale when teams are utilised. For example, a noted management consultant, Tom Peters (1987, p. 306) claimed:

> Are there any limits to the use of teams? Can we find places or circumstances where a team structure doesn't make sense? Answer: No, as far as I can determine. That's unequivocal, and meant to be. Some situations may seem to lend themselves more to team-based management than others. Nonetheless, I observe that the power of the team is so great that it is often wise to violate apparent common sense and force a team structure on almost anything.

We would not entirely agree.

Many companies have attributed their improvements in performance directly to the institution of teams in the workplace (Wellins *et al.*, 1991). For example, by using teams:

- Shenandoah Life Insurance Company in Roanoke, Virginia, saved $200,000 annually because of reduced staffing needs, while increasing its volume 33 per cent.
- Westinghouse Furniture Systems increased productivity 74 per cent in three years.
- AAL increased productivity by 20 per cent, cut personnel by 10 per cent, and handled 10 per cent more transactions.
- Federal Express cut service errors by 13 per cent.
- Carrier reduced unit turnaround time from two weeks to two days.
- Volvo's Kalmar facility reduced defects by 90 per cent.
- General Electric's Salisbury, North Carolina, plant increased productivity by 250 per cent compared to other GE plants producing the same product.
- Corning cellular ceramics plant decreased defect rates from 1,800 parts per million to 9 parts per million.

- AT&T's Richmond operator service increased service quality by 12 per cent.
- Dana Corporation's Minneapolis valve plant trimmed customer lead time from six months to six weeks.
- General Mills plants using teams are 40 per cent more productive than plants operating without teams.

Other more scientific and systematic studies of the impact of teams have found equally impressive results. Literally thousands of studies have been conducted on groups and teams and their impact on various performance outcomes. One of the first and most well-known studies ever conducted on teams was undertaken by Coch and French (1948) in the Harwood Company, a manufacturer of men's shirts, shorts, and pyjamas. Faced with the necessity of responding to competitors' lower prices, Harwood decided to speed up the line and make other process changes. Workers had responded badly, however, to previous changes in the production process, and they resisted the threat of further changes. To implement these planned changes, Harwood management used three different types of strategies.

- One group of employees received an explanation of the new standards to be imposed, the proposed changes in the production process to be implemented, and why the changes were needed. A question–answer period followed the explanation.
- A second group of employees was presented the problem, asked to discuss it and reach agreement on solutions, and then elect representatives to generate the new standards and procedures.
- In a third group, every member was asked to discuss and become involved in establishing and implementing the new standards and procedures. All members participated fully as a team.

The results of this comparison were dramatic. Despite having their jobs simplified, members of the first group showed almost no improvement in productivity; hostility towards management escalated; and, within 40 days, 17 per cent of the employees had left the company. Members of the second group regained their previous levels of productivity within 14 days and improved slightly thereafter. Morale remained high and no employee left the company. Members of the third group, on the other hand, who fully participated as a team, regained earlier productivity levels by the second day and improved 14 per cent over that level within the month. Morale remained high, and no one left the company.

Other classic studies of coal miners, pet food manufacturers, and auto workers revealed similar advantages of teams (e.g., Trist, 1969; Walton, 1965). More recently, one of the most comprehensive surveys ever conducted on employee involvement in teams was carried out among the Fortune 1000 companies by Lawler *et al.* (1992). They found that employee involvement in teams had a strong positive relationship with several dimensions of organisational and worker effectiveness. Table 8.5 shows the percentage of organisations reporting improvement and positive impact as a result of team involvement. In general, Lawler and his colleagues found that among firms that were actively using teams, both organisational and individual

Table 8.5 The impact of improvement teams on organisations and workers

Performance criteria	Percentage Indicating improvement	Percentage Indicating positive impact
Changed management style to more participatory	78	
Improved organisational processes and procedures	75	
Improved management decision making	69	
Increased employee trust in management	66	
Improved implementation of technology	60	
Elimination of layers of management supervision	50	
Improved safety and health	48	
Improved union–management relations	47	
Quality of products and services		70
Customer service		67
Worker satisfaction		66
Employee quality of work life		63
Productivity		61
Competitiveness		50
Profitability		45
Absenteeism		23
Turnover	22	

effectiveness were above average and improving in virtually all categories of performance. In firms without teams or in which teams were infrequently used, effectiveness was average or low in all categories.

In studies of self-directed teams, Near and Weckler (1990) found that individuals in self-directed teams scored significantly higher than individuals in traditional work structures on innovation, information sharing, employee involvement, and task significance. Macy *et al.* (1990) reported that the use of self-directed teams correlated highly with increases in organisational effectiveness, heightened productivity, and reduced defects. Wellins *et al.* (1991) reported that two-thirds of companies that implemented self-directed work teams could run their companies with fewer managers, and in 95 per cent of the cases a reduced number of managers was reported to be beneficial to company performance. The results of other well-known studies have produced similar outcomes (Ancona and Caldwell, 1992; Hackman, 1990; Gladstein, 1984). Many of the reasons for these positive outcomes of teams have been known for years.

Maier (1967), for example, in a classic description of the conditions under which teams are more effective than individuals acting alone, and vice versa, pointed out that teams:

Management Consultancy and Skills

- Produce a greater number of ideas and pieces of information than individuals acting alone, so decision making and problem solving are more informed and are of higher quality.

- Improve understanding and acceptance among individuals involved in problem solving and decision making due to team members' participation in the process.

- Have higher motivation and performance levels than individuals acting alone because of the effects of 'social facilitation', that is, people are more energised and active when they are around other people.

- Offset personal biases and blind spots that inhibit effective problem analysis and implementation but that are not noticed by single individuals.

- Are more likely to entertain novel alternatives and to take innovative action than individuals acting alone.

- Teams are usually more fun to work with.

On the other hand, teams are not a panacea for everything that ails organisations, nor do they represent a magic potion that managers can use to accomplish their objectives. Just getting people together and calling them a team by no means makes them a team. A leading expert on teams, Richard Hackman (1993), pointed out that mistakes are common in team building and team management.

- Rewarding and recognising individuals instead of the team.
- Not maintaining stability of membership over time.
- Not providing teams with autonomy.
- Not fostering interdependence among team members.
- Using the team to make all decisions instead of having individuals make decisions when appropriate.
- Failing to orient all team members.
- Having too many members on the team.
- Not providing appropriate structure for the team.
- Not providing the team with needed resources.

Choosing, placing and maintaining teams are the jobs of the new leaders and managers.

There are, however, many situations where teamworking is not appropriate – for example, simple, routine, or highly formalised work (e.g., stuffing Pimentos into olives) is not well suited for teams. Verespei (Iggo) observed:

> All too often corporate chieftains read the success stories and ordain their companies to adopt work teams – NOW. Work teams don't always work and may even be the wrong solution to the situation in question.

Teams, in other words, can be very powerful tools for managers in producing organisational success, but they are by no means a 'sure thing'. Survey 8.2, 'Diagnosing the need for team development', helps to identify the extent to which teams will help an organisation to improve its performance.

Teams can take too long to make decisions; they may drive out effective action with 'group think'; and they can create confusion and frustration for their members. Many people have been members of an inefficient committee, or a team dominated by one member, or have had to take responsibility for the output of a team that compromised on excellence in order to get agreement from everyone – 'to attempt to please everyone is to please nobody'.

If team failure is common, then, how can success in teams be assured? How can managers ensure the effectiveness of the teams in which they are involved? What should one learn to become a skilful team leader and team member?

However, team working is a real challenge that will not go away for management, and understanding the mechanisms of teams and their formation is a vital management skill.

Stages of the development of teams

Teams and groups

Observations on my reading history, in Library, May Nineteen, Seventeen Hundred Thirty-one:

– That the great affairs of this world, the wars, revolutions, etc., are carried on and effected by parties.
– That the view of these parties is their present general interest, or what they take to be such.
– That the different views of these different parties occasion all confusion.
– That while a party is carrying on a general design, each man has his particular private interest in view.
– That as soon as a party has gained its general point, each member becomes intent upon his particular interest; which, thwarting others, breaks that party into divisions, and occasions more confusion.

Source: Benjamin Franklin as quoted by Eric Berne (1963)

Franklin, in 1731, was echoing a fundamental truth that is now being accepted by organisations – to achieve anything effectively you need a team with a clear purpose. Without that purpose, or when that purpose is achieved, individual issues and the issues of individuals will destroy the team – if you let it happen.

Woods (1989) sees the first job of a team manager as keeping the team in touch with the purpose.

'Keeping the team in touch with the purpose' will include supplying the facilities, the controls and the direction the team needs to fulfil that purpose – a great deal of work. Should, however, the purpose be weak or unclear the manager needs to be able to take firmer control of the individuals and the group – the management style will have to move away from Consensus and Consultation and adopt a more directive approach.

Secondly the manager needs to understand the relevant needs of individuals in the group. We are not asking the manager to become a universal social worker but

Management Consultancy and Skills

499

to consider and put priority onto what is relevant regardless of his or her prejudice or personal beliefs and values.

> In the final Scott expedition to Antarctica it was relevant that Evans was under-nourished and had lost essential strength. Evans was a larger man than the others and needed more than basic rations to survive. Scott felt that he should not allow for any special pleading and with what we would now call machismo, probably con-ributed to Evans' death and the failure of the whole expedition. (Woods, 1989)

The skilful manager listens to individuals and reserves the time to understand what may be relevant.

Thirdly, the manager needs to understand the needs of the group in relation to its purpose, the facilities and the individuals within it. These are 'old fashioned' management skills but understanding the needs of the group is by no means an obvious task. We have used the word group and not team – the difference between a 'team' and a 'group' is crucial.

> **A team is a group of people dedicated towards a goal – a purpose. Every team is a group but only the rare group is a team.**

Stages of team development

Wanous *et al.* (1984) classified the stages of team development from various authors. Their work is summarised in Table 8.6. The Tuckman sequence for team formation – Forming, Storming Norming, Performing and Adjourning – will be used as our primary model. Other common names for the stages, such as Forming, Developing, Consolidating and Mature, will be mentioned as will be the Schutz's Firo-B needs of Inclusion, Control and Affection mentioned in the first chapter.

The purpose of working

People at work are motivated in two ways:

1. *The task.* Issues concerned with the quality of the work in hand.

2. *The process.* The satisfaction of the human needs to relate to the rest of the human race.

Table 8.6 Five models of team development

Schutz (1958)	Model/Faris (1958)	Whittaker (1970)	Hill and Gruner (1973)	Tuckman (1965)
	Four-stage developmental model	Integrative model	Three-stage developmental model	Integrative model

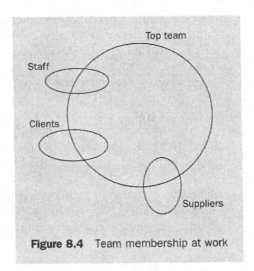

Figure 8.4 Team membership at work

We differ in the balance of our concerns for the process and the task. Some extreme individuals are motivated almost by the task alone. Others, equally extreme, are almost unconcerned with the task, and are happy provided that their human needs are satisfied. Most of us lie between these two extremes – being concerned with both human contact and with the nature of the task with which we are engaged.

Our concern to relate to other human beings can be split into three components:

1. The need for inclusion: the gregarious instinct in mankind – the need to join and to belong. (Woods 1989)

2. The need for control: the wish to know one's position in relationship to others – role and control.

3. The need for affection: the wish to relate and be accepted by others on an individual basis, the need to pair and share.

If you look back to your Firo-B scores you will see the balance of your needs. However, your 'people needs' are provided by the multitude of 'teams' in your life – home, leisure and work. Remaining at work, you may belong to teams of your own staff, your clients, your suppliers and be a junior member of the 'top team' of your bosses (see Figure 8.4).

The issue for management is that individuals – and managers are just as much a part of this 'activity' as anyone – balance our contributions to provide our chosen quantity and quality of the satisfaction of our people needs.

United Agricultural Merchants were concerned about the quality of advice given by their salespersons to farmers. The advice 'looked' as if it was to the advantage of the farmer and not of the company. Looking at the pattern of communications in their workforce they found that the company contact provided virtually no people needs for their staff. The salespersons were on the road meeting the farmers on a professional and semi-social basis. This was where the people needs were being satisfied and this was where the 'loyalty' of the staff lay.

Management Consultancy and Skills

The new trends towards home working and remote communications from laptops to head office by modems will make this issue of 'loyalty' more acute. For the home-based manager the problem of loyalty may be most acute when he or she relates to the 'top team'. He or she is unlikely to have any feeling of belonging to the 'top team' and may get all his or her human needs satisfied though colleagues or his or her subordinate teams. The dangers are obvious.

There is a logic in the order in which we require fulfilment of our human needs. Assuming that our material needs – hunger, warmth and basic security – are met, our inclusion needs come next, then control needs and, finally, our needs for affection. The same order is true for teams and provides a basis for an understanding for the stages of team development.

Unless we are skilled, we lead our teams in terms of satisfying our own level and balance of human needs. The unskilled team leader will be inclined to over-emphasise the needs he or she feels most important and underemphasise those he or she finds personally unimportant. This imbalance of leadership emphasis will have an adverse effect on team development.

The process of team development

The process of movement from group to team is in stages:

> Suppose you are invited to a social occasion – say a barbecue – and you only know the host, everyone else is a stranger. One can imagine questioning why you had been invited and feeling quite uncomfortable in spite of obvious helpful introductions by the host. There is a 'situation vacant' serving drinks and you jump at it. You have acquired a purpose and a role. As the party matures you find someone who has a mutual interest and settle down in a corner to discuss military history, the European Union, cars . . . Just as you are settled, it's time to go and you exchange cards with your new found friend, promising to 'give you a call'.

This is the forming stage where individual inclusion needs are satisfied. Our quotation from Ben Franklin drew attention to the fact that a team needs to have a purpose to distinguish it from a group. The sooner the group hears of that purpose, clearly and understandably, the better. Without that purpose or when that purpose is achieved, individual issues and the issues of individuals will destroy the team. A manager, however, at any given time needs to balance the needs of the task, the team and the individual. Adair used a Venn diagram to illustrate this point and this is shown in Figure 8.5. We need to remind ourselves continually that a team is a group of people dedicated to a goal – a purpose. Every team is a group but only rarely is a group a team.

The process of movement from group to team takes place in stages:

1. Stage 1 – the forming stage – where the inclusion, joining and belonging needs are being settled by a group of people potentially coming to work as a team.
2. Stage 2 – the developing team – where the issues of control are being settled. The issues of control may lead to dissent and hence Tuckman's nomenclature – the storming stage.

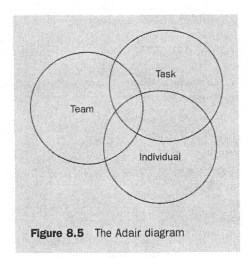

Figure 8.5 The Adair diagram

3. Stage 3 – the consolidating team – where individual relationships and norms are being established, hence Tuckman's norming stage.
4. Stage 4 – the mature or self-actualised team.
5. Stage 5 – the mourning stage where the team is disbanded.

Ideally we are looking at a smooth progression to a mature team (Figure 8.6). 'A fly on the wall' could recognise each of the stages of team development.

The eye of a fly on the wall

A 'fly on the wall' – an unbiased observer – would notice:

1. Stage 1 – the undeveloped and forming team working on fulfilling the inclusion needs of individuals.

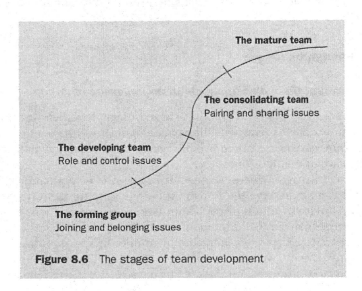

Figure 8.6 The stages of team development

Management Consultancy and Skills

503

- grumbling on immediate conditions, intellectualism
- swift 'dashes' to complete tasks
- one-sided definitions of position
- temporary and stereotyped groupings
- suspicion and a great deal of attributing blame to anyone or anything
- total reliance on them or the boss.

2. Stage 2 – the developing team working on control issues:
   - defensiveness, competition and jealousy
   - challenges to structure and task
   - experimental hostility and aggression
   - ambivalence to the appointed leader
   - 'stag fights' and 'try ons'
   - intense brittle links and cliques
   - tantrums or impatience from individuals who know that their skills already match the task.

   This stage may well justify its name – the storming stage.

3. Stage 3 – the consolidating or norming team working on affection issues. (Woods, 1989, calls these Pairing and Sharing issues):
   - potential alienation with other teams
   - blossoming of personal relationships
   - re-definition of physical boundaries
   - lack of formal leadership control
   - some uniformity of habits or dress.

4. Stage 4 – the mature team – all the needs of the team have been satisfied and the properties of a self-directed team. The reader might like to refer to Table 8.4 or the metaphor of the geese. The fly would notice pragmatic harmony.

5. Stage 5 – the mourning team – the task has been accomplished or has been lost and the members are departing. The fly would notice sadness, regret and delaying.

Managing through the stages

Stage 1: Providing the inclusion needs of an undeveloped group

When we have a group of people who have been brought together for the first time they have many concerns. They will all have the basic insecurities of not knowing exactly why they have been chosen, what is required of them and whether they are in the right place at the right time.

The leader or manager, whether or not he or she is in a command and control organisation, needs to resolve those insecurities by assuming authority and *telling* people. He or she needs to tell people about who is present and who is expected. The initial process may consist of providing name tags, places to settle in, instructions of where to get a cup of tea, guided tours round the site and introductions to key people. Only then do we need to detail what is required of the group as a whole. He or she needs to concentrate on the task, its purpose and its content (Figure 8.7).

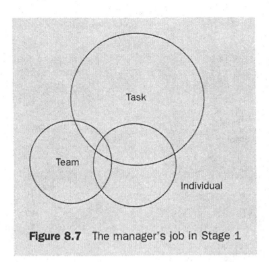

Figure 8.7 The manager's job in Stage 1

Those with high inclusion needs will be most concerned that this stage is correctly structured and will be unhappy until it is. Late comers need to be brought up to speed and introduced appropriately to the forming group.

The group and its members will stay in this undeveloped stage indefinitely if:

- the task remains unclear

- there is genuine or perceived insecurity of group membership

- the management decision-making style remains directive or authoritarian and the group depends on external decisions for its purpose and patterns to be decided – which would be quite normal in a command and control management structure.

The group will return to the undeveloped stage should any of these factors return – the task changes, redundancy threatens or people leave or join. A manager working in an authoritarian management structure or with a task that is changing uncontrollably, may well choose to keep the team in the undeveloped joining and belonging stage. The reason behind this may be that he or she is unable to provide a clear purpose to the group or because he or she wants to remain in complete control – his or her role and control needs are high.

Stage 2: Providing the role and control needs of a developing team

Once the inclusion needs of the individuals in the group are satisfied we can progress to the next set of needs. We have established a form of definition of the task, understand why we are included and now we need to establish, with clarity, the official and unofficial roles of everyone in the forming team. The formal leadership is probably accepted but the informal pecking orders are not. Consultation is possible but it is always consultation marred by suspicion : 'I'm not certain why the boss is asking her, she only graduated last year . . .' The leader/manager needs to concentrate on developing the team (Figure 8.8).

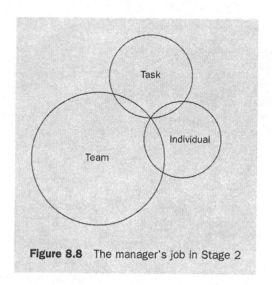

Figure 8.8 The manager's job in Stage 2

'No individual is more important than the team.'

> *Source*: Bill Shankly as manager of Liverpool Football Club in their great days

The group may stay in this rather uncomfortable developing stage if:

- the management chooses to keep competition among the group – a high-pressure sales team.

  > We were working with a company concerned with high-pressure selling to the trade. The country was divided into what seemed arbitrary divisions – all controlled by a very authoritarian marketing manager. At the sales conference it was quite obvious that a team spirit was emerging and one of the regions, with a strong emergent team, had won the 'golden rose' for sales two years running. The marketing manager chose to use the conference to announce a redistribution of the regions. As he told us: 'We don't want them getting too cocky, do we?'

- the roles demanded by functions do not fit the preferred way individuals wish to work – the hierarchy does not fit the functions necessary

- individuals in the group will not accept the principles behind the task

- individuals will not accept the values being imposed on them by the forming team – the politics or the Politics

- the management decision-making style within the organisation remains predominantly authoritarian and there is no history of consultative or consensus management.

  > This reason can lead to some very dangerous decisions. Michael Edwards in his book *Back from the Brink* (1984) describes the near collapse of British Leyland – later to become the Rover wing of BMW. When he took over the company in 1977 the workforce had become alienated from the management. In our model, management saw no reason to provide for any inclusion needs and indeed was hostile to any movement towards team working. Management was entirely authoritarian. However, a union leader

known as (Red Robbo) Robinson was able to provide group membership needs and, with this, generated a great measure of loyalty from the workforce. The consequences of this were a series of intractable industrial disputes. Edwards had to 'include' the workforce into the company processes before he was able to regain loyalty and respect from the workforce.

- the task is not clear or not ready to be defined – sometimes we need to keep a group of workers in reserve, in a 'lay-by', while other things are sorted out, and this is often thinly disguised as a training programme.

Stage 3: Providing for the human need for individual contacts – the affection or pairing and sharing needs of a consolidating team

People are working out their working relationships – norming as it has been called. Often the norming involves dressing the same.

The Charles Walls Group, a company we have mentioned previously, set up two teams with parallel functions. One team was becoming successful and the other was floundering. The 'consolidating' team had adopted a uniform style of dress for both the male and the female members – casual, decorous and in pastel colours. The other team, trapped in the developing stage and control issues, dressed competitively.

The outsider may see the consolidating team as a real team. The individuals in the consolidating team no longer need to jockey for position and are valued as members of something that can be given a discreet title – be it the 'boffins' or 'accounts'. People are in the process of finding out who they like to work with and who they can trust on an intimate level.

Obviously 'uniforms' and various forms of equipment standardisation are used on one level to encourage team development. On a more subtle level, the leader/manager needs to provide support – training, coaching and counselling – for individuals (Figure 8.9).

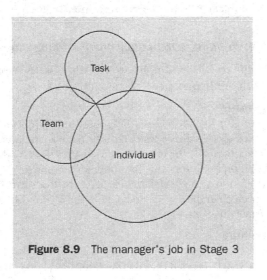

Figure 8.9 The manager's job in Stage 3

Management Consultancy and Skills

507

The process of moving from the second stage of the role and control battles to the pairing and sharing stage will most probably have involved some individuals deciding that they are not wanted or that they do not accept the roles on which the success of the team depends. In this case they will choose their moment and leave. Otherwise, the leader needs to recognise that some individuals may not like the standards laid down by the team in the previous stage – their values may not fit, and these individuals may also be encouraged to leave.

A team remaining too long in the pairing and sharing stage may well become smug. The consolidating team may never complete its progress to a mature team if:

- the group is allowed to modify the task to suit its members' preferred way of working
- management has 'forgotten' the importance of monitoring the team's processes
- the fit of personality is 'too good', and there is no 'sand in the oyster to produce the pearl'
- the team membership is static
- the management decision-making style has become the consensus as of right.

Stage 4: Establishing a mature team

The mature team is a team which takes personal and collective liability for its actions:

> I am sorry but Pat is out of the office at the moment. I can see from her notes that she would want you to buy the steelwork at that price for delivery but I cannot give you complete authority. Put in a provisional order and I will get Pat to ring back. Yes, I'm Henry Patterson, Patterson with two t's.

The manager now has to manage appropriately – bringing his or her weight for the task, the team and the individual; it is complex, is not to the taste of many who undertake it, and will be the subject of much of the rest of this chapter.

Stage 5: Allowing the team to break – managing the mourning stage

The Yorkshire clue to managing the disbandment of the team is in the word 'wake'. We have many examples from our experience and have chosen two:

Case study 1: Team in failure
Birds Eye had decided to develop a high technology route to making frozen fish portions. The technology was too advanced and the team failed. The failure was spectacular but there was no criticism of the team – it was a mature team with everything that that meant to the organisation and the individuals concerned. When everything possible had been done, the senior management of Birds Eye decided to close the project. A spectacular party was held and every stakeholder was invited. Taxis took the participants home.

Case study 2: Team in change
We were asked to advise on a very strange change. SELA, a major European manufacturer of industrial fasteners, had decided that its warehousing arrangements did

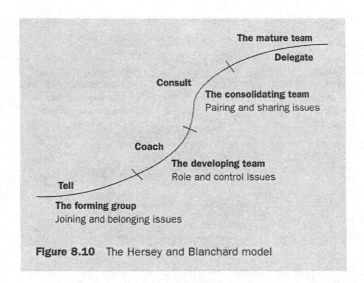

Figure 8.10   The Hersey and Blanchard model

not meet its new significance in the market. The warehouse team was mature but was unhappy and insecure about the new automated warehouse being built along-side their building which was more than 60 years old. The old warehouse had worn pine-wood trolleys and sorting pigeon holes – the new warehouse was metal and computer controlled. Nobody from the old team was to be redundant.

Our advice was to have a wake. There was a party in the new warehouse and during the party the bulldozers crashed through the old building. An old pine-wood trolley was to be presented to the assembly.

Even we were surprised that members of the 'old team' spent their weekend working with the demolition team, unpaid, to speed the work of destruction – and to rescue mementoes.

The leader/manager's job is to support the team. The mature team will survive if the task and the membership have evolved together, the management adopts a flexible and appropriate style of decision making and outside factors allow it.

The diagrams we have seen until now are from Adair. The Hersey and Blanchard (1969) model sees things in a slightly different way (Figure 8.10).

Styles of management

David Kolb, standing on the shoulders of many giants, including Jung, developed his Learning Cycle. We discussed this in some detail in the first chapter. Readers should refer back to their own responses to the Learning Style Indicator in the Survey material of Chapter 1.

The Learning preferences have been related to preferred management styles (Woods, 1989 and Figure 8.11). The reader will be able, by weighting the four quadrants, to look at the likely way he or she functions as a manager.

Management Consultancy and Skills

509

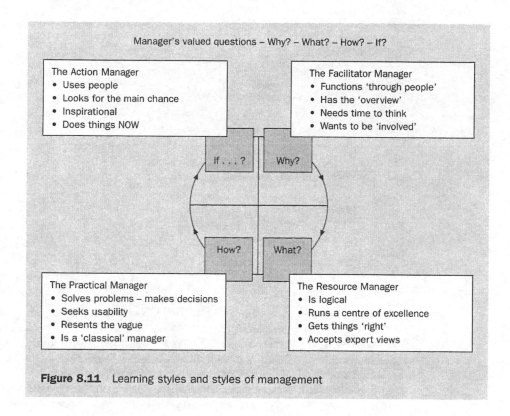

Figure 8.11 Learning styles and styles of management

The facilitator manager

This person works through his or her staff, bringing them on as individuals. They are slow to decide and inclined to need all sides of a question before deciding. They see management as a privilege and not a right – it could be said that they are not natural managers.

> Unilever Foods Research had one facilitator manager who had reached senior status, and many regarded him as a minor genius. His human management skills were such that he was given no line authority. However, the whole operations research, commanded by a resource manager, was at his disposal when he had an idea that needed study or development. He was one of the few people we have ever met who was universally liked and respected.

The resource manager

This person considers the staff to be very much as other resources necessary for the task. This does not mean to say he or she does not value them, but the valuation is in terms of professional competence. He or she works by facts, and on the advice of experts. He or she can well treat staff as a group that needs to be protected.

> One of the author's University computer department was commanded by a resource manager. The computer group was on a floor slightly below ground level

and underneath the library. Ideally suited for main frame working, the place resembled a temple and its staff acolytes. It was not suited for the casual world encouraged by the universal ownership of PC's.

The practical manager

This manager is in the 'classical' mode and is not at home in a command and control organisation. He or she is interested in the skills of the staff in relationship to the tasks they have to accomplish. The practical manager likes systems, order and competence.

When Hicksons Chemicals decided to introduce teamworking, they found that the majority of their managers were practical managers and, in the opinion of the consultants, unsuited for the new world of empowerment. This presented a major problem in recruitment, retraining, refitting, redeployment and release.

The action manager

This person is only interested in results. People are a means to an end and are judged entirely on how they achieve. He or she is often an inspirational leader, and transformational, as we will discuss later. An action manager has a clear vision but may, in the urgency and enthusiasm of the moment, forget to pass it on effectively to 'slower' colleagues.

The manager in the new organisations needs to be flexible and not rooted in one style.

Leadership in the new organisations

Warren Bennis (1997) is quoted as saying: 'Has my thinking changed? Not really. I would say what has changed is the kind of leadership that is now going to be required in organisations. It's a different form of leadership. The Lone Ranger is clearly dead.'

Over many years we have been asking students to provide a list of the people they regard as leaders. The lists are unsurprisingly the same, wherever we are; many are associated with war (Churchill, Zukov, Guderian, Haig, Joan of Arc, Foch) or with religions (Christ, Ghandi, Mohammed) or with world events (Thatcher, Nightingale, Ben Grunion) or of great evil (Hitler, Manson) or great good (Mother Theresa). Very few will be ordinary people doing a job.

Because, until recently, leadership is not associated in general with ordinary people, teaching leadership has been regarded with suspicion outside military academies or top management seminars. We are now recognising that, without leadership at all levels, our world will simply drift into anarchy. However, perhaps more importantly for this chapter, some forms of leadership can be taught. Peter Topping (1997) emphasises this point. He sees that we have gone well past the crude 'great man' theory of leadership and cites three critical factors of leadership in the present world:

Management Consultancy and Skills

1. Personal characteristics
2. The unique demands of situations
3. Actual behaviour.

Topping goes further and lists the basic ingredients of the new leadership:

- Understanding of one's self and self confidence.
- The ability to trust others, credibility and steadiness.
- The ability to foster teamwork and collaboration.
- Strong interpersonal communications skills.
- Openness to new ideas and innovation.
- Decisiveness tempered by solid analysis and problem solving.
- An awareness of relevant situational and environmental factors.
- An understanding of human behaviour in an organisational context.
- A desire to coach and teach so that others may grow.

These are the very skills that we hope to have covered in this book.

Sources of power

Imagine the scene of a Captain in command of a small warship given the task of protecting his convoy of ships from submarine attack. He is given the location of the submarine – directly underneath a number of sailors swimming towards his ship and expecting rescue. With very little hesitation he orders the attack and incidentally causes the death of all the swimming sailors. The scene is described graphically in Monsarrat's book *The Cruel Sea* (1951). What were the sources of power that gave the Captain 'permission' to make such a hard decision and be certain that it would be obeyed? Leaders without followers are not leaders. The 'sources of power' that allowed the acceptance of such a command include:

- **Experience/expertise.** At the commissioning of the corvette – a very simple ship – the Captain, his Number 1 and the Chief Engineer would know every nut and bolt of the ship. As in the novel, when the Captain was promoted to command a frigate – a much larger and technologically advanced ship – his expertise became less relevant but his experience had grown and his rank was increased to compensate.
- **Hierarchy.** The Captain has rank invested in him through the Admiralty. Later he calls a group of junior officers to order by simply patting his sleeve.
- **Charisma/credibility.** Rank, experience, expertise mean nothing if people simply do not accept your right to lead.
- **Dedication/role model.** Working harder, longer and to more purpose is expected of some leadership styles, but not all.
- **The team and followers.** The skills of the team and the presence of people willing to follow are essential to leadership 'power'. Maintaining the team is the first priority of a leader.

Management Consultancy and Skills

- **Patronage and influence.** Visible support of 'the boss', in this case the Admiral, is an essential of leadership power.
- **Clarity of purpose.** The Captain had clear written orders: 'Destroy enemy submarines and guard the convoy.' Picking up survivors was not his primary and explicitly stated concern.

Any leader needs some of these sources of power, the balance changing with time. Thus as the Captain becomes out of touch with expertise he is given more hierarchical authority – promotion.

> Andrew S. Groves, the CEO of Intel who stepped down in March 1997, saw his changing power base very clearly. His solo expertise became replaced by the ability to judge the advice and feeling he obtained by walking the plants and laboratories and judging the respect his various specialists received from their peers.

One of Topping's criteria for leadership concerned understanding the situation and the environment. The concepts of situational leadership are widely taught.

Situational leadership

Vroom and Yetton (1973) classified the decision-making styles and showed that the choice of style was entirely situational. The styles are shown in Table 8.7.

The coding of the Vroom and Yetton classification is possibly of the most elitist type, and to save the reader trouble: A stands for Authoritarian, C stands for Consultative and G for Group. The '1' is for individual and '11' for more than one. Thus C11 stands for where the manager consults more than one person at a time.

The reader might like to try a test. Forget the warship and imagine that you need to get your fellow students or workers to read the whole of our current book. This time we would like you to work on your fellow students using each of the Vroom and Yetton styles.

A1. In the A1 style you may choose to use a bald 'telling' statement: 'You will all read the book', or you may choose to soften the blow by some 'selling'. the idea: 'You will all benefit from reading the book and improve your management skills to such an extent as to guarantee promotion (or pass the exam)'

Equally, and still in A1, you could delegate the message giving to some unfortunate: 'Get them to read the book.'

A11. In A11 we need to collect information before the instruction: 'Will everyone be in the office on Thursday? Fine, now get them together and . . .'

C1. C1 allows the subordinate some knowledge of what is to come: 'I am very keen on them all reading the book. What sort of resistance are we likely to get if I tell them on Thursday? I need to make up my mind on how to proceed.'

Management Consultancy and Skills

Table 8.7 The Vroom and Yetton classification of management decision-making styles

Authoritarian styles
A1. The individual manager solves the problem or makes the decision using the information available to him or her at the time.
A11. The individual manager collects the relevant information from subordinates and then decides on a solution or makes the decision. The manager may or may not choose to tell the subordinates about the nature of the problem while he or she is collecting the information. The subordinates act as a data source and not in any way as decision makers.

Consultative styles
C1. The manager shares the problem with relevant subordinates individually, without getting them together in a group but telling them that he or she will make a considered decision which may or may not reflect individual advice.
C11. The manager shares the problem with relevant subordinates in a group, explaining that the decision may or may not reflect the suggestions and views collected.

Delegated or group styles
(G1*The manager acts as non-directive counsellor to individual subordinates getting them to work out a solution to a problem which is personal to them).
G11. The manager shares problems with subordinates in a group, giving them formal permission to develop alternatives and hopefully reach consensus on what is to be done. Using G11 the manager may or may not take on the role of Chairperson at the meeting or meetings of the group but makes it clear that he or she will accept and implement any decision or solution that has the support of the whole group.

C11. The C11 strategy could involve many of the same words as the C1 but the words would of course be addressed to a meeting of the group. The whole group would have to share their views and the views be heard in public by us before we make up our minds.

G11. In G11 you would then define the importance you give a problem and its resolution. Exactly how the group responds to the criticism, and respond it must, is not something you are going to tell them. However, if the group does come up with a legitimate, possible and agreed strategy to reduce future management mistakes, you will abide by and implement the recommendations. How much further you 'assist' in the groups decision-making process depends very much on individual styles.

Managers who are perceived as democratic may well be able to sit in for the group discussions and attempt to push their own points of view on a 'one person one vote' basis. Most managers will not be able to do this and would find that they always possessed at least 1.5 votes at the meeting. In G11 style most of us would be advised to say something like: 'I must say again that I will abide by the decision and I'm going to leave you to it. Let me know when you have decided.' The serious mistake for any manager is to indicate a G11 and then not accept the G11 recommendations of the group. A group is often flattered by being allowed a G11 process and can be helped by the process to form a team. However, a team will hit back if the manager 'betrays' it by reverting to control, i.e., A or C styles.

Often we take the gut response to decision making without checking logically whether we have a choice and whether our gut reaction is the best way. The key to effective management is clarity – if you are in A1, NEVER give the idea that you are consulting. If you are in C11, indicate that you are consulting and do not give the impression of G11. If C1/C11 or G11 does not work or cannot be completed in time and you have to move to A1/A11, explain carefully beforehand. A move from A1/A11 to G11 is virtually impossible.

Each decision-making style has short-, medium- and long-term consequences. Thus the authoritarian style might, for our example, get the job done but it is hardly a tool of constructive communication. The consultative styles still retain authority but will assist a group towards team development. The group style may well assist a feeling of team, but may not give the 'appointed' leader the control he or she needs.

The point we are making is that we all possess flexibility in our decision-making style and that pausing to look at the consequences of our choice is worth while. The Appendix contains a number of case studies for discussion (see pp. 635–7). In all the case studies certain issues have recurred in defining the situation surrounding the choice of management decision-making styles.

Factors in situational leadership

Vroom and Yetton found that the choice of decision-making style depends on a number of factors. In making each decision we have to ask ourselves a number of questions (see Table 8.8).

Vroom and Yetton prepared an algorithm (Woods, 1989) whereby the style of decision making could be arrived at automatically by asking the questions in sequence. G11 is always difficult with large groups and the accepted wisdom is that G11 without help, does not work when more than seven are involved. However, 'with help' much larger numbers can be involved.

Lada Cars – an importer of cars from the Eastern Bloc – asked us to run a G11 meeting for all middle managers. The venue of the meeting was chosen at an isolated hotel over a weekend and the meeting started with the managing director giving very stark news of the balance sheet. In the last year the company had lost half its business and was in serious trouble. A survival plan was needed. The MD then announced that he was leaving and would return on Sunday afternoon to endorse the plan developed by the group of his managers, and he left. We ran a brainstorming session for ideas and, at 200, we stopped and separated the ideas into the company functions – marketing, manufacture, distribution, accounts, etc. At the hour, on the hour, each of the groups reported to plenary and went away again to refine their ideas. When the MD returned the managers had come up with a

Table 8.8   Questions for decision makers

A. **The quality of the decision.** Do we have to get someone else's approval? Is the decision to be audited by some external authority or is the demand that we make a decision, any decision, almost regardless of its nature, and that decision will be upheld? Examples of decisions with a quality requirement would involve time, money, resources, legal implications and less easily defined factors concerned with image, precedent and correctness.

B. **Information.** Do you, as the decision maker, have enough data or expertise to decide unaided?

C. **Logical structure.** Do you, as the manager, either by experience or analysis, understand what needs to be done and what data need to be collected for a high-quality decision? Do you know how to collect the alternatives and the rules that govern their selection?

D. **Acceptance.** Do we, as the decision makers, need the commitment of others to get the decision implemented? Do others care strongly enough about the result of the decision to block or sabotage certain courses of action if they do not agree? Would monitoring of certain decisions be a problem?

   The issue occurs where others have to execute the decision using initiative, judgement, supervision is minimal and overt or covert resistance could block effective implementation.

E. **Power.** Do we have the power or the inclination to use power to enforce the decision? Power is like potential energy – power used is power lost. If you have to use raw power regularly then your power will soon become exhausted.

F. **Shared goals.** Do your subordinates share the same goals as you, the decision maker? Are their objectives, as your objectives, thinking of the organisation or group as a whole, the same as those who are affected by the decision?

G. **Conflict within the group.** Even with shared goals, certain potential solutions may be liable to cause conflict within the group.

H. **Time.** Time limits push us towards more authoritarian styles.

drastic reorganisation, well beyond the scope of anything he could have suggested without consent.

New models of management

Overall the new models of management are a challenge to the classical approaches of management put forward by Taylor, the Galbraiths, Fayol and Weber from the late nineteenth and early twentieth century and often unquestioned to the very recent past. (Burnes, 1992). The responses call for a new form of management and leadership. The issue we have to face is the role of the middle manager, or, as he or she often is now, the co-ordinator of a group moving towards the perceived ideal of a self-directed team. With the concepts of the self-directed team comes the word with almost magical significance – empowerment.

Stages of empowerment

Leadership in the new organisations has been saddled with a whole range of accepted wisdom linked with words such as 'total empowerment' and the 'self-directed team'. In our opinion both 'total empowerment' and the 'self-directed team' (Woods, 1997b) are Holy Grails whose attainment could well be a false objective.

'You are now empowered to make grommets.'
'I don't want to make grommets, I want to make dreams.'
'You are fired!'

'You are fired!' has been heard many times in so called 'empowered' organisations. We have even heard:

'I keep telling them they are empowered, but they don't listen.'

Repeating what we have already discussed in our chapter on empowerment and motivation, we see empowerment in much less idealistic terms. Charles Handy would see personal empowerment as being allowed to understand WHY a job has to be done, agreeing WHAT has to be done but being allowed to develop the HOWs for oneself – with understanding and agreement by one's manager. We would say:

Empowerment is working within a set of rules to achieve an agreed objective.

However, even in these simplistic and practical terms, the whole concept of empowerment brings stresses to managers – it's not the job that many managers signed up for.

Stages of organisational development towards total empowerment

Many of the attempts to move towards an empowered workforce flounder because they require too much of both organisations and existing managers. They are a 'bridge too far'. Table 8.9 illustrates the stages of maturity of organisations (Woods, 1997b).

Organisations are not homogeneous: some areas may be fully empowered while others may retain completely hierarchical control. Very often there is a hierarchical split of empowerment – thus the top team may well be fully empowered, as indeed may parts of the shop floor, whereas those at a sticky level of first line supervision may see themselves as at the beginning of the dialogue stage of development.

The stage of development is entirely situational. There is no universally desired level and, if there were, this would certainly NOT be the level of universal involvement or empowerment.

ND Marsden, a Japanese subsidiary making precision cooling equipment for the motor industry based in West Yorkshire, is proud of its advanced industrial relations. On our scale it is at the dialogue stage of development – in our opinion, entirely appropriate for the industry in which it thrives.

Management Consultancy and Skills

Table 8.9   Stages of organisational maturity

Stage	Organisational behaviour	Maintenance leadership behaviour	Progressive leadership behaviour
1. Awareness of the need to change	Military style culture. Training for tasks. Teams based on function, skill or 'task forces'	Top down. Procedures and manuals. A1 and A11 expected	Employee surveys. 'Tea and toilets' staff committees. Staff newsletters
2. Basic involvement	'Tea and toilets' staff committees. Staff newsletters – notice boards. 'Need to know' basis	Formal feedback on suggestions. Upward questioning allowed. C1 styles accepted	Active use of consultative committees – top team involvement
3. Established dialogue	Time for consultation – changes publicised. Customer relationship training. Consultants. Quality Circles WITHIN the hierarchy are tested. Formally analysed data – 'bench-marking' – available	Control of pace and direction of change. Appraisal systems involve real feedback. A1, A11, C1 accepted and C11 beginning	TQM discussions. Cross-departmental discussions. Departmental managers encouraged to consult
4. Participation	Matrix management in some areas. Team training starts. Information available to representatives on demand	Team working encouraged, and reassessment of managers' roles. G11 is accepted in very restricted areas	Decisions are delegated with responsibility as appropriate
5. Consultation	The teams are allowed to function with reduced supervision. The atmosphere is one of listening and hearing. Company information available on request	The symphony conductor model (see later) adopted. Setting up BPR systems. Everything and everyone is open to question. Management decision making is entirely situational	Development of open structures and a learning organisation (Senge, 1991) approach
6. Involvement or total empowerment	Self-Directed teams are the norm in the organisation. The encouragement of the learning organisation where everyone is expected and facilitated to develop his or her own skills to an appropriate level. On demand training	The football manager (see later) approach is encouraged where teams and individuals are empowered to manage their own chaos. The managers and leaders establish direction and monitor progress, arbitrate between teams and the organisation, maintain resources and provide an atmosphere of learning	Maintain the vision

Management Consultancy and Skills

Progression or regression of an organisation in the stages of development is an exercise in change management and must come from the top. In the opinion of the author **attempting to move more that one step at a time** is a delicate and often unwise exercise in change management. This is why we see impatience to reach a perceived ideal of total empowerment as being 'a bridge too far'.

A simple procedure for all management

Whatever stage of development is required, managers and leaders need to follow the same routine as discussed by Hersey and Blanchard (1969). Management is about the efficient deployment of resources, one of which is people. Managers need to define objectives, plan and then move into the soft world of people management:

- **Tell** people why things are required and **WHAT** needs doing.
- **Coach** them so that people are competent to do the job.
- **Consult** to the relevant level so that people understand what they are doing AND that they are doing it in a way that still meets your needs.
- **Delegate** given authority matched to the level of responsibility.
- **Monitor** and review what is being done – if necessary repeating the cycle of *tell, coach, consult and delegate* again.
- **Communicate** the work of the team to the 'outside'.

There is a question of balance between the **task**, the **individual** and the **team** (see Figure 8.5). The balance of task-centred activity is most intense at the beginning of any project, being added to successively by the development of the team and then the individuals. The successful manager or leader maintains the balance.

There are four dimensions of the management of people:

1. The **individual** – the more experienced and motivated he or she is, the easier it is to move to delegation.
2. The **team** – teams will move, unless prevented, to their own level of empowerment.
3. The **organisation** – overall the balance of managerial energy changes with the stage of development towards empowerment of the organisation.
4. The **manager** – the balance of control and empowerment of teams and individuals for which one has responsibility will be changed. The way in which the balance may change may well not satisfy the manager. Thus a manager brought up and comfortable in a command and control organisation where telling and monitoring are the human resource management demands of the job, may well be totally unsuited for more empowered organisations where delegation and communication may be the key elements.

We have attempted to summarise how the balance of energy between the various human resource elements of a manager's job relates to the stage of development of the organisation in Figure 8.12.

Management Consultancy and Skills

519

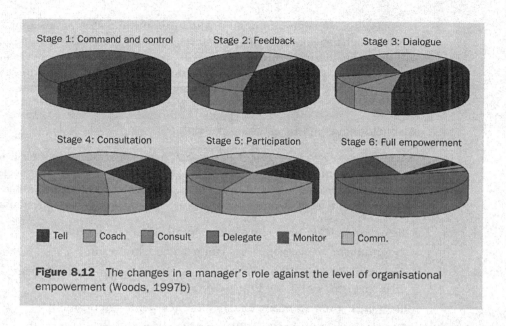

Figure 8.12 The changes in a manager's role against the level of organisational empowerment (Woods, 1997b)

Looking at the balance and the way it changes, it is easy to see the pressures on managers when organisations decide to 'empower their staff'.

Stage 1 The command and control organisations where leadership is largely devoted to telling and monitoring.

Stage 2 Where suggestion schemes have begun – telling and monitoring predominate but consulting and communication are becoming important.

Stage 3 Where meaningful dialogue is allowed and coaching and consulting become significant, although telling and monitoring are still strong.

Stage 4 Active participation where consultation in the decision-making process is beginning to be encouraged and delegation without responsibility is also beginning.

Stage 5 True consultation where coaching and communication have become most important and telling and monitoring are falling against rise in delegation – the cross-functional teams have their own controls.

Stage 6 Involvement where the self-directed teams, that are now the norm of the organisation, are left to manage their own chaos and management is largely about monitoring and communicating.

Problems from the top

Question: What are the three most import factors in managing a change in an organisation?

Answer: 1. Top management commitment
2. Top management commitment
3. Top management commitment

However, a movement towards a fully empowered organisation means progressive loss of power for the top team, and it would be unusual for all the top team to enjoy this loss of power.

> A company whose chief executive was driving the organisation towards total empowerment found that, 18 months along the journey, the Board was still split. Conceptually there was full endorsement by everyone but two directors remained with a lack of commitment on a personal level. This lack of commitment was repeatedly demonstrated as they continued to exercise their 'right' not to follow the rules that had been negotiated with all the staff (in G11). The staff, initially suspicious of the move to empowerment were now enthusiastic but the confused messages from the Board were putting the company itself in danger, until some key resignations were accepted!
>
> *A chicken may well be involved in supplying the eggs in a plate of eggs and bacon, but the pig is actually committed.*
>
> Attributed to Martina Navratilova – tennis star.

A second factor may well come from the chief executive, or at least a senior member of the top team. Driving through an organisational development requires real leadership and often a very directive style of decision making. Here lies the paradox – we call it the Claudius Paradox (Woods, 1997b). The objective of establishing Rome as a republic was *second* on Emperor Claudius's list of priorities throughout his reign, which ended when his wife poisoned him. The first priorities, jostling for pole position, were always more urgent. So it is with many managers who sincerely believe in change but also value their own survival in the present.

Managing chaos: a theory of empowerment

Imagine a scene from the daily life or your most junior and most inexperienced worker.

> Every working day he or she has to get up, prepare for work and get there. The cycle is accepted and assumed, unless the worker arrives late or is incapable of work for some reason. He or she is *delegated* the task of getting into work and allowed to manage his or her own chaos – the milk not arriving, the cat being sick, children unwilling to go to school, the car failing to start. . . . He or she is delegated – with the associated authority and responsibility – to manage this individual chaos because it would be ridiculous to do otherwise.

We are arguing that at some level it is obvious that individuals and teams **must** be left to organise their own chaos, and that the level that it is beneficial to do so is related to the stage of empowerment of the organisation or the sub-organisation being considered. We would refer the reader to the chapter on empowerment and the work surrounding the Hawthorne experiment.

The duties of the manager or leader of these new teams are, first, to decide on the 'rules' that the teams need to follow to fit into the stage of maturity of the organisation.

Management Consultancy and Skills

521

Self-directed teams

These can be formed at any stage of organisational maturity but the cage within which they operate will be different. The cage will be defined by the clarity of the task definition and the reporting period. Thus a self-directed team in a command and control organisation will have a firm objective and reporting procedures, a clear start and end date. For this reason alone self-directed teams in command and control organisations are given names such as 'ephemeral teams', 'project groups', 'task forces', etc. They are necessary, but not always found, in all organisations in recognition that the chaos of the new and unexpected is best dealt with by well-briefed, motivated and trained people on the ground. The two military examples (Hauptmann Geyer and Major Howard) were quoted previously.

Quality circles would be a more contemporary commercial example. As an organisation matures, the 'rules' can be relaxed because people can be trusted more and people are in sympathy with and understand more of the environment within which they operate.

The further strategic task is to determine the size and position for groups or teams to best handle their own chaos within their own circle of concern. Thus, for instance, in a hospital the teams may be best arranged in what remained as hierarchical levels. Often the decision was in fact a confirmation of what was known already – thus nurse teams had always IN PRACTICE organised the chaos on the ward level, the consultants at the next level, and the politicos of administration worked in their own way at the next level. In manufacturing the choice may still be in hierarchical levels but preferably at a level of responsibility and distinguished by their customer base. These are the customer-focused teams.

The manager/leader has three tasks once the self-directed team has been established:

1. *Focusing and maintaining focus for the team*. In order to allow any form of self-direction in teams the manager has to know his or her vision and transmit it in suitable form to the teams. Without this clarity and understanding of the goal and vision, the new teams cannot function independently within their circle of concern. This vision of purpose must be maintained. As Covey says: *Understand and then communicate that understanding.*

2. *Resourcing the team*. The team is essentially getting on with the task and must not be diverted to forage for supplies – be they people or materials.

3. *Maintaining the team within the total environment*. The manager or leader is responsible as spokesperson between teams and towards the organisation as a whole. The manager or leader is also responsible for fitting the team into the 'big picture'.

Monitoring results, focusing, resourcing and maintenance are the jobs for a new person – the facilitator manager for the vision and focus, the resource manager and the practical manager, all bound up in one person. This is not an easy task for the manager who values the role of controller.

New management and leadership models

The military role and control organisation saw its managers as officers in a chain of command. In the new organisations we need new models and we find two models are appropriate:

- The football manager
- The symphony orchestra conductor.

The football manager may, for very special reasons, act in a dual role of player/manager, but more normally he or she is not allowed on the pitch once the whistle has blown. All the work has to be done BEFORE the players go on the pitch and once the game has begun even slight interference can be penalised by the referee. He or she has levels of responsibility for wider 'teams', including all the support staff and the Board.

The football manager would seem to have three roles:

- Determining the tactics that meet the strategy of the Board.
- Making sure that the team have the tools to perform.
- Support and liaison with the outside world – the fans, the press, the Board, etc.

The symphony orchestra conductor has a similar function *but* is actually 'on the pitch' and remains in control. The conductor model is more comfortable for many organisations.

A manager who has grown up in a military style, command and control organisation will require a great deal of relearning before it is possible to think of his or her job in these three roles. Sometimes that type of relearning may well be seen to be impossible.

Managers and leaders

Field Marshall Bill Slim is quoted by Colin Sharman (1997) when he distinguished between managers and leaders in 1970. As a great military leader who became Governor General of Australia, he is likely to have met both.

> The leader and those who follow him represent one of the oldest and most effective of human relationships . . . Leadership is of the spirit, compounded of personality and vision; its practice is an art. Management is of the mind, more a matter of accounts calculation, of statistics, of methods, timetables and routine: its practice is a science. Managers are necessary, leaders are essential. A good system will produce efficient managers, but more than that is needed. We must find managers who are not only skilled organisers, but are also inspired and inspiring leaders.

This is the origin of what we call the *leager* – a strange hybrid between a manager and a leader, able to function as either when appropriate. However, before we get to that point we need to look at how others have distinguished the two roles.

Managers and leaders are often seen as quite distinct beings:

Management Consultancy and Skills

- Leaders chose the road for managers to drive on.
- Managers get people to do things – leaders get people to do the right things.
- Managers get people to do things – leaders get people to want to do them.
- Managers get people to do the same better – leaders get people to do better things.

A more sophisticated view is that leadership and management are on a continuum of thought. Think like a leader and you are on the way to becoming a leader. Think like a manager, and you are a manager.

- Managers think in terms of danger, strategy, rivals, authority, standardisation, policy, management by objectives, control, consistency, stability, reorganisation, systems, logic, hierarchy, scepticism, science, duty, performance, dependence, conserving.
- Leaders think in terms of opportunity, culture, partnership, customers, influence, unity, example, management by walking about, example, empowerment, commitment, crisis, rethinking, insight, proactivity, lateral thinking, equality, optimism, art, dreams, potential. To the leader these are not 'management speak' but realities, at least for a moment in time.

This leads us to certain generalities about leaders and leadership.

- **Leaders are dangerous.** The Captain Kirk's of Star Fleets rule but the Mr Spocks pick up the pieces. However, most of us are capable of thinking as leaders *and* managers when the situation calls. We may, for instance, be leaders of our team and managers for our top team – it's a safer way of working!
- **Leadership is situationally dependent.** J.M. Barrie in his play *The Admirable Crichton*, describes how a butler and his upper-class family are castaways on a desert island. Here he has the necessary aptitudes and skills to make him the natural leader. After rescue he returns to the subservient role of butler. A factual example in British twentieth-century history would be the cases of Chamberlain and Churchill. Both were leaders for their own day and not for any other. Leadership can demonstrate itself at any level of an organisation and is not in any way related to formally recognised hierarchical position.
- **Leaders need followers.** Your leadership style, at the right time and place, is a very personal affair, but in all cases is a culmination of previous circumstances. Leadership is above all about human resource skills, skills that may be developed by watching those you admire and modelling their behaviour. All of this means, as Charles Handy (1997) points out, that leaders must be given the time and space to prove themselves – 'leaders are grown and not made'.

The currency of transactional leadership

Perhaps the most contentious issue in military organisations is the way potential leaders are **made** to think as managers by the control of patronage and of credibil-

Table 8.10   The currencies of transactional leaders
There are four currencies for the manager wishing to work as a transactional leader:
• **Economic** – buying service by providing goods or money. • **Political** – protection or patronage. • **Psychological** – a shoulder to cry on. • **Customised empowerment** – rewarding desired behaviour with gaining empowerment.

ity. These two factors are outside the control of the individual. In a strictly command and control organisation very few managers are able to hire, fire or materially reward their own staff. Patronage is limited to participation in the appraisal system and the occasional award of medals. Credibility exists in such organisations by the security of status. If I do not 'get on with my boss' I will be seen to be unable to support my subordinates.

The four currencies available for the transactional leader

Table 8.10 summarises the four processes – we term them currencies – by which managers acting in the transactional mode achieve power and status with their 'followers'.

Economic   Physical rewards are often difficult for an individual manager hoping to lead and develop followers. The use of economic currency may be quite subtle – the 'blind eye' to expenses, the conference, redistribution of workload to enable overtime, various allowances. They are ways of 'buying' loyalty, however hidden.

Political   Political patronage relies on the individual 'belonging to the club'. When a manager uses this currency he or she makes an implicit or explicit contract with a follower of support. The non-verbal 'hand on the shoulder' in public or immediate access to hierarchical superiors for problem solving, often grants it. Patronage is an acceptance of a hierarchy and may easily be withdrawn should one fail to meet the requirements of the 'club'.

> In January 1994 Tim Yeo resigned as a Minister in the UK Conservative government of the time. As a politician a Minister needs to be able to lead. Yeo was Environment Minister in a political party concerned with what amounted to a crusade for 'family values'. He was unfortunate enough to have been widely publicised for having an illegitimate child. The reality of the child and its unmarried mother did not make him resign – he was finally forced to resign from office, in our opinion, because his patronage base, the constituency that elected him, withdrew support.

Psychological   Time has a high currency for the transactional manager. Giving time and concern develops 'followers'. Following the models proposed in our chapter on constructive communication is a very good start to 'banking' psychological currency.

Customised empowerment The concept is that many people work for 'space'. We suggest that the rules governing any job conform to a FRAME – a concept we discussed in the chapter on motivation. On this basis we can define empowerment as working within rules without the concept of obedience. The transaction is about allowing more scope for the individual as a reward for 'followship'.

Without being empowered ourselves we are relegated to the role of a manager. Transactions, honoured by both parties, are the currency of the transactional leader. Obligations make the world go round for the transactional leader. Your ability to function as a transactional leader depends on:

- your ability to promise and to deliver – promising to deliver and failing will reduce your personal power base
- your own status and 'membership of the club', which can be removed at any time
- your own empowerment
- your personal and interpersonal skills.

You have to be 'allowed' by others to honour your obligations.

Transformational leadership

Andrew Korac-Kakabadse and Nada Korac-Kakabadse (1997), in their recent review of Best Practice in the Australian Public Service, bring together many of the arguments we have covered. They also distinguish between transactional and transformational leaders – a distinction that has attracted considerable debate. The emerging argument holds that 'most leaders are good managers, but good managers are not necessarily good leaders' (Warburton, 1993). The world beyond the 1990s will not belong to managers, but to passionate, driven leaders who are innovative path-finders able to empower others to lead (Fairholm, 1991; Leavett, 1987; Manz and Sims, 1990; Warburton, 1993). They continue to argue that managers use transactions to maintain the balance of operations and are process- or means-oriented (Burns, 1978) – what Warburton (1993) calls 'caretakers of the status quo' and Bennis (1984) thinks of as 'replicability with a focus on control and accountability'. In contrast, transformational leaders – according to Bennis (1984), Bennis and Nanus (1985), Burns (1978), Peters and Waterman (1982) and Zaleznik (1977) – are creatively devoted to ends and not means. They think globally and seek to break moulds to create and achieve their visions (Bradford and Cohen, 1984; Henry, 1991; McAller, 1991; Selznick, 1957). Summarising, we may say that transformational leaders provide a new sense of direction. **They are change agents.**

The 'pure' manager with no pretensions of leadership is one end of the spectrum and the 'pure' transformational leader is the other. The transactional leader encroaches on both their territories. They provide vision, mobilise commitment, model and institutionalise the change they facilitate.

Providing a vision

The transformational leader, driving with personal charisma or bringing others with him or her by inspirational means has clarity of purpose that can be called vision.

- Questioning of the status quo
- A discussion of alternatives
- A presentation of an ideal.

Mobilising commitment

- Changing personal objectives into group objectives – 'all for one and one for all'
- Stimulation, drive and emotional appeal.

Modelling

- Bringing in example, symbolism and meaning with the message
- The consistency that inspires trust.

Institutionalising change

- Making the new into the norm
- Becoming the subject of legend.

The role of the Court Jester

Transformational leadership in organisations is always controversial. Unlike the transactional leader, who can be turned on or off by the patronage he or she gets from those around, and in particular 'management', the transformational leader has vision. The wrong vision for the time and place, or the right vision for too long, is dangerous for the survival of the organisation. An example would be Margaret Thatcher whose vision (in the opinion of one author) transformed a society but then became stale and dangerous. Leaders need to be able to listen to their followers and two classes of followers in particular: the Vizier and the Court Jester.

The Vizier is the loyal and able administrator who refines the vision to practical terms. Dreams cost money, detractors usually accompany followers, things take time. It is the job of the Vizier to provide substance to the vision.

The Court Jester has a quite different function. He or she, in a position without authority, tells the truth in a way that the transformational leader can hear, and process.

> Margaret Thatcher appears not to have had a Court Jester or, if she had, she did not listen. The issue was Poll Tax – a system where all citizens were taxed equally, regardless of wealth or status. For good or bad the opposition to the Tax had become united and deafening. Court Jesters, while accepting the vision of their

leaders, need to 'hear' the noise and inform their chiefs in an unchallenging way, when the noise becomes patterned (Dixon, 1994). Then the great leader changes course. Margaret did not change course and was deposed.

Churchill had a great Vizier and Court Jester rolled into one man – Auchinleck. One of Churchill's great visions was concerned with avoiding the battles of attrition that he had witnessed during the Great War. He saw the planned invasion of the French coast in 1944 as having the potential of draining so much life and asked Auchinleck to devise another plan – an invasion of Hitler's Europe through Portugal. The Auk, as he was known, did not cross the great man, which he knew would have made him more adamant and cause his own dismissal. What he did was prepare the plan in such a way as to emphasise 'impracticability' and also present a 'bill' for how much work had been involved and how working on it had damaged the grand plan for the invasion of Normandy. Churchill, a great leader, thanked the Auk and forgot the plan to invade in the South.

Really great transformational leaders:

- are in the right place at the right time
- have the strength to cultivate empowered supporters
- have the ability to stick to the vision but the flexibility to move.

All leaders need to balance:

- the needs of the task, individuals and the team
- his or her own personal needs with that of the organisation.

Work to a strategy in which you know where you want to go – or, if you prefer, have a vision. In addition:

- Plan to achieve their objective or vision using the best information available.
- Develop the resources, including the 'followers' necessary for success.
- Set up procedures for monitoring the 'advance signs' of whether the projects are on the right or wrong course.
- Remain dedicated to the objective but retain flexibility on tactics.
- If the 'signs' begin to form a cluster – review everything. Remember that your vision is rooted in a particular set of circumstances and these may have changed.
- Take care of yourself and your followers.
- Know when to quit.

A model for leadership and the learning organisation

A significant change in the role of the new leader/manager occurs when we discuss the largest change currently considered in organisations – developing the learning organisation. In a learning organisation, contrary to the irony of Scott Adams (1996) who sees all these changes as fads designed to get more work for less money,

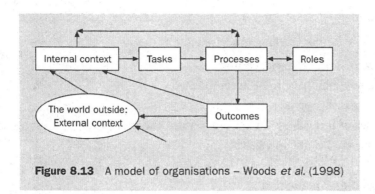

Figure 8.13 A model of organisations – Woods *et al.* (1998)

we do have a chance of facing the new world proactively. Understanding the learning organisation allows us to model management behaviour.

We will side-step the innumerable definitions of learning organisations, such as:

> Organisational learning is the process by which the organisation's knowledge and value base changes, leading to improved problem-solving ability and capacity for action. (Probst and Buchel 1997)

We will also side-step the arguments as to whether organisational learning is greater or less than the sum of the learning of groups and individuals. We are looking for a definition and a model that can be used – such niceties may only confuse. Our definition is:

> *A learning organisation has a structure and ethos that allow it and its parts – groups and individuals – to learn and adapt productively from its and others' errors and successes.*

This is the definition of an organic structure, but we see the later organisational models of Argyris and Schone (1981) as closed systems. Working models need to describe the open systems within which the new managers need to operate.

Herriot and Pemberton (1995a) proposed a further model which was modified by Woods *et al.* (1998) to provide a background to our considerations of the way we all – managers, leaders and followers – behave (Figure 8.13).

The concept behind the model is that management is about making things happen. The skills that assist us towards competencies are about making our organisations successful – however that is determined. We agree with Herriot and Pemberton in that outcomes are not merely as simple as Shea and Guzzo (1987) state:

> We believe that real world, real time group effectiveness is what matters, and it boils down to the production of designated products or the delivery of contracted services, per specification.

We see outcomes as the products, tangible or intangible, of our endeavours, functional or dysfunctional. They are what we can measure and by measuring, learn. Thus as we will see in our case study of the hospital ward, a potential risk to a member of staff is as much an outcome worthy of learning from, as a new grommet.

The model

The elements of our working model (Figure 8.13) are:

- The internal and external context
- The tasks which have to be accomplished
- The processes to achieve the tasks
- The roles of individuals and groups within these processes
- The outcomes of the processes

The principle of outcomes

The processes alone can produce **measurable** outcomes. Although other workers see **roles** and **tasks** as producing **outcomes**, we argue that this is not so. A 'role' is an abstract entity and a 'task' is merely a wish until performed – these are starting points. Thus, for instance, Belbin (1981) sees nine roles in his ideal team. We can describe one of his roles as a **Shaper** – the ideal 'tough' manager – but without the shaper in a 'context' and with a 'task' he or she does nothing. The word 'shaper' is at best a descriptor of 'how' a particular person might go about the process of a given task in a team context. Understanding the role tells us nothing about the only thing we can measure – the outcome of the task itself.

So it is with tasks. Tasks have to be performed – in our language, become **processes**, before they can produce measurable outcomes. It is outcomes alone that can be monitored and learnt from. Our model thus differs profoundly from that of Herriot and Pemberton who saw outcomes arising from the context, the tasks and the roles, in addition to the processes.

External and internal context

The **external context** is outside the immediate control of the organisation, and is the gate to the **total** environment – the world. We assume that no individual or organisation is a free agent – the external context defines the cage within which we exist and in which our behaviours are shaped. The external context comprises a world of competitors, legislators, cultures, suppliers, Unions, etc. The world is less easily defined but includes the environment.

The **internal context** is the assumptions, boundaries, tethering factors, stated or otherwise that act as our starting point for structuring the work of an organisation. They are the items we learnt to challenge in our chapter on effective problem solving.

From the internal context, tasks can be listed, new tasks arising from perceived changes and old or revised tasks to deal with what is known.

Tasks

Tasks are the response to the question of 'What needs to be done?' within the existing or changing internal context. Thus, if an organisation finds itself under increasing competitor pressure in its external context, this reflects directly on the internal context. Changed internal contexts may well demand a revision of the tasks required – money may well be seen to be tight and the tasks set of the individuals and teams within the organisation will be defensive. Another internal context could well produce an aggressive strategy reflected in tasks designed to produce new products and processes.

Processes

Processes are the practical response to accomplishing the tasks set through the internal context; however, they may well influence the internal context itself.

> Birds Eye in the 1970s was an extremely successful manufacturer of Frozen Foods for the UK market. Its domination of the market and the growth of the total market allowed it to expand some 20 per cent in its twenty-first year of operation. In the twenty-first year the market became mature. New product launches failed to meet the targets set. From experience of mature products, competitors became strong and the distributors grew in influence. From a 20 per cent growth, the growth was marginal one year later.

Prior to the downturn of Bird's Eye's business, tasks were related to producing and distributing quantity in what was virtually a seller's market – the processes reflected this. After the downturn, processes moved to cost efficiency and improved customer service.

Roles

The roles individuals and teams choose depend on the tasks they are asked to perform. Inversely, the roles individuals and teams are able or willing to adopt will feed directly back to the tasks.

> We were asked to advise on the reorganisation of two departments into one single department on a single site. The company, a family based concern, was struggling. Working with the teams concerned it was immediately apparent that strong leadership was required. Unfortunately the chief executive had a very inflexible consultative style and lacked the confidence to actually give firm orders.

In our model the tasks required for the company to survive involved the senior management adopting the role of a firm leadership, something of which they proved incapable. As they also refused to take on a strong manager to replace the CEO, the company had another reason to move towards complete collapse.

The dynamic of the model

We would affirm that learning and change are not events but a process. A learning organisation and its parts work within the inner circle of our model, recognising changes in its internal environment though monitoring the outcomes of its processes while observing the external context and working proactively with it

Management Consultancy and Skills

(Woods, 1998). We would doubt that the Zen Buddhist concept of moving towards Nivana by a series of deaths and rebirths, apply to the organisations of which we have experience; however, our observations lead us to be more modest in our claims. Most organisations at best survive by continuous and often painful change, a very few prosper. Managed discontinuous change, and learning by it, is often quoted as having about a 25 per cent chance of success (Rossiter, 1995). This does not mean that managed discontinuous change is by nature a 'bad thing' but that the response to change in the external context may be too late. Once again we return to the metaphor of Davy's Bar. Using the metaphor, many organisations are drinking in Davy's Bar and it is too late to go back that critical half-mile to refocus their business.

Our first point is that we need to accept change as a process that allows us the opportunity of learning, and that the skill of managing it lies in acting *before* we are pushed and *before* our options are reduced (Probst and Buchel, 1997). The time for organising for discontinuous change is when we have slack, and not when we are against the wall!

Using our model we see that learning – adaptation of an organisation or any subset of the organisation – can be triggered at any point.

> A training organisation was 'lucky' enough to recruit a pedantic and assertive accountant. In her **role** she was able to release the 'creative' staff from routine administration and get on with developing programmes that delighted their customers. The internal and the external contexts moved in a favourable way for the company. When she was 'head hunted' the innovative processes had to alter and the outcomes became dysfunctional, leading to an unfocused internal context and, very soon, the external context became hostile.

Our second point is that the learning organisation does not have the limitations of the command and control organisation in that change is instigated from the top. Learning organisations learn through the actions of individuals (Walsh and Ungson, 1991).

Who, then, is responsible for the attainment of goals? EVERY member of the company is responsible. Our success depends on everyone acting responsibly. To enable all members to work responsibly and to attain their common goals together and in harmony, all those in leadership must act responsibly. This is our view of responsibility in action and in leadership (Schmidt, 1991):

• The internal context can be limited to a desk or be a view from Gaia herself.

> A manager of GKN was responsible for facilitating two teams from her desk. The one team was in Wolverhampton in the industrial Midlands of the UK and the other is Westland Helicopters in Somerset. Westland Helicopters is a high technology subsidiary of GKN but Yeovil is an area based in agricultural culture. The internal contexts are totally different – difference not implying criticism. To manage the two teams requires an understanding of the internal contexts. At its crudest, an ex-farmer will do a good job in his or her good time, an ex-factory worker will do as he or she is told. Manage the two internal contexts in the same way and you will fail.

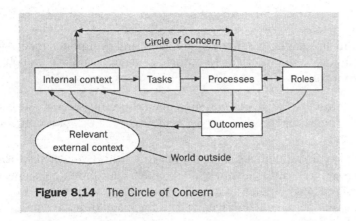

Figure 8.14   The Circle of Concern

Managing and leading within the model

What within our model is the role of the manager? We see the manager as working proactively within the Circle of Concern (see Figure 8.14). His or her job (Woods, 1997b) as a manager/leader is to:

- Convert the internal context into tasks.
- Communicate the 'what needs to be done' – the tasks – so that his or her staff can develop the processes to accomplish the tasks. Along with developing the HOW issues the manager needs to coach his or her staff so that we are not blocked by inability.
- Consult so that the HOWs meet the organisational objectives.
- Monitor the outcomes from the processes so that adjustments can be made, learn from them and, if relevant, communicate the learning and the changes to the organisation or subsets of the organisation.

Some of the outcomes will potentially develop the internal context favourably, others will be perceived as dysfunctional. We need to 'accentuate the positive and eliminate the negative' as with Kurt Lewin's process of force field analysis (1951). Looking at the roles, we see confusion. Drucker saw the role of a manager to follow the paths drawn up by the leader. No such distinction now occurs. The new manager needs to draw the path and develop processes for his or her staff to follow and understand the vision of the whole. We have therefore concocted the new role of **leager**. Leagers both lead and implement.

Richard Pascale, quoted in an AMA report (1996), states:

> Management is the exercise of authority and influence to achieve levels of performance consistent with demonstrated levels.
>
> Leadership is making happen what wouldn't happen anyway, and this is always working on the edge.

SUMMARY

The model, in its simplicity, allows individuals and groups to understand their role in a changing world and learn from the experience. We have brought forward several key concepts:

- The open nature of change and the subsequent learning process – we have presented a model that sees change and learning as a continuous process rather than an event.

- The concept of an individual Circle of Concern – within our model there are tasks, processes, roles and outcomes, all of which contribute to changing our internal context and, perhaps in a small way and maybe in a large way, affect our external environment. However, within the grand order of things, our Circle of Concern is only a subset of the whole.

  Managing effectively within our Circle of Concern involves us changing our role. The old distinction between managers and leaders, and indeed the subdivision of leadership into transactional and transformational, is no longer valid. New managers need to adopt roles primarily of visionary guide, monitor and facilitator. For this we have coined the word 'leager'.

Skill Analysis

CASE STUDY **8.1**

CHARITY MISSION STATEMENT

A charity had been established for over 100 years by a group of Methodists to provide homes for impoverished children in the northern industrial cities of the UK. A new chief executive – Joan Brown – decided to review the Mission Statement of the charity against the new world.

The old Mission Statement, found in some literature dating back over 70 years, was:

> *To provide healthy and protective homes for the homeless children of the new industrial cities and thereby lead them into the Christian fellowship.*

Her new Mission Statement was:

> *To support underprivileged parents, regardless of race, class or creed towards being able to provide a constructive life for themselves and their children.*

She now found herself in an impossible situation. The previous friendly atmosphere of the charity had vanished and people were in open and dysfunctional conflict. Work was not being done.

Discussion questions

1. What would you see as the changes that had forced a rethink of the original Mission Statement?
2. How would you expect the internal context of the team to be affected?
3. What new tasks and roles would you see the team members adopting – or indeed *not* adopting?
4. What forms of dysfunctional behaviour would you expect from the 'team'?
5. What would be the reasons for this dysfunctional behaviour?
6. What would you advise?

CASE STUDY **8.2**

HARRY GREENWAYS

Harry Greenways is a successful Leeds, West Yorkshire-based service organisation. They handle a range of services for clients ranging from arranging advertising campaigns to advising on public relations.

In 1995 the CEO – Harry Greenway, the founder and long concerned with the expansion of the organisation – was influenced to change the processes from a departmentalised system to teamworking. Using the Semler model (Semler, 1988) his new organisation consisted of a top team termed 'coaches' who were responsible for strategy and assisting the 'associates' arranged in two teams to perform the work of the organisation. A further team provided support – gardening to reception.

The new processes impacted on the roles of the associates immediately. As the Processes were based on self-directed teams, some individuals found that their role as team leader was no longer required and the consensus systems were not to their liking. After some stress, they left.

The processes led to customer-focused teams where individual responsibility to clients became collective. This was not liked by some clients and the external context of the organisation changed – clients were unhappy, reflecting on the internal context, which became more demanding. The internal context was also fundamentally altered by the 'consensus' processing of the teams. The movement of servicing teams rather than individuals was deeply resented by certain members of the organisation – as tasks altered in nature, the change in the processes became irreversible with further changes in the roles of staff and further discontent and departures.

The CEO who had implemented the change – by, it must be said, a rather authoritarian move – felt the major change in role when the changes he had imposed became organisational learning, and he moved towards a leager and not a dictator. This is the issue we have previously termed the Claudian Paradox after the Roman Emperor who always had establishing a republic as **second** on his agenda. Claudius found, as do many managers, the issues of maintaining a company pushing into number one slot ahead of their intellectual wish to empower their employees. The very people who are needed to vision and propel a change programme find it hard to delegate realistically when the changes have been learnt and implemented.

Discussion questions

1. Would you see the external context leading directly to the changes Harry Greenway decided upon for the internal context?

2. In hindsight, what could Harry have done to improve the likelihood of success for his changes?

3. Considering the duties of a manager, what could have been done to make sure that employees and customers were happy with the changes? Whose responsibility should this have been?

CASE STUDY **8.3**

THE HOSPITAL WARD

A nursing sister was accompanying the registrar on his tour round her trauma ward. At the end of the tour she attempted to explain a difficulty she was having with a patient. As she saw it, the patient was a danger to the safety of the ward and in particular the safety of her staff and the patients – her internal context.

The patient, a woman, had been admitted two days previously drunk and with a moderately serious injury from a fall. Initially passive she had become increasingly violent and threatening to her staff, the auxiliaries and other patients. The first major problem had come when a trainee nurse noticed that the patient had smuggled alcohol in her locker, and mentioned it to the patient who threw a full bedpan at her. The climax had come when the patient made a well-directed and co-ordinated attack on the team physiotherapist.

The sister wanted the patient taken to a secure unit. The registrar simply ignored the sister and went on with his review of the surgical condition of the patients. Finally the sister – in front of the final section of her ward – blocked the passage of the registrar and his party and insisted that she be heard. Her case had become slightly modified – the action of the patient was endangering the recovery of HIS patients as they recovered from surgery. The registrar took action and the problem patient was moved.

CASE STUDY **8.4**

BRUDDERSFORD

Bruddersford is an engineering company making a range of products and operating under the umbrella of a conglomerate. The whole Bruddersford company is moving into dire financial straits. Looking at the whole company, the external context had become more competitive, with unfavourable exchange rates and competitors reorganising and outsourcing. Cash flow problems and low moral dominated the internal context of the company and the response was to downsize and reduce costs. The processes for this were put in hand and unfortunately the output was further and deeper cash flow problems. The 'cash cow' of the company continued to be pressured by exchange rates and the potential star – a new product range, now starved of development cash – floundered. If the internal context continued to deteriorate for long, the bailiffs would dominate the external context.

The company was already in divisions and we decided to look at the internal context of each in turn – for the sake of this case study, the Cash Cow Division and the Potential Star Division.

The Cash Cow Division had a very small number of key industrial customers who were becoming increasingly cost conscious and demanding. Bruddersford was supplying a whole range of services to these customers, some of which had to be outsourced. Increasingly it was becoming a factoring operation with equipment idle and working at a loss when real costs were taken into account. The profits from the Potential Star Division were subsidising the operation. However, it was the foundation of Bruddersford's world and seen as its key business and provider of essential cash flow.

The Potential Star Division provided a unique product to an expanding range of industrial customers. Because of its uniqueness, price was not the main concern but staying ahead of the competition was. The Division made profits but was cash hungry. Its managers were also not in the 'Bruddersford Old Boy Network'. They were brash newcomers. The internal context of the Potential Star Division has very little in common with the Cash Cow Division.

Discussion questions

1. What would you propose?
2. What problems would you predict for your proposals?

Ancillary case studies

In subgroups consider the following three case studies: the Car Parking Problem, the R&D Laboratory reorganisation and the Production Manager's Problem. The objective is NOT to make the decision but to decide which of the Vroom and Yetton 'styles' is most fitted to solve the problem. Use Tables 8.8 and 8.9 to decide your views.

Share your individual views and reach a consensus decision. While you come to a consensus consider the criteria you and your colleagues have used in the discussion.

CASE STUDY **8.5**

THE CAR PARKING PROBLEM

You are the new manager entrusted with setting up a small office with five sub-ordinates – all of whom are of equal status. (Various ancillary workers supply functions such as cleaning, but these are not the concern of the exercise.)

The office has been created out of two terraced houses backing onto a small cobbled street with jobbing garages and similar small businesses using the access. There are two obvious parking spaces in front of the houses and a Public Car Park is readily accessible at about 400 metres with standard charges. All your staff have cars and use them to get to work. They are all recognised users of cars and claim normal company mileage rates.

You need to arrange for car parking at the office.

CASE STUDY **8.6**

THE R&D LABORATORY REORGANISATION

You are head of a R&D laboratory in the basic research department of a multinational. The programme of research in the laboratories has been arranged by your predecessor to all aspects of research – from 'blue skies' to service work. In your view the 'blue skies' work has evolved so that its commercial exploitation within the capability of the company is highly unlikely.

The skills of the 'blue skies' team are likely to be exactly what the company needs for some scientifically boring but commercially exciting projects that are appearing from the service work. The 'pure' research team are coherent and have a high morale. Their work is highly respected in the academic community and you are concerned that to get them to change goals to a less 'interesting' area, as indeed you must, will affect both their morale and their productivity.

The operating division requiring a shift in resources needs your laboratory's commitment within two weeks. The team could work on 'blue skies' projects as well as the strictly applied work but the effort of all of the team, even if only on a part-time basis, is necessary for success, so total commitment is necessary from all members of the team. The choice of the actual 'pure' research projects still to be pursued in the new environment is also completely open and you do not have the expert skills to decide the priorities.

Get it settled.

CASE STUDY **8.7**

THE PRODUCTION MANAGER'S PROBLEM

You are the production manager of an electronics company. An investment programme has not succeeded in reducing costs – quality has fallen and key workers continue to leave. To the limit of your knowledge in the industry as it is now, the systems you have installed are not defective but you do suspect that the working procedures that the robotics equipment has demanded, are not ideal. This view is not shared by your immediate subordinates, or indeed by the shop floor. Training and the confusion on bonus payments has led to poor morale and, hence, avoidable mistakes.

The situation has now come to a head and your divisional director is asking for a response by 12.00 to the quantifiable loss in productivity in the last six months. The director has confidence in you and will accept your views.

He needs concrete plans from your division to present to his Board meeting at 13.30.

The case studies are discussed in Appendix 1.

Skill Application

EXERCISE **8.1**

SUGGESTED FURTHER ASSIGNMENTS

1. List all the teams with which you are currently involved – home, leisure, work, college, etc. Classify these teams in terms of satisfying your human needs for inclusion, control and affection. Is the balance satisfactory? Is any imbalance likely to give you conflict? What can you do to avoid potential imbalance?

2. What is the stage of development of each of the teams? How do you recognise this? Is this stage of development appropriate?

3. List the managers and leaders that you respect in your world. What features do they have in common? How could you model your behaviour on these?

EXERCISE **8.2**

APPLICATION PLAN

Refer back to the 360° Feedback Questionnaire at the beginning of the chapter. The objective is to make you more effective in your chosen path. Taking not more than three items:

- What new or improved behaviours do you wish to adopt?
- What specifically do you need to do to take on these new or revised behaviours?
- What specific results would you expect from these changes in behaviour?
- How would you monitor these changes? (Remember the 'small wins' strategy.)
- With whom would it be useful to share your plans?
- Do you need additional support?
- What would be the adverse consequences of your behavioural change?
- If you still intend to go ahead – how do you celebrate success?

Further reading

Adair, J. and Thomas, N. (1998) *The John Adair handbook of management and leadership*. London: Thorogood.

Belbin, R.M. (1996) *Team roles at work*. Oxford: Butterworth-Heinemann.

Bennis, W.G. (1998) *On becoming a leader*. London: Arrow.

Hardingham, A. (1995) *Working in teams*. London: Institute of Personnel & Development.

Katzenbach, J.R. and Smith, D.K. (1994) *The wisdom of teams: creating the high performance organization*. Boston: Harvard Business School Press.

Kelly, G. (1998) *Team leadership*. Aldershot: Gower.

Wright, P. (1996) *Managerial leadership*. London: Routledge.

Notes

Notes

Notes

Notes